OBJECT ORIENTED METHODS

Ian Graham Swiss Bank Corporation, London

SECOND EDITION

▲▼ **Addison-Wesley Publishing Company**

Harlow, England • Reading, Massachusetts • Menlo Park, California
New York • Don Mills, Ontario • Amsterdam • Bonn • Sydney • Singapore
Tokyo • Madrid • San Juan • Milan • Mexico City • Seoul • Taipei

Cover designed by Hybert Design and Type, Maidenhead
and printed by The Riverside Printing Co. (Reading) Ltd.
Typeset by Meridian Phototypesetting Ltd, Pangbourne
Printed and bound in Great Britain by The University Press, Cambridge

First printed 1993.
Reprinted 1994, 1995 and 1996.

ISBN 0-201-59371-8

British Library Cataloguing-in-Publication Data
A catalogue record for this book is available from the British Library.

Library of Congress Cataloging-in-Publication Data is available

Acknowledgement
The publisher wishes to thank the following for permission to reproduce material: Kim W. and Lochovsky F.H. *Object-Oriented Concepts, Databases and Applications*, © 1989 ACM Press, Reprinted by permission of Addison-Wesley Publishing Co; Desfray P. *Ingénerie des Objets: Approche Classe-Relation Application a C++*, © 1992 Editions Masson; Coad P. and Yourdon E. *Object-Oriented Analysis* 21e, © 1991, Reprinted by permission of Prentice Hall, Englewood Cliffs; Figure 5.17 Reproduced by permission of Instromatic Data Systems Ltd; Bellman R. and Zadeh L.A. *Decision Making in a Fuzzy Environment*, © 1970; Booch G. *Object-Oriented Design with Applications*, © 1991 Benjamin/Cummings Publishing Company.

For my wife, Sue Miller

OBJECT-ORIENTED METHODS

FOREWORD

The fact that object-oriented technology has entered the mainstream of computing is without dispute. Having witnessed the steady maturation of object methods over the past decade, I am still astounded at the extent to which object-oriented technology has taken hold in so many parts of the world, and in so many different problem domains. We have seen object-oriented methods used successfully for such varied applications as the control of autonomous submarines, enterprise-wide inventory control, securities trading, semiconductor manufacturing, and even interactive computer games. Moreover, the appeal of the object paradigm is world-wide: object-oriented applications may be found in all parts of the industrialized world, and even many third-world countries – for whom the structured programming revolution passed them by – have leapt into object-oriented technology as a means of elevating their technology base.

This almost exponential rate at which object-oriented technology has penetrated the computing community is not without cost. For the uninitiated just beginning to explore the implications of objects, to the practitioner trying to make decisions about languages, databases and methods, and even to the manager trying to introduce the object paradigm into his or her organization in the face of a large base of legacy systems, the task may seem most daunting.

Ian Graham is one of those rare individuals who holds a command of the broad spectrum of object-oriented computing and is, in addition, able to articulate that vast knowledge in a form that is both understandable and approachable. In this second edition of *Object-Oriented Methods*, he provides a comprehensive and up-to-date treatment of almost everything object-oriented. His contribution is a welcome addition to the literature.

Grady Booch
August 1993

PREFACE TO
THE SECOND EDITION

When the first edition of this book appeared, there was a great deal of excitement and interest in object-oriented techniques in the information technology (IT) industry and in academia, with public seminars held almost weekly. New journals and regular conferences were being established, and the membership of special interest groups was growing rapidly. This interest has now peaked and many commercial organizations have already had their first experiences of the technology for better or worse. Still the fuss continues and, while the languages have stabilized a little, the furore over methods and life-cycle issues has, if anything, intensified. In the midst of this brouhaha most practitioners in the data processing world need to be able to answer some fundamental questions.

The objective of this book, which it shares with the first edition, is to state in a clear manner the answers to the following questions.

- What are object-oriented methods?
- Can they be used now or should one wait for further developments?
- What are suitable applications?
- What are the benefits, pitfalls and likely costs?
- What has to be done to get started?
- What special skills are required?
- What are the links to other areas of information technology (IT)?
- How can object-orientation be managed and accommodated within existing systems development practices?

The rapid acceptance of object technology since I wrote the first edition has astounded me along with even the most fervent propagandists for it. The rapid changes in the technology which have occurred during the past two years or so are less surprising, but they do mean that large sections of the original edition need to be brought up to date and some anachronisms removed. Not only have the products changed and the number of methods grown, but the conclusions that a practitioner or, indeed, a careful observer can draw are quite different from what they were in 1991. One of the most significant changes has been the acceptance, by the industry at large, of the Object Management Group and their publication of various standards for object technology. On the other hand, there is much that has not changed.

The object-oriented programmer must still, mostly, decide between C++ and Smalltalk. Thus, while the objective of the book remains the same the means of achieving it must be substantially different. This edition brings all the definitional material up to date and into conformity with newly emerging standards. It modernizes the descriptions of products and methods available and draws new conclusions based on the new facts. The most evident change is the expansion of the material on object-oriented analysis and design. Material on the OMG standards is now included and there have been major changes to the sections dealing with object-oriented databases reflecting changes in the product market and the technology itself. The bibliography has been substantially expanded, reflecting the general growth in the volume of the literature as well as the new material in this edition.

This book is essentially a survey of the whole area of object technology. It covers object-oriented programming, object-oriented design, object-oriented analysis, object-oriented databases and concerns several related technologies. There are a number of good books on object-oriented programming covering specific languages. More general coverage is provided in these books only incidentally. They give a high-level overview of the philosophy and benefits of object-orientation in general but trouble the reader with a great deal of material specifically about programming and are dependent on the syntax of particular languages. At the other extreme there are now some very good 'management surveys' available, but these are not generally of sufficient technical depth for practioners or students. The reader seeking a reasonably detailed understanding of those aspects of object-orientation not related to programming (that is, design, analysis and databases) has to turn to the research literature, conference proceedings or collections of highly technical papers. If such a reader wants to gain a general understanding of the whole field rapidly or evaluate the future rôle of object technology, there are few coherent and comprehensive sources.

My aims in putting this book together are therefore to address these gaps in the literature by:

- providing a single-source, language-independent introduction covering all aspects of object-orientation: databases, programming, design, analysis and links with other computer techniques;
- providing a high-level evaluation of the status of and prospects for object-oriented techniques and products;
- placing much more emphasis on philosophy, methods, analysis and design, databases and on the practical issues surrounding the use of object-oriented techniques in commercial environments, thus redressing the imbalance represented by the emphasis on programming languages in the existing literature;
- propagating the view that object-orientation, artificial intelligence and data modelling together (rather than separately) are required to address the central issues of IT in the 1990s;
- providing coverage of the managerial issues associated with the introduction of object-oriented technology and methods;
- providing an introduction to and evaluation of object-oriented databases and relating them to conventional database technology;

■ attempting to explode some of the myths surrounding object-orientation while retaining a genuinely optimistic evaluation of its prospects as a practical tool for software engineers;

■ supplying sufficient depth and reference material to guide students and practitioners entering the field.

The book is intended to be accessible to readers who do not have deep specialist knowledge of theoretical computer science or advanced mathematics, but at the same time it attempts to treat the important issues accurately and in depth. Incidentally to the above aims the book exposes some original work on a method for object-oriented analysis (SOMA) which is described in detail in my book *Migrating to Object Technology* (Graham, 1995). This analysis method is constructed as a combination of techniques from object-orientation, artificial intelligence (or strictly expert systems) and data modelling and is a filter for ideas taken from several other methods of object-oriented analysis and design.

The primary audience I have in mind is the IT and DP profession: software engineers and, generally, people who work with computers whether in user organizations, consultancies, universities or manufacturers. Managers and project planners will read it to gain an understanding of how the technology will affect their business practices in the immediate future to be able to plan more effectively for change. Consultants, project managers, systems analysts and designers will read it to evaluate the technology and, I hope, use the techniques explained in their day-to-day work. Programmers will read it to broaden their horizons in this area.

Two secondary audiences exist in the academic domain. First, the book could be used as a text for an introductory (probably one term) undergraduate course in object-oriented methods within a software engineering methods curriculum, perhaps complementing another course on object-oriented programming. This would be of interest to teachers of computer science, business systems analysis and possibly artificial intelligence. Secondly, researchers will be interested in the book as a survey and for the original contributions. They may also find some of the commentary scattered through the book thought provoking or even controversial.

The material in this book has been presented to several audiences at various conferences and one-day seminars and courses organized by Amdahl (UK), BIS Information Systems, the British Computer Society, the Institution of Electrical Engineers and other bodies.

MAJOR CHANGES IN THE SECOND EDITION

This edition is a substantial revision and extension of the first edition. The major changes are as follows. Chapter 1 has been modified slightly to reflect greater clarity and standardization of terminology than was present in the industry when the book was first written. Chapter 4 is revised to change the emphasis on applications since it is now much clearer what object-oriented methods can be successfully applied to. The material on object-oriented databases in Chapter 6 has been completely updated to reflect new and increasingly mature products in this area. The biggest change is to the material on object-oriented analysis and design and their management. The original chapter on object-oriented analysis and design is split into two chapters and the coverage of methods greatly increased, with mention being made of nearly 50 approaches. Chapter 9 is substantially reorganized for greater clarity of exposition and to give a far more definite prescription of the approach recommended. All other chapters and the Appendix have undergone slight revision and improvement to reflect new developments in the field and correct any errors which remained in the first edition and of which I was aware. The chapter with the fewest changes is Chapter 5, on databases in general, though even here a few changes were necessary.

The Bibliography is substantially expanded and the Glossary has been updated and improved.

Despite these drastic changes the essential purpose of the book remains unchanged and I hope it is merely a more comprehensive, detailed, up to date and accurate survey of object-oriented methods than it would have been without the alterations.

DEPENDENCIES BETWEEN THE CHAPTERS There are a number of optional reading paths through the material presented in this book. The two prime routes through the text are illustrated in the reading map. Managers and those wishing for a high-level view of the subject may take the high road through Chapters 1, 2, 4, 9 and 10, possibly diverting through Chapter 3 for a comparison of programming languages. People interested in the new analysis method must take the low road, as the original parts of Chapter 8 build on all previous chapters. However, much of Chapters 7 and 8 (the reviews of existing methods) can be read after only Chapters 1, 2, 5 and possibly 4. Chapter 1 should be read even by people familiar with object-oriented programming since it introduces terminology which may differ from that of other works.

I hope the book tells a story if read sequentially. There are certainly some key themes to look out for. These are the relative immaturity of the technologies discussed and how they may be exploited despite this, the need for object-orientation to absorb techniques and viewpoints from other areas of computing and the need to add semantic richness to the more well-understood benefits of object-orientation – reusability and extensibility.

A NOTE ON LANGUAGE AND SPELLING Since many of us are prone to strong opinions on language and spelling, and since some of my habitual usage has attracted comment from some referees of this work, I feel that it is worthwhile clarifying the principles that I have applied in this text. Also, the conventions of spelling and the rules of transformational syntax vary between English, American English and other 'Englishes'.

The principle behind the spelling is etymological. Thus words ending '-ization' are spelt that way (as is the American fashion), rather than the more usual modern English '-isation', when the Greek or Latin infinitive indicates that the former is correct. This has to be largely based on guesswork, since I have never formally learned any foreign language other than Chinese. However, I have discovered that a useful rule of thumb is to ask whether there can be an -ization. If not, as with devise, advertise or circumcise, the 's' is correct. The only exception I know of is improvisation. Connexion is spelt with an 'x' for similar etymological reasons. However, when words from foreign languages or quotations are used the

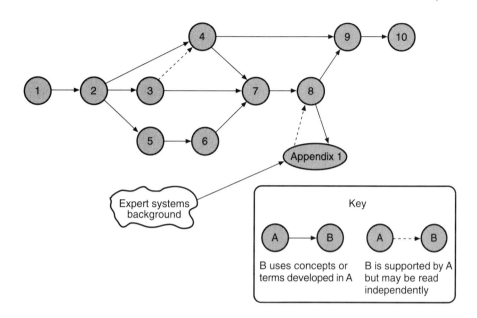

Reading map.

original spelling is retained. Thus, 'Connectionism' is used for the school of thought on neural nets, due to its American origin. Latin words are consistently italicized. Bold characters are used for emphasis and definitions.

The word data is the plural of datum and is used as such throughout. I fail to see why writers on computing should get away with their almost universal error of treating 'data' as a singular noun when writers in no other discipline do so. This is nothing to do with the differences between American and English as a brief glance a books on geography, statistics, medicine, management and so on from both sides of the Atlantic will soon demonstrate.

The word *methods* is used in three different ways in this book: in the sense of methods for doing software engineering in general (in the title), particular formal methods for doing software engineering (as with the SOMA method) and the methods (programs) representing the behaviour of objects. I have resisted the non-word methodologies on the same grounds that I would reject Physicses, or Chemistries. The OED has it that Methodology (and the capitalization is necessary) is 'the science of method' and Chambers adds 'within a science or discipline'. The plural could only be used if there had been a paradigm shift in the sense of Thomas Kuhn (a solecism in itself[1]) in our perception of the way of doing

[1] *Paradigm* really means a model or especially typical example.

things. Since many people believe that object technology is such a paradigm shift, we could correctly write the sentence: 'There is a difference between the Structured and the Object-Oriented Methodologies', meaning the that whole approach to computer science has altered. It is pure barbarism to write: 'There is a difference between the Yourdon and Jackson methodologies.' I try to avoid words like *paradigm* too.

Sexist assumptions in terminology are, of course, to be avoided. My preference is for a plural personal pronoun or s/he (pronounced 'she') instead of 'he or she'. However, I distinguish between sexual and grammatical gender; so that Man is merely short for Mankind and means the same as Humanity. Thus the term 'manday' is to be taken generically, the gender being grammatical rather than sexual. Otherwise, the French would have to start saying 'le ou la chien' and we would be obliged to use 'woperson' for 'woman'.

Split infinitives are avoided, based on pure personal preference and my belief that readability is thereby enhanced. No attempt to write in short, journalistic sentences has been made, except where clarity so dictates. I have tried to employ the *correct* word, rather than a word that everybody will know. Particularly obscure (to my referees) words, or words where the dictionary would not be adequate due to nuance, have been added to the technical glossary or defined in a footnote. The dictionaries used were the *Oxford English Dictionary (Compact Edition)* (OED) and *Chambers English Dictionary*. A certain number of words which are not in the dictionary are inevitable in a book on a technical subject of this kind. An example is workstation, as opposed to 'work station'. The latter seems distinctly wrong in the context of a local computer, where the emphasis is on its capability rather than its location. I have taken such liberties fairly thoughtfully though. Language, after all, is a living thing.

These are the theoretical principles applied. In practice there may be several grammatical and spelling errors.

ACKNOW-LEDGEMENTS Although it contains much original material, this book is largely a survey of other people's work and could not have been written without that work. I would like to acknowledge the contribution of these other authors. Also, many of the ideas contained are the result of personal interaction between the author and a number of his colleagues, clients and friends. It would be impossible to acknowledge each of these contributions individually, but I would like to thank all the people who read all or parts of the manuscript and made innumerable useful comments and criticisms. For the first edition these were: Stuart Frost of Select Software Ltd, Jane Hillston of the University of Edinburgh, David Lee of GEC-Marconi Software, Gail Swaffield, then of Ernst and Young, Jennifer Yates of BIS. Also, John Cresswell, Chris Harris-Jones, Sonia Math, Richard Seed and Richard Smith, all ex-colleagues of mine, helped by reading drafts and discussing many of the ideas. The readers for the second edition were Steve Probert and David Lee, again who made extraordinarily detailed comments all of which were useful.

A number of other, anonymous, referees made helpful and invaluable comments on the manuscript at various stages. Derek Pearce, of Logica, provided useful information on commercial applications and also was a useful sounding board for some of the ideas. Gail Swaffield helped in the development of some of the ideas, particularly those on knowledge elicitation and analysis. Tim Lamb, of Equitable Life, helped with the idea of applying object-oriented analysis to business strategy analysis. Thanks also to Peter Jones for his joint work on the development of the ideas behind fuzzy objects and for teaching me much over the years. The members of the British Computer Society Specialist Group on Object-Oriented Programming and Systems provided a valuable forum for the interchange of ideas. During the preparation of the second edition discussions with Martin Fowler, David Redmond-Pyle and several other practioners proved invaluable. Robin Crewe and Kerry Williams of Swiss Bank provided many insights and much helpful criticism in relation to SOMA. Florence Froidevaux helped me understand the Class Relationship method whose main reference source was in French. None of these people are responsible for the errors which may remain in the text. That responsibility is mine alone.

Thanks are also due to the various audiences who endured my seminars and classes during the period when these ideas were being developed and who provided valuable feedback, and occasionally – and most usefully – asked hard questions. Thanks to Tony Clifford-Winters, then of Amdahl, David Spicer of British Aerospace, Gerry Roff and Vic Wiseman of BIS and the organizers of various conferences on object technology for inviting me to give the talks in the first place.

Nicky Jaeger, Andy Ware and the other staff at Addison-Wesley reconfirmed my view of the professionalism of that firm in bringing this manuscript to a form suitable for public consumption in a very short time.

Sue Miller has now endured the gestation period of three books and put up with a partner who was largely abstracted from the concerns of everyday life, and short-tempered to boot, for long periods covering nearly three years. Sam Miller merely knows that his dad disappears to 'play with your 'puter' on many evenings and Rob is too young to do much other than smile when I make my all too rare appearances. These three get an apology as well as an acknowledgement.

I would also like to thank the thousands of people scattered throughout the world, living and dead, whose labour, by hand or by brain, created the word processing system I am now using. Without it this book would certainly not have been written.

Ian Graham
London, August 1993

BRIEF CONTENTS

CONTENTS

Trademark notice

Actor™ is a trademark of Symantec.

IBM™, IBM AS/400™ IBMPC™, IBM PS/2™ APPC™, AD/Cycle™, DB2™, Presentation Manager™, System 38™ are trademarks of International Business Machines Corporation.

Adabas™, Adabas Entire™, Natural™, Natural Expert™ are trademarks of Software AG.

ADS™ is a trademark of Aion Corp.

Apple™, Lisa™, MacApp™, Macintosh™, HyperCard™, HyperTalk™ are trademarks of Apple Computer, Inc.

ART™ is a trademark of Inference Corporation.

Automate™ is a trademark of LBMS.

Blobs™ is a trademark of Cambridge Consultants.

C++/Views™ is a trademark of CNS Inc.

Cantor™ is a trademark of VSF Ltd.

CASE*METHOD™ is a trademark and Oracle^R is a registered trademark of Oracle Corporation UK Limited.

Classix™ is a trademark of Empathy Inc.

CLU™, X-Windows™, Mach™ are trademarks of MIT.

Common LOOPS™, InterLisp™, LOOPS™ are trademarks of Xerox Corporation.

CommonView™ is a trademark of Glockenspiel Ltd.

Connection Machine™ is a trademark of Thinking Machines Inc.

COP™, Ontos™, Shorthand™, Studio™, Vbase™ are trademarks of Ontologic Inc.

dBase™ is a trademark of Ashton Tate Incorporated.

DEC™, PDP™, VAX™, VMS™ are trademarks of Digital Equipment Corporation.

Easel™ is a trademark of Easel Corp.

Eiffel™ is a trademark of Interactive Software Engineering Inc.

ENVY™ is a trademark of Object Technology International

ES/KLERNEL™, Object 1Q are trademarks of Hitachi Corp.

Excelerator™ is a trademark of Index Technologies Inc.

Express™ and Javelin™ are trademarks of Information Resources Inc.

Fact™, Generic Array Multiprocessor™, Generis™, IQL™ are trademarks of Deductive Systems Ltd.

FCS™ is a trademark of Thorn EMI Software.

G-base™ and G-Logis™ are trademarks of Graphael.

GECOMO™ is a trademark of GEC Software.

GEM™ is a trademark of Digital Research Corp.

GemStone™, GeODE™ are trademarks of Servio Logic Corp.

Genera™, Joshua™, Statice™ are trademarks of Symbolics, Inc.

GoldWorks™ is a trademark of Gold Hill Computers, Inc.

GOOD™ is a trademark of NASA.

HOOD™ is a trademark of HOOD Working Group.

HOOD-SF™, VSF™ are trademarks of Systematica Ltd.

Informix^R is a registered trademark of Informix Software Inc.

Ingres™, Simplify™ are trademarks of Ingres Corp.

Intuitive Solution™ is a trademark of Intuitive Software Ltd.

IPSYS HOOD Toolset™ is a trademark of Ipsys Ltd.

Iris™, NewWave™ are trademarks of Hewlett-Packard Inc.

ITASCA™ is a trademark of ITASCA Inc.

Kappa™, KEE™, Prokappa™ are trademarks of Intellicorp, Inc.

KBMS™ is a trademark of AI Corp.

KnowledgePro™ is a trademark of Knowledge Garden Inc.

Lego™ is a trademark of LEGO Group.

Leonardo™ is a trademark of Creative Logic Ltd.

Level 5 Object™ is a trademark of Information Builders Inc.

Lingo™, Rekursiv™ are trademarks of Linn Technologies Ltd.

Lotus-123^R is a registered trademark of Lotus Development Corporation.

me too™ is a trademark of STC plc.

Microsoft^R is a registered trademark and Windows™, Excel™, Visual (Basic)™ are trademarks of Microsoft Corporation.

Motif™ is a trademark of Open Software Foundation Inc.

Natural™, Natural Expert™ are trademarks of Software AG.

1

Basic concepts

My object all sublime
I shall achieve in time

Gilbert
(The Mikado)

It has become the case that use of the adjectival phrase 'object-oriented' has become almost synonymous with modernity, goodness and worth in information technology circles. Amidst all this hype, it is desirable to achieve a balanced view. This book will attempt, firstly, to state the case for object-orientation in theoretically pure terms but, secondly, show how limited and partial applications of these abstract ideas can contribute to real, practical advances in building useful computer systems. The approach will be independent of any particular programming language, and will avoid the syntactic niceties in favour of a high-level evaluation of the business and technical issues which arise in selecting a suitable development environment and approach. In dealing with things object-oriented we must also realize that we are entering an area that is not well bounded and where research is still incomplete in certain areas. We shall be forced to consider many other areas of current concern such as open systems, databases, CASE technology, expert systems, and much more. Occasionally, we will enter relatively uncharted territory.

The key benefits usually promised by purveyors of object-orientation are reusability and extensibility. That is, object-oriented systems are to be assembled from pre-written components with minimal effort and the assembled system will be easy to extend without any need to tinker with the reused components. We will examine both these benefits, and the extent to which object-oriented systems can actually live up to them, in detail, in the next chapter.

The phrase 'object-oriented methods' as used in this book refers to more than just object-oriented programming. It connotes a whole philosophy of systems development encompassing programming, requirements analysis, system design, database design and many more related issues. The emphasis throughout this book is going to be on this philosophy and how it can be used to address the issues that arise in constructing information systems. Benefits such as reusability and extensibility, for example, are not restricted to the reuse or extension of chunks of code. Potentially, designs and analysis documents can be stored in libraries and reused or extended over and over again, provided of course that potential users have a means to find out about their existence easily.

As I have indicated, 'object-oriented' has become an extremely overloaded term. To help clarify the issues, in this book we will distinguish between 'object-oriented', 'object-based' and 'class-based' programming, design and analysis. We shall see in Chapter 3 and elsewhere that very few commercial systems live up to the pure concept of object-orientation and that even those that do may have other disadvantages. Nevertheless, object-oriented systems do have a rôle, and it is important to ask not so much whether a system is object-oriented or not, but *how* it is object-oriented and in what way it delivers the associated benefits.

This chapter introduces the basic concepts and terminology of object-oriented methods. We begin with a short historical introduction. The motivation for and benefits of object-oriented methods and programming will be dealt with in Chapter 2.

1.1 Historical background

The rise of object-orientation reflects and recapitulates the history of computing as a whole. The earliest work in computing, going back to the late 1940s, concerned itself exclusively with what we now think of as programming. Only later did a conscious concern with design and analysis as separate issues arise. Similarly, it is object-oriented programming that first attracted attention, and only latterly did object-oriented design and, even more recently, object-oriented analysis become major areas of endeavour. In this work we thus must start with object-oriented programming before moving on to the design and analysis issues, although the latter will be our more major concern.

Although Ten Dyke and Kunz (1989) have claimed that the designers of the Minuteman missile used rudimentary object-oriented techniques as early as 1957, the history of object-oriented programming really starts with the development of the discrete event simulation language Simula in Norway in 1967 and continues with the development of a language that almost makes a fetish of the notion of an object, Smalltalk, in the 1970s. Intermediate influential languages include Alphard (Wulf *et al.*, 1976) and CLU (Liskov *et al.*, 1977). Since then there have been many languages which have been inspired by these developments and have laid claim to the appellation 'object-oriented'.

Simulation modelling is a particularly hard problem for conventional, third-generation language programmers. It requires the programmer to adapt the functional flow of control that is normal in such languages to a control flow which is more naturally described in terms of complex objects which change state and influence events from moment to moment. In object-oriented programming, this functional flow is replaced by message passing between objects which causes changes in object state. Thus object-oriented programming is an extremely natural approach since the structure of the programs directly reflects the structure of the problem. Furthermore, it is usually clear in simulation problems what the objects are: cars in a street, machines on a production line. They are usually 'real-world' rather than abstract objects and easy to identify as such. Sadly this is not always true for commercial applications as we shall see.

The term 'object-oriented' finally came into the language with the advent of the programming language Smalltalk. Smalltalk was largely developed at the Xerox research centre at Palo Alto, PARC, but it has its origins not only in Simula itself but in the doctoral work of Alan Kay which, as Rentsch (1982) records, was based on a vision of a small but ubiquitous personal computer capable of handling any kind of information management problem and capable of being used by all kinds of people. The earliest version of this was the Flex machine which, at PARC, became known as the Dynabook. Smalltalk was essentially the software component of the Dynabook and was heavily influenced by both Simula's notion of classes and inheritance and LISP's structural features[1]. Smalltalk combined the class notion from Simula with a lot of the functional abstraction flavour of LISP although, as languages, Smalltalk and LISP are quite different.

The next phase, roughly the 1980s, showed an explosion of interest in the user interface (UI). The best known commercial pioneers, Xerox and later Apple, brought the world the ubiquitous WIMP[2] interface and many of the ideas in Smalltalk are strongly tied to these developments. On the one hand object-oriented programming supported the development of such interfaces – notably in the case of the Apple Lisa and Macintosh – while on the other the style of object-oriented languages was heavily influenced by the WIMP paradigm. The most obvious effect of this is the plentiful existence of library objects for interface development, compared to a certain paucity in other areas. One of the contributory reasons for the success of object-oriented programming was the sheer complexity of these interfaces and the concomitant high cost of building them. Without the inherent reusability of object-oriented code it has been suggested that these interfaces could not have been built on such a wide scale. It has been estimated for example that the Apple Lisa, the precursor of the Macintosh, represents over 200 man-years of effort, much of which is accounted for by the development of the interface. The influence of the WIMP style was sufficiently pervasive that IBM PC and PS/2 machines are gradually being fitted out with WIMP front ends: Presentation Manager, Microsoft Windows and so on. The drive towards standardized, open systems based on UNIX is also much concerned with the UI aspects where the battle between OpenLook, OSF Motif and the like is seen as a crucial determinant of market success. In this sense object-orientation has already left its mark on the world we live in.

Also, from the mid 1970s and later, there was considerable cross-fertilization between object-oriented programming and artificial intelligence research and devel-

---

[1] LISP stands for LISt Processing. It is the language originally developed by John McCarthy around 1958 which became the language of choice for much early work in artificial intelligence.

[2] WIMP stands for Windows, Icons, Mice and Pointers and refers to a style of Graphical User Interface (GUI) which makes use of them. See Chapter 4.

opment, leading to several useful extensions of AI languages, most principally LISP. Thus we have languages such as LISP with FLAVORS, LOOPS and CLOS (Common LISP Object System). AI programming environments, themselves often LISP extensions, such as KEE and ART had their design heavily influenced by object-oriented ideas. These systems were heavily influenced by ideas on knowledge representation based around semantic networks and frames. These representations express knowledge about real-world objects and concepts in the form of networks of stereotyped objects that can inherit features from more general ones. Thus the main contribution of this input to object-orientation was the sophistication of its theories about inheritance. Object-oriented methods have still to absorb these lessons fully. AI languages and applications will be discussed further in Chapters 3 and 4.

Another stream of research in the AI world, together with research into concurrent computing, led to the notion of **actors**. Actor systems (Ahga, 1986), like blackboard systems (see Englemore and Morgan, 1989), attempt to model pools of cooperating workers or experts. An actor is a more anthropomorphic notion than an object and has defined responsibilities, needs and knowledge about collaborators. Actor languages are usually directed at real-time and concurrent applications. We will have more to say about them in Chapters 4 and 10.

Owing to the fact that they cut their teeth on user interface design problems rather than, say, database management, there were performance problems associated with early object-oriented languages when applied to other types of application. This led to the developments of new languages such as Eiffel and to extensions of existing, efficient conventional languages such as C and Pascal. Various object-oriented and object-based programming languages are surveyed in Chapter 3. Interface development also poses no significant data management problems compared to commercial applications. This meant that object-oriented programming languages often failed to provide facilities for dealing with persistent objects, concurrency, and so on. The development of object-oriented database systems is one response to this problem. These are discussed at length in Chapter 6.

The demands of many users, and in particular of financially important users like the United States of America Department of Defense (DoD), often force computer industry suppliers to change course. The demands of the DoD throughout the 1960s and 1970s have been consistently for three main things: an engineering approach to software development practice which found its expression in the so-called 'structured' methods, reusable software components (modularity) and open systems. The various system development methods adopted by many major IT suppliers represent a response to the first demand, which reached something of a climax with IBM's announcements concerning AD/Cycle and the late 1980s' furore over CASE (computer-aided software engineering) tools and IPSEs (integrated programming software environments). UNIX, X/Windows and Ada are all in some way responses to the DoD's demand that systems be 'open systems', which is to say that whatever I build and you build and whatever hardware we use we should expect to be able to make those systems interwork with minimum effort. Ada also has the character of a language designed to improve modularity. As we will see, it has been described as an object-oriented language by some. We will be exploring the extent to which this description is adequate later. More importantly we will be asking whether it and object-oriented programming in general contributes anything to these three key issues. Object-oriented programming also addresses a key DoD requirement implicit in the ones mentioned above. It promises to enable system developers to assemble systems from reusable components, thus addressing modularity and software engineering in one go.

As object-oriented programming began to mature, interest shifted to object-oriented design methods and to object-oriented analysis or specification. The benefits of reusability and extensibility can be applied to designs and specifications as well as to code. Biggerstaff and Richter (1989), Prieto-Diaz and Freeman (1987) and Sommerville (1989) have all argued, in a more general software engineering context, that the higher the level of reuse the greater the benefit. Important questions arise in this area, such as whether an object-oriented design must be implemented in an object-oriented language or whether current design methods are in fact tied to specific languages. These and related issues are covered in Chapters 7 and 8.

Just as relational databases are beginning to become respectable, if not required, technology in commercial environments, we see the major vendors introducing various 'post-relational' extensions having their origins in fields such as expert systems, functional programming and, now, object-oriented programming. Object-oriented and semi-object-oriented databases are just beginning to emerge as commercial products and one supplier has even announced an 'entity-relationship' database. What are we to make of these developments? First, the theoretical side of object-orientation has to take on concerns with such typically database issues as how to deal efficiently with persistent objects, granularity and object versioning. Second, we may interpret this development as part of the regularization of object-oriented notions. On the other hand, we have to wonder whether existing relational products will be superseded or whether they will be evolved into some sort of compromise solution. These developments have raised a number of issues concerning the relative efficiency of declarative relational query languages compared with approaches based on object identity. It is almost ironic, in the light of recent history, that the latter property is possessed not only by object-oriented databases but also by the early network and hierarchical systems. Chapters 5 and 6 will take a closer look at database theory, object-oriented databases and these issues.

Computer-aided software engineering (CASE) has become increasingly important in the development of commercial systems over the past few years. It is variously regarded with enthusiasm or scepticism. The emergence of a number of object-oriented analysis and design methods and CASE tools supporting them forces us to ask whether there is any advantage to be gained through their use. Chapters 7 and 8 deal with several design and analysis techniques claiming some degree of object-orientation. Some of these methods are supported by CASE tools and some of these are surveyed in Chapter 8.

Most recently of all, concern has shifted to standards. Object technology can only succeed against the inertia of existing practice if users can achieve the confidence in moving to it that they require from a move to open systems. If object-oriented applications are all mutually incompatible, if object-oriented databases cannot interwork with each other and with relational databases and if there are no standard notations and terms for object-oriented analysis there is little hope of this. The chief protagonist in the standards area has been an organization called the Object Management Group (OMG). The OMG is a large and growing group of influential companies committed to establishing broad agreement between vendors on both the terminology of object-orientation and on 4GL (fourth-generation language) style and interface standards – possibly based on existing technology from suppliers such as DEC, Hewlett-Packard and Hyperdesk. Companies involved at the beginning in 1989 included Hewlett-Packard, Data General, AT&T, Prime, Wang, ICL, Sun, DEC and even IBM as observers. At the time of writing, however, the OMG has grown to several hundreds, with the likes of Borland, IBM, Microsoft and most large hardware manufacturers and software houses along with some large users, big consulting organizations, AI vendors and many OO specialists as enthusiastic full members. This gives considerable cause for optimism because this level of cooperation has rarely been seen in the computer industry. Meetings of the OMG Technical Committee rotate between Europe, the USA and the far East, helping to ensure an international base. The OMG is committed to the fast production of published standards, faster anyway than the official standards bodies can operate, and has already published an architecture guide, a standard for the Common Object Request Broker Architecture (CORBA), a layered architecture for interoperation of object-oriented applications, analogous to the ISO 7-layer model for networks, and a high-level object-oriented abstract data model. Already some suppliers (including DEC, Hewlett-Packard, Hyperdesk and others) have announced Object Request Broker (ORB) compliant products and many more will soon follow. The OMG standards have yet to be made official but they already have wide acceptance. Several standards are published and more are in draft (OMG, 1991). The architecture model and the CORBA are discussed further in Chapter 10 and the OMG reference model for analysis and design in Chapter 8.

Thus the current phase of the history of object-orientation is characterized by a shift of emphasis from programming to design and analysis and by an awareness of the issue of open systems and standards. Furthermore, attention has shifted to applications where large computations or data manipulations are required; hence the emergence of object-oriented databases. One important trend is toward the incorporation of object-oriented methods into existing database management systems, into existing structured methods and into their supporting CASE tools. Another is directed to producing new purely object-oriented tools. Which will be the dominant trend has yet to be seen and there is a vast and confusing array of methods on offer; none, arguably, complete yet. Many current, medium-scale software development projects in the commercial arena are already using object-oriented programming and methods. The end result will be, I believe, the emergence of a far more practical focus. Chapters 9 and 10 will examine these questions in more depth. Chapter 4 describes several applications of object-oriented programming and its approach. The history of object-oriented methods is summarized in Figure 1.1.

The future of object-oriented methods looks very promising from our current viewpoint. With increased emphasis on distributed and open systems the object

Phase II – 1970s The Age of Invention	Phase II – 1980s The Age of Confusion	Phase III – 1990s The Age of Ripening
Discrete event simulation	WIMP interfaces	Focus on analysis and design
Simula	Xerox and Apple	Open systems
Kay: FLEX machine	LISP extensions	Applications
PARC: Dynabook	AI environments	Object-oriented databases
Smalltalk	New languages: Eiffel, C++, …	Standards

Figure 1.1 The history of object-oriented methods.

metaphor appears to be the most natural one to adopt, given its emphasis on encapsulation and message passing. Increasing concern over maintenance costs may well lead to the recognition that reusability is the key issue in programming, design and analysis. However, it is all too easy to be beguiled by object-oriented propaganda. Only a few commercial projects which have used object-oriented techniques have yet resulted in any significant amount of reusable code, though some have reported such benefits as discussed in Chapter 2.

In my view, what is required in the immediate future is not better, purer, more efficient object-oriented languages alone but better methods and notations for object-oriented software engineering. Efficient hybrid languages such as C++, with associated UI (user interface) toolkits such as InterViews and CommonView already exist, as do a few useful object libraries (or 'goody bags' as they are sometimes called). Without these libraries being widely available on a commercial basis the approach is seriously compromised. I firmly believe that this availability is a precondition for the wide acceptance of object-oriented programming. Of course, this is a vicious circle because such library modules will have to be developed during real projects. I suppose, optimistically perhaps, that a few innovative and adventurous project managers will be found to provide the initial conditions for the predicted explosion in object-oriented programming. In the meantime, I believe, object-oriented methods for design and analysis can be developed and used immediately with considerable benefit. The benefits and potential pitfalls of object-orientation are analysed in Chapter 2 after this chapter has equipped the reader with the necessary terminology and concepts.

Another possible obstacle to commercial acceptance is the lack of established object-oriented databases. The emergence of such systems can come about in two ways, either as totally new products or through the evolution of existing ones. This, in either case, is a precondition for the regularization of object-oriented technology in the commercial world. This regularization, like that of expert systems and rule-based techniques, must make object-oriented methods part of the general toolkit of the software developer along with 4GLs, databases, graphics software and so on. It is also necessary that object-orientation comes out of its ivory tower and begins to incorporate ideas from conventional IT, data modelling, artificial intelligence and other areas of computing. This process is now under way but not yet completed.

In Chapter 10 we will tentatively explore the medium-term prospects for IT in relation to these developments.

1.2 What are object-oriented methods?

As I have repeatedly emphasized, the phrase 'object-oriented methods' refers to several things, as do the terms 'object-oriented' and 'object technology' themselves. In particular, the phrase refers to object-oriented programming, design, analysis and databases, in fact to a whole philosophy of systems development based on a powerful metaphor.

Historically, as I have indicated in the foregoing, interest began with object-oriented programming and only more recently has there been great interest in these other issues. From a managerial point of view the programming issues are perhaps the least interesting, but in order to understand the basic concepts and terminology, we will have to start with a review of object-oriented programming and its associated terminology with the aim of leaving it rapidly behind. In the sequel, and especially in Chapters 7 and 8, which cover methods, CASE and related issues, and in Chapter 9 we will see how these basic concepts can be applied throughout the system development life cycle and indeed as a method of analysis for organizations. In other words, we shall proceed from the concrete concerns of programming to the abstract ones of design and analysis and then back to the concrete in a treatment of the managerial issues.

The next section introduces the terminology of object-oriented methods. The glossary summarizes this terminology as well as including definitions of some other possibly unfamiliar terms. The reader should be aware that different authors sometimes use these terms in subtly different ways. This is not altogether surprising in an emerging subject. Fortunately, standard terminology is emerging thanks largely to the efforts of the Object Management Group and the remainder of this text will refer to these standard terms. The terms used in this book represent, I hope, the emerging consensus, but also reflect the view that artificial intelligence, semantic data modelling and object-orientation must converge.

1.3 Basic terminology and ideas

Object-oriented software engineering is characterized by the following terms and concepts.

- **Objects**   The basic units of construction, be it for conceptualization, design or programming, are instances organized into classes with common features. These features comprise attributes and procedures, called *operations* or *methods*.

These objects should be as far as possible based on the real-world entities and concepts of the application or domain. Objects can be either classes or instances, although some authorities use the term *object* synonymously with *instance*. The OMG standard is to call the descriptions of classes *object types* and use the term class to refer to their implementation.

- **Encapsulation**   The data structures and implementation details of an object are hidden from other objects in the system. The only way to access an object's state is to send a message that causes one of the methods to execute. Strictly speaking the attributes are shorthand for methods that get and put values. This makes object types equivalent to abstract data types in programming, broadly speaking.

- **Messages**   Objects, classes and their instances communicate by message passing. This eliminates data duplication and ensures that changes to data structures encapsulated within objects do not propagate their effects to other parts of the system. Messages are often implemented as function calls.

- **Inheritance**   Instances (usually) inherit all and only the features of the classes they belong to, but it is also possible in an object-oriented system to allow classes to inherit features from more general superclasses. In this case inherited features can be overridden and extra features added to deal with exceptions. Inheritance is only one of the conceptual structures with which we organize the world. It is a particularly important one and its importance corresponds to the importance of the verb *to be* in language. We will examine other key structures, such as composition (corresponding to the verb *to have*), in subsequent chapters.

- **Polymorphism**   The ability to use the same expression to denote different operations is referred to as polymorphism. This occurs where + is used to signify real or integer addition and when the message 'add 1' is sent to a bank account and to a list of reminder notes; the same message should produce quite different results. Polymorphism is often implemented by *dynamic binding*. Inheritance is a special kind of polymorphism that characterizes object-oriented systems.

Abstracting from this, object-orientation in a programming language, system design or computer system is characterized by two key features, which are glorified by two impressive words:

- Encapsulation
- Inheritance

There is a tension and opposition between these abstractions. Inheritance violates reuse because sub-objects may have privileged access to the implementation of their super-objects' methods.

Other authors prefer the term 'abstraction' to our 'encapsulation' to convey the general concept. I find myself using the terms interchangeably, and do not really have a strong view on which is the better one[3]. Both words conceal a number of

---

[3] For a finer distinction see Berard (1993) and the bibliographical notes to this chapter.

important concepts. The following two sections examine these in order to clarify their meaning and establish terminology for later use. As with all dichotomies, encapsulation and inheritance are not cleanly separated: there is a tension and inter-action between them. Thus, some terms, such as polymorphism, come up under both headings and even inheritance can be viewed as a form of abstraction. The areas of overlap and the dialectic between abstraction and inheritance are examined in Section 1.3.3.

When we come to deal with object-oriented databases it will become clear that a third principle of object identity is equally important.

1.3.1 Abstraction and encapsulation

Abstraction encompasses various issues and is the more difficult of the two key terms to grasp at first. The meaning given by the *Oxford English Dictionary* (OED) closest to the meaning intended here is: 'The act of separating in thought'. A better definition might be: 'Representing the essential features of something without including background or inessential detail'. Closely associated with this notion of abstraction is the idea that abstractions should be complete in that they should encapsulate *all* the essential properties of a thing. In programming terms this means that objects should abstract and encapsulate both data and process. Things are apprehended not only through their properties but through their behaviour: by their ways shall ye know them.

The basic idea is that an object is defined by a list of abstract **attributes** (often divided into **instance variables** and **class variables**), such as size, position and colour, and a list of procedures which it is permissible to perform on these attributes, such as rotate or 'move leftwards' for a geometrical or physical object. In the purist orthodoxy of object-oriented programming the instance variables are not visible to other objects, but we will see below and in Chapter 8 that this con-dition can be relaxed and that the relaxation has important benefits for commercial applications. This idea of bundling the functions up with the data is closely related to the notion of a data type in ordinary programming languages, wherein 3 is an instance of the 'type' integer, and integers are characterized by just one attribute (their value) but by several allowable arithmetic operations. Real numbers are char-acterized by similar operations, but the actual implementation of multiplication for a floating point number is quite different from that for integers. Similarly we can treat more complex objects, such as employees of the sort normally found in data models, by specifying their attributes and **methods**, **operations** or **services** – which are the names usually used for the characteristic, encapsulated procedures. I will use these terms interchangeably with a preference for the term *method*, which is the original terminology of Smalltalk and seems to be the one generally understood. This specialized usage has nothing to do with the other usage: object-oriented methods. The latter refers to the system development methods dealt with in detail in Chapters 7 to 9. Here a **method** is defined as a procedure or function that alters the state of an object or causes the object to send a message; that is, return values.

The description or signature of a method is called an **operation**. Operations define which messages an object is able to process successfully. Figure 1.2 (a) describes a complex object or abstract data type called Employee together with some of its defining attributes and methods. Once defined, this abstraction is available to the programmer in a very direct and facile manner. Figure 1.2 (b) shows the same object using the more usual object-oriented notation, in which the instance variables are suppressed. In this book the notation of Figure 1.2 (a) will be preferred.

A **class**, in the sense used in object-oriented programming, is a collection of objects which share common attributes and methods. A class may be regarded as a template for creating instances and is also called an **object-type**, though strictly a class is the implementation of a type. The attributes and methods of an object-type are often referred to as its **features** or **responsibilities**. An attribute represents a responsibility for knowing something and a method a responsibility for doing something.

An **abstract data type** (ADT) is an abstraction, similar to a class, that describes a set of objects in terms of an encapsulated or hidden data structure and operations on that structure. Abstract data types, as opposed to primitive data types, may be defined by a user in constructing an application rather than by the designer of the underlying language. It may be noted that this idea of abstract data types bears a strong resemblance to the notion of entity type as used in data modelling methods. This is not accidental and is the basis for much of what I have to say about object-oriented analysis in Chapter 8. However, the key difference between ADTs or classes in object-oriented programming and entity types is that ADTs include methods. For example, an ADT representing lengths expressed in imperial units would include methods for adding feet and inches.

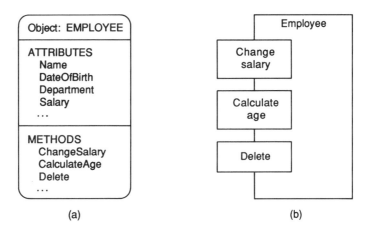

(a) (b)

Figure 1.2 (a) An object or abstract data type which captures the notion of an employee; **(b)** The Employee class in the more common object-oriented notation.

From the programmer's point of view there is a difference between classes and types, because the type information only gives a specification of an object: the class it belongs to may only be determined at run time. The difference is that classes describe specifications that may be shared among collections of objects or other classes, not just among objects with unique identity, or instances. From the analyst's point of view, however, classes and ADTs are effectively the same thing.

In programming, the ability to determine an object's class at run time and allocate its storage is referred to as **dynamic binding**. In statically bound languages the compiler allocates storage to objects and their type determines their class uniquely. Because this book is not principally concerned with programming we will routinely blur this distinction between classes and types. However, it will be important to remember that a class is not just a set. A class has members and operations whereas a set only has members. Dynamic binding is to be contrasted with **early** or **static binding**, when the allocation of types is carried out by a compiler. Dynamic binding is also known as **late binding**. Dynamic binding is the programming technique that is usually used to implement polymorphism in object-oriented programming languages.

As indicated above, in object-oriented programming it is normal to regard only instances as having unique identity, which reflects the reality of run-time instantiation in a computer system. I think this is an error outside of the context of programming and regard classes also as having unique identity. After all, there is only one class of Apples in the conceptual world. In this book, an *object* is anything with unique identity. It can be a concrete individual, real or invented, or a concept, abstract or concrete. This contrasts with many books and papers where 'object' is used as a synonym for 'instance'. I think that if we are to speak about object technology then 'object' should be a general term within that domain. Also, the OMG's Abstract Object Model (see Chapter 8) uses the term 'object type' for a class. In this way we could think of 'object' as merely an abbreviated form for 'object type' when a class is intended.

An **object** is thus to be understood as a class or abstract data type or an instance of a type. As explained above, I find it more convenient to use the term 'object' for both classes and their instances, as in Smalltalk where 'everything is an object'. **Abstract classes** may not have instances: their children are other classes. When the distinction between a class and an instance is important the term object will not be used.

An object has two aspects: an internal and an external aspect. The internal aspect describes the state, implementation and instantiation of the object. The external view, in the pure object-oriented style, shows only the names of its methods and the types of their parameters: what the object can do, as in Figure 1.2 (b). I have fudged this pure view a little here by showing the object's attributes as in Figure 1.2 (a). To return to purity, we can justify this by identifying these attributes not with internal state but with standard methods that permit access and update. However, it is convenient to talk about the attributes directly when no confusion can arise. In many books and articles on object-oriented programming this point is insisted on very strongly. However, the examples given are usually very low-level programming abstractions such as sets, bags, collections, stacks and so on. For example, a stack is described as a data structure with four methods: push, pop, top and empty. That is to say that a stack is an ordered list of things that can be added to and taken away from at one end only and can report the value held at that end. Access to the stack data is only via these methods and there is no need to describe the implementation, which might be as a linked list or as an array with an associated stack pointer. Stack has no visible attributes, although top and empty could be regarded as such. Figure 1.3(a) shows an example of a stack of integers while Figure 1.3(b) describes the protocol of a stack object.

For commercial systems the objects are far more complex and it is impossible to think of abstract concepts like 'employee' or 'invoice' without comprehending their attributes. Purists may continue to think of attributes as identified with two standard methods per attribute A: get A and put A.

Instances of objects (or strictly of classes or 'object types') are analogous to records in a database. They comprise concrete data having the properties of the object. All instances of an object have the same set of attributes and methods. This may not be true for abstract classes because class inheritance includes the potential for specializations of classes to delete or acquire extra attributes and methods. For example, a stack is a special case of a list but has no methods for concatenation. Another example might be a pet fish which inherits the attributes of fish in general but additionally has an owner.

The attributes of an instance are sometimes referred to as 'instance variables' and those of a class as 'class variables'. Class variables are shared by *all* instances of the class. For example, the number of instances of a class is a suitable candidate for a class variable. We also distinguish **class methods** from **instance methods**.

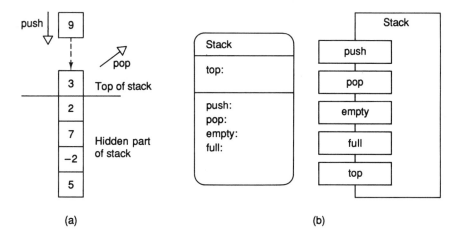

(a)   (b)

Figure 1.3 (a) Physical representation of a stack of integers; **(b)** The protocol of a stack object in two common notations. Note that the attribute 'top' has to become a method for getting the value on top of the stack to use the rightmost notation.

Again, calculating a total or average across all instances of a class would be a class method.

Under the general heading of abstraction we will encounter many seemingly abstruse technical terms such as encapsulation, polymorphism and genericity. Let us look at the meaning of some of these terms. In doing so we will uncover more of the general features of the object-oriented style.

Encapsulation or, equivalently, **information hiding**, refers to the practice of including within an object everything it needs, and furthermore doing this in such a way that no other object need ever be aware of this internal structure. Thus, in the example in Figure 1.2 the details of the ChangeSalary algorithm may be hidden inside the Employee object in such a way that other objects or even its users are unable to access the details. Similarly certain data, such as salaries, may be private to an object. The implementation of data storage is always private to the object. It is not necessary to know whether the salary is stored as packed decimal, floating point or integer to access or change it. The same applies to methods: their implementation details are private to the object, only their behaviour is visible to other objects. Objects do have internal state but it is not directly accessible. One consequence of this principle is that clients of the object are not exposed to danger when its implementation is changed as long as the interface is not also changed. The hidden or encapsulated parts of an object are its **private implementation**; the visible attributes and methods are said to be **public**.

Data are obtained from an object in object-oriented systems in one way and one way only: by sending the object a **message**. A message consists of an address (which object or objects to send it to) and an instruction, consisting of a method name and zero or more parameters. If the addressee contains a method for which the instruction makes sense then an answer is returned to the sending object. Thus I can send the integer object 3 the message 'add 5' and expect the answer '8' to come back. If I were to send the message 'report salary' to the Employee named 'Erica', I might get back either that very information or something like 'You are not authorized to see Erica's salary' as the hidden procedure may involve an access to some security tables. If the addressee does not contain a method which can process the message then a standard error message is returned. For example, such an error would result if the message CalculateAge were sent to 3, an instance of type Integer. Recall that the methods encapsulated within an object define exactly which messages that object is able to process successfully. The set of messages an object can respond sensibly to is sometimes called its **protocol**. The message's name is sometimes called its **selector**. A message may be interpreted in different ways by different receivers that decide exactly what will happen. In strongly, statically typed programming languages the compiler can ensure that objects cannot receive illegal messages. Dynamic binding implies that objects must each take on the responsibility for protecting themselves against such messages. Note that messages arrive at the interface of an object, whereas it is the hidden implementation which dispatches messages. Steve Cook (Cook and Daniels, 1992) uses the wonderful metaphor of boiled eggs, where the yolk represents the data structures, the white the implementations of methods and the shell the interface or protocol (Daniels and Cook, 1993; Graham, 1993b). Messages originate in the white, collect data from the yolk and are then sent to the shell referred to in its address.

Thus the terms encapsulation, data abstraction, information hiding and message passing all refer to much the same thing. However, some authorities distinguish between mere information hiding and what is known as 'set abstraction'. Set abstraction refers to the notion that concrete instances are regarded as objects belonging to a set with properties defined separately and inheriting those properties. For example, Fred is an instance of a man and he has brown eyes, but he inherits most of his properties from the abstract set of men including the attribute 'colour of eyes'. Another feature of objects is that they have unique identification for their entire lifetime. Object identity gives rise to some severe problems and some great benefits in database systems. This is discussed further in Chapter 6.

Other terms often encountered are **polymorphism** and **operator overloading,** which both mean pretty much the same thing: that is, they refer to the ability to use the same symbol for different purposes when the context is clear. For example, sending the message 'add 5' to an integer and to a real number actually invokes quite different procedures but it is convenient to use the same notation '+' for both purposes; it aids understanding and makes the language easier to learn and remember. Similarly 'delete' may be required to do different things to different objects, especially if some integrity checking must be performed prior to deletion of a database record. Formally, polymorphism – having many forms – means the ability of a variable or function to take different forms at run time, or more specifically the ability to refer to instances of various classes. This is illustrated in Figure 1.4. Overloading is the special case where two different operations merely share the same name, such as the operation 'open' applied to files or to windows. It is illustrated in Figure 1.5.

In point of fact, Smalltalk cheats slightly with its notion of polymorphism. The pure concept is better exemplified in functional languages, such as ML, where functions are permitted to have arguments of different types. While the understanding of polymorphism presented above will be adequate for the purposes of this text, there is a large theoretical literature on the subject in which many fine distinctions are made. Cardelli and Wegner (1985) distinguish several kinds of polymorphism. At the highest level the distinction is made between *ad hoc* and universal polymorphism. *Ad hoc* polymorphism refers to using the same symbol for semantically unrelated operations. Operator overloading fits into this category if, for example, we use the symbol + for addition of integers and matrices. Another kind of *ad hoc* polymorphism, called coercion, allows operations to work on input of mixed type, as when adding an integer to a real. Universal polymorphism splits into parametric and inclusion (or inheritance) polymorphism, the latter of which is dealt with in Section 1.3.2. Parametric polymorphism refers to the ability to substitute arguments from a range of types into a function call. It may, for our present purposes, be safely confused with genericity. The types of polymorphism are summarized in Table 1.1.

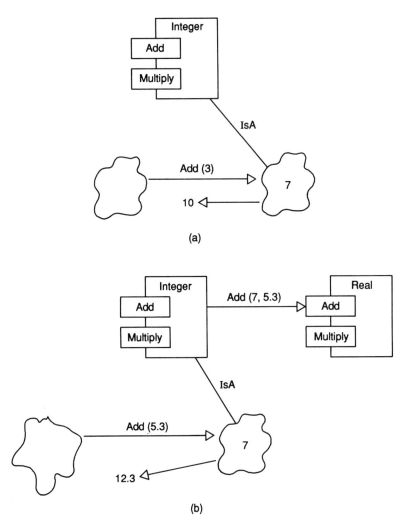

Figure 1.4 One way in which dynamic binding and polymorphism can be implemented: **(a)** The message Add(3) is sent to the integer 7, which inherits the addition procedure from the class integer; **(b)** The message Add(5.3) cannot be handled by Integer, so the routine is collected from Real.

Genericity is the ability to define parametrized modules and is found in many languages that support encapsulation, such as Ada. An example of a generic type is a list, where the list could be a list of names, a list of integers or a list of something specific like names of employees. The actual type is only determined by context. In languages such as Ada, Modula-2 and even ALGOL, it refers to the ability to define parametrized modules. Usually the parameters are types. Generic messages allow the creation of reusable components and frameworks by removing

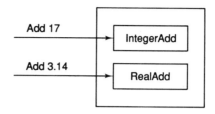

Figure 1.5 Operator overloading (*ad hoc* polymorphism) applied to addition.

the dependency of the calling routine on what is called. Genericity and inheritance may be viewed as *alternative* techniques for providing extensible and reusable modules, but genericity is far more limited in practice as we will see later. An example of genericity is shown in Figure 1.6.

The outstanding issue is how to identify objects in a real application. This issue is one that provokes deep philosophical debate and often much confusion. An empiricist view maintains that objects are out there just waiting to be perceived, and an extreme version holds that this is easy to do. In fact, the OED has it that an object is something 'thrown before the mind'. A phenomenologist view, on the contrary, recognizes that perception is an active, creative process and that objects come both from our consciousness and from the world through a dialectical process. An even richer view suggests that real-world abstractions are a reflection of social relations and human productive processes as well as having an objective basis in the real world. We will be returning to this thorny issue in later chapters. For now, we merely state that objects may be apprehended by an analyst familiar with an application in many different ways and that choosing the 'best' representation is a fundamental contribution that human intelligence always makes to computer systems. Some objects correspond directly to real-world objects such as employees, but others such as stacks correspond to invented abstractions. Abstractions sum up the relevant divisions of the domain. What is relevant may depend on the application, but this will compromise the reusability of the abstraction and so the designer should try to think of abstractions with as wide an applicability as possible. On the other hand, care should be taken not to compromise efficiency with absurdly and gratuitously general objects. Thus, when defining the Employee object we do not include 'planet of origin' among its attributes nor knowledge of galactic credits in the salary payment routines, although some future systems designer may yet exist to regret our decision. What such a designer would have to do is use inheritance, to which we now turn.

Table 1.1 Wegner's classification of types of polymorphism.

Ad hoc polymorphism	Universal polymorphism
overloading	parametric polymorphism
coercion	inclusion polymorphism

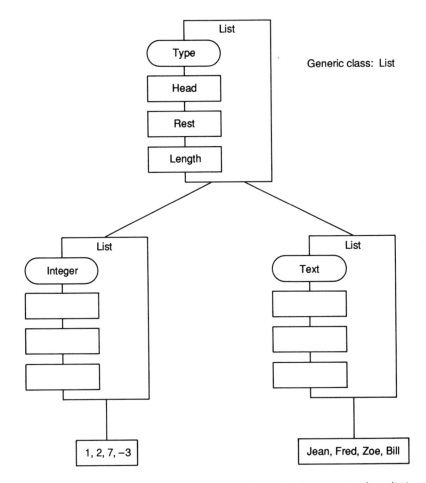

Figure 1.6 Using genericity to simulate inheritance for the generic class 'list'.

As we shall see in the next chapter the chief reason for emphasizing abstraction and encapsulation is to deliver code and specifications which are reusable. Using an object via its specification as an abstract type or class means that if its internal aspect undergoes modification, other parts of the system will not be affected. Equally, if other system objects have their implementation changed this object should not be affected.

1.3.2 Inheritance

The other primary defining feature of an object-oriented system is the way it deals with the structural and semantic relationships between instances and classes (or types) and eliminates the redundancy of storing the same datum or procedure more often than necessary. The key notion is that of an inheritance or classification hierarchy. Whereas the ideas of abstraction dealt with in the last section are largely derived from work in programming language theory and practice, the ideas of inheritance have their roots in the study of artificial intelligence (AI), where semantic networks (Quillian, 1967) and frames (Minsky, 1975) are techniques for representing knowledge about stereotypical concepts and objects, and the relationship between more general and more specialized concepts is handled through the inheritance of properties and procedures. Concepts of inheritance have also been current in data modelling, where the notion of entity subtypes is widely used.

We will consider two main kinds of hierarchy in this book, the **inheritance**, **classification**, **generalization** or **kind-of** hierarchy and the **composition**, **aggregation** or **part-of** hierarchy. In general we could consider hierarchies based on other semantic primitives, such as ownership, liking, authorship or debt, but the two chosen seem to be the main ones required for commercial systems. Next, we shall have to relax the requirement that inheritance fits into a strict hierarchy and deal with inheritance networks.

If an object has a type then it can be thought of as an instance of a class. For example, Fido is an instance of the class Dog. We can go further and notice that a dog is a special case of the class Mammal, a mammal is a Vertebrate, and so on, eventually reconstructing the entire Linnaean order. Formally, we include among the attributes of each instance a special attribute (or *slot* in the AI literature, where objects are often called *frames*) called the **IsA** slot. This attribute contains the name of the class to which the instance belongs: its parent in the hierarchy. Even classes may have parents and the convention here is to call the special attribute **AKO** (A Kind Of). The advantage of formalizing this observation in this way is that lower-level classes and objects may inherit shared properties and methods, eliminating the need to store them in every instance. For example, the attribute BirthDate is shared by all subtypes of Person, so we need not have mentioned it explicitly for Employee if we had included AKO: Person in the object specification.

Figure 1.7 illustrates a typical classification hierarchy.

There is an important difference between the kind of inheritance discussed under the heading of object-oriented programming and that supported in artificial intelligence. Normally, in object-oriented programming work, objects inherit methods and attributes from their superior classes, but they do not inherit the values of attributes. An instance inherits merely the ability to have a certain type of value. In AI and in some database applications, on the other hand, the ability to inherit values is supported. Let me illustrate this by introducing an example which we will return to regularly throughout this book.

Aardvark Leisure Products is a company that sells toys and leisure goods to the general public. It is in the process of constructing a stock and customer information system that goes under the name of SACIS. Aardvark wants to be first in more ways than its position in the telephone directory, so it has decided to take an object-oriented approach to the development of SACIS. It is also committed to making the system easy to use, so that customers and shop staff can use it in sales

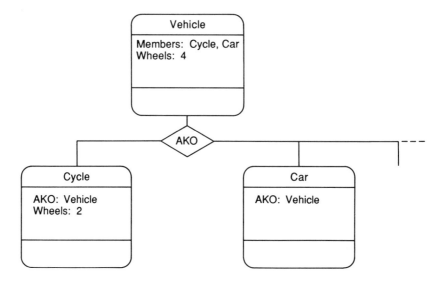

Figure 1.7 A cycle is a kind of (AKO) vehicle, as is a car. Cycle overrides the inherited value for Wheels. Car and Cycle, and possibly other classes, are members of Vehicle.

situations. This means that the user interface will be very important and that a certain amount of intelligence must be built in so that the system can give help in matching products to customer needs. Thus, SACIS will be an expert object-oriented database system. Figure 1.8 shows the high-level structure of SACIS.

Consider some object classes needed in SACIS. They must at least include Person, Customer, Adult, Child, StockItem, SportsItem, Toy, Shop, Employee and perhaps Supplier. Both Toy and SportsItem are kinds of StockItem. Suppose that there is also a class called Frisbee and that F123 is a particular frisbee. StockItem has a class method called 'report stock level' that is inherited by Toy and Frisbee. If we send the message 'report stock level' to Frisbee the inherited method looks in the StockLevel attribute and returns a number representing the number of frisbees in stock. It clearly makes no sense to send this message to F123; the method is overridden. Individual instances can deal with messages. In this case the message 'delete' might be sent to F123 when it is sold, or better for future customer support reasons, it could be sent the message 'mark yourself as sold' with the purchaser's identifier as a parameter. F123, in conventional object-oriented programming, inherits all the attributes of Frisbee but not their values. Similarly, Frisbee inherits the attributes of Toy. In an AI system we would allow inheritance of values, in particular of default values. Here is why. Toy has the attribute 'safe for children' and it is reasonable to assume that most toys are thus safe. Thus, by default, this attribute may be set to have the value 'yes'. I think it is useful for both the class Frisbee and the instance F123 to inherit this value so that the customer can enquire unequivocally 'is this one safe?' and receive the unequivocal answer 'yes'. F124 which is a customized frisbee with chains attached to the perimeter would have the

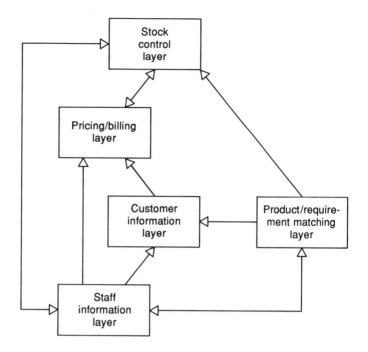

Figure 1.8 The high-level structure of SACIS.

value overridden. In languages such as Smalltalk and C++ all this has to be done in the application. In AI systems some of the work is done for you.

Classification structures of this type implement inclusion polymorphism. That is, messages sent to Toy will be understood by Frisbee and F123 unless overridden.

Not all structural relationships have the semantics of classification, however, and practical object-oriented languages need to be able to deal with situations involving compositional structures. The most typical case is a parts explosion for an object such as a car, which is composed of a body, wheels and engine. In turn the wheel may be composed of axle, spokes, rim and tyre. The notation of Figure 1.9 will be further explained in Chapter 8. Other associative structures, such as ownership or even analogy, could be modelled in the same way.

Lastly, returning to the inheritance semantics, we have to take note of the case where an object or class may have two parents. A good example is a guppy which, as a typical pet fish, is an exemplar of both the class Fish and the class Pet. A guppy should inherit the properties of both classes. This ability is referred to as **multiple inheritance.** The difficulty with multiple inheritance is that on rare occasion the properties inherited from two (or more) parents may be directly or partially contradictory. For example, over-simplifying slightly, a fish lives in the sea and a pet lives in the owner's home, so where does a guppy live? There are many solutions to this problem in practical implementations. The most usual is to allow the system to report such a conflict to the user and ask for a value for the offending

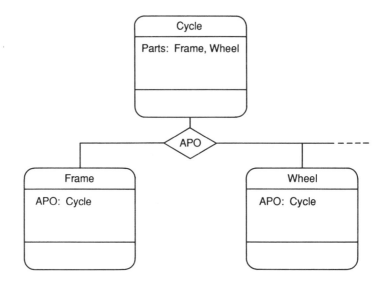

Figure 1.9 A composition hierarchy showing that Cycles are made of Frames and Wheels (and possibly other components). APO stands for A Part Of.

attribute. Alternatively, some systems allow the designer to write a procedure to resolve such conflicts automatically. There have even been suggestions for combining the answers into a composite or compromise solution; see for example the treatment given in Appendix I, which is partly based on the work of Graham and Jones (1987). Other suggestions include maximizing scepticism and assuming the values are unknown (Horty *et al.*, 1990).

Two types of conflict are possible: name conflict and value conflict. The literature on object-oriented programming usually only deals with name conflict, whereas the artificial intelligence literature tends to deal more fully with value conflict as intended in the previous paragraph. Value conflict occurs when an attribute inherits two different values from parent classes. These might be default values if the object is itself a class, or actual instance values where instance-level inheritance (IsA) is supported. Name conflict occurs when two parent classes contain different attributes or methods with the same name. Name conflicts usually arise in relation to method inheritance and Wegner (1987) lists the following seven conflict strategies used in the FLAVORS system.

- Call the most specific method.
- Call all methods in their order of precedence or in reverse order.
- Execute the first method to return a non-null value.
- Execute all methods and return a list of their results.
- Compute the sum of all returned values.
- Call all *before* demons, then call all *after* demons.
- Use the second argument to select one method or a subset of methods.

We will return to the issue of conflict strategies in Chapter 8. The notion of demons will be explained later in the text. Roughly, a demon is a procedure which fires when a datum changes and the terms *before* and *after* refer to whether the procedure fires at the beginning of a change or when it is completed; rather like pre- and post-conditions.

Inherited methods can be **overridden** in certain circumstances. An example would be the Delete method inherited by Employee from the general class Object which carries methods for most routine operations with objects of all types. If some security or authorization checking is to be maintained we may wish a special method for deletion to override the standard one.

In SACIS an example of the need for multiple inheritance might arise with the class YoungCustomer which must inherit the properties and behaviour of both Customer and Child (see Figure 1.10). Note that some children may not yet be customers and that some customers are adults. YoungCustomer inherits properties and methods from Child, which ensure that they are not sold dangerous items, and these

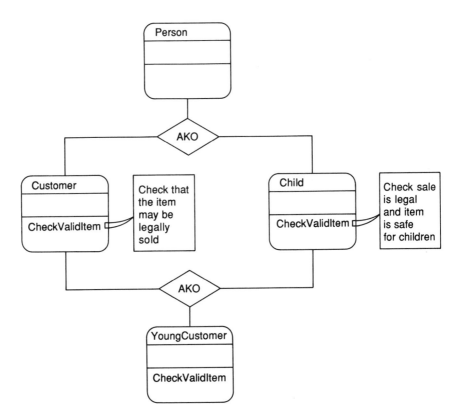

Figure 1.10 Multiple Inheritance in SACIS. Note that CheckValidItem is a different procedure for Customer and for Child, because the former checks for a legal item and the latter for a safe and legal item.

must override the more lax conditions inherited from Customer. This again shows the need for conflict resolution strategies in systems which support multiple inheritance. An example where the strategy is even more complicated arises in the case of items, such as bicycles, which are both toys and sports items. Typically a toy is a low-cost item with a short life expectation and no maintenance programme. Sports gear, on the other hand, is often costly and in need of regular maintenance.

As we have seen, the classical object-oriented programming view has it that classes inherit methods and attributes or 'instance variables' (the ability to have a value of a certain type), whereas in artificial intelligence the instances may actually inherit values. In this book we shall prefer the latter view. This means we are better able to deal with semantic notions, such as defaults. It also posits the distinction between AKO and IsA relationships. Inheritance of features by a class is treated as an AKO (A Kind Of) relationship and inheritance by instances as an IsA relationship (see Figure 1.11). Again, some treatments of object-oriented programming fail to make this distinction adequately. The distinction may be viewed as analogous to the difference between inclusion and membership in set theory.

Inheritance delivers extensibility. A new kind of object can be added without the need to rewrite existing code. Thus, our hypothetical employee from Ganymede (a moon of Jupiter) could be accommodated by a new object, 'alien employee', inheriting the properties and methods of 'employee' but adding extra features and overriding others. Inheritance thus ensures that functions are only ever coded once.

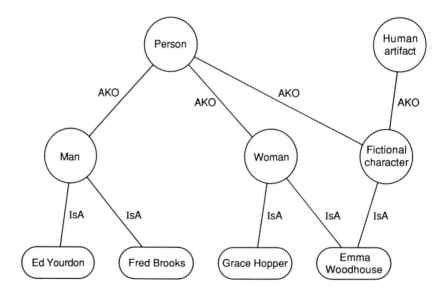

Figure 1.11 AKO and IsA links in a classification structure.

1.3.3 Encapsulation, inheritance and object-orientation

The astute reader will have noticed that Section 1.3.1 could not avoid references to inheritance ahead of time. Annoying as this may be, it shows clearly how closely the two concepts of encapsulation and inheritance are interwoven. The connexion is mediated by concepts such as polymorphism, overriding, object identity and message passing.

Inheritance is often viewed as merely a special case of polymorphism, but the concept is so rich and natural that I think this view does not do it justice. As long as we are dealing with programming languages then this type-theoretic view is sound and useful. In the context of specification and design it is more limited. Value inheritance, as discussed above, does not fit neatly into this view.

One of the key benefits claimed for object-oriented approaches is reusability, as we shall see in the next chapter. However, it is necessary to be extremely cautious about this claim. Certainly, abstraction delivers reusability but it is also true, as Snyder (1987) has argued, that inheritance can compromise this objective. The reason for this is that inheritance sometimes exposes implementation details to an object's clients. Also the hierarchy itself may be exposed so that changes to it cannot be safely made. For example, if a stack is defined as a special case of the class 'list' it may inherit the implementation of the 'head' operation as its method for 'top' and merely exclude the irrelevant operations such as 'length'. If the implementation of stack is changed to a more efficient direct one there is a danger that its clients may depend on the old implementation as a special kind of list. This problem becomes even more severe when multiple inheritance is permitted. Fortunately, as Snyder shows, careful design procedures can get round this difficulty. Page-Jones (1992) designates this problem 'polymorphism connascence' (see Chapter 8). On the other hand, inheritance is partly responsible for the possibility of reuse since without inheritance it is unlikely that many classes could be reused exactly as defined.

We should note that including APO in a composition structure or the attribute Members: in a classification structure, as in Figures 1.7 and 1.9, compromises reusability, because every time a composite changes its components or a class has new members added those attributes would have to change. Therefore, it is necessary to state that these are not part of the model, merely notational conveniences designed as an aid to navigation. It is envisaged that they are only used when automated support is available to update their values when composite objects are defined or members are added to inheritance structures.

The use of complex inheritance schemes certainly complicates a system and may compromise reusability. The compensatory benefit of extensibility is further enhanced by the capture of the structural semantics of the application. The more complex a system is, the more difficult it is to maintain, and the more semantically rich it is, the more specific and therefore less reusable its components will be. However, there are some applications where a simple solution is a bad solution. Using complex inheritance schemes may then be justified. Applications in AI and expert systems where such schemes have been developed are typical of such applications. As expert systems techniques find their way into conventional systems this issue will have to be faced by more and more analysts and designers. For example, in SACIS the problem of matching product to client is seen as requiring an expert systems solution.

Before closing this section on basic terminology we need a few more miscellaneous definitions.

Actor systems introduce an idea that is sometimes used in object-oriented ones, the idea of **delegation**. Delegation is a form of classless inheritance. It allows objects to delegate to other objects permission to perform operations on their behalf. This helps prevent the problem referred to above, in that descendants do not need to inherit the implementation of their ancestors. It enables objects to transform their behaviour without being constrained by class membership. Actor languages are usually very low-level languages compared to object-oriented programming languages.

Another key concept of object-orientation is that of **self-recursion** or self-reference. This means that objects can send messages their own methods recursively; or send messages to themselves. In Smalltalk the reserved word 'self' is used to refer to the object on behalf of which an operation is being executed, rather than the class which contains the definition of the operation. This means that the operation is bound to the object only at run time. Another way of looking at it is that an object must know its own unique identity, and be able store itself as the value of one of its own attributes. For example, in the class of employees the attribute 'ManagedBy:' for the instance 'J.Smith' may contain the value 'J.Smith', if J. Smith happens to be the managing director of Aardvark. In fact, every object must contain a reference to any object which it may send messages to.

Thus, an object-oriented system for programming, design or analysis will be expected to provide facilities for representing encapsulation and inheritance in the manner outlined above and contain a notion of object identity and self. For each object one has to declare which internal data – aspects of its state – it may alter explicitly. Its external powers are completely circumscribed by message passing.

Now we can define **object-based** programming as that style of programming supporting encapsulation and object identity; that is, methods and attributes are hidden within and private to objects and these objects have unique identifiers. There is little or no support for classes in the sense that set abstraction is not supported. In other words, objects do not belong to abstract classes which have a separate identity. Further, there is no support for inheritance. Ada is a typical object-based language.

Class-based languages, such as CLU, include the notion of set abstraction at the instance/class level but do not support inheritance between abstract classes which may have no concrete instances. Class-based systems include all the features of object-based ones: they inherit them.

Object-oriented systems are defined by inheriting the features of both object-based and class-based systems and additionally having full inheritance between classes and instances, and classes and classes; that is, both instances and classes inherit the methods and attributes of the class(es) to which they belong.

Some object-oriented systems permit instances to inherit the values of attributes set at the class level. Object-oriented systems also support self-recursion.

This equips us with all the necessary terminology to begin to look at the practical advantages and pitfalls of the object-oriented approach, before dealing with some specific languages and asking how well they match up to the theoretical ideal presented above. The Glossary may be used as a terminological *aide-mémoire* and the reader may wish to note that acronyms are expanded in the Subject Index.

☱ 1.4 Summary

In this chapter I have introduced most of the basic terminology of object-oriented methods and programming. We have also begun to discuss the technology in its historical and commercial context, looking at whence it came and the key concerns of software engineering that it addresses:

- ■ ensuring the reusability and extensibility of modules;
- ■ industrializing the software development process;
- ■ making systems with open interfaces which can share resources;
- ■ capturing more of the meaning of a specification.

An object-oriented language or system supports two main features:

- ■ abstraction or encapsulation
- ■ inheritance

Abstraction is the process of identifying relevant objects in the application and ignoring the irrelevant background. Abstraction delivers reusability through encapsulation or information hiding. Encapsulation consists in hiding the implementation of objects and declaring publicly the specification of their behaviour through a set of attributes and operations. The data structures and methods that implement these are private to the object.

Object types or classes are similar to data types and to entity types with encapsulated methods. Data and methods are encapsulated and hidden by objects. Classes may have concrete instances. The term *object* means either a class or an instance in this book.

Inheritance is the ability to deal with generalization and specialization or classification. Subclasses inherit attributes and methods from their superclasses and may add others of their own or override those inherited. In many object-oriented programming languages, instances inherit all and only the properties of their class. Multiple inheritance occurs when an object is an instance of more than one class. Inheritance delivers extensibility, but can compromise reusability. Multiple inheritance is powerful but introduces additional problems and so should be used parsimoniously.

Objects communicate only by message passing. Polymorphism or overloading increases readability and programmer productivity but may lead to slower implementations.

$$\begin{array}{lll}
\text{object-based} & = \text{encapsulation} & + \text{object identity} \\
\text{class-based} & = \text{object-based} & + \text{set abstraction} \\
\text{object-oriented} & = \text{class-based} & + \text{inheritance} + \text{self-recursion}
\end{array}$$

1.5 Bibliographical notes

The seminal works on object-oriented programming are probably Dahl and Nygaard (1966), Kay and Goldberg (1977), Ingalls (1978) and Goldberg and Robson (1983).

A number of good introductory texts on object-oriented programming and its benefits, though not on object-oriented methods in general, exist. The best in my opinion is Meyer (1988), whose main aim is describing the language Eiffel but which also has a good high-level introduction to object-orientation in general. Another excellent book of the same type is Cox and Novobilski (1991), which sets out to describe the language Objective-C, but has a good high-level introduction to object-oriented concepts and is highly readable and recommended. Neither book contains much material on object-oriented analysis or databases, but Meyer has interesting things to say about object-oriented design. Booch (1991) is a first rate introduction to object-oriented programming, concepts and design. Blair *et al.* (1991) is a collection of papers at an introductory level covering a wide range of the issues of object-orientation and is a very good introduction to basic concepts. The best management-level introductions to object technology to appear so far are both by Taylor (1992, 1992a).

Those readers who wish to delve deeper may explore the huge volume of research papers, some of which are listed in the bibliography. Two useful and accessible collections are Shriver and Wegner (1987) and Kim and Lochovsky (1989). Both contain a deal of very technical and academic material. Mandrioli and Meyer (1992) is representative of more recent collections of this type. Blair *et al.* (1991) combines several good introductory papers. The proceedings of the annual OOPSLA and TOOLS conferences are always a useful insight into the state of the art.

Berard (1993) castigates me, along with practically every other author on the subject incidentally, for confusing the concepts of abstraction, encapsulation and information hiding, as indeed I have done deliberately in this book. Information hiding (Parnas, 1972) is the principle that modules should conceal design decisions concerning themselves from each other. Berard defines abstraction as the process by which we decide what information should be visible and what hidden. Encapsulation is merely the packaging strategy used to implement these decisions. He points out that information hiding is not necessarily good and certainly is not an idea unique to object-oriented programming. While I accept these somewhat pedantic distinctions I remain convinced that to blur them in an introductory text of this nature will serve not to confuse but to clarify.

There has also been a great deal of useful material in the trade press. Two journals are worthy of mention as sources of both theoretical and application information. They are the *Journal of Object-Oriented Programming* (JOOP) and the *Hotline on Object-Oriented Technology* (HOOT). Perhaps the journal offering the broadest coverage at present is *Object Magazine*.

The distinction between object-based, class-based and object-oriented systems was originally made by Wegner in an article to be found in the volume referred to above (Shriver and Wegner, 1987), but is now standard terminology.

In the literature on programming languages some of the terms used in this book have specialized meanings, subtly different from the rather everyday sense preferred here. For example, in Smalltalk, the terms abstract class and meta-class refer to different concepts, namely the concepts of their instances having no concrete interpretation and that of a class whose instances are classes, respectively. Similarly, most other contemporary texts identify objects and instances. I have not chosen to violate this convention lightly as, I hope, the remainder of this book will show.

2

The benefits of object-oriented programming and methods

The only end of writing is to enable the readers better to enjoy life or better to endure it.
Dr Johnson (Review of Soame Jenyns' The Enquiry into the Nature and Origin of Evil)

This chapter examines the benefits usually claimed for object-oriented methods and the extent to which they are attainable for commercial system developers and users. It also points out some actual or potential limitations, problems and pitfalls associated with the technology. Lastly, we will examine some reported results from actual projects.

2.1 The benefits

Object-oriented methods in general and object-oriented programming in particular proffer several benefits to the designer and user of software. These benefits are of much the same general character as those offered by structured programming and design, but go much further in some directions and, in doing so, lead to the questioning of many of the basic assumptions of the structured methods school of thought.

Anticipating our analysis but drawing on the remarks made in the last chapter about information hiding and inheritance, the principal benefits are as follows.

- Well designed objects in object-oriented systems are the basis for systems to be assembled largely from reusable modules, leading to higher productivity. This is probably the most publicized benefit of object technology.

- Reusing existing classes that have been tested in the field on earlier projects leads to systems which are of higher quality, meet business requirements better and contain fewer bugs.
- Object-oriented programming, and inheritance in particular, makes it possible to define clearly and use modules that are functionally incomplete and then allow their extension without upsetting the operation of other modules or their clients. This makes systems more flexible, more easily extensible and less costly to maintain.
- The message-passing convention for communication between objects means that interface descriptions between modules and external systems become much easier. It also facilitates the description and construction of graphical user interfaces and distributed systems.
- Partitioning systems on the basis of encapsulated object types helps with the problem of scalability. There is no reason why effort should increase exponentially with project size and complexity as is the case with conventional systems. This topic is taken up in Chapter 9.
- In the same way the partitioning of work in a project has a natural basis and should be easier. Analysis and design by partitioning a domain into objects corresponding to a solution-oriented view of their real-world counterparts is often more natural than a top-down functional decomposition. Object-oriented systems should scale up better from small to large.
- Information hiding helps to build secure systems.
- The data-centred design approach of object-oriented analysis, because it subsumes process as well, is able to capture more of the semantics of a model in implementable form. This is very important for commercial, and especially database systems, as we will see later in Chapters 5, 6 and 8.
- Formal specification methods may be made to blend with object-oriented design. I will have more to say on this in Chapter 10.
- Object-orientation is a tool for managing complexity.
- System evolution and maintenance problems are mitigated by the strong partitioning resulting from encapsulation and uniform object interfaces.
- Object-oriented systems are potentially capable of capturing far more of the meaning of an application: its semantics. Since object-oriented methods are mainly concerned with modelling systems they can be used to carry out scenario modelling and facilitate changes within the business. This property leads to greater reversibility in the end product and enhances the possibility of reverse engineering systems and of tracing features back to requirements.
- Some applications have defeated other approaches and object technology seems to be the only way to build them efficiently. Examples are graphical user interfaces, distributed systems and workflow systems.

Software production or software engineering is concerned *inter alia* with the manufacture of high-quality systems for a reasonable outlay of effort and thus cost. Attempts to attack the issue of software quality have come from innovations in programming languages and from several structured approaches to system development. When there are claims that up to 80% of the cost of a system is accounted for by software costs, and that even skilled programmers have been generally unable to produce resilient, correct code, then something is seriously amiss. Structured methods, 4GLs, CASE tools, prototyping techniques, database systems and code generators all represent attacks on this problem. The extent to which structured methods have succeeded is questioned in a report from Butler Cox in 1990 that showed that the users of, for example, structured design were actually impairing both their productivity and the quality of the end product. 4GLs, it is claimed, may improve productivity by up to 20%, but possibly at the expense of performance. A more recent Butler Cox (now CSC Index) report confirms and refines these findings. In really complex applications some authorities have claimed that the use of 4GLs actually degrades productivity as well, due mainly to the restrictiveness of very high-level languages and the need to switch to and from 3GL coding.

The impetus to structured methods came largely from the realization that many systems were either not finished, not used or were delivered with major errors. Figure 2.1 shows the fate of a selection of US defence projects in the 1970s. It must be remembered that these systems were mainly mainframe systems written in languages such as COBOL and it is probably impossible to make a fair comparison with systems developed with modern tools in the 1990s. However, the point that something was wrong cannot be avoided.

Lietz and Swanson (1979) take up the same issue in a slightly different way and analyse the reasons for maintenance requests in a survey of nearly 500 major projects as shown in Figure 2.2. The significance of this breakdown is that most change requests are, where they are not a result of incorrect specification, unavoidable. The 'changes in user requirements' heading may of course be partly a surro-

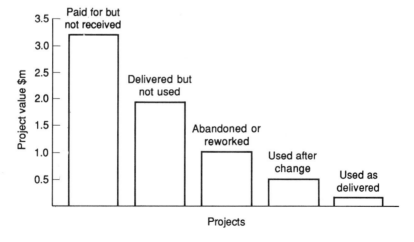

Figure 2.1 The fate of US defence projects according to US government statistics. (Source: Connell and Shafer (1989))

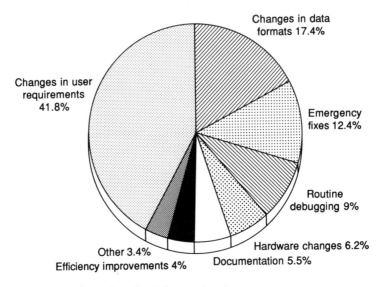

Figure 2.2 Breakdown of maintenance costs.

gate for inadequate specification, but also reflects the dynamic character of modern business. In a changing world software systems must be adaptable, and this is precisely the point addressed by the ability of object-oriented systems to be extensible and modular. Second only to these types of changes come changes in data formats, and here encapsulation offers the greatest promise as a technique for making systems resilient to changes in implementation. Recently, British Telecom changed the format for London telephone numbers. Software written in an object-oriented style suffers less from such a change since the internal implementation of 'phone_no' is hidden and the only changes that occur should be within this object, with other parts of systems not needing major changes. Of course there are always limitations to these benefits. Suppose, for example, that one's printed stationery was not physically wide enough to take the new codes and that the printing machinery was not capable (physically) of printing smaller typefaces. Another point to be made about the need for constant change relates to the way *ad hoc* or panic changes are made. Emergency fixes in conventional code often produce unexpected effects. In object-oriented systems this may still happen but, I claim, will do so less often and in a way that is eminently more traceable since the changes are either encapsulated within an object, affecting its internal implementation and visible only through the interface, or as a result of different routing of messages.

Prototyping is, I believe, an important tool for obtaining correct specifications. This is discussed in detail in Chapter 9 where we will deal with emerging trends in the management of systems development. Properly controlled prototyping can be used within conventional software developments but, when combined with object-oriented methods, offers additional benefits. Object-oriented programming languages, such as Smalltalk and certain object-oriented database systems, are good prototyping languages and the existence of reusable code modules in any language supports faster prototype construction just as it does faster final system development. When prototyping is used as a specification tool this synergy applies to object-oriented designs and specifications as well as to programming languages.

The point mentioned above about emergency fixes points, in my view, to a major problem with code generators. The idea of CASE tools which generate code and ensure adequate compatible documentation of all developments is that all changes are made in a systematic manner. If the duty programmer on the night-shift is faced with an emergency then often the only choice is to reach in and manipulate the source code directly; there just isn't time to go through the rigmarole of altering the DFDs, ER model and documentation. As time goes on, therefore, the specification inevitably moves out of line with the code and changes become harder and harder. Advocates of code generators usually respond that this is a managerial issue and that such changes should be outlawed. Real life, however, dictates that users will not tolerate their systems being unavailable for hours or days while such laudable procedures are followed. Object-oriented systems address this question by making it much easier to trace emergency fixes, so that they can be 'reverse engineered' into the specification later. While we are on the subject of CASE tools, another problem worth mentioning is a common difficulty faced by managers of very large projects using them. CASE tools of the 'code generating' sort require that most effort is spent in the analysis and architectural design stages. This leaves little time in the project plan for fixing errors that arise when the code is tested. Most project managers are not prepared to take the risk of finding that, at the very end of the project, they have to extend deadlines to deal with potentially huge unforeseen problems. The author has seen several projects abandon CASE because of this fear factor. An object-oriented CASE tool that generates code certainly suffers from the same problem, but the enforced modularity supplied by encapsulation means that modules can often be tested independently and early on in the project, giving an opportunity for a confident assessment of the cost of last-minute code fixes.

Top-down decomposition has long been advocated as a cure for many of our design ills, although I suspect that its original proponents, people such as Tom De Marco and Ed Yourdon, never really intended it as a device to guide design but advocated it as a method of *describing* systems, for which it indeed is very useful. Object-oriented methods are not top-down. They recognize that real systems often do not have a top. What, for example, is the single top-level function of an operating system? Work partitioning is accomplished by packaging objects, not by breaking tasks down into smaller and smaller components; the latter is an activity that is nearly always highly application specific and therefore leads to non-reusable modules. Within an object, of course, functional decomposition can still be used to specify a method, but more about that in Chapter 8.

QUALITY   According to Meyer (1988), Sommerville (1989) and several other authorities, the quality of a software system is to be evaluated according to several criteria. We may arguably consider the following thirteen quality issues as a comprehensive list.

- *Correctness*   Programs should meet their specification correctly.
- *Resilience and reliability (robustness)*   Programs should be robust even in abnormal conditions.
- *Maintainability*   Programs should be easy to evolve and extend as requirements alter.
- *Reusability and generality*   Programs should be built of reusable modules.
- *Interoperability*   Programs should be readily compatible with other systems; they should be 'open systems'.
- *Efficiency.*
- *Portability*   Programs should be portable across hardware and operating systems.
- *Verifiability.*
- *Security*   Data, knowledge and even functions may require selective and effective concealment.
- *Integrity*   Systems need protection against inconsistent updates.
- *Friendliness*   Systems must be easy to use for a majority of users without becoming inappropriately verbose.
- *Describability*   It must be possible to create and maintain documentation.
- *Understandability.*

Object-orientation contributes to many of these objectives, although some individual object-oriented languages may score poorly in terms of efficiency, understandability, robustness or portability. In particular, the advantages most often put forward in favour of object-oriented systems are the inherent reusability of the objects, the extensibility of object-oriented systems and the fact that formal methods of specification may be made to blend with the object-oriented approach.

Reusable code has long been a goal of systems designers. There has been limited success with reusable functions in the form of libraries of commonly used mathematical and statistical functions, but even these are often difficult to use because of the need to know a great deal about the validation of entries in long parameter lists. As far as data are concerned the picture has been uniformly black outside of the field of package software. Part of the reason for this has been the popular insistence on top-down decomposition which, in striving for a decomposition of a problem into chunks small enough for an individual to program in a short time, tends to make these chunks highly dependent on the way the decomposition itself is done. Top-down functional decompositions are by their very nature application specific. Thus the resultant modules are often not of any general applicability, and programmers constantly reinvent the same solutions in different contexts.

Some industry commentators have observed that reuse, if widely applied, could save up to 20% of development costs and that even a 1% saving gives massive competitive advantage. Other estimates claim that 70% of programmers' efforts are devoted to the maintenance of existing code and that 80% of this effort is spent on corrections rather than enhancements. The American DoD estimate that corrections cost ten times as much as new developments. Thus anything that contributes to better specification or to reusability must be high on the agenda for the software industry.

Object-oriented programming contributes significantly to the issues of reusability, maintainability and interoperability by employing three main techniques: bottom-up design, information hiding and inheritance.

A bottom-up approach to design significantly improves the potential for reuse of modules. A particularly obvious and simple example for most programmers is the way dates are handled. If it is determined in advance that some system will need to make use of dates or calculate with them, then it may be worthwhile stepping back from the immediate requirements of the system in hand to ask if it would be beneficial to provide a generic set of date routines usable by all future systems. Thus, if the present system has no need to calculate the date on which Easter falls it may still be worth including at least hooks for this function in the interface, if not a full implementation. A functional decomposition would not identify any need for this and might result in a routine where calculating public holidays involved a major change. It is encapsulation, or information hiding, that makes bottom-up design possible.

The second technique is information hiding itself. Modules implemented in an object-oriented style are accessed purely via their interface and the programmer need only be aware of this interface, which is equivalent to a specification of the function of the module. Its implementation is hidden and irrelevant to its use in the system. Information hiding can also contribute to security. A simple interface contributes to interoperability and to friendliness. In fact one of the main applications of object-oriented programming has been in the area of user interface design, as we shall see in Chapter 4.

Inheritance, genericity or other forms of polymorphism make exception handling easier and improve the extensibility of systems. In a system with inheritance, functions can be added by adding child objects that inherit their parents' specification and implementation, but still behave differently in the key areas relevant to them. In this way incremental changes become a great deal easier to conceive and implement. As was remarked in the last chapter, inheritance, if not used with care, can compromise abstraction and make systems unduly complex. On the other hand the benefit of extensibility is closely tied to that of reuse. A module that is not extensible may have a very limited range of applications in which it may be reused.

Correctness and robustness are addressed by formal specification and prototyping methods which will be discussed later (see Chapters 9 and 10) and which can be harmonized with object-oriented methods. If, and it is a big 'if', modules are well constructed with reuse in mind they are likely to be more robust. Every time they are used they are *a fortiori*[1] tested as well.

Maintainability, reusability and verifiability are all supported by the simultaneously 'open' and 'closed' nature of object-oriented systems. Meyer's 'open–closed' principle states that reusable systems should be both open, in the sense that they are easy to extend, and closed, in the sense that they are ready to use. An example of code that does not satisfy this principle can be found in almost any system which utilizes computed goto or case statements in a conventional language. Consider, for example, the following code fragment concerned with error handling in a C-like language.

[1] with stronger reason

```
Switch (n)

{case 1: error = 49;

        print("Warning - Error 49");continue;

case 2: error = 71;

        print("Execution halting due to Error 71");break;

case 3:

        break;

}
```

This code suffers from a complete lack of reusability and extensibility. Furthermore, it would be extremely difficult to document more concisely than the code itself. In order to add a new case – or handle a new error – the programmer would have to take the module off-line, make the changes and recompile. Thus, the system is not closed – it cannot be used 'as is' while the changes are made and indeed there is no guarantee that the handling of the existing functions will not be affected by some slip of the programmer. It is not open in that extensions involve changing existing code at the implementation level in order to add the new functions. Systems that employ inheritance, including object-oriented ones, do satisfy the open/closed principle. There are even object-oriented systems which permit changes to modules while the system is actually running.

The prime technique of object-oriented programming used to overcome this problem is inheritance. If we had approached the same error-trapping problem with an object-oriented point of view we would have reasoned that errors had a structure, as illustrated in Figure 2.3. In this simple case they break down into fatal errors and warnings. Both types of error inherit the attributes and methods of errors in general, and individual errors may be regarded as instances of the appropriate subclass. To add a new error, or more importantly a new type of error, we need only create a new class and a new object and specify its class. So, if we discovered a new type of error that was neither a warning nor fatal, we could make a new sub-

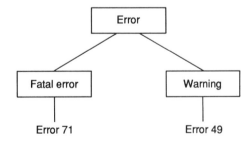

Figure 2.3 Object-oriented error trapping.

class of error describing its special features. The way existing errors are handled cannot be affected and the only compilation necessary is that of the new class.

Of course this is a trivial and unrealistic example, but it demonstrates the main point that inheritance supports the construction of extensible systems. A more realistic example is illustrated in Figure 2.4. Here a system developer may have written some code for the common features of all bank accounts, such as methods for printing statements, and dealt with the special features of deposit and current ('checking' in American) accounts in subclasses; deposit accounts, for example, need to compute interest. Now when an interest bearing current account is introduced it is easy to add a new class, either as a subclass of deposit account or of current account. Alternatively, multiple inheritance could be used to inherit features from both.

Both object-oriented and functional programming offer the programmer the opportunity to write open–closed systems. This is not the place to describe functional programming, but I will deal with it peripherally in subsequent chapters.

This apparently self-contradictory open–closed principle contributes to software maintenance, project management and especially to change control in a profound manner. Systems must be open because designers rarely foresee all the uses or effects of a module when it is being developed; new features may thus need to be added later. However, systems that are not closed off and released to users are of no use whatever. Open–closed systems imply an explicit recognition of change control procedures from the very beginning of development. Prototyping and object-oriented programming should both be viewed in the light of this observation and will be something of an implicit theme in much of the remainder of this book.

There are a combinatorially large number of ways to do a functional decomposition. The way it is done is thus likely to be highly application specific. Taking a bottom-up approach based on the metaphor of objects is likely to result in better reusability. However, this is not the easiest option. In the days when database sup-

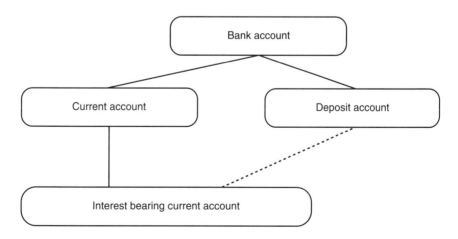

Figure 2.4 Classification structure for bank accounts.

pliers were not thoughtful enough to provide dates as built-in primitive data types, we had to write our own date arithmetic routines. I recall writing one, and thinking myself very far-sighted in incorporating an algorithm for finding the date when Easter fell. The specification of this algorithm is published in *The Book of Common Prayer*. It enabled, in those days, the computation of the dates of all UK public holidays. The trouble was, with the benefit of hindsight, that I omitted to put in routines for Ramadan, Yom Kippur and the Chinese New Year. The lesson here is that programming bottom-up, with reuse in mind, is very costly indeed, and that completely reusable code would be infinitely expensive. The solution to this dilemma is to use a combination of bottom-up and top-down approaches and to code only those functions where a potential for reuse can be foreseen. A pure bottom-up approach is, in practice, very difficult to adopt. An object-oriented system's extensibility guarantees that unforeseen functions can be added later. Object-oriented programming increases programmer productivity. The danger is that it increases it too much, and that programmers introduce un-necessary functions.

Cox (1986) has the vision of what he calls Software Integrated Circuits (Software ICs), the simile being with hardware that is literally assembled from standard components in most cases, just as are cars, radios and refrigerators. The economic benefits of this approach are well known. So why has it proved untenable and an elusive goal for software systems? Firstly, it is largely the case that the non-package software systems that represent the majority of systems, unlike most man-ufactured goods, are not mass-produced: there is but one end product. Thus, the economies of scale associated with mass production are unavailable, and project sponsors are often unwilling to invest extra effort in developing anything not imme-diately cost-justified by the task in hand. Secondly, the prevalence in the recent past of methods of top-down decomposition has led to division of labour based on an application-specific decomposition of problems. This has meant that the boundaries of modules have been defined in a way that depends on the decomposition, which in turn depends on the functional characteristics of the specific application, rather than a natural decomposition based on objects in the world: objects which would be bounded in the same way in many applications and therefore be reusable. Object-oriented methods address the latter point in avoiding the over-zealous appli-cation of the top-down philosophy. If they are to address the first point then project managers and sponsors both need to be re-educated somewhat. Project planning and costing needs to be done on the basis of future as well as current projects. The problem here is that, in a society increasingly concerned with short-term, and increasingly short-term, profits, it is nearly always easier to justify projects on an individual basis. Because of this economic reality, it is sadly likely that reusable modules will be created more by luck than by judgement, and techniques that encourage 'willy-nilly' reusability are possibly the only ones that will work. The object-oriented methods described in this book have this character, in that reusa-bility is actually easier to deliver with object-oriented methods and may add little or nothing to overall costs, although the initial development cost of a reusable module may be far, far higher than that of an application-specific module; up to ten times higher according to extreme estimates. There is always a small chance that the object-oriented style will produce reusable modules at no extra cost. This will occur when the objects are chosen well: that is, chosen to correspond to genuine, universal objects in the application domain. The notion of universal or essential objects is explained in more detail in Chapter 9.

MODULARITY   The importance of modularity has long been emphasized in the writings of software theoreticians. Parnas (1972) introduced the notion of using modules for information hiding. Meyer (1988) lays down five criteria and five principles for modularity. The criteria he names as:

(1) Decomposability
(2) Composability
(3) Understandability
(4) Continuity
(5) Protection

Decomposability refers to the software engineering and project management requirement that systems be decomposable into manageable chunks so that they can be changed more easily and so that individuals or teams can be assigned coherent work packages. The technique of top-down decomposition achieves this on the basis of a single top-level function. It is compromised by the possible non-existence of a genuine 'top' in, for example, a system such as an operating system. It is also possible to define modules with very complex interfaces to each other in this way. Object-oriented decomposition is based on a bottom-up approach and the principles of information hiding and simple interfaces.

Decomposability is strongly related to decentralization. Decentralization helps to simplify code by eliminating hidden dependencies. The latter cause large code changes to follow on from relatively small design changes. If each module in a system needs only to know about its own implementation rather than that of its servers then its code can be more readily extended internally. Design changes are thus isolated and do not automatically affect the rest of the system.

Composability refers to the property of modules to be freely combined even in systems for which they were not developed. This is fundamental to software reuse and again is supported by the principle of information hiding. Functional decomposition, as I have said, can be used to support decomposition but it has nothing to offer to aid composability. One of the strikingly unique features of the object-oriented approach is that it supports both composability and decomposability. Composability is related to the notion of extensibility, which refers to being able to add functions to a system without radical surgery. Composability and extensibility are supported by the object-oriented principles of small interfaces (see below) and especially, as we have seen, by inheritance. This argument presupposes that we are working within one language. The question arises, however, whether it is possible to compose systems from objects written in different languages.

Top-down decomposition can certainly deliver decomposability, but it cannot deliver composability except in very special circumstances.

Understandability helps people to comprehend a system by looking at its parts prior to gaining an understanding of the whole. This is a valid principle even though the whole may exhibit emergent properties not shown by its parts, since it assists learning and maintenance if treated with proper caution. Object-oriented systems are understandable in this way to the extent that it is not necessary to trace their message-passing behaviour in detail in order to understand what they do.

Continuity in a system implies both that small changes made to it will only result in small changes in its behaviour, and that small changes in the specification will require changes in only a few modules. The latter point is the one directly addressed by object-oriented methods. Once again it is inheritance and simple interfaces that deliver this benefit.

The criterion of modular **protection** insists that exception and error conditions either remain confined to the module in which they occur or propagate to only a few other closely related modules. For example, the practice in database systems of incorporating validation checks within entity descriptions supports protection in that data may not be entered incorrectly by virtue of a property of the module into which they are being entered.

The principles required to ensure these criteria for modularity are observed are identified by Meyer as these five:

(1) Linguistic modular units
(2) Few interfaces
(3) Small interfaces
(4) Explicit interfaces
(5) Information hiding

I have referred to these principles in the discussion of Meyer's five criteria above. The phrase **linguistic modular units** refers to the need for a correspondence between the modules of a system and the primitive data types or syntactic units provided by the language or method used to describe the problem. Abstract data types in particular support this principle, and it in turn contributes to decomposability, composability and protection. For example, the use of floating point primitives in most programming languages supports their reuse in widely varying programs, and user-defined types extend this benefit to other modules. Many modern software products have obtained benefits in limited applications through the application of this principle. Databases deal with whole records and tables as primitives and financial modelling systems with rows and columns. This makes certain applications much easier to develop, combine and test.

By **few interfaces** we mean that each module should communicate with as few others as possible. I have already alluded to the difficulty of tracing complex message passing. The few-interface principle contributes to both continuity and protection. It may be implemented in topologically different ways. A good analogy is a local area network where we may regard each workstation and server as objects communicating by message passing. Such a network may be implemented either as a centralized star, or as a ring in which communication is accomplished by only neighbouring nodes being allowed to communicate, although messages may be passed on in relay. Of course real networks do not work like this but the metaphor is applicable to the structure of objects within a system. A network in which every node is connected to every other one violates the principle and would evidently be difficult to maintain and change.

The principle of **small interfaces** states that the interfaces should pass as few data as possible. Again the continuity and protection criteria are addressed by this principle.

The need for **explicit interfaces** arises from the need to use objects via their specification rather than their implementation, so that in composition and decomposition the intermodule connexions are known clearly. Continuity is also addressed in that knock-on effects may be seen from the specification of modules. Data sharing may contribute to storage efficiency, but may compromise this principle if not stated clearly in the interfaces between modules.

The last three principles may be combined as the principle of **simple interfaces**. In general object-oriented systems should be written so that all communication with objects is via their interfaces (or specifications) rather than their implementations, and these interfaces should be as simple as possible: few, small and explicit. It is this combined principle to which we shall constantly refer in this book.

The principle of simple interfaces provides the basis for hoping that the criterion of composability can be met by systems written with multiple object-oriented languages. If this principle is not adhered to, such composability is likely to be a vain hope.

The principle of **information hiding** is central. It says that modules may hide the design decisions used in their construction. In the terminology of object-oriented methods this means that modules are used via their specifications, not their implementations. All information, whether concerning data or function, about a module is encapsulated within it and, unless specifically declared public, hidden from other modules. Thus, when the implementation of a module is changed its clients need not be, since they only deal with the interface.

The relationship between Meyer's five criteria and principles is shown in Figure 2.5.

The principles given above apply not only to programming but to designs and specifications as well. We shall meet these issues in detail in Chapters 7 and 8. For now, it is only necessary to state that the benefits of object-oriented design and analysis are the central themes of this book and that many of our remarks on object-oriented programming languages in the next chapter are merely laying the groundwork for this view.

OTHER BENEFITS

Another key benefit of the object-oriented approach is that it enables far better management of complexity, as is emphasized by Booch (1991). The problems modelled by computer systems, the systems themselves and the management of the development process are all inherently complex processes. An abstraction of the key elements of the problem domain and a decomposition into objects and inheritance, aggregation and usage structures based on real-world objects and concepts

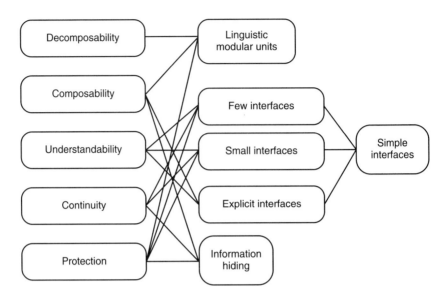

Figure 2.5 The relationship between Meyer's five criteria and principles.

helps with the management of complexity in several ways. First, the system and the problem are in close correspondence, so that the cognitive wisdom of everyday life can be mapped onto the solution. Second, encapsulation divides the problem up into coherent chunks small and simple enough for us to understand them as a whole. Third, object-orientation provides several ways to model structure and meaning: inheritance structures and so on. Lastly, the reusability and extensibility of object-oriented systems mean that complex systems may be assembled from simple ones, and that complex systems can evolve incrementally in simple steps into even more complex ones.

The pressure for more 'open' systems highlights both the benefits of and the need for object-oriented methods. Interoperability, modularity, extensibility, simple interfaces and information hiding are intimately related in the contribution they make to the development of truly open systems. Open systems are to be thought of as those which do not tie buyers or developers to particular suppliers of hardware, systems software or networks. To guarantee this ideal state of affairs, future systems will need to interoperate; that is, they must communicate and share resources. Although there are many other considerations, it is natural to think of each system within a distributed open system as an object composed of objects. Each such system needs to communicate not only with other whole systems, but with their components. The object-oriented approach supports this concept by making the interfaces that need to be defined small, explicit and few in number. Specifying communication protocols which depend only on the defined interface – not the implementation – is possibly the only way we yet know of to make open systems work. It is thus no surprise that many of the companies seriously committed to open systems have invested heavily in object-oriented technology. I will have more to say on this subject in Chapter 10. This point has also been taken up by the proponents of the idea of object request brokers which make it possible for objects or whole systems to cooperate across networks. The Object Management Group's CORBA is a standard for such products, which are beginning to emerge as I write.

A basic prerequisite for software reuse is a code library or software repository. Many CASE tools and IPSEs recognize this but fail to address the openness of the repository or the need for its components to satisfy the principles of linguistic modular units, simple interfaces or information hiding. The benefits of object-oriented programming and methods will be obtained when open code and/or specification libraries are widely available commercially. The development of such libraries, the basis for software repositories, is an urgent task for the software industry. These libraries will be all the better for being based on real systems developments as part of commercial projects.

AARDVARK
AGAIN

The aims of Aardvark, in building SACIS, are:

- to construct a system that will be both a database and an enquiry system;
- to be capable of changing and being extended with the business;
- to be able to support both conventional and expert systems components;
- to offer the option of distributed installation;
- not to lock Aardvark into any manufacturer's products;
- to have all rule-based and semantic components stored in explicit form rather than hidden in the code or normalized design; and
- to offer the possibility of using modules developed for SACIS in future systems developments.

At the outset, although it seems that an object-oriented solution is the only one even potentially capable of meeting all these requirements, the DP manager is not convinced that there is a development system that will actually do the job. What should she do? Aardvark's consultants have recommended the following cautious approach. First, the specification and business analysis should be constructed using object-oriented techniques. This means that implementation in an object-oriented programming language will be straightforward if a suitable one can be found by the end of the analysis stage, but if not the system can still be implemented in a conventional language. The benefits of having a specification with extensible and reusable components remain. In view of the uncertainty surrounding the final development platform, the specification is to use throwaway prototyping for which it is natural to use an object-oriented language. Smalltalk was considered, but owing to existing skills and because the prototype might still evolve into the full system, it was eventually decided to use C++ with suitable libraries. The developers will receive basic training in object-oriented concepts and in Smalltalk, to help overcome any residual prejudices from their days working with C. While the specification stage is proceeding, Aardvark is investigating options for the database components. We will follow this development in subsequent chapters. Aardvark's caution is justified because object-orientation is not without drawbacks. In the next section we examine some of them.

⊟ 2.2 Some problems and pitfalls

Caution is needed in assessing the benefits of any new technology. Object-oriented methods are not a panacea and there is a profound need to state the areas where the claimed benefits may not be delivered, and a need to identify those which may only be delivered in certain circumstances. I have claimed software reuse, for example, as a key benefit. In fact, reusable data structures have proved an elusive goal even where object-oriented methods have been used. One of the reasons for this is that designing reusable modules actually adds to the cost of a project and there is always a temptation to get the job in hand done as quickly as possible even at the expense of future reusability. I have already remarked on the economic short-termism which seems to characterize post-industrial society, especially in periods of high interest rates. In such a milieu, it is extremely difficult to make a case for extra investment in reusability, and although object-oriented methods make reusable systems *less* costly they do not remove all extra costs. The extra cost can only be justified in terms of future reuse savings which are discounted back to present-day prices. This may prove to be a serious impediment to the delivery of this promised and much vaunted benefit. The author has conducted an informal survey of colleagues who have carried out object-oriented projects by asking them what reusable components emerged from their projects. In a straw poll of about six projects, only one did not remark to the effect: 'Oh! We really didn't have the time to sort that one out. No, nothing really emerged we would ever use again.' However, and against this, several staggering successes with reuse are reported in the next section.

Another problem I have already alluded to is the lack of commercially available object libraries. Without such libraries of modules, developed in anger on real projects, the true benefit of reuse cannot be delivered in volume. On the other hand in the absence of such libraries, why should any company take the technology up? It seems that we are caught on the horns of a dilemma. Unless pioneering companies take considerable risks, possibly motivated by benefits other than reuse, useful libraries will not emerge and the technology will not mature. The success of commercially developed reusable components depends on the willingness of project sponsors and investors to allow for the extra cost of their development, and to be prepared to recover investments over a longer period. In Chapters 7 and 8 we will look at the issue of higher-level reuse: the reuse of designs and specifications. Here too, good libraries and good tools to navigate these libraries will be needed.

If libraries are to be useful we must find ways of navigating through their volume and complexity. Even when useful object libraries, and classification and navigation techniques for them, are developed and become widely available, another problem still has to be faced. How are developers going to know that a particular library contains just the object they need in this particular case? Here is a potentially huge information overload difficulty. People just cannot be expected to know what is in every library and it is inconceivable that every library could contain all, or even most, of the objects that a typical developer is likely to need. Several solutions to this problem are possible. Service companies may act as information brokers. Expert systems containing the information may be developed and sold commercially. Group work and techniques for the classification of objects will be needed. High-level languages will be needed to describe the interactions among objects in the library. The use of libraries may never go beyond those restricted to programming and interface-level objects such as those that already exist. It is even conceivable that a successful vendor might be able to create one big product with most of the useful classes created by others, but this seems a very remote possibility. I suspect that vertical, industry-specific libraries will emerge as the property of product and consultancy companies and be used in contract developments. The obstacle to this happening soon is the fact that these companies, or at least the consultancies, have been traditionally reluctant to make this kind of investment.

The management of large component libraries for object-oriented programming is still a significant unsolved problem. Two chief ways of organizing such libraries have been explored. The classes in the library can be organized hierarchically, which permits browsers to be used. Alternatively, retrieval can be accomplished by storing keywords with the classes in the manner of a conventional information retrieval system. It turns out that neither approach is ideal and the current thinking is that a combined approach is best, but there are still no commercial software products to assist with this severe problem and manual methods are in use at most sites.

The problem of emergency fixes referred to above is yet another serious point against the widespread adoption of object-oriented techniques. The reusability of an object may be seriously compromised if a zealous programmer fixes a bug in it in an incorrect way: 'The best laid schemes o' mice an' men gang aft a-gley'. Configuration management systems can be used to alleviate this problem partially, but, as with CASE code generators, it is not always possible to enforce managerial controls strictly in the hurly-burly of real system operation.

We also need to develop protocols for change and version control for systems of complex objects with multiple interconnexions. Work on formal specification of objects' interfaces is required so that composability languages can be developed to allow library modules to be configured to meet a specification. There is also some current interest in building tools that can estimate the impact of a changed interface on other objects in a system (see Hood, Kennedy and Muller, 1987). These are deep research issues that indicate just how immature the field is at present. I do not expect to see these issues resolved until the second half of the 1990s.

Most object-oriented programming languages do not support the notion of persistent objects: that is, objects which, stored on disk, persist unchanged between executions. Thus, data and object management is not well supported by object-oriented programming. The emergence of object-oriented databases is beginning to address this deficiency, but there is still a wide gulf between the object-oriented programming and database communities, and some purists, such as Wegner, claim that persistent objects defy the basic philosophy of object-orientation. A programming style that cannot tolerate persistence, however, is merely doomed in my opinion. Object-oriented databases will be dealt with in detail in Chapter 6.

The efficiency of object-oriented programming languages with their support for dynamic binding and garbage collection (see Chapter 3) is in doubt. For applications, perhaps real-time applications, where efficiency or sheer scale is of major concern, these languages are simply not a viable proposition, although a few small-scale, real-time applications have been written in such languages. Hybrid languages, on the other hand, may be more efficient but they often compromise object-oriented principles and benefits. A similar paradox in the field of expert systems, which at one time were often written in the similarly inefficient language LISP, has now been effectively resolved by the emergence of mature hybrid development systems. Such a maturation of object-oriented programming environments is necessary before the benefits of object-oriented programming can become widely realized.

As pointed out in Chapter 1, inheritance compromises reuse unless fairly strict procedures are adhered to. Thus, inheritance-free or object-based approaches as advocated by Jackson, advocates of Ada, advocates of actor-based systems and others have a distinct place in the armoury of the software developer.

Reusing parts of applications still requires a large helping of creativity. It requires developers to separate the functionality of different domains from that of applications built to model them. This is something that we can never provide an exhaustive set of rules for, automate or de-skill. A bad programmer can produce unusable, never mind unreusable, systems just as easily in an object-oriented style as in any other. As the old adage has it: real programmers write FORTRAN, and can do so in *any* language.

Inheritance structures are only one form of semantics. As we will see in subsequent chapters, other forms include client/server relationships, association and part structures, data multiplicity and modality constraints, business rules and control rules. It is my contention that including any semantic information in a system potentially compromises the reusability of its components. The reason is that the more you say about something, the more specific you are, the more you have related it to its context. On the other hand, a non-specific object will be a poor model of a real-world object which is always perceived and used in a context. The trade-off between reuse and semantics must become an important concern of object-oriented designers, analysts and programmers. In certain applications, such as graphical user interfaces where the objects themselves are largely computational artefacts, the context is tightly circumscribed and this problem arises less sharply. In general commercial systems, and even in simulation problems, this is not so.

I have commented that sometimes it becomes necessary to trace the behaviour of a system, in order to debug it, by tracing the passage of messages from one object to another. This tracing of message-passing behaviour in understanding or debugging a system can be enormously difficult and remains, in my view, a very serious defect of object-oriented systems. One envisages future generations of software engineers criticizing their counterparts of the 1990s for 'spaghetti message-passing structures' or some such.

The field is developing rapidly and current products may be superseded rapidly. For example, full support for multiple inheritance is not available yet in any single system in the sense that it was defined in the preceding chapter. That is, no system in wide commercial use supports class and instance-level inheritance of methods, attributes and attribute values with explicit, user-defined rules for conflict resolution. I think this is a deficiency and that there will be new or extended languages which address it. From the point of view of someone building a large system in an object-oriented programming language this possibility must be worrying, since the organization will ill be able to afford to switch languages mid-stream. Fortunately, this problem does not apply to object-oriented analysis or design.

I have emphasized the benefits arising from simple interfaces and information hiding. I have claimed that when a module's implementation changes, its clients will not be affected. There are, however, circumstances when this euphoria is ill justified. Suppose, for example, that the change is so large or profound that the interface itself changes. For example, suppose that we have lived comfortably with the notion of 'employee' and that all our systems and databases contain a uniform interface to 'employee' objects. Now workers' self-government, or slavery, or some completely different social system is introduced. Surely our notion of the interface of the employee object must undergo radical change. What are we to make of employees who receive no salary, for example – or directors who take no profit?

Function libraries, especially in scientific programming, have been quite successful as a reuse strategy but are often considered hard to use because of the need to remember long parameter lists, or 'common blocks' in FORTRAN, and to understand the inner working of the functions in some cases. It remains to be seen whether this will be posterity's judgement on object libraries. For the reasons given in the previous section, I think not.

The principal additional costs in adopting object technology are the investment in new hardware, software and methods that may be required, the costs of the essential training and re-education of both developers and management and the extra costs of developing reusable components and managing libraries. This point is explored further in Chapter 10.

It is also the case that reusable components may cost a great deal more to write than conventional estimates would indicate. Jacobson *et al.* (1992) estimate over ten times as much and most experience indicates a factor of at least six. For some applications, such as GUI (graphical user interface) development, class libraries or application frameworks can be purchased commercially. This at least removes the cost of component development, but few domains receive this treatment at present. Having written or purchased a suite of classes, the problems do not end. Managing component libraries is difficult and costly.

One of the most difficult problems to face up to is the organizational and cultural changes that must follow the adoption of object technology if it is to be fully beneficial. We are used to rewarding analysts and programmers according to the amount of code they produce (scaled according to the language generation they work with, of course) rather than the amount of other people's code they reuse. This implies a change in the reward structure that may well be resisted. Furthermore, project managers are paid to make projects come in on time and not to write code for the benefit of subsequent projects. This too could be a big shock and some workers have suggested that class development should be totally separated from application building. However, this is often impractical and not always feasible since so many development ideas come from direct involvement with users. My book *Migrating to Object Technology* (Graham, 1994) explores such issues further.

The final problem with object technology I want to raise arises from the view taken by its more extreme proponents that it is the last word in software engineering: the so-called silver bullet. Major investments in object technology (OT) may be impeded by the more sensible view that it will eventually be succeeded by an even more powerful metaphor, just as relational databases – once also the last word – are now being superseded by newer approaches (see Chapters 5 and 6). An indication that improvements over and above OT are possible is given by the emergence of new metaphors based on new languages like BETA (see Section 3.6). Fortunately, it appears that such developments will incorporate, rather than displace, the object-oriented metaphor, so that investments made now should be secure against technological change.

2.3 Case-studies

In this section we will examine very briefly some of the benefits that have been reported by users of object technology.

Perhaps the oldest and best-known case of the large-scale, beneficial application of object technology is the one at Brooklyn Union Gas, where a customer management system consisting of 1.5 million lines of PL/1 was replaced by a system written using an object-oriented preprocessor. The new system is very large, with 850 on-line users, a 100-gigabyte database and 10000 code modules. The benefits reported include a 40% reduction in code size due mainly to reuse, low maintenance costs (12 people in the team), trouble-free installation and above all great flexibility and extensibility. These benefits were not free. The developers had to invent their own object-oriented development methods and standards as these were not available in the development period from 1987 to 1990; traditional methods were found seriously wanting.

Another application where striking benefits were noted was a maintenance management system developed for General Motors. This system helped the company schedule repairs and maintain the parts inventory. The old system consisted of 265000 lines of PL/1, took 12.5 man-years to develop and used 13.6 Mbytes of mainframe memory when running. A replacement was written in Smalltalk 80 in less than a man-year and consisted of only 22000 lines of code and used a mere 1.1 Mbytes of memory. Remarkably the performance of the two systems was roughly the same and the overall productivity gain was estimated at 14:1. Admittedly, building a system for the second time is nearly always easier to do, but the ratio is still very impressive.

Although I have argued that reuse is a hard benefit to achieve, compared with extensibility, some companies have been able to realize it. Petroleum Information supplies geographic data to the oil and gas industry. They built a geographic information system (*Sorcerer's Apprentice*) using CLOS and report a figure of 80% for code reuse. This has led in turn to much shorter development times and to the developers tackling problems that would have previously been thought intractable.

Guiness Peat Aviation wrote an aircraft furniture and fittings purchase-scheduling system using a combination of Actor and Gupta's SQL server under MS Windows. They too report high levels of reuse, a 200-fold improvement in the ease of modification to screens and productivity gains of up to 8:1 over conventional 4GL tools.

Other large-scale applications include Midland Bank's WiTTE, a financial trading environment written in Smalltalk V and C; several front-office trading systems written in Objective-C under NeXTstep at Swiss Bank Corporation; Wyatt Software's WyCASH+ portfolio management system written in Smalltalk V; and Hambrecht and Quist's *Phoenix* brokerage system written in Object Pascal.

Harmon and Taylor (1993) describe 20 of the 225 case-studies entered for the 1992 Object World competition for the most beneficial use of object technology. These include an accounts and administration system for the Southern California Gas Company, an object-oriented analysis (OOA) simulator for Boeing and a software engineering environment for a hospital.

The themes that emerge from these experiences are that reuse is achievable though more than a good object-oriented programming language is required to achieve it. What is required is the determination to succeed, good project management, sound methods, attention to the problems of education, training and change management and a modicum of luck. Given these factors reuse is attainable but only at a cost. Reusable code naturally takes a little longer to write and test. However, the immediate benefits that arise from extensibility often push reuse into second place as a consideration. As argued in Chapter 10, extensibility is one of the key characteristics that businesses require from systems. Thus, even if reuse is not an option you may still gain greatly from object-oriented methods.

⊟ 2.4 Summary

This chapter has concentrated on the tangible benefits arising from the use of object-oriented programming and to a lesser extent, object-oriented methods in general. The benefits of the latter, object-oriented analysis and design, are more fully explored in Chapters 7 and 8. We take a closer look at the particular benefits of object-oriented databases in Chapter 6. We have also noted certain disadvantages of the object-oriented approach.

The benefits may be summarized in the formula:

$$\text{encapsulation} + \text{inheritance} + \text{Identity} \Rightarrow \text{reusability} + \text{extensibility} + \text{semantic richness}$$

Reuse, extensibility and other object-oriented benefits apply to designs and specifications as well as to programming.

Top-down decomposition can lead to application-specific modules and compromise reuse. The bottom-up approach and the principle of information hiding maximize reuse potential. Encapsulation delivers reuse.

Inheritance makes exception handling easy and therefore leads to more extensible systems. The open–closed principle is supported by inheritance. Inheritance delivers extensibility but may compromise reuse.

Semantic richness is provided by inheritance and other natural structures, together with constraints and rules concerning the meaning of objects in context. This also compromises reuse and must be carefully managed.

Meyer's five criteria for and five principles of object-oriented design were explained.

Other benefits identified in this chapter include:

- Well-designed objects in object-oriented systems are the basis for systems to be assembled largely from reusable modules, leading to higher productivity.
- Reusing existing classes that have been tested in the field on earlier projects leads to systems which are of higher quality, meet business requirements better and contain fewer bugs.
- Inheritance makes it possible to define systems that are more flexible, more easily extensible and less costly to maintain.
- Message passing means that interface descriptions between modules and external systems become much easier and support GUI development and client/server systems.
- Object-orientation is a key tool for managing software complexity. Object-oriented systems should scale up better from small to large. Encapsulation helps with scalability as project size and complexity increase.
- Partitioning of work has a natural basis and should be easier. Analysis and design by partitioning a domain into objects corresponding to a solution-oriented view of their real-world counterparts is often more natural than a top-down functional decomposition.
- Information hiding helps to build secure systems.
- Data-centred design captures more of the semantics of a model in implementable form.
- Formal specification may be blended harmoniously with object-oriented methods.
- System evolution and maintenance problems are mitigated by the strong partitioning resulting from encapsulation and uniform object interfaces.
- Object-oriented systems are potentially capable of capturing far more of the meaning of an application. Object-oriented methods are about modelling and facilitate changes within the business and more reversible systems.
- For some applications there is no sensible alternative to object technology.

The benefits we claim are not unqualified and there are a number of pitfalls in the object-oriented approach. These include:

- Tight project deadlines may mean that reusability is not delivered.
- Object libraries must be developed and knowledge about them disseminated.
- The field is developing rapidly and current products may be superseded rapidly. For example, full support for multiple inheritance is not yet available in any single system.

- When inheritance or other semantic constructs are used, strict controls are necessary if reuse is not to be compromised.
- Issues such as persistence, concurrency and performance have still to await the benefit of consensus.
- Messaging topology is important and it is quite possible to write bad object-oriented systems.
- Reusable components may cost a great deal more to write than conventional estimates would indicate.
- Managing component libraries is difficult and costly.
- Culture change is necessary and everyone hates it.
- There are unavoidable costs associated with training and re-education.
- Object technology may not be the last word in software engineering.

Several commercial users have reported real benefits including reduced code size and maintenance, high levels of reuse and good extensibility. There is a widespread belief that the approach scales up better than traditional approaches but little empirical proof of this yet. A small number of quite large projects do support this belief in scalability.

2.5 Bibliographical notes

The clearest exposition of the business motivation for and the benefits of object technology as a whole is to be found in Taylor (1992). He also provides a large amount of valuable case-study material. Further case-studies may be found in Harmon and Taylor (1993) and Wilkie (1993).

Bertrand Meyer's excellent book (1988) is a particularly clear exposition of the reasons for and benefits of an object-oriented approach to programming and design, although it concentrates on Meyer's own language, Eiffel, in explaining the concepts. I have borrowed from it extensively in this chapter and recommend the serious student of object-oriented programming to read it. Brad Cox (Cox, 1986; Cox and Novobilski, 1991) also provides an extremely down-to-earth assessment of the benefits of object-oriented programming and concentrates on the issue of software reuse. Cox's language for examples is his own Objective-C. Booch (1991) discusses the benefits of object-oriented design. A second edition is now available. There is not yet, to my knowledge, a good popular exposition of the benefits of object-oriented programming based around the popular C++ language. I hope that this will be remedied soon, as C++ seems to be emerging together with Smalltalk as one of the most popular commercial object-oriented languages (see Chapter 3).

Most books on object-oriented analysis and design offer a study of the general benefits of object technology but the list is too long to give here.

3

Object-oriented and object-based programming languages

Language is the dress of thought.
Dr Johnson (Lives of the English Poets)

Chapter 1 gave a fairly informal introduction to the main concepts behind object-oriented programming and methods. In dealing with programming languages, this chapter introduces a little more in the way of technicalities and rigour.

Although this is not intended to be primarily a book on object-oriented programming languages, the importance of the latter in the development of object-oriented ideas means that it is obligatory to give at least a brief treatment. We shall, however, be concerned later with future directions in software development and the languages presented in this chapter will be discussed from the point of view of their likely commercial adoption.

There are well over 100 object-oriented and object-based programming languages. Naturally, there is not the space even to mention all of them here. Readers wishing to learn an object-oriented programming language are directed to the many good books offering such tuition mentioned in the bibliographical notes at the end of this chapter.

3.1 Object-oriented languages

It is probably impossible to give a complete, watertight definition of what a truly object-oriented language is. However, we know from Chapter 1 that object-oriented at least means class-based plus inheritance and self-reference. This section deals with languages which fit this mould and which most people would agree are object-oriented. Scholastic arguments about whether languages are 'truly' object-oriented are particularly sterile, especially in view of the fact that there is no formal theory as with logic or functional programming. Until such a theory appears there can be no object-oriented equivalent of, for example, Codd's twelve rules for relational databases (Codd, 1985).

3.1.1 Simula

Simula, formerly Simula 67, was probably the first language to introduce the notions of classes and inheritance into general-purpose programming. Its origin in 1967 (Dahl and Nygaard, 1966; Dahl, Myrhaug and Nygaard, 1968) was based on earlier work on a specialized language, Simula 1, for discrete event simulation and this influenced many of its features. Simula 1 and its descendants were all, in turn, strongly influenced by ALGOL with its notion of program blocks.

Simula came out of work on discrete event simulation and operational research dating back to 1949, when Nygaard was working on the design of nuclear reactors. The differential equations involved in such problems were too hard for even numerical solution, so alternative techniques had to be developed from first principles. A successful technique is to simulate a world which moves (transforms its state) in discrete steps corresponding to time intervals. With such simulations, which can be run and rerun on a computer, the effects of different parameters can be observed rather than calculated. This is analogous to the use of spreadsheets for business 'what if' analysis. However, the languages available in the 1960s were not particularly suited for simulation. Whereas the abstractions of conventional languages like FORTRAN attempted to describe processes in the computer, Simula, with its abstractions, essayed to describe real-world processes.

The seminal simulation problem involved objects which were neutrons and absorbent rods in a nuclear reactor. A more readily understandable example is the simulation of traffic passing through a complex intersection which involves random arrival rates, saturation flow rates, traffic light settings and queuing. The vehicles are generated and tracked through the system as it passes through discrete time steps, rather like time-lapse photography, and the behaviour can be observed, at each time step, in terms of queue lengths, delay times, junction locking and similar features. It is also possible to observe global phenomena such as stability or convergence to a stable state. The system, once constructed, can be tested under different assumptions on such variables as volume, signal linking or cycle times.

Simula, which still has many active users, is an ALGOL-like programming language with a built-in notion of classes and hierarchical inheritance. Multiple inheritance is not supported. Information hiding is accomplished by 'protecting' a feature, which in effect prevents it from being inherited downwards. Polymorphism in the form of overloading is supported. Type checking can either be carried out statically at compile time, for efficiency, or at run time if a feature is declared 'virtual'. The system needs to perform garbage collection from time to time while running. That is, it has to reclaim the memory occupied by instances which were assigned but are no longer being used. This, in common with most other object-oriented languages, is a feature which militates against run-time efficiency, but, as we have seen, the main application influence behind Simula came from problems of simulation where performance is seldom the key issue. Simula has a library of special classes that contain most of the primitives required for discrete event simulation; in most other object-oriented languages these would have to be written. Another consequence of Simula's simulation background is that it has a set of unique features addressed to supporting applications where concurrency is important; 'co-routines' can be invoked and left to run while the main process continues uninterrupted until it needs the results from the co-routine. The features of Simula are summarized in Table 3.1.

The emphasis is on processes rather than data but Simula is responsible for many of the ideas which informed its descendants, especially those of classes, instances and inheritance. The idea of abstraction is implicit, but notions like message passing had to wait for the arrival on the scene of Smalltalk. Currently, the developers of Simula are working on a new language BETA (Kristensen *et al.*, 1987) which is an object-oriented language that also includes the features of functional and constraint-based programming and is further described in Section 3.6.6. The same group is responsible for a strongly typed, object-oriented formal specification language called ABEL (Dahl, 1987).

Table 3.1 Simula features.

Type checking/binding	Late or early
Polymorphism	Yes
Information hiding	Yes
Concurrency	Yes
Inheritance	Yes
Multiple inheritance	No
Garbage collection	Yes
Persistence	No
Genericity	No
Object libraries	Simulation

3.1.2 Smalltalk and its dialects

To this day the language which is widely considered as the purest representation of the object-oriented ideal is Smalltalk, which exists in two dialects: Smalltalk 80 and Smalltalk V (not a Roman numeral, and pronounced 'vee' for Virtual). Smalltalk came about as a result of work by Alan Kay, Adele Goldberg, Daniel Ingalls and others at Xerox PARC throughout the 1970s. In fact Smalltalk is not just a language but a complete programming environment, with editors, class-hierarchy browsers and many of the features of a 4GL. It was Smalltalk which established clearly the idea of message passing as the main and only way that objects could communicate. Influenced by Simula, its designers took the notion of objects to an extreme and declared that everything should be an object, including classes themselves. In Smalltalk even the humble integer is an object. Because of this decision there is a need to deal with classes of classes, metaclasses, and some authorities have commented that the rather odd notion of metaclass in Smalltalk tends to make the language difficult to understand, at least for beginners. Also treating numbers as objects is all very well for consistency, but it is not necessarily very efficient and is puzzlingly strange to most programmers used to other languages. Smalltalk is not a strongly typed language so that errors, which arise when an object receives a message it cannot deal with, for example, are processed entirely at run time. It also needs to garbage-collect and all binding is done only at run time. All these characteristics mean that Smalltalk is by no means a fast language in execution terms. It makes up for this by being an excellent environment for development, especially prototyping, and is perhaps best known for its distinctive iconic or WIMP interface which has influenced so many other systems.

The work on Smalltalk not only introduced the term 'object-oriented' into the language, but was largely responsible for the ideas behind the iconic interfaces to be found in many modern systems from the Apple Lisa onwards. Perhaps the ease with which such interfaces are built in Smalltalk is responsible for the predominance of graphical interfaces among the applications of object-oriented programming and the fact that few object libraries aimed at other applications are yet available.

It has been estimated that the Lisa project consumed over 200 man-years of effort. Clearly, a company such as Apple cannot afford to expend this much resource every time a new machine is released. The benefit of reusable software is therefore not merely a benefit but a necessity in such applications. This point will be expanded upon in Chapter 4.

One important and influential notion introduced by Smalltalk is the notion of metaclasses. A metaclass, in ordinary parlance, is merely a class of classes, which cannot be instantiated, and therefore represents an abstract concept from which more concrete concepts may inherit. In Smalltalk, the above notion is called an abstract class and a metaclass is defined as a template for class construction: something that can create classes. This is almost certainly a result of the influence of LISP on the language, and makes it possible to describe the language within the language and indeed to extend and change the structure of the language. In Smalltalk each class is the sole instance of its metaclass and a metaclass is created when the class is. Each metaclass is an instance of the class Metaclass and subclasses of the class Class. The class methods are actually stored in the metaclass. This can make the language difficult to understand for beginners. The language has no built-in types (other than 'object') and some commentators regard classes as user-defined types. This reflects another strong influence from LISP and functional programming on the language.

Smalltalk has no built-in control structure: any such structure must be built from message passing. For example, enclosing an expression in square brackets – called a 'block' – defers evaluation of the expression. Most control structures are implemented as messages to objects which take blocks as arguments.

Some current versions only support single inheritance, and applications requiring multiple inheritance have to be designed in a possibly unnatural way to overcome this limitation. According to Meyer (1988) this often involves much code duplication and makes heavy use of dynamic binding.

Change control is an important issue in Smalltalk environments since programmers can, in principle, modify each other's work. The Smalltalk browser supports good communication amongst the team and other change-control tools are provided. One key weakness here is Smalltalk's lack of any notion of persistent objects. Another is its essentially single-user character. The ENVY development environment is a partial answer to this deficiency. ENVY provides a shared code repository that provides editions, versions and releases of classes, methods and associated persistent objects. This makes multi-programmer projects feasible by enabling configuration management in a distributed environment. The alternative, before such products emerged, had been file-oriented check-in/check-out systems that were clumsy to use.

Although Smalltalk is a comprehensive, productive environment for programmers, garbage collection, dynamic binding and the lavish graphical user interface all make heavy demands on hardware. Also Smalltalk is a complete environment which cannot readily interwork with other languages, so that it cannot be easily integrated with existing code. These are two of the main factors impeding its acceptance.

The advantages of Smalltalk are:

- its conceptual uniformity in making everything an object;
- a superb run-time environment including symbolic debuggers, browsers and full access to the class hierarchy;
- dynamic binding supports polymorphism, therefore great flexibility;
- it is easier to understand and tune the overall design than in conventional languages;
- the fact that it is very hard not to write in an object-oriented style, making Smalltalk an excellent pedagogical tool. That is, it can be used to teach the key concepts, so that programmers get into the habit of writing in an object-oriented style even in languages such as C++ where the style is not enforced.

The disadvantages include:

- efficiency and memory requirements;
- no support for persistent objects;
- no consistent way of dealing with multiple users or change control without additional products such as ENVY;
- messaging errors can only be detected at run time.

The features of Smalltalk are summarized in Table 3.2.

Table 3.2 Smalltalk features.

Type checking/binding	Late
Polymorphism	Yes
Information hiding	Yes
Concurrency	Poor
Inheritance	Yes
Multiple inheritance	No
Garbage collection	Yes
Persistence	No
Genericity	No
Object libraries	Mostly graphics

Of the two dialects of Smalltalk, the classic is Smalltalk 80 which is based on the original Xerox work and is now supplied by Parcplace Systems, largely under UNIX. Smalltalk V from Digitalk is an excellent and fast PC implementation that also offers some support for multiple inheritance. The 'V' in Smalltalk V indicates the perhaps surprising fact that this package implements its own complete virtual memory management system on top of DOS. Hardly the most efficient way to implement a language, but one encouraging portability between platforms! Smalltalk V is available on a number of platforms such as the PS/2 and Macintosh and also under Windows and PM (Presentation Manager).

Since Smalltalk there have been many attempts to produce object-oriented languages which attempt, at the risk of compromising Smalltalk's purity and consistency, to overcome efficiency problems and maintain the key benefits of object-oriented programming. These attempts fall into a number of different categories and must be evaluated along a number of different axes. First, there is a split between languages which emphasize abstraction at the expense of inheritance or vice versa. Next, there is a split between languages descended from the artificial intelligence tradition and those which emanate from the cogitations of computer language specialists. Finally, we have a three-way split between logic programmers, functional programmers and the rest. A large section of the conventional programming camp has taken the route of extending existing languages with object-oriented features. It is to these that we now briefly turn.

3.1.3 C extensions

One approach to efficient object-oriented programming that has been popular is to extend an existing language to include object-oriented features. C is an example of an efficient base language that has been extended in this way. There are essentially two ways in which this can be done, exemplified by the languages Objective-C and C++. Objective-C (Cox, 1986; Cox and Novobilski, 1991) extends vanilla C by including one additional data type in the form of a C structure within a function library with, in essence, the functionality of Smalltalk. AT&T's C++ (Stroustrup, 1986) on the other hand actually changes the C compiler and extends the syntax with a new primitive data type for classes.

OBJECTIVE-C   Objective-C is a language based on ordinary C with a library offering much of the functionality of Smalltalk's language elements. It introduces a new data type, object identifier, and a new operation, message passing, and is a strict superset of C. Objective-C operates as a preprocessor which transforms statements into a form acceptable to the ordinary C compiler.

Cox's terminology differs from that of Smalltalk. Storage is managed by 'factory' objects, which represent classes and are created at compile time. Factory objects all have a method called 'new' which creates instances of their class at run time, by responding to a message of the form:

thisObject = [Object new]

Such objects encapsulate methods and state variables which are inherited by instances. The instances encapsulate state values and have a unique identifier. Inheritance may be overridden by the existence of a variable or method with the same name in the instance or subclass. Multiple inheritance is not supported, but can be implemented by the programmer.

Objective-C is supplied with a number of built-in classes such as those for objects, arrays, collections, sequences, sets, and so on. Class libraries are also available. It is bundled with the NeXT machine as standard and has been used for some of the biggest object-oriented programs ever written.

The features of Objective-C are summarized in Table 3.3.

C++   C++ is a genuine modification of the C language itself rather than an extension. The principal change is the introduction of a new genuine primitive data type 'class'. It has no high-level data types or primitives and relies, as with C, on libraries to provide such extensions. Thus, new types are defined in the language itself. The main

Table 3.3 Objective-C features.

Type checking/binding	Late or early
Polymorphism	Yes
Information hiding	Yes
Concurrency	Poor
Inheritance	Yes
Multiple inheritance	No
Garbage collection	Yes
Persistence	No
Genericity	No
Object libraries	A few

inspirations for the language came from C (and its noble ancestor BCPL) and from Simula. C++ is designed with both portability and efficiency in mind. In fact it was certain weaknesses in Simula 67, in terms of efficiency, which led to its development. It also emphasizes the goal of being able to incorporate the large quantity of existing C code and strives to be a superset of C, although some incompatibilities do exist. Thus, although it is much harder to do so by accident than in C, in C++ the programmer can violate the data protection and typing rules and data may then be accessed in inconsistent ways. C++ is a compromise between the object-oriented ideal and pragmatism.

C++ supports abstraction, inheritance, self-reference and dynamic binding. Both static and dynamic typing are supported. The type system, unlike Smalltalk's, is not organized as a single-rooted tree structure but as a collection of relatively small trees. Therefore C++ tends to encourage broad and shallow class structures compared with the narrow and deep structure enforced by Smalltalk, where everything is a subclass of Object. This observation may be of some use in determining application suitability.

Class declarations are divided into a public and a private part. Ordinary C structures (structs) are regarded as classes where every method is public. In a class, the private data and methods are only available to the object's own methods, while the public ones are available to any other object or function. Methods in C++ are called 'member functions'. Message passing corresponds to function calls. Instance variables ('private member variables' in the terminology) store data. Data can be stored at the class level, in a limited way, by allocating store when the program is loaded. Thus, such data are fixed for all instances of the class.

One novel feature of C++ is the ability to give a function access privileges to the private parts of several classes of which it is not a member. This is done by declaring the function to be a 'friend' of these classes. This can be used to simplify the description of an operation on two types. For example, if we wish to define multiplication of vectors by matrices, defining multiplication as a friend of these classes allows their implementation to be accessed. Friend functions need an extra argument to point at the object to which the operation is applied. Friends support the facility of being able to call C++ functions from normal C programs. This feature needs to be handled with great care if encapsulation is not to be compromised.

As with Smalltalk, the same name can be used for different methods. Thus, for example, multiplication of integers or matrices can use the same symbol. The reader will recall from Chapter 1 that this facility is called 'operator overloading', a form of *ad hoc* polymorphism.

Inheritance is implemented though the definition of subclasses. In C++ subclasses are referred to as 'derived classes'. Derived classes inherit all the properties of the base class in terms of which they are defined as public. Complete hierarchies are possible since a base class may itself be a derived class. Inherited methods may be overridden. Versions after 2.0 have a multiple inheritance mechanism and a full exception-handling mechanism is promised (see Koenig and Stroustrup, 1990).

By default, binding is established at compile time, as in a conventional language, either as a global variable or one scoped within a program block.

Alternatively the object can be created in the free store and created and destroyed under program control. With these techniques, the types of the arguments of a function must be known at compile time. Dynamic binding is implemented by 'virtual functions' defined in a base class but which can be redefined in derived classes. In this way the types of arguments can be determined at the time a function is applied.

C++ has no automatic garbage collection. Any such feature would have to be implemented by the programmer or provided by an environment with suitable code libraries.

The features of C++ are summarized in Table 3.4.

Whilst it is possible to use C++ as an object-oriented programming language, it is equally possible to ignore or misuse all (or some) of its object-oriented features. A particularly sobering statistic is that, of the very many C++ programs in existence within AT&T, it is estimated that fewer than 1 in 10 contains even a single class. This perhaps suggests that C++ programmers, migrating from C, should be forced to do a stint of Smalltalk programming (perhaps prototyping the projected C++ implementation) where they may lose some of their more deeply ingrained habits and will be forced to think in terms of objects. It also suggests a need for sound object-oriented design and analysis methods.

The language now exists in a number of different versions, some of which are public domain – g++ for example – on a wide range of machines.

As we remarked, C++ is a compromise, but it is a sensible compromise. It gives low-level control over the hardware when required and the benefits of object-oriented programming when required – and enforced. The worst things that can be said about C++ are, first, that it is a very difficult language to use well and, second, that many programmers continue to use it as simply a 'better' C. It is currently one of the most successful object-oriented programming languages in commercial applications on workstations and PCs, and looked likely to remain so for the foreseeable future until IBM announced Smalltalk as an SAA language and began to implement parts of Presentation Manager in it. Another new factor is the emergence of Eiffel into the public domain (see Section 3.1.5). At the time of writing there are already projects involving 100 staff, about 100 000 lines of code and in excess of 2 000 classes. Its long-term success is predicated on the development and availability of good quality, useful function libraries. We shall revisit this issue in Section 3.4.

Table 3.4 C++ features.

Type checking/binding	Late or early
Polymorphism	Yes
Information hiding	Yes
Concurrency	Poor
Inheritance	Yes
Multiple inheritance	Yes
Garbage collection	No
Persistence	No
Genericity	Yes (templates)
Object libraries	A few

3.1.4 Other languages with object-oriented features

There are a number of languages which, while they do not have the purity of
Smalltalk, do have object-oriented features. Generally speaking these emphasize
either abstraction or inheritance. Languages such as Ada, Modula-2 and perhaps
even Object Pascal fall into the former category. Several products with an artificial
intelligence genealogy such as KBMS, ProKappa or Leonardo fall into the latter,
and we often hear the term 'frame-based' in that case. We deal with the latter in
Section 3.3 of this chapter and in Chapter 4.

Languages such as Ada, and to a lesser extent Modula-2, exemplify languages where data abstraction and the benefit of reuse are the key concepts. As discussed in Chapter 1, such languages are referred to as object-based.

In Ada, and similar object-based languages, packages are not first-class
objects in that they may not be passed as parameters. This means that Ada does not
fully support data abstraction. It does, however, support operator overloading and
provides garbage collection as an option.

Ada has no direct support for inheritance but generic packages can be used
to implement a limited form, as shown in Figure 1.6. Although subtypes and
derived types can be defined by restriction, Ada cannot extend existing types by
adding new attributes and methods. This leads to the need for code duplication and
seriously limits any extensibility benefits. The latter benefits are also compromised
by the enforced early binding of this language. Ada emphasizes early binding and
strong typing for efficiency and safety.

Ada, due largely to DoD fiat, has become the language of choice for most
defence-related work. Recently, it has begun to penetrate commercial developments
as well. One common and major criticism of Ada has nothing to do with its lack
of object-orientation. It is a very rich language and its critics claim, with some
justification, that this makes it very difficult to learn and use well, owing to the
sheer number of primitive statements. This also makes it compare poorly with lean
languages like C in terms of the compiler's space requirements.

There are now some unofficial variants of Ada available commercially. A
typical one, such as Classic Ada, offers object-oriented constructs such as class
hierarchies, (single) inheritance, dynamic binding, method overriding at both class
and instance levels in addition to standard Ada features. Classic Ada, which is currently an Ada preprocessor, also supports rapid prototyping better than Ada does
and is equipped with automatic trace facilities.

Object Pascal (Apple) is a successor to a language called Clascal, which was
used to develop some of the Apple Lisa and Macintosh interface. It is essentially a
simple superset of Pascal. Objects are Pascal records encapsulating procedures and
functions. Object Pascal supports only single inheritance and does not offer garbage
collection as a built-in feature. Borland Turbo Pascal is an extension of Pascal with
many object-oriented features but lacking any multiple inheritance facilities.
Ultimately, the Pascal extensions will be attractive to organizations that already
have a heavy investment in Pascal code and wish to move to object-oriented
programming.

The features of Ada, Object Pascal and Turbo Pascal are summarized in Tables 3.5, 3.6 and 3.7 respectively.

CLU was an advanced language developed at MIT in the late 1970s (Liskov *et al.*, 1977). Its central unit of abstraction is the 'cluster', a concept identical to a Simula class. In contrast with the ALGOL-like nature of Simula, procedures and data structures may not be defined outside of a cluster in CLU. CLU coexists with a separate class-based formal specification language designed for it. The design

Table 3.5 Ada features.

Type checking/binding	Early
Polymorphism	Yes
Information hiding	Yes
Concurrency	Difficult
Inheritance	No
Multiple inheritance	No
Garbage collection	No
Persistence	As any 3GL
Genericity	Yes
Object libraries	Not many

Table 3.6 Object Pascal features.

Type checking/binding	Late
Polymorphism	Yes
Information hiding	Yes
Concurrency	No
Inheritance	Class-based
Multiple inheritance	No
Garbage collection	Yes
Persistence	No
Genericity	No
Object libraries	A few

Table 3.7 Turbo Pascal features.

Type checking/binding	Early
Polymorphism	Yes
Information hiding	Yes
Concurrency	No
Inheritance	Yes
Multiple inheritance	No
Garbage collection	No
Persistence	No
Genericity	No
Object libraries	A few

method calls for the description of the algebra of each data type's operations and supports genericity. Inheritance between classes and their instances is supported but not inheritance between metaclasses and their subclasses.

Another object-oriented programming language, Lingo, developed at Strathclyde University, forms the basis of the Linn Rekursiv machine (Harland, 1988; Pountain, 1988) which, along with the NeXT machine, probably represents the first generation of object-oriented computers. IBM and Apple have created a company called Taligent to produce an object-oriented machine and operating system with a broadly similar profile to the NeXT but, it is to be hoped, with greater compatibility with other systems and standards.

A claim could also be made for the operating systems of the IBM System 38 and AS/400 machines as a zeroth generation, since object-oriented ideas clearly influenced their design. Once again, 'object-based' is probably the right term for such developments.

3.1.5 Eiffel

Eiffel (Meyer, 1988) is a purpose-written object-oriented language that consciously attempts to address the issues of correctness, robustness, portability and efficiency.

Unlike Smalltalk and Objective-C, in Eiffel classes are not objects. This enables static typing to help eliminate run-time errors and improve efficiency.

A class describes the implementation of an abstract data type. It is defined at compile time and can create instances of the type (objects) at run time. The terminology differs from that of other languages in that methods are called 'routines'. Classes encapsulate both routines and attributes, which are referred to collectively as 'features'. Features may be private or public (exported) in the same way as in C++ or Ada.

An important feature of Eiffel is the ability to specify the formal properties that an object's operations must obey by writing 'assertions'. Assertions may express preconditions, postconditions or invariance conditions. Preconditions force a check whenever a method is called, postconditions are guaranteed to be true when the method terminates or returns values and invariance conditions are always true once an object is created or a method called. These features are provided to help towards the goal of producing proofs of correctness and reflects Meyer's background in software engineering and formal methods. This sort of feature can be added to Smalltalk with a little effort, as has been shown in the Fresco project at Manchester University.

Assertions permit Eiffel to incorporate exception-handling features. A violation can cause a message to fail or may invoke a 'rescue' procedure contained in the offending method. Assertions may be viewed as a formal contract between a server and its clients.

As in Ada there is a notion of generic classes – classes with parameters representing types; although, unlike Ada, full inheritance is supported. Pre- and postconditions may be specified to create secure modules. Multiple inheritance is supported but inheritance conflicts are not dealt with because attributes or methods inherited from two parents must be renamed in the descendant. Note that in all the languages dealt with so far the values of attributes are not inherited, only the ability to have a value. Inclusion polymorphism is supported by allowing type checking to authorize more specific objects but not more general ones. In Eiffel, a notion of deferred classes allows inherited methods to be overridden.

Applications are compiled into C for efficiency and portability. A library of classes is provided. Importantly for efficiency, garbage collection is optional. When it is used, Eiffel garbage-collects incrementally using a novel algorithm.

Eiffel can be used, like Ada, as a design language or program description language (PDL). The design is implemented as a set of high-level classes and the methods are filled in later. This reduces the risk of errors when translating formal design notations into code.

Although Eiffel appears to be an important extension of the concepts of object-oriented programming, its early versions received some bad press as a system for commercial developments. At the ECOOP'89 conference it was suggested (Cook, 1989) that Eiffel was not type-safe, although this is contested through an appeal to the existence of compiler errors. Leathers (1990) reports that the 4GL supplier, Cognos, abandoned a key redevelopment using Eiffel because of both performance problems due to an early version of Eiffel and a certain lack of surrounding tools (browsers and so on) but, more importantly, because of the errors made in managing the unfamiliar technology. Some important lessons which Leathers points to are lack of staff experienced in object-oriented product development, lack of management understanding of the technology and failure to apply conventional project management disciplines. The most important observation to emerge from this experience is that prototyping is essential. A throwaway prototype, as a first phase to the project, would have enabled more rational decisions to have been taken concerning the final development. In Chapter 9 we will take up the issue of prototyping and its management in detail.

Recent developments are new, much better releases of the original proprietary compiler and the fact that the language is now in the public domain with a number of very good third-party compilers becoming available. This and the novel features of the language make it likely that there will be a surge of interest in Eiffel. In particular, the notion of assertions has been taken up vigorously by a few object-oriented methods proponents, as discussed in Chapter 8.

The features of Eiffel are summarized in Table 3.8.

Table 3.8 Eiffel features.

Type checking/binding	Early
Polymorphism	Yes
Information hiding	Yes
Concurrency	Promised
Inheritance	Yes
Multiple inheritance	Yes
Garbage collection	Yes
Persistence	Some support
Genericity	Yes
Object libraries	A few

⊟ 3.2 Functional and applicative languages

Some authors have emphasized the distinction between object-oriented and value-oriented programming. MacLennan (1982) points out that values (such as the number 17) are applicative and read-only: they are timeless abstractions. Objects, that is, instances, exist in time and can be created, destroyed, copied, shared and updated. Values are referentially transparent: whatever refers to them will always be using the same value. In part, this implies a major criticism of the approach taken in Smalltalk, where everything is an object. The failure to make a proper distinction leads to several dangers. Data structures unwittingly shared may be updated erroneously, or there is a potentially costly duplication overhead. Given all the advantages of applicative or value-oriented programming, why should we need objects at all?

Firstly, simulation of the world in a computer system is vastly simplified if the data structures used correspond to real-world entities. Files are objects and cannot be described by algebras. Variables in ordinary programming languages are objects, identified and differentiated by their locations regardless of their current values. A value is said to belong to a type, whereas an object belongs to a class. The essential difference is that two objects with the same description may be different objects, whereas there cannot be two values with the same description. For example, there can only be one integer with the value 17, but there may be two identical copies of the Mona Lisa. That the converse is not true can be seen by considering two objects with different descriptions, the morning and evening stars, represented by the same physical object, the planet Venus. Many languages obfuscate this issue. For example, files in Pascal may not be assigned to or used in expressions, even though they are declared in the same manner as other types. Programmers simulating systems must deal with 'state' and changes of state, they must deal with time and (at least in artificial intelligence) with possible worlds. Applicative programming is not designed for this but for dealing with timeless mathematical abstractions.

What is needed, then, is a clear distinction between values and objects and a language that supports the distinction and allows the most appropriate models (values or objects) to be used. A classification structure for programming languages is shown in Figure 3.1.

Functional programming is a style exemplified by languages based on formal logic and mathematics, such as LISP or ML.

Conventional programs work by assigning values to variables which represent storage locations in memory. Any prior value stored in that location is overwritten and lost forever, unless steps have been taken previously. Applicative languages such as LISP do not use this destructive assignment process. Applicative, as opposed to imperative, programming does not permit assignments or side-effects. In practice this means that the processor has periodically to do some garbage collection to get rid of values no longer required in order to save on storage. Another common feature is 'lazy evaluation' whereby values are not compu-

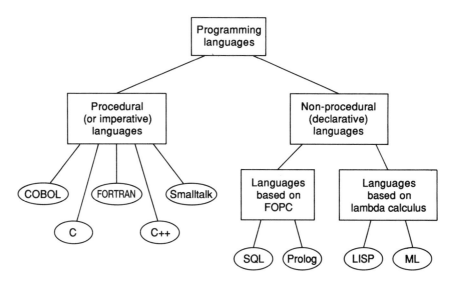

Figure 3.1 A classification structure for programming languages.

ted until a function requires them. Such languages are based on function application and composition and depend on a logical system known as 'lambda calculus' which will be described below. Applicative programming becomes functional programming when it maintains 'referential transparency', which is to say that every expression or variable has the same value within a given scope; all variables are local. This implies that we can always substitute an expression with one of equal value without altering the value of the whole expression. This property is useful in theorem proving and database enquiry where rewriting expressions and substitution are fundamental operations. Although this scoping rule is reminiscent of object-oriented languages, functional programming does not allow objects to have state.

A procedural language instructs a computer how to carry out a particular task. A non-procedural one tells it only what to do, not how to do it. Consider the following database enquiry, which asks how many employees are working in each department, and in those groups, what the total and average salaries are.

```
SELECT        DNAME, JOB, SUM(SAL), COUNT(*), AVG(SAL)

FROM          EMPLOYEES, DEPARTMENTS

WHERE         EMPLOYEES.DEPTNO + DEPARTMENTS.DEPTNO

GROUP BY      DNAME, JOB
```

This query in fact produces correct output but the results need not concern us here. The language is SQL. Notice that nowhere is the computer told how to answer the question. This would involve obtaining a list of employees, sorting it by department and job and then computing the count and average and total salaries. Finally, department name must be substituted for department number in the output. That would be a fairly complicated procedure involving reading records and saving intermediate results at each stage. The non-procedural language SQL, based on relational calculus which we will cover in Chapter 5, makes all this unnecessary. In actual implementations of SQL there are built-in functions which introduce an element of procedurality. Purity is a rare boon.

The term declarative is a slightly more general one than non-procedural, because it includes purely descriptive languages. It is more to do with the way data are represented than with any particular programming style. The opposite of a declarative language is usually referred to as an imperative one, but this usage is falling back under the onslaught of the snappier but less euphonic 'non-procedural'. The language Prolog also has a declarative and non-procedural style. Let us now turn to the logics which make such languages possible.

Both Prolog and SQL are based on the first-order predicate calculus, a form of mathematical logic, with SQL being based on a smaller subset and thus being less expressive. Such languages are commonly called logic programming languages only when they are as expressive as Prolog. Functional languages are based on another logical system, the lambda calculus, and are not usually referred to as logic programming languages, even though they are rooted firmly in logic.

There are a number of distinct benefits usually associated with functional programming languages, including:

- their formal basis;
- the fact that they are easy to extend by adding extra, reusable functions;
- the uniform programming metaphor, whereby everything is a function;
- the fact that higher-order constructs (functions of functions) are easy to express; and
- their support for polymorphic types (as in ML) or a completely type-free style (as in LISP).

HEALTH WARNING   The remainder of this section on functional programming is slightly more advanced than the rest of the chapter and may be omitted by people with an aversion for mathematical notation. Understanding it in detail is not a prerequisite for understanding the rest of the book.

The lambda calculus originated in the 1930s and was principally due to Alonzo Church. His original motivation was to provide a foundation for all of mathematics based on rules; that is, the idea of a function being a process of passing from argument to value rather than Dirichlet's more modern notion of functions as graphs (subsets of relations). It is possible to think of such functions or rules as being given by natural language sentences applied to arguments (also expressed in words), or as computer programs that may be applied to other computer programs or structures. In both cases the language is type-free, which is to say that there is no distinction between the sort of objects that constitute a function and those which can be its possible arguments. In particular, a function can be applied to itself. Self-recursion is thus supported. The axiom of foundation makes this impossible in ordinary set theory and the logic which it models: FOPC[1]. Church's original theory was shown to be inconsistent by the discovery of the Kleene-Rosser paradox, but he managed to salvage a consistent sub-theory which forms the basis of current research and of a number of programming languages, the most prominent of which has been LISP, which first originated in about 1956 (McCarthy, 1960).

In LISP, which stands for LISt Processing, as with the lambda calculus there is no distinction between program and data, both of which are expressed as hierarchically structured lists.

The lambda calculus represents a class of partial functions – that is, functions not defined on their entire domain – defined on the integers which turn out to be the recursive functions, and these are equivalent to the Turing computable functions. Based on this equivalence the Church–Turing hypothesis states that the ordinary, intuitive notion of a function that can be computed by a terminating algorithm is equivalent to the notion of a recursive function. Thus the interest of computer scientists in this subject is not surprising. Church soon discovered that the lambda calculus was undecidable. The problem concerned whether the terms of the lambda calculus have a normal form; in the language of Turing machines these are functions that have no unpleasant infinite loops, and are equivalent to Turing's 'satisfactory' machines.

In order to achieve completeness Church introduced the abstraction operator 'lambda' which lets us create or 'abstract' a function from terms of the language. Thus, (lambda x.M)a is the function that is equal to the result of substituting a for all occurrences of x and applying the function M. For example, we can make a function of one argument as follows.

$$g=(lambda \ x.2*x+3)$$

So that $g(1)=5$, $g(2)=7$, $g(3)=9$, and so on. Additionally, the lambda calculus supports an operation based on a term which takes the values 'true' and 'false', which permits conditional expressions to be included in function definitions. For example:

$$g=(lambda \ x.if \ x>5 \ then \ f(x) \ else \ -f(x))$$

Function abstraction and application are the primitive operations of this logic. The operator lambda extends the type of the language in a universal way which is analogous to the way that introducing inverse elements x^{-1} extends the language of elementary group theory, or negative numbers extends that of natural number arithmetic. However, Curry showed that lambda is not absolutely necessary, although it is intuitively appealing in a mathematical context. Modern dialects of LISP have begun increasingly to drop the explicit lambda notation, but it is still implicitly present as is apparent from the care that has to be taken with variable bindings in difficult programs.

---

[1] First-Order Predicate Calculus.

Formally, the language (of lambda calculus) is defined as follows:

The alphabet consists of variables x,y,z,... together with symbols for reduction →, equality = and abstraction λ. The terms are defined recursively as follows:

Variables are terms

Application of two terms yields a term

If M is a term and x is a variable the N (lambda xM) is a term

The well-formed formulae are defined by saying that if M and N are terms, M → N and M = N are formulae. The reduction, equality and abstraction operators are defined by requiring that they satisfy certain axiom schemes.

A variable is **free** if it is not in the scope of a lambda x and **bound** otherwise. In this way lambda is analogous to the universal quantifier of predicate logic or the definite integral of school calculus.

All of the many dialects of the LISP language rest on the lambda calculus. LISP is in some ways a very low-level language resting on very few primitives, which can be thought of as specifying a virtual machine. The most fundamental primitives are CAR, CDR (pronounced coo'der), ATOM and LAMBDA (or PROG). The only primitive data type is the list. A list consists of a head and a tail (physically a pointer to the head of another list). CAR returns the head as an atom and CDR the tail as a list – modern terminology usually refers to 'head' and 'rest'. Thus, the head of the list (apples, bananas, carrots) is (apples) and the rest is (bananas, carrots). Atoms refer to values in store and are the raw material from which lists are built. CONS constructs new lists by adding a new head to a list. There are, in addition, several control structures and arithmetic and relational operators. Like C and Pascal, LISP is a recursive language.

Logic programming as exemplified by the various dialects of Prolog is based on a particular form of mathematical logic known as the first-order predicate calculus (FOPC). The term 'first-order' is important. It represents the idea that the logic cannot deal directly with statements about statements but only with statements about objects of primitive (atomic) type. Although it can be shown mathematically that first-order systems can express higher-order notions, this expression is often otiose and extremely unnatural. Functional programming may also be regarded as a form of logic programming but the underlying logic is a different one: the lambda calculus described above. The interesting point about both kinds of logic programming is that they are based on a formal theory whereas object-oriented programming is only based on a metaphor: there is absolutely no formal theory. This means that it is very difficult to prove anything about object-oriented applications. There have been continuing attempts to remedy this apparent defect. EQLog (Goguen and Meseguer, 1986) and its sister language OBJ2 (Futatsugi *et al.*, 1985) are based on yet another kind of logic – equational logic – and OBJ2 sets out consciously to seek a unified formal basis for logic and object-oriented programming (Goguen and Meseguer, 1987). FUN (Cardelli and Wegner, 1985) represents another such attempt. We take up some of these research efforts in Section 3.6.5. However, my feeling is that the lack of a formal theory is not only not an encumbrance to commercial developments but may actually be a positive benefit, as we shall see in the remainder of this book and especially in the chapters on databases.

Other important functional languages include ML (Milner, 1978), Hope (Burstall *et al.,* 1980) and Miranda (Turner, 1985). Natural Expert is an extension to Software AG's Natural 4GL that is designed to help embed expert systems in ADABAS applications. It is unusual in not being a rule-based language, and could be described as 'ML with lazy evaluation'. BETA (Kristensen *et al.,* 1987) is a modern language being developed in the Simula tradition by some of the original Simula team. It aims to combine the ideas of constraint-oriented logic programming with object-orientation.

In the research literature there have been a number of attempts to unify object-oriented programming with functional programming, and indeed with logic programming. One of the basic difficulties here is that logic programming based on FOPC seems to be fundamentally incompatible with object identity, although abstraction and inheritance can be modelled readily.

One of the most long-lived and popular functional programming languages, however, is LISP. In the next section we turn to the various object-oriented extensions of LISP.

☰ 3.3 AI-based systems

The treatment of AI-based, object-oriented developments in this section is divided in two. It treats first of LISP extensions and then of modern expert systems development environments, which are not all based on LISP.

3.3.1 LISP extensions

For many years LISP has been the main language for academic research in artificial intelligence. LISP provides much of what is needed for the implementation of an object-oriented language in the Smalltalk style. It has garbage collection, dynamic binding, editors, debuggers and a uniform typeless style. There are also large numbers of reusable functions available, some in the public domain. Therefore it is natural that there have been several object-oriented extensions of LISP.

The artificial intelligence influence shows chiefly in the inheritance systems of some LISP extensions, where not only attributes but their values can be inherited, multiple inheritance is usually supported and demons, or event-driven processes, are supported. Demons (or triggers in the database literature) are operations that are attached to data structures and which fire when the structure is accessed.

Thus, there are 'if needed' and 'if updated' demons. These two are sometimes called backward and forward chaining demons respectively. We also find them described as 'when needed' and so on in some systems. These operations are usually attached not to objects, but to the attributes of objects. This can be viewed as making such attributes into separate objects in their own right or as breaking the principles of encapsulation, according to whether you are an opponent or a supporter of this kind of system. The key point about this approach, as I will argue, is that it captures much more of the semantics of an application.

The emerging standard for LISP extensions is CLOS, the Common Lisp Object System (Moon, 1989). CLOS is a LISP extension based on the ideas of generic functions, multiple inheritance and method combination. Meta-objects enable the user to alter the basic structure of the object system itself. It was designed, like Smalltalk, at PARC.

In AI systems, the notion that corresponds most closely to that of an object is a frame. A frame is a structural abstraction that tries to capture the idea of a stereotypical object. Frames consist of an extensible list of *slots* which are equivalent to attributes, or class variables. Slots may contain both state and process description, and methods are attached to a particular slot. Slots containing state may also have *facets* (in addition to 'value'), which are methods for determining search, default values and triggers. Part of a frame is shown in Figure 3.2. In CLOS each object has a unique identifier, and the slots contain pointers to other objects representing the state of the entire object. Every instance object belongs to a class, and every class is a type. Slots may either be type restricted or free; that is, they may only be allowed to take values of a specified type, or they may be permitted to take any value whatsoever regardless of type. Generic functions, in Common LISP, work on objects of several types. Methods, in CLOS, are specified to determine what generic functions do when called with particular arguments. The mapping between a generic function and its corresponding set of methods is part of a mapping between functional and object-oriented programming. Methods are defined by specifying a generic function, conditions under which it applies to objects, parameters, inheritance rules and code.

Methods are of several types. *Accessor* methods give access to, or update, the value facet of a slot. They are the special methods we referred to in Chapter 1 which make it possible to talk directly about attributes in an object-oriented environment. This means that the implementation of state is hidden behind standard accessors such as get and put value. This will be an important concept in Chapter 8. An important difference between CLOS and many object-oriented programming languages is the provision for facets (that is, sub-slots) other than 'value'. An attribute or slot of an instance may have a value; for example, the value of BirthDate for Employee 'Ian Graham' may take the value 19480813. Proper classes may have attributes with default values that may be inherited, so that, in Figure 3.2, an employee whose department is unknown may be assumed to be in the sales department. In CLOS, subclasses may add slots, methods and type and initialization conditions to those inherited from superclasses. In this respect CLOS is similar to Smalltalk. The close association between LISP and artificial intelligence

```
 ┌─────────────────────────────────────────────────────────────┐
 │  Name:  Employee                                             │
 ├─────────────────────────────────────────────────────────────┤
 │  AKO:  (Person, Taxpayer)                                    │
 ├─────────────────────────────────────────────────────────────┤
 │  Slots::                                                     │
 │      Age:                                                    │
 │          Facets – Value:                                     │
 │                  Default:                                    │
 │                  IfNeeded:  run AgeRelatedEntitlements       │
 │                  IfUpdated:  run CalculateAge                │
 │                                                              │
 │      DateOfBirth:                                            │
 │          Facets – Value:                                     │
 │                  Default:                                    │
 │                                                              │
 │      Salary:                                                 │
 │      Department:                                             │
 │          Facets – Value:                                     │
 │                  Default:  Sales                             │
```

Figure 3.2 Part of a frame (not necessarily a CLOS frame) for Employee. Note that each slot has facets for its value, default value, and if-updated and if-needed demons. The if-updated demons are procedures (or rules) which fire whenever the value (or sometimes default) facet changes. The if-needed demon searches for a value to fill the value facet when it is accessed and contains no value at that point in time.

makes it unsurprising that CLOS supports multiple inheritance. Like FLAVORS, an earlier object-oriented LISP extension, CLOS inheritance conflicts are resolved by defining an order of precedence in the list of superclasses in a class's definition. This is a flexible system but not as general as the scheme described in Chapter 8 for general object-oriented specification purposes. The class precedence list determines which characteristics of a slot to inherit when name conflicts arise. When more than one method is inherited, CLOS allows methods to cooperate by a complex technique called 'method combination' based on the FLAVORS notion of 'mixins'. How best to do this is not a fully resolved issue at present, although it represents an important advance over the approach of other object-oriented programming languages. We will return to this issue in Chapter 8 in a context free of particular language considerations. Just as slots may have defaults, there may be default methods, which may be overridden. Backward and forward chaining demons may be specified to simulate pre- and postconditions, triggers and side effects. CLOS, like Smalltalk, regards everything as an object, including its own language constructs, with constructs called meta-objects which provide particularly good facilities for extending the language itself. Like all LISP systems, CLOS garbage-collects, sometimes at inconvenient moments. Dynamic binding is supported using the same mechanism that LISP uses to allocate storage at run time. Since slot names are encapsulated but not hidden, CLOS classes are not true abstract data types, but this disadvantage can be overcome by good programming disciplines. The features of CLOS are summarized in Table 3.9.

CLOS applications as diverse as the production of animated graphics for television commercials, geographic information systems and telephone network control have been written and used.

Various object-oriented extensions to LISP emerged piecemeal within the artificial intelligence community through the 1970s and 1980s. LOOPS, Common LOOPS, FLAVORS, KEE and New FLAVORS represent typical such attempts. CLOS represents the emerging standard that synthesizes all these approaches in the LISP world.

A particularly interesting such extension is CommonObjects, developed by Snyder (1987). This system emphasizes the importance of not allowing inheritance to compromise encapsulation. This is accomplished by preventing the inheritance of attributes: only methods may be inherited. An alternative and, I think, preferable suggestion is to have two distinct inheritance hierarchies for methods and attributes (see Danforth and Tomlinson, 1988) or, better, for interface and implementation. The AI notion of inheritance and the LISP culture tends to oppose this kind of protection and, as we have seen, the protocols for protection suggested by Snyder could be imposed by good programming practice rather than by compilers. This is one of the issues which is unresolved and leads me to believe that object-oriented programming is still a somewhat immature discipline.

The number of different object-oriented extensions of LISP is too large for them to be enumerated here, let alone described. They include, in addition to those already mentioned, Ceyx developed at INRIA, LOOPS (Bobrow and Stefik, 1983) and CommonLOOPS (Bobrow *et al.*, 1986) developed at Xerox, Oaklisp (Lang and Perlmutter, 1986) and many more.

As the engineering discipline of expert systems emerged from the academic one of artificial intelligence, a number of higher-level programming environments for this kind of work emerged, not all based on LISP. We now turn to these.

Table 3.9 CLOS features.

Type checking/binding	Late
Polymorphism	Yes
Information hiding	Yes
Concurrency	Difficult
Inheritance	Yes
Multiple inheritance	Yes
Garbage collection	Yes
Persistence	No
Genericity	Yes
Object libraries	A few

3.3.2 Other AI-based development systems

KEE, ART and Joshua are all LISP-based expert systems development environments designed originally for specialized workstations. They all support an object-oriented style to some extent. We will take KEE as a surrogate for all three. Its main claim to object-orientation derives from the fact that its *units* support attribute and method inheritance and multiple inheritance. Slots in the units contain *facets* which can be used to determine the control regime under which inheritance takes place; for example, to determine whether inheritance takes precedence over defaults or the type of multiple inheritance regime. KEE is not, however, so strong in terms of encapsulation and the user may obtain direct access to the state of a unit from LISP.

Kappa, Nexpert Object and GoldWorks represent attempts to provide similar facilities in a PC environment. Kappa and Nexpert are written in C and GoldWorks in LISP and the main effects of this difference are in terms of performance. ProKappa is a UNIX version of Kappa. Tricky programming in GoldWorks, as with KEE, is usually accomplished in LISP itself. Taking Nexpert as a representative of this type of package, we note first that while multiple inheritance is supported among classes, an object can be an instance of no more than one class. In general these packages have similar features to KEE and ART but some compromises are made in view of the memory limitations of PCs. Hitachi's ES/KERNEL and Expersoft's XShell are both expert system shells with a strong object-oriented content. The latter is written in C++ and emphasizes distributed implementation. Both products are unusual in offering facilities to incorporate fuzzy logic. ObjectIQ is a Romanized version of ES/KERNEL with these fuzzy facilities removed.

KBMS is a second-generation expert systems development system which is particularly interesting for its close coupling with popular database systems such as DB2. It is similar in architecture to Leonardo (described below) but slightly stronger on object-oriented features, in offering method inheritance and support for encapsulation. A bizarre (because I can't think of an application for it and it sounds dangerous) feature of KBMS is that it not only supports multiple inheritance but allows the inheritance network to be changed at run time. ADS, from the same supplier as KBMS, is another second-generation expert systems shell; that is, it is an expert systems development environment. The exact definition of a 'shell' will be presented in Chapter 4. It was originally a rather simple rule-based, backward (and secondarily forward) chaining system, but recent enhancements have provided support for encapsulation and classes whose slots can inherit both attributes and methods. Instances can be created at compile or run time. As with KBMS, it offers integration with several database systems. ADS does not support multiple inheritance. Both systems run on mainframes and PCs.

Level 5 Object is yet another system of this general type and supports encapsulation, inheritance and when-needed and when-updated demons attached to attributes.

Leonardo is an expert systems development system which, while it cannot be described as truly object-oriented, does have a number of object-oriented features. Multi-level, multiple inheritance of attributes (not methods) is fully supported and rulesets, procedures, screen layouts and other components are treated as objects with some browsing facilities supplied. However, encapsulation of procedures is not supported and the built-in procedural language is conventional in design. In Leonardo's present form (Version 4.00), although attribute inheritance is fully supported, method inheritance is not.

All the AI-derived systems tend to major on their support for inheritance and be rather deficient in terms of encapsulation. They also offer a semantically rich form of inheritance that differs from the one found in most object-oriented programming languages like Smalltalk. Although C++ permits the inheritance of default values, in most object-oriented languages this is not so. In the frame-based AI systems, values (in particular default values) can be inherited as well as attribute names. This means that dealing with multiple inheritance is a more complex problem, but this merely reflects the general principle that semantically complex systems make tougher demands on programmers and designers. My view is that the AI people have got it right and that this kind of inheritance will gradually penetrate the world of object-oriented programming. Object-oriented programmers have a lot to learn from other computing disciplines including AI and, as pointed out by Roger King (1989), from work in the area of semantic data modelling. This will be a recurrent theme in this book.

At present, there are no ideal object-oriented expert systems development tools, though there are some very good ones. One reason is the need to implement efficient reasoning algorithms, such as the RETE algorithm, which is easier to do when objects are created as a by-product of processing rules rather than having rules attached to objects in mini expert systems. In this respect Kappa and XShell come closer to the object-oriented way of doing things than do Nexpert and KBMS, say.

Thus, we have seen that, among the vast number of languages claiming to be object-oriented in some way, there are considerable differences of emphasis and function. One is tempted to suspect that the use of the term 'object-oriented' is often motivated as much by marketing considerations as by veracity. In other words it has become fashionable to describe almost any product as object-oriented in order to make a spurious differentiation from its competitors. Journalists call such usage 'hype'; *caveat emptor!*[2]

3.4 Object libraries and application frameworks

An object library is a collection of complete, tested, documented, reusable objects, available either as a commercial package or as part of an in-house software library. Object libraries are key to object-oriented developments because without them any reuse benefits cannot be obtained. Most object-oriented programming languages are

---

[2] Let the buyer beware!

delivered with basic, generic object libraries, but these are seldom adequate for productive application development. For that reason there are now a few commercially available libraries which can supplement a language.

ObjectWorks (ParcPlace Systems) is an environment which can be based on C++ or Smalltalk. In the C++ version it provides an interface to UNIX, incremental compilation, source-level debugging and graphical browsing/editing facilities. It is type-safe and supports multiple inheritance, which C++ and Smalltalk did not always do. In the Smalltalk-80 version it includes a library of over 300 classes and several thousand methods. It runs unchanged across a variety of machines from DOS PCs to UNIX workstations, and is source compatible across this range.

Object libraries for building graphical user interfaces in C++ are gradually becoming available on a commercial basis. A number of systems, such as CommonView from Glockenspiel and Intuitive Solution 2 (a forms-based development environment developed in CommonView), are available under Presentation Manager. There are also libraries integrated with the Microsoft Windows environment such as C++/Views. Among the best known (or at least most aggressively marketed) at the time of writing were Classix and InterViews. Typically, all these libraries offer classes dealing with relatively low-level programming abstractions such as stacks or linked lists, and graphics concepts such as rectangles, buttons or windows. Visual BASIC, an otherwise conventional language, incorporates a library of graphical objects which can respond to messages but does not yet support inheritance. Libraries with classes which will be needed for specific vertical commercial systems developments do not yet exist, and this, I believe, is a major issue facing this maturing field.

Another important system running under Presentation Manager is Easel from a company originally called Interactive Images, though now expressing a fuller commitment to the product as Easel Corp. Easel is a complete 4GL with particularly good, CUA-compliant, user interface graphics facilities, an SQL interface and a procedural programming language. Easel is mentioned in IBM's AD/Cycle announcements and has been partly funded by IBM. The original DOS version was largely icon driven, although the OS/2 versions show more sophistication and the MS Windows implementation promises the same level of functionality and perhaps will not make the same demands on memory (1 Mb for just the run-time system). The important aspect of Easel is its compliance with IBM's standards such as CUA and LU 6.2 and support for database access and network protocols such as APPC. Easel is not fully object-oriented but does support inheritance. Easel Corp. now also sells a fully object-oriented 4GL called ENFIN/2 that is based on Smalltalk. ENFIN is among the first of a new generation of object-oriented 4GLs based on the client/server model of computing. Such products provide application frameworks for commonly required types of computer system. These frameworks bolster productivity for applications with significant demands for graphical user interfaces programming, database access and client/server links. They usually offer visual programming and extensive class libraries for windows programming and database interfaces along with the usual low-level foundation classes. Sometimes they include report-generator classes and other useful tools. ENFIN is fairly typical of such application framework 4GLs. Others include GUI Master and Choreographer, and the NeXTstep environment includes several.

LispWorks is a commercial programming environment for workstations incorporating CLOS. Access to X windows is via an extensible set of 'widget' classes; that is, classes of predefined window elements corresponding to the hardware in question.

In the mainframe arena there are few libraries or object-oriented 4GLs as yet. The Sapiens application generator has some object-based features as rules (or more exactly, constraints) are attached to data objects, but fully fledged object-oriented 4GLs are under development. At the very least, as we have seen with Cognos, 4GL suppliers are writing their systems in object-oriented programming languages.

Without object libraries object-oriented programming becomes intensely and unnecessarily tedious. One of the strengths of C has always been its ability to include libraries of functions, and adding libraries of objects is a natural continuation of the progress of the language which will probably increase its commercial acceptability. However, there is a negative side to systems that rely heavily on libraries of either sort, as the history of C has indeed demonstrated. That is to say, every inclusion from a proprietary library decreases application portability. This is often not important for one-off applications but is very important for package developments. Furthermore, since one of the main reasons for the use of object-oriented programming is reusability, one is forced to wonder whether this benefit itself is compromised by a lack of portability. System developers should consider this trade-off early in the planning phase of each new project.

A major difficulty with class libraries is the sheer difficulty of knowing what the library contains and what its classes do. It is estimated that it takes a good programmer about a day to become fully conversant with a class. Thus, to become familiar with a typical class library (Smalltalk 80 has about 350 classes in its library) takes over a man-year. Against this it is estimated that the production of a fully tested and debugged class at the right level of granularity takes, on average, about two man-months of effort: about sixty years for a 350-class library. Of course, no program is likely to need every class in the library. These observations point to the need for group work. Teams should meet regularly to review code being developed. The advantage of this is that someone other than the developer may well know of a class which could be used to speed development. Group work techniques should be already familiar to FORTRAN programmers used to working with large function libraries, such as the NAG library of FORTRAN mathematical procedures. They are essential for object-oriented programming.

In the presence of large object libraries change control becomes an especially critical issue. The matter is further complicated by the existence of complex objects that consist of more than one interconnected object. If one of the components changes, how does this affect the whole? Theoretically, in perfectly encapsulated languages, a changed implementation should not have any effect, but if inheritance is allowed this may not be the case and, worse still, we can never really guarantee that the interface of an object may not have to be changed. One way round the problem is suggested by module interconnexion languages, such as DeRemer and Kron's MIL75; metalanguages that make the connexions among objects explicit. To achieve the benefits of software reuse we need a composability language that can be used to specify module interfaces, so that ultimately re-usable modules can be configured to meet a specification and the implementation language of each module can be independent. Further, object classification techniques are needed to help programmers understand the libraries they are dealing with. There is thus a profound need for a tool that can estimate the impact of changing an interface – that is, change prediction (Hood, Kennedy and Muller, 1987). The general absence of such tools and techniques in the commercial domain is only one indicator of the immaturity of object-oriented programming. However, the emergence of such tools may be an index of its maturation. We have already discussed the fact that component management is a difficult and unsolved problem in Chapter 2.

The absence of existing high-level class libraries for most commercial appli-cations is a serious obstacle to the widespread adoption of object-oriented pro-gramming. Here is a vicious circle: without such libraries development is too costly, and good library modules can only emerge from real projects. Companies wishing to obtain the benefits of object-oriented programming will have to cost-justify projects in terms of long-term reuse, which is especially hard to do in a period of high interest rates. This suggests that the first commercial libraries will be sold by companies that have built systems and wish to recoup some of their development expenditure; and these libraries may, initially, take the form of tailorable application packages.

Buyers of such packages will need further assurance that the quality of the modules is sufficiently high; that is, that they have been designed and written to support reuse from the outset, and not just sold as a means to recoup development costs thought of later.

3.5 Selecting an object-oriented language

How then are we to choose a tool or language that will deliver the benefits we seek from object-oriented methods? The answer is complex. First we must look at the characteristics and requirements of each application and try to choose the tool best suited for the job, as there is no object-oriented panacea. For example, in choosing between C++ and Smalltalk, we might consider whether classification structures discovered during the analysis stage are broad and shallow or narrow and deep. Second, we must ask ourselves seriously about the organizational impact of our choice; will it fit in with other systems standards or be acceptable to existing staff? Much of the motivation for using languages such as Ada or C++ is predicated on the last point. The alternative is to step back from the problem slightly and ask if the benefits can be better obtained through the use of object-oriented analysis and design, deferring the choice of programming language till later or even implement-ing the design in COBOL, FORTRAN or some 4GL.

As we shall see in the next chapter, the construction of complex GUIs is practically impossible without a language that supports a high level of reuse and extensibility. Thus, organizations contemplating the construction of a GUI should seriously consider adopting an object-oriented programming language for this purpose. Similarly, if the application is simulation of some sort then an object-oriented programming solution is strongly indicated.

Selecting a particular language or set of languages depends on enumerating the known features of the application and predicting what features may be needed in the future. The language features can then be checked off. The difficulty with this approach is that it is almost impossible to guarantee the prediction's accuracy or completeness. This leads to a search for a language with the maximum number of features, to insure against future change. This would be a fairly simple matter if there were a language with *all* desirable features and if some features were not at odds with others. For example, in terms of maximum features, there is no object-oriented language with both comprehensive data abstraction features and totally flexible multiple inheritance. Even the Smalltalk dialects that do support multiple inheritance do not have the flexibility of the AI-derived systems mentioned in the foregoing. In terms of contradictory features, we have seen that there is no language that is 'fully object-oriented' and at the same time capable of high-volume, multi-user, real-time performance.

At present, I recommend people to gain experience first by prototyping in a language like Smalltalk then, if developing on workstations, to move the same team over to develop the application in something like C++. If a mainframe implementation is called for, I usually advise them to wait and see. The next section gives my view on what they should be waiting for.

Since object-oriented programming is a maturing, as opposed to mature, technology, any language selected now runs a risk of being superseded by some as yet unwritten language that is destined to become an industry standard. Here again is a conundrum. Should we wait for this mature technology and then have to begin to learn how to use it, or should we plunge in now, knowing that some of our results may be redundant? I think that companies entering the field now must do so on the basis that what they learn will be more valuable than the programs they write. In that sense selecting an imperfect language may not matter much. The object-oriented metaphor may well prove more important than the final language. The philosophy of this book is that analysis and design for reusability and extensibility will have a lasting value and enable users of the object-oriented metaphor to gain the benefits of mature languages when they arrive.

In subsequent chapters we take up these questions in some detail, looking at object-oriented analysis and design as a separate issue from implementation and going into some depth on object-oriented databases. In the next chapter, for example, we survey the sort of applications that have been typical for object-oriented programming systems and try to determine how to map an application's requirements onto a suitable language.

☰ 3.6 Other developments

One of the most important current developments is the emergence of an object-oriented version of COBOL, a language that exists but is still the subject of a standardization effort. Further, a number of hardware suppliers have adopted specific languages.

3.6.1 Object-oriented COBOL

The Codasyl standards committee has already begun to lay the basis for an object-oriented version of COBOL under pressure from user groups advocating open systems and stressing the importance of software reuse as projects get larger. It is not clear yet what this will look like but it may not appear until 1995/6 according to current plans. It is likely that a stop-gap will be released sooner by suppliers such as Micro Focus and Realia. Certainly, Object COBOL of some sort is urgently needed by users who want the benefits of reuse and extensibility while needing to protect a huge investment in existing code: an estimated 70 milliard lines of code worldwide.

At the time of writing two or three Object COBOL compilers are released in beta-test versions. In an atmosphere where the standards bodies seem not to be in a hurry, it is inevitable that such products will establish *de facto* standards. Several names for the language have been suggested, including OO-COBOL, COBOL++ and COOBOL. My suggestion is SmallBOL, but no one is expected to take that seriously.

Early releases indicate that OO-COBOL will provide the following features:

- user-defined types based on COBOL record structures;
- encapsulation;
- classes as templates for abstract data types;
- classification (instantiation by loading a program);
- message passing as program calls via the USING verb;
- inheritance using the COPY verb;
- polymorphism using multiple entry points and the READ statement;
- the ability to use objects written in other languages;
- garbage collection for single objects using the CANCEL verb;
- upward compatibility from COBOL;
- better support for prototyping.

The first features to appear will concern encapsulation and only later, I think, will really useful inheritance features appear in COBOL. Having predicted this, I hope that it will not be the case. The appearance of a genuinely object-oriented version of COBOL is a prerequisite for the development of mainframe applications on any really wide scale and for the maturation of the technology. Although it is unlikely that really leading-edge applications will be written in COBOL, the emergence of Object COBOL is to be welcomed and embraced. The maturity of a programming style is to be recognized when it is applied to the mundane, not the esoteric.

3.6.2 Trellis

Trellis/Owl (Schaffert *et al.*, 1986) developed at DEC was rare in being a strongly typed language and data management system combined. It was strongly influenced by CLU and supported multiple inheritance, concurrency and genericity. It also incorporated a data model and may influence the future design of Digital's database product Rdb. Object-oriented and other types of database are discussed in Chapters 5 and 6.

Currently, DEC has opted to support the Trellis Object System under DEC Windows. It is integrated with Rdb under VMS via SQL and includes a library of tools for browsing, debugging and programming. It provides garbage collection and persistent objects. It also provides for concurrency using multiple threads of control, multiple inheritance and overriding. Trellis is supplied with source code, although DEC will not support it if altered. DEC's attitude to Trellis is reminiscent of their attitude to the OPS-5 rule language, where for many years they built up in-house skills and some large applications in a language not widely used on other hardware. The advantages are that the language is tuned to the environment and very detailed support is available. The disadvantage, for the user at least, is a potential lack of portability.

A number of other so-called 'persistent object' languages are described in Rosenberg and Koch (1990). PS-Algol, a persistent version of ALGOL, is described by Gray *et al.* (1992).

3.6.3 Other languages

Actor (Whitewater Group, 1989) is an object-oriented language and environment which seems to have been inspired in name only by the actor model (Agha, 1986). It is designed to support developments under Microsoft Windows and contains an extensive class library for this purpose, along with a browser and debugger. The language supports encapsulation, single inheritance, late binding, incremental compilation and garbage collection. Actor was acquired by Symantec in 1992.

Actor languages are dealt with in Chapter 10 in connexion with concurrency. Actor languages such as Act 3 and ABCL/1 implement inheritance without using classes, so it is difficult to decide whether they should be called object-oriented or not. In practice, they deliver the same benefits as encapsulation and inheritance and so the distinction is baroque, though actor languages tend to be very low-level. Actor is an object-oriented language, not an actor language.

3.6.4 Object-oriented programming in conventional languages

If software development is, as I believe, to be dominated by the sort of object-oriented analysis and design techniques discussed in Chapters 7 and 8, then many users worried about the performance characteristics and difficulty of learning object-oriented languages may consider implementation in a conventional language. Most purists in the field are scathing about this option. In this section we consider whether this is a practical possibility.

Although there are specifically object-oriented (or at least object-based) versions of Pascal, implementing an object-oriented specification in ordinary Pascal is very difficult. This is chiefly due to the language's main strength, its block-structured nature. Such a structure emphasizes decomposition by process, and although abstraction features such as enumeration data types are provided, the overall control structure is most naturally functional in nature.

Implementing an object-oriented design in COBOL is, at best, a bizarre prospect. The remarks made in relation to Pascal also apply to COBOL to some extent.

With both FORTRAN and C it is quite possible to implement object-oriented designs, and in fact there is an existence theorem in the sense that Objective-C is implemented in C. However, it is difficult and costly and, in FORTRAN, the lack of dynamic arrays means that assembler extensions will probably be required and some other programming constructs in the language would obstruct such developments.

If, as the saying goes, real programmers write FORTRAN, then the *really* tough guys write assembler. There have even been a few attempts to write assembly language in an object-oriented style. Dorfman (1990) lays down some guidelines for doing this.

In Ada and Modula-2 object-oriented programming is only partially possible unless considerable trouble is taken and extra documentation is usually necessary. They have already been discussed as object-based rather than object-oriented languages, and of course the encapsulation aspects of object-orientation are provided for. Genericity can be used to simulate a limited form of inheritance, but this is not the natural way to proceed.

Rumbaugh *et al.* (1991) give a number of useful heuristics for implementing an object-oriented design in a conventional language. A revised version of these guidelines which I have found useful is as follows.

- Classes are converted to data structures: structs in C; records and packages in Ada; arrays and common blocks in FORTRAN; records in Pascal.
- Messages are converted to function calls.
- Storage for objects is allocated to global or stack variables.
- Inheritance hierarchies are 'flattened' by making each non-abstract class a structure and reimplementing inherited methods in each one, usually by sub-routine calls.
- Polymorphic references are resolved at compile time by identifying the class of each object and at run time by testing each instance or by using select/case statements.
- The associations of the data model are mapped to pointers or implemented as data structures themselves.
- To preserve encapsulation global variables should be avoided (but see above), scoping should be parsimonious and access methods should be used to access fields of different classes. They should not be accessed directly.

The existence of large investments in programs written in conventional languages such as COBOL has to be recognized. An important concept, which can protect this investment during the move to object-oriented programming, is that of 'object wrappers' (Dietrich *et al.*, 1989). It is possible to create 'object wrappers' around existing code which could then be replaced or allowed to wither away. An object wrapper enables a new, object-oriented part of a system to interact with a conventional chunk by message passing (see Graham, 1992a; 1993a for a discussion of the issues concerning wrappers).

Many commentators, especially the specialists in object-oriented programming, think that implementing an object-oriented design in a conventional language cannot be done, or at least is inadvisable. As we remarked above, there is an existence theorem here in the form of Objective-C. Clearly it can be done but it is a question not of possibility but of productivity. After all, we could do object-oriented programming in machine code since that is what all systems, even interpreted ones, end up as. The real question here is how easy it is to produce and maintain the code.

3.6.5 Type theories and object-oriented programming

Up to now object-oriented programming has developed without the guidance of any rigorous mathematical theories of syntax or semantics. Object-oriented programming is a style or metaphor rather than a formal method, but it is a very powerful metaphor indeed. For this reason there have been a number of attempts to provide more rigorous foundations. These attempts divide into explorations intended to unify object-oriented programming with either functional or logic programming, or both, and attempts to supply rigorous type theories (for a survey of these approaches see Danforth and Tomlinson, 1988) or even denotational semantics (Cook, 1989).

Functional and logic programming share a feature with object-oriented programming in that they all attempt to divorce the description of computation from its details. They try to model the real-world problem rather than the computational process as in conventional languages like COBOL or FORTRAN. Functional and logic programming are usually based on formal theories of logic that are first-order and untyped. Current research in this area includes the development of algebraic languages such as OBJ2 (Futatsugi *et al.*, 1985). These efforts are also directed at constructing provably correct compilers. Theories based on algebraic models, such as OBJ2, make a strong distinction between values and operations, whereas those based on higher-order logics, such as SOL (Mitchell and Plotkin, 1985), FUN (Cardelli and Wegner, 1985), DL (MacQueen, 1986), Russell (Demers and Donahue, 1979; Hook, 1984) and Poly (Matthews, 1983) allow functions and even types themselves to be treated as arguments (values); in other words, as first-class objects.

Type theories for programming languages are useful because they enable compilers to carry out a lot of checking at compile time and thus avoid many run-time errors. Borning and Ingalls (1982) suggest that the type of an object in Smalltalk could be taken to be its nearest superclass. In Emerald (Black *et al.*,

1986) a subtype belongs to a type X if it provides all the operations of X via the same argument list and issues results of the same type.

This whole area is the subject of much deep and active research and it will be some time before all the disputes are sufficiently resolved to lead to a model acceptable for broad commercial purposes. In the meanwhile we will have to make do with the object-oriented metaphor without the comfort of a universally agreed formal basis. However, the fact that such formal theories are within the grasp of the researchers is encouraging.

I believe that the absence of a formal theory is not an obstacle to the development of commercial applications, except maybe in safety-critical and security-sensitive domains. The reason for my belief is a strong conviction that the real world can never be captured in a single formal theory.

3.6.6 BETA and Mjølner

I have mentioned BETA as a research project earlier in this chapter. This language is now commercially available within a development environment called Mjølner[3] (Knudsen *et al.*, 1993) which is sold by a Danish company, Mjølner Informatics. BETA (Madsen *et al.*, 1993) is based on a more general model than Smalltalk and provides greater conceptual modelling abilities by allowing objects and methods to be detached from classes. It is derived from Simula and appears to be a significant advance over object-oriented programming providing, perhaps, an indication of future directions in languages.

In BETA, objects are regarded as physical, real-world entities. Each has unique identity and may be an aggregate of other objects. A clear distinction is made between being part of something and being a property of something, as exemplified by my car having a wheel and having a colour. Unlike Smalltalk numbers are values and not first-class objects, which overcomes a major objection to Smalltalk. The language's most powerful concept is that of a **pattern**. A pattern could represent a class, a record type or a procedure: for example, a car, a log entry or a 20000 mile service. Patterns can represent almost any phenomenon such as variables, data structures, co-routines or procedure activations. Objects are instances, not of classes, but of patterns, and patterns participate in inheritance networks. It is interesting that workers in object-oriented analysis have also discovered the usefulness of patterns independently. Coad (1992) suggests looking for repetition in classification and composition structures and Jacobson *et al.* (1992) use inheritance not only for objects but for use-cases (see Chapter 8).

BETA has been implemented by Nokia Telecommunications, a Finnish company, on a digital telephone switch. BETA and Mjølner are available in versions for the Macintosh and UNIX workstations. The latter include a CASE tool for early parts of the life cycle. The tool includes code generation and visual programming facilities and programs are reversible to the diagrams. I will argue in subsequent

---

[3] Mjølner was Thor's magical hammer. The perfect tool capable of producing thunder.

chapters how important reversibility is for software engineering. No other language known to me seems to offer such support for it. As in Smalltalk, there is a meta-programming feature whereby the environment itself can be altered.

These developments point the way to enhancements of the object-oriented metaphor itself, but at present they have not gained any widespread commercial acceptance and BETA is little used outside Scandinavia. However, I suspect that the good ideas of BETA will begin to penetrate other languages and, even more rapidly, structured methods.

▭ 3.7 Directions and trends

There are two key objections to object-oriented systems usually advanced: they do not scale up, and they are inefficient. Experience shows that big systems can be built, the biggest, at the time of writing, having up to 900 000 lines of code and 3500 classes. These applications include maintenance management, real-time train control systems, decision support systems, financial trading systems, hardware diagnostic, CAD products, customer management systems, a system for tracking container movements through Singapore's docks and a CT[4] scanner. This latter is an interesting example of an object-oriented system in a safety-critical domain. With conventional systems there seems to be a qualitative change at about 100 000 lines of code where everything gets harder out of all proportion to a small amount of extra functionality. Experience suggests that this just does not happen with object-oriented systems. Although this evidence suggests that the above objections are not serious, it is noteworthy that these successes apply to a limited range of application types. The real question is not whether object-oriented programming is inefficient or scalable, but what applications it can be applied to. This question will only be answered on the basis of experience, although, as we have seen, this experience will be coupled with the emergence of new languages with new features and new class libraries and application frameworks.

It has to be admitted that some real-time systems do exhibit insuperable performance problems. Fast real-time systems are feasible though, in certain application areas.

Libraries should be tested on real applications. Some people believe that classes should be delivered in binary to support reuse. Such binary classes are expected to appear soon from Digitalk, the supplier of Smalltalk V. Particular testing problems arise because of inheritance, since it gives rise to side effects and can expose a class to the implementation of a parent's instance variables. The test harness must automatically test through all the inheritance levels. Such a test harness soon repays its cost on even quite small projects. Testing strategy is

---

[4] Computer tomography: A CT scanner is a sort of X-ray scanner that works by focusing on a series of narrow planes.

summed up by 'try to kill the worst bug first'. Testers should ask themselves: 'If there were such a bug, where would it be?'. Object-oriented programming has demonstrated that it can achieve very good error rates if properly managed: up to twice as good as the industry average. Generally, object-oriented systems just seem to be more reliable.

Apart from GUI development, the most important application area at present is in manufacturing. General Electric (GE) has done a lot of useful work, and one unnamed company claims to be committed to have every line of its code object-oriented by 1999. This aim may not be realistic, but it is an important indicator of the seriousness with which the technology of object-oriented programming is being taken by some leading players. Several other large (and formerly very conventional) DP organizations known to me are making object technology a central plank in their downsizing and distributed systems strategy.

Another thing that recent experience has shown is that there is real need for project managers to realize that they must train object-oriented programmers properly. It takes about six months to become comfortable with the object-oriented style. The best way to learn is on the job with experienced people, as a sort of journeyman. A common beginner's mistake is designing objects with far too fine a granularity.

It must be realized that the development life cycle for object-oriented systems is fundamentally different, as is the structure of project organizations. Object-oriented projects have more in common with mathematical modelling than with traditional business systems projects. The whole feel is that of simulation rather than analysis and design. The waterfall model is no use for this sort of project and prototyping is important. For software reuse, there must be a technical review of every single line of code. This is partly because it is very hard for any programmer to know what is in all the code libraries and also because of this it has been found that group work helps considerably – someone else might know that 'just the class you need' is in such and such a library.

There is no experience yet of large-scale commercial reuse. Although there are many reusable classes of a type where a theory can be advanced as to their ideal structure, such as for programming constructs like stack or for graphics, classes suitable for, say, payroll systems have not emerged commercially. Such a development would be a turning point in the regularization of object-orientation.

The two main obstacles to the proliferation of the object-oriented style are performance problems and the habit of trying to apply traditional life-cycle and design techniques.

In the meantime, project managers wishing to make a migration would be well advised to create object wrappers around their existing code which could then be gradually replaced. Big companies are now taking up the cudgels, lured by the promise of a 24:1 productivity gain. With the steady improvement of hardware, languages like Smalltalk may catch on. One project I know of switched from Pascal to Smalltalk and the system actually ran faster because in an object-oriented environment it is possible to gain a better understanding of the whole system and this makes it easier to do global optimization.

For the present, C++ and Smalltalk look like becoming the most successful, practical, general-purpose object-oriented programming languages, at least in the world of workstations and downsizing. Their long-term fortunes, however, will be intimately tied to those of UNIX and will also depend on the development of new coherent semantic and type theories. C++ was once expected to lead the field but the fortunes of Smalltalk and, to a lesser extent, Eiffel are reviving rapidly. The emergence of Object COBOL will be of critical importance for the future of object-oriented programming in the world of mainframes and commercial systems.

An alternative path for the COBOL community would be to switch to a new object-oriented language that preserves the good features of COBOL while dropping some of its idiosyncrasies. This route will obviously meet with more resistance than the Object COBOL option, but nevertheless has much to recommend it. The question with Object COBOL will be exactly which object-oriented features it supports: will it emphasize abstraction or inheritance?

Object-oriented programming languages are powerful but immature, in the sense that they are acquiring new features rapidly, and new languages are still emerging. For certain applications, such as GUI development and distributed computing, they are absolutely indispensable, as we shall see in the next chapter.

3.8 Summary

There is a vast range of languages which are connected to the idea of object-orientation. These range from 'pure' object-oriented programming languages like Smalltalk to object-based languages like Ada. No firm classification is appropriate. We have made an *ad hoc* classification as follows, although the following is not intended to be a complete list.

- Pure object-oriented languages
    - CLOS
    - Eiffel
    - Simula
    - Smalltalk
    - Prolog++ and DLP
- Extended conventional languages
    - C++
    - Objective-C
    - Object Pascal and Turbo Pascal
    - Modula-3 and Classic Ada
    - Object COBOL
- Extended LISP and AI environments
    - KEE, Joshua and ART
    - KBMS and ADS
    - Nexpert Object and Level 5 Object
    - ProKappa, Kappa, ObjectIQ and XShell

■ Object-based languages
  – Ada
  – Modula-2
  – Ellie
■ Class-based languages
  – CLU

Object-oriented designs can be implemented in conventional languages, but it is difficult and many of the benefits may be lost.

Object wrappers can be used to migrate to object-oriented programming and still protect investments in conventional code.

Object-orientation is a metaphor backed by no formal theory, but research work is proceeding on this topic.

Strict waterfall life cycles are not appropriate for object-oriented programming. Prototyping is essential and group work is highly advisable where class libraries are being used. This is further discussed in Chapter 9.

It appeared until recently that C++ would become the most successful, practical, general-purpose object-oriented programming language, at least in the world of workstations and down-scaling. Increasingly, interest is turning to Smalltalk and perhaps Eiffel. Where NeXT machines have penetrated business Objective-C is in wide use. The emergence of Object COBOL will be of critical importance for the future of object-oriented programming in the world of mainframes and commercial systems.

Object-oriented programming languages are powerful but immature, in the sense that they are acquiring new features rapidly, and new languages are still emerging. For certain applications, such as GUI development, they are sufficiently mature and absolutely indispensable. For others, class libraries will have to be developed as part of flagship projects for major users. We await the emergence of object-oriented 4GLs and object-oriented databases to enable object-oriented programming in the context of routine DP.

⊟ 3.9 **Bibliographical notes**

The original reference on Simula is Dahl and Nygaard (1966), but there are several modern introductions now, including Kirkerud (1989).

There are also many introductory texts on Smalltalk including the seminal one by Goldberg and Robson (1983) and many other more recent books too numerous to list. I like Gray and Mohamed (1990) as a simple tutorial. One of the most comprehensive tutorials on Smalltalk 80 is Lalonde and Pugh (1990, 1991). For Macintosh users, Schmucker (1986) contains useful guidelines for the use of Object Pascal and MacApp (Apple, 1988), its class library.

Stroustrup (1986) describes the C++ language in detail along with a philosophical justification for its approach. Other primers include Dewhurst and Stark

(1989), Eckel (1989), Lippman (1989), Mullin (1989), Hansen (1990), Pohl (1989), Pinson and Weiner (1988) and Weiner and Pinson (1990). Winder (1993) is a good, popular text emphasizing the newer features of C++ such as the use of templates. Coplien (1992) is widely considered the best book for advanced C++ programmers. Cox and Novobilski (1991) provides a general introduction to object-oriented programming illustrated heavily with examples written in Objective-C but comparing it with other languages.

Undoubtedly, the best reference on Eiffel is the book by Meyer (1988) referred to in the last chapter, which again provides comparisons with other languages. Meyer also has a lot to say about the difficulties of doing object-oriented programming in conventional languages.

The future of Object COBOL is discussed by Adams and Lenkov (1990) and Belcher (1991). McCabe (1992) discusses the object-oriented extension of Prolog and logic programming in general. Eliëns (1992) describes a research language DLP with far more power than Prolog++ that also addresses issues of parallelism. The advanced object-based language Ellie is introduced by Andersen (1992). BETA and Mjølner are succinctly described by Durham (1992) and in more detail by Knudsen *et al.* (1993) and Madsen *et al.* (1993) respectively.

Booch (1991) gives detailed worked examples of object-oriented designs based around C++, CLOS, Smalltalk, Object Pascal and Ada.

Tello (1989) deals with some of the artificial intelligence-related languages such as Nexpert Object, GoldWorks, ART, KEE, LOOPS and CLOS, but is slightly out of date now.

Tomlinson and Scheevel (1989) and Yonezawa and Tokoro (1987) describe concurrent object-oriented programming and actor languages.

Shriver and Wegner (1987) covers some of the more obscure issues in object-oriented programming language theory. Cardelli and Wegner (1985) is the classic paper on polymorphism. This paper also includes an exposition of the research language FUN mentioned in Section 3.6.5.

Moon (1989) is an excellent introduction to the ideas behind CLOS, and Snyder (1987) introduces Common Objects. Both papers give important advice on how to use inheritance without compromising abstraction and its main benefit, reusability.

Danforth and Tomlinson (1988) give an excellent and penetrating survey of research into type theories for object-oriented programming languages along with many interesting general comments on object-orientation. Further references on the languages mentioned in Section 3.6.5 will be found in this paper.

The object-oriented Rekursiv machine is described in an introductory manner in Harland and Drummond (1991).

Tom Love's *Object Lessons* (1992) is full of practical experience and commercial wisdom concerning object-oriented programming and its applications.

The *Journal of Object-Oriented Programming* is a useful source of more up-to-date material, with more language-specific material being available in *The C++ Report* and *The Smalltalk Report*.

4

Applications

These things are beyond all use,
and I do fear them.

W. Shakespeare (Julius Caesar)

As we saw in the last chapter, applications of object-oriented programming are gaining ground rapidly in certain areas. These areas presently exclude much of mainstream DP, but are nevertheless quite diverse. The most active industry sectors have been manufacturing and the computing industry itself. As with all new technologies, object-oriented programming is met with a certain amount of scepticism from the established practitioners of the IT industry. To overcome this resistance, it is necessary for successful applications to become visible.

In this necessarily terse chapter, we will take a look at some applications of object-oriented programming and the features which make applications suitable both for the approach and for existing languages. Also addressed are some of the questions facing project managers using object-oriented programming languages.

Although there are still, at the time of writing, only a few large, well-known systems outside of the user interface area, a small number of pilot flagship projects have shown that significant object-oriented systems can be built, the biggest having around 900000 lines of code and 3500 classes. The applications already mentioned in Chapters 2 and 3 included customer management, maintenance management, geographic information systems, financial trading, real-time train control systems, container movement tracking systems, a CT scanner and the production of animated graphics for TV commercials. Others include various simulation games, three-dimensional drawing packages, budgeting and telephone network control. A few applications of object-oriented databases are mentioned in Chapter 6. Object-orientation is being applied routinely in the design of new hardware and operating systems, from the IBM AS/400 to the Rekursiv machine, as well as in software development. There are various object-oriented operating systems for conventional machines, such as UCLA Secure UNIX for the PDP-11. I even remember encountering, some years ago, an object-oriented operating system for the IBM 370 aimed at high-security applications. What made it so memorable was its name, GNOSIS. GNOSIS, now renamed I believe, stood for Great New Operating System In the Sky. Encapsulation makes it inherently easier to build secure operating systems.

Secure computing has thus been an application of object-orientation for some time.

Software houses such as Borland and Microsoft claim now to be fully committed to developing their applications with object-oriented techniques and languages. The benefits of reuse are particularly pertinent to the needs of such developers who can sell millions of copies of an application. The needs of end users who may only produce one copy of an application are very different from those of software houses and the benefits of extensibility and flexibility will often override those of reuse. Thus, both kinds of organization can benefit from object-oriented methods but in different ways.

This will be a concise chapter for two main reasons. First, it seems inappropriate in a text of this nature to report at length on current applications which may well be quite old hat by the time of publication. That is the proper task of the press. Secondly, and more importantly, the field is, in my view, still immature and its immaturity is chiefly shown by the inward-looking nature of most current applications. In other words, with the exception of simulation models and the sort of thing mentioned above, the main use of object-oriented programming to date has been to produce software development environments of one kind or another, rather than systems for the direct benefit of end users. We must immediately make a further exception to this sweeping claim. Many companies have used object-oriented programming to write user interfaces to systems that are not themselves object-oriented. Thus, the most important application of object-oriented programming is currently in the area of the user interface, and we begin by looking at this area.

4.1 Graphical user interfaces

The reason that the most popular application of object-oriented programming up to recently has been user interface (UI) design is partly the pervasive influence of Smalltalk, which emphasized the user interface and office automation applications from the early days of the Dynabook, and partly because of the complexity of the typical graphical user interface (GUI).

The approach was pioneered at Xerox not only in Smalltalk but in InterLisp, their proprietary dialect of LISP. The influence of this early work on the later development of the Apple Lisa and Macintosh user interfaces is well known. In turn, in the current generation of workstations, this iconic style of user interface is almost totally pervasive, from the various UNIX windows environments – OpenLook, Motif, and so on – to MS Windows, Presentation Manager and NeXTstep.

One study, carried out by US consultants Temple, Barker and Sloane in 1990, found that GUI users completed 35% more work per unit time compared with users of command-based interfaces, and completed 91% of assigned tasks compared with 74%, an improvement of nearly 23%. The survey also attempted to measure attitudes. The index of frustration for GUI users was found to be about half that for people using commands. These are average figures for users, rather than systems professionals, and should be applied with care. Personally, I resisted GUIs compared with well-designed command languages for a long time, but that is probably due to many years of indoctrination. Most users and professionals will become more productive quite quickly in front of a GUI, though I still believe their main benefit is consistency rather than ease of use until the learning curve has been ascended.

Clearly, the proliferation of such interfaces directs attention to efficient ways of building and maintaining them. Since the early Xerox work was so intimately tied up with the development of object-oriented programming, it is hardly surprising that developers have tried to exploit the benefits of this technique in the design of user interfaces.

WIMP interfaces are tremendously expensive to develop. If over 200 man-years of effort were required for the development of the Apple Lisa, of which most went on software development, and a considerable amount of that was concerned with the interface, it is inconceivable that Apple could move on to the Macintosh and then the Macintosh II without reusing some of the Clascal code used for the Lisa. As the pace of hardware development accelerates, suppliers cannot afford a new 200 man-year development every few years. This applies not only to the developers of the computing environment but to its users as well. Most of the current GUIs just could not have been written without the use of object-oriented techniques. Furthermore, applications programming in such environments becomes almost impossible without libraries of reusable and extensible graphical objects. Under Microsoft Windows a simple 'hello world' program takes about 83 lines of C code excluding the reuse of the Windows API code, and often has to be edited, compiled and linked outside the Windows environment. The applications programmer interface (API) in such systems is huge, and the event-driven style of user interaction makes programming doubly difficult. The object-oriented programmer need not fight so hard with the API if new types of windows, scroll bars, radio buttons and so on can be defined as instances of existing classes that understand how to respond to events (messages) and whose methods can be inherited. The object-oriented style, or some style that supports reuse and extension, is really essential for productive programming in such environments. Maintenance is also eased by the use of object-oriented programming. Thus, there is a profound need for object-oriented solutions to the problems of the construction, maintenance and use of GUIs. With a good class library to hand, object-oriented programming can speed up applications development in a system such as Windows by up to 75%. Visual BASIC, while not an object-oriented language, contains built-in UI objects that have changeable attributes and empty methods which correspond to interface events. For example, a command button object has a method called Click that can contain the code to be executed when the mouse is left-clicked over the button area. Additional objects of this type can be written in C or purchased from third parties. At present (Version 2.0) inheritance is not supported but this may change. Visual BASIC is an example of how the object-oriented style can be usefully embedded in a conventional language as an application framework. There is now a host of properly object-oriented application frameworks for GUI development based usually on C or C++. Typical products include Borland's ObjectGraphics, Tigre and Zinc.

Object-oriented programming is not only used by GUI developers and application programmers, it may be used by users to facilitate their tailoring of applications to some particular purpose. With the first generation of object-oriented interfaces, such as the Macintosh I, neither the user nor the application programmer had access to the icons as objects. With later systems, such as the NeXT machine and the HyperCard system, programmers have limited access and can make extensions to the interface. Winblad *et al.* (1990) believe that the trend is to giving users this level of access.

Typical applications of object-oriented programming to user interface development include UIMS – a complex user interface management system designed for electronic design applications written in C++ (Raghavan, 1990), and GLAD – a visual database interface written in Actor (Wu, 1990). Apple Computer has developed a user extensible visualization system, DoubleVision, which helps scientists produce flexible colour plots of two-dimensional data (Mock, 1990).

Another application of object-oriented programming is the Simplify front-end to the Ingres relational database management system, which offers users a WIMP interface, based on AT&T's OpenLook X-Windows product, to most database functions. The object-oriented extensions of Ingres are discussed in the next chapter.

Many windowing environments now include usable class libraries. Good examples are NeXTstep, the NeXT machine library, and NewWave. One thing that makes NewWave particularly interesting is its facilities for developing object wrappers, so that existing, conventional UI code can be utilized. Hewlett-Packard's NewWave, which started life as an extension to Microsoft Windows, is an object management facility with a special API for several GUIs. It enables objects from several different applications to be used together and applications (running in different windows) to be permanently linked. NewWave supports the idea of object wrappers by permitting non-object-oriented applications to be embedded, and is particularly suitable for developing multimedia user interfaces. This philosophy is also evident in the Object Management Group's CORBA standard and, to a lesser extent, in Microsoft's OLE. OLE is being used to make word processors, spreadsheets, graphics packages and other packages work together by sharing objects. For example, the same spreadsheet could be used by two users and easily embedded in a document with one user's changes being reflected in the other's document.

The Andrew toolkit (Borenstein, 1990) is a programming system that is designed to assist in the construction of complex multimedia applications in a C environment. It is a sort of application-specific Objective-C which, like Objective-C, extends C with a preprocessor to provide the features of object-oriented programming in general and concentrate on support for multimedia graphics applications.

The benefits of object-oriented programming which apply specifically in the UI area are as follows.

■ The ease with which a consistent interface between 'desktop' objects may be used and reused.

- The fact that interfaces sport relatively few classes.
- The fact that the desktop metaphor maps relatively easily onto the object metaphor.
- Because of the establishment of the technology in this area, there is a plentiful supply of useful object libraries in existence, and Smalltalk and some other languages actually include such features as standard.
- The sheer complexity of modern GUIs makes object-oriented programming a necessity rather than a luxury; if it did not exist then GUIs would have forced us to invent it.

Much of what has been written about the benefits of object-oriented programming has concentrated on this area for illustrative examples. For that reason we will not dwell on it at great length here. It is noteworthy, however, that many current popular systems may never have been written were it not for the influence of the object-oriented paradigm and indeed its enabling technology. Certainly, most windows systems have been implemented (or at least prototyped) in this way. The use of graphical object libraries also contributes significantly to the quality and robustness of these systems, which are themselves likely to be used over and over again.

In trying to generalize these benefits to other application areas, practitioners have often come up against the problem that real business systems are often much more complex. They contain many more objects, those objects have several and complicated attributes, they may have equally complex and numerous methods and, worst of all, the object classes may be quite volatile compared to the items which may appear on a user's screen. We will be taking up such applications in the remainder of the text.

▤ 4.2 Hypermedia, multimedia and group work

A technology closely related to UI technology is now emerging under the general heading of hypermedia.

The term hypertext refers to an idea first advanced by Doug Englebart – the inventor of the mouse – as early as 1963 (Englebart, 1963; Englebart and English, 1968), and to a number of computer systems embodying this idea. Even earlier, Roosevelt's wartime science adviser, Vannevar Bush (1945), had suggested similar ideas. The term itself came into use much later in the work of Ted Nelson (1980, 1981) when machines had become powerful enough for a reasonably fast implementation. Nelson's XANADU interactive reference, writing and conferencing system is still available on UNIX workstations. Hypertext systems are directed to two main aims, better navigation of complex information retrieval systems and improved user interfaces. The idea behind XANADU is more far-reaching still. Nelson's vision is of a huge, publicly accessible repository of data, connected to international networks, which can respond to requests for information from relatively untutored users in any medium: text, graphics, film or sound.

Typically, a hypertext system may be viewed as a network of text fragments linked together by a complex network of pointers. A hypertext document is not read sequentially, like a novel, but according to content, like an encyclopaedia. One reads the text, spots a relevant or interesting term or concept and then is able to go directly to the text explaining the term, usually by pointing at – or clicking a mouse over – the phrase or icon concerned. Such a system will usually make use of a WIMP interface and often contains support for multimedia data including text, graphics and, these days, even music fragments or moving video images. Thus the more general term 'hypermedia' is to be preferred to 'hypertext'. Sometimes the data can be distributed across a network of machines, offering the user simple unified access to multiple data resources. Often the user has access to editing, linking and development tools within the system, so that externally developed programs can be invoked from the system on demand or even when certain links are processed. For example, if I wish to access text concerning an individual whose date of birth is stored I might wish the retrieval pointer to cause the age to be calculated and displayed.

Hypertext fragments are referred to as 'nodes', 'cards' or 'pages' and the pointers as 'links'. Nodes can be given a 'type' if required, to indicate the subject matter or the form of the page: text or graphics, say. Nodes may be combined into composite nodes for increased modularity. Links are of two types: 'from' links and 'to' links. The unique 'from' link at a node refers to the node last visited, and a set of 'to' links record the node currently available for the next step in the journey through the information world. A link between nodes is normally created by the user who highlights an item and records what it points at. Some hypertext systems create links dynamically or automatically. An example of this might relate to the production of a document contents list or index. Graphical browsers are often provided. From these features it is readily seen that object-orientation has had a strong influence on the design of hypertext systems and object-oriented programming languages are often the bases for their development. It is worth noting in passing that the artificial intelligence notion of semantic networks has also had an influence.

At present, the four main applications of hypertext technology are literature reference systems, problem exploration systems, browsing systems and hypertext development environments.

Literature reference systems are large on-line libraries with interdocument links. Nelson's XANADU system is an example envisioned as a network ultimately capable of holding all the world's literary treasures.

Problem exploration systems, such as IBIS (Norman and Draper, 1986), are interactive systems providing fast response to a set of specialized commands and amplifying communication among people involved in complex problem-solving and decision-making activities. A related, although not specifically hypertext, approach is represented by Action Technologies' The Coordinator (Winograd and Flores, 1986) which is an earlier example of the groupware discussed fleetingly in Chapters 6 and 10. Groupware, software to support group work or computer-supported cooperative work (CSCW), promises to be one of the important technologies of the 1990s. CSCW is a generic term covering studies of how people

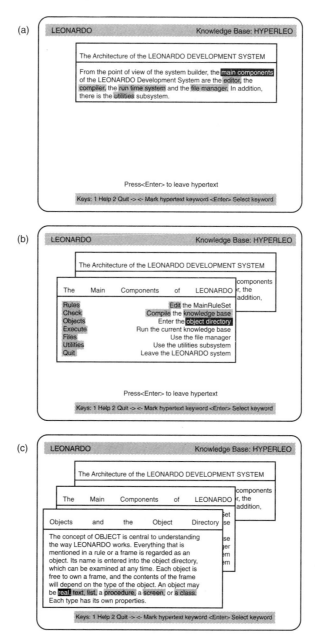

Figure 4.1 A fragment of documentation concerning the Leonardo system implemented as a hypertext application in Leonardo itself. (**a**) The top level: a number of words are highlighted as hypertext pointers to other pieces of text. The cursor is over 'main components'; (**b**) The button is selected and the explanation of 'main components' pops up with more highlighted words. The cursor is over 'object directory'; (**c**) Information on the object directory pops up with more highlighted keywords. The cursor is positioned on 'real'. (By kind permission of Software Directions.)

work in groups and the enabling hardware and software technologies. It combines various computer technologies, from electronic mail, shared databases and video conferencing to complex decision-support aids which keep track of document versions, user commitments and actions, with several human factors theories. It is a multi-disciplinary field drawing on computing, group psychology, sociology, anthropology and much more. Key theories involved include organization theory, speech act analysis, team theory, decision theory and ergonomics.

Browsing systems are aimed primarily at the reader rather than the writer. They provide easy access to large volumes of information where ease of learning and usability are important, such as on-line policy and procedure manuals or maintenance handbooks. Typical such systems are ZMS from Knowledge Systems and the University of Maryland's Hyperties. Within this category fall help systems for software. Hypertext help is now standard in many MS Windows products and is easy to write using the Microsoft Help Compiler or similar products.

Hypertext development environments are general systems aimed at helping with the construction of information retrieval and/or user interface systems. Notecards, from Xerox, is LISP-based and allows LISP applications to be constructed around its open architecture. HyperCard, which is distributed free with the Apple Macintosh, and Guides, which will run on PCs, are possibly the best-known hypertext systems. HyperCard includes a procedural language, HyperTalk, which enables routines to be attached to buttons. If it is deficient at all, it is in the area of database management as links to other systems have to be built to handle large problems. Neptune, from Tectronix, is a system which includes a client/server approach whereby the back-end is an abstract hypertext machine handling node and link transactions efficiently while Smalltalk handles the front-end interface management.

Hypertext systems, which allow the attachment of procedures to their links, raise naturally the question as to whether some knowledge processing could be done at this point in order to simulate 'intelligent' traversal of the information network. This has led to the emergence of hybrid 'expertext' systems combining the features of hypertext and expert systems. A typical such system is KnowledgePro from Knowledge Garden which allows rule-based programs to be attached to links. A number of expert system environments such as Nexpert Object and Leonardo have now adopted hypertext help systems within themselves. My feeling is that there will be a general convergence of expert systems and hypertext technologies over the next few years and that this process will be accompanied by the universal adoption of object-oriented techniques for the development and design of these systems.

Hypermedia, to re-emphasize the point, refers not only to the manipulation of text objects but to that of images, moving pictures and sounds; in fact, to any kind of object with unique identity, state and behaviour. Put this way, there seems no alternative to object-oriented programming as a development platform for hypermedia. For hypermedia systems, with their graphical style and message passing between 'cards', it is natural, if not essential, to build them using object-oriented programming systems and integrate them with the latter.

One of the biggest opportunities for hypertext/hypermedia systems is in office automation. In fact, hypermedia is going to be a very important technology indeed in many application areas. There are strong and obvious links between the development of true, mass-market hypermedia applications and networking technology. The key obstacle to hypermedia is probably the bandwidth of existing (and projected) communications channels.

Multimedia technology is the basis for manipulating structured text, images, sound and video subject matter on computers and across networks. It is becoming a standard feature of computers as windowing systems are gradually fitted out with such facilities. For example, Microsoft Windows now includes, as standard, access to sound synthesizers and video disks. Much of the technology behind this is being constructed with object-oriented languages, as is much of the underlying network management technology now supporting workgroup applications. For example, NYNEX's Multimedia Broadband Communications Systems, a platform for multimedia workgroup applications including electronic conferencing, is constructed largely in C++.

Object request brokers will be needed to support this kind of application when its component software comes from several suppliers.

4.3 Client/server and distributed systems

Client/server computing became popular as networked workstations proliferated. It is one of the most important applications of object technology partly because message passing is the most natural metaphor to use to describe networked, cooperating systems and partly because existing approaches have failed significantly in practice. Although many organizations are convinced that the client/server approach is safer and more flexible than earlier centralized or distributed approaches, recent experience at some companies has indicated that the reality of delivering the approach is not so easy. Working out where data should be handled for efficient processing, storage costs due to partitioned servers, where the business rules should be stored, locking problems when data are kept on the server and locking delays due to two-phase commits all make life harder. The approach really requires much more intelligent networks, which will be able to work out who handles what based on current loadings and know when to call the server and when to bundle requests. Not all applications are suitable for this approach, but for those that are object-orientation offers the most promising approach to design, for there is still no methodological framework for building client/server systems. Thus while savings of the order of 30% are possible over a five-year period, according to a CSC Index report, without object-oriented methods they are unlikely to be realized.

A particular kind of client/server system arises when companies wish to use a GUI running on a workstation to access an existing system running on some other machine, typically a mainframe. This kind of application combines the features of distribution and GUIs and an object-oriented approach is strongly indicated. Several proprietary tools exist for this purpose and combine graphical tools with APIs to handle network and database protocols. Some of these tools, such as Easel, are conventional while others, such as Choreographer, GUI Master and ENFIN include object-oriented languages with specialized extensions. It is generally accepted that the object-oriented products are more flexible. There are also a number of class libraries and application frameworks for this purpose such as CommonView for PM, ObjectWorks and Zinc. If a package is not appropriate, a low-level object-oriented language with a built-in GUI class library such as Actor or Smalltalk may be used. In any of these cases what is required first is a sound way of *describing* the system to be built. The naturalness of the metaphor makes object-oriented analysis and design techniques singularly appropriate if not essential for this.

Another suggestion is that instead of specialized frameworks and products being used the network should itself take on more of the responsibility for intersystem communication by becoming more intelligent. Many people now believe strongly that object request brokers are the right way to overcome the problems of client/server implementation. ORBs are discussed further in Chapter 10.

It is clear that object technology is the natural way to describe and deliver applications involving any kind of distributed computing. Where these applications involve several media, hypermedia linkages, graphical user interfaces or a client/server architecture this is even more the case. In particular, many object-oriented databases have features specifically designed to help store multimedia objects and support group work. Chapter 6 will describe some of these products.

4.4 Artificial intelligence and real-time systems

Another application area where object-orientation has been influential for a long time is artificial intelligence and its commercial offspring, expert systems. We have already dealt with the debt which object-oriented programming owes to simulation, and thus it is natural that there has been interest in applying object-oriented techniques to real-time problems. In this section we look at these two areas together, as there has been some overlapping of interests.

As we saw in the last chapter, LISP can be extended to deal with objects in a reasonably natural way. Thus, it is natural that people already building AI systems and expert systems in LISP should use object-oriented techniques whenever simple and appropriate. Many applications in the general area of artificial intelligence can be viewed as applications of object-oriented programming.

4.4.1 Expert systems

Artificial intelligence (AI), strictly speaking, is about using computational models to help understand the workings of the human brain. Expert systems (or knowledge-based systems) technology on the other hand is about using some of the lessons learnt from AI to solve practical problems. In particular an expert system does not set out to model general problem-solving capability but to simulate the behaviour of an 'expert' in some narrow discipline. One of the earliest systems, the well-known MYCIN system (Buchanan and Shortliffe, 1984), simulated the diagnostic abilities of a physician in the area of infectious diseases of the blood.

For many years the language of choice for AI research was the functional language LISP. It turns out that LISP can be easily extended to deal with objects and messages – in fact LISP is one of the easiest languages to extend for *any* purpose. For this reason AI researchers were among the first to exploit the benefits of object-oriented programming. In doing so they largely reinvented the subject – it has to be said also that OOP workers got many of their ideas from AI – and still use a slightly different terminology. In particular AI people talk about 'frames'. Frames were invented to represent stereotypes (Minsky, 1975) of objects, concepts or situations, but implementations of frames look almost indistinguishable from the objects of object-oriented programming, especially in terms of their inheritance features. To understand frames we must understand the basic architecture of expert systems.

Expert systems are not only defined by what they do but how they do it. In a typical modern expert system the 'expertise' or 'knowledge' is stored separately from the reasoning strategy, often in the form of simple if/then rules. These rules can be readily changed, which means that expert systems are easier to maintain than some other kinds of computer system. This is important when it is realized that the majority of software cost these days goes toward the maintenance of existing systems rather than the construction of new ones. Furthermore, this architecture permits the systems to explain their reasoning to users, which can be important if humans are to act confidently on the basis of a computer's advice in critical or sensitive areas.

Expert systems attempt to represent domain knowledge within a computer system. Rules are good at representing causal knowledge, but there are many other types of knowledge: process knowledge, object knowledge, intuitive knowledge, and so on. Representing knowledge about the shape and properties of a motor car's distributor cap, for example, would be unspeakably tedious, if not quite impossible, using if/then statements. A much better way, as we know, is to represent the object as a series of attributes and methods: as objects and classes of objects. In the world of AI such objects are sometimes called units, or scripts for procedural abstractions, but usually *frames*. Expert systems with rules and frames have the same expressive power as logic programming languages but are far easier to use, due largely to their ability to deal with higher-order constructs and inheritance structures.

Frames, from the beginning, have been closely connected with notions of inheritance, as explained in the last chapter. A frame is a structure with an extensible set of 'slots' which contain the attributes of a concept or object. A slot may have various *facets* such as a value, constraints, a default value and attached procedures. Thus, methods are not viewed so much as an interface, but as means to fill the value facet or to initiate action in the system. Some slots have the special purpose of determining inheritance. For example, the employee frame may have an AKO slot containing its superclasses: classes from which it may inherit. This slot too may have facets, representing inheritance from different perspectives. For example, from the dominant perspective of a payroll system, an employee is a kind of taxpayer, but from the point of view of zoological classification an employee might be usefully regarded as a mammal. What this suggests is the superposition of multiple non-interacting inheritance hierarchies for different purposes. In AI, frames (objects) inherit values; in object-oriented programming objects normally only inherit the ability to have a value. Frames contain pointers to attached procedures and these too are inheritable, though the attached procedures are not properly encapsulated and may be accessed independently of the frame. Also in AI, multiple inheritance is the norm rather than the exception. Frames, I assert, are semantically richer than objects, but objects give far better encapsulation. Recent work has tended to emphasize the convergence of the concepts of frame and object. In Chapter 8 I will offer a version of the converged theory.

Another characteristic of expert systems is their ability to work with vague or judgemental statements. This is required by systems which need to represent the sort of knowledge used by human experts, such as 'invest in companies whose stocks are greatly undervalued' where the term 'greatly' has no precise meaning but is still perfectly understandable. There are several technologies available for this uncertainty management. One that is popular in Japan but less so in the West is fuzzy logic. Other methods abound and include probability theory, various belief theories and numerous *ad hoc* and descriptive methods. For an introduction to uncertainty and fuzzy logic in knowledge-based systems, see Graham and Jones (1988). Appendix I describes a fuzzy extension to the SOMA object-oriented analysis method.

Summarizing, an expert system consists of a 'knowledge base', containing the objects and rules corresponding to specialist knowledge of the application, an 'inference engine', which is a program that applies the knowledge in the knowledge base to the data presented to the system, and some means of managing uncertainty. If the system is emptied of its application-specific knowledge and given the means for developers to insert easily some other knowledge base it is called an 'expert system shell'. Such shells are highly productive development environments for builders of expert systems.

Expert systems are now helping companies across the world in such diverse areas as insurance underwriting, financial trading, bank loan authorization, the control of complex plant such as cement kilns and blast furnaces, the diagnosis of faults in vibrating machinery, database optimization, the selection and combination of chemical coatings, the configuration of computers and telecommunications machinery, planning and scheduling, chemical product formulation, laying out the Yellow Pages, the diagnosis of faults in an interbank payments system, and many others. Another key area of application is in data processing itself, with packages already available for project estimation and structured methods support (as part of CASE tools). The 'hype' about expert systems which characterized most of the

1980s is now supplanted by a burgeoning number of real applications. Graham and Milne (1991) report some modern applications of expert systems, especially in manufacturing.

A number of expert systems 'shells', which are programming environments containing built-in inference and uncertainty handling methods and some means of adding knowledge, contain object-oriented features. The systems discussed in the last chapter, such as ADS, ART, Kappa, KBMS, and Nexpert, are all expert systems development environments with more or less of the features of object-orientation. Their suppliers are now prone to repositioning them as 'object-oriented development environments', with varying degrees of justification. Usually, their strength lies in their inheritance features rather than their abstraction facilities. This makes them suitable for applications with complex process semantics or business rules – as opposed to data semantics. It thus carves out a set of niche applications that are usually, although by no means always, expert systems. Such applications are characterized not by being knowledge intensive (although they may be that as well) but by involving inheritance structures where the behaviour of the conflict resolution strategies reflects something important about the application.

AARDVARK   In the case of SACIS, for example, we envisage a definite requirement for matching customer characteristics to product features. Aardvark's policy is to only sell toys that are safe. This is not as simple as it seems at first. A product that is safe for an adult (for example, a sword swallowing kit) might not be safe for a ten year old. A toy safe for a ten year old (for example, a bag of marbles) should be considered decidedly risky in the hands of an infant with a natural penchant for swallowing things. What is required, within SACIS, is an expert systems component capable of matching product to client on the basis of rules and the properties of complex structures of product and customer types. Without attempting to describe the whole application, let us observe the inheritance structures involved (see Figure 4.2).

Customers are classified in advance as Child, Teenager and Adult, rather than merely encapsulating age. Child admits a further classification as Infant and Junior. Defaults and constraints on age, or date of birth, are encapsulated within the structures. Toys may be similarly classified according to their functional properties. Note that Marble inherits multiply from both Toy and from SmallItem. Small items are those with overall dimension under, say, 30 mm. This means that Marble inherits an additional property of being small and additional methods concerned with the manipulation of small objects within the stock system: they are stored in bins. Now we may encapsulate the rule 'if toy is small then safe is false' within the Infant object, without having an impact on other objects and eliminating much redundant code. We will return to the issue of encapsulating semantics in Chapter 8.

Almost any application written in these AI systems could be said to be an application of object-oriented programming, and there are hundreds. To list them would be merely tedious. On the other hand, it has been claimed that expert systems have been written in Smalltalk. Here the difficulty is in getting everyone to agree that the system in question is 'really' an expert system. This debate is just about as sterile as the one over whether a particular language is 'really' object-oriented.

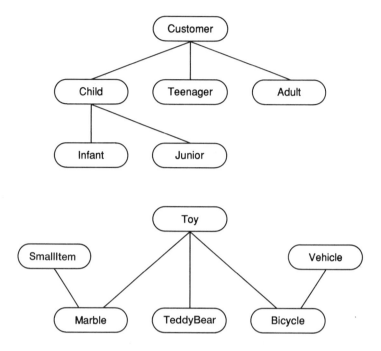

Figure 4.2 Fragments of inheritance structures in SACIS.

Picking up a theme from the last chapter, if you want to implement an object-oriented design then you might consider, in addition to a fully fledged object-oriented language and conventional ones, an expert systems development environment. Today it is a viable option.

4.4.2 Actor and blackboard systems

An important control technique in artificial intelligence is referred to under the heading of blackboard systems. In complex systems, and especially in real-time systems, there may be many sources of knowledge and many plans and procedures. Typical application areas are fighter battle systems and financial trading rooms.

Blackboard systems have been applied in a military context where, for example, a fighter pilot has to process a vast amount of incoming data in order to select from a limited range of actions. The model is one of several independent knowledge-based systems monitoring the input and advising the pilot when some-thing interesting occurs; for example, when a real target or threat is identified among many dummy targets or threats. The financial trader is in a similar position, being the recipient of a vast amount of data from several information feeds, all of them in need of analysis to determine (a) if anything interesting has occurred requiring further analysis, and (b) what the appropriate action should be.

A blackboard system is so called because it imitates a group of highly specialized experts sitting around a blackboard in order to solve a problem. As new information arrives it is written up on the blackboard where all the experts can look. When an expert sees that s/he can contribute a new fact based on specialist knowledge, s/he raises a hand. This might be to confirm or refute an hypothesis already on the board or to add a new one. The new evidence will now be available to the other experts who may in turn be prompted to contribute to the discussion. The chairman of the group monitors the experts and selects their contributions in order, according to an agenda visible on the board. Common storage is the blackboard, and the agenda is under the control of a specialized inference program. In the trading context, our experts might be represented by a technical analysis expert system, a fundamental analysis system, an option strategy adviser, and so on. If, for example, new price information arrives from the wire, the chartist might detect a possible reversal but need to await confirmation before a sell signal is issued. However, the fundamental analyst only needed this small piece of confirmatory evidence to suggest a flagging in the security's fortunes. The combined evidence may be enough to generate a valid signal and thus, incidentally, beat all the pure chartists to the winning post. Perhaps also this action of selling the security will attract the attention of the option strategist who now sees a need to modify positions in order to maintain a risk-free hedge or to avoid an otherwise unexpected exercise in now unfavourable market conditions.

If the components of a blackboard system need to communicate there are essentially two methods of achieving this. Actor and object-oriented systems allow objects to send and receive messages that have definite destination objects when sent. In blackboard systems the messages are posted to a common data area that is accessible to other objects. This is useful when messages have to be broadcast rather than sent. Sometimes the blackboard is partitioned into pigeonholes. Usually, messages must be dealt with according to the order in which they arrive and the state of the receiving object at that time; thus all such systems tend to look like real-time systems and would benefit greatly from parallel hardware architectures. Having said this, one of the earliest blackboard systems was Hearsay-II which was addressed to the problem of speech understanding, which is only implicitly a real-time problem. Most applications since then have been in military real-time communication, command and control systems, so that little has been published openly. Recently, however, work has begun on blackboard systems in plant process control and complex currency-dealing decision support systems, nearly always using some object technology.

Blackboard systems run into problems in continuous reasoning because of the accumulation of information in the common data area and the global accessibility of that data. Actor systems, on the other hand, need to know in advance which objects will need to communicate. For these reasons there have been attempts to combine the formalisms in some systems. One programming environment, BLOBS, was developed along these lines by Cambridge Consultants Ltd and applied to such problems as ship positioning control. BLOBS supports an object-oriented programming style, so that instead of passing data to a program for manipulation, messages are sent to objects. Objects are synchronized with a real-time clock and an 'agenda' object may be set up to schedule processing. An object (unsurprisingly in BLOBS) is called a 'blob'. Here is an example of a blob:

```
static blob Biggles

        private vars x,y,dx,dy

        on_message fly_north with s=speed do

                o —> dy; s —> dx;

                send 'biggles flies north to base';

        enddo

        ...

        on_message tick with t=time interval do

                x+t*dx —> x;

                y+t*dy —> y;

        enddo

        on_message where_are_you with s=sender do

                send 'biggles is at', x=x,y=y, to (s);

        enddo

    endblob
```

A typical way to implement a blackboard system is to set up a family of frames representing a community of cooperating experts. Each frame has a slot containing a 'trigger' and one indicating priority of execution of the procedures attached to the frame. Some frames will fire their procedures on the trigger value denoting the start of processing and these are, *ceteris paribus*[1], executed in order of priority. The priorities may be subject to dynamic alteration as earlier procedures write facts on the blackboard. Demons may be used to detect critical changes to the blackboard's data and amend the appropriate frames. Other frames are triggered directly by certain values in the database.

Object-oriented programming is a programming style rather than a control or knowledge representation strategy. It is designed to promote modularity and reusability of code as well as facilitating better representation in the user interface. However, in looking at systems like Xerox's LOOPS, which combines object-oriented programming with InterLisp, high-quality graphics and a number of facilities for encoding knowledge-based systems, it is difficult sometimes not to end up con-

---

[1] Other things being equal

fusing the two. If a generic object can inherit from multiple parents it is sometimes called a *flavour*. If all the attributes and methods associated with an object, flavour or blob can be filled in, then there is a case to be made for saying that we *understand* the object. The property attachment and procedural inheritance features lead us to a notion of meaning being inherent in an object-oriented description. Object-oriented control and meta-control strategies clearly have an interesting future. Much will depend on the theoreticians sorting out the terminological mess wherein there is no clear distinction between objects, frames, semantic nets and so on.

Other influences from artificial intelligence on object-oriented languages have been dealt with in the treatment of functional languages in Section 3.2.

4.4.3 Military, real-time and simulation applications

The European Fighter Aircraft Project used an object-based design method, HOOD, and an associated toolkit from Ipsys to design its computer systems to construct a set of systems implemented in Ada. This £2,000 million project involved a consortium of European companies and, as with many defence projects, standardized on Ada. The European Space Agency's (ESA) Columbus space station, Hermes space plane and Ariadne rocket projects also used Ada and HOOD, which is not surprising since ESA actually commissioned the development of HOOD. Details of HOOD are given in Chapter 7.

Objective-C was used to develop a system for military situation assessment at SRI, SITMAP (Knolle *et al.*, 1990). It automates the labour-intensive process of plotting symbols on maps by presenting map backgrounds and real-time tactical overlays. ART has been used for similar applications.

Because of the dominance of Ada in the defence sector, this pattern is common for military applications. The Electro Optics Division of Thorn EMI Electronics has also adopted Ada and HOOD for the construction of an air defence alerting device (ADAD) based on thermal imaging technology. The conventional Yourdon method was used for the analysis. Although the project is regarded as a success, it is not clear, according to one of its managers, that any reusable code has emerged from it.

An application to the simulation and control of manufacturing systems is described by Glassey and Adiga (1990). They used Objective-C to rebuild a fairly large (6000 lines of C) system for the simulation of wafer fabrications which includes treatment of task and resource planning.

Simulation of complex systems has been an application of object-oriented programming since the earliest days of Simula. Traffic systems, nuclear reactors, integrated office systems, financial systems and manufacturing processes have all been successfully subjected to the approach.

Nierstratz and Tsichritzis (1989) discuss the essential characteristics of an object-oriented office systems simulator. Sim City is an educational game which simulates city planning situations and allows players to explore the consequences of various budgeting, pricing, traffic control and environmental decisions.

4.4.4 Neural networks and parallel computing

Hardware design itself has already fallen under the influence of the object-oriented philosophy. It is claimed that the IBM System 38 and AS/400 machines are object-oriented in precisely the sense that the hardware and operating system were designed using object-oriented techniques. The operating systems of the NeXT and Rekursiv machines are also object-oriented. With the emergence of various models of parallel computation and the hardware based on them, object-orientation is a very natural way to model message passing between hardware units. Also, the Rekursiv offers direct hardware support for message passing, dynamic binding and so on. Parallelism comes in various levels of granularity, from simple four-processor transputer surfaces on PC cards up to massively parallel machines such as Fahlman's Connection Machine. The most massively parallel device in the known universe is the human brain. Neural networks are a kind of massively parallel machine loosely based on the structure of the brain. I will use them to illustrate how the object-oriented metaphor maps onto the implementation, or indeed simulation, of parallel architectures. First we must understand what a neural network is.

The study of neural nets is at least as old as the computer itself and can be traced back to the work of McCulloch and Pitts in the 1940s. As with AI, when commercial data processing came to dominate the use of the world's computer power, research in this area retired to the university. Nevertheless, it remained an active and promising area. Ross Ashby's influential books *Design for a Brain* (1960) and *Introduction to Cybernetics* (1956) show that the same set of ideas which we discuss below was being vigorously pursued by the cyberneticians in the 1950s. Neuroscientists also expressed much interest, as well as posing many interesting problems for verification by means of neural models.

Probably the most significant early practical application of the idea came with Rosenblatt's PERCEPTRON and this device gives us an opportunity to explain the basic ideas behind neural computing.

Essentially, the idea is to design a computational device which, in place of the monolithic single processor of the Von Neumann machine, has many very simple processors rather like the neurons in the animal brain. These distributed processors or neurons have to work together in order to achieve anything but the most trivial computational tasks. To do this, organic neurons seem to send messages through an immense tangle of interconnexions, and a neural network system taking this as inspiration proposes that its processors too are connected in as complex a way as is needed. The PERCEPTRON is a simple example which is based on a model of the visual cortex and designed to be able to 'learn to see' coherent physical objects presented to it (in 2D) via a TV camera or similar. To see that this is in fact a very difficult problem, consider how hard it is to recognize a familiar object from a photograph taken from an unusual angle or close position. Some frame of reference is required. In the case of the PERCEPTRON and similar devices this is achieved by the introduction of a teacher who can tell the system when it has and has not recognized the object correctly.

The original PERCEPTRON is a relatively simple device compared to modern neural nets. (Technically, it is a one-layer network – see below.) Modern networks have been shown to be at least as powerful as digital computers (Turing machines). Nevertheless, important theorems can be proved about the PERCEPTRON's ability to learn to recognize patterns.

Conventional computers usually consist of a single, monolithic central processor together with various peripheral devices. Information is processed sequentially in accordance with a stored program of arbitrary complexity. This model of information processing differs radically from the structure of the human brain which, so far as we know, consists of millions (roughly 10^{11} it is believed) of very simple processors called neurons connected to other neurons by an even larger number of synaptic connexions. To compensate for the simplicity of the neurons as computers and the slow rates of information transfer across synapses, the brain carries out its processing in a massively parallel fashion. These discoveries of neuroscience inspire attempts to construct computing machinery that mimics this parallel distributed kind of information processing. Implementations of this idea are thus often called neural networks.

The connexions in a neural network permit the units (neurons) to send very simple excitatory or inhibitory messages. Since an individual unit may receive many (in the brain, many thousand) signals it is necessary to propose that a 'weight' is given to each input and used to derive the total effect on the unit.

In detail a neural network consists of:

- A set of n units, which are simple computers capable of computing the 'activation' of the unit as a function of the input signals and weights and an output function of the activation.
- A rank n vector representing the current activation of each unit
- An $n \times n$ matrix representing the connectivity and the weight distribution in the network. Note that a weight of zero is equivalent to 'no connexion'.
- A learning rule by which weights are modified in the light of experience.

This is a slightly simplified account but the interested reader may refer for more detail to the classic text by the PDP research group (Rummelhart and McClelland, 1986).

Figure 4.3 illustrates a simplified fragment of a neural network. Looking at a single unit j we take some function of the weights w_{ij} and the output values o_i of all the incoming connexions to arrive at the net input net_j. The simplest way to do this is to take the weighted sum of the input to j. Next we compute the new activation a_j of j as some function of the old activation and net_j. Usually this function will be a simple sigmoid function of net_j, as shown in Figure 4.4 (a) which ignores the old value of a_j, but this will depend heavily on the properties required of the target application. The final step is to calculate the output which will be propagated to the units connected to j, which is often done by a simple threshold model as illustrated in Figure 4.4 (b). That is, the net input has to reach a certain level before the neuron will 'fire'.

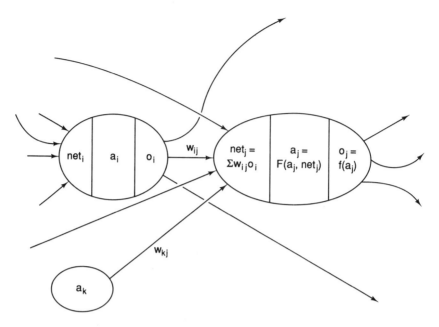

Figure 4.3 The structure of a neural network (after Rummelhart and McClelland).

The learning algorithm models the ability of the brain to construct useful groupings of neurons which act as symbol recognition units or feature detectors. There are many ways in which this can be done, the oldest being the Hebbian learning algorithm which I shall describe in outline.

The Hebb rule strengthens the weight on the link between two units if both are active in proportion to the product of the activation of the second unit and the output from the first. Thus

$$w_{ij} = ko_i a_j$$

A more complicated version of this rule allows for a 'teaching input' which is the activation resulting from a successful pattern match and is compared with the actual activation so that

$$w_{ij} = k(t_i - o_i)a_j$$

This is one of many possible similar learning rules and is known as the Delta or Widrow-Hoff rule. Another popular idea is to regard learning as a process of minimizing the 'energy' or generalized cost of the network which is defined as a function of the weights and activations summed across all the connexions. The weights are altered by relaxation towards the local minimum and additional steps are taken to ensure that the global minimum is found with very high probability. These techniques are closely related to the genetic algorithms (Goldberg, 1989) found in machine learning systems on conventional hardware.

The details of which learning rules are best at what tasks need not detain us. This is in fact a topic of continuing research, but enough is known about some algorithms to show that real systems can be built with them.

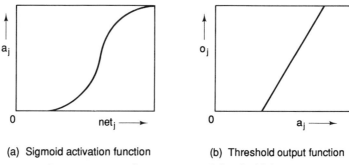

(a) Sigmoid activation function   (b) Threshold output function

Figure 4.4 Typical activation and threshold functions.

It is convenient to divide the units of a neural net into hidden (or internal), input and output units. The input and output units are the only ones visible to the user and the hidden units are usually organized (at least conceptually) into layers. The idea here is that units at level n+1 represent the activation of abstract features represented by the activation of groups of units at level n. For example, we may want our network to be able to recognize printed words. The input units may take letters from an OCR[2]. Suppose there is only one output unit which fires if and only if the input sequence is a word. It is necessary to postulate hidden units that act as valid sequence detectors. The first layer is devoted to recognizing the letters. This, of course, is a simplification, and we should really include a layer of feature detectors for the components of the letters. If the input matches a letter unit then that unit is excited and all other letter units are inhibited. The letter detectors are connected to units in the next layer which will represent words. If all or some of the letters in a word are active then the word will become active. How these units evolve is either a matter for the learning algorithm (and the teacher) or the designer may hard-wire the appropriate excitatory links.

A typical such scheme is shown as Figure 4.5.

Neural networks are good at pattern completion as well as pattern recognition. For example, in some of the early research work, it was found that some neural nets could learn to recognize partly obscured words, as shown in Figure 4.6 (a). They could even learn to guess at non-words as indicated in Figure 4.6 (b), possibly by having learnt some 'looks like a word' rules. Another important feature of these networks is that, as with the brain, if a few processors are damaged they can still continue to function, even if only to a limited capacity. This property is known as graceful degradation. Monolithic computer systems degrade most ungracefully when they go down.

The main observation to be made here is that neurons are evidently objects with encapsulated behaviour and which communicate by passing messages. What better than an object-oriented programming language to simulate such a system? Blum (1992) provides the basics of an object-oriented framework for neural systems and gives source code for a C++ class library containing several learning algo-

[2] Optical Character Reader

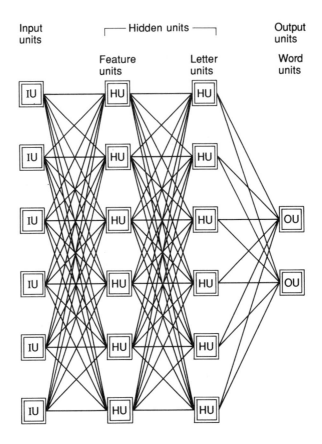

Figure 4.5 A multi-layer neural network.

rithms. The second observation is that, although short-term memory resides in the units as activation, long-term memory resides in the weightings: in the system as a whole. This, I think, leads to some interesting conclusions about the global properties of object-oriented systems where the message-passing topology may be viewed as containing unencapsulated control information. This observation has influenced the treatment of methods in Chapter 8.

4.5 Geographic information systems

Geographic information systems (GIS) are essentially computer systems that replace or automate aspects of analogue, paper-based cartography and record keeping. They typically comprise subsystems for:

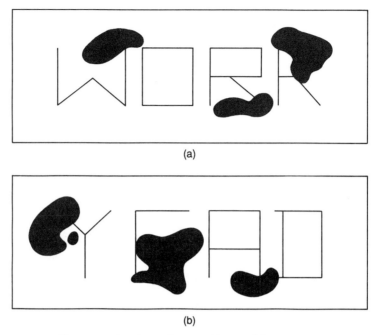

Figure 4.6 (a) A word recognition problem;
(b) A similar non-word recognition problem.

(1) data capture from existing maps, remote sensors, satellite images and so on;
(2) data storage and retrieval of spatial data in a form which supports fast retrieval for analysis and rapid updates;
(3) database management systems for handling information about the attributes of spatially defined features;
(4) reporting and map display.

At a more detailed level, a typical GIS product will support the overlaid presentation of several line maps on a background map and the fast retrieval of information about the adjacency and proximity of polygons, such as those representing postal sectors or counties. Also it is often necessary to store attribute data for polygons, nodes and links and support quick panning, zooming and plotting. GIS can store information on demographics which could be useful for marketing purposes or on routing for the optimization of travelling costs. Most GIS store two kinds of data: mapping data and data concerning the attributes of the objects to be mapped. The performance of relational systems is poor on mapping data because of their inability to store complex, structured objects and their need to do joins to reconstruct them. For this reason the mapping data are usually stored in a proprietary file system. The attribute data are often stored in a relational database and also often shared with other applications. In many applications a change to mapping data must be reflected in changes to the attributes and vice versa. This close coupling has been a significant task for product developers. Relational systems that support BLOBS can be used but they cannot interpret the data.

The history of GIS has been compared to that of civil aviation (Peuquet and Marble, 1990). For the latter, it is claimed that there have been only three significant events: the Wright brothers' first flight, the first civil airliner – the DC3 – and the Boeing 707. The simile is constructed by noting that the first successful geographic information system, CGIS – the Canadian Geographic Information System – succeeded in being used where most others failed to get off the ground at all owing to either poor design or bad software engineering practices. This occurred in the days when computing was almost exclusively a matter of batch-processing mainframes taking punched cards as input and was a remarkable achievement in itself. The development of interactive computing in the 1970s made it possible for a revolution in geographic information systems to take place, and the equivalent of the DC3 was ARC/INFO. Its authors took an existing pseudo-relational database (INFO) to hold attribute data and added a proprietary topologically structured database (ARC) to hold the map data. The analogue of the 707 is yet to appear, and we may safely assume that this will happen in the near future for two major reasons:

(1) the huge amount of money being invested in this technology at present, which all market surveys predict will increase;
(2) the new possibility of constructing both the attribute and the map databases in an efficient but unified database management system using object-oriented technology. In particular, modern object-oriented databases combine the efficiency of the network, pointer-based approach with the flexibility of the relational as will be seen in Chapter 6.

We can expect to see a new generation of GIS products emerge that will be based on a single object-oriented database that will provide an effective standard for data exchange among different GIS. In this way the current generation of products will become outdated in two major respects: lack of a data storage standard and reliance on inflexible topological storage schemes.

Current GIS rely heavily on CAD and database technology and usually operate on non-standard, proprietary file-management systems. To see the reason for this it is necessary to understand that there is a fundamental reason why topological data may not be retrieved efficiently from a relational database. Cartographic data may be represented in a number of different ways: as analogue (paper), raster (bit maps) or vector images. Vector images are particularly suited to the storage of network data and this may be done with one of two basic data models: 'spaghetti' models and topological models. Spaghetti models give very efficient retrieval but are badly adapted for analysis. Modern products almost always adopt a topological model. Such a model stores not only the locations of points and lines but information about adjacency and intersection. This is accomplished by storing pointers linking the topological entities – points, lines and polygons – and sometimes by encoding the coordinate pairs locationally so that they are stored in a proximity-ordered manner. A typical technique is the Peano ordering which stores points as numbers constructed by interlacing the bits from the binary representation of the longitude and latitude of the points. This makes zooming and nearness calculation very fast since points can be stored sorted in order of proximity. The problem with relational databases is that such systems need to store data in normalized tables and that these tables need not correspond to anything physical like a line or polygon. Such objects must be reconstructed at run time by joining several tables. Unfortunately a join operation is about the slowest thing a relational database can be asked to do. Network databases can be up 100 times more efficient for this kind of application. On the other hand network databases are horribly inflexible and difficult to manage in the face of schema evolution. For this reason data concerning the attributes of map features, such as the capacity of a road, are best stored in a relational database because it is these data which are the most vulnerable to changes in the schema. The map data, however, are not so vulnerable and may be stored in a purpose-built network database. This is the way nearly all products since ARC/INFO have been constructed. Object-oriented databases offer the possibility of storing all the data in one database for the first time. Pacific Bell implemented a pilot system for network maintenance using an early version of ObjectStore (see Chapter 6). The most recent geographic information systems, such as Smallworld, have opted for an object-oriented approach to storing mapping data. The authors of Smallworld chose to create their own persistent version of Smalltalk and object-oriented database because no commercial OODBs existed at the time they started. Vendors starting now have a much better choice.

Most non-Windows PC products use the AutoCAD DXF standard to store maps. These range from full AutoCAD implementations such as Addmaps to Geo/SQL, which latter uses Oracle to store attributes and its image database. This leads to suspicions about its potential performance. AutoCAD is used for display only and provides the user interface.

We have seen in Chapter 2 that GIS systems have been built using object-oriented languages. Also several object-oriented databases have been used to build geographic information systems, as we shall see in Chapter 6.

4.6 Other commercial systems

Currently, many user organizations are developing workstation components of mainstream systems using object-oriented technology. These include a number of manufacturing companies, software houses, banks and insurance companies to my knowledge. As with any new technology, there is a certain amount of secrecy surrounding the details of these applications. The trouble is that object-oriented programming can be applied to almost anything, and sweeping generalizations are difficult and misleading. A good feel for the sort of thing that can be done is given by notional examples such as the SACIS application in this book. Booch (1991) describes, in enormous detail, the design of several notional applications, including systems for real-time control of a home heating system, ray tracing in geometrical optics, cryptography and traffic management. Wirfs-Brock *et al.* (1990) describe an on-line documentation system and Rumbaugh *et al.* (1991) describe the design of notional systems for ATMs (automatic teller machines).

Other application areas which have been reported include environments for visual programming, CASE tools, computer integrated manufacturing (CIM) systems, electronic publishing systems, quite a few CAD/CAM systems, where issues related to object-oriented databases are paramount, and computer-assisted learning systems. The new windows interface to the Ingres DBMS has been built using object-oriented principles, as have a number of projected new 4GLs such as the Cognos development referred to in the last chapter. GEC-Marconi Software Systems are using a method of object-oriented design (HOOD) to develop PCTE+, the extension of the European Portable Common Tools Environment (PCTE) which is, to some extent, a response to the idea of repositories. The same company is also using HOOD to add function points analysis (Albrecht and Gaffney, 1983) to their GECOMO project cost estimation tool. HOOD is discussed further in Chapter 7 and repositories in several subsequent chapters.

The interface component of decision support and executive information systems (EIS) is very important, and object-orientation is evidently a key technology. Systems for building such interfaces, such as Macroscope, already exist. Apple's internal management decision support system MacDSS is built with MacApp and Object Pascal.

Systems with the feel of what might be called object-oriented spreadsheets, such as Javelin, have been around for some time and more are currently emerging. The advantages of such systems include the possibility of maintaining real-time consistency across multiple views, so that graphic and numerical views change together, and the ease with which complex types, such as subarrays, may be manipulated.

Booch (1991) describes in detail the design of a notional problem-reporting MIS for a software development company, written in C++.

Applications to the problems faced by software developers, in DP itself, have been fairly common. One such application is a branch path analyser for C programs (Pinson and Wiener, 1990). This program, written in Smalltalk, identifies branch paths; that is, blocks of code whose execution may be conditional on the value of one or more parameters. It also maintains statistics on which paths were used during test runs. Significantly, the system was re-implemented in C++ and Objective-C for greater efficiency.

The SACIS example we have been discussing needs a database, which means that it is not suitable as an application of existing object-oriented programming languages *per se*, unless they offer some means of coping with persistent data – which most of them do not. The next two chapters investigate the issue of what kinds of database systems are suitable for semantically rich applications like SACIS.

Object-oriented methods can be used for organizational modelling or simulation as discussed in the case-study in Chapter 8. This enables strategy studies to be conducted by simulation, so that alternative scenarios may be tested and compared.

The situation where object technology is limited to non-critical or fringe applications cannot change much until two key developments occur. The first, and most important, is the resolution of various issues concerning object-oriented databases. The second event we are waiting for is the emergence and acceptance of Object COBOL. Until then, I will argue, commercial organizations can obtain considerable benefits from the use of object-oriented methods for systems analysis. This will put them in an ideal position to exploit object-oriented technology as it matures in programming, databases and design.

4.7 Choosing a language for an application

The first question a potential convert to object-orientation should ask is: why use object-oriented programming at all? If the benefits of reusability and extensibility do not matter, as with a totally one-off, organization- and application-specific development, or an application where performance is so critical that the natural development language is assembler, then object-oriented programming is likely to be an encumbrance. If we can eliminate such considerations then we must look at the features of the application and available development environments to determine application suitability. In this section we will examine some guidelines.

A suitable application for object-oriented techniques and languages should contain complex objects but not too many of them. Without complex objects the power of the approach is not realized. With millions of classes to model there is a small element of risk, in that we have no concrete evidence yet that the approach scales up, though informed opinion suggests that it should scale up even better than conventional software engineering. There should be reuse potential; that is, it should be anticipated that some of the classes will be actually reused at least six times. Particularly volatile applications, ones with event-driven interfaces, are especially suitable. If low productivity in a conventional language has been experienced, as with Windows application building, then the approach is likely to be suitable. Systems involving a lot of concurrency also indicate an object-oriented approach. Applications in engineering CAD, CASE tools, office automation, group working, simulation and modelling are often suitable for object-oriented methods.

We have seen that GUI developments benefit greatly from the use of OOP. Thus, the type of user interface is an important thing to consider. Need it be flexible? How important is ease of use? Will it be used by a variety of people with differing skills and knowledge? If the answer to any of these questions is positive then an object-oriented solution is indicated.

Developers should consider carefully the potential for reuse, extension and resale of objects. Reusable objects cost more to develop and investment in them is repaid over a longer period. Will future projects need to utilize similar objects? Are the objects of this particular system central to the business or only to this application? Could the objects be sold to other developers? All these factors, not easy ones to evaluate, influence the decision. Also, extraneous factors need to be taken into account. For example, in a period of high interest rates or economic and political uncertainty, long-term investments are resisted more strongly, partly owing to the effects of discounted cash flow.

Some companies are convinced of the benefits of this kind of investment already. Bill Gates, founder of Microsoft, has been quoted as saying that Microsoft is not going to be in the business of selling software for much longer. It will be in the business of selling objects.

The business objectives of a development will determine which of reusability, extensibility or semantic richness are the most important features. The language chosen must reflect these priorities. Applications involving complex objects (whether complex in terms of attributes or methods) will need languages that can express this complexity. Applications where re-engineering is envisaged as a requirement will require languages that are computationally rich and explicit. Chapters 5 to 8 examine some database systems and design and analysis methods with different degrees of expressiveness in these respects.

Booch (1991) has argued convincingly for the view that object-orientation is a means of managing complexity, one of the hardest problems facing any software engineer. If the systems under consideration are complex and must evolve with the business then object-orientation is worthy of very serious consideration, almost regardless of cost. Modern businesses can only exist on the basis of flexible computer systems. Decision makers aware of this will naturally turn to object-orientation in the absence of any competing solution to the problem of managing complex software projects. I do not know of any such competing technology.

Having decided that object-oriented programming is appropriate, there is no escaping a detailed, comparative analysis of the actual language features against the application requirements. The sorts of issues that will arise here include performance – in terms of memory use, storage utilization and speed – coding effort, portability and the features of each surrounding programming environment. The purchasers must ask what libraries and tools are available and what change control and other facilities for effective library class use are available. Does the proposed system have facilities for linking to databases and other systems, and how easy are these facilities to work with? These are just a few of the important questions that must be asked. Much will depend on the application.

Other, more commercial, considerations also usually arise. For example, object-oriented programming languages may be classified into multi-vendor languages, such as C++, Object Pascal or CLOS, and proprietary language standards such as Actor or Objective-C. An organization must decide whether it is prepared to be exposed to the risk of a language's single vendor ceasing to trade or take defensive measures such as source code escrow agreement or the like. It may also be important whether the company's chief supplier of hardware has taken a view on suitable languages within some overall hardware, network or systems development strategy. Even if this is not the case, the existence of industry standards may be considered an important issue.

I do not offer a recipe to resolve all these issues, but merely invite the reader to consider them along with the many factors which cannot be anticipated in a general work of this nature.

4.8 Project management issues

Management commitment is a key to success for every project and an object-oriented one is no exception. There must be a serious attempt to justify the benefits accruing from the use of object-orientation and relate them to the real needs of users. This, and other strategies for obtaining management commitment, must be pursued with great vigour. Otherwise object-orientation will be seen as a solution in search of a problem.

The training of object-oriented programmers has been recognized as a key issue. As has been remarked already, C programmers are quite capable of writing C++ without using its object-oriented features – it used to be said that real programmers wrote FORTRAN, and could do so in *any* language. What this means is that training has to be taken seriously, and properly budgeted for. Training C++ programmers in Smalltalk may be viewed as an unjustified expense by senior management. Project managers will have to understand why it is essential (if it is) and be prepared to go into battle on the issue.

Prototyping is another expense that has to be justified, especially throwaway prototyping. This book has argued, and will argue further in Chapter 9, for the importance and benefits of prototyping. Project managers must understand the arguments and be able to sell the benefits to management. Prototyping must be managed properly if it is not to go out of control. Chapter 9 offers guidelines on the management of projects which use prototyping and object-oriented methods.

It is widely accepted that sound structured methods and techniques are beneficial. Whether this is true or not, methods must be managed, and that means that project managers must understand them fully. Chapters 7 and 8 discuss object-oriented methods and their incorporation within existing structured methods. Chapter 9 looks more closely at the managerial issues.

4.9 Summary

There is an increasing number of applications of object-oriented programming, but up until recently the majority have been concerned with the production of effective user interfaces or simulation models. Widespread commercial use is not yet a reality.

The main areas of application divide into those where much has already been achieved – user interfaces, hypermedia, multimedia, distributed and client/server systems, GIS, simulation and process control and AI – and those where there is merely a potential for successful applications – data processing, database, EIS and business modelling.

Object-oriented programming languages are immature but improving rapidly. In choosing an object-oriented language the key features to look for are the way the language handles encapsulation of the attributes and methods of complex objects for reusability, the way inheritance is used to support extensibility and the richness of the language for expressing application semantics. The application should be examined to determine whether a flexible UI is required and which of reusability, extensibility and reversibility are the most important.

More recently the trend has been to use object-oriented programming in the development of programming environments and CASE tools themselves.

Management commitment is a key to success. Training is an important issue. Prototyping is essential. Project managers must understand the technical and commercial issues.

4.10 Bibliographical notes

There are too many books on GUIs, hypermedia, AI and expert systems to mention here. Graham and Jones (1988) reflects some of my own views on expert systems and is quite a good bibliographical source. Feigenbaum *et al.* (1988) reports on several live applications of AI and their benefits. Tello (1989) looks at some of the object-oriented AI programming systems. Englemore and Morgan (1988) is a comprehensive source book on blackboard systems. The essential reference on neural nets is Rummelhart and McClelland (1986), while Aleksander and Morton (1990) is a practical tutorial introduction to the topic. Blum (1992) shows how object-oriented programming may be applied to building neural nets. The AI notion of frames is explained in Winston (1984) and very lucidly in Shadbolt (1989).

Some of the applications mentioned in this chapter are covered, though with the exception of GUIs not in great detail, in Winblad *et al.* (1990). Khoshafian and Abnous (1990) discuss the issue of object-oriented UIs in some detail, and describe many of the interface applications and products mentioned in this chapter. Pinson and Weiner (1990) describes six of the applications we have mentioned in detail and includes useful remarks on the suitability of the various languages used and on project management issues. Taylor (1992) discusses 18 real applications of object-orientation.

Wilson (1991) reproduces a short report prepared for the UK government's computing watchdog, the CCTA. The report itself defines and explains CSCW and comprises less than half the text. The remainder is taken up with appendices that list current research projects throughout the world, with contact addresses, and describe a few available products. Khoshafian *et al.* (1992) describe an object-oriented approach to office automation with detailed information on multimedia, client/server, network, GUI and groupware technologies. Graham (1994) also gives more detail in these areas. Peuquet and Marble (1990) is a first rate introduction to geographic information systems and includes some seminal papers in that area.

Booch (1991) shows how to design five applications in great detail. Wirfs-Brock *et al.* (1990) describe the design of notional systems for an ATM network and program documentation.

Harland and Drummond (1991) discuss the architectural support for object-oriented programming provided by the Rekursiv machine and its systems programming language, Lingo.

Tom Love's *Object Lessons* talks obliquely, but from direct experience, about several important commercial applications.

Object Magazine is a good source of application descriptions and news.

5

Database technology

I have a cat named Trash ... If I were trying to sell him (at least to a computer scientist), I would not stress that he is gentle to humans and is self-sufficient, living mostly on field mice. Rather, I would argue that he is object-oriented.

Roger King (My Cat is Object-Oriented)

These days, if you want to sell a software product, you tell the world that it is object-oriented. Once upon a time you had to say that it was relational. In this chapter we look at this shift of emphasis, or shift in fashion, as the more cynical might put it.

The relational database was not inflicted on the commercial world without justification. I was one of the people in the late seventies and early eighties who proselytized on behalf of the relational gospel. In this chapter we will look at the positive reasons for the emergence of the relational approach, but also at some of its defects. To make this discussion possible we first have to understand something of the nature and history of databases and data modelling.

All database systems are distinguished from other programs by their ability to manage persistent data and to access very large quantities of these data efficiently and safely. Other common features of database systems, identified by Ullman (1988), include:

- support for an abstract data model;
- support for high-level access or query languages;
- support for transaction management in a multi-user environment;
- support for controls on access and data ownership;
- support for data validation and consistency checking;
- support for consistent data recovery from system and hardware failures, which minimizes loss of data.

We will examine only the first two of these issues and not delve into the remainder, which are the proper province of texts on database systems *per se*. Some appropriate references are given in the bibliographical notes at the end of this chapter.

☱ 5.1 A potted history of data models

If we can skip over that period in computing when we still programmed with plug boards, the beginning of data storage was the sequential file. One read through the file from the beginning until the required datum was matched and then rewound the tape in readiness for the next access. As more sophisticated storage devices such as drums and disks emerged, programming languages were extended to include statements enabling direct access – sometimes called for some incomprehensible reason 'random access'. This soon led to the realization that access speeds could be improved by hashing or storing index files.

The existence of indexed files made it possible to conceptualize a structural relationship among these files that would capture some of the structure of the real world or of the application. Since class membership is such an obvious and ubiquitous structural component of the world the first database products imposed a hierarchical structure among their files. In business systems, this often came about in the form of 'occurrences' of a type; for example, a company with several addresses. Hierarchical databases such as IMS were both popular and efficient. However, many business relationships did not fit into neat hierarchies and more general networks often emerged from the investigations of systems analysts. This led to the development of network databases exemplified by products such as TOTAL and IDMS and enshrined in the standards of the CODASYL committee. Network systems were nearly as popular and nearly as efficient as their hierarchical forebears. Both types of system, however, depended on fixed pointers and were very difficult to change or extend in response to business reorganization. All these products developed in response to practical requirements and without the benefit of a formal theory: there was no explicitly worked out 'network data model' or 'hierarchical data model'. In this respect object-oriented programming seems to be recapitulating the history of databases as an *ad hoc* technique lacking a formal theory.

The next development was the introduction of the first formal data model, Ted Codd's relational model of data (Codd, 1970). It was based on the first-order predicate calculus (FOPC) and, equipped with this theoretical basis, it supported a relationally complete, non-procedural enquiry language. The *de facto* standard now established for data definition and data manipulation, SQL, is loosely based on the relational calculus (one of the possible non-procedural languages). The highly redundant syntax of SQL owes as much to IBM's early language GIS as to the relational calculus, but its great benefit as a standard for enquiry, update and, indeed, communication between databases is well established. This great advantage is supplemented by the flexibility of the relational model and database management systems based upon it. Attributes can be added or removed without the need to reconstruct complex pointer systems, and relational databases make it possible to redefine business systems and organizational structures to better achieve competitive edge in an increasingly international, competitive and complex market.

It was soon realized that the relational model was not the only possible formal data model, and that other models might have certain advantages.

In general terms, a data model is a mathematical formalism consisting of a notation for describing data and data structures (information) and a set of valid operations which are used to manipulate those data, or at least the tokens representing them. The functional model of Shipman (1981) is one of the most successful in theoretical terms, while Chen's entity-relational model is one of the most widely used commercially although it lacks a coherent theory about the operations on data. The ideas of the functional model are closely related to ideas of semantic networks in AI and to functional programming. The underlying logic, thus, is closer to the Church–Curry lambda calculus than to first-order predicate calculus. Languages exist which exploit this model: Daplex and Adaplex. In Daplex two entities with the same component values can still be distinguished by having distinct references: they have 'object identity'. This cannot be accomplished in the standard relational model and extensions to the latter have been suggested by Codd and others which introduce unique identifiers for tuples so that an expression can denote a unique object that exists separately from its components. This is related to the idea of 'call by reference' in programming languages, as opposed to 'call by value'.

As with LISP, the functional approach removes the distinction between data and function (or program) and permits abstract data typing; that is, types are defined implicitly by the operations used. For example, the type List could be defined by the operations CAR, CDR and CONS. New types can be generated by generalization (IsA or AKO) and aggregation, so that entities can be defined and arranged in hierarchies or networks. The functional model thus holds the promise of new developments, especially with the advent of parallel and dataflow hardware architectures when the overhead of non-destructive assignment can be regarded as less important.

Various extended relational models, starting with Chen's entity-relationship (ER) model, have been proposed to overcome shortcomings in the relational model. The chief among these shortcomings, in my opinion, was the difficulty of capturing data semantics in relational implementations. It is increasingly realized that semantic models have to attempt to capture functional semantics as well. Other suggestions for data models include the binary relational model, where all relations have only two attributes and Codd's own RM/T (for details of both these models see Date (1983)). These were all attempts to deal with widely recognized deficiencies in the relational model. For a long time entity-relationship models were treated as purely analysis and design tools. As we shall see, recently there have been several attempts to construct complete DBMSs based on the ER model or even some deductive model capable of incorporating functional semantics (business rules) in the code. For example, the abstract Fact machine, which was based on an extension of the binary relational model, was implemented in the Generis product discussed in Section 5.6 below.

The development of formal data models both led to and was encouraged by the commercial development of relational database management systems

(RDBMS). Today nearly all database systems that are not performance critical are being developed as relational systems. Where efficiency is important and the scale is large, as with modern airline reservation systems, the hierarchical and network systems persist.

There has been a detectable tendency to promote a *post facto* rationalization of the CODASYL work, as though there were a hierarchical or network data model. The functional model turns out to map very well onto the network databases and provides just such a rationalization. It so happens that IsA links and functions correspond closely to the owner–member links and 'sets' of a CODASYL database.

Current interest has now turned to the possibility of object-oriented database systems and models. Ullman (1988) defines a preliminary object-oriented data model also capable of representing the hierarchical and network databases. Before turning to these in the next chapter, let us examine the relational model and its predecessors in more detail.

▤ 5.2 Weaknesses of early databases

The early hierarchical and network databases suffered mainly from their inflexibility. In the hierarchical model only certain kinds of structural relationships were expressible, namely, single inheritance or subtyping. The network systems allowed more general graphs to be constructed, but still it was very hard to change these relationships once the system had been designed. Adding or removing an attribute also often involved a major redesign exercise. In this section we introduce a part of database theory and look briefly at the style of these early approaches.

The simplest non-primitive data structure we can consider is a list, followed closely by lists of lists and the kind of tree-structured lists found in languages like LISP. Anyone who has written a computer program will have opened a file of data and read through it, record by record, until some condition was satisfied. This is just like looking down a list, or list of lists if the file stores more than one kind of symbol. For example, consider a computerized telephone directory that stores name, address and telephone number for some defined population. If you have the name and address, it is then easy to look up the number. Not so if you have the number and address and want the name. This is because lists or files have logical structure: the structure of being sorted in a particular order. To facilitate our task we would have to read the file in a different order. The telephone book is a list of lists that can be viewed as a table. The situation can be more complicated in that lists of lists of lists, and so on, can arise. For example, our reverse phone book might have the structure shown in Figure 5.1.

There are three extensions in the PR department of ABC Ltd, so we have to include a 'repeating group' consisting of a list of extensions and contact names. A little thought will show that this arrangement has the logical structure of a tree

Phone_No	Company	Dept.	No_Of_Exts	Extension	Contact
999-8888	Aardvark	Sales	1	102	S. Jones
777-1234	ABC Ltd	PR	3	110	J. Doe
				111	A.N. Other
				133	E. Codd
123-4567	Blue Inc	Mkting	1	2001	P.C. Plodd

Figure 5.1 A file with a repeating group.

or hierarchy. The use of repeating groups in early databases derived from the restriction to sequential storage devices, such as tape, in early computers.

The next level of complexity occurs when we have more than one file. Given direct access technology, in the above example we do not need to keep the repeating groups in the same file. We can, instead, arrange for the company file records merely to contain logical pointers to the extensions file. The structure is now something like that shown in Figure 5.2.

There are two files with a common field to link them. Logically, this link could be represented differently. It is logically a one-to-many relationship between departments and extensions. An extension cannot be in two departments in this scheme of things, which shows up one major limitation of the hierarchical approach to data structure: the difficulty of dealing with general, many-to-many relationships. More complex hierarchies may easily be envisaged.

The astute reader will detect that I have oversimplified in this example, in that two companies may possess the same department code. The key in the second file should, strictly speaking, be interpreted as a company-department code. However, the idea should still be clear despite this slight abuse of language.

To get a feel for the complexity of the network model, let us suppose that our SACIS database is to contain the information about particular stock items and their suppliers contained in Figure 5.3. The relationship represented is stated as 'for every part there may be many suppliers and for every supplier there may be many parts'. Item i4 has no current supplier.

The detailed network is shown in the diagram in Figure 5.4.

FILE-1

Phone_No	Company	Dept.	Dept_Code
999-8888	Aardvark	Sales	17
777-1234	ABC	PR	23
123-4567	Blue Inc	Mktg	24

FILE-2

Dept_Code	Extn	Contact
17	102	S. Jones
23	110	J. Doe
23	111	A.N. Other
23	133	E. Codd
24	2001	P.C. Plodd

Figure 5.2 Decomposition to eliminate repeating groups.

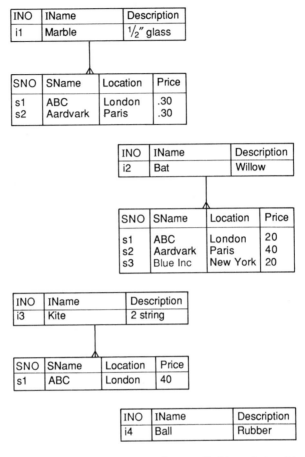

Figure 5.3 Data representing the supplied-by relationship.

Notice the ring structure of the links and that there are two ways to retrieve the answer to the query 'Find the description of part i2 made by s2': either start with the company and look along the pointers for a connector linked to the part, or start with the part and look for the company. It is completely non-trivial to decide which is the more efficient strategy.

Most people seeing a diagram such as that in Figure 5.4 for the first time would surely agree that it looks a frightful mess. The maintenance costs associated with practical network databases seem to bear this view out. However, access via pointers is very efficient.

Relational databases overcome some of the limitations of hierarchical and network systems in terms of flexibility, as we shall see in the next section.

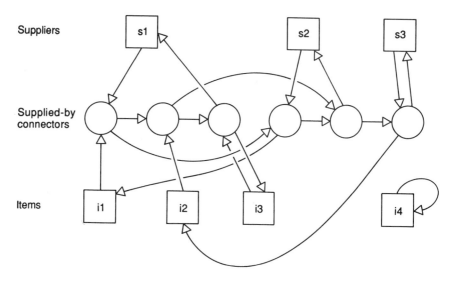

Figure 5.4 Network pointer structure for the supplied-by relationship of Figure 5.3.

⊟ 5.3 The relational model and how it helps

Owing to the commercial importance and theoretical basis of the relational model we must briefly review its main ideas.

The relational model of data was motivated by several aims, among them the desire to use formal methods in database design, enquiry and update; the desire to be able to prove the correctness of programs based on non-procedural descriptions; and the urge to meet Occam's razor: that a theory should be as simple as possible while retaining its expressive power. The basic idea is that data are represented as a series of tables or 'flat files'. No repeating groups or implicit hierarchies are to be allowed, and no fixed structural links are to be a part of the database. Logical relationships between the data are constructed at run time or are held in tables themselves. Thus the same type of object is used to represent both entities and relationships. Also these 'cross-reference' tables can be rebuilt without the need to reorganize the basic data. This is a great advantage in databases which model enterprises subject to much organizational change. It is amazing that, even today, many systems development methods still place emphasis on labelling datasets or entities as to whether they are subject to change over time. In a relational database, the assumption is that everything can, in principle, change over time unless some exogenous fiat dictates otherwise. This is typical of the extent to which the relational model has been misunderstood by its proponents as well as its enemies. The chief source of misunderstanding is the confusion between logical and physical data models. The relational model is a logical one. On the other hand there was no real, motivating hierarchical or network model in the logical sense. These are physical designs. In fact, relational database products can be implemented as network databases for efficiency. The logical relational model allows users to view one data structure in many different ways, through so-called user views, and thus one important benefit of relational databases is a higher degree of user acceptance.

Relational databases have been introduced fairly informally so far. This common practice has often led to misconceptions so we now turn to a slightly more precise development. The reader who already has a thorough understanding of relational theory or who, perhaps, has a broad practical understanding and an aversion to even a little mathematics, may comfortably skip to Section 5.4, or skim the remainder of this section.

The relational model consists of two intrinsic and two extrinsic parts. The first of the intrinsic parts is a structural part which uses notions of *domains, n-ary relations, attributes, tuples* and *primary* and *foreign keys*. The second is a manipulative part whose main tools are relational algebra and/or calculus and relational assignment. The extrinsic parts include an integrity part in respect of both entities and reference. The fourth component normally considered as within the relational model, although this is not strictly the case, is the design part consisting of the theory of normal forms. We will explain some of this terminology as we go.

A relation, mathematically defined, is any subset of a Cartesian product of sets. Given a list of sets $A_1, \dots, A_n$, their Cartesian product is the set of all lists or bags[1] of n elements of the A_i where there can be only one element in the bag from each A_i. Such a bag is called an ordered n-tuple, or just a **tuple.** The relation is sometimes said to be **n-ary** if there are n attributes. Each A_i is called a **domain** when viewed as a set of elements from which an attribute may take its values and an **attribute** when viewed as a label for that set. These concepts are illustrated in Figure 5.5

An equivalent notion is that of a table, and it is this one that is most often used in the context of computers because of the strong physical analogies.

The next order of structure in a database concerns the relationships between relations. These, of course, are relations themselves. Chen (1976) uses the terminology 'entity-relations' and 'relationship-relations' to distinguish them. We will talk about 'links' as a shorthand, implying no connexion with the links of a CODASYL database. Both kinds of relation must conform to certain integrity constraints. Every entity must have specified at least one **primary key** set of attributes that uniquely identifies each tuple at any given time. Furthermore, it must be in first normal form; that is, the attribute values cannot be complex structures (repeating groups, lists, and so on) but must be atomic data types (numbers, strings, and so on). This is no restriction for data processing applications but in list processing, text and image storage and knowledge processing we will see that extensions are going to be needed. The links have two kinds of property, multiplicity and modality. The *multiplicity* (sometimes called cardinality) of a link may be one-to-one or many-to-one and the *modality* may be necessary or possible. This level of structure is added to the relational model and is not strictly a part of it. Integrity, multiplicity and modality constraints are usually coded in the application and nearly always in some

---

[1] A *bag* is a list wherin elements may be repeated, as opposed to a *set* where repetition is not permitted.

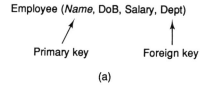

Employee (*Name*, DoB, Salary, Dept)

Primary key   Foreign key

(a)

Name	DoB	Salary	Dept
R.L. Stevenson	1/1/1850	10,000	Shipping
C. Dickens	25/12/1812	4,000	Curiosities

(b)

Employee — Name → Character strings

Employee — DoB → Dates

Employee — Salary → Money

Employee — Dept → Department names

(c)

Figure 5.5 **(a)** A 4-ary relation with its four attributes, one primary and one foreign key; **(b)** The domains of the four attributes; **(c)** Some tuples from the Employee relation.

exogenous procedural language. Thus we will refer to this part of the theory as *extended* relational analysis (ERA).

As Figure 5.6(b) illustrates, there are 16 possible link types connecting two entities or relations. The links are interpreted directionally in such a way that the second modality/multiplicity icon pair is the one read. In the figure we read the outer symbols as multiplicity symbols and the inner ones as modality symbols. The multiplicity symbols are a crow's foot – read as 'many', a bar – read as 'one' and no symbol – read as 'zero'. The zero option is rarely used and is excluded from the 16 possibilities, otherwise there would be 36. The modality symbol for possibility is O – read as 'may be' or sometimes more barbarously 'are optionally'. The symbol for necessity is a bar, | – read as 'must be'. Thus, in Figure 5.6(a) we interpret the link from left to right by 'for every employee there must be exactly one department', and from right to left as 'for every department there may be many employees'. The Chen ER notation, discussed later in this chapter, is very similar. Several other data analysis notations with the same semantics exist. For example, the

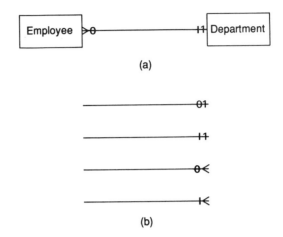

(a)

(b)

Figure 5.6 ERA notation.

Oracle CASE*METHOD notation (Barker, 1990), which derives from the Bachman tradition, uses a dotted line to denote possibility.

We will also need the definition of a **foreign key**; that is, an attribute which is the primary key of some other relation. The integrity rules specify what happens to related relations when a table is subjected to update or deletion operations.

We now turn to the manipulative part of the model; that is, to the means by which queries and update requests can be expressed. There are essentially two methods and various hybrids of them. The two methods are known as the relational calculus and the relation algebra. A manipulation language is said to be *relationally complete* if any possible operation over the database may be prescribed within a single (and *a fortiori* non-procedural) statement of the language. This provides us with an operational definition of a relation calculus. A language permitting all feasible operations over a database to be prescribed, but in more than one statement of the language (and therefore a procedural language), is operationally defined as a relational algebra.

The first method to emerge with Codd's original paper was the relational calculus, which is a retrieval and update language based on a subset of the first-order predicate calculus. Later, the Berkeley QUEL language used in Ingres was based on it.

In relational calculus, retrieval is done via a tuple-variable which may take values in some given relation. An expression of the tuple calculus is defined recursively as a formula of predicate calculus formed from tuple variables, relational operators, logical operators and quantifiers. In this sense relational calculus is non-procedural. Consider the following statement of predicate calculus:

$(\exists x,y)(t \in \text{ITEMS}) \land x=\text{INAME} \land y=\text{DESCRIPTION} \land \text{INAME}='\text{Kite}'$

This can be regarded as a query which should return the name and description of all items whose name is 'Kite'. Note that the tuple variable, t, is free and the bound variables, x and y, correspond to the attributes. In QUEL the syntax would be

RANGE OF T IS ITEMS

RETRIEVE(INAME.DESCRIPTION)

WHERE INAME='Kite'

A similar syntax permits update operations of arbitrary complexity in this non-procedural style.

The alternative approach is to regard enquiries and updates as expressed by a sequence of algebraic operations. This is more procedural and comes closer, if not very close, to the physical implementation, since the results will depend on the order of evaluation. In actual implementations, a query optimizer will usually attempt to select the optimal order of evaluation making use of the referential transparency of algebra. Relational algebra is based on four primitive operations: selection, projection, union and join. These operations are illustrated in Figure 5.7. Selection on a predicate yields those tuples that satisfy the predicate; it corresponds to the comprehension schema of set theory, $\{x: p(x)\}$[2], and may be thought of as a horizontal subset operation. The corresponding vertical subset operation is just the projection out of the Cartesian product. If two tables have the same attributes, their union may be formed by appending them together and removing any duplicates in the primary key. The join of two relations A and B over a relational operator (or dyadic predicate) p is obtained by building all tuples that are the concatenation of a tuple from A followed by one from B such that p holds for the attribute specified. Duplicates are eliminated here too. The derivative operations such as difference and intersection will not be covered here. This account of relational algebra has been slightly oversimplified for brevity. For the full details the reader may consult Elmasri and Navathe (1989) or Date (1981). Relational algebra can be regarded as defining the scope for operations such as retrieval, update, view formation, authorization and so on. Purely algebraic languages are extremely rare in practice. Gray (1984) gives a syntax for such a language, ASTRID.

Several hybrid languages based partly on calculus and algebra exist, the most notable being those based on the IBM System-R language, SQL. SQL was partly derived from the motivation to produce a 'structured' language. Later it was found necessary or convenient to add in most of the power of algebra and calculus, so much so that SQL is a highly redundant and thus inelegant language. However, it has become the *de facto* industry standard so we will introduce its syntax and use it in examples.

The query given above, in SQL, would be

SELECT INAME,DESCRIPTION

FROM ITEMS

WHERE INAME='Kite'

---

[2] Read as: the set of all elements, x, such that statement p about x is true.

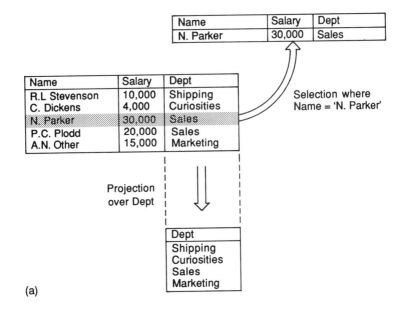

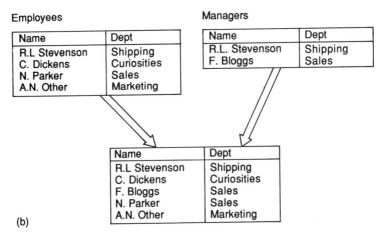

(b)

Figure 5.7 Operations of relational algebra. (a) Selection and projection operations; (b) The union of two (compatible) relations; (c) The join of two relations over the predicate: Employee.Dept=Manager.Dept. Note that the tuples with null values are eliminated.

The reader is warned not to confuse this SELECT with the selection of algebra defined above. This query might be regarded as saying: Project ITEMS over INAME and DESCRIPTION, and select under the predicate INAME='Kite'.

Note that relational query languages operate on tables, or sets of tuples. A query always returns a table. Strictly speaking one should refer to such a language

Employees

Name	Salary	Dept
R.L. Stevenson	10,000	Shipping
T. Smolett	11,000	Shipping
L. Sterne	9,000	Shipping
I. Graham	13,000	IT
C. Dickens	4,000	Curiosities

Managers

Name	DoB	Dept
R.L Stevenson	1/1/1850	Shipping
C. Dickens	25/12/1812	Curiosities
N. Parker	13/3/1956	Sales
F. Bloggs	8/11/1977	Sales
A.N. Other	29/2/1948	Marketing

Employee Name	DoB	Salary	Dept	Manager Name
R.L. Stevenson	1/1/1850	10,000	Shipping	R.L. Stevenson
C. Dickens	25/12/1812	4,000	Curiosities	C. Dickens

(c)

Figure 5.7 (cont'd)

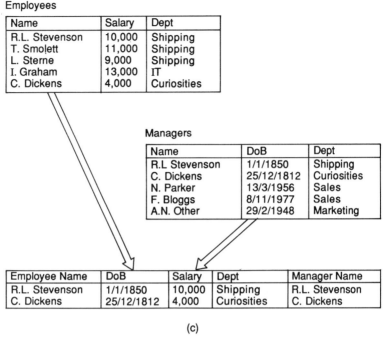

as a tuple-relational calculus. It is also possible to construct domain-relational cal-
culi, where variables range over the domains of attributes. In contrast, in the tuple
calculus variables range over tuples. For example, taking the query about kites we
have been working with up to now, we could express it in a domain calculus language as follows:

RETRIEVE x,y FROM ITEMS(p,'Kite',q,r,y)

where the relation schema is:

INO	INAME	SNO	PRICE	DESCRIPTION

and all variables are regarded as free variables. Notice the positional style and the
similarity with IBM's Query By Example. The latter is, in fact, based on the
domain calculus.

   We have said that relations must be in first normal form. In fact this condition sits at the bottom of a hierarchy of normal forms as shown in Figure 5.8, of
which the most important are the third or Boyce–Codd normal forms. The theory
of normal forms is merely a way of formalizing the common-sense notion of a
'good design'.

   To facilitate the definition of the various normal forms we have to define
what it means to say that one attribute of a relation is functionally dependent on
another. An attribute is functionally dependent on another if and only if each value

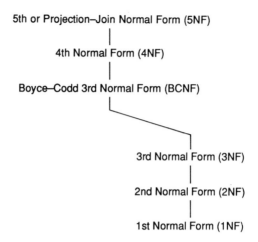

5th or Projection–Join Normal Form (5NF)

4th Normal Form (4NF)

Boyce–Codd 3rd Normal Form (BCNF)

3rd Normal Form (3NF)

2nd Normal Form (2NF)

1st Normal Form (1NF)

Figure 5.8 The hierarchy of normal forms.

of the second one uniquely determines the value of the first. In other words the projection of the relation onto these two attributes is a function (that is, a single valued, everywhere defined relation).

Functional dependency is not symmetrical. For example, if the relation is the set of all points on a parabola, then the y-axis is functionally dependent on the x-axis but not vice versa, as illustrated in Figure 5.9. For a more concrete example, in most company relations the telephone number will be functionally dependent on the company number (this assumes no party lines). Date (1981) points out, interestingly from our present point of view, that a functional dependency is a special form of integrity constraint; in other words it is a legality condition relating to the semantics of the situation.

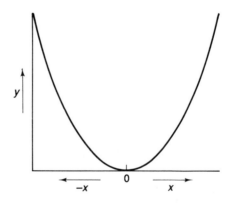

Figure 5.9 The relation on real numbers defined by a parabola $(y=x^2)$.

Relation 1

SNO	Location	Currency	INO	Price
1	London	£	1	30
1	London	£	2	20
1	London	£	3	40
1	London	£	4	20
1	London	£	5	10
1	London	£	6	10
2	Paris	FF	1	30
2	Paris	FF	2 ·	40
3	Paris	FF	2	20
4	London	£	2	20
4	London	£	4	30
4	London	£	5	40

Relation 2

SNO	Location	Currency
1	London	£
2	Paris	FF
3	Paris	FF
4	London	£
5	New York	$

Relation 3

SNO	INO	Price
1	1	30
1	2	20
1	3	40
1	4	20
1	5	10
1	6	10
2	1	30
2	2	40
3	2	20
4	2	20
4	4	30
4	5	40

Relation 4

SNO	Location
1	London
2	Paris
3	Paris
4	London
5	New York

Relation 5

Location	Currency
London	£
Paris	FF
New York	$

Figure 5.10 Normalizing relations.

Functional dependencies express concrete relationships in the real world and require an understanding of the application. Functional dependencies in general cannot be discovered by an automatic process, only by a skilled systems analyst.

Intuitively, a relation is in (third) normal form if and only if the primary key uniquely identifies a tuple and the other attributes are independent from one another and are all functionally dependent on the key. These attributes are properties or descriptions of an entity. In fact, it has been said that, for a third normal form entity, the value of an attribute depends upon 'the key, the whole key and nothing but the key'.

Formally then, a relation is in first normal form if and only if all attributes can only take atomic values, usually numbers or strings, but this actually depends on the underlying logical language. It is in second normal form if and only if, in addition, every non-key attribute is functionally dependent on the primary key and on no proper subset of that key. Second normal form designs overcome certain anomalies in respect of the operations of insertion, deletion or modification of tuples. For example, consider the following five relations shown in Figure 5.10.

In Relation 1 of Figure 5.10 it is not possible to record the existence of a supplier by its supplier number (SNO) until it supplies an item, unless we allow the key field INO to take null values. Even worse, if the ninth tuple is deleted we lose all the information about supplier 3. This phenomenon is often referred to as 'the connectivity trap'. If we try to amend the location of supplier 1 then all the tuples referring to that supplier must also be amended or the database will become inconsistent, an error that could easily be made in practice. Relation 1 shows our database in first normal form but not in second. Decomposing it into Relations 2 and 3 achieves second normal form and overcomes all these problems. Note, incidentally, that if the layout is conceived of as representing physical storage we may have saved some space on secondary storage too. The reader should also note the functional dependencies implicit in this database: Currency depends on Location, which depends on SNO, and Price depends on both the supplier and the item numbers, which together form the primary key of Relation 1 and separately the primary keys of Relations 2 and 3. We have not, with our new design, overcome all problems. It is not possible to record the currency of a location until a supplier with that location is entered in the database. Similarly if we delete the last tuple of Relation 2 we lose information about dollars. Since this table still contains some redundancy there are update problems that remain also. To recover from these symptoms we note that the functional dependency of Currency on SNO arises by composing the other dependencies: it is a *transitive dependency*. If we rearrange the database into Relations 3, 4 and 5 we remove all transitive dependencies and thus overcome all the anomalies mentioned.

A relation is in third normal form if and only if it is in second normal form and every non-key attribute is non-transitively dependent on the primary key. There is a slightly stronger version of this definition due to Boyce and Codd as follows. A relation is in (Boyce–Codd) third normal form if and only if every attribute on which others depend is a candidate key (that is, could be the primary key). This definition is not couched in terms of first and second normal forms and is thus slightly more elegant. It can be shown that it implies all the normal forms defined so far, with the possible exception of the first (Ullman, 1981).

Note that the join of Relations 4 and 5 recovers Relation 2 and the join of Relations 2 and 3 recovers Relation 1 without any loss of information in the sense that no spurious tuples are introduced. This need not be the case, although it can be shown that any relation admits such a lossless decomposition. Care must be exercised in database design and manipulation to avoid operations of projection followed by join which lose information in this way. For example, projecting Relation 2 over (SNO,Currency) and (Location,Currency) would give a 'lossy' join over Currency.

To overcome this lossy join problem, and other minor problems, fourth and fifth normal forms have been introduced. Their precise definition is a fairly complex matter and would be out of place in this text. The reader is referred to the works specified in the bibliographical notes to this chapter for these definitions. An informal definition is given in the next paragraph.

It may be useful to provide a crisp summary of the above description of normal forms. First normal form, or 1NF, insists that attribute value entries are 'atomic'; that is, there are no 'repeating groups' or lists and values must be primitive data types rather than pointers. This means that values may not represent complex objects with their own structure. Second normal form, or 2NF, says that tuples are uniquely defined by a primary key. Note that this is not the same as unique object identity because two records with the same attribute values but different identity cannot be stored. In relational systems object identity is faked by introducing unique identification fields such as Employee No. The most useful form of 3NF (Boyce–Codd NF) says that every determinant is a candidate key. In other words, every string of attributes that uniquely identifies a tuple could be the key. I like to think of this normal form as a sort of institutionalized common sense, because it is how a seasoned relational designer would write the relations down from the beginning. 4NF helps to avoid redundancy and 5NF prevents what are called lossy joins; that is, if you join two (or more) relations and then decompose to the original form no data are lost.

The theory of normal forms is an aspect of 'bottom-up' design and is complementary to top-down design methods. It is not, strictly, a part of the relational model. The whole theory of integrity is also not a part of the model.

One striking weakness of the usual relational point of view, when it comes to business applications, is the unnatural way in which it handles relations which are directly perceived in multidimensional form. The very best example of this is in the domain of financial modelling. The refusal to recognize as atomic any object of higher type (lists, vectors, and so on) makes the relatively trivial tasks of spreadsheet modelling tortuous within a relational model. The ease of use of such packages as Lotus123, Excel, FCS, System W and Express derive from the richness of the data structure and its good match with the way in which the problem is generally perceived by humans. In practice, most organizations will store raw data in relational tables and aggregate them in various ways before passing the results to such packages for modelling and decision support applications. This makes it seem as though the relational model is about handling bulk, unrefined data, but this is patently not the case. Some very high-level decision support applications do suit the relational organization of data perfectly.

This problem can be addressed partly within the relational model by moving from a tuple calculus to a domain calculus. An example of this approach is to be found in the financial modelling system Express. The Express system literature refers to the product as supporting a relational data model. This is justified in the sense that the data model is a logical one and that the algebraic operations, such as move, project and so on, are supported. However, the version of the relational model present in these systems differs in important ways from the model described above, thus meeting certain practical needs and pointing to deficiencies in the latter. The enquiry language is based on domain relational calculus.

Express, along with several other decision support systems, provides a logical data model to the user that differs from all of the network, hierarchical and relational viewpoints. It is a multidimensional data model; that is, it is concerned with variables scoped over several dimensions which may be thought of as a hypercube. For example, in a financial model, the dimensions of a pertinent 6-dimensional hypercube might be: Time, Balance Sheet Items, Companies, Regions, Products and Currencies. These dimensions need not map into the real line, as in Cartesian geometry, but may themselves be sets. In fact, this data view is simply a transform of the relational model, where instances in a dimension are equivalent to attribute values drawn from a domain.

The benefit of the Express representation lies, of course, in the syntactic ease with which operations over projections of the relations may be expressed. A typical query of this type might be: 'List all the balance sheets of companies in region A'.

Relational systems have great strengths. They make changes to the data structure easy and they protect users from complexity with non-procedural enquiry languages which can be optimized automatically. Performance problems have been gradually overcome. After initial resistance, relational databases have now achieved such wide acceptance in industry that most systems planners no longer even consider hierarchical or network solutions, except for the sort of large transaction intensive applications mentioned already. IBM recommends DB2 even for large applications, and most planners are only faced with the choice between a few relational products such as Informix, Ingres, Oracle, Supra or Sybase. The decision criteria are usually only factors such as support, portability or even marketing effort.

5.4 Semantic data models and data analysis methods

As has been pointed out already, a data model is a mathematical formalism consisting of a notation for describing data and data structures and a set of valid operations which are used to manipulate those data. Data models also help a designer eliminate redundancy in storage and inconsistencies in the structural design.

There are several extended data models and associated notations, including ERA, a notation within the broad Chen tradition, which we have already described and which we will use again in this book. The general term for these richer models is *semantic data models*.

There is a distinction between models based on predicate logic, such as the relational model, which support a declarative access language and a generally declarative style, and others. Such models are value-oriented and do not support object identity. The other class of data model may be thought of as object-oriented in the sense that object identity, and usually inheritance, is supported. These 'object-oriented' data models include the implicit models of the old hierarchical and network databases. Ullman (1988) has argued that there is a fundamental trade-off between declarativeness and object identity, and thus object-orientation.

In a model based on relations and only relations, the type of the result of an operation is always the same, so it is a candidate for input to some further operation. Thus operations can be composed easily. In models that support abstract data types this is fundamentally not the case, since object identity introduces type variation and an operation may result in a totally new type. Such a new type may need totally new operations defined on it, although in an object-oriented system it may well inherit them.

Semantic data models started with Abrial's (1974) binary relational model. The schemata of the binary model are essentially semantic networks restricted to classes. Chen's (1976) notation was introduced originally purely as a notation for design. It had quite different goals from the relational model, which attempted to separate the physical and logical description of data and develop powerful non-procedural enquiry languages. Semantic data models were intended to permit the modelling of relationships and integrity. Modern semantic models also include very sophisticated means of dealing with inheritance, composition structures, instantiation and subtyping. The general idea is to be able to model data at appropriately high and low levels of abstraction and to capture as much meaning as possible.

Smith and Smith (1977) showed that the relational model was insufficiently expressive to capture all of an ER model. Also, pure relational databases cannot support complex objects of any sort including abstract data types. This is prevented by 1NF. Object-oriented design allows as many types as necessary and permits full inheritance between them

Thus there is an obvious need for object-oriented databases to permit the design to be implemented easily. This is the topic of the next chapter. In the remainder of this one we examine other approaches that have emerged and are emerging.

The most widely used semantic data models are the entity-relationship (ER) models. Various ER models arose from attempts to analyse and model data independently of the database software that would be used to implement the design. The principal such models and notations were those due to Chen (1976) and Bachman (1977). ER models have two aims: to classify relations into types and to enforce business rules such as rules for referential integrity. The Chen ER model only has two types: entity-relations and relationship-relations. Schmid and Swenson (1975) proposed five types, but one is forced to wonder what is special about the number 5. There have been several, semantically richer, extensions of the basic ER model, some of them with similar names. The extended entity-relationship model (EER) introduced by Teorey *et al.* (1986) includes notations which differentiate generalization and subset hierarchies. The enhanced entity-relationship model (also EER) was introduced by Elmasri and Navathe (1989) with the aim of being a superset of most other ER proposals. To achieve their aims, Teorey *et al.,* and Elmasri and Navathe especially, are forced to introduce classes or abstract types into their EER models much in the manner of object-orientation. It is instructive that these authors seem driven inexorably towards this introduction of classes. Possibly this indicates that the notion of abstract classes with inheritance is canonical; that is, a sort of 'best' way of dealing with higher-order notions about entities and concepts in a data modelling context.

Figure 5.11 shows a typical EER notation. Note that the ternary relationships can be factored out by allowing relationships to have attributes corresponding to the third entity. For example, we might create an entity called 'project assignments' with attributes Employee, Project and Location.

It is worth noting that relationships, in the ER model, can be first-class objects in as much as they can have attributes themselves. Figure 5.12 shows an example where the relationship 'uses-car' may need to store attributes showing the valid range of dates for which a particular car was used by a particular employee.

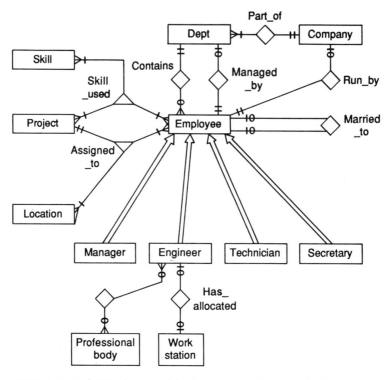

Figure 5.11 A typical EER data model of a personnel and project system, showing binary and ternary relationships and inheritance (the thick arrows).

In fact, there are three ways of representing a relationship in ER models. An object may contain an attribute whose domain is another object representing the relationship; two objects may both contain attributes with each other as domains; or there may be a specific object for the relationship. For example, referring to the data in Figure 5.12, the employee object could instead have a CarUsed attribute, or the Car object have a UsedBy attribute as well. The reason for choosing the third representation is precisely when the relationship itself has several important attributes.

The current Chen and Bachman style notations are in wide use and usage permits a variation in notation. One of the most interesting aspects of some versions of the Chen notation is their very explicit way of dealing with the semantics of inheritance and other structures. In particular, subtype relationships may be of four types, denoted as follows.

E/M   Exclusive/Mandatory

E/O   Exclusive/Optional

I/M   Inclusive/Mandatory

I/O   Inclusive/Optional

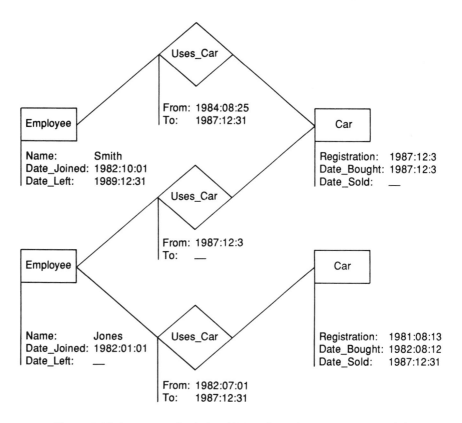

Figure 5.12 Instances of relationships with attributes in an ER model.

The term 'mandatory' indicates that a member of the supertype must be in one of the subtypes; that is, the subtypes are an exhaustive list or *partition* of the type. The 'exclusive' indicates that each subtype's intersection with the other subtypes is empty. 'Optional' indicates that the list is not exhaustive: there may be more, as yet unidentified, subtypes. 'Inclusive' indicates that the subtypes may overlap. A notation for this is illustrated in Figure 5.13. This notation is important and will be assumed in Chapter 8.

The traditional ER models either cannot, or make it extremely difficult to, cope with CAD/CAM database objects such as images, geometric drawings or structure-free text. It is this practical consideration, I believe, that drives data modellers towards object-oriented data models, for much the same reason that database vendors have been forced to introduce object-oriented constructs into their otherwise relational products.

There are two further important observations to make about ER models. In ER models, because not only entities but relationships themselves can have attributes, relationships represent first-class conceptual objects. The second observation is that Chen ER models tend to produce 3NF relations as a matter of course.

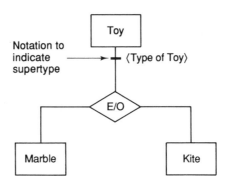

Figure 5.13 Inheritance in ER notation.

There are a number of systems development methods whose data modelling subsystems are largely based on the relational model, such as parts of IE and SSADM, CASE*METHOD, and several extensions to the relational model itself. A significant extension of this type is Codd's RM/T, which incorporates null values into the relational algebra and adds some of the abstractions from ER models, including subtypes and multiple inheritance, integrity rules, support for multiplicity and modality constraints and database operations and a distinction between two types of relation. E-relations represent the existence of entities and P-relations their properties.

There are two broad approaches to semantic data models. The first emphasizes the use of functions or attributes to relate objects, and the second emphasizes the use of type constructors. The first is represented by the functional data model and the second by the various ER models and their extensions. The key difference between the two philosophies is that in the type construction approach relationships are themselves types: first-class objects.

The functional data model (Shipman, 1981) is based on the lambda calculus described briefly in Chapter 3. The primitive concepts are entities and 'functional' relations and their inverses. Functional relations are single-valued relations: many-to-one relations. Inheritance is implemented by function composition. One of the nice things about the logically based functional model is that a formal type theory exists for it. A number of, mainly experimental, systems such as Daplex and Adaplex exist, as we have already seen. We have also seen that CODASYL or network databases can be given a formal foundation based on the functional model. Figure 5.14 shows part of a data model in typical functional notation. Daplex, according to Gray *et al.* (1992), is suitable for representing objects and computationally rich, but it is not complete. Completing it takes one in the direction of persistent object languages and object-oriented databases, which we will examine in the next chapter.

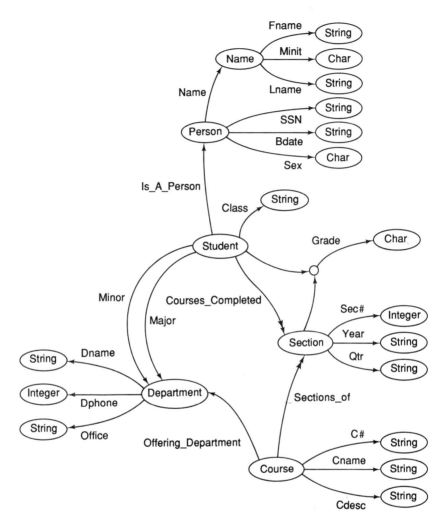

Figure 5.14 Part of a data model in typical functional notation concerning university course enrolments. The ovals are objects (sets) and the arrows represent functions. (After Elmasri and Navathe (1989).)

The generic semantic model (GSM) (Hull and King, 1987) is an attempt to superset most semantic data models, although it was developed primarily for tutorial purposes. SDM is another model proposed by Hammer and McLeod (1978, 1981). In SDM a database is a disjoint set of classes and instances and distinguishes classes from names and values. A value could be an instance of some class or a primitive *name*. It supports inheritance and includes a predicate language for specifying relationships and derived data in the manner of deductive data-bases.

A commercial implementation of SDM called SIM exists (Jagannathan *et al.,* 1988).

There have been several attempts to build real database systems on the basis of full semantic data models. Adaplex is an early such attempt to do this on top of the functional model by embedding a semantic database language, Daplex, within Ada. The Distributed Data Manager (Chan *et al.,* 1983) is a distributed semantic DBMS based on an extension of Adaplex. Generis is a semantic, or 'deductive', database based on an extended binary relational model. There are also systems now called entity-relationship databases based on the Chen model and some *ad hoc* extensions to relational database management systems, such as Ingres, incorporating features from both semantic models, object-orientation and artificial intelligence. These are discussed later in this chapter.

Object-oriented models include behavioural abstractions (methods) rather than the purely structural abstractions of data models. They seldom support the rich type constructors of semantic data models, such as the ability to model set-valued functions. Constructed types are arrived at by aggregating attributes, as when we construct the type Name from Style, Forename and Family_name, or by grouping into sets, as when we construct sets of items of similar type. The inheritance methods associated with the two approaches also tend to be different. Data models, as with AI systems, often allow the inheritance of defaults at the class level, whereas object-oriented models only allow attribute names to be inherited. Also, in data models inheritance tends to be restricted strictly to subtypes, while in object-oriented programming the inheritance of methods can take place between unlike types. For example, textual objects might inherit a 'display_self' method from Geometric_Object, although, in my view, this is bad practice.

King (1989) has emphasized the differences between semantic data models and object-orientation. He says:

Semantic models focus on the recursive definition of complex objects, and on the inheritance of structural components (aggregations) and relationships. Object-oriented models focus on the definition and inheritance of behavioural capabilities, in the form of operations embedded within types, and also support simpler capabilities for structuring complex objects; but this distinction is not as sharp as it might seem.

However, my interpretation is that there is a strong need for object-oriented databases, and object-oriented methods in general, to absorb the structural modelling features developed by data modellers along with, I think, good ideas from artificial intelligence research and development. In Chapter 8, I will attempt to demonstrate how this can be done at the analysis level. Object-oriented database researchers seem to be pursuing similar goals, and the ORION and ITASCA systems discussed in the next chapter is an example of a project with such goals.

The artificial intelligence, or strictly knowledge-based systems, extensions I have in mind are principally to do with the way defaults and inheritance conflicts are handled, but it is also true that rule-based programming has a significant contribution to make to system development. This will be explained more fully in Chapter 8.

For commercial applications, such as SACIS, where there is a strong data modelling element, it is beneficial, and even necessary, to build an object-oriented modelling system that incorporates the elements of semantic data models and object-oriented programming. A similar convergence of both object-orientation and semantic data modelling with AI models is also likely to be beneficial because of the richness of the inheritance, grouping and, especially, the meta-structural features of the latter, whereby the structure of data may itself be a property of those data. On the other hand the AI frame models have much to learn about encapsulation from object-oriented programming and about aggregation and abstraction from data modelling.

Let us now examine why the relational model is not appropriate for such developments.

5.5 Weaknesses in the relational model

The great strength of the relational model is its basis in a formal theory: first-order predicate logic. This is what makes it possible to have a relationally complete, non-procedural enquiry language such as SQL or QUEL. The logic ensures that certain things about this language can be proved mathematically. Another notable and very real benefit is that the database structure can be easily changed without completely redesigning the database. The other much vaunted benefit is the rigorous normalization theory that has emerged.

No one, with the possible exception of a few overzealous and commission-hungry salesmen, claims that the relational model is without difficulties. The difficulties I want to deal with include the difficulty of dealing with recursive queries, problems related to null values, lack of support for abstract data types and, most importantly in my view, severe shortcomings in the representation of data and functional semantics; there is no real support for business or integrity rules. I also want to point out some problems with the theory of normalization. Let us now examine this normalization theory a little more critically, and have a slightly deeper look at the other issues mentioned.

5.5.1 Normalization

There are a number of problems with normalization which are quite obvious to anyone thinking about object-oriented systems. First, normalized relations rarely, if ever, correspond to any object in the real world. The decomposition is driven by considerations of computation or logic, rather than modelled on the structure of the application. This prevents normalized relations being reusable in isolation and prevents any progress towards the assembly of systems from components. Not only do the normalized tables correspond to absolutely nothing in the application, but normalization also hides its semantics completely. One reason for this is that normalization conceals the application knowledge which is represented by functional dependencies among attributes. This means that normalization removes any possibility of full reverse engineering and that the process of normalization is effectively irreversible. For example, in the normalized relations of Figure 5.10, is it possible to tell from them that suppliers set prices in the currency of the state in which their town is located? Clearly not, and the loss of this information, or functional dependency, prevents its recovery. If the rules about currency were to change, as they might well do in post-Maastricht Europe, the systems would be difficult to redesign.

We have discussed some of the deficiencies of normalized data models. Not everything about normalization is bad. The elimination of redundancy in data storage delivered by 4NF cannot really be faulted in design terms although retrieval efficiency may be affected. In an object-oriented system there is an analogous need for a normalization theory for methods. In fact, encapsulation of methods does provide a sort of normalization automatically. For example, in terms of entities and relationships, if we consider the relationship 'sold to' in SACIS this relationship must ensure (via one of its methods) that the objects related consist of a valid customer and an item which is suitable for that customer. It would be redundant to store these integrity checks in the Customer or StockItem classes. Normalized behaviour requires that they are stored in the SoldTo class, which is the most natural place anyway.

Experienced data modellers instinctively remove many-to-many relationships from their models as part of normalization. This introduces entities which often have no correspondence to things in the real world. In an object-oriented context this seems quite wrong. The usual example given is that of Orders and Items which are related in a many-to-many fashion. A new entity called Order-line is used to resolve the relationship into two one-to-many relationships, as shown in Figure 5.15. This strategy is fine when there is a real, physical thing like the printed order line to observe. However, in other cases it is absurd. Consider that a legal regulation may apply to many products and that a product may be subject to many regulations.

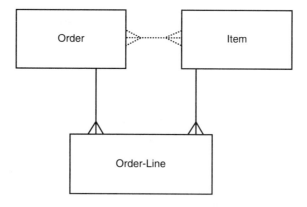

Figure 5.15 Resolving many-to-many relationships.

What is the equivalent of Order-Line? Is it Product-Regulation-Incidence? Similarly, cars may be painted many colours and colours applied to different models. What is the equivalent of Order-Line here? The over-zealous normalization of models is to be carefully avoided in an object-oriented context.

For those who are still worried about update anomalies, it is worth pointing out that these anomalies arise precisely because of the lack of object identity in relational systems where tables and tuples may not correspond to a single object.

5.5.2 Integrity and business rules

Integrity rules are semantic rules which assert that it is incorrect, for example, to delete a supplier reference because that supplier does not supply any part at present. In relational terminology we may state the rules for entity and referential integrity as follows.

Entity integrity: No primary key may include an attribute which may take null as a value.

Referential integrity: If a relation R contains a foreign key whose values are taken from the primary key values of a relation S then every occurrence of the foreign key in R must either match a primary key value in R or be null. R and S may be the same relation.

Note that entity integrity is not the same as object identity because a tuple is identified by its key value, not an unchangeable identity independent of attribute values.

Business rules are rules such as 'if an employee has over five years' service then award an extra day holiday' or, less crisply, 'long-standing customers who pay regularly deserve special attention'. Business rules relate the attributes of entities.

In most relational system integrity rules are usually coded in each client application, which makes changes very difficult to control. A more recent trend has been to provide facilities in the database server itself to overcome this difficulty. In such 'client/server' database implementations, it is often also possible to store 'triggers' in the server, procedures which update tables automatically when certain data change their values. This gives limited support for business rules, but they are still written in SQL or a procedural extension of SQL which makes understanding and changing them non-trivial. Support for rules of any kind is an extra, not a part of the relational model itself.

5.5.3 Null values

Null values in tuples present a difficulty of interpretation. A null can be taken to mean the logical value 'unknown'. They can mean that a value is just not applicable to particular tuples, or they could merely mean that no values have been supplied yet. Date (1983) suggests disallowing them altogether, but has then to introduce a complex superstructure of new logical operators and defaults. However, null values are a very natural way to deal with incomplete or exceptional data. The difficulty arises because FOPC is a 2-valued or Boolean logic: the only values allowed are true or false. Allowing null values immediately means that one must work in a 3- or 4- or even infinite-valued logic. Thus, against the evident benefits of working within a formal theory, we have to recognize that any such theory imposes limitations that real-world problems soon force us to go beyond.

As with rules, the problem of null values is one of the semantics of the application. The relational model is a purely syntactic model: it contains no intrinsic support for any kind of semantics. Data semantics have to be added on, and there is a huge literature on how to do this in the area of semantic data modelling. Functional semantics are also important. The rules by which a business operates are part of its functional semantics.

5.5.4 Abstract data types and complex objects

First normal form forbids the storage of complex objects, so that abstract data types cannot be dealt with by the relational model. This means that queries over databases which must store BLOBs (Binary Large OBjects), such as those involving structured text, engineering drawings or graphics, may be impossibly slow, since all the structure of a retrieved object must be recovered in the application at run time. It also means that methods cannot be stored ready for use in the database.

Even though relationships can be stored in relational or network databases, they are static: created at the time the database is designed. Furthermore, there is no natural way for relationships to have attributes: they are not first-class objects. The attributes of relationships are useful for such tasks as recording the time-span for which a relationship holds, such as when the 'supplies' relationship holds only at certain times of the year. For example, Christmas crackers are usually available only between September and December, although sadly this period seems to get longer year by year.

5.5.5 Recursive queries

Another negative effect of 1NF is that it disallows recursive queries; that is, queries about relationships that an entity has with itself. An example of such a relationship is the parenthood relation on the person entity.

Recursive queries have been the subject of study at the IBM laboratory in Heidelberg under the umbrella of its ten-year Advanced Information Management (AIM) research project. The researchers report (Dadam, 1988; Linnemann, 1987) that a short recursive query of the form:

```
SELECT    x

FROM      x IN Employees

WHERE     x.Emp_ID = 'W09867'
```

can take as many as 18 lines of SQL to express. The project is exploring an extension of the relational model where relations can be normalized but do not have to be in 1NF. They call them NF^2 databases. Unnormalized relational models have been applied to office automation by Kitagawa and Kunii (1989). Note that the definition of Boyce–Codd NF does not depend on the definitions of either first or second normal form, so a normalization theory is still possible for such databases.

One way to implement recursive queries is as a search of an inheritance hierarchy. As an example, consider the following query in Adabas Entire, which is discussed in the next section.

```
Find person

 Referencing recursively

  via Child

   person = 'George'
```

This query finds all of George's ancestors. In other words we are searching an inheritance hierarchy upwards, or backwards. Forward, or downward, search is accomplished with the syntax 'Referenced recursively'.

Notice that there is only one relation. All types are stored in the PERSON relation via the explicitly stored relation 'child of' which is stored explicitly since Adabas Entire is an entity-relationship database.

It is worth noting that another consequence of first normal form, and consequently of flat file structures, is that foreign-key joins must be performed to reconstruct complex entities in an application. This can be very expensive in terms of processing time.

▤ 5.6 Entity-relationship and deductive databases

Apart from genuinely object-oriented databases, which are discussed in Chapter 6, there are several product sets which address all or some of the problems we have examined. These may be broadly classified as semantic databases. Commercial semantic databases are of four main kinds: entity-relationship databases, deductive databases, extended relational databases and functional databases. We will look at examples of the first three of these.

5.6.1 Entity-relationship databases

Adabas Entire represents an emerging trend in being an entity-relationship database wherein the relationships between entities are stored explicitly, rather than being implicit, and are thus recoverable. In fact the Adabas product has never insisted on relations being in 1NF, despite the claim that it was a relational database. In fact, you can use Adabas as if it were relational, merely by putting all relations into 1NF. This puts a burden on the database designer to choose the correct path, for NF^2 databases, like all more powerful systems, are more difficult to design. Much more knowledge and understanding are required. However, for complex problems the NF^2 solution is often far easier to express.

Adabas Entire is directly based on the Chen ER model. Its extra functionality is achieved by a very small extension to the syntax of Natural, the Adabas 4GL and enquiry language. Storing the relationships explicitly not only permits recursive queries, but automatically enforces referential integrity. Typically, ER databases such as Entire have no notion of classes and inheritance, nor do they offer advanced facilities for storing business rules either explicitly or in the server.

To overcome this deficiency, Software AG have also announced Natural Expert as an extension to Natural. Natural Expert is sold as a means of incorporating expert systems into Natural applications, but is particularly unusual in that it introduces functional programming (a form of lazy ML in fact) instead of the more usual production rule style. Functional programming when combined with the entity-relationship database could address quite a few of the deficiencies in relational databases alluded to in the foregoing.

The convergence of ER and functional concepts represented by Adabas is also evident in the functional database camp, where proponents of systems such as Daplex are now regarding a lot of their work as object-oriented. A project exemplifying and illustrating this convergence of ideas and styles is reported in Gray and Kemp (1990).

Adabas Entire is by no means the only product in this area. ZIM from Zanthe is another early ER database management system, and IBM's Repository Manager is beginning to look very much like an ER database if not an object-oriented one, even though its data storage mechanism is still DB2.

5.6.2 Deductive databases

Alongside the development of ER database systems, and mainly influenced by developments in AI and expert systems, a number of systems best described as 'intelligent' or deductive databases have been launched. Many of these systems have all or some of the features of object-oriented databases alongside features more usually found in expert systems. Some are discussed in the next chapter owing to their emphasis on object-oriented features. Here we look at just one powerful deductive database, Generis, as a representative of this kind of system.

Generis, formerly called Fact, is a deductive database system based on an extension of the binary relational semantic model first introduced by Abrial (1974), the generic relational model (McInnes, 1988), and rooted in the AI tradition. It supports the explicit storage of facts (A is X), rules (If P then Q), relationships, triggers and complex data structures as well as raw data. It supports classes and multiple inheritance via the assertion of facts of the form: A is a B. It does not contain any significant features for encapsulation, although one 'method' may be encapsulated within certain object types. An extremely powerful query language, IQL, which can fill in missing information in the query using facts stored in the database, makes programming very productive. To illustrate, the SQL query:

SELECT   EMPLOYEE, SALARY, DEPARTMENT

FROM   EMPLOYMENT, DEPARTMENTS

WHERE   LOCATION='LONDON'

AND   JOB_TITLE='SALESMAN'

AND   EMPLOYMENT.DEPARTMENT=DEPARTMENTS.DEPARTMENT

becomes simply:

DISPLAY SALARY SALESMAN AND DEPARTMENT FOR LONDON

The result is the same, but in Generis the relationships (such as 'works in DEPARTMENT of employee') are retrieved and printed as column headers, as illustrated in Figure 5.16. In other words, the class structure, or the knowledge contained within it, is used to fill in the missing links. Generis also supports recursive queries.

Generis also has features that make it particularly suitable for intelligent text retrieval applications, and has been applied to a number of such applications, particularly in healthcare. The architecture and facilities of Generis are summarized in Figure 5.17.

Generis is a curious and powerful hybrid formed from relational, object-oriented and expert systems ideas. It extends the relational model with data semantics and supports recursive queries and inheritance, but not abstract data types or full encapsulation.

EMPLOYEE	works in DEPARTMENT of employee	located in LOCATION of department	earns SALARY of employee
A. Langham R. Biter	Sales Production	London London	27000 15000

Figure 5.16 Generis standard report format.

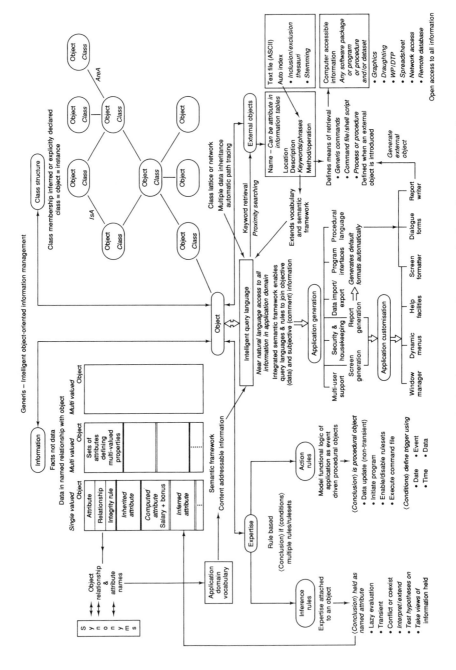

Figure 5.17 Generis features (by kind permission of Instrumatic Data Systems Limited).

From a practitioner's point of view, one of the most interesting potential applications of such semantically rich languages is specification prototyping, which is discussed in Chapter 9.

There are several other approaches to deductive databases. Many proceed by adding the power of logic programming to an existing RDBMS, using a language like Prolog as a database extension. Bell *et al.* (1990) offer a study of this approach. Other deductive databases are discussed by Gray *et al.* (1992) and their approach compared to that of object-oriented programming.

5.6.3 Relational databases with object-oriented extensions

A number of vendors of relational database management systems, under the influence of developments in object-oriented programming and expert systems, have made significant semantic extensions to their products.

Sybase is a relational DBMS with two novel features. First, it is based on a client/server architecture whereby the data integrity and business rules may be stored in the server, the database, rather than in each individual application. This has extremely beneficial consequences for maintenance, because when such a rule changes this does not mean that every application must be checked. The rules are implemented as triggers, active or data-driven rules that fire when data are changed, and stored procedures. The difficulty is that these rules are written as SQL or procedural code, and are thus not necessarily easy to understand or change. The vehicle for this is a non-standard procedural extension of SQL, Transact SQL, which includes control structures, procedures, assignment and other general-purpose programming constructs. Sybase offers some modest, but important, extensions to the vanilla relational system, some of which lean in an object-oriented direction. Adding stored procedures to database tables is certainly a step closer to object-orientation since data and processes are thereby combined. However, true encapsulation is not achieved since the data may be accessed directly and the tables need not be modelled on domain objects owing to normalization.

Ingres Version 6 offers similar extensions in the form of a multi-client/multi-server architecture, which is important for performance and distributed database reasons, and support for rules and triggers. However, Ingres – at least at the time of writing – goes beyond Sybase and other relational systems in offering explicit support for abstract data types and rules, with inheritance promised soon. Sybase and Ingres share common historical roots, in the sense that some of the early workers on Ingres, after a period working on database hardware, wrote Sybase. Evidently there is a lot of cross-fertilization of ideas in this community. Undoubtedly, the various database products will keep on leapfrogging each other in the race to be the best, most object-oriented system.

It is important that Ingres has decided to disrupt the calm acceptance of the relational model as little as possible, for those companies with large resources committed to the relational approach. The object manager is implemented as a separate layer that can be used, but Ingres may still be used as a pure relational database.

Ingres also has a knowledge manager, also implemented as a separate layer for the same reasons. The performance implications of this approach have yet to be established.

Oracle Corporation too has begun to add object-oriented features to its product. It is announced that Oracle Version 8 will be 'fully object-oriented'. More likely than not the SQL/3 language will reflect these developments closely.

The Committee for Advanced Database Function (CADF) consists of a number of leading figures in the database world who have come together to define the desirable functions of the next generation of databases. Many of the features they identify are essentially the features of object-oriented database systems which we discuss in the next chapter, where we will also examine these features in more detail.

Commercial systems, typically, have large amounts of data but the operations performed on them are relatively simple. For this reason the expressive power of most data management languages is very limited. Complex procedures are implemented by recourse to a general-purpose language such as COBOL, C or FORTRAN. Databases that have to deal with more complex relationships, such as VLSI design or CAD databases, need much greater generality in the access language. This is the significance of the requirement for computationally rich languages; that is, languages which permit any procedural or non-procedural computation to be expressed concisely.

Abstraction in databases means that fewer data have to be retrieved because the server understands more of the semantics of the object rather than regarding it an undifferentiated string of bits (a BLOB?) and having to retrieve the whole structure leaving the application to use its semantic knowledge to extract the relevant data.

Recursive queries and abstract data types are supported by Ingres Version 6, Adabas Entire and most deductive and object-oriented databases. The latter will be discussed separately in the next chapter.

5.7 Summary

The relational model was the first formal data model. Relational databases based on it were inherently more flexible than earlier, pointer-based, hierarchical and network systems. However, to achieve this flexibility relational databases cannot support object identity, which was a positive feature of earlier systems. Also, pointer-based systems were more efficient. There is a contradiction and consequent trade-off between object identity and non-procedural enquiry capabilities.

A data model is a mathematical formalism consisting of a notation for describing data and data structures (information) and a set of valid operations which are used to manipulate those data. Several more or less formal models emerged after the relational model. The functional model is one of the most successful in theoretical terms, while the entity-relational model is one of the most widely used commercially.

The functional model is a formal model which can be used to describe network systems. There are also a number of semantic models and extensions to the relational model which add semantic capabilities. Most important among these are various extended ER models, which support hierarchical and network structures for subtypes, grouping and aggregation.

Object-oriented models include behavioural abstractions (methods) rather than the purely structural abstractions of data models. They seldom support the rich type constructors of semantic data models. The inheritance methods associated with the two approaches also tend to be different. Data models, as with AI systems, often allow the inheritance of defaults at the class level, whereas object-oriented models only allow attribute names to be inherited. Also, in data models, inheritance tends to be restricted strictly to subtypes, while, in object-oriented programming, the inheritance of methods can take place between unlike types.

There is a need for object-oriented databases, and object-oriented methods in general, to absorb the structural modelling features developed by data modellers along with ideas from artificial intelligence. A convergence of both object-orientation and semantic data modelling with AI models is also likely to be beneficial.

Relational databases present difficulties in dealing with recursive queries, null values, abstract data types and the representation of data and functional semantics; there is no real support for business or integrity rules.

Normalization hides and destroys semantics. Normalized relations rarely if ever correspond to any object in the real world and normalization conceals the application knowledge that is represented by functional dependencies among attributes. This means that normalization removes any possibility of full reverse engineering. The process of normalization is effectively irreversible.

There have been several attempts to build real database systems on the basis of full semantic data models.

ER and deductive databases are useful hybrids, capable of addressing many database problems for which the relational systems are unsuitable. Deductive databases are especially useful for specification prototyping.

The object model, now emerging, combines many of the features and benefits of the extended relational, deductive and ER models and pointer-based systems. It is also, I will argue, the location for a convergence of ideas from semantic data modelling, artificial intelligence and object-oriented programming, design and analysis.

Developers now face a choice between pure object-oriented and deductive databases and extended releases of relational systems. Desiderata for this choice are discussed in the next chapter.

▤ 5.8 Bibliographical notes

Ullman's (1981) first text on database theory was the first comprehensive pedagogical introduction and analysis of the relational model, but was superseded as a standard text by Date (1981). Ullman's later two-volume text (1989) covers knowledge management and object-orientation, but remains a sound introduction to relational concepts as well. A very readable and comprehensive introduction to all aspects of database theory is the book by Elmasri and Navathe (1989), which also introduces object-oriented databases. All these volumes cover normalization theory thoroughly.

Semantic models are discussed in Date (1983), Elmasri and Navathe (1989) and Ullman (1989). Some important seminal papers on data models are collected in Zdonik and Maier (1990).

Hull and King (1987) and Peckham and Maryanski (1988) are excellent surveys of semantic data modelling techniques, with the former providing a comparison with object-oriented and AI models. Teorey *et al.* (1986) is an excellent survey of ER models and introduces one influential extended version and a design method associated with it.

King (1989) discusses the differences between semantic models and object-orientation. Brodie, Mylopoulos (1986) and Brodie and Mylopoulos and Schmidt (1984) cover various issues related to semantic, intelligent and deductive databases, and to combining insights from database theory, artificial intelligence and object-oriented programming.

The Postgres papers (Stonebraker and Rowe, 1987) provide insight into the design decisions involved in extending a relational database with knowledge-based and object-oriented features.

The connexions between semantic data models and object-orientation are discussed by Hughes (1991) and even more fully and profoundly by Gray *et al.* (1992) who gives a first-rate introduction to semantic models.

6

Object-oriented databases

It's like sitting at the water's edge at low tide
praying you won't get wet. You can either jump in now,
run in the other direction, or wait until the tide
surrounds you.

Chris Stone of the Object Management Group

So far, in this book, we have seen some advantages offered by object-oriented programming languages, some of the limitations of conventional database management systems in this respect and some suggestions for overcoming them. However, object-oriented programming languages also have their limitations. In particular, languages like Simula, C++ and Smalltalk offer no explicit support for persistent objects; that is, objects which are stored off-line on secondary storage devices and whose state persists from moment to moment and from session to session. Such languages have no effective means for dealing with persistent objects in the manner of a database. It is not possible to send messages to objects stored off-line. The best that can be done in Smalltalk, for example, is to store the entire session image off-line and reload it at the next session. Clearly, this is totally inadequate for any application with large amounts of important stored data, a feature that characterizes practically all commercial applications.

Persistent languages do not help with issues such as concurrency, security and recovery. In such languages the programmer must still write extra code to handle them.

The question then is how we may obtain the advantages of an object-oriented approach to systems development, retain the ability to store and manage persistent objects off-line and deal with issues such as concurrency and recovery in as facile a manner as we have come to expect with relational database management systems. Several approaches to resolving this issue have emerged under the banner of object-oriented databases.

There are three reasons why we might consider that an object-oriented database is required: to facilitate a clean interface with an object-oriented programming language; to tackle an application that requires the flexibility of a relational database but for which the performance of the latter is inadequate; or to tackle totally new kinds of application where the message-passing metaphor seems particularly appropriate. The remarkable fact is that object-oriented databases may be over 100 times faster for the right application and still retain the flexibility of a relational implementation in terms of schema evolution.

The commercial need for fully integrated object-oriented systems has led to the development of a number of systems described as object-oriented database management systems. These were mainly experimental systems for a time, but products such as GemStone, Ontos, Versant, ObjectStore, Objectivity, POET and ITASCA are now emerging as fully fledged commercial products. As we saw in Chapter 5, there are also a number of novel database systems with object-oriented features, including deductive and semantic databases, which are not fully fledged object-oriented database systems but share many of their features and benefits. Some conventional RDBMSs, such as Ingres, now include object-oriented features, and it is likely that most of this class of products will do so in the fullness of time. The object-oriented movement has even led to a revival of interest in hierarchical and network databases. The ER database, Adabas Entire, is ultimately implemented as a network database. Ullman (1988) points out that hierarchical and network databases such as IMS and the CODASYL family do support object identity, although they do not have the other features of the object-oriented model. Their main limitation, inflexibility in the face of schema evolution, is due to the manner in which object identity is implemented as fixed pointers.

In this atmosphere, the key question for systems strategists and planners is whether they should embrace the new object-oriented databases, do nothing or opt for a strategy based on extensions of the relational products. In this chapter we will attempt to arrive at a solution to this dilemma.

▤ 6.1 What is an object-oriented database?

Recall from Chapter 1 that an object-oriented programming language has three key features:

- encapsulation – the ability to deal with complex objects and encapsulate methods and data structures within them;
- inheritance – the ability for objects to participate in networks and share both attributes and methods thereby;
- self or object identity – something we have not paid much attention to until now.

We have seen that the common object-oriented programming languages do not support some basic functions required by a data-intensive application. In particular there is no support in such languages for:

- persistence of objects;
- management of very large amounts of data;
- data and transaction integrity;

- sharing and concurrent multi-user access;
- access or query languages;
- recovery;
- security.

Persistent objects are those which continue to exist after a session terminates. Objects can be created and destroyed in memory by an application or compiler. If some of them are to be persistent, there are two ways to handle their storage. They can be stored in a conventional database or directly as objects. The former would mean that the objects are not ready for use: they must be constructed from the files retrieved. If an object-oriented database is used, and the objects are stored directly as objects, then a retrieved object is ready for use immediately after retrieval. Persistence is closely related to object identity, because if objects are related via references to unique identifiers, then the relationships among objects persist as well as the objects.

The ability of a system to differentiate objects, throughout their lifetime, according not to their components or attributes, but by a unique identifier, is known as **object identity**. There are three conventional techniques for identifying objects: by physical locations in memory (pointers), primary keys or user-defined identifiers. In a relational system, if the primary key changes the object (tuple) identity may change too. In such systems, identity has to be simulated by surrogates or unique identifiers, such as Supplier_No, but so long as these are not under system control this does not guarantee against violations of identity. An object may be accessed in different ways: bound to different variables. There is no way to determine whether two variables refer to the same object. Using the idea of primary keys is also problematical. Primary keys are not permitted to change. If the key happens to represent a property that can change (are there any that cannot?), this can cause severe problems. Further, if we wish to merge two systems that use different keys for the same object, say 'name' and 'employee number' for employees, then the resultant change may break the continuity of identity. Such keys are not usually unique across the whole system, only within relations. For example, if Sam is both an employee and a shareholder in the same company, he may be stored as two entities rather than as one, leading to the possibilities of inconsistency and redundancy. How many times have you wondered why you receive the same mailshot three or more times?

There are several ways in which object identity can be implemented. The most common is the use of a system-generated unique identifier. This overcomes the problems mentioned above and is common in both object-oriented databases and languages. The identity of an object will not depend either on its location or its properties, just as an object in the world can have all, or most of, its properties change one by one but remain the same object throughout. A good example is a river which, in geological time, can change its source, route and contents, but still be the Amazon.

Object identity clarifies and extends the notion of pointers used in hierarchical databases and conventional languages like C. Relationships between objects can make use of a stored identity, or use a value-oriented expression as in SQL. Thus, the object-oriented database approach, in a sense, unifies value-based and identity-based access.

An **object-oriented database** system (or data model) is a database system (or model) – in the sense that it has all the features of databases discussed in the last chapter, including access languages, the ability to manage very large amounts of data, persistence, data and transaction integrity, concurrency, security and recovery – which additionally supports abstraction, inheritance and object identity. Additionally, with a modern object-oriented database, we usually expect some form of versioning system. The latter is largely an historical accident. While relational databases were substantially developed in the days of the stand-alone mini-computer or mainframe, object-oriented databases emerged in the days of the networked workstation. This meant that these new products were developed within a cultural setting where passing work to colleagues across the network for modification was quite normal. Transactions of this kind are called **long transactions**. They occur frequently in engineering design and document production contexts but not in the sort of applications to which conventional database management has been mostly applied. Traditional databases can only manage short transactions. For example, imagine what happens when the transactions of two automatic teller machine users withdrawing cash collide or reach deadlock. Normally, one of the transactions is aborted and the ATM user must rekey the instruction; irritating perhaps but not disastrous. Now imagine the equivalent situation when two engineers have spent months on their designs and want to commit them to the database simultaneously. If there is a deadlock I suspect that most engineers would feel quite suicidal were their transactions to be aborted and lost. The requirement here is to create a temporary version of the transaction automatically and commit that rather than merely abort it. Thus, control over versions was seen to be essential and was built into object-oriented database products from the earliest designs.

Objects can store relationships represented as links to other objects, and methods. These relationships are often regarded as objects in their own right and, as such, may have attributes and methods. For example, a use relationship may be time dependent: my use of the office telephone may be restricted to certain times, or zones. In this example, the use relationship might involve methods concerned with reporting overseas calls to management for certain grades of staff. Thus, object-oriented databases contain much of the functionality of semantic data models although, as we have seen, there are some inheritance features which are not always supported in the object model. Object-oriented databases go beyond semantic models insofar as they capture behavioural abstractions: methods. This means that they can represent and even normalize behaviour.

Conceptually, an object in an object-oriented database stores both attributes, which may themselves be complex objects, and methods together. In an actual implementation, complex objects and method code may not be physically stored with the object identifier, but pointers to the physical location may be stored. It is important that any enquiry language copes with this question of physical storage quite transparently, so that the user or designer of the database application may proceed as though the physical storage were in accordance with the conceptual model. Only a few of the commercial object-oriented databases actually store methods in the database. The majority only store the data structures and methods are dealt with by the run-time system in the conventional manner. Perhaps this justifies the use of the term *object-oriented database* as against the otherwise preferable but never used *objectbase*. A consequence of this is that most products are tightly coupled with a particular object-oriented programming language, as we shall see in Section 6.4.

In object-oriented programming, the emphasis is on behavioural abstraction. As far as structure is concerned, this means that the emphasis is on the inheritance of encapsulated methods. In object-oriented database systems, there is a much stronger requirement to model the structural properties of data and make explicit inheritance and aggregation structures. This kind of structure can arise in several different ways. Objects can be grouped in classes according to their common structural and behavioural properties; this is **classification**. For example, employees and customers can be grouped as people, and people, animals and plants can be grouped as living things. There is no unique way of classifying objects, and objects may be classified as belonging to more than one class. Classification structures (or networks) represent generalization and specialization. Vehicles are generalizations of cars, and specializations of artefacts. Closely related to classification is **association**. Here, concrete instances are grouped into a class according to some property that they share. An example of an association of objects that is not a classification of them might be the set of all things that are red or the set of things that weigh more than one tonne. The distinction, and how to use it in data analysis, will become clearer after you have read Section 9.2, where a distinction is made between essential (classificatory) and accidental (associative) objects. Classification sometimes represents a subset relationship and association a membership relationship. Something that is an instance in one application can be a class in another. For example, in a database of scientific terms, hominid is an instance, while in an anthropological database hominids may have several instances, or indeed subclasses. Objects can be grouped as components of some composite object in two ways: as a parts structure or as a set of attributes. This is **composition** or **aggregation**. For example, a car is composed of wheels, transmission, body, and so on. We call this notion 'composition structure'. Aggregation structure is more general and includes the possibility of conceptual composition as well as physical composition. For example, a computer is a concept aggregated from concepts including name, operating system, other software, location, access rights, and so on. Note that these components can in turn be aggregates; 'other software' for example. Aggregation of attributes and methods is how objects are formed conceptually in object-oriented programming.

It is important to note that classification and aggregation networks can interact. An object which is an aggregate of several objects contains (inherits?) their attributes and methods. An object that inherits attributes and methods from a supertype also inherits their aggregation structure. This issue does not arise often in object-oriented programming, but in databases it is crucial. The theory of this interaction is not yet fully worked out but the theory of semantic data models has much to offer.

Another kind of structure which is important in the design of complex data management systems is the structure of **usage**, or client/server, relationships between objects. These structures represent the message-passing topology of systems and measure the complexity of their control structures. This will be dealt with in the next two chapters.

As we will discuss more fully later, every verb could give rise to an association structure. The ones we have mentioned, to use, to aggregate and to be a kind of, seem to be particularly important. In AI, where semantic nets are used, other structures sometimes emerge, based on relationships like ownership. Attempts to lay down fixed sets of 'conceptual primitives', as for example Schank and Abelson (1977) tried to do within their theory of 'script' objects and Lenat and Guha (1990) are still attempting to do, have generally failed. I think this reflects a general philosophical issue: the theory of categories. Aristotle gave a set of fixed categories of thought, which were taken up and modified by Kant. The need to revise the set leads us to the observation that these categories are dynamically, socially and historically determined, and cannot be fixed. Human practice determines the canonical ones. In this case, DP practice has further determined that composition, classification and usage are canonical categories or structures. The semantic data models discussed in the last chapter, such as the EER and GSM models, are expressive enough to capture the semantics of classification, aggregation, association and use, but are weak in behavioural terms. They form the basis for schema descriptions in object-oriented databases. The need for complex, interacting structures of this kind arises because they represent structure in the real world and are part of the semantics of a database application. However, exposing attributes and methods via these structures makes it very hard to enforce the principle of information hiding. An object-oriented database, therefore, is required to do much more with data structures than an object-oriented programming language.

To fill out this loose definition it is important to make a few comparisons between object-oriented and relational databases. First, as Ullman (1988) argues cogently, there is a trade-off between non-procedurality (or non-declarativeness) and object identity. Relational systems offer non-procedural, that is declarative, access languages based on logic which are subject to query optimization. Object-oriented systems are fundamentally procedural and non-declarative in the mode of access via explicitly declared relationships between objects and classification and aggregation structures. However, for the same reason such systems require less optimization, and for enquiries on complex objects can be massively more efficient.

The mismatch between table-oriented languages such as SQL and ordinary record-oriented programming languages means that a separate data manipulation language (DML) is required for access. In a relational system, the unit of currency is the table: every SQL query returns a table. In a conventional programming language the unit of currency is the variable. Database programmers usually have to write code to move a 'cursor' across tables to resolve this problem and map cells to variables and *vice versa*. This **impedance mismatch**[1] (see Figure 6.1) between

---

[1] So called because an impedance mismatch in an electrical interface prevents optimal power transfer.

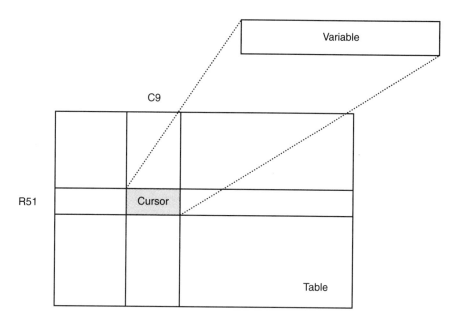

Figure 6.1 The impedance mismatch.

declarative and procedural styles and between the type systems of the application language and the database, causes a loss of information at the interface and impedes automatic type checking. 4GLs try to, but can only overcome these problems partially. In object-oriented database systems there is a match between programming and enquiry languages based on the notion of an object. Computationally rich DMLs can be constructed easily, or the application language can be extended to include the type system of the database. The distinction between the two languages can almost disappear. The Versant object-oriented database system, for example, does all enquiries in standard C++. We will see later (Chapter 8) that this applies to the distinction between languages and methods as well: the language and model impose the method. Resolving the impedance mismatch supports client/server architectures, where more of the semantics is stored in the database. This means that accesses are reduced, and that integrity is better maintained. Also, having a single type system leads to a more natural and uniform data model so that logical database design becomes the same as class library design and no special data analysis methods are needed.

Object-oriented databases do not often need to do joins, the slowest operation that a relational system can ever have to perform. Since objects are stored as coherent wholes, retrieval of an object is a single, simple, although maybe large, operation. In a relational environment, an application derives the structure of the database at run time from disconnected tables, whereas in an object-oriented database the structure is stored directly. So instead of performing joins, the application follows pointers from object to object. This is reminiscent of the structures found in network databases, but object-oriented databases are more flexible in terms of schema evolution. This is because the object metaphor means that data are stored in coherent chunks; often the pointers are restricted within a single file. It also reflects the benefits of information hiding, because, in a network database, the programmer needs to know whether connexions between record types are implemented as a linked list or as an array of pointers, different commands being used in each case.

Relational database management systems (RDBMSs) can store objects, in the form of attributes or tables, but the amount of traffic between an application and such a database is increased because of the need to reassemble objects after retrieval and vice versa for storage. Typically, many normalized tables are necessary to represent a real-world object, and this leads to the need for joins to reconstruct coherent objects. This is especially true when the objects are complex ones such as graphical images, documents, balance sheets, and so on. This issue of performance is related to the old arguments about network versus relational databases, but now the argument can take place on the level of logical concepts, rather than at a physical level, where empirical results are the only proofs that can be bandied. Typical RDBMSs are optimized for the large joins which characterize their usual commercial applications. Further, these products have had over ten years of refinement and tuning. This makes them more efficient than current object-oriented databases (OODBs) for constructing accounting and stock control systems and the like. It is the applications that need to carry out many small joins, such as complex bills of materials, the management of structured documents, geographic information systems, CASE and CAD, which give them the most trouble. All these applications need to store complex objects and OODBs are usually far more efficient for this kind of work.

In an OODB, integrity constraints can refer to instances, unlike relational systems, where only entity (or class level) constraints may be expressed. In an OODB the semantics of the application, such as functional dependencies, are not hidden in the normalization of tables. Redundancy is dealt with by storing pointers to objects.

Relational systems usually have a limited set of primitive data types: integer, money, date, and so on. Some systems support extended types such as text or BLOBS (binary large objects), but these have no accessible internal structure or semantics associated with them. Object-oriented databases allow user-defined types with semantics attached via the class system. This is what makes it possible to use an object-oriented programming language as both the access language and DML.

In object-oriented programming, there are two ways to define subclasses: by forming unions of types or by defining a subtype explicitly. The second approach is better in database systems because it does not permit *ad hoc* types to be constructed from semantically unrelated types, and it extends naturally to types with encapsulated methods.

Object-oriented databases are important because they address some key issues for the application of information technology. They promise to deliver the benefits associated with object-oriented programming, reusability and extensibility, and to add the benefits of database systems. In doing so, a wider range of applications can be addressed and the promise of vastly improved performance and storage economy over relational systems, while retaining the latter's flexibility, is borne out by early experiences. Perhaps most importantly of all, they promise to deliver the benefits associated with semantically rich languages, in the manner of semantic databases and expert systems. In my opinion, object-oriented databases and their associated 4GLs will find their apotheosis when they are able to combine object-oriented programming, semantic data models and expert systems in one unified framework.

▤ 6.2 Benefits of object-oriented databases

The benefits that users are looking for from object-oriented databases mirror those to be obtained with object-oriented programming: reusability, increased modularity and extensibility. Also we would like to think that the flexibility of relational systems can be retained and combined with the efficiency and semantic expressiveness of pointer-based systems.

It is convenient, for exposition, to group the benefits arising from the use of object-oriented databases into three categories as follows: those arising from a need to use an object-oriented programming language or environment; those arising from the enriched semantic capabilities of an object-oriented database; and those arising directly from the capabilities of the object-oriented database design itself.

6.2.1 Benefits arising from a need to use object-oriented programming

If an organization has already decided, for reasons which we need not discuss here, that it needs the benefits of object-oriented programming and has to manage persistent data, there are several benefits that accrue from linking the application programming language and environment to an object-oriented database system. These may be summarized as follows:

- An object-oriented database minimizes the need for paging objects in and out of memory when using object-oriented programming. The other such benefits are those associated with database systems in general, but OODBs are particularly pertinent to sharing, distribution, security and versioning.
- Object-oriented databases help to close the semantic gap between real-world objects and concepts and their representation in the database. They also attack the impedance mismatch between the application programming language and the DML, which gives the developer less to learn and a more uniform mode of expressing designs.

6.2.2 Benefits arising from enriched semantic capabilities

These benefits are, principally, as follows:

- It is possible to store both the relationships between objects and the constraints on objects in the server, rather than in the client application. This can have enormous implications for both maintenance and application integrity. A change need only be made once and the possibility of multiple, inconsistent changes is removed, or at least minimized.
- An object-oriented database or model can express whatever the entity-relationship model can express, supersets the hierarchical model and the network model and enriches all of them semantically. The efficiency of hierarchical systems is approached, but dynamic binding of methods and garbage collection can compromise this potential for efficient access.
- There is, at least potentially, support for 'rules' (active objects) in an object-oriented database. All current proposals for this are *ad hoc*, but one can foresee the emergence of a standard protocol for encapsulating rules. A suggestion along these lines is contained in Chapter 8.
- Object-oriented databases offer the possibility of earlier type checking of *ad hoc* enquiries, compared to relational systems. This is accomplished via the user-defined type system, which can be used to reject incorrect types before making an actual database access. The relational compromise is to compile frequently used enquiries in advance, as in Ingres.

In a sense, the semantic capabilities of programming and database systems are an end in themselves. It has long been a goal of software engineering to be able to carry out reverse engineering; that is, to take a piece of executable code and discover enough about its purpose and function to rewrite it in another language or on a different machine, and to do this automatically if possible. As things stand, reverse engineering in this sense is quite impossible. The best that can be done is to recode small modules individually, and that with a lot of manual intervention. Although there are some good automated tools supporting the activity, it still takes a great deal of skill even to do that. The reason for this state of affairs is that programs do not contain, in an explicit form, the semantics contained, say, in a functional specification. For me then, a benefit, if not *the* benefit, of the object-oriented approach is that it promises to make reverse engineering possible for the first time. If we can capture the semantics of objects and encode them in explicit, readable form – as rules and classification structures perhaps – then we can recover them and use them to generate new code which need not mimic the physical architecture or module structure of the original system. This is imperative for specification (or throwaway) prototyping as dealt with in Chapter 9.

6.2.3 Benefits of object-oriented databases as such

Object-oriented databases combine the speed of a network database with the flexibility of a relational one. The Sun Cattel benchmark (Cattel and Skeen, 1990) shows typical 100-fold performance improvements for certain kinds of engineering database retrievals and updates. The more advanced object-oriented database products such as ITASCA support dynamic schema evolution just as well as any relational system and most OODB products will do so eventually, I suspect. This means that a whole series of applications which were not amenable to attack with a DBMS can now be tackled straightforwardly. Support for long transactions using persistent locks and for automatic version control makes these products the basis for a new approach to distributed computing. The fact that most products have supported distributed update from the outset is another consequence of their origin in the network and workstation culture. Relational systems have only recently, and after much difficulty, added such capability. Also the message-passing metaphor is a natural one to use to describe distributed systems.

OODBs give generally better performance when complex objects and complex relationships must be dealt with. This is mainly because there is no need to break up large objects for storage in normalized tables and reassemble them at run time via slow join operations. This is especially true in applications involving engineering drawings and complex graphics. Further, the amount of disk space occupied may be far less, because of the need to store many more index files in relational systems.

The object metaphor supports multimedia applications in a natural way. Objects with the properties of shapes, with temporal behaviour (videos and sound), text and other concepts may all be modelled, and stored, within a unified conceptual scheme.

The benefits of reuse do not need to be restated here. Extensibility is a key benefit that arises directly from the classification structures of an object-oriented database. I would not claim reuse as the key benefit, since complex structures may compromise encapsulation. However, reuse is a key benefit of object-oriented programming languages, and the benefits of a small, smooth interface between an object-oriented language application and an object-oriented database mean that the benefit of reusability can be better delivered in the application itself. OODBs support extensibility since data types can be extended using their inheritance features. New subtypes may be added without the need to restructure existing portions of the database. Aggregation is easier to model and objects can be treated as individuals or as collections within the model.

Mature object-oriented databases may simplify concurrency control and a sound method of query optimization may emerge from current research, but this is an unresolved issue at present.

Object-oriented databases give generally better navigational control over queries, because pointers to related objects are stored in objects.

Object-oriented databases have built-in referential integrity and generally richer semantics than other systems. They share these benefits with systems based on the semantic models, and entity-relationship and deductive databases. Object identity solves the problem of dangling tuples[2] and means that there is no need for referential integrity checks, because objects are not referred to but addressed directly. The richer semantics is based on the ability to construct types and encapsulate constraints within objects at any level in the type network, including the possibility of overriding and exception constraints.

Physical clustering of objects on disk is a problem for designers of relational systems. They must ensure that tables which are frequently joined reside on the same device or close to each other in storage, to minimize disk accesses. The only basis for clustering is empirical study of common queries. In object-oriented systems there is a more logical basis for clustering based on class and aggregation hierarchies. Objects that form groups are stored together as composite objects, and, in a well-designed system, classification structures are used as the natural basis of clustering. This is not just an implementational convenience: the clustering reflects the semantics of the application, and therefore it is likely, although not guaranteed, that common queries will refer to nearby physical locations on disk.

Not having a separate DML means that developers have only one language to learn. This is possible because the type systems required in the application and those stored in the database can be made to match. One way of doing this, for example, is to use C++ classes to extend the type system of the language to include the types that would normally be unique to the DML, such as 'relation' in a relational DML.

The possibility of having class libraries of common database and application-dependent structures helps to speed development. However, it is necessary to beware of the difficulties of awareness and navigation of libraries mentioned in previous chapters in relation to object-oriented programming. Browsers and class librarians are essential tools if this benefit is to be exploited. Here too, group work is an asset.

Although locking is easier to conceptualize in an object-oriented model, because the natural unit of locking is the object, with a single lock on all relevant data rather than multiple locks scattered among unrelated tables, locking has proved a quite severe problem in practical systems. As we shall see, it is easy to lock large hierarchies and so bring the system to its knees in performance terms. Multi-user access is still a problem in object-oriented systems, and purchasers will be wise to ask for concrete demonstrations to allay any doubts in the context of a particular application.

Object-oriented databases map very well onto client/server and distributed architectures. Sending a message to the encapsulated methods of an object supports a client/server architecture, because it is not necessary to repeat the functionality across many applications. The example used in Chapter 1, where a method for calculating the age of an employee, or in fact any person, is stored with the object, illustrates this idea. We do not have to copy age routines to several applications, since if they are stored centrally, the danger of the system accidentally evolving

---

[2] Dangling tuples are tuples that are not represented in all the (normalized) relations that contribute to the representation of an object, and that can thus be lost when a join operation is performed.

several different ways of doing the calculation – say as 'age next birthday' in some places and 'age last birthday' in others – is removed.

I have argued for the ability of computer systems to capture more of the semantics, both data and functional, of an application in explicit form. This theme is expanded upon in Chapter 8.

The object-oriented metaphor is a unified conceptual model covering design, programming and enquiry. The benefits of a unified metaphor or 'paradigm' are easy to see. It is to be hoped that such a style will lead perhaps to higher productivity and flexibility, but ultimately this will depend on how well programmers understand the metaphor. Although there is a lot to be said in support of extended relational databases, extending SQL as in the Ingres approach does not address this issue.

6.3 Problems with object-oriented databases

As with other aspects of this technology, there are pitfalls as well as benefits. We will consider some of these in this section.

At a purely theoretical level it is a problem that there is no universally accepted object-oriented data model. However, there have been a lot of suggestions in this direction. Ullman (1988) describes a primitive and quite general model. Other excursions include Beech (1987), Lecluse et al. (1988) and Manola and Dayal (1986). This disbenefit is not one that should worry the commercial practitioner greatly: it will probably be resolved within a year or two anyway and the OMG is working toward this goal.

Object identity is all very well in theory, but real-world objects do not always have accessible unique identities. Not only is it possible for Sam to be stored twice as a shareholder and as an employee in a relational database: if he does not volunteer the information that he has an alias (Lord Lucan, say) then our object-oriented database may have two representations of an object that does have unique identity though we cannot find out about it. One way round this is to model only the identity of rôles rather than the objects playing them.

One cannot do query optimization in an object-oriented database without compromising the goals of object-orientation, especially the principle of information hiding, because optimization requires looking at the implementation. On the other hand, queries over complex objects are much faster anyway. Object-oriented databases based on the functional model can carry out query optimization, however. Gray et al. (1992) show how this can be done in an object-oriented extension of Daplex. Kim (1990) claims that it is likely that only minor changes to existing optimization techniques will be required but admits that it is still essentially a research area.

Yet another problem is the difficulty of modelling relationship types in an object-oriented database. It is also hard to compose operations, because they are not all table-valued as they would be in a relational system: they may return values of any type. The result of an operation may even be of the type of a new ADT with no operations yet defined on it.

Another potential problem arises because of the many different versions of multiple inheritance supported by different database and language products. It seems inevitable that anyone wishing to exploit this aspect of object-oriented technology will need to ensure that the programming language and the database are compatible in this respect.

As with distributed relational databases, distributed object-oriented databases give rise to problems that have yet to be solved. Not only do all the traditional locking and commit strategy issues arise anew, but there are extra problems. For example, no one knows how to guarantee network-wide object identity yet. Any system that employs two-phase commits to handle update, as do all current distributed systems, will inevitably be slower than a centralized database. Only parallel implementations can address this problem. Another potentially insuperable problem is that of deciding where to put the data. Practical experience shows that there is very rarely a perfect distribution strategy: one user's need for local storage to perform complex analyses may be contradicted by another's requirement to combine the very same data with others for regular reports.

There are several other unsolved problems concerning concurrency, schema evolution, locking and query optimization. The reader is referred to more technical references such as Khoshafian and Abnous (1990), Kim (1990), Gray *et al.* (1992) and Zdonik and Maier (1990), and to other works mentioned in the bibliographical notes at the end of this chapter, for details on these problems and current research aimed at overcoming them.

Although the logic of a locking protocol is easier to understand in an object-oriented system, it is not obvious that locking can be accomplished efficiently in a multi-user environment. There are very severe locking problems associated with inheritance hierarchies.

There is a general lack of standards for object-oriented access languages. Without standards no serious commercial organization will take this technology seriously, except for non-critical applications. The key standards issues at present involve defining what exactly an object-oriented database is and defining language extensions for SQL and even standard data management extensions to languages like C++, at least at the level of custom and practice. Both ANSI and ISO are examining possible standards for an Object SQL and for a new version of standard SQL which will allow the relational vendors to introduce more object-oriented features. The goal of this work on SQL3 is to make evolution more possible. It introduces a notion of type and distinguishes this from tables so that tuples may have a type different from the table that contains them. Subtyping is permitted and one can make new tables of a given type using the syntax:

Create table PartTimers **of** Employees

Non-1NF tables are permitted. Object identity is supported by having the system generate an uneditable surrogate and foreign keys are superseded by REF types which enables attributes to be typed. Lastly types can contain function definitions or methods that can be written in the procedural part of SQL3. Attributes can be private or public, as can functions. Beech (1992) claims that SQL3 removes any conflict between the relational model and encapsulation.

Most commercial OODBs are tied to a particular object-oriented programming language. However, these usually offer APIs for other languages. This means that integrating existing code with the database can be a little more troublesome than need be.

The view that object-orientation in databases and commercial systems is going to be a permanent feature of the software industry is supported by the appearance of self-appointed standards bodies representing influential players in the market. On the one hand there is the Object Management Group (OMG) and on the other the Committee for Advanced DBMS Function (CADF).

CADF is a group of influential individuals from the database world who published a sort of advanced database manifesto in 1990 (Stonebraker *et al.*, 1990) which laid down a number of principles which an advanced database management system ought to meet in the near future. These principles, perhaps analogous to Codd's famous 12 rules for relational systems, include the following.

- Object-oriented databases should have all the facilities of a conventional DBMS, including high-volume data management, concurrent multi-user access, high-level access languages, simultaneous access to distributed data, support for efficient transaction processing and full recovery and security features.
- Object identity should be supported.
- There should be support for at least one form of inheritance.
- Support for transparent distributed access and update.
- Support for complex objects via encapsulation or abstract data types and classes.
- The provision of computationally rich languages compared to SQL.
- Support for dynamic binding.
- Support for user defined functions (for example, sum and average).
- Type checking and inference capabilities.
- Effective version and configuration control.

CADF originally included such figures as Mike Stonebraker and Larry Rowe – the principal architects of Ingres, David Beech – technical adviser at Oracle, one of the designers of IRIS and now closely involved with the definition of SQL3, Jim Gray – author of Tandem's Nonstop SQL, Phil Bernstein – director of Digital's DBMS laboratory, Bruce Lindset – architect of DB2, and Michael Brodie of GTE, a leading researcher in knowledge-based management systems.

The OMG, on the other hand, is committed to establishing broad agreement between vendors on both the terminology of object-orientation and on 4GL style and interface standards. This group too subscribed to an object-oriented database manifesto (Atkinson *et al.*, 1990).

In the world of conventional, commercial IT there is little experience to build on yet and few successful commercial products in wide use. For this reason there are a host of unanswered questions in relation to commercial applications. For example, it is not clear whether an object-oriented database can be used effectively from a conventional language like COBOL.

Whatever benefits object-oriented technologies may be capable of delivering, design and implementation issues do not go away. For example, the designer still needs to ponder on the construction of indexes, caching, and so on. This needs good, experienced people. It also needs good management. We will look at some of the management issues in Chapter 9.

Object-oriented databases do not yet constitute a stable, mature technology. Necessary features from the wish-list are still being added to products. However, the maturation process is proceeding very rapidly. There is no formal model universally accepted yet and no equivalent of Codd's 12 rules. Among the several 'object-oriented' database products dealt with below, some are good for some types of application while some are good for others. If you are building a multimedia database, for example, you might consider GemStone. However, for a database extension of a GUI application coded in C++, Ontos might be a more natural choice. Worse still, there are no firm rules yet for making the choice, because there is not enough practical experience to distil the rules from.

6.4 Survey of existing products

In a short work of this nature we cannot possibly do justice to all of the object-oriented database and semi-object-oriented database products in existence. Our main aim will be to discuss the general use of this technology and future prospects, giving an indication of the desiderata for using or avoiding it. As with object-oriented programming languages, however, we cannot avoid a brief survey.

6.4.1 GemStone

One of the earliest, and probably the purest, object-oriented database in existence as a commercial product is GemStone (Maier and Stein, 1987; Bretl *et al.*, 1989), which is built on top of an extension of Smalltalk called OPAL. OPAL (Servio Logic, 1989) can deal with persistent objects. Unlike ObjectStore, Ontos and Versant (see below), which are intimately linked to C++, it is not so closely tied to a particular language. Although the DML is OPAL, GemStone can be accessed from other languages such as Smalltalk or C++. GemStone is aimed mainly at CAD/CAM applications by its vendor, Servio Logic Corporation. It has been a commercial product longer than any of its competitors and is one of the most mature products.

OPAL has a class library covering a few basic but intricate data structures and supports all of the key object-oriented features: abstraction, inheritance and identity. It is, by default, like Smalltalk, a typeless language. Unlike most common database languages, even primitive operations, such as insert, delete and update, must be declared explicitly for each class defined, which is a nuisance. This reflects the strong encapsulation philosophy behind Smalltalk. Multiple inheritance is not supported. Any system based on Smalltalk, with its garbage collection and enforced late binding, must be approached with some scepticism concerning performance issues. Another minor potential problem is that the GemStone access language forms queries and indexes over object attributes. This can be used to violate encapsulation. Attributes and classes can be optionally given a type or *kind*, but this does not prevent run-time failures due to polymorphism.

The architecture is based on the client/server model and supports distribution. The Stone is the database server or object manager and is accessed via multiple versions of the Gem, a virtual machine that compiles and runs OPAL methods. The Stone is responsible for garbage collection. GemStone is one of the few products that stores methods in the database. This, and the client/server structure, is what makes it possible to access GemStone from other languages including C, Pascal, and C++.

Objects cannot be deleted from OPAL except by garbage collection and each object's location is stored in a table. This makes relocation easier. GemStone's locking strategy involves database shadowing for recovery and a combination of optimistic and pessimistic regimes for concurrency control. Each client maintains a shadow of the object table.

GemStone, in common with most other object-oriented databases, lacks facilities for semantic data modelling including aggregation structures, exceptions, rules, constraints, triggers and the like. It also lacks support for many-valued attributes, set-valued relations, one-to-one relations, inverses of relations and keys. Gray *et al.* (1992) discuss this weakness of object-oriented databases at length and present a system called ADAM which addresses some of them.

GemStone is easy to use for Smalltalk programmers. Other may be helped by GeODE, the GemStone Object Development Environment, which is a 4GL that provides a powerful forms and schema design tool, interactive queries and a highly visual programming language.

6.4.2 Ontos and Versant

Ontologic's Vbase was also one of the first proper object-oriented databases to emerge within a C/UNIX environment. It was strongly influenced by CLU, and emphasized strongly typed ADTs. It also attempted to perform as much binding as possible at compile time. Vbase had its own proprietary type definition language, TDL, and used COP (C Object Processor), a proprietary object-oriented extension of C, for access. Its withdrawal from the market and subsequent replacement with a new product, Ontos, points to a number of generic issues or problems with first-generation OODBs. First, in the world of commercial databases, SQL is so well established and well understood that introducing a new language such as TDL, however good, is almost certainly a doomed enterprise. Further, there was no room in the market for yet another object-oriented extension of C, let alone a proprietary one like COP. Second, but even more significantly, early users of Vbase found that there were severe performance problems due to Vbase's locking mechanism. In any system that supports inheritance this is a potential trouble spot. Suppose, in SACIS, that a particular item belongs to the class ModelCar which, in turn, is a subclass of Toy, Car, StockItem and so on. This item inherits behaviour and data from its superior classes. Suppose now that one of these classes undergoes an update. Surely, everything below it in the hierarchy must be locked. If the updated class is sufficiently general we can soon end up effectively locking the whole database. In a multi-user database this is quite unacceptable. This difficulty is not unique to Vbase and was a problem for several early object-oriented databases. In fact there is a parallel problem in relational systems that support triggers for integrity control, where uncontrolled updates can propagate through the database, locking as they go.

To overcome, or at least limit, these difficulties, Ontologic released a second-generation product, Ontos, again aimed mainly at the engineering and CASE markets. For this kind of application where complex objects proliferate, huge performance improvements over relational systems are possible. In Ontos, TDL is replaced with an object-oriented extension of SQL, called Object SQL or Ontos SQL, which adds object query syntax to standard SQL. COP is replaced by C++. The locking problem is addressed by giving the designer control over the locking strategy, allowing a choice between pessimistic and optimistic protocols. Although still closely linked to C++, it is now planned that Ontos will be accessible from other languages and Version 2.0 introduced a 4GL called Shorthand, a windows front-end and a report and forms generator called Studio. It also supports multiple inheritance and has a graphical browser and a graphical tool to generate C++ header files and the schema. Methods are not stored in the database so that links between methods and their data have to be maintained. The schema is stored in the database and is accessible to programmers. Special classes are provided to model composition structures, exception handling and keys. Distribution across LANs is supported using a client/server model. Performance is enhanced by disk clustering and caching techniques. The company, renamed Ontos Inc., released Version 2.2 in 1993 with extended support for workgroup applications, better event notification and global deadlock detection, enhanced productivity tools and triggers. Most UNIX platforms are supported and VMS and MS Windows versions are projected but not released at the time of writing.

As it stands, Ontos enhances C++ with persistent objects. The extended environment automatically moves objects, or groups of objects, between store and memory. Class libraries are provided, as is an exception-handling mechanism. (Recall that C++ does not have one yet.) A very important feature of Ontos in particular, and this type of product in general, is the provision of support for object version histories and shared transactions, taking databases a step closer to CASE tools and to supporting groupware applications. The company also plans to release a series of application-specific class libraries. Ontos has been one of the more successful products, in the commercial sense, and is now supported by a number of CASE tool code generators. Ontos Inc. claimed over 400 active users worldwide in 1993.

Versant, the object-oriented database product from Versant Object Technology, is another UNIX-based system that uses C++ as the primary access language, although access from Smalltalk is possible. Object SQL is also supported. It may be regarded as a direct competitor to Ontos in most respects. A unique feature (at least among the C++-coupled products) is event notification, which assists with interprocess communication and groupware applications. It is based on a multi-client/multi-server architecture like Ingres and scores very highly on the Cattel benchmark. Versant provides gateways to conventional systems such as Oracle, and a number of development tools for GUI development under Motif and report writing. It is used as the repository for the Rational ROSE CASE tool (see Chapter 8).

Other features of Versant include good support for composition structures, multiple inheritance and versioning. The class library resembles the NIH library. Versant's particularly strong transaction management features support cooperative work well.

6.4.3 ObjectStore and Objectivity/DB

ObjectStore (Attwood, 1991) is yet another object-oriented database management system with close ties to C++. It was the first product of its type to run under MS Windows rather than in UNIX environments, which it also does. Like Versant, performance is very good on the Cattel benchmark and the architecture is multi-client/multi-server to support distribution. Class libraries are provided to support versioning, configuration management and composition structures. The class libraries also support object indexing and clustering, associative queries, relationship management and iteration over sets. There is a danger that associative queries may violate encapsulation. There is no Object SQL; the idea is that removing the impedance mismatch and providing classes makes programming so easy that there is no need for the complexities of an Object SQL. ObjectStore has, at the time of writing, fewer productivity tools than Ontos or Versant, with only a graphical schema designer and class browser.

Efficiency is addressed by the use of pointer swizzling techniques. Pointer swizzling means that global object references are converted to local memory addresses when an object has been loaded into main memory. Swizzling techniques are used to bring attribute access time down to levels close to that of programming language memory structures. An alternative approach is to partition the object space. Then object identifiers within a single segment need no translation. Static or dynamic clustering of connected objects on disk also helps access efficiency. Some of the things one can do with pointers in ObjectStore, such as pointing at persistent objects directly in virtual memory, seem a little dangerous to me, but power is rarely obtained without risk. This product too has very good versioning, multiple inheritance and transaction management features and would support group work.

The first major, mainstream hardware manufacturer to endorse a commercial object-oriented database management system was Digital, who are making

Objectivity/DB the basis for their future CASE and repository offering under VMS. This product too is coupled to C++ and supports distribution, long transactions and versioning. Special features have been developed to support electrical and mechanical CAD applications, though others are not ruled out.

6.4.4 ITASCA and ORION

The papers on the ORION object-oriented database contain some of the most profound thinking on the subject to be found anywhere. The ORION research project at MCC concentrated on schema evolution and produced a descriptive semantics and a set of rules which must be followed if a type network is to remain consistent as attributes and methods are added to or removed from a class. These rules are different from those usually adopted in database systems. The schema of an object-oriented database is dynamic and may evolve in the following ways without any need for recompilation.

- Changes to the description of an object: adding, deleting or updating attributes or methods.
- Changes to the objects represented by the system: adding, deleting or changing the identity of an object. Deleting a class usually results in all its subclasses acquiring all the superclasses of the deleted class as parents rather than themselves being deleted.
- Changes to the structures of the database: adding, deleting or modifying an inheritance, composition, use or associative relationship.

Schema evolution is complicated by the presence of inheritance. If a super-class changes then everything below it in the lattice has to be checked for dependencies. Other structures (composition and use) similarly complicate things. It is important to note that object identity is and must be preserved throughout all schema changes in an object-oriented database. For that reason, it is assumed that schema changes are reasonably gradual. This issue is closely related to that of version control, and most object-oriented databases offer some sort of version control at the instance, class and schema levels. In ENCORE, for example, there is a class called History-Bearing-Entity which contains attributes such as previous-version, next-version and member-of-version-set, which can be inherited by any object requiring version control. The version set is an association containing all versions of the object.

Although ORION was inspired largely by Smalltalk, there are a number of important extensions in the model. Multiple inheritance is supported, and there are three built-in methods for conflict resolution: either a 'left first' rule is used whereby the first superclass in the list of superclasses is used to inherit the conflicting method or attribute from; or the user may specify the choice which the object should make; or the user may specify that the object should inherit both properties and rename one of them. Attributes may have defaults at the class level. We will see the importance of this feature in the next chapter. Even though class-level multiple inheritance is supported, an instance is only allowed to belong to one class. Another profound aspect of the ORION work is the recognition that classification (AKO) and composition (APO) structures are often closely coupled, and a semantics for this coupling has been developed. The notation used in ORION to show this coupling is shown in Figure 6.2, where the body of a vehicle is owned by one specific vehicle and cannot exist without it. The AKO links are lines emanating from class attributes that indicate such dependencies. ORION also has a semantics of and a protocol for version control and important ideas on locking. As ORION was a research system there were still problems in such areas as type safety and garbage collection, but the ideas referred to above are, in my opinion, key ones and many have been carried forward into the commercial successor to the ORION prototypes.

In his book on ORION, Kim (1990) argues strongly for the provision of non-procedural enquiry languages for object-oriented databases but does not explore the position held by many others (such as Ullman): that there is a fundamental trade-off between declarativeness and object identity. He justifies this with a mention of research into non-first normal form databases. In defining the query model, Kim states that the structure of an object-oriented query 'is basically that of a relational query', and I cannot help but wonder whether the truth of this statement depends on the compromises that ORION has made to support a non-procedural approach to queries – joins and all. The strength of the query model, on the other hand, should not be ignored. It is practical and even necessary if object-oriented data-bases are to become accepted commercially. Kim's discussion offers thoughtful treatment of how both composition (parts) and classification (inheritance) hierar-chies or structures affect query processing and optimization.

ITASCA is a commercial product based on the ORION research prototypes. Both ORION and ITASCA were written in Common LISP, but the latter runs on UNIX workstations as well as the original Symbolics development platform. It shares all of the features of ORION and is unusual in storing and activating

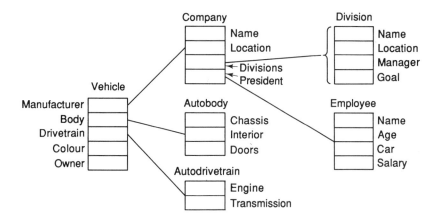

Figure 6.2 ORION class schema (by kind permission of the ACM Press).

methods directly in the database, which makes it possible to embed methods written in any language, currently only LISP, CLOS, C, C++ and FORTRAN. ITASCA is based on a distributed multi-client/multi-server architecture and has no centralized name or data server so that there is no single point of failure. Dynamic schema evolution is supported and there are good security, recovery and concurrency services. Authorizations can be inherited, which should reduce the overhead of database administration considerably. Composition structures are well supported and event notification can either be flag-based or message-based. In this way both triggers and workflow applications can be supported. As with Versant, the database can be partitioned into a shared part and various private databases with no need for the user to know where a particular datum is physically stored; ITASCA is thus locationally transparent. Class indexing is used to improve performance and, where possible, queries are executed in parallel on different networked machines. Query optimization uses database statistics in a manner reminiscent of the Ingres optimizer. Associative text searches are also possible.

The only apparent major defects in ITASCA are lack of support for encoding business rules and constraints except as methods or triggers, lack of a suite of 4GL development tools and some doubts as to performance. While I suspected immediately that the LISP implementation limited performance, the supplier, ITASCA Systems, has assured me that 'any slowness is due the rich features of the product and not LISP'.

In a comparative study of object-oriented databases in the context of engineering applications, Ahmed *et al.* (1992) found that ITASCA had better feature provision than any other product surveyed and represented the best value for money. They conclude that it had 'very sophisticated features and is relatively easy to use for LISP programmers, though the LISP environment incurs some overhead in run-time efficiency'. The features used in the comparison and some of the subjective ratings given to each product and overall (unweighted) scores achieved are shown in Table 6.1.

6.4.5 Other products and systems

IRIS

IRIS (Fishman *et al.* 1989) is another system that offers an Object SQL (OSQL). It was developed as an experimental system at Hewlett-Packard, and its data model is based on the functional, rather than a strictly object-oriented, model. It is very relational in style and shows strong Prolog influences. The underlying storage manager is similar to the one used in System R, the precursor to DB2. Multiple inheritance is supported and the type of an object can even change at run time. This is a powerful but dangerous facility. Versioning is also supported. In addition to Object SQL, access from Objective-C and LISP is supported. Support for multimedia databases in IRIS is accomplished via specialized data managers rather than by storing all sorts of objects in a single type system, as with other OODBs. Because the

Table 6.1 Comparison of object-oriented database product features for engineering use (source: Ahmed *et al.*, 1992, but the first two rows' values are modified in the light of more recent information).

Feature	GemStone	Ontos	Versant	Object-Store	ITASCA
Platforms	9	9	9	10	9
Availability and support	8	8	8	8	8
Price/performance	6	6	7	7	8
Multiple inheritance	0	8	10	10	10
Composition structures	1	1	2	4	10
Dynamic schema evolution	5	3	3	2	10
Storage management	9	10	10	10	10
Lock management	6	6	8	6	9
Event notification & communication	1	1	3	1	8
Version management	0	0	10	10	10
Flexible concurrency management	4	3	6	5	6
Group work facilities	4	3	6	5	6
Query management	9	9	7	8	9
Security & authorization	8	0	3	2	9
Multimedia support	0	2	2	2	10
User interface	2(OPAL)–10(Smalltalk)	6	5	6	8
External language interface	5(C++) –10(Smalltalk)	9(C++)	7(C) –9(C++)	5(C) –9(C++)	6(C) –10(LISP)
Average	5.29	4.82	6.24	6.06	8.24

transaction manager of IRIS is based on that of System R the locking of the inheritance hierarchy is a problem. The ITASCA approach of having special locking protocols for inheritance networks is far better. A commercial version of IRIS is released under the name Open ODB.

I have a niggling doubt about systems like Ontos and IRIS that offer an object-oriented extension of SQL. First, there is a contradiction in the notion of Object SQL. We have seen that object-oriented databases cannot support a non-procedural access language in anything like a natural way: access is fundamentally procedural. Relational systems, on the other hand, offer a model basis for query optimized non-procedural access using, say, the relational calculus which underpins SQL. Now, procedural extensions of SQL already exist in several relational systems, such as Sybase and Ingres, but a voice in my head screams that this mixture is unnatural and dangerous: it compromises both the relational model and the object metaphor. It must, in the long run, make programming harder. Furthermore, it is difficult to see what the benefits of such compromised OODBs are over the extended relational systems, which are also a compromise but are at least based on mature proven systems. Further, while the syntax of OSQL may be similar to that of SQL the semantics are quite different, leading to potential confusion for users already used to SQL. The next worry is that there will be a proliferation of Object SQLs. How many Object SQLs are there already? The answer is hard to give, owing to the difficulty in agreeing over just what constitutes an Object SQL, but there are several on almost any measure. The only hope here is that standards for Object SQL may emerge, perhaps through the good offices of the two self-appointed standards groups, the Committee for Advanced Database Function or the Object Management Group, if not one of the official standards bodies such as ANSI. Even in this case, it is difficult to see how a standard can be at once broad enough to capture all the functionality required in such diverse applications as CAD/CAM, CASE, hypermedia and commercial systems. The best we can hope for, I think, is a core standard with innumerable application-specific extensions. Loomis (1991) offers an interesting discussion on these matters and strong arguments in favour of Object SQL.

PCLOS   PCLOS (Persistent CLOS) is an attempt to build a tightly coupled interface between an object-oriented database (IRIS) and an object-oriented programming language (CLOS).

STATICE   Statice (Symbolics, 1988) is an extension of the Genera programming environment for Symbolics machines and of Common LISP. It supports the definition of objects with multiple inheritance, object identity and encapsulation of methods. These objects are persistent and sharable. The same reservations about the performance of LISP-based systems expressed in relation to ITASCA apply to Statice, although if you must LISP, you had best do it on a Symbolics box, which is optimized for the language. Statice is now being ported to other workstations and to run under UNIX.

O_2 O_2 (Lecluse *et al.*, 1988; Deux, 1990) was developed at GIP Altair and supports multiple object-oriented programming languages and its own dialect of C, CO_2. It comes with a graphical browser, programming environment, debugger and a form of Object SQL. Development is done in interpretative mode, during which schema evolution is possible. The final system is compiled and schema evolution halted thereby. O_2 supports class hierarchy indexing and disk clustering.

POET   POET, from BKS Software in Germany, is a low-cost object-oriented database for DOS, MS Windows, UNIX, NeXT and other environments. It has close coupling to C++ and is fundamentally a C++ pre-compiler that adds persistent classes and other extensions to the language and comes with a graphical browser and query optimizer. Schema evolution and version control are supported. The programmer works in a large, partitioned virtual address space and database access is handled by the system. Like many other object-oriented databases support for security, concurrency and recovery is very limited.

G-BASE   G-Base was an early object-oriented database developed in France by Graphael and based on LISP; it came equipped with a closely coupled Prolog-like expert systems development language called G-Logis. It could also be integrated with ART.

ODE   ODE (Agrawal and Gehani, 1989) is a research system coupled to C++ in the same manner as Vbase and Ontos. It provides versioning, iteration, query processing, constraints and triggers with time-outs. In ODE a procedural extension of C++ called O++ handles all data manipulations analogously to the way COP in Vbase does so.

OTHERS   On the fringe of the object-oriented database world, there are a few unified object-oriented programming and data manipulation languages such as Vision and DEC's Trellis/Owl. Vision from Innovative Systems Techniques (Insyte) is intended to be simple enough for use by users in the context of financial planning and decision support. Data dependencies in this kind of application rely on time and temporal relationships. To address this kind of problem efficiently Vision adopts a functional style and, although it is not a genuine object-oriented database, this permits the handling of both inheritance and temporal relationships. It uses the notion of prototype objects which blurs any distinction between instances and classes. Vision has been applied in financial applications such as pension fund management.

LOOM (Kaehler and Krasner, 1983) represents an alternative solution to the problem of making a single user language persistent. It effectively makes the disk drive into a vast virtual memory for Smalltalk. There are several similar products extending Smalltalk.

In the last chapter we introduced some alternatives to pure object-oriented databases: hybrids, such as Generis, and extended relational systems, such as Ingres Version 6. Generis and Ingres both support rules, which most object-oriented databases do not do, at least not directly. Generis supports inheritance but not abstraction or object identity. The Ingres product supports user-defined types, so that simple tasks like the addition of feet and inches are simple to deal with. Inheritance is promised, but it is difficult to see how Ingres can support object identity fully on its relational basis.

6.4.6 Research issues

In addition to the products mentioned above, there are a number of research systems which may spawn or influence future products. Typical such systems are ObServer/ENCORE (Elmore *et al.,* 1989; Zdonik and Wegner, 1985, 1985a; Skarra and Zdonik, 1986), OOPS (Schlageter *et al.,* 1988) and PDM (Manola and Dayal, 1986). These systems are test beds for new ideas and ironing out problems with the current generation of products, and their evolution should be closely watched by anyone interested in object-oriented database theory and implementation. ObServer is a general-purpose object server developed at Brown University. ENCORE (Extensible and Natural Common Object REsource) is its DDL and DML. This system has many of ORION's features and a better transaction manager for supporting group work.

A new generation of what Parsaye *et al.* (1989) call 'intelligent' databases is emerging in parallel with the object-oriented revolution. The roots of these developments lie in various attempts to combine database technology with ideas from artificial intelligence and especially expert systems. Some of the early work on Postgres (Stonebraker and Rowe, 1987) – some of which has emerged as part of Ingres – is situated in this tradition, as are several early attempts to achieve this unification by placing Prolog front-ends on databases to enrich the semantic expressiveness of SQL. The deductive databases mentioned in the preceding chapter also combine work from expert systems and database theory. It is suggested by Parsaye *et al.* that the next generation of database systems will be an amalgam of features from four areas: expert systems, object-oriented programming, traditional databases and hypermedia. I would add semantic data modelling, but generally agree. There is some indication that a few database vendors will incorporate these ideas in future product releases.

At present the only way to achieve expert systems capabilities in a data-intensive application is to use the fairly limited knowledge representation capabilities of systems like Ingres, employ a deductive database or build a loose coupling between a database and an expert system shell of some sort. The problems with such loose couplings arise when there is a large amount of traffic between the application and the database. If, instead of generating database calls in SQL, the shell loads whole segments of the database for processing there are then integrity and concurrency problems. Thus, applications that need knowledge and also need very frequent database access must look towards the emergence of these 'intelligent' databases. Exactly the same remarks apply to hypermedia applications, where a system like HyperCard must be loosely coupled to a database. Building these couplings involves a great deal of effort and heartache too.

As if the situation was not bad enough, with an immature object-oriented database technology and the prospect of a proliferation of different Object SQLs, we now face a further proliferation of 'intelligent' SQLs, incorporating rules.

A great deal of work is also going on in the tradition of conceptual modelling and functional databases. Gray *et al.* (1992) describe two systems, P/FDM and ADAM, in this area.

6.5 Applications of object-oriented databases

The applications to which object-oriented databases are best applied are those where relational systems perform poorly or those where the object metaphor is appealing. These include distributed and client/server systems, workflow and group work automation, enterprise integration modelling, multimedia databases, voicemail, geographic information systems (GIS) and product data management. Some complex bill-of-materials applications may benefit too.

Early, widespread applications of genuinely object-oriented databases were to VLSI design and other CAD applications. Previously, due to the inadequacies of relational systems these applications all had their own purpose-built file systems, which made development costly and sharing of information across systems impossible.

In typical CAD applications, where complex objects representing the design components and the logical relationships between them need to be stored, an object-oriented database helps performance by optimizing the physical location of frequently related data. If the whole design is stored as a single object, this will reduce the number of access operations needed to view or update the design.

Computer-aided software engineering (CASE) is another area where complex objects and relationships are important. CASE tools may be divided into two types, known as 'upper' and 'lower' CASE. Upper CASE tools, or IPSEs, handle tasks throughout the software development process, from project planning and management to configuration management and maintenance. Lower CASE tools, usually included with upper CASE systems, merely support documentation, diagram production and structured development methods. In upper CASE, the time dependencies which hold between objects – in relation, say, to version control – are complex networks, and the objects are often complex software modules consisting of code, parameters, file structures and documentation in words and pictures. In lower CASE, the diagrams and documents have a complex, far from tabular structure. (Note that my terminology is at variance with the way some CASE vendors use the terms *lower* and *upper* CASE. For example, for some vendors, lower CASE covers analysis while upper CASE covers design. They then use the term *vertical* to cover tools which support specific techniques for design, analysis, testing and so on, and *horizontal* for life-cycle support tools. In object-orientation, where logical analysis and design largely merge, this usage is singularly inappropriate.)

Further, following the guidelines of a method involves rules, as does consistency and completeness checking of diagrams. Thus, expert systems technology is incorporated in most major CASE products these days. The complexity of the objects, the existence of structural relationships among objects, the complex time dependencies and the need for CASE repositories to be open to many development environments means that object-oriented and knowledge-based technologies are a fairly obvious choice for developers of such tools. Since the data storage component is so important, object-oriented databases are being used to develop several CASE systems; even more so, since versioning is standard within many object-oriented databases.

I have already mentioned the use of Eiffel at Cognos. One may presume that the next generation of Cognos products will be based on an object-oriented database, although it is not possible to give details at the time of writing. Ontos has been used successfully by Index Technologies, suppliers of the Excelerator CASE tool, in crafting the next generation of their product range. IBM's Repository Manager is ultimately based on the relational database kernel of DB2, but recent announcements indicate a shift to a fully object-oriented repository manager. Amdahl's Huron repository product appears to be based on an object-oriented database, and Digital has announced a similar intention within their COHESION strategy, using Objectivity/DB.

Ontos has been applied to telecommunications network management systems, simulating accidental gas releases at chemical plants, multimedia voice and video editing, geographic information systems and configuration management. Versant has been used in network management, CAD, geographic information systems, office automation, workflow automation and financial services. IBM used GemStone for a complex manufacturing database. Other applications have been reported in the areas of computer-assisted publishing, materials requirements planning (MRP) and, to a small extent, artificial intelligence.

What all these applications have in common is that they are all concerned with problems that involve very complex objects, and where the relationships among the objects – both in time and in space – are as important as their individual structure. Not only are these objects complex structurally but they also often exhibit complex behaviour. For example, an engineering drawing may be viewed as plan, elevation, side elevation or isometric projection, and these views may be rotated and scaled. Storing behavioural abstractions, the key feature of object-oriented databases, is therefore important in such applications.

Applications in DP, apart from building CASE tools, will depend on the recognition that businesses also have complex objects, such as informal management and communication networks, but this is not the critical issue. The reasons for using object-oriented databases in commerce, where – to be fair – most objects are just not as behaviourally complex as those in CAD and GIS applications, will hinge on the semantic abilities of object-oriented databases. Semantically rich systems offer a potential for reverse engineering which was not previously available.

Some people would argue that the requirement is not for reverse engineering but for correct, zero-defect forward engineering, based on sound analysis and design methods. This argument contains some sense, but still makes the rather idealistic assumption that there will never be circumstances where a company wishes to back out of implementation or analysis decisions.

6.6 Strategic considerations

Should a company considering the benefits of object-oriented databases go for a totally new object-oriented database product such as ITASCA, Ontos, ObjectStore or GemStone; or should it, rather, choose an extended relational system such as Ingres or even wait for Version 8 of Oracle and SQL3?

In fact, these are not the only options. Semantic or deductive databases offer many of the advantages of object-oriented systems, and robust commercial products exist and have been used. Companies can also stay with their standard relational products and embed object-oriented constructs in the host language, although we have seen some of the disadvantages of this approach. They may choose an application-specific embedded database such as in a CAD/CAM system or in a CASE system, as with the Team*work* configuration management system.

However, for many companies the leading question will be the choice between improved and extended relational systems and genuine object-oriented ones. In either case, these companies will have to realize that there is bound to be a divergence from industry standards, especially in relation to SQL. Instead of one SQL there will be many, each with absolutely indispensable functions added – at least this is what their vendors will claim – such as Ingres SQL, Oracle SQL, and so on, all with a standard core and non-standard extras to lock you in to the product.

In the world of object-oriented databases too, it is far from clear whether there will be a truly standard Object SQL, nor is it clear, as I have argued, that it will work. If you are going to be object-oriented, I suggest you will do best to use an object-oriented language for access.

In the medium term, I predict that mainstream DP applications will need to build on existing systems and will go for extended relational solutions. The main reason for this is that the approach protects investment in existing code and staff skills. The whole issue of migration strategies for organizations is discussed fully in Graham (1994).

Small, perhaps small-business critical, applications or special-purpose applications in fringe areas can safely adopt the pure object-oriented products. Text retrieval, image, CAD and graphics applications are typical of such fringe applications.

Some relational vendors have effectively answered the performance criticism by implementing their products on massively parallel machines but there is no reason why object-oriented products should not be similarly parallelized and speeded up. On the contrary, the object model is highly suitable for distributed and parallel implementation.

Prospective purchasers of database products should look at what standards, including open systems standards, the products they are considering support. Relevant standards in this area include the Object Management Group's CORBA, Microsoft's ODBC, the draft Object SQL and SQL3 standards and the X3/SPARC/DBSSG/Object-Oriented Database Task Group's Object Data Management Reference Model.

Facing up to the conundrum posed by Chris Stone at the beginning of the chapter, the answer for most organizations must not be to jump in unprepared and get wet, neither to sit still and be drowned nor to run away. The answer must be for them to take some swimming lessons. In other words, explore the technology on small, but important, projects and prepare the people for the skills they will require in the long run.

You have by now, dear reader, if you have read sequentially, accompanied me through six chapters in which I have told you often that object-oriented programming is an immature technology. Now I am telling you that object-oriented databases represent yet another immature technology. Of course, I am emphasizing commercial IT here and not geographic information systems, multimedia or CAD/CAM applications, where there is more experience, but some of the problems I have mentioned are still present – even in these domains. I hope that I have also displayed and conveyed my enthusiasm for this extraordinarily promising technology, since I am convinced that object-orientation is the way of the future. If it is so immature, what is left for the serious commercial practitioner? Preparation, education and application to a few rather novel areas? By all means! However, I think that object-orientation can be used right now. We shall see how it can be exploited immediately in the remaining chapters.

▤ 6.7 Summary

A database management system supports:

- persistence of objects;
- management of very large amounts of data;
- data and transaction integrity;
- sharing and concurrent multi-user access;
- access or query languages;
- recovery;
- security.

An object-oriented database management system combines database facilities with those of object-oriented programming – encapsulation, inheritance and object identity – so that:

Object-oriented database = database + object-orientation.

Object-oriented databases combine some of the features of semantic data models and object-oriented programming. They should add expert systems features, but often do not. They embody at least two kinds of orthogonal but interacting structures: classification and aggregation structures.

Relationships between objects can themselves be regarded as objects with state and behaviour.

There is a tension between database systems that support non-procedural enquiry languages and query optimization, such as RDBMSs, and those, like OODBs and network databases, that support object identity. Object SQL is a contradiction in terms, but may be a useful practical compromise.

The main benefit, so far as commercial systems are concerned, is the possibility of capturing application semantics explicitly, thus better enabling reverse engineering and prototyping. A further important benefit is that of extensibility. Reuse is harder to achieve.

OODBs remove the 'impedance mismatch' between application and enquiry languages. Compared to relational systems, they remove the need to perform expensive joins when objects are used in an application. This makes them potentially much more efficient for applications involving complex objects. OODBs, while much more efficient, retain the flexibility of relational systems. They add support for long transactions and automatic version control. Some offer dynamic schema evolution and support for multimedia and group work.

OODBs have a number of other advantages over RDBMSs, but there are unsolved problems concerning non-procedural enquiry languages, query optimization and locking.

There are still many problems with current-generation object-oriented database systems. Products are still maturing. There is no universally agreed formal model behind them, and there are no standards yet. OODBs achieve many of the aims of semantic data models, but are not as structurally rich yet. They also omit many of the features of knowledge management. They are evolving towards a new generation of systems combining semantic models, expert systems, object-orientation and hypermedia technology.

There is a small, but growing, number of commercial object-oriented database products. These have been mostly applied to applications where complex objects predominate, such as CASE tools, multimedia databases, geographic information systems and CAD/CAM systems. Commercial applications are in their infancy.

There are several ways to achieve benefits, apart from pure object-oriented databases: semantic databases, deductive databases or extended relational databases. Eventually, the latter will offer object-orientation via SQL3.

Key applications of object-oriented databases include those which need to do many small joins to reconstruct complex objects, support distribution and versioning and handle multiple media and cooperative work.

Commercial users should consider object-oriented databases for small or 'fringe' applications, and extended relational systems for mainstream systems, especially extensions of existing systems. These fringe applications may be business-critical. Extensions to languages like SQL endanger standards, but standards will eventually emerge.

Object-oriented database is an immature but rapidly maturing technology of great significance to information technology in general.

⊟ 6.8 Bibliographical notes

Two texts specifically about object-oriented databases worth consulting are Gupta and Horowitz (1991) and Hughes (1991). Other surveys include Brown (1991), Chorafas and Steinmann (1993). Gray *et al.* (1992) present two sets of subject matter. The first is an overview of modern database theory and practice, emphasizing the need to incorporate ideas from semantic data modelling and artificial intelligence research into object-oriented databases. The ensuing critique of object-oriented databases descended from the pure object-oriented programming tradition is first-rate. The second subject is a report on the rather specialized research of the authors' group into experimental database languages and systems and the construction of a complex protein structure database application. The gloss on this contains important insights of quite general applicability. This book is essential further reading to anyone serious about object-oriented databases. Cattel (1991) includes coverage of the extended relational products. Ahmed *et al.* (1992) provide a comparison of six products from the point of view of engineering applications.

Kim *et al.* (1989) is an introduction to the main features of ORION. It is contained in the excellent collection of papers edited by Kim and Lochovsky (1989) which also includes material on GemStone and a prototype object-oriented database called OZ+ aimed at office automation applications. Kim (1990) is a general text on object-oriented databases but concentrates almost entirely on ORION for examples and may be best regarded as a first-rate introduction to the principles behind ITASCA.

Winblad *et al.* (1990) give a high-level overview of object-oriented databases. Khoshafian and Abnous (1990) provide a deeper discussion, including a treatment of the architectural issues which are not included in this text, which is after all a wide-reaching survey with a focus on methods.

Vbase is described in Andrews and Harris (1990), and in Elmasri and Navathe (1989), which is also a first-rate textbook on databases in general. Another excellent text on modern database theory (Ullman, 1988, 1989), describes the GemStone language OPAL in detail.

Persistent programming languages are surveyed in Atkinson and Buneman (1987) while Rosenberg and Koch (1990) gives a glimpse of current research in this area. The influential persistent programming language Galileo is described in Albana *et al.* (1988).

Zdonik and Maier (1990) contains a representative sample of the seminal papers on object-oriented databases, although material on the important topic of schema evolution is omitted. The editors include introductory material that is comprehensive and informed. Interesting material on schema evolution can be found in the papers on ORION, such as Kim *et al.* (1989) and Nguyen and Rieu (1989) who introduce some AI techniques for automatic propagation of changes and the dynamic classification of instances. Other research papers may be found in Meersman *et al.* (1991). Cardenas and McLeod (1990) is a collection of seminal papers whose theme is the integration of object-oriented and semantic data models.

As an aside, Zdonik and Maier (1990) is part of a series of 'readings in' different areas of computing. They all contain seminal papers on their subjects and, next to the excellent ACM journal *Computing Surveys,* are a good way to become familiar with the broad 'advanced computing' horizon without any risk of vulgarization.

Among several surveys of work on integrated knowledge and database systems (Brodie, Mylopoulos and Schmidt, 1984; Brodie and Mylopoulos, 1986; Ullman 1988, 1889) and a number of volumes in the Morgan Kaufmann 'readings in' series edited by Minker, Stonebraker, and Mylopoulos and Brodie are worthy of mention. Parsaye *et al.* (1989) is an introduction to most of the related technologies and describes a particular model developed by the authors.

Object Magazine and *JOOP* are good sources of current, fairly high-level discussions on the topic.

7

Object-oriented design

The will
And high permission of all-ruling heaven
Left him at large to his own dark designs,
That with reiterated crimes he might
Heap on himself damnation.

Milton (Paradise Lost)

In this chapter and the next we step back from tools, languages and implementation issues in order to determine whether object-oriented methods have a genuine place in the analysis and design of systems that may eventually be written in conventional, value-oriented languages, object-oriented languages or hybrids. We will also look at the usefulness and the shortcomings of several object-oriented design and analysis methods that have been suggested, and suggest a set of requirements for a practical analysis technique. Following the historical treatment I have adopted so far, this chapter concentrates on object-oriented design insofar as it can be separated from object-oriented analysis because interest in design preceded interest in analysis *per se*.

In previous chapters we have examined the various object-oriented implementation technologies. This one surveys several object-oriented design methods and notations before moving to a higher level of abstraction and dealing with analysis in the next. These two chapters are the central chapters of this book. Their purpose is to unite several threads which run through other chapters. These themes – of object-oriented programming and its benefits, expert systems and knowledge engineering and data modelling and database management – are united in the requirements for practical object-oriented software engineering. The strategic problem posed by the maturing technologies of object-oriented programming and databases is addressed by an approach to analysis and design which should permit the phased, gradual exploitation of the benefits of object-orientation at the analysis level, thus laying firm foundations for the exploitation of maturing language and object management technologies. Chapter 9 takes up the managerial and life-cycle issues raised in this way.

In the world of object-orientation, techniques developed for design are often useful for analysis, and *vice versa*. Thus, the reader interested in one may not omit a study of the other. Furthermore, the decision as to whether an approach which contributes to both areas should be dealt with under analysis or under design is sometimes difficult and the result rather arbitrary. Therefore these two chapters should be read together. If you are wondering why the design chapter precedes the one on analysis then I should explain that this organization follows history rather than logic, since object-oriented analysis is a much more recent innovation than object-oriented design.

7.1 Programming, design or analysis?

The development of computer science as a whole has proceeded from an initial concern with programming alone, through increasing interest in design, to a current concern with analysis methods which pushes interest in languages into the background. Reflecting this perhaps, interest in object-orientation also began, historically, with language developments. It is only more recently that object-oriented design methods emerged. Object-oriented analysis methods are also emerging but have not settled down yet.

Object-oriented methods cover methods for design and methods for analysis. Sometimes there is an overlap, and it is really only an idealization to say that they are completely separate activities. Hodgson (1990) argues that the systems development process is one of comprehension, invention and realization, whereby a problem domain is first grasped or apprehended as phenomena, concepts, entities, activities, rôles and assertions. This is comprehension and corresponds entirely to analysis. However, understanding the problem domain also entails simultaneously apprehending frameworks, components, computational models and other mental constructs which take account of feasible solution domains. This inventive activity corresponds to the design process. Of course, most conventional thinkers on software engineering will be horrified that I suggest that understanding the answer precedes, to some extent, understanding the problem, but that is precisely what I am saying. All other cognitive processes proceed in this way, and I see no reason why software engineering should be different. These considerations also enter into the realization process where these frameworks and architectural components are mapped onto compilers and hardware. Advocates of prototyping have long argued that it is beneficial not to make a rigid separation between analysis, design and implementation. On the other hand, managerial and performance considerations lead to serious questions about the advisability of prototyping in commercial environments. Graham (1991) suggests a number of ways in which prototyping can be exploited but controlled, an argument which is summarized in Chapter 9. At the root of this debate are ontological and epistemological positions concerning what objects are and how we can apprehend them or know about them. These too are discussed further in Chapter 9.

The various structured-methods schools have tried to appropriate whatever they regard as useful from object-orientation and incorporate it within their existing framework. This is possibly a sound approach in that there can be a reasonably smooth transition for organizations already committed to some method or other, but clearly there are dangers, and some methods camps have ridden roughshod over the basic contributions of object-orientation in their zeal to be able to use the buzz-word. Some consulting firms are following the path of incorporating object-orientation into mainstream methods with a view to obtaining the benefits of smooth transition without losing sight of the fundamental object-oriented objectives.

Biggerstaff and Richter (1989) have suggested that less than half of a typical system can be built of reusable software components, and that the only way to obtain more significant gains in productivity and quality is to raise the level of abstraction of the components. Analysis products or specifications are more abstract than designs. Designs are more abstract than code. Abstract artefacts have less detail and less reliance on hardware and other implementation constraints. Thus the benefits of reuse can be obtained earlier in a project, when they are likely to have the greatest impact. However, the less detailed an object is the less meaningful it becomes. Where extensibility or semantic richness is important greater detail may be required, and this may compromise reuse to some extent. This leads us to ask if object-oriented analysis and design techniques exist which can deliver the benefits of reuse and extensibility. In the face of an immature object-oriented programming technology, this question attains even more significance: can we gain these benefits now, pending the appearance of more mature, more stable object-oriented programming languages? I think we can. However, the subsidiary question of which methods of design and analysis we should use is harder. We must examine several proposed methods of design and analysis critically, and synthesize a method that will serve not only GUI applications or Ada systems but a wide range of commercial projects.

Software houses and consultancies ought to be particularly interested in reusable and extensible specifications. The reason for this is pecuniary. What the people employed by software houses and consultancies do, to earn their livings, is work with clients to understand their businesses and their requirements and help them produce software solutions to their problems. Having gained all this valuable experience, consultants then go on to the next client and sell what they have learnt, perhaps for a higher fee justified by the extra knowledge. Some firms go further. They try to encapsulate their experience in customizable functional specifications. BIS Information Systems, for example, has a product called the 'mortgage model', which is a functional specification of a mortgage application, based on a number of such projects and capable of being tailored to the needs of a particular client. The trouble is, for BIS at least, that the mortgage model cannot be sold to greengrocers or washing machine manufacturers, even though some of the entities, such as account, may apply to all these businesses. What is required, then, is a set of reusable specification components that can be assembled into a functional specification suitable for *any* business. Object-oriented analysis, and to a lesser extent design, promises to deliver such a capability.

To fix terminology, let us begin with a vastly oversimplified picture of the software development process or life cycle. According to this simplified model, development begins with the elicitation of requirements and domain knowledge and ends with testing and subsequent maintenance. Between these extremes occur three major activities: specification and logical modelling (analysis), architectural modelling (design) and implementation (coding and testing). Of course this model permits iteration, prototyping and other deviations, but we need not consider them at this stage. Prototyping, along with the managerial issues it raises, is dealt with in detail in Chapter 9. In real life, despite what the textbooks tell us, specification and design overlap considerably. This seems to be especially true for object-oriented design and analysis because the abstractions of both are modelled on the abstractions of the application, rather than the abstractions appropriate to the world of processors and disks. Design may be divided into logical and physical design, as is well known. In object-oriented design the logical stage is often indistinguishable from parts of object-oriented analysis. One of the major problems encountered with structured analysis and structured design methods is the lack of overlap or smooth transition between the two. This often leads to difficulties in tracing the products of design back to original user requirements or analysis products. As we shall see in the next chapter, the approach adopted in object-oriented analysis and design tends to merge the systems analysis with the process of logical design, although there is still a distinction between requirements elicitation and analysis and between logical and physical design. Nevertheless, object-oriented analysis, design and even programming, through working consistently with a uniform conceptual model of objects throughout the life cycle, at least *promises* to overcome some of the traceability problems associated with systems development. One of the chief reasons for this is the continuum of representation as the object-oriented software engineer moves from analysis through design to programming. In these transitions the unit of currency, as it were, remains the same: it is the object. Analysts, designers and programmers can all use the same representation, notation and metaphor rather than having to use DFDs at one stage, structure charts at the next and so on.

7.2 Object-oriented design methods

The benefits of object-oriented design are perhaps obvious to the reader who has absorbed the remarks in earlier chapters, but specifically include the following.

- Required design changes are localized and unexpected interactions with other program modules are unlikely.
- Object-based design is suitable for distributed, parallel or sequential implementation.
- Shared data areas are eliminated, reducing the possibility of unexpected modifications or other update anomalies.

Object-oriented design methods share the following basic design steps although the details vary quite a lot.

- Identify objects and their attribute and method names.
- Establish the visibility of each object in relation to other objects.

■ Establish the interface of each object and exception handling.
■ Implement and test the objects.

There are quite a few emerging object-oriented design methods, the oldest of which is probably due to Grady Booch, whose paper (1986) sets out what is chiefly a method for using some of the features of Ada in an object-oriented style. From this point of view object-oriented design is based on the principle of information hiding, rather than either the composition of functions (as with traditional methods) or a fully object-oriented approach embracing inheritance. This encapsulation can be readily implemented using Ada packages or Modula-2 modules, whereas inheritance and polymorphism are unnatural constructs in these hierarchically structured languages. Message passing can, however, be easily simulated using function or procedure calls which implement the constructor and access operations of an object. Booch has more recently published a much extended and improved method that is not closely tied to Ada. It is discussed separately below.

Booch's original method begins with a dataflow analysis which is then used to help identify objects by looking for both concrete and abstract objects in the problem space that will be found from the bubbles and data stores in the dataflow diagram (DFD). Next, methods are obtained from the process bubbles of the DFD. An alternative but complementary approach, first suggested by Abbott (1983), is to extract the objects and methods from a textual description of the problem. Objects correspond to nouns and methods to verbs. Verbs and nouns can be further sub-classified. For example, there are proper and improper nouns, and verbs to do with doing, being and having. Doing verbs usually give rise to methods, being verbs to classification structures and having verbs to composition structures[1]. Transitive verbs generally correspond to methods, but intransitive ones may refer to exceptions or time-dependent events: in a phrase such as 'the shop closes', for example. This process is a helpful guide but may not be regarded as any sort of formal method. Intuition is still required to get hold of the best design. This technique can be automated, as some of the HOOD tools described below and Saeki *et al.* (1989) show.

For example, a SACIS requirements statement transcript might contain the following fragment:

> If a *customer* <u>enters</u> a *store* with the intention of <u>buying</u> a *toy* for a *child*, then *advice* must <u>be available</u> within a reasonable *time* concerning the suitability of the toy for the child. This will depend on the *age range* of the child and the *attributes* of the toy. If the toy is a *dangerous item*, then it is unsuitable.

I have italicized some candidate classes (nouns) and underlined some candidate methods (transitive verbs). The process could be continued using the guidelines set out in Table 7.1.

---

[1] One point of caution here is that verbs include stative verbs (verbs that indicate that a state of affairs holds) which are compound constructions in English; 'to be present' is a stative verb whereas 'to increase' is not. This suggests perhaps that Chinese, where stative verbs are distinguished, is a good intermediate language for object-oriented design, and it is probably easier to learn than Ada.

Table 7.1 Guidelines for textual analysis.

Part of speech	Model component	Example from SACIS text
proper noun	instance	J. Smith
improper noun	class	toy
doing verb	operation	buy
being verb	classification	is an
having verb	composition	has an
stative verb	invariance-condition	are owned
modal verb	data semantics, precondition, post-condition or invariance-condition	must be
adjective	attribute value or class	unsuitable
adjectival phrase	association	the customer with children
	operation	the customer who bought the kite
transitive verb	operation	enter
intransitive verb	exception or event	depend

Most of the methods descended from Booch's work use some form of textual analysis of this sort. Booch's notation represents objects as blobs, as shown in Figure 7.1. Arrows indicate which objects use the services (or methods) of other objects, thus defining client/server (or usage) relationships and message handling.

Groups of objects are partitioned into 'subsystems' of manageable size corresponding to the levels or layers of a DFD, as pictured in Figure 7.2(a). Classes are identified with Ada packages and drawn as shown in Figure 7.2(b). Booch does not see any need to denote attributes in his notation as all access to the object's interface is via a method, or operation, although Ada itself permits access to the data structures within a package specification. The shaded area represents the implementation of the package or package body, and an unshaded rectangle (or parallelogram for generics) denotes the specification. The unshaded ovals represent a package's name or type declaration and the unshaded rectangles each denote a method.

The icons shown in Figures 7.2(b) and 7.3 have become known as Gradygrams. Booch distinguishes between two kinds of client/server relationship

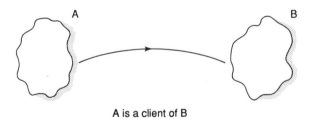

A is a client of B

Figure 7.1 Booch notation for the client/server relationship between objects.

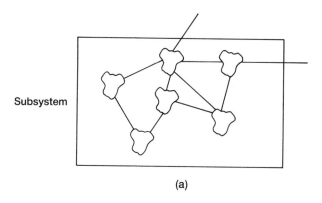

Subsystem

(a)

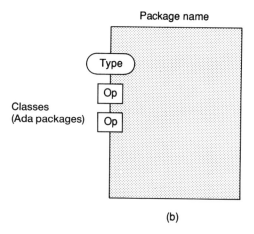

Package name

Classes
(Ada packages)

Type

Op

Op

(b)

Figure 7.2 (a) Layers in Booch notation; **(b)** Classes are identified with Ada packages in Booch notation and only the type and the methods are shown.

between objects as illustrated in Figure 7.3. If the arrow starts from the shaded rectangle that represents the body of the object A then the implementation of A depends on the services offered by B. If the arrow originates from the type declaration oval then only the specification (or interface) of A depends on B. This reflects the concern with design rather than analysis.

Sommerville (1989) uses Ada as an all-purpose design language. This is a common approach for authors of method-based code generators who use an Ada-like program description language (PDL) as an intermediate stage between pictorial or textual design and actual code. In Ada, classes are identified with abstract data types and correspond to packages that, in the argot of Ada programmers, export limited private or private types. Instances correspond to instances of private or limited private types or packages that serve as abstract state

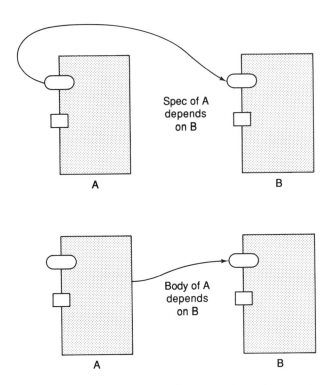

Figure 7.3 Booch notation distinguishes between clients that use the specification or interface of servers and those that use their implementation.

machines. Methods correspond to subprograms exported from a package specification. As a rule of thumb, if a single instance of a class is required it should be defined directly as a package, but if a number of instantiations are needed it should be defined as a class. If the object's state need be accessed by other objects, it should be defined as an instantiation of a class. Inheritance is difficult in Ada but a limited form can be implemented through derived types or generic packages.

Booch appears to have undergone something of a conversion since this early work. His more recent work (1991) shows a broadened perspective on object-oriented design, no longer tied to any specific language such as Ada. His revised notation and method support implementation in Smalltalk, CLOS, C++, Ada or most object-based or object-oriented languages. He also has evolved quite general guidelines on object recognition and the management of object-oriented design and programming projects. We discuss his revised method in a separate subsection below.

Following Booch's pioneering work a number of specifically design-oriented methods have emerged which are closely coupled to systems developments using the Ada language, such as GOOD, HOOD and MOOD. We will look at two of these. Several other design methods and notational conventions, which are not tied to Ada, have followed close on the heels of the Ada methods. We will look fairly closely at two: OOSD and Booch's more recent work. Three others are discussed briefly. These are OODLE, JSD and a borderline analysis/design method which I will designate CRC. Other methods and notations, not discussed, include a widely used one due to J.A. Buhr (1984) which is used in the team*work*/Ada CASE tool and in the Texel method (Section 8.2.10) and influences methods such as OODLE.

7.2.1 GOOD

The General Object-Oriented Design (GOOD) method was developed at NASA by Seidewitz and Stark (1986). It covers both requirements specification and design of Ada projects. The method proceeds, as with Booch's, from a preliminary layered set of dataflow diagrams to an identification of the objects involved. One looks in the DFDs for externals, data stores, control interfaces and control stores. Classes are discovered by examining the flow of data and control. Examination of the main processes leads to an abstract model of the system's function, and by tracing the incoming and outgoing flows attached to these processes a set of layered diagrams can be constructed. These diagrams emphasize control and data relationships among entities. Thus the entities and entity groupings become the objects and the original data transformations become their methods. As with Booch's method and other Ada-derived methods, this approach enforces a top-down seniority hierarchy among objects, based on how objects use each other.

7.2.2 HOOD

The notion of a seniority hierarchy is picked up by another method, HOOD. The 'H' in HOOD in fact stands for Hierarchical – the reader will be able to infer by now what the 'OOD' stands for. This method is also very much directed at Ada development and was developed at the European Space Agency. It was directly influenced by GOOD and also draws on the Abstract Machines method of Matra Espace and techniques originated at CISI Ingénière, both French companies. Like GOOD it emphasizes compositional (part-of) hierarchies, but has nothing what-soever to say about classification (inheritance) hierarchies. In HOOD, objects are either 'passive' or 'active'. Passive objects can only use the services of other passive objects but active ones can use any object's services. HOOD is a top-down method that proceeds by decomposing a top-level object and then further decomposing the resultant objects. In effect, then, there are two hierarchies in HOOD: the compositional hierarchy and the usage hierarchy. The usage hierarchy may, in fact, be a network.

Diagrammatically, HOOD follows a Booch style, Gradygram notation. A typical notation is shown in Figure 7.4, which also indicates how the inclusion or composition hierarchy is denoted by icon inclusion. Seniority or usage relationships

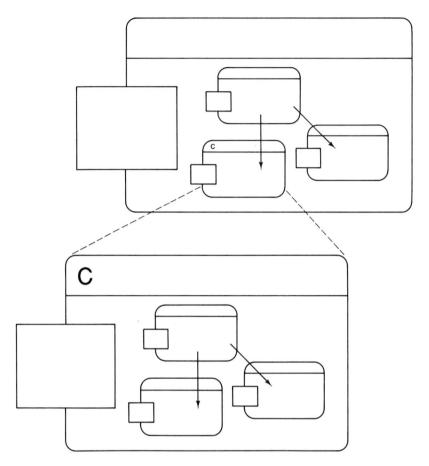

Figure 7.4 HOOD decomposition of objects with use and inclusion relationships. The arrows may be interpreted as 'uses' and the enclosure of a package in the diagram denotes that it is part of the enclosing object.

are shown by arrows with the arrowheads pointing at the more junior partner as in Figure 7.5(a). Figure 7.5(b) gives a notation for the 'implemented by' link, which is shown as a dotted line. The parent operation 'start' is implemented by the operation 'begin' of the child object A, which delivers all the functionality expected of 'start'. The 'implemented by' link is a very useful decomposition technique to which we will have cause to return in Section 8.3.

The HOOD method uses a number of steps to decompose each object, starting with a basic design step which might involve diagramming techniques from other structured analysis and design methods. The concepts so derived are mapped onto objects and external interfaces. This step breaks down into stating the problem, usually as text, and then analysing and structuring the data. The Abbott idea

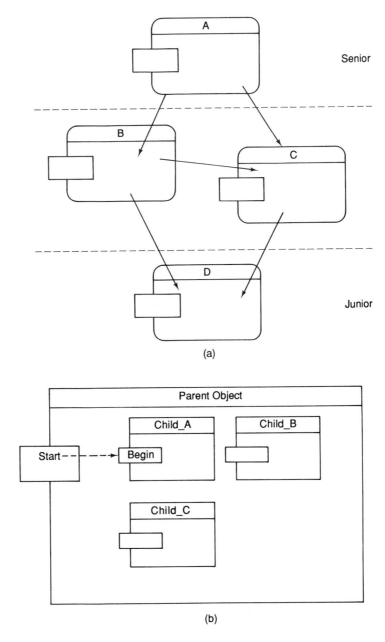

(a)

(b)

Figure 7.5 HOOD use relationships and implemented_by links: **(a)** The seniority hierarchy with use relationships; **(b)** The parent method Start is said to be 'implemented by' the method Begin of Child_A which supplies the functionality of Start. Implemented_by links in HOOD are shown by a dotted arrow. Other usage relationships are not shown on this diagram.

of using nouns and verbs to identify objects and methods, mentioned earlier, is supported. As an example of how conventional techniques can help in identifying objects, consider how to map concepts from the conventional Yourdon structured design method. Context diagrams give hardware objects and external interfaces. DFDs give abstract data types and data pools. The information model also gives data types. State transition diagrams give active objects and object-based control structures.

The next step is to produce an informal solution strategy. This breaks down into a number of tasks: an outline in natural language, rough HOOD diagrams and a description of the current level of abstraction. The third step is to formalize the solution strategy. This is done in stages by identifying and describing the objects and their operations, grouping them and producing HOOD diagrams showing parent–child relationships and operations (the composition hierarchy), usage (client/server or seniority) hierarchies, 'implemented by' links, dataflows and exceptions. Lastly, any design decisions must be justified. It is also advisable to record links to the original requirements specification for future traceability.

A note on terminology is necessary at this point. HOOD calls methods 'operations' and 'implemented by' links refer to the need of operations in parent objects to call operations in a child object.

Now the solution strategy is formalized, the next step is to formalize the solution itself. This consists in refining the object definition skeleton (ODS) of parent objects by defining types, constants and data, refining the ODS of terminal objects by defining their internals and operation control structure (OPCS), checking for inconsistencies, producing documentation and generating and testing Ada code.

As noted already, usage relationships are indicated by arrows. Exceptions are denoted by a bar across the arrow, as shown in Figure 7.6, but are not dealt with explicitly. That is, the direction of flow of the exception is not shown (it is

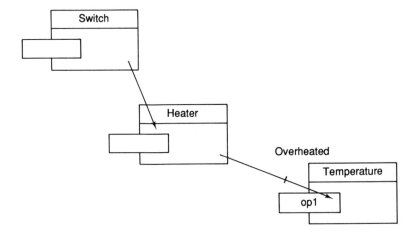

Figure 7.6 Exception flow in HOOD. The exception Overheated is raised by the object Temperature and processed by Heater.

implicitly the reverse of the use arrow) and the exception is dealt with in relation to the object as a whole rather than attached to a parameter or dataflow. In this example, if the temperature exceeds some limit, or a breakdown in the temperature sensor occurs, the exception 'overheated' can be raised.

Dataflows can also be recorded using the notation illustrated in Figure 7.7, which is based on structure charts (Yourdon and Constantine, 1979).

This has been a very brief description of the HOOD method. One of the attractions of HOOD is that it is a published and supported method in the public domain, rather like SSADM.

Common criticisms of HOOD are identified by Hodgson (1990) as follows.

- There is no support for genericity, inheritance or polymorphism. Generics are commonly used by Ada programmers and so this is a serious deficiency even for an object-based method.
- There is insufficient separation of the definition of an object from its use and little support for reusability.
- The graphical formalism is both incomplete and inconsistent. HOOD diagrams do not explicitly show which operations are used by which objects, what flows are defined on each operation, how exceptions are propagated and what data are encapsulated by objects. The notation depicts subprograms as objects and control structure is also shown as a subprogram that passes control to a task. The parent object is depicted with the same notation as the child.
- There are difficulties with the strict parent–child seniority hierarchy. In real-time systems, events and exceptions may affect the execution of a deeply nested sub-object and it is inefficient to pass control through many enclosing objects.

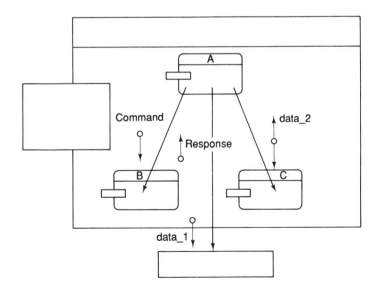

Figure 7.7 Dataflows in HOOD.

Additionally, many people feel that HOOD, while appropriate for many real-time military applications, is less so for commercial ones. The lack of support for inheritance makes it object-based rather than object-oriented. Thus, reuse is supported but not extensibility. The rôle of data structure (entity attributes) is played down in favour of concentration on functional abstraction. In the next section we will examine a notation which partially meets some of these shortcomings.

7.2.3 OOSD

Some of the criticisms listed above are dealt with in another design method, Object-Oriented Structured Design (OOSD), introduced by Wasserman, Pircher and Muller (1990). OOSD is, strictly speaking, not a method but a notation to which methodological rules can be added. This notation is probably the closest of all the methods encountered so far to the spirit of object-orientation, in that it supports inheritance as well as abstraction. Although it is much closer to object-oriented principles, it still bears the marks of the influence of Booch and the Ada-ites. It also provides a more gradual transition for developers familiar with structured design, on which it is partly based.

OOSD is a non-proprietary notation for architectural design that combines top-down structured and object-oriented design. It is aimed at supporting general object-oriented goals such as reuse, modularity, extensibility and the representation of inheritance and abstraction. It also aims to support visual representation of interfaces among design components, code generation, language independence, communication between designers and users, and a variety of approaches. Ambitious aims!

OOSD once again uses a notation derived from Booch's but it is also influenced by structure charts (Yourdon and Constantine, 1979) and its support for concurrency is based on Hoare's (1974) notion of monitors. Classes are shown as rectangles with smaller superimposed rectangles denoting their methods. Attributes are not explicitly mentioned in the OOSD literature but the ostensibly private storage pool could be used for this notational purpose. Attributes are also implicit in dataflows, which are indicated by arrows originating in unfilled circles. These flows are enumerated explicitly, as illustrated in Figure 7.8, in a similar notation to that of structure charts. In OOSD angle brackets denote indirection or parameters as usual.

Client/server relationships are shown by thicker arrows between objects. If one of these arrows has an output dataflow as in Figure 7.9, this indicates that the client object (save_state) instantiates the object.

Unlike HOOD, OOSD declares exceptions explicitly. The notational convention is diamond-shaped areas overlapping the object body. The exception parameter passing is shown in the same notation as that for dataflows but with filled diamonds at the arrow butts (Figure 7.10).

Hidden operations are catered for in the manner shown in Figure 7.11, where 'is full' is used by the externally visible push method.

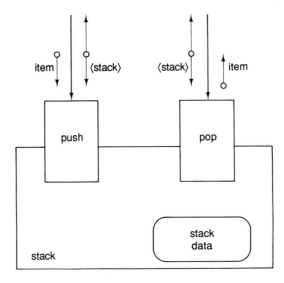

Figure 7.8 An OOSD object representing a stack.

Generic classes are dealt with in the same way but the rectangular class body outline is drawn as a dotted line. Inheritance between classes is indicated by a dotted arrow and multiple inheritance is permitted. Concurrent or asynchronous processes are catered for by monitors, which are shown as parallelograms as in

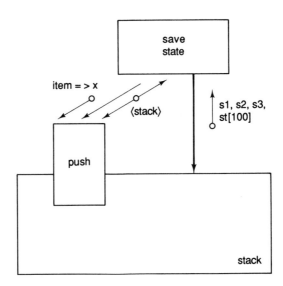

Figure 7.9 The class save_state instantiates 103 objects of type stack and may use its methods.

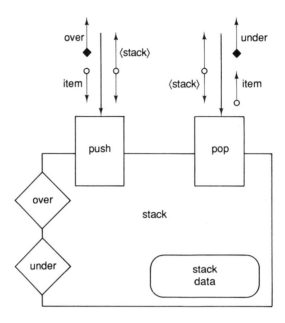

Figure 7.10 Exception handling for stack.

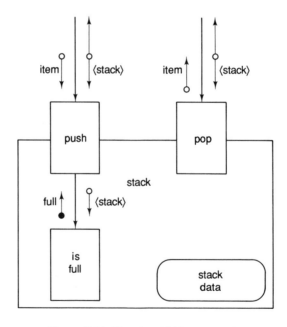

Figure 7.11 Showing hidden operations.

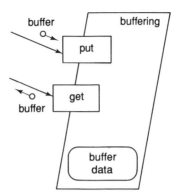

Figure 7.12 A buffering monitor.

Figure 7.12. This notion of a monitor is rather like that of a class but its data are shared out among its various methods. In the case illustrated more than one process (as with network interrupts) may put or get data. These operations need exclusive access to the hidden buffer data.

The entire set of OOSD symbols is shown in Figure 7.13. The reader requiring a deeper understanding may consult the paper by Wasserman *et al.* (1990), from which this summary is largely taken, for a very clear detailed exposition.

OOSD is not so much a method as a notation to support object-oriented design methods in general. The user of OOSD can add design rules according to the particular method in use. Where these design rules are explicit, this may be formalized easily, but where vague rules, such as HOOD's insistence that objects should have 'a low fan-out', are involved the designer's judgement is required – pending perhaps the use of expert systems technology for this purpose. OOSD is intended to be language-independent and is not tied to Ada or any other language. This means that some of the notions of OOSD will not be explicitly supported by the target language. Implementing classes is a lot easier in C++ than in FORTRAN, although possible in both. Again, languages such as FORTRAN with no support for concurrency make it harder to implement designs that include monitors. Equally, some of the detail of languages is not captured by OOSD. For example, there is no equivalent to Ada's limited private types or C++'s virtual functions or friends. Another important point to note is that OOSD is a notation for architectural design rather than detailed, physical design. This means that it offers little help with the physical clustering of files on disks, the most suitable hardware, meeting service levels or the optimal use of memory.

Other notable points concerning OOSD are its ready acceptance by developers already familiar with structured design and its suitability for real-time systems because of the monitor concept. The arrows in an OOSD diagram, for example, are

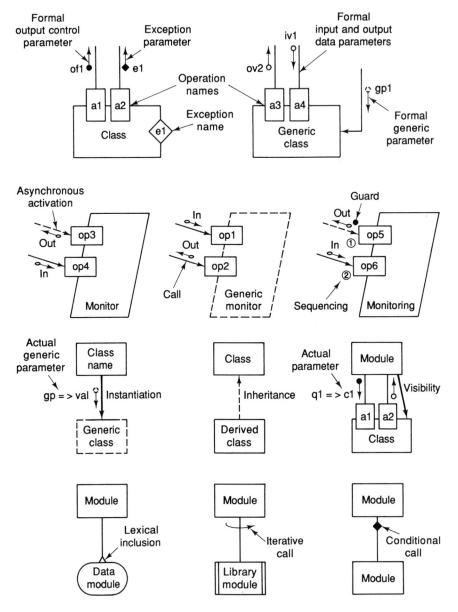

Figure 7.13 The complete OOSD notation.

interpreted exactly as in a structure chart. It makes a distinction between the definition of an object and later reference to it by other objects. This means that the notation does not require all the details of an object to be displayed each time it is used. The protocol for overriding methods in multiple inheritance is also significant. If a method may be inherited in two ways, it must be named to make clear which way is preferred, or overridden. For example, in the domain of geometry, the class of geometrical objects may have subclasses 'regular figure' and 'solid'. A regular solid is in both these classes. Now, all geometric objects have a method called 'invariant rotation', but for general solids this is a far less complicated method than for regular figures. Thus regular solids must inherit a method designated as 'regular figure invariant rotation' or override with its own method, according to the requirements of the problem. In OOSD, methods may be added to a subclass or overridden. They may not be dropped.

OOSD is one of the more advanced hybrid, low-level object-oriented design notations. It seems unlikely to be extensible to a consistent analysis notation because of the difficulty of dealing with large numbers of methods and the absence of a way of dealing with very complex data structures and attributes. On the other hand, it is more suitable for architectural or logical design than physical design.

7.2.4 JSD and OOJSD

Jackson Structured Design (JSD) (Jackson, 1983) is an object-based rather than fully object-oriented method. JSD models are decomposed in terms of events or actions and their time dependencies. Within these events the JSD approach first defines objects. The next step constructs a specification in terms of communicating sequential processes that can access each other's state – violating thus the principle of information hiding. The method may be useful if the object-oriented design is to be implemented in a conventional language.

A number of similarities between JSD and object-oriented design methods can be identified. JSD contains useful techniques for entity and method identification in its modelling stage. Also, the time-ordering analysis technique of JSD may be regarded as a means of documenting classes. JSD and object-oriented design use the concept of objects similarly though their terminologies are different. JSD can give guidance on which objects and operations are likely to be relevant to a problem. This is especially so where the time ordering of events is important. Otherwise, the links are fairly tenuous.

Jackson has declared his concern with the problem we discussed in Chapter 1: that inheritance violates encapsulation and therefore reusability. One might expect therefore that JSD will evolve towards a more fully object-based, though not object-oriented, style. Jackson's ideas have certainly been extremely influential on the development of other object-oriented methods.

More recently, object-oriented versions of JSD have begun to emerge. The section of Chapter 8 dealing with Systems Engineering OO illustrates an example of such a method. In a similar way, attempts have been made to create object-oriented extensions of conventional methods that use JSD-style entity life history (ELH) techniques such as SSADM where, for example, effect correspondence diagrams are suggested as a means of showing visibility. The more extreme suggestions have even claimed that inheritance is nothing more than a one-to-many relationship and can thus be accommodated within SSADM data modelling techniques.

All the methods dealt with so far are extremely weak in the area of semantic data modelling, and none of the diagramming techniques allow for detailed description of object attributes. To correct this we turn in Chapter 8 to emerging data- and object-centred analysis methods. First, it is necessary to examine the later thinking of Grady Booch.

7.2.5 Booch '91

Booch's (1991) revised design method and notation consists of four major activities and six notations. The first steps deal with the static aspects of the system, both logical and physical. The dynamics are dealt with using the existing techniques of state transition and timing diagrams. Schematically, this may be shown as:

> Logical structure
> > Class diagrams
> > Object diagrams
> Physical structure
> > Module diagrams
> > Process diagrams
> Dynamics of classes
> > State transition diagrams
> Dynamics of instances
> > Timing diagrams

Booch suggests that Abbott-style linguistic interpretation (as outlined in Table 7.1), conventional structured analysis techniques or object-oriented analysis are all suitable precursors to object-oriented design, but warns that developers using structured analysis must resist 'the urge to fall back into the abyss of the structured design mindset'.

Both classes and instances are shown as formless blobs in the manner of Figure 7.1, but classes have a dotted outline. If these blobs have shadows, as in Figure 7.1, this indicates that they denote free subprograms, which some languages permit.

A fairly rich notation for the relationships between classes is added, which uses different kinds of line to indicate usage, inheritance and other relationships. Figure 7.14 shows these symbols. Booch recommends a form of layering, so that classes are organized into 'categories' containing several related classes. These layers are shown as rectangles. Arrows between these rectangles denote visibility or usage relationships.

Each class, in Booch's method, is described by filling a standard template which includes identity, attributes, methods and the following extra design information.

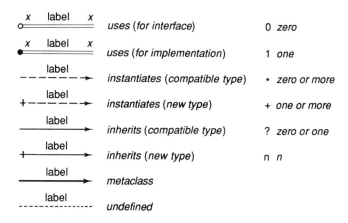

Figure 7.14 Revised Booch class diagram relational icons.

Documentation (text)
Visibility (exported/private/imported)
Multiplicity (0/1/n)
Superclasses
Used classes
Generic parameters
Interface implementation (public/protected/private)
State transition diagram
Concurrency (sequential/blocking/active)
Persistence (static/dynamic)
Space complexity (text)

Note that there are some data semantics present but no process semantics, although the state transition diagram associated with each class can represent this information. Some items, such as concurrency and space complexity, are related to quite low-level physical design, and their details are not relevant to the argument presented here.

Class and object diagrams and their associated templates describe the logical, static design of a system. The physical design may differ from the logical. For example, data may be clustered for efficient access, or processes clustered according to related usage to prevent thrashing. To enforce this distinction, which is not made in his earlier work, Booch distinguishes between classes and modules, the latter corresponding to program segments, which could be separately compiled functions in C++ or complex Ada packages. The notation for modules is based on the earlier Gradygram notation shown in Figure 7.2(b). Process diagrams, which are really simple block diagrams, show the communication relationships between physical devices and processors.

The dynamics of a system must also be described. This is accomplished in two ways. The state transition diagrams show the dynamics of classes, which is a technique shared with several of the object-oriented analysis methods discussed in the next section. The instance-level dynamics are shown by timing diagrams borrowed from the field of hardware design. These timing diagrams show the methods of each instance commencing and terminating in relation to each other, as shown in Figure 7.15.

The problem with state transition diagrams is that, while they may be fine for systems with a small number of states – as with controllers – they are hopeless for systems with large numbers of, or even continuous, states. An object with n Boolean attributes may have 2^n states. Most commercial system objects have several, non-Boolean attributes. For this reason, it is necessary to focus on states that give rise to data changes significant to the business. This means that both the states and their related changes must be apprehended at the same time. In work at BIS, it has been found that a modified entity life history, or state change notation, is preferable to both state transition and entity life history diagrams because it enables both states and events to be perceived at once. Figure 7.16 shows such a state change diagram (SCD). SCDs differ from state transition diagrams in that the arrows have no meaning in themselves, and from entity life histories in that they show how activities trigger state changes. In the figure each icon shows, in the centre, a process or activity, valid prior states at the top, and resultant states names and numbers at the bottom. Branches imply a level of control, not shown on the diagram, which chooses the activity according to the terminal state of the previous activity. The right-hand side of the diagram shows the triggers of the activities; that is, the events. Jane Hillston (personal communication) has pointed out a similarity between SCDs and the activity diagrams of Birtwistle's DEMOS (Birtwistle, 1979).

Timing diagrams, for similar reasons, may only be manageable for reasonably small systems, depending on the complexity of interaction among processes. The Objectory method discussed in Section 8.2 offers a similar method for handling the dynamics of instances. A different approach is described in the subsection on Ptech.

Booch's method is one of the best-worked-out design methods, and is superior to GOOD and HOOD in not being tied to Ada and in having a much more general notion of structure. Against the conventional wisdom, these richer semantic

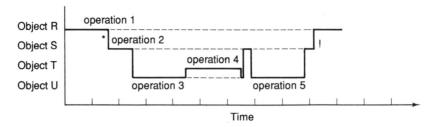

Figure 7.15 A timing diagram as used by Booch. The asterisk (*) indicates the creation of an instance and the shriek (!) its destruction.

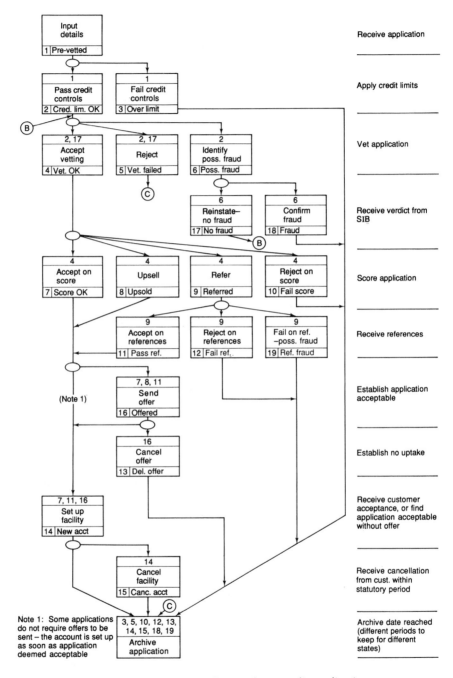

Figure 7.16 Life history for a credit application.

properties of the method mean that it overlaps the territory of the analyst as well as that of the designer. This is justified by the incremental approach to software engineering which Booch advocates, for, in prototyping, analysis and design are often closely interwoven. The main weakness of Booch's method, and it has this in common with other object-oriented design methods, is that the global dynamics are tagged on almost as an afterthought. Further, there is no serious attempt to deal with business rules and other such process-semantic aspects of specification.

One of the central problems of software engineering is that of coping with complexity. Object-oriented design methods address precisely this issue. Waterfall models and other bureaucratic or 'cookbook' approaches to system building fail to recognize that managing complexity requires great flexibility. Risk-driven and incremental approaches recognize the need for sound but adaptive methods. Booch recommends what he calls 'round-trip gestalt design', that is, a process of incremental complete designs at different levels of abstraction and refinement, proceeding neither strictly top-down nor bottom-up. This process proceeds roughly in the following order.

- Identify classes and instances.
- Define their semantics.
- Find relationships among them.
- Implement the design as a prototype.
- Examine the system for cohesion and consistency.
- Redefine classes, instances, semantics and structures on the basis of what has been learnt.

The process stops when it is believed that all the key abstractions and functions have been defined, and is highly non-linear. Defining an object's methods and interface may affect the protocol of another object or a classification structure. Equally, discovering a structure may lead to the perception of new objects. Lastly, we should note the obvious: there is never a best or optimal design. Different designers will produce different models and they may be equally suitable for their purpose.

This method stresses that identifying objects and their classes is a logical design decision independent of their organization into modules, which is a physical design decision.

Booch's method distinguishes client/server, seniority or usage relationships and containment or parent–child relationships. At the class level, containment has two senses: classification (the concept is contained) and composition (the thing is contained). The Booch design method makes the distinction but gives no guidance on how these two kinds of structure are interrelated.

Usage relationships define the control structure of a system, or its message-passing topology. Any means of doing this is a step forward for object-oriented design methods, but the practice of explicating every single message is not a good one. It leads to impenetrably complex representations. What is required is a notation which summarizes the control structure, or flow of control, in a manner simple enough for direct apprehension of the design's complexity and easy comparison between more or less complicated designs.

Booch distinguishes three rôles for objects. **Actors** or active objects can initiate behaviour in other objects but not be acted upon and **servers** can only be operated upon by other objects. **Agents** do both. In my view the client/server relationship is better viewed as a relative notion. An object can be a server in one respect but an actor in others. This usage has no connexion with the actor systems discussed in Chapters 4 and 10.

In this method, and in general, there is a trade-off between use and containment structures. Containing an object (say having it as an attribute value) reduces the number of objects which are visible to the enclosing object. Obversely, containment restricts the easy use of an object by other parts of the system and may compromise its reuse potential. This observation points to an important design decision. The granularity of objects is one of the key design decisions and, as has been remarked, beginners tend to get it wrong. They tend to make the granularity too fine.

The Booch method is undergoing further development and an improved version is anticipated sometime in 1993 and eagerly awaited by many (see Bibliographical Notes to this chapter).

7.2.6 OODLE and recursive design

The Shlaer/Mellor approach to object-oriented analysis and design is described in Shlaer and Mellor (1992). In this section we examine two of its design-oriented components.

OODLE

OODLE (Object-Oriented Design LanguagE) is a design-specific component of the Shlaer/Mellor method whose approach to object-oriented analysis is described in the next chapter. It prescribes four types of diagram interrelated by a layering scheme to help with documentation and potential automated support. The notation is said to be language-independent though there is a small hint of Ada in the notation and the support for friends is reminiscent of C++. The diagram types are as follows.

- **Dependency diagrams** show usage (client/server) and friend relationships between classes.
- **Class diagrams** show the external view of a class in a manner similar to Buhr (1984).
- **Class structure charts** show the structure of the methods of a class and the flow of data and control.
- **Inheritance diagrams** depict inheritance.

Figure 7.17 shows all three notations in outline. In the dependency diagram single arrows denote messages while double ones show friendship violations of encapsulation. In the class diagram, the top box is the class name and the other inner rectangles are its methods. Hexagons drawn outside the icon and connected to a method show parameters passing. If drawn inside the icon they depict hidden data structures. In class structure charts, rectangles denote methods and hexagons parameters passing between them in much the manner of OOSD. OODLE is a

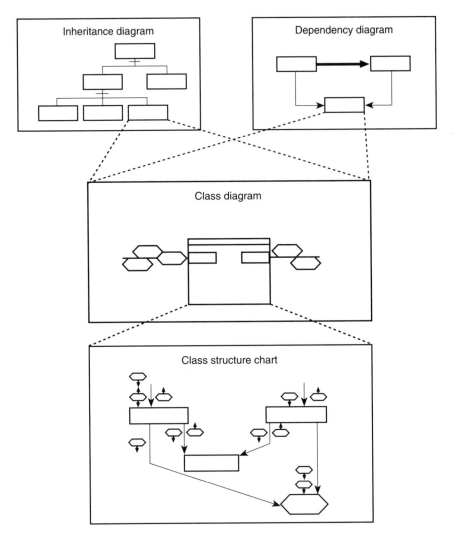

Figure 7.17 Simplified OODLE diagrams and their relationships.

much richer notation than these simplified diagrams indicate, with support for the representation of such things as polymorphism, exceptions and so on.

RECURSIVE   Several problems have motivated the idea of recursive design. Often classes do not
DESIGN   fit together well. Also, despite the fact that reuse is based on external interfaces only, different styles of implementation across different objects lead to maintenance difficulties. Design therefore should be recursive rather than iterative. It should also be done using a method with precise semantics whenever possible. Recursive design is an abstract, general design principle rather than a design process in itself.

The basic idea, and a good idea it is too, is that the performance and maintainability of a system should be addressed by applying a set of general rules across all code modules rather than by low-level tinkering to tune systems. The latter approach makes every component into a special case. There is wisdom in this and it contrasts with much existing practice in object-oriented projects. However, it could be objected that when reuse is really carried out, new developments are exactly special cases. Recursive development requires that the application is separated from various reusable domains at different levels and that formal bridging techniques are constructible between domains at different levels. For example, we might construct a standard bridging technique between low-level UI designs and a particular operating system. The key domain is the 'architecture domain' which insulates application domains from particular implementations, as illustrated in Figure 7.18. Curiously this is exactly what the designers of NeXTstep and the Taligent machine are trying to do at the machine level. HOOD offers such a bridge, but only to one architecture, that of Ada tasking. This is not general enough for most purposes.

Lastly, recursive development can be contrasted with iterative development, as shown in Table 7.2.

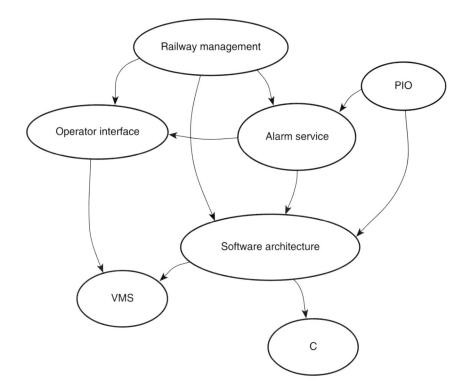

Figure 7.18 A typical Shlaer/Mellor domain chart.

Table 7.2 Iterative versus recursive design.

Iterative	Recursive
FOR EACH requirement DO	FOR EACH requirement DO
analyse	analyse
design	execute analysis model (test)
code	END DO
execute code (test)	define design rules
END DO	test rules
integrate software	apply rules to 'generate' code

From this it may be deduced that the time for all stages of iterative development is proportional to the complexity of the requirement, whereas for recursive development design and code costs fixed and, after an initially higher investment, reuse benefits accrue to each successive project.

The term 'generated' here could refer to code hand-generated from the rules, but it is hard to see the argument other than as supporting the ICASE bandwagon. Further, and in my opinion, recursive design principles could just as readily be applied to conventional development.

The Shlaer/Mellor method emphasizes evolution from current practices over revolutionary object-oriented approaches. It is discussed further in Section 8.2.

7.2.7 CRC and RDD

A responsibility-driven approach to analysis and design using class, responsibility and collaboration (CRC) cards, due to Beck and Cunningham (1989) and described fully in Wirfs-Brock *et al.* (1990) is useful for documenting object-oriented designs and also for teaching the basic concepts. This technique is often known as RDD (responsibility-driven design). It has the singular advantage of using nothing more expensive than a box of index cards as a CASE tool, although originally the idea was to use a hypertext system. Cardboard was found to be more effective in practice.

The CRC approach assumes the existence of a written requirements specification and proceeds by using an Abbott-like textual analysis to name the key objects. For each object representing a class, a card is prepared containing the class name and lists of superclasses and members. Next, a further textual analysis finds the 'responsibilities' or methods required by the class. These methods are further refined by examining three kinds of structure: classification, composition and, novelly, analogy structures. The use structure is determined as a list of classes which each class 'collaborates' with, and these are added to the cards. Once again the composition structures are examined to identify usage, along with 'has-knowledge-of' and 'depends-on' relationships. Collaboration helps with granularity as classes with no collaborations are factored out at this stage. The structures are now analysed to differentiate between abstract and concrete classes and a set theoretic notation is used to picture shared methods. The classes are also organized into layers, or subsystems, which are assigned contractual relationships with other subsystems and lists of delegated tasks. Lastly, all the components – classes, methods, subsystems and contracts – are designed in detail.

This approach emphasizes responsibilities, or methods, over attributes, or data, to help defer as many implementation decisions as possible, but it still acknowledges the existence of attributes. It is usable at both the design and analysis levels and, notation aside, can be regarded as a valuable set of guidelines which may be added to other object-oriented analysis approaches. Alone, it gives scant help in identifying objects or describing overall control structures. The contracts can be used to define pre- and postconditions, which helps with some of the control structure, but there is little to support business rules and functional semantics.

Formally, responsibilities are divided into attributes that represent **responsibilities for knowing**, or the state of the object, and **responsibilities for doing**, or the operations the object can perform. **Collaborations** are requests to a server to help fulfil a client responsibility and constitute visibility or usage relationships at a detailed level. General associations are not well handled by CRC. A **contract** is the set of messages that a client can send to a server and constitutes the high-level usage relationship. Contracts are sometimes used to group related responsibilities.

Figure 7.19 shows a typical CRC card and a subsystem card. Listing the members or subclasses is not a good idea since it compromises encapsulation and thereby reuse. Collaborations may be shown graphically using a collaboration graph, using the notation shown in Figure 7.20. The method uses these graphs to extract coherent subsystems based on containment and contractual groupings. For anything but trivial systems these graphs become very cluttered indeed, and while the idea is good it is not easy to apply in practice. Other methods of layering and grouping must be found.

As it stands, the method requires a written requirements statement as input and proceeds through the following steps.

(1) Identify objects (from the nouns in the specification) and organize them into classification structures.
(2) Find responsibilities (from the verbs in the specification).
(3) Assign responsibilities to classes.
(4) Examine the structures to refine responsibilities.
(5) Find collaborations.
(6) Discard classes without collaborations.
(7) Refine the structures.
(8) Group responsibilities into contracts.
(9) Use collaborations to define subsystems.
(10) Fill in the details.

Many users of CRC use walkthroughs to validate their model and discover the global dynamics of the system: something that few other methods do well,

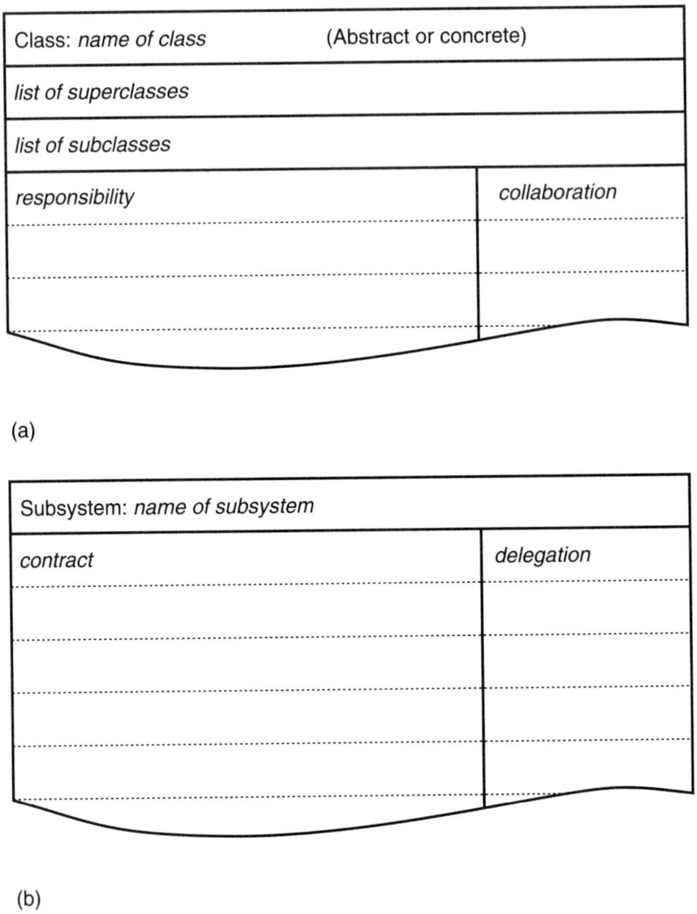

Class: *name of class*	(Abstract or concrete)
list of superclasses	
list of subclasses	
responsibility	*collaboration*

(a)

Subsystem: *name of subsystem*	
contract	*delegation*

(b)

Figure 7.19 **(a)** CRC class card; **(b)** CRC subsystem card.

incidentally. This often done by organizing a workshop where people rôle-play the objects, which is at least great fun and often highly revealing.

CRC is a simplistic but very practical method. Much of its notation is poor and it does not cover all the issues. It is usually used as a precursor to the use of other notations. I use it at the requirements capture stage and as a pedagogical tool as it does get people to understand the behavioural emphasis of object technology quite quickly. An enhancement of the CRC technique in the context of requirements capture and analysis is exposed in Chapter 9.

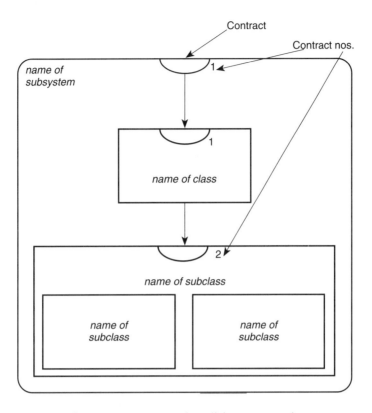

Figure 7.20 An example collaboration graph.

☱ 7.3 Summary

Object-oriented analysis and design cannot be cleanly separated. Design is architectural modelling. It adds detail, precision and implementation-dependent features to the analysis models. Design can be divided into logical and physical design. The Object Management Group call physical design 'implementation modelling' and define design modelling as providing 'rigorous specifications of the interfaces provided by a set of object types'. Implementation modelling is then carried out to develop an implementable solution including its distribution characteristics. It is logical modelling that merges most with object-oriented analysis.

The original object-oriented design method was Booch (1986). The main object-oriented and object-based design methods and notations in current use are the Booch (1991) method, OODLE, HOOD and OOSD. Many of them use Abbott textual analysis as a starting point. STDs are widely used to represent the dynamics of objects. Booch '86 and HOOD are really only suitable for Ada developments. OOSD is not a method but a notation to which the rules of a method may be added. It is language independent, as is Booch '91. JSD is moving towards being object-based and object-oriented versions have appeared. A refined Booch method which will emphasize analysis much more is due *circa* 1993 (see Section 7.4). CRC is transitional between analysis and design and is simple, practical and a good teaching aid, but it is incomplete in some areas, such as not dealing with composition structures.

CASE tools for object-oriented design methods will be dealt with in Section 8.4.

7.4 Bibliographical notes

Booch's paper (1986) has been mentioned extensively in the foregoing and was very influential. His more recent book (Booch, 1991) is probably the most profound and comprehensive view of object-oriented design you are likely to find. It contains a large number of insights and heuristics about what constitutes a good design, how to apprehend objects and how to use and manage the technology. It is the most essential further reading to this book. Wasserman *et al.* (1990) describe OOSD fully and compare it with HOOD, GOOD and MOOD. A good source of information on HOOD is by Robinson (1992) which contains the complete HOOD Version 3.0 manual, an excellent tutorial and a version of the paper by Hodgson quoted at the start of this chapter. The Version 3.1 manual is now published by Prentice-Hall.

OODLE and recursive development are described in Shlaer and Mellor (1991). The CRC cards approach is well described in Wirfs-Brock *et al.* (1990), which contains two useful worked examples. Lorenz (1993) presents a method and notation which has much in common with the approach of Wirfs-Brock *et al.* but covers more issues, though in less depth. Lorenz's method does make use of collaboration graphs. This book also gives a useful worked example and plenty of sound practical advice.

Just as this book was going to press, details of the 1993 revision of the Booch method became available to me. There are a number of significant additions and improvements including a slightly greater emphasis on analysis, a much simplified and improved set of relational icons compared with those illustrated in Figure 7.14, increased compatibility with other notations and methods (notably OMT and Objectory) and a cut-down version of the notation known as 'Booch Lite'. Interestingly, the second edition of Booch's book concentrates almost exclusively on the C++ language rather than the five languages that he used for illustrative purposes in the original book.

8

Object-oriented analysis

Present themselves as objects recognized,
In flashes, and with glory not their own.

Wordsworth (The Prelude)

Analysis is the decomposition of problems into their component parts. In computing it is also to be understood as the process of specification of user requirements and system structure and function independently of the means of implementation or physical decomposition into modules or components. Analysis is traditionally done top-down using structured analysis, or an equivalent method based on functional decomposition, combined with separate data analysis. Often the high-level, strategic, business-goal-driven analysis is separated from the systems analysis. Here we are concerned with both and will eschew any distinction between business and systems analysis. This is necessary for sound systems analysis and possible because object-oriented analysis permits the system to be described in the same terms as the real world: the system abstractions correspond more or less exactly to the business abstractions. In the next chapter this distinction is reintroduced from the viewpoint of project management, where it is convenient.

Object-oriented analysis is analysis, but also contains an element of synthesis. Abstracting user requirements and identifying key domain objects are followed by the assembly of those objects into structures of a form that will support physical design at some later stage. The synthetic aspect intrudes precisely because we are analysing a *system*, in other words imposing a structure on the domain.

There are three primary aspects of a system. These are respectively concerned with: (a) data, objects or concepts and their structure; (b) architecture or atemporal process; and (c) dynamics or system behaviour. We shall refer to these three dimensions as data, process and control. Object-orientation combines two of these aspects – data and process – by encapsulating local behaviour with data. We shall see later that it is also possible to encapsulate control. Thus, an object-oriented analysis can be regarded as a form of syllogism moving from the particular (classes) through the individual (instances) to the universal (control).

In this chapter we shall examine some approaches to object-oriented analysis which have been put forward and attempt to synthesize a method of sound practical value from the suggestions contained in these approaches. The resultant method, SOMA, is not to be regarded as cast in concrete. SOMA is a filter for ideas present in other conventional and object-oriented methods. It recommends a notation but is actually neutral on the shape and design of icons and so on. The idea is that the user can use the notation s/he is most comfortable with and extend it with the extra expressive power of SOMA. It is evolving with my day-to-day work and may be modified by the reader if s/he sees fit. A more formal and complete description of the SOMA notation, method and life cycle will be found in *Migrating to Object Technology* (Graham, 1994). Unlike most other methods SOMA includes prescriptive techniques for requirements capture and the discovery of objects. We shall discuss the problems of identifying objects, and techniques for doing this, in Chapter 9. The reader is assumed to have read Chapter 7.

The next section discusses software engineering in general and the one after is a wide ranging and fairly detailed survey of extant methods of object-oriented analysis. The chapter concludes with a discussion of CASE technology and emerging standards for object-oriented analysis and design.

8.1 Software engineering

The conventional wisdom in software engineering holds it as self-evident that a system must be described in three dimensions: those of process, data and dynamics or control (see Figure 8.1). The data dimension corresponds to entity-relationship diagrams (ERDs) or logical data models. The process models are represented by dataflow or activity diagrams of one sort or another. Finally, the dynamics is described by either a state transition or entity life history notation. To ensure that these diagrams are consistent, structured methods usually insist that some cross-checking documents are created to 'glue' the model together. For example, to check the consistency of a model between the entity-relationship and dataflow views, a CRUD matrix might be constructed. CRUD stands for Create, Read, Update or Delete, and checks which processes use which entities and how they are used. This approach creates a potentially enormous overhead in terms of documentation alone. However, it does ensure that all aspects of a system are covered, assuming the knowledge elicitation is not deficient. It also has the advantage that where two techniques are used to reach the same conclusion then, if the results agree, the level of confidence in them is raised.

Data-centred approaches to software engineering begin with the data model while process-oriented approaches start with DFDs. Some real-time approaches begin with finite state machines or STDs, but this is unusual for commercial systems developers. Data are more stable than functions and so data-centred approaches are to be preferred in most cases.

As we have seen in Chapter 5, there is a rich theory of semantic data modelling going far beyond the normal use of ER diagrams. This theory encompasses

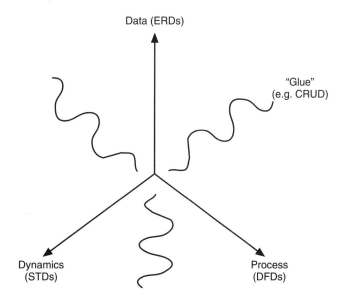

Figure 8.1 The three dimensions of software engineering.

many of the concerns of object-orientation such as inheritance and abstract types. It also illuminates our understanding of relationships or associations between entities by highlighting the fact that they may be ternary as well as binary and that they may themselves have attributes and states. Until recently much of this work has been ignored by workers in object technology and in AI as thoroughly as these two areas have ignored each other.

Object-oriented analysis and design methods fall into two basic types, those which mimic existing structured methods by having three separate notations for data, dynamics and process, and those which assert that, since objects inherently combine processes (methods) and data, only one notation is required. I will call these two approaches **ternary** (or **three-pronged**) and **unary** respectively.

Three-pronged approaches have the advantage that existing practitioners of structured methods will be broadly familiar with the philosophy and notations, and proceeding in this way helps to ensure a smooth transition to object-oriented approaches for those already skilled in traditional methods. Against this, unary approaches are (a) more consistent with the metaphor of object-orientation and (b) easier to learn from scratch.

Of the ternary approaches the clearest examples are OMT (Rumbaugh *et al.*, 1991), the modified Ptech of Martin and Odell (1992) and OSA (Embley *et al.*, 1992) all discussed in the sequel. Of the unitary ones the best known are CRC (Wirfs-Brock *et al.*, 1990) and Coad/Yourdon (Coad and Yourdon, 1990, 1991, 1991a) also discussed below. There is also a growing number of hybrid methods of both types, such as that of Henderson-Sellers (1992) and SOMA.

Looking at the existing object-oriented analysis methods available and published certain things are noticeable. Some, such as Coad/Yourdon are simple but lack support for describing system dynamics. Some, such as Rumbaugh's OMT and Shlaer/Mellor are richer but very complex to learn. Methods like OMT also offer little to help express business rules and constraints. Embley's OSA and Martin and Odell's synthesis of IE with Ptech are slightly simpler three-pronged approaches. OSA allows the analyst to write constraints on the diagrams as a sort of afterthought. None support rules and you will search in vain for advice on how to combine the products of the three separate models into a coherent single model, though OMT does provide more help than others in this respect. In an attempt to address some of these weaknesses in these otherwise attractive methods I was led to the SOMA method. SOMA combines a unitary notation for object-oriented analysis with knowledge-based systems-style rules for describing constraints, business rules, global system control, database triggers and quantification over relationships (for example, 'all children who like toys like each other'). It also addresses in this way the issue of reversibility and thus is ideal as the analytic precursor to prototyping.

Although SOMA seems to be unique as an analysis method in combining objects and rules, several software products already do this, notably expert systems shells such as Nexpert Object, Kappa, KBMS, ADS, XShell and ObjectIQ/ESKernel and a few database products such as Ingres and Generis. There seems to be no suitable analysis approach for such products. One of the weaknesses of all existing object-oriented analysis methods is in the way rules and constraints are added almost as an afterthought. It turns out, as we shall see, that extending the object model to encapsulate not only attributes and methods but rules is a profound step. It enables an object-oriented description of rule-based systems, advanced databases and enterprise models with the attendant benefits of reuse and extensibility and also increases the semantic richness of descriptions of conventional systems. SOMA is also unique in supporting fuzzy classification, which is important for requirement specification in some domains such as enterprise modelling and process control, though unfashionable in many software engineering circles.

8.2 Methods of object-oriented analysis

Recently, several of the most well-known software development methods thinkers have produced object-oriented extensions to conventional systems analysis and design methods, most notably Constantine, Jackson, Mellor, Page-Jones and Yourdon. Other less well-known thinkers have also contributed. It is widely agreed that these methods are all more or less incomplete and it has been remarked that they are not so much methods as suggestions for methods. This section examines several of these suggestions and some hybrids.

The CRC approach to object-oriented design, discussed in the last chapter, could equally be regarded as an analysis technique. Since it has been adequately described it will not be included here, though we will revisit the ideas in Chapter 9. In fact, there is a general problem in distinguishing object-oriented analysis methods from object-oriented design methods which does not arise for conventional methods. Because of the continuum of representation and philosophy from analysis at least up until logical design, it is often hard to tell where one begins and the other ends or, indeed, if there is any difference at all. This is good news for the developer and maintainer but bad news for the project manager and estimator because it is harder to construct a work breakdown structure. In this chapter we will take the view that there is little real difference between analysis and logical design. In Chapter 9 we will be more careful about the distinction.

8.2.1 Shlaer/Mellor OOSA

An early example of object-oriented analysis was due to Shlaer and Mellor (1988), but this method could not really be regarded as object-oriented for several reasons, including the complete absence of any notion of inheritance. As described in their book it was little more than an object-based extension of data modelling. However, a later book by Shlaer and Mellor (1991) introduced inheritance (entity subtyping) and the idea that methods could be discovered by modelling the life cycles of entities with STDs. Their stance on object identity is still suspect, though, because they regard identifiers as sets of attributes or keys. Further, normalization rules (rules of attribution) are applied to objects, regarding them as little more than relational tables. We have seen in Chapter 5 why this is dangerous and undesirable.

The first step in Shlaer and Mellor's method is the definition of objects and their attributes. The entity modelling notation is descended from the Ward/Mellor notation. Emphasis is placed next on defining object life histories, using Moore-style state transition diagrams and the corresponding tables. These are then used to define operations. The notation for the state models is also fairly standard. Global dynamics are handled by coordinating object life cycles annotated in object communication models which show events (or equivalently, messages) passing between entities. Relationships are also given life-cycle models.

A novel idea is the definition of reusable domains, such as illustrated in Figure 7.18, which helps impose a layered approach to software engineering and encourage reuse.

This method may be classified as ternary and proceeds by creating an information (or data) model showing objects, attributes and relationships. Next, a state model describes the states of objects and transitions between states. Finally, a DFD defines the process model. The method is influenced strongly by relational design: objects are in first normal form and object identity is not a natural feature of designs. Users of the method tend to be users who have migrated from the Ward/Mellor approach and the applications I have heard of seem to have a real-time or process control flavour rather than a commercial DP flavour, but this may be a historical accident. It is a complex method covering analysis and design which has had a controversial history but which is in quite wide use. The design aspects of this method and its notation were discussed in the last chapter and need not be revisited here.

This method is partially supported by the team*work* CASE tool. David Lee of GEC-Marconi has suggested to me that the free bundling of this OOA method with an existing CASE tool has encouraged many software engineers to try it out. This is supported by the use of familiar modelling tools using ERDs, STDs and DFDs and the method's compatibility with the earlier Ward/Mellor approach, which is widely used in the real-time community.

8.2.2 Coad/Yourdon

An approach to emerge from the 'Yourdon' camp, which owes a lot to the tradition of entity-relationship modelling, is summarized in Coad and Yourdon (1990, 1991, 1991a) and was primarily interesting as the first widely published account of a reasonably complete, practical, object-oriented analysis (*qua* analysis) method and supporting notation, suitable for commercial projects. Coad and Yourdon introduce a less clumsy notation than that found in Booch, Shlaer/Mellor or most of the design-oriented approaches dealt with in the previous chapter. They shift the emphasis very much to analysis as opposed to design. Ada data structures, decomposition into modules or other language-level constructs play no part in their method, which is remarkable for its simplicity though incomplete in some areas. However, the ideas are useful enough to form the basis of a method that, even if it evolves over time, can deliver real benefits in terms of reusable and extensible specifications.

One of the most notable features of the Shlaer/Mellor and Coad/Yourdon notations is the explicitness of attributes. We have already explained how this violates the traditional object-oriented principle that objects are specified by their methods alone. However, we also saw that attributes can be identified with standard methods that access their state, such as 'put salary' and 'get salary'. In my view the complexity of the data structures present in most commercial systems is what leads to the need to make attributes explicit.

There were two editions of the analysis book by Coad and Yourdon published within a year of each other. In what follows I shall freely mix the notations and terminology of both editions, according to what I feel is both correct and useful.

Coad and Yourdon suggest that analysis proceeds in five stages which they label:

- *Subjects.* The problem area is decomposed into 'subjects' which corresponds to the notion of 'levels' or 'layers' in dataflow diagrams and to Booch's subsystems or class categories. These subjects should be of a manageable size in that they contain only about five to nine objects.
- *Objects.* Next, the objects are identified in detail by searching for business entities in much the same way as a data analysis would be performed. Coad and Yourdon give little additional guidance on how to perform this task.

- *Structures.* Two completely different structures are identified, classification structures and composition structures. This is where inheritance is dealt with as the classification structures are merely specialization/generalization trees. Coad and Yourdon say little about how these trees are processed or interact (see below).
- *Attributes.* As in conventional data analysis, attributes are detailed and modality and multiplicity relationships specified using a version of extended relational analysis (ERA). In this there is a departure from some other object-oriented design methods which only specify methods.
- *Services.* This is the Coad/Yourdon word for operations. Each object type must be equipped with methods for creating and deleting instances, getting and putting values and with special methods characterizing the object's behaviour.

Coad and Yourdon offer the mnemonic 'SOSAS' to aid the remembrance of these steps.

Coad's (1991a) object-oriented design adds to these five activities (or layers as he calls them) four components. Principally, his OOD consists in refining the products of OOA into what they call the Problem Domain Component of the design (by adding new solution space classes) and adding three new components called the Human Interaction (HIC), Task Management (TMC) and Data Management Components (DMC). These components allow design-specific issues – such as threads of control, specific processors, package software and so on – to be included in the OOA diagrams. Great emphasis is laid on the similarity of notation for analysis and design and the way this smoothes the transitions so sharply felt in traditional methods. This work on OOD addresses some criticisms which were made of the OOA method. For example, trigger and terminate constraints are introduced for Services. However, no real distinction between logical and physical design is made. Also, Coad is evidently aware of the oft-levelled critique that his OOA cannot handle dynamics. Hence, perhaps, we find on page 151: 'simulation of the behavioural dynamics being modelled. Inbound and outbound Message Connections may be highlighted, based on the selection of a Service or Services. Alternatively, threads of execution can be displayed – one at a time, or all together, using different line patterns for each thread – once they have been defined'. It is not made clear whether this requires every single message instance to be enumerated or how completeness can be checked.

We have already used the diagrammatic notation defined by Coad and Yourdon in Chapter 1, which shows an object type as a triple icon as shown in Figure 8.2.

It is useful to think of the two lower boxes, where the attributes and methods are displayed, as scrolling windows, since it is rarely possible to write all the details in a small box. This points clearly to the need for automated support for this notation, and indeed a low-cost tool called OOATool has been produced for sale by Coad's company, Object International.

The possibility of message passing between objects is shown in the same way as the original Booch notation, by arrows. In this area, Booch is in some ways

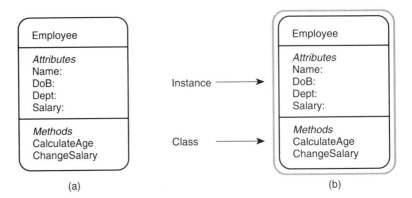

Figure 8.2 (a) Coad/Yourdon notation for a general object; **(b)** the revised notation draws a grey outline around objects that may have instances.

actually a lot clearer than Coad and Yourdon and I prefer his terminology of clients and servers. His later notation, shown in Figure 7.14, is definitely superior. Coad and Yourdon, like Booch, actually permit analysts to enumerate messages. In using the method I have found that this is useful at a first attempt at analysis, but that it results in a dreadful mess when things get complex. In fact the resultant spaghetti is redundant because the method names show which messages will be processed if passed. All we have to show is visibility: whether a message *may* be passed (see Figure 8.3).

In the second edition of their book, Coad and Yourdon cave in to criticisms that they had failed to distinguish classes and instances in the first. They now draw a grey outline around the class icon to indicate its typical instance, if it has any

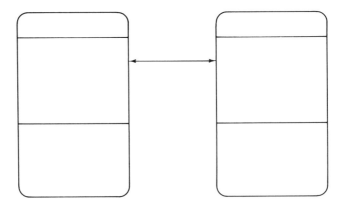

Figure 8.3 The possibility of messages passing between objects is indicated by the arrowheads.

instances. This is useful but obfuscates some issues of data semantics unless used with care, as we shall see below. Messages are regarded as being sent to instances and end on the outer box. The use structure is also muddled, since these arrows show actual implementation message passing rather than client/server relationships between *classes*.

Layering into 'subjects' is a process that takes place at various stages of analysis and can be used for an initial decomposition at the start or to organize the model after objects have been identified or refined. A similar process is usually associated with dataflow diagrams. Layers or subjects are represented by square boxes and message passing by arrows as though the layers were objects (Figure 8.4). However, in this method subjects are arbitrary decompositions to aid understanding and have no clear semantics. Worse, it is possible to have messages or even inheritance links crossing the boundary of a subject though this is ill-advised.

Some subjects arise quite naturally, as objects are assembled into classification or composition structures.

Coad and Yourdon propose the notation shown in Figure 8.5 for inheritance hierarchies and that in Figure 8.6 for composition. The arrowhead denotes composition. The other notations on the links refer to data semantics, which is discussed below.

Regarding these structures as subjects, messages sent to the subject are normally regarded as being sent to the top of a composition structure and the bottom of a classification structure. However, there will always be applications where this is not the case. Messages and relationships are shown only between instances. A problem introduced with the second edition is a distinction between three kinds of composition: part–whole, container–contents and collection–members. This represents a fundamental misunderstanding about semantic primitives. The last two are merely extra structures, not special cases of composition. Such structures may be used but should not be confused with composition structures. There may indeed be other important structures in a particular application. For example, a database concerned with anthropological research might well employ kinship as a fundamental structure.

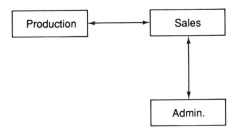

Figure 8.4 Layers are groups of, ideally, between five and nine objects or possibly coherent classification or composition structures.

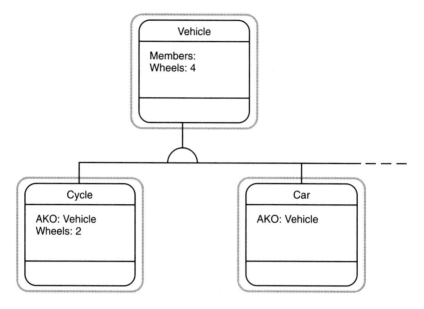

Figure 8.5 Classification or inheritance hierarchy in Coad/Yourdon notation. AKO = A Kind Of.

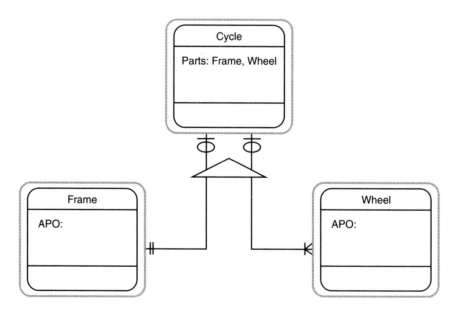

Figure 8.6 Composition hierarchy in Coad/Yourdon notation (instance level). APO = A Part Of.

When defining attributes, exactly the same considerations apply as in any data modelling exercise. The analyst is able to take advantage of inheritance and assume that unspecified elements are inherited where this makes sense. Multiple inheritance of attributes, or of methods, is not supported by the 1990 version. In the second edition, multiple inheritance is notationally permitted, but there is nothing to help with conflict resolution short of annotating every single attribute and method with such instructions as may be necessary. This leads me to assert that even the revised method does not genuinely support multiple inheritance.

Method, or service, definition is the stage where the functional aspects of the system are specified. A method is a procedure that alters the state of an object (that is, the values of its attributes) or causes the object to send messages. Methods define exactly which messages an object can process. Thus, as we have noted, it is rarely necessary or useful to label all the 'message' arrows on the diagrams, as the legal messages can be read off from the Methods window. It is necessary at this stage to record the exception-handling and parameter-passing behaviour of the object. This must be textual as there is no notational support for exceptions.

One of Coad and Yourdon's useful suggestions concerns the use of standard object and method description templates. Their method is based on the formal specification language, Ina Jo (Wing and Nixon, 1989), but any program template style will help enforce a communicable style of documentation and assist in making both object and method specifications complete. The template must name the object and list the attribute and method names in the interface just as in the diagrammatic notation. However, it must also indicate features of the attributes, such as whether they are always or only occasionally derivable, annotate the object with the designer's intentions and remarks on traceability, criticality, sizing constraints and so on. For each method the template specifies its purpose in the form of English or structured English statements. Of course, the text may be annotated with diagrams when this is helpful. Fundamentally, each method is specified in the same way that analysts have always specified system components. The only difference is that these details will be hidden within the object and only accessed via their interfaces.

Coad/Yourdon is weakest when it comes to specifying the dynamics of systems, but a state transition approach is suggested for object dynamics though no notation for this is defined. There is no explicit support for specifying business rules.

Defining the data semantics is usually not addressed by object-oriented design methods such as HOOD and OOSD. This reflects the latter's concern with really quite low-level programming abstractions and their genesis in real-time applications where complex data management problems either do not arise or are dealt with separately. Further, object-oriented programming languages have not been noted for their handling of persistent objects, and some authorities (for example, Wegner, 1987) even go so far as to say that persistent objects contradict the very spirit of object-orientation, while others such as Meyer insist that it is

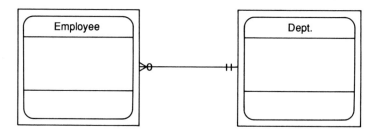

Figure 8.7 Data semantics. Note that numbers may be used instead of the 'crow's feet' symbols used here.

fundamental to the approach. An analysis method aimed at commercial systems must, however, worry about these issues.

The extended relational analysis (ERA) notation, described in Chapter 5, is similar to that recommended by Coad and Yourdon (1990) and is probably as good as any other. This notation helps to specify two aspects of relationships: their multiplicity and modality. Recall that multiplicity refers to whether relationships are one-to-one, one-to-many or many-to-many and modality refers to whether they are necessary or possible (optional) and is closely connected to the issue of referential integrity, also discussed in Chapter 5. Figure 8.7 defines a many-to-one relationship at the instance level. Relationships of this kind are not shown as first class objects in the Coad/Yourdon notation. This can arise in some applications, although it is rare. For example, it may be useful to regard a marriage relationship as an object with its own properties, such as date, and methods, such as annulment.

There are certain other defects in the Coad/Yourdon approach. Under the influence of the relational database movement, they insist that attributes should be 'atomic'. This is wrong. Object-orientation is about modelling complex objects which need not be atomic, as we saw in Chapter 5. They also talk about keys rather than object identity and about normalization, although these issues are dismissed as 'deferred to design'.

Figure 8.8 shows most of the features of the Coad/Yourdon notation as it appears in the second edition of their analysis book. In this diagram, which represents an analysis of vehicle registrations, there are two layers, one composition structure and several classification structures. The heavy arrows represent message passing.

The method is not perfect but it is simple and unary. Contrast it now with a ternary notation of considerable richness and complexity: OMT.

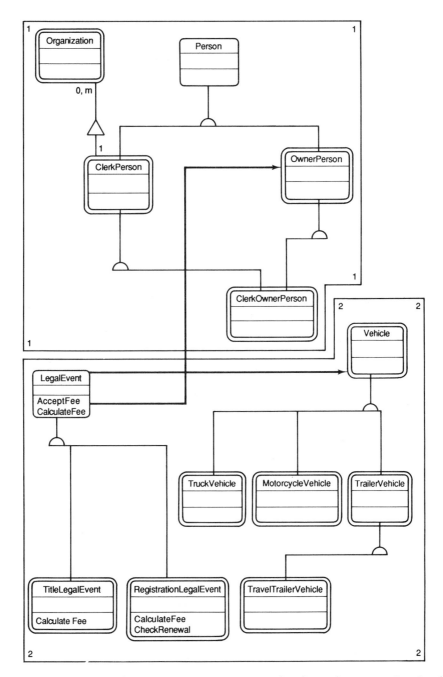

Figure 8.8 Coad/Yourdon OOA notation. (From Coad and Yourdon (1991). Reprinted by permission of Prentice-Hall, Englewood Cliffs, NJ.)

8.2.3 Rumbaugh – OMT

The Object Modelling Technique (OMT) is widely regarded as one of the most complete object-oriented analysis systems so far published. It originates from the work of James Rumbaugh (1991) and his colleagues at General Electric. It is a three-pronged approach with strong roots in traditional structured methods and offers an extremely rich but frighteningly complicated and detailed notation. Automated support is therefore advisable and a number of tools support the notation. The complexity is partly paid for by the ability of some of these tools to generate code automatically. The method is relatively language-independent though it is more usually associated with C++ than Smalltalk developments.

OMT breaks down into three main phases or activities: analysis, system design and object design. **Analysis** assumes that a requirements specification exists (or at least provides no techniques thereto) and proceeds by building three separate models using three different notations. The first to be built is the Object Model (OM), which consists of diagrams similar to those of Coad/Yourdon, and a data dictionary. The notation is fundamentally that of ER modelling with operations and other annotations added to the entity icons. Next, for every object a Dynamic Model (DM) is built consisting of STDs drawn in an extended Harel notation and global event flow diagrams. The third step is not used by every practitioner and then only at the highest level of abstraction by most of those who do. This is the Functional Model (FM). The FM is indistinguishable from a DFD to all intents and purposes. Operations discovered in both the DM and FM are then added to the OM and a walkthrough is performed, after which the analysis report including all the above deliverables is produced.

The basic object modelling notation is shown in Figures 8.9 to 8.11. It is a much richer notation than Coad/Yourdon. Note in Figure 8.9 that attributes are typed and operations given argument lists and return types, and that instances have round corners and bracketed names. Although analysts are usually more interested in classes than instances, OMT allows such instance diagrams. Figure 8.11(a) shows that ternary associations are allowed but associations with attributes are often expanded into first-class objects, as in Figure 8.11(b) and 8.12. Associations are annotated with rôles and may have a qualifier. The latter is occasionally very useful. For example, if Class-1 is Directory, Class-2 is File and the qualifier is Filename in Figure 8.10, then it is the filename which specifies the uniqueness of a file within a directory. The one-to-many relationship between Directory and File is thus effectively reduced to one-to-one.

Classification structures are shown as in Figure 8.13, from which it can be seen that the notation is richer than that of Coad in expressing exclusivity and optionality.

Composition structures are shown as in Figure 8.14. A particularly strong feature of OMT is the ability to represent recursive composites, as in Figure 8.15. Figure 8.16 is included to give an idea of just how complete – and complex – this notation is; and we have not finished yet. The Dynamic Model notation, based on Harel (1987) state charts, is even richer.

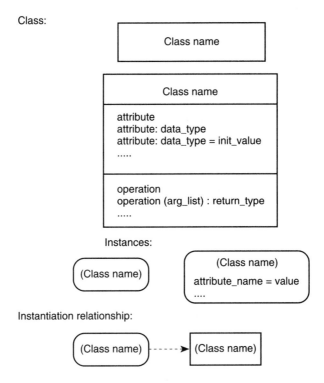

Figure 8.9 Classes and instances in OMT.

Figure 8.17 shows a global event trace for the activity of making a phone call. An object of interest, the phone line in this case, is placed at the centre and a sequence of events traced as shown. There could be several such sequences. From an analysis of this external behaviour an internal state model of phone line is built as shown in Figure 8.18. The notation used is based on Harel state charts and explained further by Figure 8.19. Events, which may occur with attributes, cause actions that may be guarded by conditional statements (preconditions). On completion of the action the object enters the target state. When a state is entered the 'do' activity is performed. Actions are instantaneous but activities take time. When the system leaves the state the activity ceases. With the Harel notation, states can have substates and exist concurrently. The entire DM notation, in all its complexity, is shown in Figure 8.20.

The final modelling stage is the production of the FM. This is not always done and most practitioners sccm to use it at a high level, roughly as a conventional analyst would use context diagrams (level zero DFDs). As we shall see when we discuss Ptech, this attitude to process (or architectural) modelling is common. In fact the notation is hardly distinguishable from a DFD notation. It is illustrated completely in Figure 8.21. Having completed the three (or two) models the operations discovered are copied to the OM and we can move on to system and object design.

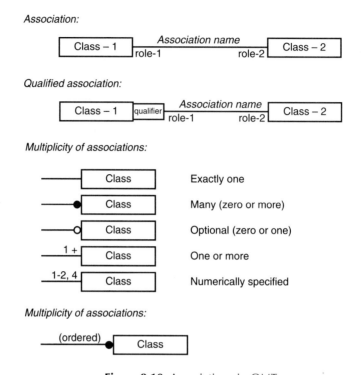

Figure 8.10 Associations in OMT.

System design proceeds by organizing the objects into subsystems, identifying concurrency from the DM, allocating subsystems to processors or tasks, deciding on whether data are to be stored in files, memory or a database management system, deciding on the use of peripherals and global resources, deciding on control structures, setting boundary conditions (start/end/fail) and setting trade-off priorities. This too is documented in a design document.

Object design involves converting the information in the DM and FM to OM operations. The remaining steps are to:

(1) design algorithms;
(2) optimize access paths;
(3) implement control;
(4) adjust structures;
(5) design attribute details;
(6) package structures into modules;
(7) write the design report, including a detailed OM, DM and FM.

OMT is intended to be a method for both analysis and design, but although it contains a fairly complete method for analysis it tends only to give heuristics for design. OMT covers more issues than most other methods but it remains

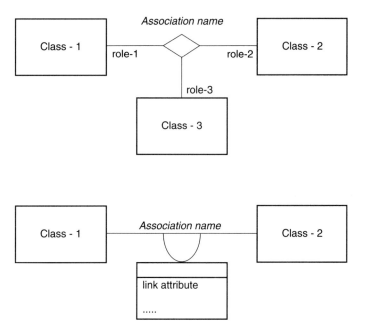

Figure 8.11 **(a)** Ternary associations and **(b)** associations with attributes in OMT.

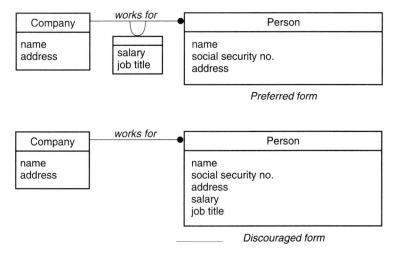

Figure 8.12 Associations should be expanded into objects in preference to adding attributes to existing objects.

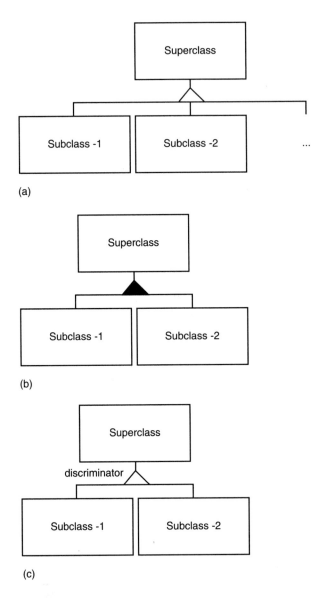

Figure 8.13 Classification in OMT. **(a)** More subclasses exist; **(b)** Subclasses have overlapping (non-disjoint) membership; **(c)** Discriminator is an attribute whose value differentiates between subclasses.

incomplete in some areas and it is very complex to learn and use the notations. The omissions include the ability to model business rules at a high level or control rules at all. We will return to this point in Section 8.3. OMT comes from a real-time background and this is reflected, I think, in its emphasis on STDs. This

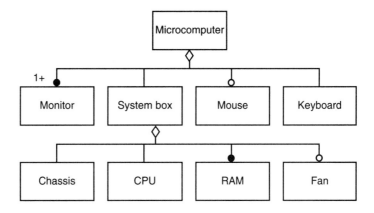

Figure 8.14 An OMT composition (aggregation) structure for PC assemblies.

fails to recognize explicitly that in many commercial applications there are objects whose behaviour does not depend on the substantive state in which they are. For example, when the Employee object reports the value of Age it would be silly to model this as depending on transitions based on time. On the other hand, unlike some other methods that emphasize STDs, such as Shlaer/ Mellor and Texel, the OM does permit the analyst to just write operations in at that stage.

Rumbaugh *et al.* (1991) gives some sound heuristics for implementing object-oriented designs in relational databases and in conventional languages. Language heuristics have already been discussed in Section 3.6.4. The guidelines given for relational database implementation are as follows.

- Implement object identity using primary keys, preferably machine-generated surrogates.
- Classes are tables and instances tuples.

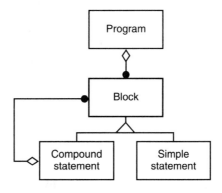

Figure 8.15 Recursive composition structure showing how programs are built up.

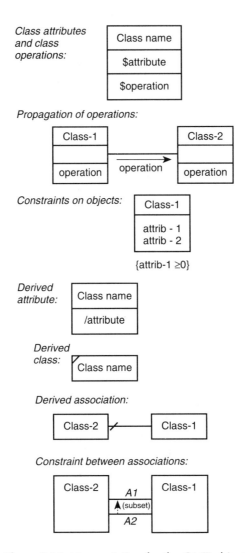

Figure 8.16 More notation for the OMT object model.

■ Associations are tables.
■ Inheritance links are shared identifiers with a secondary index.

Generally speaking, third-generation relational databases such as Ingres and Sybase and semantic databases give better facilities for object modelling, but the above guidelines will work for most products.

Already, although we have only looked at two notations in any detail, we can see that there are contradictory notations for classification and composition and that

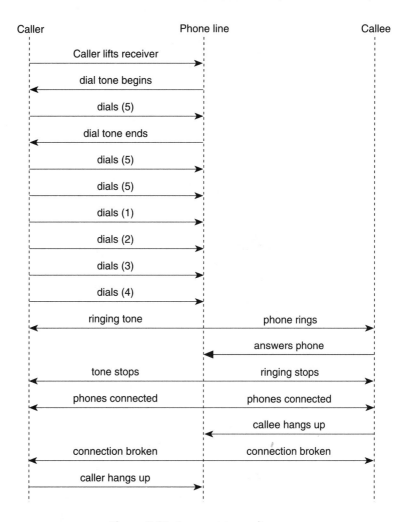

Figure 8.17 An event trace diagram.

they do not conform to anything in conventional notations. In Section 8.3 a resolution of this problem will be attempted.

8.2.4 Martin/Odell – Ptech

Ptech, from Associative Design Technology, is a proprietary set of methods and tools covering both analysis and design. It has enough features in common with object-oriented approaches to make it worth including here. The Ptech CASE tool also generates code for C++ and Ontos.

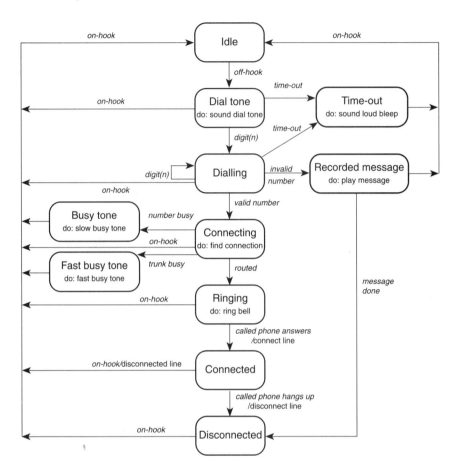

Figure 8.18 OMT state model for the Phone_line object.

The ideas behind Ptech are based on the metaphor of process engineering as the production of systems by assembling reusable components, an approach that of course separates analysis and logical design from implementation. The emphasis is therefore on what is done rather than how it is done. In that sense Ptech is process-oriented rather than strictly object-oriented, although the approaches have many features in common. Ptech combines this process-driven view with the abstraction features of more data-centred, object-oriented design and some ideas from set theory and artificial intelligence.

Edwards (1989), the author of Ptech, stresses the need for a formal basis for any object-oriented method and criticizes what he calls 'naive' methods of object-oriented analysis such as Coad/Yourdon or even OMT. The emphasis, in Ptech, is on prototyping throughout. Edwards also thinks that executable specifications are

Figure 8.19 OMT state transition diagram notation.

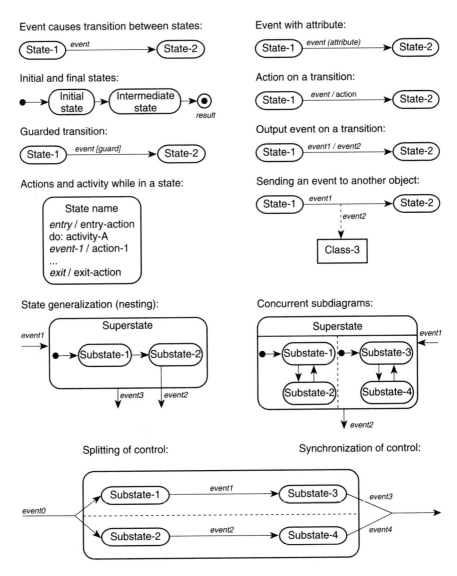

Figure 8.20 OMT dynamic model complete notation.

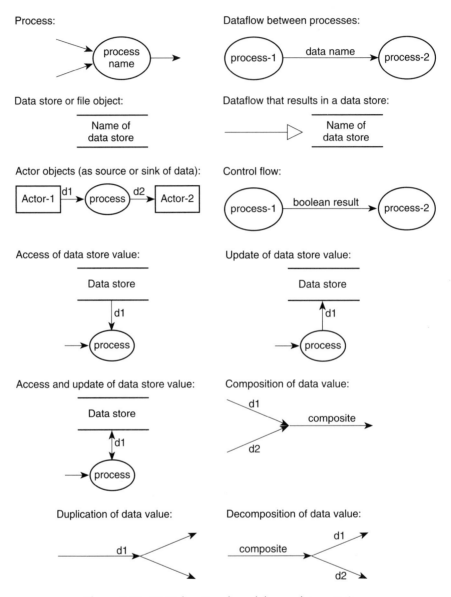

Figure 8.21 OMT functional model complete notation.

prerequisites for reverse engineering and maintenance. I agree, and will discuss this in the next chapter.

Ptech is described in a book by James Martin and Jim Odell (1992).

The Ptech notational system consists of three types of diagram: concept diagrams (broadly equivalent to extended entity-relationship diagrams in the general

Bachman style) called object schemata or concept schemata; event diagrams or schemata (which fulfil the rôle of state transition diagrams); and activity/function diagrams (with much the same purpose as DFDs). The first two diagramming notations are supported by formal languages, the class calculus and the event calculus. Figure 8.22 summarizes the main architectural components of the method.

Concept diagrams show the static aspects of processes and event diagrams their dynamics. It is possible to illustrate how instances are created and terminated and how they move in and out of classes using a combined concept and event diagram. The activity diagrams give a high-level functional view broadly analogous to that given by a dataflow diagram. Concepts are regarded as sets and set theory is used to describe concepts using simple set operations such as union, intersection and difference. Inheritance is shown, à la Bachman, by inclusion of icons as in Figure 8.23, and non-exhaustive partitions by an extra bar. Thus, in this figure, a token can be either a slug, a 5-pence piece, a 10p or a 50p, and nothing else. These four subtypes *partition* the token concept. The last three form a partition of the coin concept. A value can be represented by a coin or something else as yet unspecified. This is represented by the double line at the bottom of the class outline. Personally I do not like the conventions, especially the Bachman style of showing subclasses by inclusion, though it is powerful enough in the hands of a skilled analyst. Nor do

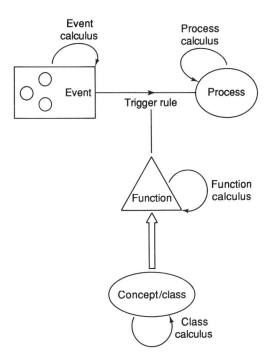

Figure 8.22 The Ptech process engineering metaphor.

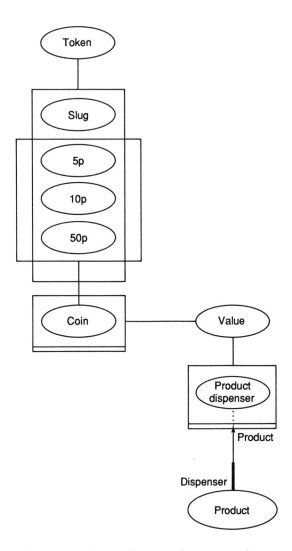

Figure 8.23 Ptech concept schema showing inheritance and partitioning inheritance.

I like showing classes as sharp-cornered rectangles. I like to think that instances have sharp corners because if you drop them on your foot they hurt, whereas classes can't hurt anyone and therefore have rounded corners. Ptech shows events with round-cornered boxes. The other notation shown in Figure 8.23 is Ptech's version of data semantics (the function calculus) and need not concern us here. This figure and Figures 8.24 and 8.25 refer to a fragment of the design of a vending machine.

Events are n-place concepts – that is, objects with n attributes – which have definite pre- and postconditions. The postconditions imply that every process has a

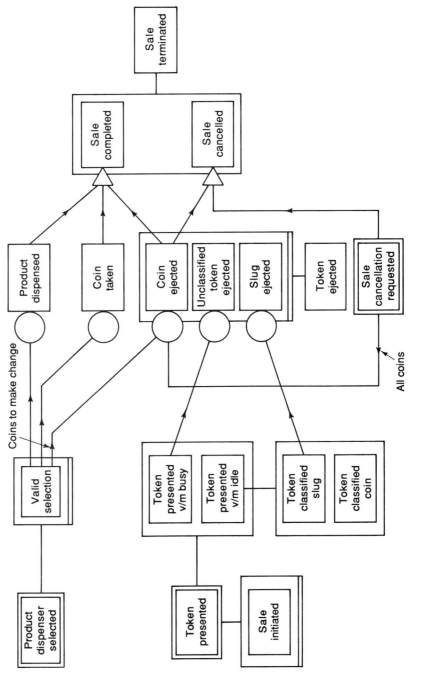

Figure 8.24 Ptech event schema.

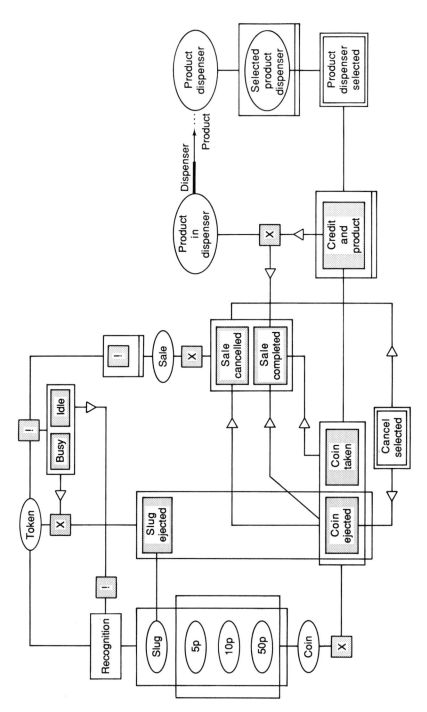

Figure 8.25 Combined concept and event schema for the vending machine example.

definite goal. With events, the set theoretic class calculus is paralleled by a function calculus based on the lambda calculus. This permits the definition of triggers and business rules. Figure 8.24 illustrates an event diagram from the vending machine design. The rectangles represent events and arrows terminating in circles represent trigger rules or preconditions. The triangles represent postconditions or decision processes which evaluate to true or false, depending on the outcome of the preceding processes (the incoming arrows).

The Ptech event modelling notation is, broadly speaking, a finite state machine notation with enriched semantics to deal with constraints, preconditions and the like. This is undoubtedly a useful notation but the recommended notation for matching these diagrams to the object model, which involves drawing rough outlines round event icons and linking them to class icon in a separate object diagram with arrows, is extremely messy. The main flaw in the approach is summed up in the remark: 'Operation reusability is a key factor in OO specification and implementation'. I disagree and think that class reusability is the key and this is why integrating the object and behaviour models is so critical. Ptech event diagrams are especially useful in grasping the control structure of a system. They add something essential and lacking in many object-oriented approaches. However, regarding concepts as sets violates the spirit of object-orientation, because concepts with methods are much more than sets: they are algebras at least. Ptech focuses much more on events than objects. This is both its strength and its weakness, since true object-oriented methods focus on reusable objects but are usually weak in global dynamic modelling. However, in Ptech events are objects too and they can participate in classification structures. The Ptech behavioural model is well thought out and simpler to comprehend but not as detailed as that of OMT.

Ptech concept and event diagrams can be combined as shown in Figure 8.25. Here double boxes represent events external to the system. An ! means creation, and an X means termination. Note the similarity to ! and * in Booch timing diagrams.

The final diagram type in Ptech is the activity/function schema or object flow diagrams. These are introduced to give 'a high-level functional view'. As with the object flow models of OMT, I expect that few practitioners will make much use of this technique as it provides nothing more than top-down modular decomposition, and a more object-oriented levelling approach, such as that found in HOOD or SOMA, is far more appropriate. Figure 8.26 shows such a schema describing process flow of control in a fast-food restaurant. The circles are processes and the rectangles are the products of these processes. The arrows represent dataflows or dependencies.

In methodological terms, Ptech consists of four main activities: object structure analysis, object behaviour analysis, object structure design and object behaviour design. Object structure analysis (OSA) involves building concept schemata showing classes, associations, classification and composition. Object behaviour analysis uses event schemata and shows state transitions, event types, trigger rules, control conditions and operations. Object structure design adds

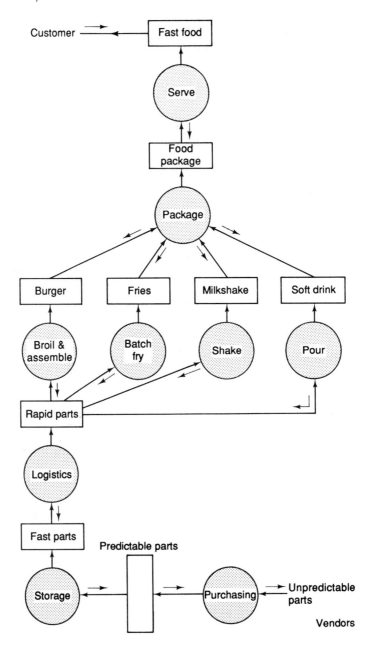

Figure 8.26 Activity/function diagram for a fast-food application.

implementation dependent aspects to OSA and object behaviour design adds the details of the methods. The behavioural model has sufficient expressive power to denote preconditions but not, so far as I can tell, invariance conditions. Business rules can be expressed as preconditions and a declarative syntax is permitted albeit allowing single rules rather than full rule-sets. This would require the specification of a procedural process. The notational convention for tying the behavioural aspects to the structural ones, which we are told by Martin and Odell is 'very important', is clumsy as exemplified by Figure 8.27.

We have only been able to scratch the surface of the Ptech approach in this brief exposition. It is a very rich and expressive notation and method. In fact, the worst point that can be made about Ptech is that it is, as a theory and as a tool, horrendously complicated. It takes a real expert to use it well. However, Ptech evidently does work and has been used successfully in the NHS as described below, but if you are not an expert user it is clumsy and potentially as bureaucratic as most conventional structured methods. Some of the ideas it contains, especially the event schemata, are invaluable and should find their way into every serious software engineer's tool kit.

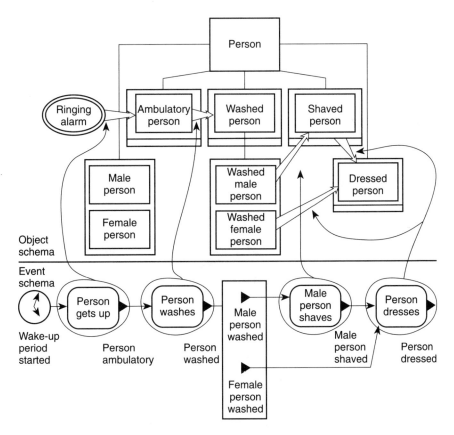

Figure 8.27 Cross-referencing the Ptech event and object (concept) schemata. (Reprinted from Martin and Odell (1992) by kind permission of the authors.)

For details of Ptech the reader should refer to Martin and Odell (1992), w. contains some deep insight into how object-orientation contributes to business enterprise modelling. The contribution here is that business rules and constraints should not be left as an afterthought, as they are in most extant object-oriented analysis techniques, nor should they be 'buried in multiple COBOL programs'. In other words object technology should support adaptable businesses.

CASE-STUDY   The Ptech method has been used successfully in the UK National Health Service for modelling in clinical healthcare, although sufficient cause was found to make modifications and extensions (Fowler and Capey, 1991). The application is not a traditional data processing one but concerned the technical domain of storing and retrieving information on patients' treatments. At the start of the project several piecemeal systems already existed in domains such as transplant surgery, diabetes, and so on. It was desired to construct a process model to unite these separate systems. The methods background was that SSADM and later IE had been used.

Teams were small and, most interestingly, consisted typically of one or two analysts and one or two clinicians (doctors, nurses, and so on). The clinicians were given training in the analysis technique and, in time, became the best analysts. This was only made possible because the object-oriented approach makes direct models of the real-world medical domain.

Of the three Ptech views, the architectural view (the equivalent of data flow) was only useful at the highest level. In contrast, the subtyping notation was rich and expressive in practice. Most object-oriented methods that have state models are good at describing the internal dynamics of objects. Ptech event schemata were found to give a better view of the global dynamics. Certainly flowcharts are a very poor tool in this respect and event schemata combine process and data together, giving an ideal tool for modelling the entire enterprise in an event-driven manner. It was found that the use of OO emphasized the clinical knowledge and operational business rules and their separation.

However good Ptech was, some gaps were discovered. The most important was that no advice is given on how to proceed from a completed analysis to actual screens and so on. This led to the introduction of view classes that give a simplified and more concrete picture of a particular application based on the core model, which is highly abstract. Presentation classes further separate the view processing from the interface and permit different GUIs to use the same views.

Several tools, including Generis, were tried and abandoned. Current work proceeds using GemStone and Smalltalk in a client/server environment. This has been productive and successful to the extent that the doctors now not only analyse but cut code. Version 1 of the Ptech tool was abandoned early on in this project. Subsequently a Macintosh drawing tool was used quite successfully, pending evaluation of the new version of the Ptech tool which was expected to be better than Version 1.

8.2.5 Objectory and OOSE

Object-Oriented Software Engineering or OOSE (Jacobson *et al.,* 1992) is a method for object-oriented analysis and design derived from Jacobson's Objectory (from Object FactOry). Objectory is a proprietary method and OOSE is a simplified version which is said to be inadequate for use in production: 'You will need the complete ... description which, excluding large examples, amounts to more than 1200 pages.' (Jacobson *et al.,* 1992). You will probably also need to buy consultancy and the OrySE CASE tool from Jacobson's company, based in Sweden. Having said this the method is powerful and full of interesting and useful ideas. Jacobson is one of the most experienced practitioners of OOA in the business and his many insights based on numerous projects cannot be ignored. Objectory is unusual among OO methods in attempting to address the entire software development life cycle. It was originally derived from experience in building telephone exchange systems at L. M. Ericsson using block design techniques and is one of the oldest object-oriented methods. It has its other roots in object-oriented programming and data modelling.

The underlying enterprise philosophy has it that **tools** provide support for activities in three categories: architecture, method and process. **Architecture** signifies the choice of techniques to be utilized, the **method** makes explicit the procedures to be followed and the **process** provides for scaling the method up. All this is by way of analogy with what goes on in the building trade. Development is progressive, involving iterative cycles of analysis, construction and testing. Each iteration is regarded as a change to an existing system involving version and documentation control at the module and system levels. In terms of the life cycle OOSE recommends stages of analysis, construction and testing; construction is further divided into design and implementation. Requirements elicitation precedes analysis and is outside of OOSE. Delivery and maintenance (production) follow testing. Each of these activities produces models. Analysis results in requirements and analysis models, construction in design and implementation models and testing in a test model.

Many of the ideas of OOSE are similar to those of other OO methods, but one original idea stands out: the use case. Use cases are descriptions of how users interact with a system. These can be viewed either as the process bubbles in a DFD-style context diagram or as scripts of the kind found in AI research. Scripts (or use cases) can have subscripts to deal with exceptions. The advantage of this approach is that requirements can be traced right through the life cycle, and this is what OOSE emphasizes. Also it is straightforward to generate test scripts from use cases. On the other hand, it is known that it is seldom possible to predict scripts for all cases of system interaction: imagine predicting your daily interaction with a complex word processor, for example. Subscripting may also introduce 'modes' into a system, making it harder for users to predict the behaviour of the system for any given input without maintaining a model of the system's internal state at all times (see Thimbleby, 1990). Nevertheless the idea is a useful one and has re-emerged in several other methods, such as OBA, which emphasize the cooperation between objects over extracting the objects from the terminology of the domain. Another feature of the method is a better than usual way of organizing models into subsystems.

Use cases first make an appearance in the requirements model along with actors. Actors are external entities with which the system interacts. For example, an actor could be a certain rôle that the users play such as 'cash depositor' for an ATM. The use case model specifies the complete (*sic*) functional behaviour of the system as a whole. This approach may be compared with the layer grouping technique of SOMA where the visible operations of a layer correspond to use cases though no claims about completeness are made. The actors are used to find the use cases and are instantiated in actual interactions with users. Another point to note is that the same event can initiate different use cases depending on the state of the system (mode) and the purpose and subsequent behaviour of the user. The users need not know which use case they are going to perform at the outset, only that eventually closure will be achieved on completion of some use case. We will see that this is a useful approach to high-level system scoping. It is better than DFDs partly because it requires that we ask what the system expects of the user as well as vice versa; that is, the behaviour of the users is regarded as objects and not merely which data flow from them. OOSE does not really take the use case idea to this logical conclusion, which is of immense significance for the specification of UIs. Instead it exploits use cases to the full as a source of quality control. In Chapter 9 we will see how this idea can be adapted for requirements elicitation. A top-level use case diagram is shown in Figure 8.28.

The use case model is used to generate a domain object model with objects drawn from the entities of the business. This is then converted into an analysis model by classifying the domain objects into three types: interface objects, entity

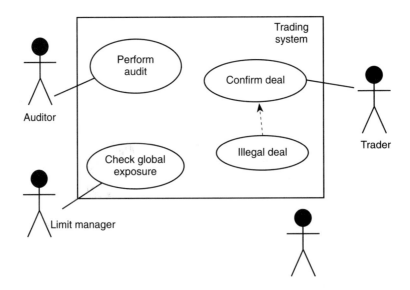

Figure 8.28 Top level use case diagram for a financial trading system showing a sub-use case for deals that fail to confirm due to a breach of regulations.

objects and control objects. These entity objects emphasize storage and are stable in the sense that they normally persist longer than a use case and may be compared to the domain objects of SOMA or shared objects of LBMS's Systems Engineering-OO (see Section 8.2.9). Control objects emphasize behaviour. Splitting up objects into types is said to help with functional changes and, I think, is a good idea closely related to the classical ideas of data independence. The rationale behind this split is said to be that if every object had to be a 'real-world' entity then control and presentation behaviour might be split across several objects thus making changing the behaviour harder as requirements evolve. This is a good idea as long as it is only used for really exceptional behaviour in a use case that does not belong to a business object. For greater traceability, each function of a use case is tied to an analysis model object. In practice several use cases can have objects in common as shown in Figure 8.29.

The analysis model supports inheritance and instance associations which are also used to record aggregation. Associations are directed arcs, which helps preserve encapsulation.

The analysis model is then converted to a design model expressed in terms of 'blocks' that are implementations of one or more objects. Blocks can be typed as entity, interface and control, and new blocks introduced to represent implementation domain concepts. Blocks are next converted to modules of the target language. These blocks are connected using interaction diagrams. This is an interesting technique, similar to Booch's timing diagrams, which addresses one of the weaknesses in most other methods: their ability to express global dynamics. The next step is to generate annotated source code as the implementation model and then proceed to testing. A big danger with OOSE is the assumption that all sequences can be expressed in use cases and here again in interaction diagrams. For many complex systems and almost all expert systems

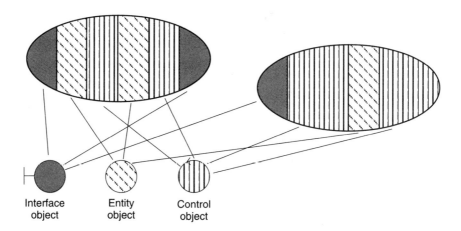

Figure 8.29 Mapping use cases to domain objects in OOSE.

this cannot be done. In fact if it could it would imply a modeless user interface, and Thimbleby (1990) has shown how rare this is in practice and indeed how it may be undesirable in general. However, the interaction diagram is useful and adds to our knowledge of the global dynamics, even if not exhaustively. It also traces back to the use cases of the requirements stage directly. An interaction diagram is shown in Figure 8.30.

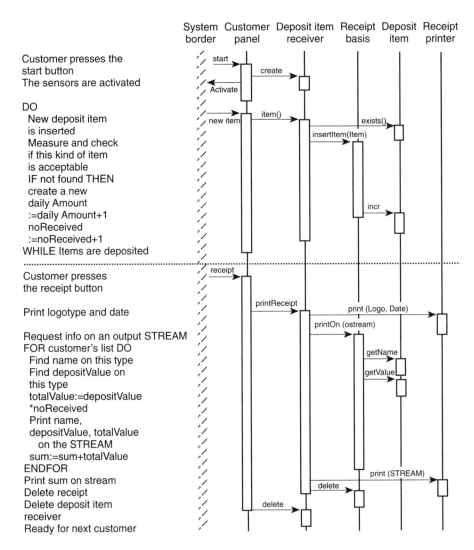

Figure 8.30 An interaction diagram for a use case representing the process of returning items to a recycling machine. (Reprinted from Jacobson (1992) by kind permission of the ACM Press.)

The internal dynamics of blocks are described with Mealy STDs in a similar manner to Booch '91. This has the strength of enabling simple code generators to be written but does not help with objects whose state is not significant to their behaviour and, one suspects, would be unmanageable for objects with very many states.

Objects are organized into subsystems in both the analysis and design models. At the lowest level these are regarded as 'service packages' that are either delivered whole or not at all.

The implementation model converts blocks or modules to specific language constructs (C++ classes, Ada packages, and so on) and consists mainly of annotated source code.

The test model consists of a test specification derived from the use cases and a test result or report. OOSE has adapted many useful ideas from the conventional testing literature (particularly Myers, 1979) to object-orientation. Classes, blocks and subsystems (service packages) are unit tested first and then integration tests are performed on all except classes. Both white- and black-box techniques are applied to unit testing. Testing will be dealt with in Chapter 9.

OOSE can be adapted to both real-time and relational database systems. As with OMT, heuristics are given to assist in translating classes to tables, dealing with inheritance and so on.

OOSE has a good simple notation with only nine node and six link symbols. This is both its strength and its weakness compared to a method like OMT. It is not clear that OOSE supports prototyping as an approach except for the UI, although incremental development is encouraged as is sound risk analysis and the collection of metrics. In the case of incremental development a time-box of between 3 and 6 months is normal and would typically implement between 5 and 20 use cases.

An appendix to Jacobson *et al.* (1992) describes the application of Objectory *per se* to enterprise modelling.

8.2.6 OORASS

OORASS (Object-Oriented Rôle Analysis, Synthesis and Structuring) was developed by Reenskaug (1989, 1990) and others at Taskon AS in Norway and remains proprietary. It covers analysis and design and is unusual in emphasizing the rôles played by objects and addressing several areas in an evolutionary life cycle.

Analysis starts with the discovery of **areas of concern**, which are effectively high-level business functions and the unit for forming coherent subsystems. Next cach area is modelled using collaborating agents and objects which may take on various **rôles**. The rôles are obtained from all the objects with the same position within the structure of an area of concern. Rôles are interpreted in a similar way to the rôles of the agents of Objectory but the idea is extended to the internals of a system rather than restricted to external agents. Different objects may adopt different rôles in different contexts. Rôles have resource requirements (references to servers), competence (things they know), duties and rights (operations). Rôle X may 'know about' rôle Y; that is, contain a reference enabling messages to be sent. These client/server links are refined by **port** symbols as shown in Figure 8.31. The single circle port indicates that rôle X knows about zero to one instances of rôle Y. The double circle port says that Y knows about zero to many instances of X. No port symbol indicates that the rôle at that end of the link does not know about the other rôle. This introduces the multiplicity semantics of entity modelling into usage diagrams and may be useful for high-level requirements capture in a similar way to the manner in which use cases in OOSE are used with inheritance.

Each port symbol may have associated to it a set of operations called a **contract** that defines what the visible rôle has to be able to offer. OORASS is neutral on the notation to be used for object representation.

Analysis is regarded as a top-down, but not hierarchical, process and there are analogies with the layering approach of SOMA in this respect, though rôle models are not decomposed as such. The modelling is complete when the analysts fully understand the area of concern and the model is stable. If not, or if the area does decompose, the analyst should redefine the area and repeat the activity.

Types, or object types, are synthesized from rôles and this defines the visible behaviour of some objects. **Synthesis** creates new objects by inheriting behaviour from simpler ones. Terminologically, OORASS defines classes as the implementation of types and allows type networks to differ from class networks. Multiple inheritance is permitted. Structuring uses a meta-model to specify the run-time behaviour of objects as they are bound to each other during instantiation. This capability is remarkably absent from most other object-oriented analysis methods. More formally, synthesis begins with an area of concern and looks for events and responses. These map onto messages and operations. Candidate objects are identified, though no formal techniques are proposed within OORASS, and then CRC cards are used to identify and assign operations and collaborations. Next, message sequence diagrams are drawn followed by rôle diagrams. Last, the message sequences are used to identify the contracts with constraint and invariants.

The advantage of this approach is that analysts are allowed to construct simple rôle models representing object interaction and then combine them in a uniform way to create larger models. This is claimed to enhance the reusability of the products of analysis and design and is similar in philosophy to the use-case

Figure 8.31 OORASS rôle diagram.

approach of Objectory. It addresses a major weakness of many other methods in specifically addressing the run-time dynamics of systems at the analysis level.

OORASS is supported by a CASE tool called OORAM, also available from Taskon. The method is aimed at building systems emphasizing message passing and distribution.

8.2.7 Desfray – class-relationship method

Desfray (1992) describes the class-relationship method for object-oriented analysis and design currently marketed by a French company, Softeam, in the context of C++ projects for which it is specifically designed. The method is notable for its use of a notation derived from Chen entity-relationship models and therefore potential compatibility with Merise, the structured method widely used in France. It is also notable for paying attention to formal methods through the use of Eiffel-like assertions. A CASE tool, Objecteering, is available and this will generate C++ code.

The class-relationship method is a 'three-pronged' approach in that there are three separate models for each system: an object/entity model, a state-transition model and a dataflow model. As with other three-pronged approaches such as OMT, it is often difficult to see the utility of the dataflow model and models of message passing are richer than DFDs. Be this as it may, this is a respectable way of doing object-oriented analysis and will easily stand comparison with OMT. Some improvements, such as a further refinement of the notion of 'abstract relation', are still possible and the dataflow model specifies the linking of processes and contains a notion of events and their ordering. Softeam is committed to improving this model to move beyond mere dataflows, but this is reported as work that was still in progress in 1992. The entity-relationship and state-transition notations are simpler and more natural and the ability to use assertions addresses a fundamental deficiency of most other methods (the exceptions being BON, Ptech and SOMA). The sequence of techniques is similar to OMT: build the data/class model, find the assertions, use the dynamic model to deal with events and the sequencing of methods and finally use the DFDs if required. The concept of encapsulation is emphasized far more than in OMT. Desfray suggests that the state-transition model could be improved by the introduction of specific states and a mechanism for state synthesis. In terms of what the method covers, the entity-relationship models include full support for inheritance in addition to all familiar data modelling constructs. While relationships can be regarded as objects, Desfray makes an important distinction between classes and relationships. 'Relationships never possess methods. Their unique function is to connect classes.' A little thought shows that this is a valid distinction and one not made in earlier work on the subject; although in contrast OMT specifically permits 'link operations', I have never found a valid use for them. This helps with the distinction between attributes and classes. A relation is a directed link between two classes that allows a class to know about the other class's instances. Bi-directional relationships are discouraged. He also states that 'a relationship is part of the definition of the concept that a class represents'. The next innovation is the introduction of inheritable class invariants corresponding to a limited form of business rules. Classes are regarded as being formed from a composition or aggregation of their attributes, regarded as object types. A general rule in entity modelling is that the only authorized attributes are those that belong to a base class. This helps avoid confusion arising from merging domains or from multiple inheritance: an element is not allowed to be part of two classes in this method. Classes are organized into schemata corresponding to Coad/Yourdon subject areas but in common with that approach these schemata appear to lack the semantics of classes, as messages may not be sent to them. 'A schema is the representation of a domain. It is composed of a group of classes. It constitutes the specification of a particular domain. A class belongs to one and only one schema. An application is thus partitioned into schemata' (p.86). 'The Class-Relationship method permits [mutual] usage relationships (message passing) between classes but forbids them between schemata.' (p.91) – provided, that is, that the classes are part of the same schema. Ameliorating this situation, certain classes may be declared as 'interface classes' for the schema. Schemata also possess invariants defined as the union of all the invariants of contained classes plus 'some general clauses' (p.93). To clarify this, mutual usage is defined as follows: if classes C1 and C2 can use each other's services the relationship is mutual. The latter can only happen within a schema. However, if schema S2 can use S1 then S1 is forbidden from using S2. Desfray gives guidelines for eliminated schema-level mutual relationships. There are three categories of usage relationship between classes:

(1) *Operational usage:* C1 uses C2 only to allow a method of C1 to execute to completion.
(2) *Context usage:* C1 uses C2 as a parameter of a method of C1.
(3) *Characteristic usage:* C1 uses C2 when C1 inherits from C2. Schema S1 has a usage link with another schema S2 when at least one of S1's classes uses at least one of S2's. S1 classes can only access the interface classes of S2 and not its 'body' classes. This brings schema quite close to the 'layers' of SOMA. In addition, schemata may have inheritance links between them.

The most important innovation is the use of assertions, although these are restricted to preconditions and postconditions. Invariance conditions are not mentioned, which only affects the applicability of the method to systems where parallelism is important. Class invariants are supported, however.

8.2.8 OSA

OSA (Object-Oriented Systems Analysis) is an approach developed at Hewlett-Packard and similar to Rumbaugh's OMT in that the method follows the conventional tripartite division of analysis into three separate (but related) activities with a notation for each. It differs in being a slightly simpler notation and in a number of other ways. It is described by Embley *et al.* (1992).

OSA begins with an entity-relationship notation (the object relationship model or ORM) which permits the description of attributes, classification and aggregation structures and data semantics in the form of associations. More general constraints are merely written on the diagrams in note form next to the object they relate to and thus constraints have no relation to inheritance. The claimed advantage of this approach is that it does not constrain the analyst. However, Embley *et al.* (1992) say that 'Since notes do not constrain object classes or relationship sets, an ORM diagram has the same meaning with, or without them.' (*punctuation as original*). Thus, it appears that information is lost by the final model. The complete set of notations available within the ORM is shown in Figure 8.32.

A state transition notation allows the analyst to describe the behaviour of each object. This object behaviour model (OBM) defines the methods for the object, but the ORM may not be extended to include them. Triggers, real-time constraints, exceptions and events are all handled within the OBM and it is here that the similarity with OMT is most apparent, although the emphasis is on modelling the internal behaviour of the objects rather than the interactions between objects. Figure 8.33 illustrates the OBM notations.

Finally, message passing is described in a dataflow-like object interaction model (OIM). The advantage over OMT is that this model deals more evidently with message passing than with atemporal data flows but it could be argued, by those who support such views, that logical dataflows are not catered for at all. In some sense the OIM combines dataflow and state transitions. Figure 8.34 shows the permissible OIM notations.

Good levelling facilities allow the analyst to move between high- and low-level views of a system. Views are classified as *dominant* or *independent* according to whether the high-level view is the name of an existing class or one with separate identity, respectively. Decomposition rules are given for both ORMs and OBMs and it is claimed that the ability to structure all modelling constructs consistently with high-level views is a unique feature of OSA. A lot of this notation seems unnecessarily complex from some points of view, but the ideas are undoubtedly useful. Each of the ORM, OBM and OIM can be levelled in this way and the notation is indicated in Figure 8.35. In Embley *et al.* (1992) detailed diagrams contain a great deal of supplementary annotation of such things as constraints, exceptions and transition priorities.

The OIM notation is perhaps the most useful in so far as it differs from other OOA methods. However, it would not be easily grafted onto other approaches as the analyst is able to link messages to the internal states and transitions of each object. Some of the things one would do in the OMT dynamic model are done here in the OSA approach.

OSA is 'model-driven' in the sense that a model is constructed rather than asking analysts to follow a fixed series of steps – characterized as a 'method-driven' approach. This evidently maps well onto much practice in the OO community. As with Ptech and OMT, it remains unclear how the three independent analysis results are to be combined into a single object model, although some attention is paid to consistency and conformance between diagrams. It is claimed that OSA makes no

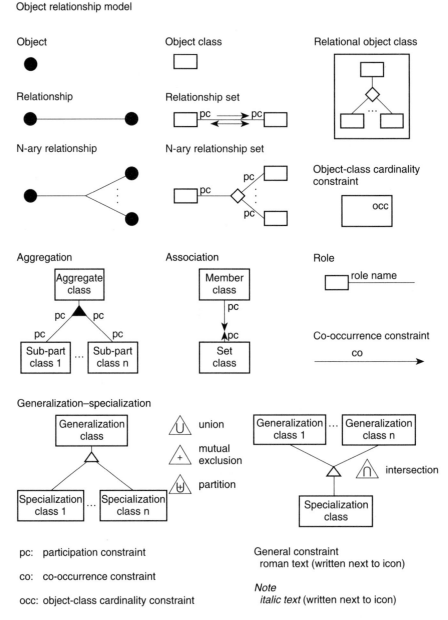

Object relationship model

Object

Object class

Relational object class

Relationship

Relationship set

N-ary relationship

N-ary relationship set

Object-class cardinality constraint

occ

Aggregation

Association

Role

role name

Co-occurrence constraint

co

Generalization–specialization

Generalization class

∪ union

+ mutual exclusion

⊎ partition

Generalization class 1 ... Generalization class n

∩ intersection

Specialization class 1 ... Specialization class n

Specialization class

pc: participation constraint

co: co-occurrence constraint

occ: object-class cardinality constraint

General constraint
roman text (written next to icon)

Note
italic text (written next to icon)

Figure 8.32 OSA object relationship model. (Adapted from Embley *et al.* (1992))

distinction between classes and attributes and that this helps enforce consistency. This is a hard claim to accept given the immense philosophical significance of the object/attribute problem. OSA permits multiple inheritance notationally but, in common with Coad/Yourdon, omits any treatment of conflict resolution.

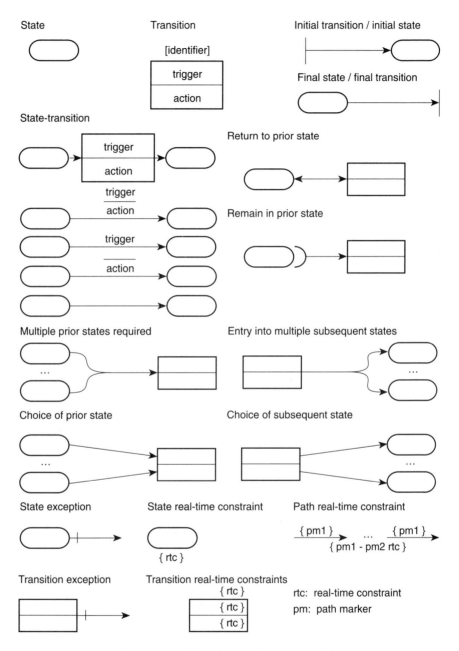

Figure 8.33 OSA object behaviour model.

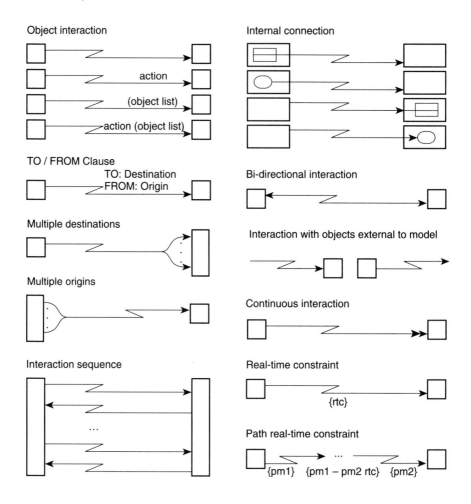

Figure 8.34 OSA object interaction model.

The appendix to Embley *et al.* (1992) sets out a logical formalism for the ORM component of OSA. A small worry is that presenting an object-oriented model in a first-order language seems to throw away one of the chief simplicities of object-orientation: the ability to express complex structures directly in higher-order terms.

OSA is a reasonably complete ternary method which bears comparison with OMT and has, in my view, a slightly better notation. However, the popularity of OMT and the lack of OSA CASE tools may preclude it from great success.

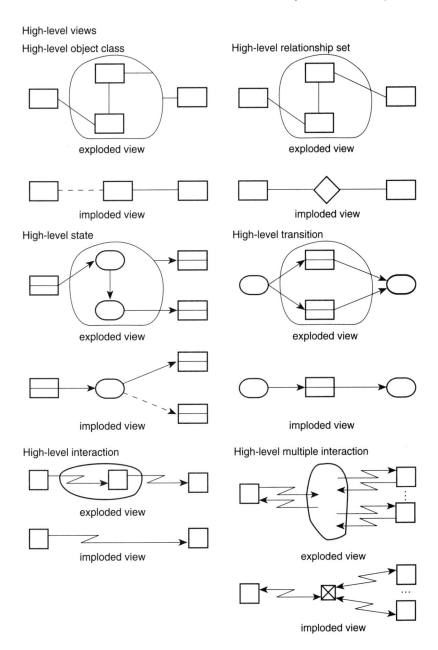

Figure 8.35 Levelling in OSA.

8.2.9 Systems Engineering OO

LBMS Systems Engineering OO or SEOO is the method supported by the UK company LBMS. It has four aspects:

(1) Work breakdown structures and techniques
(2) A shared object modelling method
(3) Specific GUI design techniques
(4) Relational database linkages

A method is viewed as a process model plus techniques with their rules and end products. The proposed life cycle is a standard rapid-development one and emphasis is placed on ending stages with something executable that can be evaluated by users.

One of the great advantages of a conventional database management system is the separation of processes and data which gives a notion of data independence and benefits of flexibility and insulation from change, because the interface to shared data is stable. The data model is to be regarded as a model of the statics of the application. With object-orientation, processes and data are integrated. Does this mean that you have to abandon the benefits of data independence? Already in client/server relational databases we have seen a step in the same direction, with database triggers and integrity rules stored in the server with the data. With an object-oriented approach to data management it therefore seems reasonable to adopt the view that there are two kinds of object, which I call **domain objects** and **application objects**. Domain objects represent those aspects of the system that are relatively stable or generic (in supplying services to many applications). Application objects are those which can be expected to vary from installation to installation or from time to time quite rapidly. This approach resurrects the notion of data independence in an enhanced, object-oriented form. A conventional data model is a view of the domain objects, which latter also include constraints, rules and dynamics (state transitions, and so on). The goal is to make the interface to this part of the model as stable as possible. The domain objects form the shared object model. Most interaction between components is via this model and for this reason SEOO designates them **shared objects**.

Cameron (1992) argues that in structured methods for data processing systems data modelling has proved to be a highly effective technique for analysis and design. However, much of the semantic richness available to the analyst is lost in the representation. Further, he claims that in rejecting process–data separation many object-oriented analysis approaches lose the benefits of data modelling, and he proposes the shared object modelling technique as a direct successor to data modelling. The technique is intended to be object-oriented yet retain the advantages of data modelling, and be well suited to commercial data processing applications.

Data modelling is successful because:

■ Data analysis is used as a modelling tool. Analysts use data models as a basis for understanding functionality. The data model is stable relative to the information requirement that it supports.

- Processing components, either whole subsystems or individual transactions, interact via the shared data described by the data model and held in the database. To isolate and stabilize most of the important system interfaces so early is a huge benefit.
- There is a direct route from a data model to a preliminary database design.

On this view, data modelling should be generalized to a form of object modelling and the split between persistent data and all processing replaced by a split between shared objects and the other objects. Object-orientation provides a more powerful modelling medium than data. The shared objects similarly form the important interfaces between subsystems. There is still a direct route, albeit slightly longer, from shared object model to database design.

It is the instances (analogously the data) that are shared, not just the classes (analogously the data definitions). Sharing, possibly across many systems, imposes a discipline on the range of methods a shared object should support. Processing specific to a particular application should be excluded. Otherwise the class definition of widely used objects, for example Customers, would be continually under review as applications are added and modified. Creating separate subtypes of Customer for each application does not help, because it is the individual objects that are shared, and they cannot change their type for each application.

Application-specific functionality is modelled outside the shared object model, in terms of other objects (for example, user interface objects) which use services provided by shared objects.

One benefit of a system developed around a shared object model is that applications can be relatively independent, in exactly the way that several programs can independently interact with a database. One application can be extended with new or modified objects, or have objects removed, with minimal effect on other applications, provided that the shared object interfaces are not changed.

Few of the widely known object-oriented analysis and design methods make or place importance on the distinction between shared and other objects. Yet it seems a prerequisite for the success of an object-oriented analysis method in business computing.

The diagram in Figure 8.36 describes the shared object modelling technique in more detail. The high level of integration is important. The individual parts have equivalents in most structured methods. A data model is equivalent to a view of the object model. The dynamic behaviour of the objects is another useful view of the object model. These descriptions are developed as views of an integrated whole rather than as separate models to be integrated later, if at all. This integration distinguishes shared object modelling from structured methods, and even to an extent from, say, the OMT approach.

GUI modelling is regarded as a special kind of analysis activity. Context diagrams and something rather similar to use cases are used to define tasks and output. Further design principles (such as IBM's CUA, 1991a; 1991b) are applied. The window design is separated from user object design, resulting in a three-layer model in which there are windows using the services of user objects in the next layer that in turn use the services of shared objects.

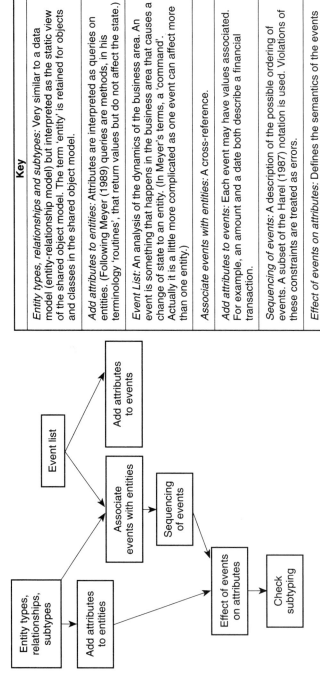

Key

Entity types, relationships and subtypes: Very similar to a data model (entity-relationship model) but interpreted as the static view of the shared object model. The term 'entity' is retained for objects and classes in the shared object model.

Add attributes to entities: Attributes are interpreted as queries on entities. (Following Meyer (1989) queries are methods, in his terminology 'routines', that return values but do not affect the state.)

Event List: An analysis of the dynamics of the business area. An event is something that happens in the business area that causes a change of state to an entity. (In Meyer's terms, a 'command'. Actually it is a little more complicated as one event can affect more than one entity.)

Associate events with entities: A cross-reference.

Add attributes to events: Each event may have values associated. For example, an amount and a date both describe a financial transaction.

Sequencing of events: A description of the possible ordering of events. A subset of the Harel (1987) notation is used. Violations of these constraints are treated as errors.

Effect of events on attributes: Defines the semantics of the events (commands) by specifying their effect on the attributes (queries). This is usually done informally and often selectively, because most of the effects are obvious.

Check subtyping: Check that the substitutability rule for subtyping is obeyed by the events and the sequencing constraints. Review the type hierarchy in the shared object model. (Substitutability means that a client of objects of type A should be satisfied with objects of a subtype of A.)

Figure 8.36 Shared object modelling.

For relational database interfaces a mechanism akin to database views is used to overcome the problems associated with joins: 'many short-lived objects implement one long-lived object'.

Systems Engineering OO is a hybrid method which is important for its contribution of a layered, shared object model and emphasis on evolutionary migration from existing technologies.

8.2.10 Texel

Texel is an object-oriented analysis and design method with strong roots in the Ada development world, although it is claimed that C++ developments can also be supported and inheritance is not neglected as in HOOD. The method is supported by P.P. Texel and Co. of New Jersey and the originator Putnam Texel. The company also provide training and can call on a large number of case-studies. Although most of these are military or real-time applications it is claimed that MIS applications are equally well supported.

The activities within Texel are as follows.

First, nominate candidate object types (called object classes), attributes, and so on. This may take as input a written specification, system documents (such as DFDs and data dictionaries) or domain-expert interviews. Every noun, verb, and so on is written down uncritically at this stage. No specific interviewing or object identification techniques are recommended. 'Disposition keys' are added to each phrase showing whether it is thought that the entry is a class, attribute, duplicate, descendant, process and so on. This process converts the 'candidate object class list' to the 'disposition list'. The next product is the 'baseline object class list' (BOCL) which represents the likely list of classes at this stage. Traceability is emphasized throughout. From the BOCL, an ER diagram similar to a Shlaer/Mellor information structure diagram (entity model) is produced showing associations but not aggregation. The ER notation is semantically incomplete showing multiplicity and modality but not exclusivity or partitioning. The diagram is refined by adding attributes, aggregation, trace correlations and system boundaries. There are no specific techniques for class or attribute placement (see Monarchi and Puhr, 1991). Finite state machines are used for behaviour placement later; that is, after the production of the overview object class analysis diagram (OOCAD) and the derivative object class analysis diagram (OCAD). Figures 8.37(a) and 8.37(b) illustrate the OOCAD and OCAD for a sealed environment monitor (SEM). Two documents, the object class specification (OCSD) and the relationship specification (RSD), are then produced, ending the static phase of analysis. The first documents the classes of the OCAD. The second documents the links in this diagram descriptively. These are partially illustrated in Figures 8.38 and 8.39 using the same example of a SEM.

Phase I of the Texel method is illustrated schematically in Figure 8.40. Phase II of analysis results in state models for each class. This activity takes a similar approach to that of Shlaer and Mellor (1991). The purpose is to identify events and methods for each object. This of course does not help much for objects without

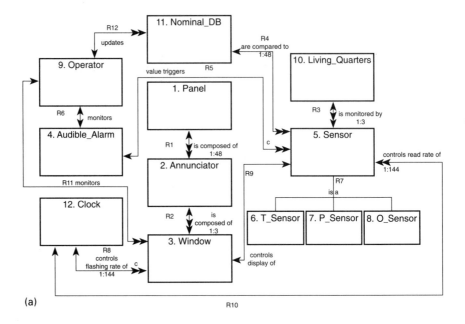

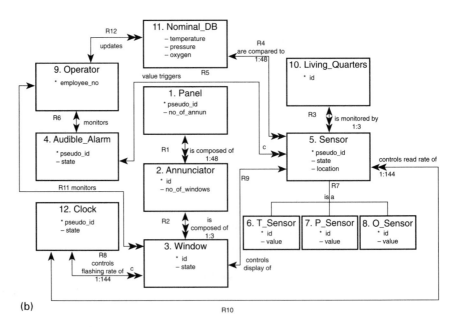

Figure 8.37 (a) OOCAD diagram for a sealed environment monitor; **(b)** corresponding OCAD diagram.

---

4. Audible_Alarm

Audible_Alarm (Pseudo_Id,State)
Description: The Audible_Alarm is a device that will notify the HCC Operator when the value of one of the environmental conditions deviates from the normal value by 3% or more.

There is only one Audible_Alarm associated with the HCC SEM.

The Audible_Alarm is turned on by the SEM and turned off by the Operator.

4.1 Audible_Alarm.Pseudo_ID

Description: ......

Figure 8.38 Part of an OCSD – Audible_Alarm.

significant state, which occur commonly in business models, which is one of the reasons why methods such as Fusion eschew state models. The Texel solution is to produce a bogus state for the offending objects, though in practice it is admitted that they may be just written down. One of the best features of the method is that the object class communication model (OCCM) produced at this stage permits message and event flow to be analysed. A distinction is thus made between internal events (identified first) and external events. Messages are shown explicitly, however, so that the notation may not scale up to really complex commercial systems. Figure 8.41 shows the OCCM for the SEM example.

The final analysis step is the production of state models for each class as illustrated in Figure 8.42(a). Figure 8.42(b) shows just how complex these state models can become even for straightforward things like windows.

R5.   Sensor (TRIGGERS) Audible_Alarm (Mc:1)
      Audible_Alarm (IS TRIGGERED BY) Sensor

      The severity of the deviation between the actual value read by a sensor and its counterpart in the Nominal_DB dictates whether or not the alarm should sound.

      Condition: If the deviation between the value read by a Sensor and the nominal value in the Nominal_DB is 3% or higher then, and only then, is the Audible_Alarm sounded.

R6.   Operators (MONITORS) Audible_Alarm (1:1)
      ......

Figure 8.39 Part of an RSD.

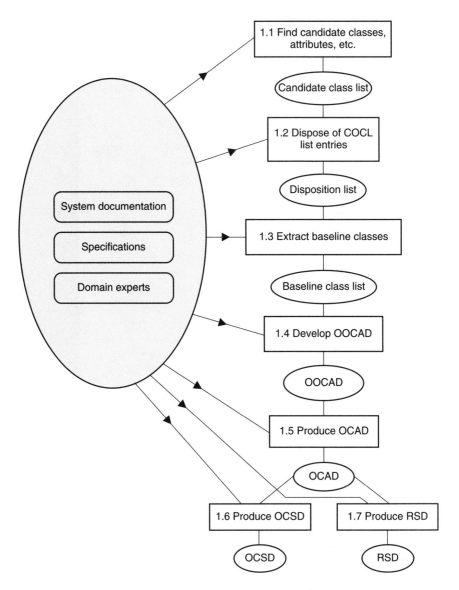

Figure 8.40 Texel analysis process, Phase I.

Multiple inheritance is forbidden. Complex constraints and rules are not representable non-procedurally and assertions are not part of the design stage.

Design proceeds via an informal strategy similar to that of Booch. Classes that will become the objects (Ada packages) of the design are defined and linked by an outline main algorithm. Inheritance is flattened away using variant-discriminated record types in preference to generics. Ada structure charts conceptually

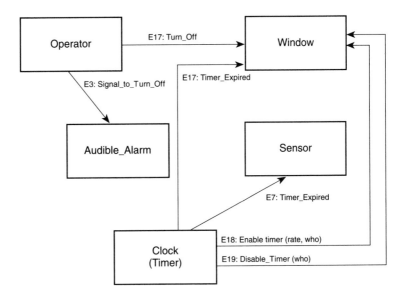

Figure 8.41 Example OCCM.

similar to those of Buhr are used to represent the design graphically and then an Ada PDL is produced or generated.

Throughout the process great emphasis is placed on producing traceability matrices linking requirements to analysis and design products. I find this disturbing because the whole point of object-oriented analysis and design is surely that traceability is incremental and traces should be reconstructed dynamically by linked steps.

Texel is classified as a ternary modelling system with separate ER, STD and message flow models. Its real-time roots are evidenced by the centrality of the use of STDs where normally it is not permitted to define operations prior to obtaining a state model. It is closely related to the Shlaer/Mellor approach and draws on Booch. Like most methods, it does not cover all aspects of the OMG reference

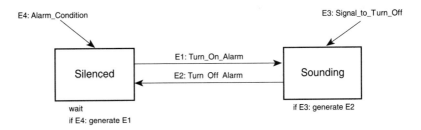

Figure 8.42 (a) Texel state model for Audible_Alarm; **(b)** Texel state model for Window.

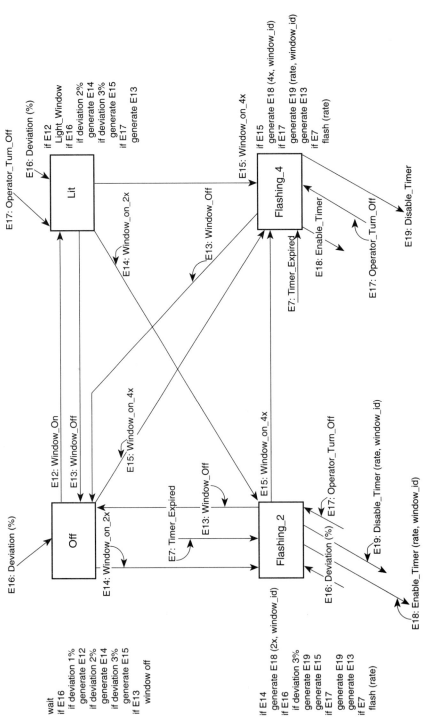

Figure 8.42 (b)

model and there is nothing on object identification, component management, metrics or testing – except for the use of CRUD-like requirement/object matrices that are further annotated with events. Group and view concepts are very limited except for a concept similar to Coad's Subjects. The process model is latent and no specific iteration or prototyping management techniques are visible in the documentation.

The main problem with this method is that it is difficult to see how it would be useful in designing for a language dissimilar to Ada such as Smalltalk, Eiffel or an object-oriented 4GL[1]. The second problem applies to business systems, where one suspects that methods deriving from domains such as telecommunications, real-time, military and the like are less suitable than those derived from the semantic data modelling tradition. Clearly this is still a contentious point, but I would lump Texel with Shlaer/Mellor, Booch, Objectory and, to a lesser extent, OMT, and oppose it to CRC, Coad/Yourdon, Fusion, Ptech and SOMA. The SOMA position is that state models are fine when they help but are a subsidiary tool only. The difficult and important thing is to get hold of the methods and find a way to represent global system dynamics.

Texel is provided with CASE tool support in the form of a single user tool called Texel-SF and implemented in the VSF meta-CASE system.

8.2.11 BON – Nerson

BON (Better Object Notation) is described in Nerson (1992) and is one of very few methods to take the importance of business rules and class invariants seriously. It derives from the Eiffel school of thought and therefore the inclusion of assertions is less surprising. It was developed under European ESPRIT II funding and is influenced by Booch, Coad/Yourdon, Page-Jones and Constantine, Shlaer/Mellor, OMT, OOSD, CRC and work on object-oriented Z (Duke *et al.,* 1991), making BON a true hybrid. Emphasis is placed on such issues as the continuity of analysis and design, scalability, reversibility, traceability, static and dynamic models and component management. The activities within BON are:

(1) *Define the system boundary* This involves identifying external events.
(2) *Identify candidate classes* BON classes are defined by attributes, operations, constraints and relationships with other classes. No specific object identification techniques are included.
(3) *Group classes into clusters* Clusters are subsystems that have no clear semantics but are definitely not regarded as objects. They are used to group cohesive sets of classes.
(4) *Define candidate classes in terms of questions, commands and constraints* Analysts must ask: 'What data can be asked for?' Questions become

---

[1] C++ can be written in an Ada-like way but this is not necessarily the right way. As the saying goes, you can write FORTRAN in any language.

attributes or Eiffel 'functions'. Commands are operations and constraints are either assertions or class invariants. Class invariants may be thought of as rules and all constraints as describing the knowledge maintained by the objects. Analysts must ask whether objects behave similarly to tease out classification structures. Associations are recorded in a rather odd textual manner.

(5) *Define the behaviour of each class in terms of events, object communication protocols and object creation charts*   Events can be external or internal. Internal events are usually time related and lead to the discovery of communication protocols and assertions related to global system control. The notation for describing classes includes special symbols for depicting inward and outbound data flows. Pre- and postconditions and class invariants are written in a formal logic notation. An example class invariant stating that corporate customers should not be given weekend discounts is expressed as:

client.is_corporate $\Rightarrow \forall$ l∈documents • ¬l.discount.weekend_rate

which could perhaps be more readily expressed in structured English. Object creation charts show which classes create instances of other classes.

(6) *Define class features, invariants and contractual relationships*   Class features may correspond to internal events. Static and dynamic relationships are shown on separate charts using an unusual and fairly idiosyncratic notation.

(7) *Refine the class descriptions*   Here reuse opportunities are sought.

(8) *Develop classification structures.*

(9) *Complete and review the architecture.*

Class indexing is used to aid future retrieval from libraries using a standard header template. BON has several strengths not found in many other methods such as the emphasis on component management and rules. However, I find the notation unappealing. It will be of great interest, however, to Eiffel developers since it supports that language's constructs directly while remaining language-independent. BON is close in spirit to SOMA, described in the next section. A CASE environment based on a PCTE-compliant repository and called EiffelCase is under development using Eiffel. There are two tools, a drawing tool and a component management system. Some of the BON notation is illustrated in Figure 8.43.

8.2.12 Fusion – Coleman

The Fusion Method (Coleman and Hayes, 1991; Coleman *et al.,* 1994) is a hybrid method developed by a team led by Derek Coleman at Hewlett-Packard Laboratories in the UK. HP did a survey of methods in use within HP and generally extant in 1990, resulting in a set of requirements for an object-oriented analysis and design method. The chief requirement identified was for a model of usage with a simple notation. No method met all HP's needs. OMT gives a process for analysis but only heuristics for design. Thus Fusion was constructed by borrowing ideas from other methods. It is still being developed in this way. The main influences have been OMT's notation, CRC's interaction modelling, ideas from Booch '91 on

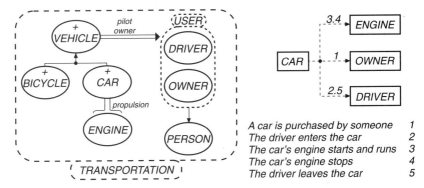

A car is purchased by someone   1
The driver enters the car   2
The car's engine starts and runs   3
The car's engine stops   4
The driver leaves the car   5

Static model (left side):
- Clusters are represented with rounded corner rectangles drawn with dashed lines and are tagged with a name.
- Classes are represented as a name inside an ellipse, with optional annotations: deferred classes are topped with a star sign, non-deferred descendant classes are topped with a plus sign, reused classes have an underlined name.
- Inheritance relationships are represented with a single line ending in an arrowhead oriented from the descendant to the parent. Client–supplier relationships are represented by a double line ending in an arrowhead in case of association and with an open curly bracket in case of aggregation. The double line may be tagged with class feature names involved in the client–supplier relationship. Relationships are defined between classes and can be extended to clusters.

Dynamic model (right side):
- Objects are represented inside rectangles. A shadowed rectangle denotes multiple instances.
- Communication protocols are represented with dash lines, labelled with numbers. These numbers are then referred to in commented scenarios.

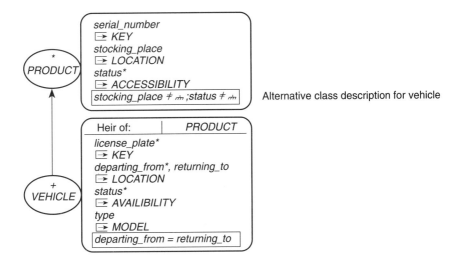

Alternative class description for vehicle

Figure 8.43 (a) Fragments of the BON notation.

Figure 8.43 (b) Class descriptions for a car rental system.

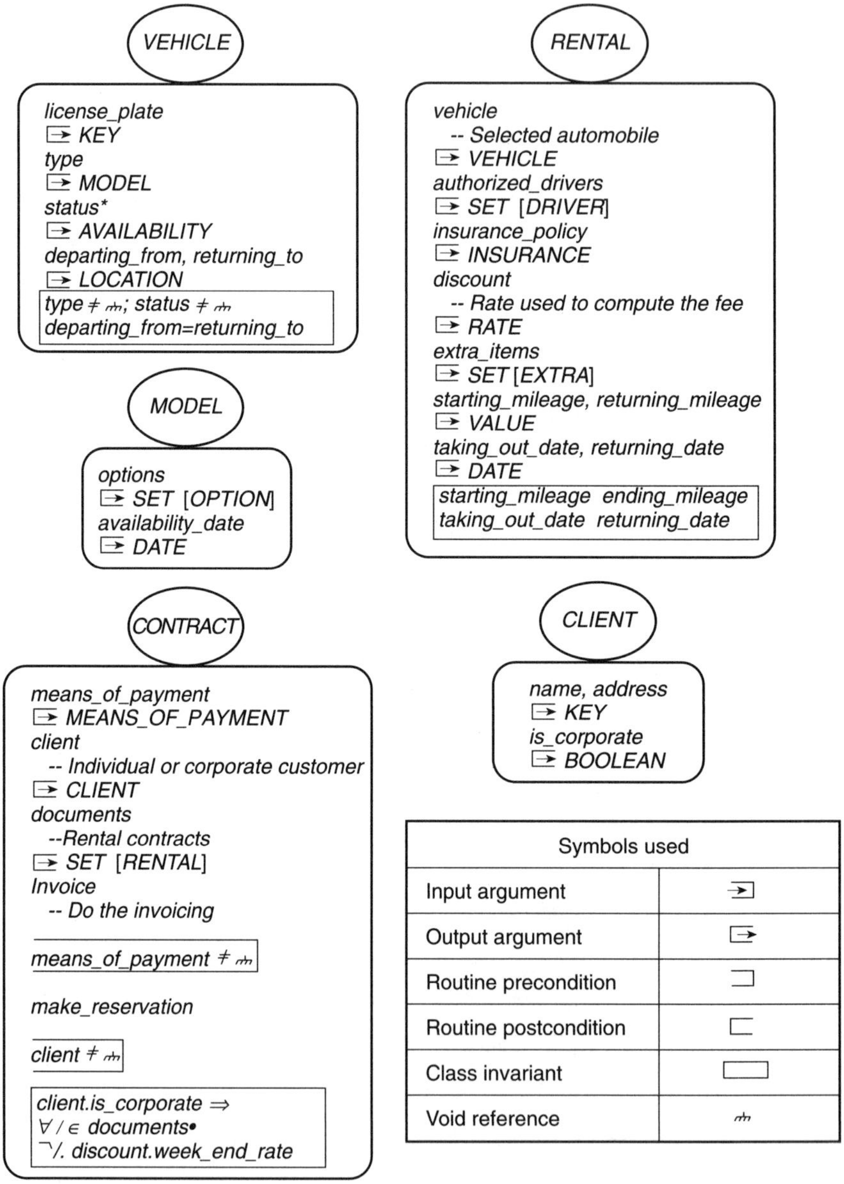

VEHICLE

license_plate
  ⇨ KEY
type
  ⇨ MODEL
status*
  ⇨ AVAILABILITY
departing_from, returning_to
  ⇨ LOCATION
type ≠ ⌙; status ≠ ⌙
departing_from=returning_to

MODEL

options
  ⇨ SET [OPTION]
availability_date
  ⇨ DATE

RENTAL

vehicle
  -- Selected automobile
  ⇨ VEHICLE
authorized_drivers
  ⇨ SET [DRIVER]
insurance_policy
  ⇨ INSURANCE
discount
  -- Rate used to compute the fee
  ⇨ RATE
extra_items
  ⇨ SET [EXTRA]
starting_mileage, returning_mileage
  ⇨ VALUE
taking_out_date, returning_date
  ⇨ DATE
starting_mileage ending_mileage
taking_out_date returning_date

CONTRACT

means_of_payment
  ⇨ MEANS_OF_PAYMENT
client
  -- Individual or corporate customer
  ⇨ CLIENT
documents
  --Rental contracts
  ⇨ SET [RENTAL]
Invoice
  -- Do the invoicing

means_of_payment ≠ ⌙

make_reservation

client ≠ ⌙

client.is_corporate ⇒
∀ / ∈ documents•
⌐/. discount.week_end_rate

CLIENT

name, address
  ⇨ KEY
is_corporate
  ⇨ BOOLEAN

Symbols used	
Input argument	⇥
Output argument	⇨
Routine precondition	⊐
Routine postcondition	⊏
Class invariant	▭
Void reference	⌙

visibility and some ideas from the Z and VDM schools of formal methods. The use case idea from Objectory is now being incorporated too. The Fusion process model is illustrated in Figure 8.44.

The dynamic model of OMT (and that of other methods such as Shlaer/Mellor) was not found to be useful in practice and is not used. This is an encouraging if remarkable finding compared to the conventional wisdom, which makes me suspect that excessive emphasis on state models is the result of telecomms and real-time application backgrounds. Dataflow diagrams are not used for the functional model because they are too operational. Pre- and postconditions are used instead though I have always found that these are very hard for users to understand. Methods are not introduced until the design stage. Concurrency is not supported and so there are no invariance conditions in the method yet. Because these assertions are not attached to classes they cannot be inherited.

One tricky problem for some practitioners of object-oriented analysis is to know when to stop doing analysis. It is claimed that Fusion helps with this problem. Visibility is introduced at design time. Interactions define which objects

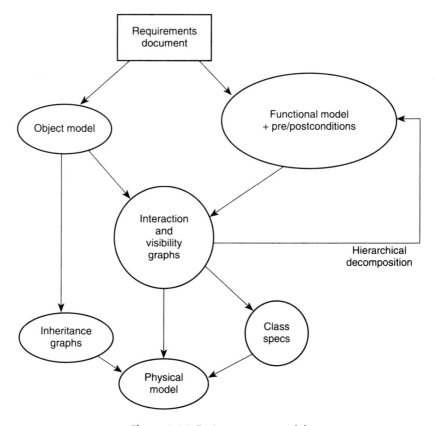

Figure 8.44 Fusion process model.

need which methods – again at design time. CRC is used for the interaction model although contracts are not used. This can be done in rôle play sessions.

8.2.13 Other methods

OBA or Object Behaviour Analysis is described by Rubin and Goldberg (1992). OBA is a method that starts by eliciting scripts from interviews or documents (which are similar to the use cases of Objectory) and developing a context model. Next, the participants and their responsibilities are identified and initiators distinguished. Modified CRC cards are used to record the details of objects and discover classification and usage structures and other associations, though aggregation is not emphasized. Finally Harel state transition models are developed for each object. OBA has more to say about requirements capture than most other methods but is not particularly remarkable in other areas. The SOMA approach to requirements capture outlined in Chapter 9 incorporates some of these ideas.

Frame-Object Analysis or FOA (Andleigh and Gretzinger, 1992) is a method deriving from conceptual modelling in advanced database and artificial intelligence work and emphasizes the use of semantic nets. It covers quite a lot of the life cycle from requirements to testing and is unusual in emphasizing business rules. In this method a frame is a major component of an information system identified with a semantic net consisting of objects and associations. Effectively frames are subsystems or layers and are collections of objects. Each object has identity, attributes and operations. Frame diagrams are used to depict containment, classification, associations, dataflow, sequencing and state transitions and it is far from clear how one is to avoid confusing classification and composition or state transitions with dataflow. The strength of FOA is its emphasis on business rules and the use of database constraints and triggers to represent them, though there is little additional notational support for this. The method is most suitable for database system construction where C++ is to be used as the development language and an advanced relational system as the storage manager.

CGI Yourdon is the name often given to a modern version of the original DFD-centred Yourdon methods family that is now maintained by CGI. They have proposed an object-oriented extension to the Yourdon structured methods (Marden, 1990) and offer training in it. A very similar approach is described by Sully (1993). The approach relies heavily on the use of DFD notation to describe the internal behaviour of objects. The approach derives objects from DFDs, ERDs or STDs if such conventional models have been built. This is useful for people already steeped in the Yourdon philosophy but strange in that most other object-oriented methods play down the significance of dataflow and no other method uses dataflow to record the description of objects themselves. The external view of an object is represented with a Gradygram notation showing the identity of the object and its visible operations. Inheritance and associations are represented with Chen-style diagrams and usage (object dependency) diagrams are also drawn where appropriate, with a style similar to HOOD seniority diagrams. Internally, the structure of the object is represented as a traditional DFD, with dotted lines showing control flows. Where there are control transformations, these are represented using STDs, decision tables or state tables. In contrast with most well known OOA methods, this does help distinguish objects with complex significant states but I am not convinced that the emphasis on DFDs is otherwise very helpful. Other methods tend to use DFDs only for context modelling and even then I have found it necessary to expand the concept of a dataflow to include a notion of expected return values (see Chapter 9).

Page-Jones and Weiss (1989) developed the Synthesis approach to OOA/D. More recently Page-Jones, Constantine and Weiss (1990) have introduced what they call a **Uniform Object Notation** in the context of a general approach to object-oriented analysis and design, with much in common with conventional software engineering practice. The notation is similar to several other object-oriented analysis and design notations discussed in this book with clear influences from Booch and Structured Design. Even more recently Page-Jones (1992) has generalized Constantine's classic notion that good design minimizes coupling and maximizes cohesion by defining connascence[2] and three different kinds of encapsulation. Level 0 encapsulation represents the idea that a line of code encapsulates a certain abstraction. Level 1 is the encapsulation of procedures into modules and level 2 is the encapsulation of object-oriented programming. Two elements of a system are connascent if they share the same history and future or, more exactly, if changes to one may necessitate changes to the other. Good design should eliminate unnecessary connascence, minimize connascence across encapsulation boundaries and maximize it within them. For level 0 and level 1 encapsulation this reduces to the principle of coupling and cohesion. As pointed out in Chapter 1 inheritance compromises reuse. The connascence principle tells us that inheritance should be restricted to visible features or that there should be two separate hierarchies for inheriting the implementation and the interface as suggested in Chapter 3. It would also discourage the use of friends in C++. Page-Jones classifies several kinds of connascence as name, type, value, position, algorithm, meaning and polymorphism. Polymorphism connascence is particularly interesting for object-oriented design and is closely related to the problems of non-monotonic logic. For example, if FLY is an operation of BIRD and PENGUIN is a subclass of BIRD then FLY may sometimes fail and sometimes succeed. This causes maintenance problems should the system be changed. I think that rules, as described in the next section, may be used to avoid this problem, as may the fuzzification of objects and inheritance discussed in Appendix I. The principle of connascence is a profound contribution and should be adopted by every object-oriented designer.

Henderson-Sellers gives his name to the method outlined in his (1992) book and other publications. The notation is influenced by the Uniform Object Notation referred to in the previous paragraph but is simpler. The method is a hybrid method for object-oriented analysis based on earlier published work from several authors and emphasizes the need to incorporate existing structured methods where possible. I think this is indicative of a current trend towards such hybrid methods. Like most

---

[2] Literally, connascence means being 'born together'.

other methods there is scant help on identifying objects. Notation is provided for all the important structural features of an object-oriented system. Rules are not supported. The most important new contribution is the 'fountain' life-cycle model, wherein deliverables bubble up and shower down on you rather than spinning out of the vortex of a spiral model. Showing classification and other associations on the same diagram, as other methods do, is (correctly) discouraged. The case-studies described in Henderson-Sellers (1992) confused me a little. For example, a bibliography object is decomposed into objects with names like 'sort' and 'quit' which the text had taught me to think of as methods if I understood it correctly. The only time I would reason otherwise is if I were trying to reuse components from an existing function library. The method includes guidelines for implementation in various object-oriented languages. This method has recently been extended and refined as MOSES.

MOSES (Henderson-Sellers and Edwards, 1994) stands for Methodology for Object-Oriented Software Engineering of Systems and is based on an extension of the Uniform Object Notation, though it is claimed that other notations are permissible. It provides a comprehensive life-cycle model and emphasizes the continuum of representation, project management guidelines and extensibility. The fountain model is incorporated in this work.

ADM3 (Firesmith, 1993) is an extension of an earlier Ada-oriented method, ASTS, with an emphasis on real-time system development. It consists of notations for state modelling, control modelling and time modelling and uses ideas from semantic networks. It is a complex ternary method reminiscent in some respects of both Booch '91 and OMT.

Berard (1993) offers a reasonably comprehensive object-oriented life-cycle model reminiscent in some respects of MOSES. Again a semantic net influence is present in the form of Berard's object and class specifications. These consist of a 'precise and concise description' (a sort of executive summary for the object), various graphical representations including semantic networks and state transition diagrams, lists of required and suffered operations, constants and exceptions. The notation is detailed and more in tune with the mind-set of a designer than that of an analyst in my opinion. There is no provision for rules.

Syntropy is a proprietary method developed by Steve Cook, John Daniels and their colleagues at Object Designers Limited, though I understand it may be published soon. The method claims to be notation-independent but uses the popular OMT notation by default. The emphasis is on a behaviour-oriented approach, making much of the notion of behavioural specialization (classification). Some of the mechanisms of Syntropy are taken from Booch '91 and we may safely classify the method as a hybrid.

Other methods abound. COOSD is method developed by Aksit who are based at the University of Twente in Holland. It is based on composition in the style of the functional data model. The key novel ideas are those of rôle participation and abstract communication types. ORCA (OO Requirements Capture and Analysis) uses Frameworks and DONT diagrams. Space does not permit an exhaustive coverage of these ideas, but it is certain the emerging hybrid methods will pick up and synthesize them as the field matures. Other methods that cannot be covered in detail include ALEX-OBJ, MOOD, OSDL, OSMOSYS and SYS_P_O.Several other methods are mentioned in the bibliographical notes below. At present there are probably well over 60 more or less complete object-oriented methods in existence. This is clearly an unsustainable situation, especially as none of them is complete and many merely represent opinions on what is important at various points in the life cycle. At present users will have to synthesize a complete method from fragments of the published ones. The method described in the next section is the result of just such a synthesis, arrived at from using some of the methods described in this book on projects.

8.3 SOMA – A semantically rich method for object-oriented analysis

Among the thirteen or more methods described so far there is considerable variation. They range from the complex and difficult notations of OMT, Ptech and Shlaer/Mellor to the simpler ones of CRC and Coad/Yourdon, from an emphasis on process to an emphasis on representation and from language dependence to the giddiest heights of abstraction. We have also looked at some hybrids. None of these methods is complete in the sense that all issues of the software development life cycle are addressed or that every conceivable system can be easily described.

This section presents an approach which started life as an extension of the method and notation advocated by Coad and Yourdon but which now incorporates so many ideas from other object-oriented analysis and design methods that the connexion with Coad/Yourdon is quite tenuous. In principle other base notations, such as that of OMT, could be extended with SOMA constructs – making SOMA more of a methods *filter* than a method. It also incorporates ideas and techniques from the fields of artificial intelligence and semantic data modelling. It is intended to be particularly suitable for commercial systems development. This chapter covers the representational side of SOMA. Its life-cycle model is briefly described in Chapter 9. Graham (1994) offers a more rigorous treatment of SOMA than is appropriate in this survey.

SOMA is intended to be a semantically rich method for object-oriented analysis. In its basic form, described here, it is intended to retain the simplicity of notation of the Coad/Yourdon method but add extra activities and refine the semantics of subjects (called layers in SOMA). It also modifies the notation to bring it into conformity with Chen-style entity-relationship modelling conventions. Like Coad/Yourdon, classification and composition structures are supported along with general associations. Pre-, post- and invariance conditions are also supported. Lastly, it adds expert-system-style rules to objects to enhance the semantic richness of the analysis models in all cases and to help model the analysis of advanced database and knowledge-based systems. At design time these rules are converted to logical assertions. SOMA is unique in providing support for fuzzy objects and inheritance, as described in Appendix I.

The seven activities within SOMA are as follows:

- Identify layers.
- Identify objects.
- Identify usage, classification and composition structures.
- Define data semantics and associations.
- Add attributes to objects.
- Add operations to objects.
- Add the declarative semantics of the objects (rule-sets).

First, let us establish some notational points. Objects in SOMA are displayed in the form shown in Figure 8.45(a). If the icon has square corners it represents an instance, if round a class. Thus an object has an identifier and three lists: attribute names, method names and rule names. Each of these has additional information attached as we shall see.

Surrounding a class icon with a box as in Figure 8.45(b) says that the class is not an abstract class, in the same manner as Coad's grey outlines. In other words the class may have concrete instances that might not be classes. This also tells us that any subclasses that there are do not form an exhaustive list of possible subclasses.

The explicit treatment of attributes violates the principle of information hiding. However, as we have seen, the complexity of the data structures present in most commercial systems, compared to simple programming abstractions like windows or stacks, leads to the need to make attributes explicit and visible. Thus in this method we retain the attributes window. To retain some object-oriented purity, we regard each attribute in this window as a shorthand for two standard methods. For example, the attribute Name: is short for the methods GetName and PutName. Special versions of these methods may be included in the methods window, in which case they override the standard methods. Each method is regarded as containing standard security checks, which may be overridden. Validation conditions must be specified for each attribute.

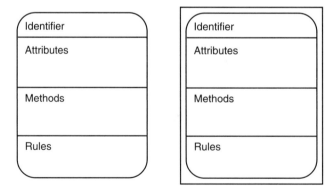

Figure 8.45 (a) A SOMA class; (b) A SOMA class with instances.

Thus, an object icon must display, at least, its identity, attribute names and method names. Rules do not always exist. Each part of the icon is called a window. The same icon may be used for classes or instances, but the identity window must make the distinction clear by the name (perhaps brick-12) or by appending the letter I in square brackets. I use the convention that rounded corners denote classes while sharp ones designate instances.

The operation name may contain – along with the details of the method's function, parameters and type information – invariance, pre- and post-conditions that must hold when the method is running, fires and terminates respectively. In this way, a part of the control structure is encapsulated in the object's methods.

8.3.1 Layers

Layers in SOMA are not just a convenient way to decompose the problem domain as in most other methods: they are bona fide objects in their own right, with the semantics of objects. Layers differ from other objects in two ways: (a) they exist at the top of a composition structure; (b) each of their methods must be implemented by a method of some object within that structure. This means that layers can be arrived at top-down, as in Coad/Yourdon, or bottom-up during the Structures activity. Further, the requirement that every method must have a properly terminated implemented-by link (an idea borrowed directly from HOOD) assists in completeness checking during top-down design. Equally the analyst can ask, during a bottom-up analysis: 'What does this method implement for the layer?'

Notationally, layers may be shown in the notation of Figure 8.45 but a 'Gradygram' notation as in Figure 8.46 is preferable since it is easier to show implemented-by links in this way.

For example: a commercial system might have the layers Marketing, Sales, Accounts and Production. The Accounts layer is an object representing the Accounts Department as a whole and may have a method called ProduceSalesInvoice. Accounts is composed of three objects or layers: PurchaseLedger, SalesLedger and NominalLedger. The ProduceSalesInvoice method is implemented-by the ProduceInvoice method of the Sales object, denoted Sales.ProduceInvoice.

In the context of a traditional top-down analysis, we might well start with a DFD-style context diagram showing external objects and dataflows crossing the system boundary. The system is then the top-level object (layer) with methods defined by these dataflows. Each method is then examined to determine if it could be implemented by a lower-level object.

What happens when a component object needs to send a message outside its container? While messages sent to layers are dealt with at the layer interface and delegated thereby to the components' methods along implemented-by links, it is less obvious what should happen when a component requires the services of an object outside its containing layer. Considering Figure 8.46, we can observe that there are two cases.

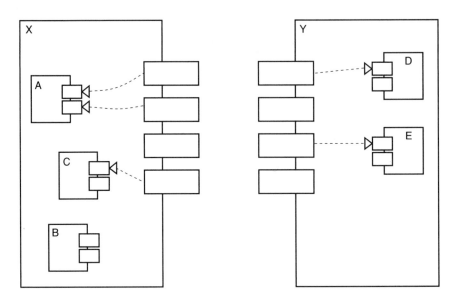

Figure 8.46 Layers and implemented-by links in SOMA.

Case 1 occurs when a class B with no implemented-by links needs the services of E, say. In this case B should be removed from the composition structure since it implements no services for it. This may involve a minor redesign, but is good practice in most cases.

Case 2 is the case where a subclass A needs the services of either Y or E. Here A is either performing a service for X, in which case the request to send a message to E should be relayed through X recursively, or on its own behalf. If the latter, it seems quite permissible to entertain a direct correspondence or collaboration, but the semantics of the design should be examined carefully to see if the anomaly can be removed, for the diagrams may get a little messy. In other words, layers can contain object references in their components.

The notation for layers needs to be relaxed sometimes as layers really have a dual aspect. They can be regarded either externally, as coherent entities, or internally as collections of objects that may receive communications from the outside world on an individual basis. I have found that both viewpoints arise quite naturally during analysis. Thus when the internal viewpoint is adopted, the arrows may penetrate the layer and seek out individual objects. In my view, layers should, if possible, be regarded in the same way as object wrappers: in other words, as high-level objects themselves. Such objects receive and send messages and, on receipt, delegate responsibilities to objects which they encapsulate.

By default, the wrapper object's methods are the union of all its component object's methods. It is the responsibility of the wrapper object itself to resolve polymorphic references. For example, if two objects within the layer have the same method and the sender has not specified which applies, a rule is required in the layer object to determine how to resolve the conflict.

8.3.2 Finding objects

Objects are identified as usual using the methods of data modelling, those suggested by Coad and Yourdon or Shlaer and Mellor, the Abbott textual analysis technique as used within Booch, HOOD and CRC, or in any other way (perhaps from examining DFDs or Jackson event diagrams as suggested by Ince (1991)). SOMA adds object identification techniques taken from knowledge elicitation and HCI practice. Specifically these include: structured and focused interviews, Kelly grids, topic analysis and task analysis. A new refinement technique called analysis of judgements is added. (All these techniques are described in Chapter 9.) These techniques are most helpful when a written requirements statement does not exist and interviews are necessary.

Where no specification exists another useful technique used within SOMA is based on Objectory use cases. A context diagram showing external entities and actors is constructed and use-scripts prepared for each actor. Exceptions are defined as subscripts and the resultant text used to prepared extended CRC cards. These may then be used to conduct walkthroughs with users and analysts. The details of this method are described further in Chapter 9 and in *Migrating to Object Technology* (Graham, 1994).

In practice, I also use some of the techniques of CRC (Wirfs-Brock *et al.,* 1990) to identify objects and to refine their definition and organization when a written specification of requirements is available. This is a good way to start but requires the additional techniques of SOMA when the system is complex or semantics is important. I have also found CRC to be an excellent vehicle for teaching object-oriented analysis concepts to beginners.

State models of systems can also be used to identify and refine objects as in OMT or OSA. The response of objects to system events can be designated by entity state change, state transition or life-history diagrams with effect correspondence diagrams taken from SSADM Version 4. The use of multiple techniques is recommended to boost confidence in their products, which should be the same, or at least equivalent, whichever technique is used.

The SOMA notation is merely the final repository for all the information discovered and unifies the static object model with the dynamic behavioural model using assertions and rules.

8.3.3 Structures and data semantics

The structures to be identified are of three main kinds: usage, classification and composition structures. Usage structures show the permissible message paths through the system, classification structures show inheritance of features and composition structures show the formation of aggregate objects and layers.

Usage structures record the message passing topology of the system or, equivalently, the visibility or client/server relationships. This structure generalizes the HOOD seniority hierarchy. The objective is to minimize the 'homology' or complexity of the structure and this homology may be a useful metric to collect. The homology is found by counting the number of 'holes' in the structure, regarding double-headed arrows as two single-headed arrows. In Figure 8.47 the homology is 2.

Here it is quite permissible to build separate behavioural models for objects and for their interactions. SOMA is neutral on the notation to be used as the global behavioural model is discarded later and the results embedded in SOMA objects. Local state change diagrams may be embedded in the objects. Possible notations and approaches to behavioural modelling include those of Booch '91, OMT, OSA, SSADM ELHs, Martin and Odell's object behaviour model notation or Harel (1987) state charts. This means that existing CASE and diagramming tools can be used for this activity. The results are consolidated using SOMA notation.

Messages may be shown explicitly with labels in the very early stages of analysis. The formal diagrams, however, are compiled under the rule that an arrow joining two icons represents the possibility of any message being passed, the actual legal messages being determined from the methods window of the receiver. These arrows are thus equivalent to usage structures or client/server relationships. Illegal polymorphic messages must be explicitly declared in the method description or as a comment in the rules window. For example, it may be necessary to permit

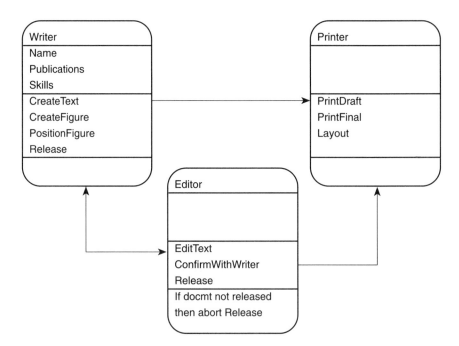

Figure 8.47 A fragment of a usage structure. Writers may ask a printer to print a draft and editors may ask them to print a final copy. Writers can release text to an editor and editors check changes with the author, who can approve them. Not all attributes, methods and rules are shown.

'user' objects to send messages to 'employee' class objects, but to forbid the user to discover an employee's age. It is proposed that tools which support SOMA should include facilities for dynamic simulation of events/messages using an augmented Petri net: augmented because each object needs to stack the tokens that it has passed. Failing this, manual walkthroughs or state diagrams are to be used.

CLASSIF-
ICATION
STRUCTURES

The notations of some methods are sometimes ambigious, due to lack of expressiveness, or a little clumsy. An example is the Coad/Yourdon notation for classification and composition given in Figures 8.5 and 8.6. A suggested alternative to both is shown in Figures 8.48 and 8.49.

The notation inside the diamond is interpreted exactly as outlined in Chapter 5. That is, E/O stands for 'exclusive/optional' and I/O means 'inclusive/optional'. Recall that the term 'exclusive' indicates that each subclass's intersection with the other subclasses is empty, and that 'inclusive' indicates that the subclasses may overlap. The 'optional' indicates that the list is not exhaustive: there may be more, as yet unidentified, subclasses. An M, for 'mandatory', indicates that a member of the superclass must be in at least one of the subclasses; that is, the subclasses are an exhaustive list or *partition* of the class.

Classification can be shown either in this manner, in OMT or Coad/Yourdon notation or, more simply, as simple trees or fern diagrams as in Figure 8.52. An X against an attribute or method (on the left) records the fact that it may not be

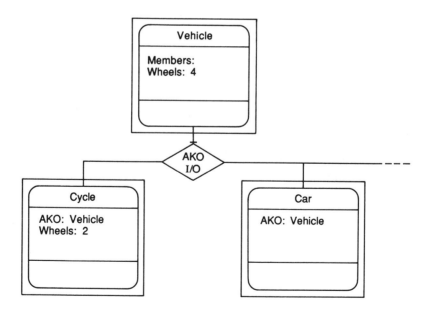

Figure 8.48 (a) An improved classification notation. Note the special attributes Members: and AKO: (A Kind Of); **(b)** Informal tree diagram recording a classification structure.

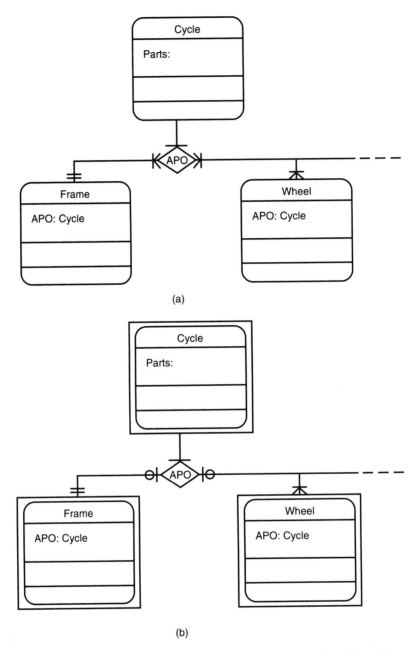

Figure 8.49 An improved composition notation. Note the special attributes Parts: and APO: (A Part Of) which records the structural link at either end **(a)** Class level; **(b)** instance level.

inherited from a superclass. The attribute windows of classes that participate in classification structures must contain the special attributes AKO: and Members:. Instances must contain the special attribute IsA:. If desired, a distinction may be made between the special attributes 'Members:' and 'Subclasses:', although the context always makes this clear. Clearly, if the Members: attribute is regarded as part of the specification, it compromises reuse, because every time a new member is added it must be changed. However, if we envisage automated support for this method this problem evaporates, since it is an entirely mechanical procedure to update the Members: attribute automatically every time a member is added or deleted from the class. Strictly, Members: is not part of the specification but merely a convenient navigational aid.

It may also be argued, by those committed to an object-based approach to analysis, that inheritance is an implementation issue which should not enter into the analysis process, and that users may be confused by it and distracted from the goals of the system. This is a genuine argument but suffers from two weaknesses. First, it confuses the elicitation of requirements with the conceptual analysis process which seeks to abstract the key concepts of the application independently of the perceptions of users. In the latter, the structural features of the domain are revealed, including natural notions of specialization and generalization. Secondly, inheritance, and other, structures are an important part of the domain semantics: the way objects are classified defines the domain, and often the purpose, of the application. For example, the objects of sociology and history are the same, people and organizations, but in history we would not classify by socio-economic group but by social class or perhaps nationality. The structures represent the *purpose* of the analysis.

Classification, inheritance or generalization/specialization structures permit the analyst to record the semantics of classification. Inheritance is only used in this sense in SOMA and any kind of *ad hoc* polymorphism or inheritance merely for the purposes of code sharing is banned at the analysis stage. The notation for these structures follows the Chen style of ER modelling. Thus a diamond connector marked AKO (A Kind Of) indicates that the objects attached participate in a classification structure. A bar on a connector indicates a link to a superclass and its absence a link to a subclass. The bars can be named if desired. In the case of multiple inheritance there will be two or more such bars. Normally, multiple inheritance is conjunctive; that is, the subclass is a kind of all its superclasses. In rare cases disjunctive inheritance is useful. In this case, where the subclass is a kind of one of the superclasses, a double bar is used. This too can be named and annotated.

Implicitly all AKO relationships are many-to-one associations of a special kind denoting classification. However, including this redundant multiplicity information not only adds nothing to our understanding of the problem but is usually highly confusing.

Certainly the Chen style for dealing with multiple inheritance works much better than the Bachman style adopted in, say, CRC, ORACLE*CASE and Ptech, where subclasses are shown by inclusion. This is even true for single inheritance when the hierarchy is deep and we have boxes, within boxes, within boxes and so on. Martin and Odell (1992) fudge this by allowing the fern diagrams produced by Kappa to be used as well as inclusion boxes.

COMPOSITION STRUCTURES Any composition structure is a layer. Classification structures are viewed as orthogonal to these and are neither layers nor are they usually shown on the same diagram as composition. Messages arrive at the outside of layers and are delegated to sub-objects via implemented-by links. Messages can arrive anywhere in a classification structure but do so most often at instances. Thus in use structure diagrams, classification structures are expanded but composition structures are not.

Other notations interpret composition links as instance-level connexions. I have found it useful, very occasionally, to permit a class-level interpretation as well. In Figure 8.49 a particular wheel (an instance) may belong to only one cycle at any one time. However, that type of wheel (its class) may be a part of several models or types of bicycle. At the instance level, for every wheel there is at most one bicycle that it is part of. However, at the class level, for every wheel type there may be many bicycle types which incorporate it.

The attribute windows of classes or instances that participate in composition structures must contain the special attributes: Parts and APO. Exactly the same remarks apply to the APO: attribute of parts as apply to the Members: attribute of superclasses. They are navigational aids which must be updated automatically when the Parts: attribute is added to or subtracted from, otherwise every time a composite object was restructured the specification of its parts would have to be altered. The E/O, E/M, I/O and I/M notations may be used but parts do not usually overlap.

SOMA has been criticized for using the same diamond symbol for classification and composition as this may be confusing but I find the distinctions clear enough in practice.

ASSOCIATIONS Other kinds of associations and their static semantics must be catered for. Data semantics are normally only annotated at the instance level. In SOMA it has been found useful to permit class-level connexions of this type as with composition structures. This serves to enrich the semantics. Connexions of this sort may be thought of as **associations**; that is, structural relationships other than usage, classification or composition. In some cases these associations have properties and should be expanded into objects in their own right. In others the association may be so important for the application (for example, kinship in anthropology) that a fourth or fifth structure must be added to the model. Data semantic links indicating multiplicity and modality may be used on composition structure links.

Elements of the rich notation of OMT are used for recording complex composition structures and associations. In particular the notation for recursive composition shown in Figure 8.15 is recommended.

At this point it is possible to raise the issue of whether a particular concept is to be included as an object type or merely as an attribute of another object. The usual data modelling considerations apply, and generally objects with one or very few attributes and/or methods are better treated as attributes of other objects. The guidelines for identifying objects given in Chapter 9 are helpful in this context. It is also worth remarking that, as with sound data analysis practice, object ownership and validation should be specified as clearly as possible.

Normalization into third normal form provides valuable guidelines in making the decision about whether to treat something as an object or as an attribute. 3NF is the normal form which eliminates most update anomalies. However, normalization is definitely not part of the object model and should only be used as an heuristic guide. Recall from Chapter 5 that ER models tend to produce 3NF relations. Here too it will be found that what is most natural tends to look like 3NF. The rule is: model the real world and think about potential redundancies and anomalies.

Note that when a relationship is represented explicitly with its own attributes and/or methods, the normal four-window object icon is used rather than the diamond notation of ER models. The latter is reserved for preliminary data analysis sketches and structures. Following Desfray, we do not normally permit relationships to have operations though they may, rarely, have rules.

ATTRIBUTES AND OPERATIONS Attributes are discovered using standard data modelling techniques. Two special list-valued attributes are used: AKO: and Parts:. The AKO: attribute is list-valued and contains the superclass names for the object. The Parts: attribute contains a list of objects that compose the object. Where automated support is available the dual attributes, Members: and APO:, may be employed to aid navigation through the model, but these must be updated automatically otherwise reuse is compromised.

In SOMA every attribute has a type which must be a valid user-defined or primitive class in the system. The analyst is free to decide what is primitive but must list these. Typical primitives will include real, integer, string, list, date and so on. Attributes also store associations. For example, if we have the semantic relationship which says that employees must work for exactly one department while departments may employ zero or more employees, then we might record

WorksIn: (DEPT,1,1)

as an attribute of EMPLOYEE and

Employs: (EMPLOYEE,0,n)

as an attribute of DEPT or produce the equivalent 'crow's foot' diagram. In fact, we regard attributes as split into two classes: pure attributes and attributes representing associations.

The extent to which such associations compromise reuse has been widely debated, but the requirements of commercial systems development seem to have brought the consensus round to their acceptance, and associations are even part of the OMG Abstract Object Model. These linkages are inherited along classification links in the following default manner.

Superclass	Subclass
One-to-many	Zero-to-many
Zero-to-many	Zero-to-many
One-to-one	Zero-to-one
Zero-to-one	Zero-to-one

These default assumptions may be overridden. In the case of overriding the diagrams must show the replaced composite link as in Figure 8.50.

Also, attributes store the usual defaults, security, ownership and access codes and range constraints which are not defined by their type.

Methods or operations! Here is where SOMA borrows almost everything from other object-oriented and conventional methods. STDs may be used as in OMT and OSA. Even SSADM ELHs may be employed. DFDs may be used as follows. Take a data store and find the objects that encapsulate it. Identify the immediately linked processes as candidates for methods. Repeat for each data store and refine the results. The HOIST method (an extension of HOOD) and the CGI-Yourdon approach offer refined versions of this technique. SOMA is deliberately neutral on the technique to be used because in this way practitioners may build on their previous experience. As with ternary approaches to analysis the question arises as to whether STDs refer to the whole system or to individual entities. OMT tends toward the former view and OSA to the latter. The philosophy of SOMA, shared with Coad/Yourdon and OSA to a lesser extent, is that the conventional structured techniques are used internally on an object-by-object basis and not for global system description. The latter is the function of the usage diagrams in object-oriented analysis. However, cross-checking the products of a global DFD with the methods identified within SOMA can act as an additional check on completeness and is not discouraged where doubts exist.

When the behaviour of the object is very complex state transition diagrams have proved an effective tool for identifying operations. All the traditional techniques for specifying computer systems are also to hand for the specifier of each method: dataflow diagrams, Petri nets for concurrent methods, state transition diagrams, decision trees and even good old top-down functional decomposition.

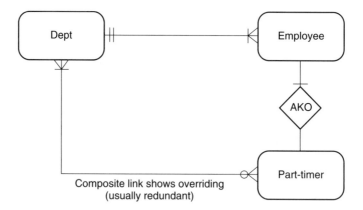

Figure 8.50 Overriding the default semantics given to a composite classification link. In the absence of the override the default would state that part-timers worked in zero-to-one departments.

Operations have a parameter list and a return type. Pre-, post- and invariance conditions may also be attached to each operation and are inherited.

It is essential to make a distinction between operations that apply to instances, such as calculating a person's age from their date of birth, and operations which apply to entire classes, such as calculating the average age of all employees. If the distinction arises then these types of method are called *instance methods* and *class methods*, respectively. *Class methods* are preceded with a $ sign, following the convention of OMT.

8.3.4 Rules

In performing object-oriented analysis and building a model, a large number of lessons can be learned from AI systems built using semantic nets and from semantic data modelling. Specifications that exhibit reusability and extensibility are all very well, but do not necessarily contain the meaning intended by the analyst or the user. To reuse a specification of an object we should be able to read from it what it is (data structure), what it does (operations), why it does it and how it is related to other objects. It is my position that this semantic content is partly contained in the structures of classification, composition and usage, and the rules which describe their behaviour.

The Coad/Yourdon notation for composition or parts hierarchies for example, as I have remarked, does not take account of search strategies. This is not merely an implementation issue but a question of the application semantics. Inheritance hierarchies use the knowledge implicit in them in a manner analogous to search, and search can occur in a backward or forward chaining manner, just as in expert systems. Backward chaining descends the hierarchy, looking for values, while forward chaining assembles properties from the components of the hierarchy.

The fact is that all semantics compromise reuse. We saw in Chapter 1 that inheritance does so, and so does anything that makes the *meaning* of an object more specific. In system specification both aspects are equally important and the trade-off must be well understood and managed with care, depending on the goals of the analysts and their clients.

Defining data semantics is best kept separate from the definition of both objects and attributes. We should regard it as an important separate task. As remarked already, relational DBMSs often require much of this information to be thrown away or incorporated in application programs. Thus, one justification for object-oriented databases, or even extended relational or semi-object-oriented databases, is that these semantics can be captured in the target development environment as well as in the analysis in completely explicit form. Explicitness delivers flexibility in that when the data semantics or the business rules change the application can evolve. If we are going to build executable, reversible specifications, it is crucial that information is not lost in coding. This includes all types of semantic information. Data semantics may be captured in relationships and stored explicitly in object-oriented or deductive databases. Functional semantics may be captured explicitly as rules. We turn to the issue of rules and their representation next.

In my opinion, the most serious defect of many methods of object-oriented analysis is their lack of support for functional semantics, global control description or business rules. We now turn to this whole area, which I term **declarative semantics** because procedural semantics are encoded as methods.

It is necessary at this stage of an analysis to record business rules and the exception-handling and parameter-passing behaviour of the object. The Coad/Yourdon method lacks a notation for exception handling. This is not always important but, for those applications where it is, a notation similar to OOSD can be used in annotations to each object without doing violence to the simplicity of the notation we recommend. I suggest below a method of annotating exceptions in a non-procedural fashion to be contrasted with the procedural notation of HOOD or OOSD.

Object-oriented methods surveyed so far may obviously be extended to deal with multiple inheritance although this is not included in their description, except at the notational level. This extension must include provision for annotating the handling of conflict arising when the same attribute or method is inherited differently from two parent objects. It must also permit different semantics for subclasses which partition their superclasses into an exhaustive set of subclasses and those which are incomplete, in the sense that presently unspecified subclasses may still be added.

The obvious suggestion to cover these declarative semantics is to add rules to SOMA objects which can not only disambiguate multiple inheritance but also define priority rules for defaults and demons. A demon is a method that wakes up when needed: when a value changes, or is added or deleted. That is, these rules can determine how to resolve the conflict that arises when an attribute inherits two different values, or perhaps specify whether the default value should be applied before or after inheritance takes place or before or after a demon fires. They may also specify the relative priorities of inheritance and demons. These rules themselves may have defaults. Business rules specify second-order information, such as dependencies between attributes, for example, a dependency between the age of an employee and his or her holiday entitlement. Lastly, global pre- and postconditions that apply to all methods may need to be specified as rules. A typical business rule in a personnel application might include 'change holiday entitlement to six weeks when service exceeds five years' as a rule in the rules window of the Employee object. With this extension the notation can cope with analysis problems where a relational or deductive database with object-oriented features is envisaged as the target environment.

These rules are encapsulated within objects, instead of being declared globally as is the case with all current implementations in object-oriented programming languages. They may also be inherited and overridden. The benefit of this is that local variations in control strategy are possible. Further, the analyst may inspect the impact of the control structure on every object – using a browser perhaps – and does not have to annotate convoluted diagrams to describe the local effects of global control. If such a global view is desired then STDs or Ptech event diagrams may optionally be used. Genuinely global rules are contained in a top-level object, called 'object', and will be inherited by all objects that do not override them. Just as state transition or state change diagrams may be used to describe the procedural semantics of methods, so decision trees may be found useful in describing complex sets of rules.

One must also be aware of the need to decide whether rules belong to individual methods or to the object as a whole. There is no principled reason why methods cannot be expressed in a rule-based language. However, the distinction to be made here is not between the form of expressions but the content of the rules. Rules that relate several methods do not belong within those methods, and rules which define dependencies between attributes also refer to the object as a whole. Conversely, rules that concern the encapsulated state of the object belong within one of its methods. The most important kind of 'whole object' rules are control rules which describe the behaviour of the object as it participates in structures that it belongs to; rules to control the handling of defaults, multiple inheritance, exceptions and general relationships with other objects.

The declarative semantics (rules) activity is the most novel aspect of SOMA. It enhances the usual object model by adding a set of rule-sets to each object. Thus while an object is normally thought to consist of identifier, attributes and methods, a SOMA object consists of identifier, attributes, methods and rules. Rules can be further subdivided into types. This has a number of interesting consequences, the most remarkable of which is that those objects that are local entities can encapsulate the rules for global system behaviour, rather as DNA is supposed to encapsulate the morpheme.

Another consequence is that rule-sets can be regarded as objects for expert systems developments. In that case one natural approach is to regard rule-set objects as having a small number of attributes and methods. For example, we might have the attribute Goal_variable: and the method Backward_chain: inherited, of course, from the general rule-set object.

As with attributes and methods, the interface of the object only displays the name of a rule-set or rule. In the case of a backward chaining rule-set this might well consist of the name of the value being sought: for example, If Route: needed SEEK Route:.

Away from this specialized use, rules may be of several different types. For instance, we may have triggers, business rules and control rules. Business rules typically relate two or more attributes and triggers relate attributes to methods. For example:

> Business rule:
>   If Service_length > 5 then Holiday=25
> Forward Trigger:
>   When Salary + SalaryIncrement > 20000 run AwardCoCar

Business rules specify second-order information, such as dependencies between attributes, for example a dependency between the age of an employee and her holiday entitlement. Lastly, global pre- and postconditions which apply to all methods may need to be specified. A typical business rule in a personnel application might include 'change holiday entitlement to five weeks when service exceeds five years' as a rule in the rules window of the Employee object. With this extension the notation can cope with analysis problems where a relational or deductive database with object-oriented features is envisaged as the target environment. Quite complex rules can be expressed simply as rule-sets. For example the InsuranceSalesman class might contain the rules for giving the best advice to a customer in the form:

> If client is retired and Client.RiskAverse: is false
> then BestProduct: is "Annuity"
> If client is young and Client.RiskAverse: is false then
> BestProduct: is "Endowment"
> If Client.RiskAverse: is true then
> BestProduct: is "Bonds"
> If Client.Children: > 0 then
> Client.RiskAverse is true

The rules fire when a value for BestProduct: is needed. Note that these rules do not compromise the encapsulation of Client by setting the value of Risk.Averse in that object. The Salesman is merely making an assumption in the face of missing data or prompting the Client for that information. If the Client.RiskAverse: attribute is already set these rules never fire.

Integrity rules are regarded as part of the data semantics and stored as part of the type information. More interesting is what happens with control rules.

Let us examine a simple but amusing example involving multiple inheritance and default values of attributes. Suppose that we wish to construct a text-based adventure game. Let us agree to call it 'Quest'. In an adventure of the type represented by Colossal Cave we usually have the following sorts of entities: locations, actors and things. The game has locations that may contain movable objects (we will call them 'things' to avoid confusion) listed in the contents attribute or have mysterious properties described by methods. The attributes of locations also describe the various entries and exits. There are players, and the computer pretends to contain an anthropomorphic guide who, if you ask it to eat the snake, say, will reply with something like 'I just lost my appetite'. These actors may be conveniently regarded as persons and, lo and behold, we have our first inheritance structure as shown in Figure 8.51. Note that the guide is not allowed to pick up objects (indicated by the X) but inherits the ability to move from place to place. Players can issue commands such as 'eat snake', 'take torch' or 'go north'.

Life gets interesting when we examine the Thing layer for structure. Things can be classified into treasure, which has value in points, weapons, which do not, and utility items such as food, bags and the like. A provisional structure is shown in Figure 8.52, where it can be seen that multiple inheritance has intruded: the jewelled sword is both treasure and a weapon. Treasure has positive value in points, and weapons have none. So what is the value of the jewelled sword which could inherit from both weapon and treasure?

There are several strategies for handling inheritance conflicts of this type. The system may report the conflict to the user and ask for a value, and this is the most common strategy. Unfortunately, stopping runs in a batch environment is usually more than merely annoying: it is costly. All other approaches require that the

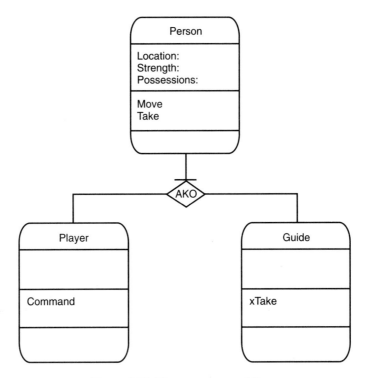

Figure 8.51 The actor layer of Quest.

system is coded with some of the semantics of the application. Touretzky (1986) and others have suggested various 'shortest path' (or longest path) strategies based on the idea that the most direct inheritance represents the most specific knowledge. This can be useful but the assumption is not always justified and the strategy breaks

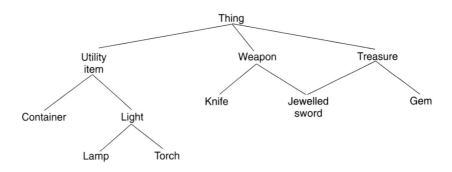

Figure 8.52 The structure of things.

down when the path lengths are equal. Other work by Touretzky (Horty *et al.,* 1990) suggests that conflict implies ignorance and means we should inherit the null value 'unknown'. The problem with this is that it reproduces all the logical problems that arise with null values in databases discussed by Date (1983) and in Chapter 5, but in some applications it makes sense. It may also lead to run-time errors. If possible, the inheriting object can be given the answer in advance and told, by the default control rule, for example, not to allow inherited wealth to override existing resources. Lastly, in the case of attributes rather than methods, the inherited values can sometimes be combined. One could, for example, take the average or weighted average of two numerical inherited values. Appendix I describes a sophisticated scheme for combined value inheritance of this type. It also shows how to implement partial inheritance (inheriting something to a certain extent – a bit like inheriting your mother's singing voice) and even how to inherit partial properties (like being a bit rich), using notions from artificial intelligence and fuzzy set theory. But we still have not resolved the problem of the jewelled sword. A good practical suggestion in this case is to embody the rule 'If conflicts occur on the Value: attribute, combine values by taking their maximum' in the thing class. This ensures that the sword gets its points and can still kill the troll. Figure 8.53 shows an example of a conflict-breaking rule.

Rules are used to make an object's semantics explicit and visible. This helps with the description of information that would normally reside in a repository, such as business rules for the enterprise. It can also help with interoperability at quite a low level. For example, if I have an object which computes cube roots, as a client of that object it is not enough to know its methods alone: I need to know that what is returned is a cube root and not a square root. In this simple case the solution is

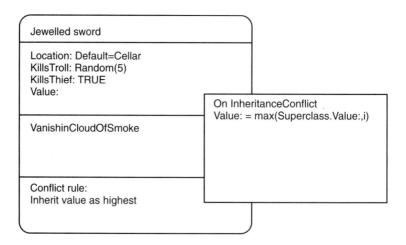

Figure 8.53 SOMA object notation including a conflict breaking rule.

obvious because we can characterize the cube root uniquely with one simple rule: the response multiplied by itself twice is equal to the parameter sent. If this rule is part of the interface, all other systems and system components can see the meaning of the object from its interface alone, thus removing some of the complexities of repository technology by shifting it into the object model. Tools that do this properly have yet to emerge.

It is sometimes possible, in simple cases, to specify rules that must be obeyed by all control strategies for multiple inheritance. In the case where objects are identified with only abstract data types – that is, constructed types representing relations, say, are not permitted – we have a clear set of three rules for inheritance:

(1) There must be no cycles of the form:

x is AKO y is AKO z is AKO x

This rule eliminates redundant objects.

(2) The bottom of an AKO link must be a subtype, and the top must be a subtype or an abstract type (that is, not a printable object; not an attribute).

(3) It must be possible to name a subtype of two supertypes. This rule prevents absurd objects, such as the class of all people who are also toys: toyboys?

These rules are recommended as design checks.

As we have seen, control rules are not the only rules in an application. We have mentioned business rules already. In both cases encapsulating these rules in objects makes sense and enhances reusability and extensibility. System-wide rules belong in the most general objects in the system: the top of the hierarchy (or hierarchies if there is no catch-all class as there is with Smalltalk's 'object'). Both kinds of rule are stored in the fourth box of the object icon.

The rules which appear in the rule window may be classified into several, not necessarily exclusive, types, as follows.

- Control rules
- Business and exception handling rules
- Triggers

Rule-based extensions to object-oriented analysis help enrich the semantics of models of conventional commercial systems. This makes these models more readable and more reversible: more of the analysts' intentions are evident in the model. It also provides a truly object-oriented approach to the specification of advanced database and knowledge-based systems.

It may be enlightening to know that I was first motivated to add rules to the Coad/Yourdon method when using it not to describe a computer system but to build a model of an organization. This kind of activity, known these days as enterprise modelling, brings to the fore the need to record business rules, often expressed at a high level or vaguely – just the sort of thing knowledge-based systems builders are used to. The recent agreement between James Martin's company and Intellicorp to use ProKappa as an enterprise modelling CASE tool in conjunction with ADW and object-oriented concepts from Ptech confirms the view that object-oriented analysis combined with ideas from expert systems is ideally suited for such work.

MOVING TO DESIGN – FORMAL CONDITIONS VERSUS RULES   Everything that can be expressed as rules can, in principle, be expressed as a combination of pre-, post- and invariance conditions. However, doing so can be complex and unreadable. The advantage of rules is clarity and conciseness. The analyst will be able to judge which is best in individual cases. As an example, the rule about holidays could be expressed as a postcondition on the length of service attribute, so that whenever its value changes in any way a method is called which updates Holidays:. This is really a postcondition on the method for updating length of service, not on the attribute. Since this standard method is not usually exhibited, this adds to the difficulty of maintaining its conditions and the rules approach seems much cleaner on balance. In implementation this decision may be easily reversed. Where formal correctness is an issue, rules should be avoided because of the possibility of side-effects and the lack of a formal proof theory. I find that this is rarely an issue for commercial systems, where rules are usually the best form of clear expression for analysis purposes.

Unless implementation is to be in a rule-based language, SOMA designers will replace the rules of SOMA analysts with assertions. This is more precise but less communicable to users, so it is important to trace the conversion or even automate it.

In SOMA classes consist of an identifier, pointers to superclasses, pointers to component classes, attributes, methods and rule-sets. Attributes may be simple place-holders for objects or may denote relationships with appropriate multiplicity and modality information. Attributes are shorthand for their standard get and put methods. Methods may specify assertions of three kinds: preconditions, post-conditions and invariance conditions. Attributes, methods and rules may be inherited. Rules and rule-sets may be of six kinds, as follows:

(1) *Rules that relate attributes to attributes*   Example: if Service >5 then Hols=Hols+1. This could be expressed as a postcondition on put.Service causing put.Hols(Hols+1) or as a precondition on get.Hols.
(2) *Rules that relate methods to methods*   These are naturally expressed as assertions rather than rules anyhow.
(3) *Rules that relate attributes to methods*   Example: these may be expressed as if_needed (pre.get) or if_changed demons (post.put) or as pre- or post-conditions.
(4) *Control rules for attributes*   Example: behaviour under multiple inheritance conflicts and defaults (preconditions on gets).
(5) *Control rules for methods*   Example: behaviour under multiple inheritance conflicts (postconditions on gets).
(6) *Exception handling rules*   Example: overheated sensor (invariance or post-condition on temp).

I assert that there are exactly these six kinds of rule and that there is a mechanical way to convert from rule form to assertion form. Research is under way to prove this assertion and to define a formal language for expressing the rules (a BNF style, perhaps) and assertions (Z or VDM, say).

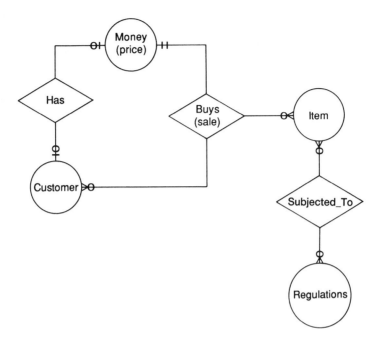

Figure 8.54 Part of the SACIS data model.

Note that the assertions attached to each method are inherited, and that integrity rules are part of the data semantics.

SACIS
CASE-STUDY
For a more concrete and realistic example, we will examine some objects in SACIS with their rules. The scenario involves a particular kind of event, a sale. A sale involves a customer, who may be an adult or a child, and a list of items, which may be of various types. There is a bar-code reader that reads and updates the stock system and a system whose task is to ensure that the sold items are suitable for the customer's purpose. The term suitable encompasses various 'fitness for purpose' criteria, one of which is safety. Let us assume that a particular customer is trying to buy a tube of glue. The conventional data model is outlined in Figure 8.54. The decision as to whether the relationships shown as diamonds in the figure should be objects or not is deferred for the time being.

Note that there are a number of multiple inheritance structures involved: specifically, those for glue and customer shown in Figure 8.55, which also illustrates that it is sometimes convenient to designate disjunctive multiple inheritance when a subclass is either an A or a B. The convention is that a double bar is used above the AKO icon. This is to be avoided if possible.

The question is how to model the derivation of safety for this tube of glue. Since glue inherits from office supplies and toy there should be no safety issue.

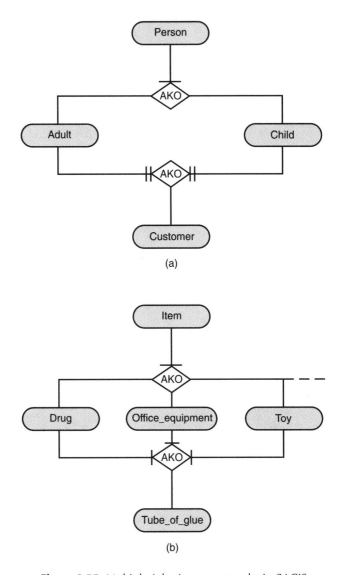

Figure 8.55 Multiple inheritance networks in SACIS.

However, the structures illustrated show that we have modelled the fact that glue can be abused as an intoxicating drug. Most shops now decline to sell glue to children for this reason; the structural modelling of this fact represents a business rule for such shops. However, it is also possible that there is a bona fide reason for a child purchasing glue, perhaps if a model that must be glued has been purchased. In such a case the system should either permit the sale or, more strictly perhaps, refuse to sell either the glue or the model (which is useless without the glue in any case).

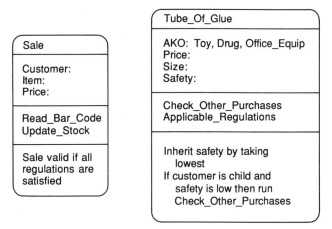

Figure 8.56 Part of the object-oriented analysis of SACIS.

To implement this, the system should flag the value of glue safety as low and scan the entire transaction to look for glue-related purchases. Figure 8.56 shows two of the objects that must be recorded during the analysis of this problem to convert the outline data model to object-oriented form.

In summary, SOMA extends Coad and Yourdon's SOSAS mnemonic to a more comprehensive slogan: LOSAAMR. In other words, analysts should proceed by identifying:

- Layers
- Objects
- Structures:
  - Usage structures
  - Classification structures
  - Composition structures
- Associations and their data semantics
- Attributes with notation to represent type, validation, security and defaults
- Methods with notation to represent exception handing, assertions and parameter passing
- Rules:
  - Control rules
  - Business rules
  - Triggers

The recommended method is to deal with these steps in roughly the order given, although layering is an activity subject to revision at most stages. The model may be regarded as a waterfall with iteration or, preferably, I think, as a spiral.

The process is risk-driven, as with most spiral models. The issue of such life-cycle models will be discussed in Chapter 9.

We now take a brief look at the current state of CASE tools and life-cycle models in relation to object-orientation.

☰ 8.4 CASE tools and life-cycle models

Computer-aided software engineering (CASE) became fashionable during the 1980s along with object-oriented programming. In parallel there was an increasing emphasis on structured development methods, such as Information Engineering (IE) and Structured Systems Analysis and Design Method (SSADM), which incorporate a series of notational and design techniques and rules for using them. The claimed benefits for structured methods are well known. They are designed to avoid the chaotic production of undocumented, poorly costed and justified, unmaintainable systems. On the other hand they are often bureaucratic and inflexible and tend to undervalue the creative aspects of software production and de-skill the labour force, leading to problems when the unexpected occurs – as it usually does. In fact, a survey of 600 projects carried out by Butler Cox (1990) found that projects using structured techniques (about one-sixth of the total surveyed) had 15% lower productivity than average, and error rates 40% above average during testing and the first month of operation. Projects using modern 4GL software products fared better, with screen painters giving improvements of up to 40% in development times. Some methods developers, such as the CCTA who defined SSADM, have made attempts to update their methods to incorporate 4GL and prototyping techniques, but we must ask whether methods incorporating object-oriented ideas have a rôle to play in restoring the balance between discipline and creativity. Certainly, object-orientation does offer a philosophy of system development that can be described by a method, as we have seen. In my view object-oriented techniques will penetrate methods gradually. IE and SSADM are already under pressure to offer some such extensions. In the meantime we are at least faced with several object-oriented techniques, which are the building blocks of methods.

Systems for automatically checking the completeness and consistency of a diagram or which apply heuristics to a design are clearly helpful to both the neophyte and the seasoned designer. The only danger is that the tool may impose a method or notation too strictly to permit the exercise of creativity, or inhibit dealing with a different sort of application, where the rules may not be appropriate.

A lot of the benefit that some CASE tools deliver is due to their ability to generate code automatically. This means that project managers have to have the confidence to allocate very little time to the coding stage. If something does go wrong at the coding stage there is then no time to correct it. Further, code generation without reverse engineering is very dangerous. The duty programmer who makes an urgent midnight patch is unlikely to go off and fix all the design and analysis diagrams, even if the managerial controls insist that s/he should. Current-generation CASE tools only support a very limited form of reverse engineering, if they do at all. Systems that capture semantics are required to make fuller reverse engineering possible. This suggests that it is possible that object-oriented databases with versioning and object-oriented diagramming front-ends may completely replace the current generation of CASE tools. Certainly, leading CASE vendors, such as Index Technology, are building their next-generation products on top of object-oriented databases.

At least for small, for example decision support, systems it is likely that object-oriented databases will supersede both conventional RDBMSs and CASE tools, although this trend may be overwhelmed if most RDBMS vendors include enough of the object-oriented tool-set in their products.

It is manifestly reasonable to ask if there are any CASE tools supporting object-oriented methods and techniques. At present there are only a few such tools although the situation is likely to change rapidly. Until this happens system developers will have to construct their own diagramming tools with whatever comes to hand. Likely platforms for such developments are Smalltalk and HyperCard. However, as there are a number of tools emerging, we attempt a brief description and evaluation of these next. The use of graphical and CASE tools is recommended to enhance productivity. Any tool used, however, should not entail a commitment to the implementation language unless it is known with complete certainty what the target environment will be and that it will never change. Since methods are undergoing very rapid evolution at present it may be wise either to use very low-cost tools that can be replaced or adopt a meta-CASE approach. The latter is more expensive but more adaptable and the tools should be less likely to need replacement as methods settle down. This gives advantages in terms of training and the continuity of large projects.

System Architect (from Popkin Software & Systems Inc.) is a comprehensive CASE tool running under Microsoft Windows that supports several diagramming techniques such as ER, state-transition and dataflow diagrams. As an optional extra it supports a diagramming technique based on Booch's (1991) object-oriented design, and there is some flexibility in that icons may be designed by the user. Coad/Yourdon is also supported on this low-cost tool.

ROSE is a tool dedicated to supporting the Booch methods solely and fully and is supplied by Booch's own company, Rational. It runs under UNIX.

HOOD is supported by a growing number of tools, including IPSYS's HOOD Toolset, VSF's HOOD Software Factory, Cadre's team*work*. The IPSYS HOOD tool kit emerged from work at Software Sciences on PCTE (Portable Common Tools Environment) and the ECLIPSE CASE tool. It consists of eight tools: a graphical editor, informal and structured text editors, a design checker, a code generator for C, C++ and Ada, a document generator, a facilities window and a customization tool. Context-sensitive help for both HOOD and the tools is provided.

HOOD-SF is a tool kit written in Virtual Software Factory (VSF), available from a UK company called VSF Limited. The latter is a tool for constructing CASE tools: a 'meta-CASE tool'. It uses a Prolog-like formal description language called Cantor to describe methodological and structural rules. Diagramming notation and rules are defined within a graphics editor. Constraints and data semantics may also be defined. Thus, syntactic checks, such as not permitting unmediated connexions between data stores in a dataflow diagram, or semantic checks, such as not allowing low-level dataflows which have not been defined at a higher level, can be enforced. Cantor additionally permits the definition of code generators for 4GLs and other languages. Traceability between analysis, design and coding stages is also supported, helping with potential reverse engineering approaches. The data/design repository is implemented as an inverted semantic net, which gives roughly linear performance degradation with size, unlike the relational approach embodied within IBM's Repository and similar products, where an exponential curve can be expected. This superior approach suffers only from its proprietary nature and perhaps the difficulty of learning Cantor. The commercial designer would, I suspect, have considerable difficulty with the unusual syntax of Cantor. VSF has been used to build CASE tools for several methods other than HOOD, including SSADM. The HOOD version provides support for Issue 3.0 of HOOD. The flavour of the notation used can be garnered from Figure 8.57.

The latest addition to VSF's method support at the time of writing was the Texel method described in Section 8.2.10 and a variant of Ptech.

Object Maker is a meta-CASE tool that runs on several platforms, including PCs, with support for a huge range of conventional and object-oriented methods including Booch, Coad/Yourdon, OMT, Firesmith's ADM3, CRC, Shlaer/Mellor and others. Paradigm Plus from Protosoft is a similar meta-CASE product and supports many object-oriented methods.

SELECT, from Select Software Limited, is another CASE tool that has the cost advantage of running on PCs. SELECT supports several real-time methods such as Ward/Mellor, Hatley and MASCOT and SSADM support is projected. It supports HOOD Issue 3.0 and OMT already, and the authors intend to provide support for other object-oriented analysis and design methods. The underlying database is Btrieve, so that interface with other systems, including expert systems, is possible. The most remarkable thing about SELECT is its very low price and the PC platform.

Software through Pictures (StP) from Interactive Development Environments (IDE) offers support for OOSD and other object-oriented design methods, including Booch, CRC and OMT, as well as conventional approaches. Although it does not have the configurability of VSF, it does allow annotations to objects which could in principle be used to add rules and so on. IDE are committed to making it more of a meta-tool. Nevertheless, StP provides users with the ability to customize their environment, traceability features, code generation, and good interaction with other tools. It is intended by IDE to make StP gradually more like a meta-CASE tool. The philosophy implied by the name, writing software entirely by drawing pictures, is very beguiling. Graphical notations are under the user's control and

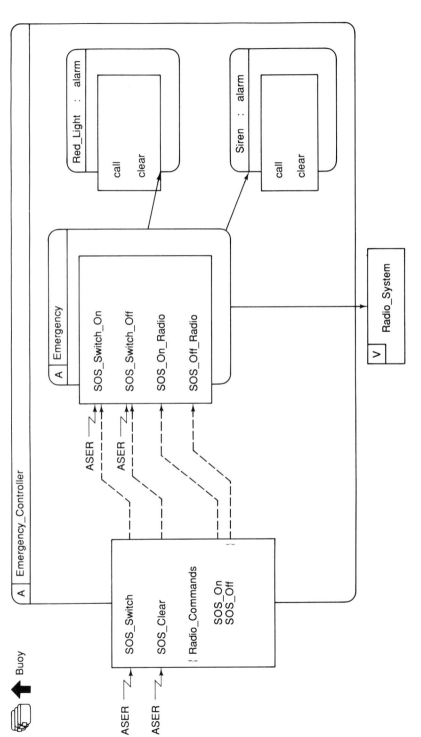

Figure 8.57 Part of a HOOD-SF design for a radio buoy simulation. ASER stands for ASynchronous Execution Request, solid lines show the use hierarchy and dotted ones the 'implemented by' relationship.

automatic documentation is possible. OOSD is a very detailed notation suitable for designers rather than analysts and it does not support directly the recording of things like business rules and so on. Secondly, the main strength of StP is code generation capability and specific support for the C++ language. This violates the principle stated above that analysis should be implementation-independent.

Cadre Technologies' team*work* analysis tool partially supports Shlaer/Mellor and provides support for HOOD. It is also worth noting the use of object-oriented programming in the recent development of the product. Like Cognos, it is reported that Cadre encountered some early adoption problems with the approach.

Ptech is a tool as well as a method. It has been described in the foregoing, but is worth rementioning as a complex but powerful CASE tool and code generator in its own right. Early versions generated C; the end product with Version 2 is C++ and Ontos calls. Of especial interest are the features which support object wrappers, so that existing code and code patched in by software engineers can be separated out from generated code. This is an essential feature possessed by very few code generators and CASE tools. Original development was for Silicon Graphics hardware but a SparcStation version now exists. The Ptech code generator is incorporated in DEC Design, a meta-CASE tool which at the time of writing supports Ptech and Coad/Yourdon.

Coad/Yourdon OOA is supported by OOATool from Object International. GE have a UNIX tool supporting OMT.

Having said that there are few commercial CASE tools supporting a genuinely object-oriented approach, we can yet specify a set of minimum requirements for such tools. These include the sort of flexibility provided by Object Maker, Paradigm Plus, VSF and IPSYS, user-defined method rules and graphics, good external interfaces to databases, spreadsheets, text processors and expert systems tools, multi-user support and an open repository. Systems like Ptech and VSF, which are essentially single-user tools, are severely limited because of this. CASE tools without multi-user support, version control and some notion of work packages are virtually useless except for the smallest project. Multi-user support is essential for any large project and especially so when development teams are geographically distributed. This is emphasized by prototyping and the particular problems of evolving extensible systems.

Diagramming tools are essential for object-oriented analysis. Flexibility and user-defined rules and graphics are an obvious aid to companies unwilling to tie themselves to methods which may change or become inappropriate. Good external interfaces to databases, spreadsheets and text processors allow existing systems and practices to be accommodated and let all contributors to a project work in the way they find most comfortable and productive.

The significance of IBM's AD/Cycle and Repository Manager announcements is not to be underestimated owing to the likely commitment of many large users to these products when they emerge and stabilize. CASE tools, whether they support object-oriented methods or not, will have to tolerate interfaces with a repository even if they support more efficient data and knowledge representations.

Interfaces to expert systems tools permit deficiencies in the way methodological rules are implemented to be corrected. The latter will be important when in-house methods are developed and there is a need to impose new consistency or method-following rules on the CASE tool. The alternative is to embed rule-based languages in the tools. Users could define expert systems which could apply various checks and constraints to their designs. This possibility emphasizes the need for an open repository, so that the expert system may access it directly through a known interface. Examples of CASE tools with such an open architecture are DesignAid and SELECT, which both use Btrieve as the primary database for text and graphics. An expert system shell with a Btrieve interface, such as Leonardo, could be used, in principle, to implement any additional rules that a system designer wanted to specify. Often a mainframe repository is required to ensure consistency and wide availability, which militates against tools without open architectures. The advantages of a mainframe over a micro or workstation network are to be evaluated against the power, flexibility and cost effectiveness of the latter. This is further discussed in Chapter 10.

Method independence is a controversial issue. On the one hand it is said that, to be of real value, a CASE tool has to be used within the context of a structured method and life-cycle model to which the organization is totally committed. Further, most users and suppliers agree that an expert on the particular method used must be attached to the project almost full-time to guarantee success. On the other hand, as has been pointed out, rigid adherence to methods is often bureaucratic, stifles innovation, does not apply equally to all types of project and can increase costs by large amounts. Analysts who follow formal rules blindly do not always develop the skill of being able to deal successfully with the unexpected. Thus there will be a need on some projects to adapt and alter even the best of methods. This indicates a strong requirement for tools which are useful independently of any particular method: tools where any appropriate diagram type or documentation style can be used. An alternative is to develop tools, such as Object Maker and VSF, which can be adapted to different methods. However, this is not the same as the mix-and-match approach which is sometimes found to be efficacious. Also, the cost of such adaptation can be significant and inappropriate for a minor diversion from a method within a project which is mostly conformant to it. Thus, for many projects the so-called 'vertical' or 'lower' CASE tools may be preferred to ones which incorporate a full life-cycle model and method. Here productivity is enhanced by powerful diagramming and consistency-checking tools, but creativity is less restricted. The downside is that the systems engineers have to be able to follow a method, whether formal or in their heads, without the guidance and support of the tool. The correct answer, I believe, is to make the decision in the light of the peculiarities of each individual project.

An additional requirement for a CASE tool for object-oriented projects is the provision of class-library navigation tools. Such tools imply the need for a librarian analogous to a data administrator in every software organization.

No existing CASE tools meet all these requirements. At present I would advise either choosing a very low-cost tool that can be abandoned and replaced as the field matures or, if this is unacceptable, investing in a meta-CASE tool.

Business analysis methods which map onto object-oriented designs easily are still rare. Methods such as IE are data-driven but still separate the functional design in the, often vain, hope that the project team will find time to construct entity life histories or process/entity matrices to complete the combination of function and data. BIS have attempted to incorporate object-oriented design and analysis methods within SSADM, IE and other mainstream methods. Several other consultancies are pursuing this path actively. It is certainly to be recommended that any object-oriented approach should not neglect the lessons learnt from the last 30 years of system development experience. It is important that development organizations are able to build on their existing data modelling, DFD and other skills.

Booch (1991) thinks that expert systems technology may be employed to help designers invent new classes to simplify a class structure and with similar creative design acts, although he opines that this is unlikely to be possible in the near future owing to the problem of incorporating common-sense knowledge. I do not think it is possible at all, partly for ontological reasons and partly because I believe that intelligence is a social phenomenon and therefore not replicable by machines, but this is not the place to give the arguments in detail (see Langham (1993)).

With the development of object-oriented database products and similar extensions to RDBMS-based 4GLs, a large part of the functionality of CASE tools may become redundant. The reason for this is that much of the justification for diagramming techniques boils down to two things: implementation independence and the difficulty of reading the structure of a system from its code or agreeing it with non-computer-literate users. Implementation independence has been an important issue in systems design for some time. An implementation-independent representation, say in the form of structured English and/or dataflow diagrams, allows the analysis and design to be carried out prior to the choice of implementation language and hardware and can act as a medium for transporting applications from one machine to another. Thus, even prototypes are often usefully converted into 'paper models', as illustrated for example by the case-studies mentioned by Bodkin and Graham (1989). Now, a high-level language is precisely one where the gap between conception and implementation is narrower and if we can generate code automatically from pictures – and after all that is precisely what screen painters and code generators in CASE tools often do – then we can, in effect, code in the intermediate representation. In a 4GL based on a database for example, pictorial software generation is already available to some extent with forms-based report and screen designers. As 4GLs of this type move closer to the idea of non-procedural, pictorial programming the distinction between analysis, design and programming blurs. In some high-performance applications this will never be a tolerable approach owing to inevitable performance overheads, but in many large commercial systems the extra cost of computer power (getting cheaper) will be overcome by the decreased cost of development and maintenance which depends on skilled human labour power (getting scarcer). For the time being, however, methods will remain an important issue in software development. Further, object-oriented databases now automate issues like version control which would have to be added to conventional products.

At present, I think that CASE is an immature technology that will evolve rapidly under the influence of object-oriented ideas and methods.

Prototyping and the use of formal methods and proofs of correctness both contribute significantly to the quality and reliability of systems. Detailed discussion of these important life-cycle issues is deferred to the next chapter.

▤ 8.5   The OMG abstract object model and OOA/D reference model

The Object Management Group have defined a high-level reference model for object-oriented analysis and design. Its purpose is to cover all imaginable issues in object-oriented software engineering but it is not a method in itself but a framework within which methods may be evaluated. Schematically the reference model is described in Figure 8.58.

Object modelling provides a set of terms and concepts for representing everything within the scope of analysis and design as an object. It defines standard terms. SOMA, as described in Section 8.3, is concerned with object modelling.

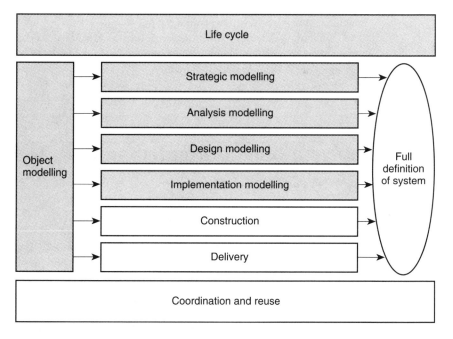

Figure 8.58 The OMG reference model. Only the shaded areas are within the scope of the model.

Strategic modelling covers enterprise and business modelling, requirements capture and development planning. **Analysis modelling** covers the process of obtaining a description of the problem domain. Chapter 9 describes some of these aspects of SOMA, together with the life cycle. **Design modelling** (called logical design in this book) consists in adding non-public information to class specifications and producing a solution to some particular problem including system objects. **Implementation modelling** is physical design and involves designing modules, the distribution strategy and taking account of the software and hardware to be used.

There is minimal normative structure in the reference model. You can use a waterfall or prototyping approach. You can start at any point from business strategy modelling to code. The OMG special interest group who developed the reference model considered over 30 methods and none of them were excluded by the result. Interestingly, the SIG viewed functional models as being to do with grouping and views rather than as a part of the analysis model. The reference model embraces the OMG object model for object-oriented analysis and design which is now fairly comprehensive and quite widely agreed. The need for the object model arose because of the large variance in meaning given to terms like 'object' and 'method' in the literature. Does 'object' mean instance or class? The object model now declares that **object type** shall be the correct term for class. Some of us will continue to say 'object' for short, just as data modellers say 'entity' for entity type. **Methods** are defined as the implementation of **operations**. This book has used this standard terminology as far as possible and pointed out any deviations. Table 8.1 sets out the terminology of the object model and the various specialization relationships between terms.

One of the beneficial side-effects of the activities of the OMG's object-oriented analysis SIG has been to prompt methodologists to extend their methods into more areas of the reference model.

▤ 8.6 Applying object-oriented analysis to business modelling – a case-study

Object-oriented analysis can be applied not only to the analysis of computer systems but, in principle, to the analysis of any 'system'. We will illustrate this with a case-study showing how the method is applied to modelling the structure of an organization and the information flows within it, with the aim of providing a model of the business that could be used to simulate different organizational strategies. This case-study is based on one carried out by the author for the office services department of a life assurance office. The project used an adaptation of the Coad/Yourdon method. Although business rules did not have to be used because of the relatively high-level nature of the exercise, a more extensive study would almost certainly have had to use them.

Table 8.1 The OMG abstract object model concept hierarchy.

Term	Specializations
Value	Object Non-object Concept
Non-object	Relationship
Concept	Modelling concept Object model concept
Modelling concept	Strategic modelling concept Analysis modelling concept Implementation modelling concept Deliverable Activity type Technique
Object model concept	Rule concept Object behavioural concept Group and view concept Object structure concept
Rule concept	Constraint Assertion
Object behavioural concept	Operation Event State Transition Message
Message	Request
Group and view concept	Diagram Schema Quality concept Strategic model G&V concepts Analysis model G&V concepts Design model G&V concepts Implementation model G&V concepts
Object structure concept	Attribute type Object type Relationship type
Object type	Strategic model object type Analysis model object type Design model object type Implementation model object type
Relationship type	Association Aggregation Specialization Instantiation Usage

One of the problems the department faced was the option to move to full electronic publishing. It already ran a sophisticated printing operation but typesetting was carried out on old-fashioned composing workstations and paste-up was done manually. Figure 8.59 shows the high-level structure of the department and its interactions with other departments as seven layers. Each layer is shown as an object and the links represent possible message passing.

Each layer may be viewed externally or from an internal point of view, as is illustrated for the printing and graphics division in Figure 8.60.

The external view defines permissible message passing between the departmental object and other organizations. The internal view indicates that there are two subdivisions, each of which is represented as an object. The Graphics area has a manager, a graphic artist, a plate-maker and so on (its composition structure) and required functions are partly listed in Figure 8.60(b). It communicates with the printshop whose structure is partly exposed by Figure 8.60(b) by, for example, sending completed negatives for printing. The detailed internal structures are not shown. Because the introduction of desktop publishing equipment was contemplated, we drew the message-passing structure of Graphics both before and after its introduction. This is depicted in Figure 8.61 where it can be seen how the process is simplified by the removal of a separate paste-up rôle, the graphic artist now being able to combine WYSIWYG typesetting (not available on the old workstations) with graphics and to produce PostScript output for direct input to the plate-making machinery.

It should be noted that, while this notation proved very expressive and useful for most areas of the business, it was sometimes more natural to use dataflow dia-

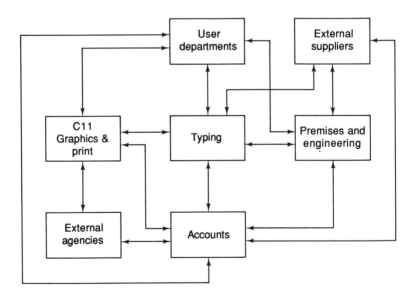

Figure 8.59 Layered representation of office services.

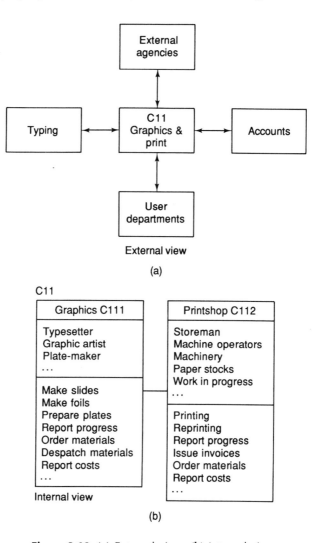

Figure 8.60 **(a)** External view; **(b)** Internal view.

grams and this was done on a few occasions, reflecting the view that rigid methods stifle innovation and inhibit productivity. The use of dataflow diagrams in information systems strategy planning is discussed by Eastlake (1987). In all, the object-oriented analysis method was helpful in clarifying the problems and solutions and communicating the results to management who, we found, understood the notation readily with a little explanation.

In this case the modelling was done entirely on paper with no more sophisticated technology than a word processor. This showed up one difficulty, referred to earlier, in constantly having to redraw boxes to contain more attributes and operations. This characterizes business models and commercial problems and an

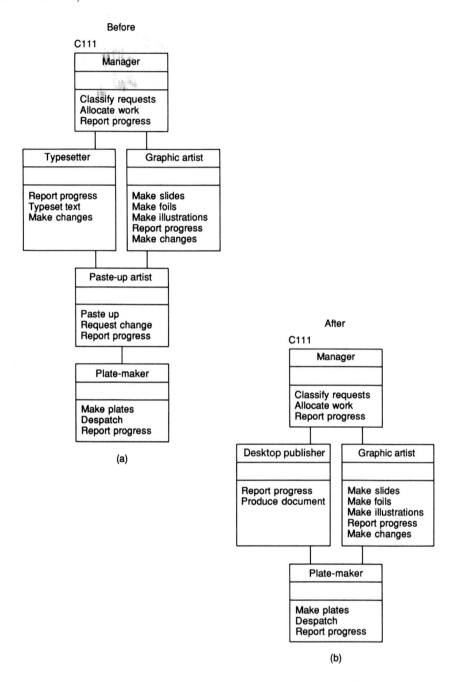

Figure 8.61 (a) Before the introduction of desk-top publishing; **(b)** After its introduction.

adaptable drawing tool would have been useful. Since performance was not critical, we considered using Smalltalk or HyperCard, but a copy was not to hand and deadlines dictated that we did not in fact exercise this option.

⊟ 8.7 Summary

The benefits of object-oriented programming apply equally to object-oriented analysis and object-oriented design and are even amplified. Object-oriented specifications and designs have the potential to be just as reusable and extensible as object-oriented programs. This is especially true of specifications as they are often less specific to a purpose. The benefits are potentially greatest at the analysis level.

Object-oriented design and analysis overlap more than design and analysis in conventional approaches, owing to the fact that they both try to model real-world objects. This is especially true of the distinction between analysis and logical design. This helps close the traceability gap and is closely bound up with a prototyping approach to systems building.

Object-oriented analysis exists in several forms, with over 50 published suggestions. The approaches are ternary or unary, cover different fragments of the life cycle and vary according to the degree of emphasis placed on state models. Most are weak on issues such as business rules. The SOMA approach recommended here emphasizes simplicity and semantic richness. It adds rules, fuzziness, layers with clear semantics and permits designers to convert rules to assertions. It proceeds using seven activities:

- Layers
- Objects
- Structures
  - Usage structures
  - Classification structures
  - Composition structures
- Associations and Data Semantics
  - Modality and multiplicity
- Attributes
  - Types, defaults, validation, security
- Methods or operations
  - Parameters and their types, assertions
- Rules
  - Control rules
  - Business rules
  - Triggers

Semantic primitives other than specialization and composition may be required for certain applications. The emphasis on explicit attributes arises more in commercial systems than in technical domains. The emphasis on semantics and data models arises from similar considerations. The method of handling exceptions and business rules presented in this text is essentially non-procedural and is to be contrasted with the procedural exception handling of HOOD and OOSD. The activities enumerated above need to be regarded as subject to iteration. The specification itself must be prototyped.

Object-oriented analysis must include techniques and notations which are semantically rich. That is, it must address not only object identity, abstraction and inheritance, but the declarative semantics of objects. I have suggested that rule-based techniques are appropriate for this purpose and shown how they can be notationally included.

The many object-oriented methods surveyed represent opinions rather than mature methods. Hybrid methods based on synthesized ideas from these suggestions, conventional methods, AI and semantic modelling are emerging. A rationalization of the current position is expected to happen soon with a few market leaders emerging. There is no clear candidate for market leader yet. As an example of the confusion, consider the many notations for classification structures on offer. Just a few of these are illustrated in Figure 8.62.

The prospects for object-oriented analysis look bright at the time of writing, especially because of the consensus developing rapidly around the OMG models. The benefits of reuse and extensibility are a strong driving force for its widespread adoption. There are currently at least two distinct styles of notation, one deriving from the Booch tradition and represented by HOOD and OOSD, and notations of the type described in this chapter derived from data modelling. There will probably be a convergence between these two styles as designers tackle bigger, more commercially oriented systems and business analysts take on more problems involving multimedia, concurrency and real-time operations. CASE tools supporting the notations and method are a necessity to enable analysts to use the methods effectively and efficiently.

CASE tools capable of handling object-oriented concepts are emerging. Object-oriented databases and 4GLs may supersede CASE tools for some purposes, including configuration management.

Object-oriented analysis can be applied to organizational strategy as well as to systems development.

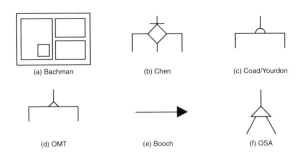

Figure 8.62 Some of the suggested classification structure notations.

☰ 8.8 Bibliographical notes

There is a huge number of sources claiming to offer object-oriented design and analysis methods although few bear close examination as complete methods. Coad and Yourdon (1990, 1991, 1991a), Desfray (1992), Embley *et al.* (1992), Jacobson *et al.* (1992), Martin and Odell (1992), Rumbaugh *et al.* (1991), and Shlaer and Mellor (1991) are among the exceptions and have been discussed extensively in this chapter. BON is described in Nerson (1992), OBA in Rubin and Goldberg (1992). Without particularly endorsing or criticizing any of their methods, I should also mention the suggestions of Ackroyd and Daum (1991), Alabiso (1988) , Bailin (1989), Champeaux *et al.* (1993), Colbert (1994), Davis (1993), Dillon and Tan (1993), Gorman and Choobineh (1989), Halliday and Weibel (1993), Ilvari (1991), Kappel (1991), Kilov and Ross (1994), Lee and Carver (1991), Leiberherr *et al.*, (1988), McGregor and Sykes (1992), Page-Jones *et al.* (1990), Ward (1989) and Wilson (1990). Dedere (1994) describes his MERODE method. Meyer and Mandrioli (1992) covers recent advances. The methods of Wirfs-Brock *et al.* (1990) and Lorenz (1993) mentioned in Chapter 7 both use CRC cards as a prime modelling technique. Lorenz also contains a notion of use cases. Both these methods may be regarded as analysis rather than design techniques.

Winblad *et al.* (1990) give a survey with a different emphasis from that given herein, and no suggestions for extensions to the methods described. Wilkie (1993) surveys several methods including the OSMOSYS method developed by Winter Partners. A really first-rate survey and classification of over 20 methods is given by Monarchi and Puhr (1992). Henderson-Sellers and Edwards (1993) updates Henderson-Sellers (1992), provides a survey of several methods and introduces a comprehensive life-cycle approach called MOSES.

Martin and Odell (1992) describe a method for object-oriented analysis based on a sort of merger of Martin's IE and John Edwards' Ptech methods. There is an apparent schism between the object-oriented principles expounded in the early chapters and the method presented later. Principally this is because both IE and Ptech model the world using three quite distinct notations: entity models, state change models and dataflow diagrams – although these are now fashionably renamed object structure, object behaviour and object flow schemata. Search as you may, it is never made clear if or how these separate viewpoints can be combined into a single model of the objects of a system including both their structure and behaviour. This does not mean that the method will not work. The final (rather good) chapters give advice on how to convert the notation into an implementation in an OOPL, but this is never done at the pre-design level. The equivalent advice on non-object-oriented implementation is similar to OMT. Other interesting ideas include viewing relations as 'immutable' composition structures in an attempt to rescue some of the relational model within the OT framework. Chapters 26 to 28 discuss design and implementation and are well worth reading for the advice contained, which appears to be based on sound practical experience. There is a particularly interesting discussion of a technique called *object slicing* which helps resolve multiple inheritance in languages that do not support it. The discussion of event scheduling will interest GUI builders particularly. The four appendices dealing with the relationship between object-oriented and entity-relationship modelling are among the best and most thought-provoking in the book and offer interesting new perspectives on some well-known concepts. For example, the state of an object can be viewed as either the collection of its associations or as its collection of superclasses. This book should not be confused with James Martin's *Principles of Object-Oriented Analysis and Design* with which it shares several common chapters. The latter omits much of the more interesting material to be found in the Martin and Odell version but does contain one innovation: rules. Unfortunately these rules are dealt with in a non-object-oriented fashion. They are merely 'written on the diagrams' and thus cannot be encapsulated or inherited.

Jacobson *et al.* (1992) had already become a classic a year prior to its long-awaited publication, partly because of the standing of the authors and the age of their Objectory method. OOA specialists will profit from reading it but for the general reader the proprietary nature of Objectory and the sheer length of the text will probably put them off. However, the chapter on testing is one of the best treatments to be found in the literature. The explanation of OOSE is somewhat verbose and I found that the two case-study chapters were far more enlightening than the abstract description. It also contains some good advice on issues such as how to distinguish objects from attributes (which may vary from application to application) and how to assign operations to objects.

Andleigh and Gretzinger (1992) describe their Frame-Object Analysis method and provide much useful background information on software engineering, databases and distributed processing. The method is applied in some detail to the design of a financial trading system.

Booch (1991) contains a large number of insights and heuristics about analysis in a book ostensibly concerned with design, how to apprehend objects and how to use and manage the technology. Berard (1993) also offers many insights and clarifications along with a detailed discussion of the application of Constantine's ideas on cohesion and coupling to object-oriented systems, though I prefer the briefer treatment of Page-Jones (1992).

Lenzerini, Nardi and Simi (1991) surveys the different interpretations of inheritance in knowledge engineering and object-oriented programming. It provides useful insights into the problems of multiple inheritance.

Object Magazine, JOOP and *ROAD (Report on Object-Oriented Analysis and Design)* are good sources of up-to-date information on object-oriented analysis. The September 1990 and September 1992 issues of the *Communications of the ACM* were both devoted to object-oriented analysis and design and contain a great deal which would be of interest. The paper on connascence by Page-Jones in the 1992 issue is highly recommended reading for all object-oriented designers, as is the description of BON in Nerson's paper.

9

Managing object-oriented methods

He will learn to his cost that to bring a science by criticism to the point
where it can be dialectically presented is an altogether different thing
from applying an abstract ready-made system of logic to mere inklings
of such a system.

Marx to Engels, 1 February 1858

Companies introducing object-oriented technologies, whether object-oriented programming, databases, design or analysis, will need to manage projects using any or all of these. The question that must be asked is whether existing management practices, structured methods, CASE tools and so on will work unchanged or whether new practices, styles and metrics must be adopted. This chapter sets out to answer this question and provide guidelines for managing object-oriented projects.

The principal distinctive features of all the object-oriented technologies, from a managerial viewpoint, are the way objects model real-world features, the possibilities of reuse, the easy extensibility of such systems and their richer semantic content. This entails spending more effort early on in projects, so that estimating practices must change. Other changes will be discussed in Section 9.1. This section describes, in outline, the recommended SOMA life-cycle and process model.

Most object-oriented analysis and design methods omit to prescribe methods for identifying objects and Section 9.2 introduces a range of techniques for doing this which are an integral part of the SOMA method but which may be usefully used in any methodological context.

Perhaps the most significant change which must, I believe, accompany a move to object-oriented methods is the use of prototyping. Prototyping is much misunderstood and much maligned. Furthermore, I believe that even the proponents of prototyping have misunderstood its use and function. Therefore, one of the tasks of this chapter is to explain what prototyping is, what it is not and how it is best used. This is done in Section 9.3.

The Object Management Group reference model described in Chapter 8 provides a framework against which the model outlined in this chapter may be evaluated. The areas of the reference model covered here to different extents are the life cycle, strategic modelling, analysis modelling, design modelling and coordination and reuse.

9.1 Managing analysis and design

This section presents some project management guidelines for projects using object-oriented analysis and design, and possibly planning to use object-oriented programming. These comments are divided among seven stages, from project initiation to delivery.

Although an object-oriented approach throughout the life cycle is ideal since the same concepts and notations are dealt with throughout, it is possible to use object-oriented design and programming with conventional structured analysis or indeed mix technologies in several different ways, as illustrated in Table 9.1.

Table 9.1 The feasibility of combining object-oriented and conventional approaches.

Analysis	Design	Coding	Feasibility
Conventional	Conventional	Conventional	High
Conventional	Conventional	Object-oriented	Low
Conventional	Object-oriented	Object-oriented	Medium
Object-oriented	Object-oriented	Object-oriented	High
Object-oriented	Object-oriented	Conventional	Fairly high
Object-oriented	Conventional	Conventional	Medium

A conventional design will not usually map well onto an object-oriented language, though we have already seen that there are clear heuristics for implementing an object-oriented design in a conventional language. Converting the products of object-oriented analysis to conventional design or vice versa is perfectly feasible but introduces an extra layer of complexity owing to changes in notation. This section will assume that a purely object-oriented approach has been selected.

9.1.1 Project initiation and set-up

One of the most important and urgent issues for this sort of project is proper training. Analysts should be fully trained in the sort of object identification and knowledge elicitation techniques discussed in Section 9.2 and in object-oriented analysis, design and programming concepts. This helps them to uncover latent knowledge and requirements and to map these onto objects. Managers should be trained in object-oriented concepts as well. At least one manager and one analyst should be trained and/or experienced. Other staff can be used in journeyman rôles to transfer the skills more widely. Where in-house experience is not available many organizations have found that bringing in an external mentor is highly beneficial.

It is critical, for object-oriented projects that focus on user needs – as they should – to get total senior management commitment. This will not only ensure the budget, but guarantee the allocation of the necessary time commitment from users and domain experts. The first task of the project manager is to identify key users, domain experts and sponsors and get them involved, committed and enthusiastic. Techniques for achieving this include establishing and agreeing clear objectives, terms of reference and benefits. Asking users to place measures on their objectives and prioritize them is very helpful in refining them

Once users and experts are identified they must be interviewed, either individually or in workshops. This is where the training in knowledge elicitation comes in. Good knowledge engineers plan every interview or workshop and establish its objectives. Preliminary interviews should be short and top-down through the organizational hierarchy.

Project planning is affected by prototyping and the intent to reuse system components. Both intentions mean that project planners must allow much more time for analysis and design, although coding prototypes is included in these activities. Coding should be quick and straightforward, or even non-existent as a separate activity. This does not mean there is no division of labour between designers and programmers. Thus, in planning and negotiating with sponsors, one should plan to invest in thorough analysis and design, before even beginning prototyping, and allow more time for it.

Picking up the point made earlier about training and the experiences mentioned in Chapter 3, it is often wise to prototype in a pure object-oriented language, such as Smalltalk, at first. This helps prevent C++ programmers programming in C style, which is easy to do in C++. Quality control should be warned to look for this trait. One metric they can use is the number of classes defined per week, or per n lines of code.

It is recommended, not only for object-oriented systems but in general, that managers organize their projects into small teams, because the results are generally better. In object-oriented analysis one can use layers to partition the work. In this way the project structure should reflect program structure and *vice versa*. This approach reduces management overhead because tasks are well defined and bounded, and everyone knows where they stand. A small team is probably formed from about two to five souls. It has been the consistent experience of early projects that the object-oriented style of software engineering simplifies management.

Waterfall models of software development do not permit the exploitation of prototyping or support the construction of systems where reusability and extensibility are important goals. Adopt a risk-driven spiral model, such as that suggested by Boehm (1981), instead, or even a 'fountain' model such as that of Henderson-

Sellers and Edwards (1990, 1993). Incremental development, if feasible and properly managed, will help users with the transition to the new system and distribute testing resources more evenly across the project. It also improves morale among both users and developers and may permit some coding to proceed in parallel with design, which enables tight deadlines to be met more easily.

Reuse does not happen automatically. Objects may be reusable, but that is only their potential. To get the benefits of reuse, it is necessary to actually reuse the reusable. This means that the resource of a library of objects has to be carefully managed. The process of managing objects involves matching existing objects to requirements and then either reusing them or customizing them. If no suitable library class exists one will have to be built. New and customized objects then need to be examined for reusability by as many people as possible before being granted the status of library objects.

It is a good idea to work within the context of a standard process model; which is to say the components of a development environment comprising the following layers:

- Modelling
  - Business object models
  - Application object models
  - Foundation classes
- Methods
  - Techniques and notation
  - Life-cycle model
  - Rôles
  - Team structures
  - Standards and metrics
  - Etc.
- Tools
  - CASE tools
  - Project support tools
  - Standard metric collection procedures
- Authoring systems
  - GUI authoring tools
  - 4GLs
  - Languages
  - Databases
  - Application Frameworks/Class libraries

If possible, this should be standard across all projects.

9.1.2 Problem investigation and requirements capture

The first task of requirements capture is to identify key users and domain experts more accurately and assess their suitability, availability, willingness, and so on. To anticipate potential conflicts and hold-ups, it is also wise to appoint lead users and experts who will resolve disputes. Remember that interview and workshop schedules need to be flexible and slightly elastic, since busy users cancel meetings. On the other hand, users who are not busy are to be suspected of not being particularly knowledgeable or good at their jobs either.

The key skill here is interviewing. A few points should be noted about interviewing and the resources it consumes.

Successful one-shot interviewing usually requires two people, one to talk – that is keep the conversation going – and one to write and sketch. This is true at first; once a rapport with users is established, one-to-one contact works well. A rule of thumb I use is that an hour-long interview will consume between half a day and a day to complete the write-up and analysis. Tape-recording interviews is highly beneficial, but permission should be sought and the interviewers must be sensitive. For example, the tape should be stopped when the phone rings: it may be a personal or sensitive subject that is being discussed. Do not bore users, or domain experts, by exposing your techniques. There is nothing that bores people as much as Kelly grids, card sorts or phenomenology (see Section 9.2). Use questioning techniques covertly, in a natural conversational style. Good training and experience will develop this skill.

The alternative to interviewing people individually is to conduct workshop sessions, often called JAD (joint application development) workshops. These can be split into scoping sessions and refinement sessions if possible.

The scoping sessions must establish the project's terms of reference and define and prioritize objectives. This involves placing a rough forecast of the expected benefit to be derived by achieving each objective. Further, it tends to reveal grouping among objectives: when one objective cannot realize its benefits without another being also achieved, say. The most important benefit of this prioritization is that, in later project phases, it enables project managers to place emphasis on the critical modules. This is especially important where prototyping or rapid development is contemplated. The priorities should be traced through to modules, therefore, wherever possible. The first major task when the SOMA approach is adopted is to produce a context model emphasizing message flow. This is similar to obtaining a Level 0 DFD but takes longer and gives more information. Facilitators and analysts must understand that objects with responsibilities are being sought and not functions. Dataflows should be regarded strictly as message flows between the system object and the external entities, which may be actors (that is users playing a particular rôle), external systems or anything else that interacts with the system. It is important that message flows are related to events at this stage. The format should be:

Message name	Trigger event	Source	Information sent/received	Expected result	Target

Diagrams need not show every such relationship between clients and server as long as this table is complete. That is, where there is more than one message flow between the same source and target then only one arrow need be drawn. As an example, consider a counterparty who phones an equity trader to make a sale of equities. We might then record the message as 'external sale request' between counterparty and trader and specify that counterparty identity, instrument, limit price and quantity are passed as parameters. The result is a trade confirmation and an instruction to Settlements. The trigger is random action by counterparty. Note further that these messages can be classified. External sale requests could be for equities, bonds, foreign exchange and so on. This should be exploited by the facilitator to elicit more of the context model objects and to find gaps in the model.

We have looked at the external interactions; now we look at the interactions internal to the business area and posit a 'system' within it. To this context model, use or **task scripts** (and subscripts to note exceptions) are added. These are roughly similar to the use cases used in Objectory, from where this idea is borrowed. Once the external environment has been discovered the first step is to identify the actors. Actors are users adopting a rôle to interact with the system for some purpose. These actors now communicate with the system as external entities. Object-oriented requirements capture and analysis has much in common with HCI design in this respect (see Johnson, 1992). Purposes may be viewed as goals with sub-goals, which may in turn be found from scripts. The question is: what sort of people or systems will make use of any proposed system and how will they expect it to behave? In other words, what responsibilities does the system have towards its users? For each message flow in the environment model, it should be established what the rôle player or external agent would normally expect to happen in the form of a script beginning with an event. For example, when a 'request to raise invoice' event occurs in an accounting system, the actor who does this might expect the system to check the credit limit and, if OK, print the invoice, send it to the client, file a copy and send a confirmation. No more detail is required at the scoping stage and it is probably sufficient that the system has a 'produce invoice' operation attached to some entity responsible for invoicing. Each script states what the system is normally expected to do. However, to emphasize exceptions it is advisable to record subscripts corresponding to exceptional conditions. Referring to Figure 8.28, the 'confirm deal' script may have an 'illegal deal' or 'check position' subscript and various objects will be required to implement the script. The script might read: 'To confirm a deal the trader enters the *counterparty* and *security* details and checks the limits on his *position*. If the limits are OK the deal is struck and confirmed'. Here there are at least three objects (in italics). Implicitly, for a computer system, there is also a 'screen' object handling the interaction. An exception subscript is far more useful. For example, the 'settle trade' script might read 'on receipt of ticket, match trade and record data'. When the match fails, a subscript such as 'alert exception manager and print letter' must be added. Another point to note is that task scripts may be classified just like objects. For example, a script for 'confirm equity trade' may inherit features from 'confirm trade' and add extra features specific to equities. This completes the scoping phase of the workshop. A matrix of events and objects affected should be produced if time permits.

The task script texts are then analysed to find both external and internal entities and the responsibilities of (a) the system and (b) the users. The results of the scoping session should be examined with a view to discovering as many object types and operations as possible. The main technique used is textual analysis of the task scripts and other pre-existing documents. Abbott textual analysis was explained in Section 7.2. Recall that, roughly speaking, nouns are candidate objects and verbs are candidate operations. These should be listed fairly uncritically as a basis for discussion. Subsequently questioning and discussion is used to refine the model and produce classification and composition structures which in turn are used to refine the model. During discussions the aims will be to:

- eliminate duplicates;
- classify objects as within or outside the system;
- eliminate 'accidental' objects (see Section 9.2) and demote them to attributes;
- insert relationship objects (if any);
- detect nouns used as stand-ins for verbs.

Now we have some objects (nouns) we must identify their responsibilities (that is, the services they provide to other components or actors) or the operations (methods) they can perform. To do this we may examine the verbs present in the scripts. These operations must then be attached to a suitable object type. The guiding principle is encapsulation: objects should contain and hide their data behind their operations. For example, a share register hides registrations behind an interface that permits it to send certificates to new registrants, pay dividends and so on. In the refinement workshops the functions will be tied to these and further objects.

Key questions that should be asked are:

- Who is involved in an interaction to carry out the responsibility?
- What exceptions may occur? (for example, credit limit exceeded)
- What services must be provided to execute the interaction?
- Which objects may provide such services?
- Which data does a service need to access? (These should be encapsulated by the object to which the operation is tied if possible)

The task scripts that were identified in the scoping stage should be further refined and checked for completeness. Have all potential actors and uses been identified? Have all exceptions been covered sufficiently? The task scripts should be further examined for entities and operations and the operations attached to the entities where possible.

Rough SOMA diagrams are produced including classification and composition structure diagrams where possible. The objects in the model are the basis for preparing CRC cards, one per object. For each of the operations on these cards we next identify collaborations (usage relationships). It has proved highly beneficial to use rôle-play to walk through the model and produce a usage diagram. Where objects with complex and significant states are discovered we produce a state model, though this is often done after the workshop session owing to lack of time. Another important activity that can be deferred until later is to check that all objectives are met by some object's operations, using a matrix technique. Risk identification should be attempted at this stage if time permits. Entities should be classified into interface objects (if any) and system objects. System objects should be further divided into application objects and domain objects. Domain objects are persistent and likely to be fairly stable in structure throughout the lifetime of the application, though their instances may change rapidly. Typical examples might include Share-Register, Client-Database, and so on. Application objects are more volatile. They contain the operations which are not firmly tied to long-term stored data. Making this separation helps with the maintainability of the system in future and corresponds to the traditional notion of data independence. For those familiar with Sybase, then roughly speaking, a Sybase server table with stored procedures will correspond to a domain object. The client would store the operations of application objects.

Each operation can now be provided with a process description exactly as in a conventional method, but these **must** be attached to an object.

Rules and constraints that connect attributes and operations to each other and specify things like conflict resolution strategy are also written down. For a system where declarative rules are important, such as trade-matching rules in a settlement system, this step is highly significant for two main reasons. First, recording the rules to which an object must conform directly as rules matches the way users think about the problem and is far easier to use as a communication tool. The alternative would be to record these rules as preprocessing steps within procedures, which is much harder to understand and, worse, makes implicit assumptions about the style of implementation. Secondly, where there is a corpus of declarative knowledge expressed as rules, it may be advantageous to implement these rules directly in a knowledge-based systems component of the final system with considerable benefits in terms of both rapidity of development and maintenance as regulations, say, change in future. Objects with many rules can be implemented directly as the rule-sets of an expert systems development tool. It is recommended that a simple IF/THEN syntax is used to record rules, as described in Section 8.3. The ordering of a set of rules is not significant. If it is, in the real world that is, then an operation should be defined instead. If an expert systems implementation is not desired then the rules can be converted to assertions and then to operations mechanically at design time. As pointed out in Chapter 5, some advanced relational databases provide for the storage of rules.

A modified CRC approach is most beneficial at this stage and the next step is to conduct a brainstorming session to elicit further key entities. Their names are written on large index cards. For each entity we add its responsibilities. These come from the preliminary analysis and the brainstorming. They are written on the index cards that represent the entities that perform these operations. Next it must be established which other entities collaborate with each entity to carry out each operation identified. During this process an attempt is made to organize the cards into classification and aggregation structures. Facilitators will use questioning techniques to elicit these structures, including the ones based on Kelly grids (see Section 9.2).

At this point rôle-playing may be carried out. Each participant takes one or more cards and acts its part. The facilitator issues events based on the task scripts and the messages are passed round verbally, noting changes of state on the back of the cards. In this way the responsibilities and collaborations are 'debugged' and issues exposed. Whether this works well will depend on the personalities of the participants to some extent.

Finally any constraints and rules that the objects are subject to should be recorded on the cards. The format for a SOMA class card is shown in Figure 9.1.

Classes are either application or domain objects as described above. Classes are either abstract or concrete. Abstract classes have no instances. Attributes have a type which is an object type or a primitive, for example, DoB(Date). Attributes that represent relationships have multiplicity and modality constraints, for example, WorksIn(Dept,0,1). It is important to note that relationships are to be regarded as one-way pointers **out** of the object and not as two-way links between objects. If a

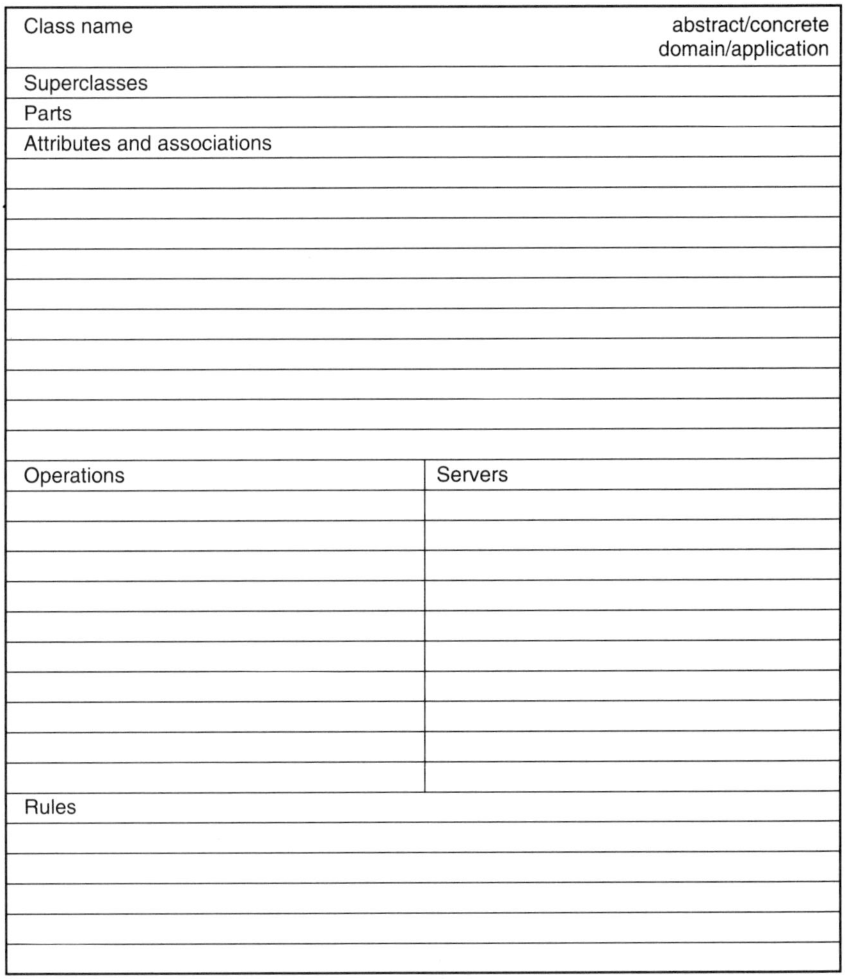

Class name	abstract/concrete domain/application
Superclasses	
Parts	
Attributes and associations	

Operations	Servers

Rules

Figure 9.1 A SOMA class card.

two-way link is required then an object representing the relationship must be defined, especially if the relationship has attributes itself.

The output from this stage consists of the completed cards and a series of event traces documenting the walkthroughs.

Object types should be divided into those with significant states and others. Where the states are complex a state transition model should be used to discover further operations. As an example, a trader probably does not have significant state, his behaviour only depending on his position (which he may not encapsulate), whereas a counterparty may and a device such as a funds-transfer system (SWIFT, say) always will. Whether this technique is useful depends largely on the application. In a settlement system, a trade is a likely candidate for having a complex life history in this way whereas a security is not. A state transition diagram is a good way to identify the responsibilities of an object like 'trade' and check for completeness. The CRC walkthrough establishes the global dynamics of the whole system while this technique looks at the internal dynamics of a complex object.

The task scripts relate to quality and will be used to produce test plans later. A short paragraph on quality should be included in the documentation. Matrices relating scripts to objects and objects to objectives are useful too. The use of existing systems and databases should be considered as early as possible. A paragraph on transition to design should also be appended.

Normally, JAD workshops are a precursor of rapid development, which is discussed in detail in Section 9.3.

The use of graphical and CASE tools is recommended to enhance productivity. Any tool used, however, should not entail a commitment to the implementation language unless it is known with complete certainty what the target environment will be and that it will never change. Since methods are undergoing very rapid evolution at present it is recommended that organizations either use very low-cost tools that can be replaced or adopt a meta-CASE approach. The latter option is more expensive but more adaptable and the tools should be less likely to need replacement as methods settle down. This gives advantages in terms of training and the continuity of large projects.

Deliverables from the workshops are as follows:

(1) Project name, description, participants and terms of reference.
(2) Objectives with measures and priorities where possible.
(3) Context model. This records message flows between the proposed system, regarded as an entire object, and the external agents and entities. The events triggering messages should be identified along with parameters passed and results returned.
(4) Task scripts defining the high-level behaviour of the system in response to interactions with external actors. Subscripts denoting exceptions or exceptional paths. Any diagrams illustrating them.
(5) List of nouns and verbs extracted from the task scripts for further analysis.
(6) An object model showing relationships, multiplicity, modality, partitioning, exclusivity and subtyping (inheritance) or some of these.
(7) Class cards with superclasses, parts, responsibilities, servers and rules.

(8) A matrix relating objectives to objects and their operations (used to prioritize implementation).
(9) A set of classification and aggregation structure diagrams.
(10) A usage (message passing) diagram showing the system boundary.
(11) A state diagram for each object type with complex and significant internal states (optional).
(12) For each operation a process description.
(13) Quality report (relating task scripts to objects).
(14) Transition to design report (distinguishing application, domain and interface objects).
(15) Event/object matrix (optional).
(16) Risk analysis (optional).

Deliverables from this stage when the workshop approach is not used include interview transcripts or summaries and paper models, which include task scripts, key objects in the domain, structures, application objectives and critical success factors. State diagrams may also be included. The project's design goals and principles should be published and discussed within the team and with sponsors. For example, simple interfaces may be a design goal. This includes the examination of the commercial importance of design goals such as reusability, extensibility, and so on. Quality control should check the products of the project against these agreed goals.

At this stage a peer review of the paper model is required. After the first review, prototype construction can begin. The prototype should be tested and then reviewed with users and/or experts before reconstructing the paper model.

As we have seen, regular group-work sessions with peers to review reuse, use of library objects and goals contribute to productivity.

Another key task in this stage is estimation. Most traditional estimation methods rely on either experience, using comparison with similar projects, or metrics which depend on first estimating the number of lines of code to be produced. Neither method is appropriate for the estimation of object-oriented systems. The heuristic methods will not work, simply because there is not yet enough experience of this kind of project in the world, and some people claim they lead to bias even in conventional projects. Secondly, the measure of lines of source code also relies on experience and is impossible to use except for a language, such as COBOL, in which many applications have been written within the same industry or organization. The obvious unit of estimation for object-oriented programming, or design for that matter, is the object. A concrete technique with appropriate metrics for object-oriented estimation has been proposed by Laranjiera (1990). The only conventional estimation technique likely to be at all useful is Function Points Analysis (Albrecht and Gaffney, 1983). This method may give a rough first estimate if used with care and judgement.

The only relevant metric quoted in this book is the very rough guide that a tested object of the *right* granularity costs about two man-months. However, this is based on non-commercial projects (CAD, CASE, process industry, and so on) and no one yet knows how to define the right granularity for commercial systems.

9.1.3 The analysis stage

Once the elicitation stage has been initiated, as above, proper analysis begins. This covers definition of domain objects and behaviour, structures, users, business rules and business process modelling at the domain level. Analysis was covered extensively in the previous chapter and the main tasks were covered there, so need not be repeated here.

Build the paper model following the steps outlined in Section 8.3 or using your favourite analysis method. Use the layers that emerge to define work packages and analysis teams for very large projects. Continue refining or rewriting the prototype to implement the paper model as it evolves. Impose a time-box discipline (as described in Section 9.3) on the iterations and evaluate the risks and rewards of changing the schedule in the light of new information. Make sure that each new prototype module is tested before review with users or experts.

Analysis is the first opportunity for the identification of reuse of existing component classes and identification of classes that may be suitable for entry into the component library.

In object-oriented analysis it is necessary to integrate new modules as they are developed. Version control procedures must be established for this purpose. Layers or classes are the units of configuration management as well as of work packaging.

Review both the prototype and the paper model with users and/or experts. Workshop sessions are valuable and efficient at this stage too, and can be run pretty much as described in Section 9.1.2, but go into more detail and involve fewer users. Interviews at this stage are typically focused rather than structured.

Release current public versions of prototype and paper model for discussion and criticism by users. This helps with transition to the new system and aids credibility and communication.

Continue to use group work sessions within the analysis and prototyping team. These sessions will be looking at reusability, use of library classes and duplication of function among classes.

If the project is converting from an existing system, use object wrappers to protect investment in existing code and smooth the transition. Languages like C++ help accomplish this and thus decisions made at this stage affect the choice of languages and class libraries.

9.1.4 The design stage

Design modelling involves the addition of system and HCI objects and their behaviour to the analysis model and the addition of more detail. Again, the design process has been covered already in terms of representation. In SOMA the key step in moving to logical design is to convert rules to assertions. One purpose of the design stage is established by the need to review the analysis products for technical feasibility. Therefore, the project may have to iterate at this point, and re-analyse. This is inevitable and should be planned for.

The products of design modelling include object diagrams, instance diagrams, structures, layers, modules, message-passing topology and so on, depending on the design techniques adopted. Document every new library object fully. Physical design or implementation modelling includes module definition and distribution strategy and interpretation of hardware and language constraints. The SOMA design stage at present only covers design modelling.

There should be a defined strategy for mapping the model onto the target language. This involves introducing language-specific constructs such as friends in C++, flattening inheritance structures in the case of non-object-oriented languages and converting rules into language features in non-rule-based ones.

Choose class libraries carefully. The choice may influence the design significantly. The project team members should be encouraged to invest time in learning about the libraries. Such investment will be repaid quickly.

Group work continues to be valuable during design. Hold design reviews to establish that all key abstractions have been identified and comment on their likely reuse.

Classification structures may have to be refined during implementation, as instances become known. Again, this is inevitable and must be planned for.

Design may be largely accomplished within prototype iterations, though prototyping should not start without some preliminary analysis and outline design. Even then, the design should be documented using an object-oriented notation.

9.1.5 The coding stage

At this stage, developers have to refine the prototype with performance in mind, or rebuild it from scratch if necessary. If a rebuild is contemplated then assign layers or individual objects with low connectivity to programming teams. Test and document every object thoroughly and review its reusability.

Report reuse and extension problems and use these to review the use of library objects. Refine classification structures during implementation, as instances become known.

Programming is much more efficient if powerful tools are available. In object-oriented programming, good debuggers and class hierarchy browsers are essential. The budget should include provision for their purchase. Incremental compilers are almost essential. They remove tedious and costly recompilation delays. Avoid languages which do not support incremental compilation. Test every object as it is produced, and again as it becomes part of a classification structure.

Group work becomes invaluable during coding.

9.1.6 Testing

Testing object-oriented systems, as with conventional ones, involves verification and validation. Verification means ensuring that the code meets the specification and validation checks that the result actually meets current requirements. Testing often takes place in the reverse of the order in which the system is produced. Thus, unit tests of modules or classes occur first and whole system tests last, with integration tests of whole layers between. After delivery, regression tests check that functions supported by the original release are still supported by subsequent fixes. Usually a test harness is built to automate regression tests.

Jacobson *et al.* (1992) point out that polymorphism makes it harder to count the number of paths through a code module, which in turn makes it harder to be sure that test coverage is complete: every sequence of mouse clicks is a potential path. The solution is to use the task scripts to represent potential paths through the system. If possible, paths should be grouped into equivalence classes that can be tested as if one path. Another problem is that an inherited method may not work in the context of the subclass even though it worked properly in the superclass, meaning that the entire structure should be integration tested top-down. This can happen when the subclass has different values for attributes that the method uses and if multiple inheritance conflicts or overriding have modified the methods in some way. Perry and Kaiser (1990) discuss object-oriented unit testing further.

With an object-oriented language, testing should have been carried out during coding as each class is completed, preferably by a separate team. This includes integration testing of either each layer or the whole system with the new classes added. Thus the testing is largely completed by the testing stage, which must only look for unexpected effects of the system working as a whole.

It is highly advisable to build a test harness: a suite of applications and user dialogues which are known to work as expected along with test runs. Do this at least as soon as prototypes are released to users. User feedback can be used to design the harness. It will pay for itself very quickly indeed, unless your programmers always write error-free code.

Follow all the usual, good, conventional testing practices (see for example Myers (1979)). State matrices and decision tables remain useful. The main difference with object-oriented testing is that unit testing begins far earlier in the life cycle.

Since object-orientation emphasizes the interface rather than the implementation of objects, it might be expected that black-box testing techniques, where only the specification is used to construct tests, would suffice. This has been found to be empirically false in studies carried out at Hewlett-Packard (Fiedler, 1989), where white-box testing, which examines the implementation, was shown to increase the number of defects detected significantly. This implies that class designers and implementers must be intimately involved in the testing at the white-box stage as independent testers may be unfamiliar with the way low-level functions work.

The SOMA life-cycle model implies that the sequence:

(1) prototype,
(2) white-box test,
(3) incorporate library classes,
(4) black-box test,
(5) document,

(6) train,
(7) user test

is the norm.

Test servers prior to client objects, because defects in servers may be propagated to their clients.

9.1.7 Delivery and acceptance

Acceptance testing has been carried out continuously since prototypes were released to users. This minimizes final acceptance-testing work loads. However, some last minute changes may be expected.

The object-oriented approach using prototyping described in Section 9.3 and recommended here is designed to ensure that what is delivered is very close to the real requirements, not only the stated requirements or the requirements as they were twelve months ago or longer. Thus, the developers should not expect a flood of change requests on delivery. They should know what the rate of change of requirements is from the experience of prototyping. Thus, it is possible to estimate a flat rate of change requests and to anticipate fulfilling them owing to the ability to extend the system by adding new classes and the growing number of reusable classes in the library.

Training and documentation are critical to acceptance. I regard documentation as part of the user interface, deserving the same attention and careful design.

I have presented the ideal picture. At present we do not have the robust, mature object-oriented languages and databases to support this ideal. We do have the possibility to achieve an approximation using object-oriented analysis and design though. Language and database support is very close, and a one-year project starting with object-oriented analysis may be confident that language and database technology will be maturing by the end of the project.

9.2 Identifying objects

The discussion of how to go about identifying objects has been deferred until now, apart from a mention of Abbott's (1983) textual analysis method in Chapter 7. The reason for this is that object identification is recognized as a key, possibly *the* key, bottleneck in applying both object-oriented design and analysis. In this respect the topic deserves the attention of a separate section, in which I will try to show that the object identification bottleneck is as chimerical as the famous Feigenbaum knowledge acquisition bottleneck. Techniques exist to help apprehend objects, mostly those in use already in data modelling and knowledge engineering, and good analysts do not, in practice, stumble badly in this area.

The methods surveyed in Chapters 7 and 8 give scant help in identifying objects. HOOD, CRC and some other methods use Abbott textual analysis but otherwise there are no precise, normative techniques. Coad and Yourdon (1991) say that analysts should look for things or events remembered, devices, rôles, sites and organizational units. The Shlaer/Mellor method offers five categories: tangible entities, rôles, incidents, interactions and specifications. This is all very well, but rather fuzzy and certainly not complete. This section provides several, quite precise, normative techniques for eliciting objects. They are founded in knowledge engineering, HCI practice and philosophy.

The dominant philosophical view in Western scientific thinking has been, for a very long time, empiricism. I believe that this clouds our view of what objects are in various subtle ways and must be overcome by the object-oriented analyst. For example, empiricism holds that objects are merely bundles of properties. As pointed out in Chapter 1, an empiricist would maintain that objects are out there just waiting to be perceived, and an extreme version holds that this is easy to do. A phenomenologist view, on the contrary, recognizes that perception is an active, iterative, creative process and that objects come both from our intentions and from the objectively existing world in an ever repeating dialectical process. When we see a tree we bring our ideas about trees to bear before we make the perception. As the leading biologist J. Z. Young (1986) puts it, when we look 'we know already what we are going to see'. An even richer view suggests that real-world abstractions are a reflection of social relations and processes, as well as having an objective basis. We perceive the tree as mediator of our own human processes of production both of wooden artefacts and of ourselves – as when we enjoy the tree for its beauty. Ehn (1988) and Winograd and Flores (1986) explore these issues in relation to computer systems in general. Objects may be apprehended by an analyst familiar with an application in many different ways and choosing the 'best' representation is a fundamental contribution that human intelligence always makes to computer systems. Some objects correspond directly to real-world objects such as employees or chairs, but others, such as stacks or quarks, correspond to invented abstractions. Abstractions sum up the relevant divisions of the domain. What is relevant may depend on the application, but this will compromise the reusability of the abstraction and so the designer should try to think of abstractions with as wide an applicability as possible. On the other hand, care should be taken not to compromise efficiency with over-general objects. The more high-level our systems become, the more they are to be regarded as tools for enhancing communication between humans. The more the human aspect is emphasized, the more the subjective factor in object identification comes to the fore.

As I have suggested, most object-oriented analysis methods give little help with the process of identifying objects. I have suggested already, following both Abbott and the approach of HOOD, that a very reasonable semi-structured approach is to engage in the analysis of nouns, verbs and other parts of speech in an informal written description of the problem discussed in the preceding section. Rules of thumb here include: matching proper nouns to objects, and improper nouns to objects or attributes; adjectival phrases qualifying nouns, such as 'the employee who works in the salaries department', indicate relations or may indicate methods if they contain verbs as in 'the employee who got a rise'. Guidelines for this technique were given in Table 7.1 (p.198).

The Abbott technique is useful, but cannot succeed on its own. This semi-structured approach is only a guide and creative perception must be brought to bear by experienced analysts as I have already emphasized. Using it involves difficult decisions. Analysts and designers can learn much from two key branches of philosophy: epistemology and ontology. Epistemology is the theory of knowledge: what knowledge is, how it is possible and what can be known. Ontology is the science of being: what is and how it comes about. These two sciences are intimately related because we are interested in true knowledge: knowledge of what really is. Both disciplines are concerned with the nature of objects, and are therefore directly relevant to the identification of objects in object-oriented analysis and design. This view is taken by Wand (1989), who proposed a formal model of objects based on Bunge's mathematical ontology. Unfortunately, this ontology is atomistic: it conceives things as reducible to irreducible components. Nevertheless, the principle of an ontologically based model, albeit not a formal model, is a sound one.

Fred Brooks (1986) notes the difference between essence and accidents in software engineering. The distinction is, in fact, a very old one going back to Aristotle and the mediaeval Scholastics. The idea of essence was attacked by modern philosophers from Descartes onwards, who saw objects as mere bundles of properties with no essence. This gave rise to severe difficulties because it fails to explain how we can recognize a chair with no properties in common with all the previous chairs we have experienced. A school of thought known as phenomenology, represented by philosophers such as Hegel, Brentano, Husserl and Heidegger, arose *inter alia* from attempts to solve this kind of problem. Another classical problem, important for object-oriented analysis, is the problem of categories. Aristotle laid down a set of fixed pairs of categories through the application of which thought could proceed. These were concepts such as universal/individual, necessary/contingent, and so on. Kant gave a revised list but, as Hegel once remarked, did not put himself to much trouble in the doing. The idealist Hegel showed that the categories were related and grew out of each other in thought. Finally, the materialist Marx showed that the categories of thought arose out of human social and historical practice:

> My dialectic method is not only different from the Hegelian, but is its direct opposite. To Hegel, the life-process of the human brain, i.e. the process of thinking, which, under the name of 'the Idea', he even transforms into an independent subject, is the demiurgos of the real world, and the real world is only the external, phenomenal form of 'the Idea'. With me, on the contrary, the ideal is nothing else than the material world reflected by the human mind, and translated into forms of thought. (Marx (1961))

So, we inherit categories from our forebears, but also learn new ones from our practice in the world.

All phenomenologists and dialecticians, whether idealist or materialist, acknowledge that the perception or apprehension of objects is an active process. Objects are defined by the purpose of the thinking subject, although for a materialist they correspond to previously existing patterns of energy in the world – including of course patterns in the brain. A chair is a coherent object for the purposes of sitting (or perhaps for bar-room brawling) but not for the purposes of subatomic physics. You may be wondering by now what all this has got to do with object-oriented analysis. What does this analysis tell us about the identification of objects? The answer is that it directs attention to the user.

User-centred analysis requires that we ask about purpose when we partition the world into objects. It also tells us that common purpose is required for reusability, because objects designed for one user may not correspond to anything in the world of another. In fact reuse is only possible because society and production determine a common basis for perception. A clear understanding of ontology helps to avoid the introduction of accidental, as opposed to essential, objects. Thus, Fred Brooks, in my opinion, either learned some ontology or had it by instinct alone.

Some useful tips for identifying important, rather than arbitrary, objects can be gleaned from a study of philosophy, especially Hegelian philosophy and modern phenomenology. Stern (1990) analyses Hegel's concept of the object in great detail. The main difference between this notion of objects and other notions is that objects are neither arbitrary 'bundles' of properties (the empiricist or Kantian view), nor are they based on a mysterious essence, but are conceptual structures representing universal abstractions. The practical import of this view is that it allows us to distinguish between genuine high-level abstractions such as Man and completely contingent ones such as Red Objects. Objects may be judged according to various, historically determined, categories. For example 'this rose is red' is a judgement in the category of quality. The important judgements for object-oriented analysis and their relevant uses are those shown in Table 9.2.

Table 9.2 Analysis of judgements.

Judgement	Example	Feature
Quality	this ball is red	attribute
Reflection	this herb is medicinal	relationship
Categorical	Fred is a man	generalization
Value	Fred should be kind	rules

The categorical judgement is the one that reveals genuine high-level abstractions. We call such abstractions **essential**. Qualitative judgements only reveal contingent and accidental properties unlikely to be reusable, but nevertheless of semantic importance within the application. Beware, for example, of abstractions such as 'red roses' or 'dangerous toys': they are qualitative and probably not reusable without internal restructuring. Objects revealed by qualitative judgements are called **accidental**. Accidental objects are mere bundles of arbitrary properties, such as 'expensive, prickly, red roses wrapped in foil'. Essential objects are universal, in the sense that they are (or belong to) classes which correspond to objects that already have been identified by human practice and are stable in time and space. What they are depends on human purposes: prior to trade, money was not an object. Reflective judgements are useful for establishing usage relationships and methods: being medicinal connects herbs to the sicknesses that they cure. Value judgements may be outside the scope of a computer system, but can reveal semantic rules. For example, we could have, at a very high business analysis level, 'employees should be rewarded for loyalty', which at a lower level would translate to 'if five years service then an extra three days annual leave'.

Attributes are functions that take objects as values; that is, their ranges are classes. They may be distinguished into attributes whose values are abstract (or essential in the sense alluded to above) objects like employee, and those with printable, that is, accidental, objects as values like redness. This observation has also been made in the context of semantic data models by Hull and King (1987).

For business and user-centred design, the ontological view dictates that objects should have a purpose. Methods too should have a goal. In Ptech this is accomplished by specifying postconditions. These conditions should be stated for each method (as in Eiffel) and for the object as a whole in the rules window of a SOMA object.

Lenat and Guha (1990) suggest that instances are things about which something definite can be said, but point out the danger of relying too much on the structure of natural language. They suggest that a concept should be abstracted as a class if:

- several interesting things can be said about it as a whole;
- it has properties shared by no other class;
- there are statements that distinguish this class from some larger class it belongs to;
- the boundaries of the concept are imprecise;
- the number of 'siblings' (for example, complementary classes whose union is the natural generalization of this one) is low.

They also emphasize the point I have made: that purpose is the chief determinant of what is to be a class.

A useful rule of thumb for distinguishing essential objects is that one should ask if more can be said about the object than can be obtained by listing its attributes and methods. It is cheating in the use of this rule merely to keep on adding more properties. Examples abound of this type of object. In a payroll system, an employee may have red hair, even though this is not an attribute, or be able to fly a plane, even though this is not a method. Nothing special can be said about the class 'employees who can fly' unless, of course, we are dealing with the payroll for an airline. What is essential is context sensitive.

Very long methods, objects with hundreds of attributes and/or hundreds of methods, indicate that you are trying to model something that normal mortals could not apprehend in any conceivable perceptive act. This tells me, and I hope your project manager, that you have not listened to the users.

It is not only the purposes of the immediate users that concern us, but the purposes of the user community at large and, indeed, of software engineers who will reuse your objects. Therefore, analysts should keep reuse in mind throughout the requirements elicitation process. Designing or analysing is not copying user and expert knowledge. As with perception, it is a creative act. A designer, analyst or knowledge engineer takes the purposes and perceptions of users and transforms them. S/he is not a *tabula rasa* – a blank sheet upon which knowledge is writ – as older texts on knowledge elicitation used to recommend, but a creative participant.

Johnson and Foote (1988) make a few suggestions for desiderata concerning when to create a new class rather than add a method to an existing class, which seem to conform to the ontological insights of this section.

Epistemology has been studied by knowledge engineers involved in building expert systems. Many of the lessons learnt and the techniques they have discovered can be used in building conventional systems, and this is now routine in my work. In particular, they can be applied to HCI design (Johnson, 1992) and within object-oriented analysis and design.

Several of the methods which have been developed by knowledge engineers trying to elicit knowledge from human beings with the aim of building expert systems can be used to obtain concepts in any domain. These concepts often map onto objects. This is not the place for an exegesis on methods of knowledge acquisition, but we should mention the usefulness of methods based on Kelly grids (or repertory grids), protocol analysis, task analysis and interviewing theory. The use of the techniques of Kelly grids for object identification is explained later in this section. Protocol analysis (Ericsson and Simon, 1984) is in some ways similar to the procedure outlined earlier of analysing parts of speech, and task analysis can reveal both objects and their methods. Task analysis is often used in UI design (Daniels, 1986; Johnson, 1992).

Broadly, task analysis is a functional approach to knowledge elicitation which involves breaking down a problem into a hierarchy of tasks that must be performed. The objectives of task analysis in general can be outlined as the definition of:

- the objectives of the task;
- the procedures used;
- any actions and objects involved;
- time taken to accomplish the task;
- frequency of operations;
- occurrence of errors;
- involvement of subordinate and superordinate tasks.

The result is a task description which may be formalized in some way, such as by flowcharts, logic trees or even a formal grammar. The process does not, however, describe knowledge directly. That is, it does not attempt to capture the underlying knowledge structure but tries to represent how the task is performed and what is needed to achieve its aim. Any conceptual or procedural knowledge and any objects which are obtained are only elicited incidentally.

In task analysis the objective constraints on problem solving are exploited, usually prior to a later protocol analysis stage. The method consists in arriving at a classification of the factors involved in problem solving and the identification of the atomic 'tasks' involved. The categories that apply to an individual task might include:

- time taken;
- how often performed;
- procedures used;
- actions used;
- objects used;
- error rate;
- position in task hierarchy.

This implies that it is also necessary to identify the actions and objects in a taxonomic manner. For example, if we were to embark on a study of poker-playing we might start with the following crude structure.

> Objects: Card, Deck, Hand, Suit, Player, Table, Coin
> Actions: Deal, Turn, See, Collect

One form of task analysis assumes that concepts are derivable from pairing actions with objects, for example, 'See player', 'Deal card'. Once the concepts can be identified, it is necessary to identify plans or objectives (win game, make money) and strategies (bluff at random), and to use this analysis to identify the knowledge required and used by matching object–action pairs to task descriptions occurring in task sequences. As mentioned before, this is important since objects are identified in relation to purposes.

As a means of breaking down the problem area into its constituent sub-problems, task analysis is useful in a similar way to dataflow analysis or entity modelling. Although the method does incorporate the analysis of the objects associated with each task, it is lacking in graphical techniques for representation of these objects, and therefore remains mostly useful for functional elicitation.

The approach to cognitive task analysis recommended by Braune and Foshay (1983), based on human information processing theory, is less functional than the basic approach to task analysis as outlined above, concentrating on the analysis of concepts. The second stage of the three-step strategy is to define the relations between concepts by analysing examples, then to build on the resulting schema by analysing larger problem sets.

The schema that results from the above analysis is a model of the knowledge structure of an expert, similar to that achieved by the concept-sorting methods associated with Kelly grids, describing the 'chunking' of knowledge by the expert. This chunking is controlled by the idea of expectancy according to the theory of human information processing; that is, the selection of the correct stimuli for solving the problem, and the knowledge of how to deal with these stimuli. As pointed out by Swaffield (1990), this approach is akin to the ideas of object modelling owing to the concentration on the analysis of concepts and relations before further analysis of functions/tasks.

The method of hierarchical task analysis can be better understood through the use of an example. Figure 9.2 is based on a project I once ran, concerned with the selection of input technology for a financial trader. The overall task to be described is that of recording a deal when the trader, in this case an equities trader, agrees to buy from or sell to some counterparty (the person at the other end of the transaction in 'dealerspeak').

The diagram in Figure 9.2 is to be interpreted from the top level, which represents the overall task of striking a bargain and recording it, downwards and from the left-hand side. Note that the hierarchy is represented as a network at some points. This is only to avoid repetition of common subordinate operations and recursion.

We decompose the top-level task into ten steps starting with the initial contact. This task is complex but does not impinge on the deal capture process and so is not expanded further. This, of course, refers to the receipt or initiation (usually by telephone) of a communication in which a dealing situation is identified. Once this complex activity is initiated the next step (possibly carried out in parallel) is to establish to whom the dealer is talking, and it is here that computer systems have a rôle to play. Thus, this task requires further decomposition. For example, 2.1 could refer to recognizing someone's voice or spotting their identity from the lights on a dealer board. Next, the counterparty identity must be validated as an authorized one by finding its code. This can be done either from the dealer's memory, from a paper list kept at hand, from a screen display or by calling out to a colleague who, in turn, may have all these resources available. Thus, there are recursive processes implicit in the diagrams but which have not been expanded. If the code is not obtained either the process can terminate (1.10) or a new code can be created. Having acquired the code it must be entered into the record-keeping system, computerized or manual. This is the first point where there is significant interaction with the technology of deal capture, and the heavily drawn box indicates this interface. Further decomposition in terms of *inter alia* finger, arm and eye movements is not shown in the diagram precisely because it will now depend on the selected technology. The code must now be validated and if incorrect we either return to 2.1 or correct the entry (2.4) before re-entering stage 2.3. At this point we can return to level 1 and proceed to a similar process in order to identify the instrument being traded. Notice that this process revisits stages 2.1 through 2.4, which explains the tangle of descent paths in the diagram. The remainder of the diagram may now be interpreted in a similar fashion.

Note incidentally that 2.8 descends from 1.5 directly and that 1.8 refers to the verification of the entire transaction.

It will be seen that most of the tasks involve complex cognitive processes, especially perhaps 1.1, 1.4, and 1.5. However, the benefit of the task analysis is that it enables abstraction of those tasks where there is an interface with the deal capture technology from this background.

This rather detailed example is included here to give a feel for the practical problems in applying task decomposition. It should be clear, in particular, that there is value in using task analysis for designing systems and user interfaces, but we

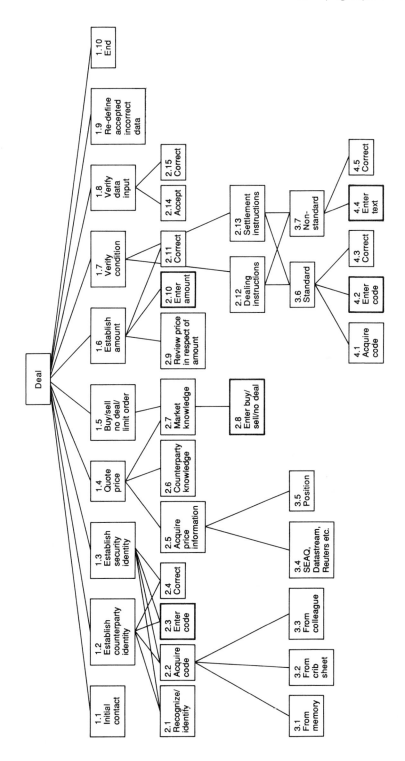

Figure 9.2 A task decomposition of an equity trader's dealing task. Note that both objects and actions are identified.

assert that other applications where it is necessary to conceptualize procedural knowledge can benefit from the approach. The example also shows the way in which task analysis can reveal the presence of objects, such as price information and settlement instructions, quite incidentally to its analysis of tasks. Thus in applications where the functions are more immediately apparent to consciousness than the objects and concepts, task analysis is a useful way of bootstrapping an object-oriented analysis. This is often true in tasks where there is a great deal of unarticulated, latent or compiled knowledge. Task scripts can be deepened into task analysis tree structures where this is helpful.

Task analysis will not help with the incorporation of the many psychological factors which are always present in deal capture or similar processes, and which are often quite immeasurable. Other incommensurables might include the effects of such environmental factors as ambient noise and heat, and the general level of distracting stimuli.

Readers familiar with Jackson Structured Design may notice a similarity between the task decomposition of Figure 9.2 and a JSD entity structure diagram. It could have been obtained from considering the time-ordered actions of the life history of a 'deal'. Any common sub-tree can be 'dismembered' (to use the JSD term) and regarded as either a separate group of actions or as a new object in its own right. It can then become the result of a JSD 'operation' or, in other words, a method. I am grateful to David Lee of GEC for pointing out this similarity to me. One striking thing about this observation is how it shows that different disciplines within IT keep reinventing the same wheel under different names.

In some ways it could be held that the use of a formal technique such as task analysis in the above example can add nothing that common sense could not have derived. However, its use in structuring the information derived from inter-views is invaluable for the following reasons. Firstly, the decomposition of complex tasks into more primitive or unitary actions enables one to arrive at a better understanding of the interface between the tasks and the available implementation technology, as will be seen in the above analysis. This leads to a far better understanding of the possibilities for empirical measurement of the quality of the interface. The second factor is that the very process of constructing and critiquing the task hierarchy diagrams helps to uncover gaps in the analysis, and thus remove any contradictions.

Task analysis is primarily useful in method identification rather than for finding objects, although objects are elicited incidentally. We now turn to methods borrowed from knowledge engineering which address the object identification problem more directly.

Basden (1990 and 1990a) suggests, again in the context of knowledge acqui-sition for expert systems, a method which may be of considerable use in identify-ing objects and their attributes and methods. He offers the example of a knowledge engineer seeking for high-level rules of thumb based on experience (heuristics). Suppose, in the domain of gardening, that we have discovered that regular mowing produces good lawns. The knowledge engineer should not be satisfied with this because it does not show the boundaries of the intended system's competence – we do not want a system that gives confident advice in areas where it is incompetent. We need to go deeper into the understanding. Thus, the next question asked of the expert might be of the form: 'Why?' The answer might be: 'Because regular mowing reduces coarse grasses and encourages springy turf'. What we have obtained here are two attributes of the object 'good turf' – whose parent in a hierarchy is 'turf', of course. Why does regular mowing lead to springy turf? Well, it helps to promote leaf branching. Now we are beginning to elicit methods as we approach causal knowledge. To help define the boundaries, Basden suggests asking 'what else' and 'what about' questions. In the example we have given the knowledge engineer should ask: 'What about drought conditions?' or 'What else gives good lawns?'. These questioning techniques are immensely useful for analysts using an object-oriented approach.

One of the most useful knowledge engineering techniques for eliciting objects and their structure is that of Kelly, or repertory, grids. These grids were introduced originally in the context of clinical psychiatry (Kelly, 1955). They are devices for helping analysts elicit 'personal constructs': concepts which people use in dealing with and constructing their world. Constructs are pairs of opposites, such as slow/fast, and usually correspond to attribute values in object-oriented analysis. The second dimension of a grid is its 'elements', which correspond to objects. Elements are rated on a scale from 1 to 5, say, according to which pole of the construct they correspond to most closely. These values can then be used to 'focus' the grid, a mathematical procedure which clarifies relationships among elements and constructs. In particular, focusing ranks the elements in order of the clarity with which they are perceived, and the constructs in order of their importance as classifiers of elements. The details can be found in any decent book on knowledge acquisition; for example, Hart (1989), Graham and Jones (1988).

To illustrate the usefulness of Kelly grids, suppose we need to interview a user. The technique involves first identifying some 'elements' in the application. These might be real things or concepts, but should be organized into coherent sets. For example, the set {Porsche, Jaguar, Rolls Royce, Mini, Driver} has an obvious odd man out.

Given a coherent set of elements, the user is asked to take any three and specify a concept that applies to two of them and not to the third. For example, with {Porsche, Jaguar, Mini}, top speed might emerge as an important concept. Users are asked for the opposites of the identified concepts and to give names for higher-level concepts: 'Can you think of a word that describes all the concepts {speed, luxury, economy}?' might produce a concept of 'value for money'. This technique is known as laddering, and elicits both composition and classification structures. Users may be asked to sort elements into groups and name the groups. This is known as card sorting. All these techniques are first-rate ways of getting at the conceptual structure of the problem space. An example of a Kelly grid is shown in Figure 9.3.

There are several computer systems which automate the construction and focusing of these grids, such as ETS (Boose, 1986) and its commercial descendant

ELEMENTS

CONCEPT	Rolls Royce	Porsche	Jaguar	Mini	Trabant	OPPOSITE
Economical	5	4	4	2	2	Costly
Comfortable	1	4	2	4	5	Basic
Sporty	5	1	3	5	5	Family
Cheap	5	4	4	2	1	Expensive
Fast	3	1	2	4	5	Slow

Figure 9.3 A Kelly grid. Scores are between 1 and 5. The left-hand pole of the concept corresponds to a low score for the element and the right (its opposite) to a high one. The grid is not focused.

AQUINAS (Boose and Bradshaw, 1988). These systems convert the grids into set of rules. It is curious that these automated tools throw so much of what is captured by the repertory grid analysis away. It is clear that laddering and sorting produce classification structures, for example. These are then disguised as production rules with a consequent loss of information. I predicted in the first edition of this book that tools would evolve which would capture such structural information directly. That this has begun to happen is illustrated by the latest work of Gaines and Shaw (1992; Shaw and Gaines, 1992), but the work is not yet commercialized. In the interim the technique must be used manually, and preferably informally, for object-oriented analysis.

Object templates have been used in knowledge acquisition for expert systems. Filling in the templates is a structured method for gathering semantic information which is of general applicability. The knowledge engineering approach emphasizes that classes should correspond to concepts held by users and experts. High-level classes represent abstractions that may be reusable across several similar domains. The abstraction 'object' is universal in all domains, but 'account' is usable across most financial and accounting applications. Mortgage account is more specialized and therefore reusable across a narrow set of applications. The key skill for analysts seeking the benefit of reuse is to pitch the abstractions at the right level. Prototyping and interaction with users and domain experts all help to elicit knowledge about objects.

Thus, ontology and epistemology help us find objects and structures. They should also help us know how to recognize a good object when we meet one, either in a library or as a result of our own efforts. The third requisite tool for this purpose is, of course, common sense. A few common-sense guidelines for object identification are worth including at this point.

Always remember that a good reusable object represents something universal and real. An object is a social animal: its methods may be used by other classes. If not, ask what its function is or delete it from the model. Although an object should not be so complex as to defy comprehension, it should encapsulate some reasonably complex behaviour to justify its existence. A method that does not make use of its current class's own attributes is probably encapsulated in the wrong object, since it does not need access to the private implementation.

Measuring the quality of an abstraction is very difficult. Guidelines can be taken from an analogy with the design of machinery. As with a machine, there should be a minimum number of interchangeable parts and the parts should be as general as possible. Suggested criteria, with their corresponding metrics, include several that we have already met in the context of object-oriented programming. Interfaces should be as small, simple and stable as possible. The object should be self-sufficient and complete; the slogan is: 'The object, the whole object and nothing but the object'. As a counter-example to this notion of complete objects, consider a class for objects whose names begin with the letters 'CH'. In other words avoid accidental objects. Objects must not need to send lots of messages to do simple things. In other words the topology of the use structure should be simple.

Similar guidelines apply to methods. Methods too should be simple and generative. For example, the method 'add 1' generates a method 'add n' for all n. Look for such commonalities. They should be relevant; that is, methods must be applicable to the concept, neither more specific nor more general. Methods should depend on the encapsulated state of the containing object, as mentioned above. A very important principle of object-orientation is the principle of loose coupling or the Law of Demeter[1] which states that 'the methods of a class should not depend in any way on the structure of any class, except the immediate (top-level) structure of their own class. Further, each method should send messages to objects belonging to a very limited set of classes only' (Sakkinen, 1988). This helps classes to be understood in isolation and therefore reused.

Analysts should avoid objects arising solely from normalization or the removal of many-to-many relationships. The rule is: if it is not a real-world entity then it is not an object. For example, the many-to-many relationship between ORDERS and INVOICES may be removed by introducing a new class ORDER-LINE. This is fine, the lines are real things; they get printed on the invoice. On the contrary there seems to be no such natural object that would remove the many-to-many relationship between cars and the colours they may be painted or products and the regulations that apply to them.

The last point I wish to make is that analysts should not be expected to get it right first time. They never do. This is the mistake of the waterfall model, and we know all too well that the costs of maintaining incorrectly specified systems are high. Prototyping and user-centred design, if properly managed, allow the analyst to get it right – but third time round. We will examine this and the management of prototyping in the next section.

---

[1] The Greek goddess of agriculture and therefore of cyclical rebirth.

9.3 Prototyping and structured methods

The deliverables from object-oriented requirements capture and rapid analysis should form input to a planning process that will set up a project lasting about three months, elapsed time during which a small team will prototype the objects representing the objective with the highest priority. Evaluation of the prototype should be based on the views of an independent evaluation team and upon the task scripts developed at that stage. This section details the SOMA approach to prototyping, though the approach could be added to other object-oriented analysis techniques.

It is believed by many software engineers that prototyping is only appropriate for small systems and that the methods used to build them do not scale up to large commercial systems. This section looks at prototyping from the point of view of the traditional system development life cycle, shows how the latter can be modified to incorporate fast prototyping in building large or small systems and examines certain questions concerning object-oriented programming languages and prototyping.

In fact, much has been written concerning the benefits of prototyping by thinkers on conventional software engineering (Brooks, 1973; Boar, 1984). Less has emerged on the incorporation of prototyping into structured methods (but see Connell and Shafer (1989)).

9.3.1 Types of prototyping

There are, in my view, three kinds of prototyping, which I choose to designate evolutionary, revolutionary and revelationary.

Evolutionary prototyping is used when the target system may be constructed in the original prototyping language, with suitable lower-level language extensions. It is particularly appropriate when the requirements are expected to change rapidly and continuously over time, and thus has been the development method of choice for executive information systems, for example, and for expert systems.

In other circumstances, for example when the target language is not yet determined or when there are no sufficiently powerful prototyping tools available for the target hardware, a **revolutionary** or 'throw-away' approach may be usefully adopted. The disadvantage of this approach is that a new system must be developed from scratch and the users may have to accept that features available in the prototype will be too expensive to provide in the language eventually employed. If such an approach is to be used, therefore, much more effort must be put into documenting the agreements reached as to functionality between prototypers and their clients. The user may be disappointed when the pretty pop-up menus and interactive (that is, asynchronous) style evaporates in the eventual implementation. This potential problem, therefore, must be anticipated and explained. The revolutionary approach is to be regarded as identical with system specification and is also known as **specification prototyping.**

The third, **revelationary** or **exploratory**, method is the one associated by many opponents of prototyping with hacking and many early expert systems developments. This method too has its place as a generator of ideas in the research labs, but cannot be sanctioned in a commercial environment where proper budget and life-cycle controls are essential. LISP or Smalltalk environments are superb for this kind of activity, but it will be admitted by even the most sibilant LISPer or object-fixated programmer that there are serious worries about the performance of commercial systems which involve dynamic binding, resource-hungry graphical interfaces or garbage collection. For these reasons I would suggest that revelationary – that is, research oriented – prototyping should be declared a *strict* subset of revolutionary prototyping by fiat of the software community. In this way those methods developed for revolutionary prototyping may be applied with suitable extra controls and stages to the good ideas that emerge from R&D.

Evolutionary prototyping is often confused with rapid development. Although there are strong connexions, this is a mistake because prototyping is merely a tool for rapid development. In this chapter we shall see that rapid development is a set of managerial controls that may be used to control prototyping, rather than a technique, as prototyping is. Similarly, revelationary prototyping is often confused with incremental development. This is an error of the same kind. Both evolutionary and revelationary prototyping can be used within an incremental approach, but the latter can be attempted, albeit at some risk, without prototyping at all.

9.3.2 Why is prototyping necessary?

I will argue for three positions concerning the necessity of prototyping. First, prototyping produces 'better' user interfaces. Secondly, a prototype is a specification which acts as an amplifier of communication between users and analysts (and even designers in the evolutionary case). Third, executable specifications can be tested and, if they are sufficiently semantically rich, used to generate new implementations. Let us begin with the interface design issue.

Conventional software engineering has had too little to say about the design of the user interface (UI). Incorrect interfaces account for many complaints from users and every complaint, if converted into a change request, converts in turn into a cost. Prototypes force analysts to confront the user with an interface and good analysts will use this as an opportunity to experiment and converge on a facile and powerful interface. Thus prototyping helps to design good UIs. One of the key contributions of expert systems software here has been the ease with which 'intelligent' dialogues can be built. We call a dialogue 'intelligent' in this context when unnecessary questions are not asked and when the order of asking is not too stupid. Object-orientation helps as well by providing very easy ways to validate input and even inherit the validation from existing objects. The key point about object-oriented methods is the provision of objects which are used via their interface or specification rather than their implementation. This exegesis of course begs the question as to what is a good or correct interface. In the plainest terms, such an interface is one that users can operate in a natural way and are comfortable with, but which enhances their ability to do the job at hand. In the Heideggerian terminology of Winograd and Flores (1986) a good interface is one that makes the system as 'ready-to-hand' as possible. A tool is ready-to-hand if it is not present in the forefront of consciousness when the job is being done. For example, when using a hammer you do not have to think about the process of hammering, it is only necessary to concentrate on the nail (and of course the adjacent thumb).

In measuring the goodness of an interface we must consider two dimensions: the satisfaction of users and the consistency and conformity to standards of its design. User satisfaction is measured by both asking them if they are satisfied and observing them at work with the system. Often, unreported frustrations are readily observable to an experienced analyst. Consistency applies to issues which may be reported by the users and to the application of DP standards, or both. For example, if menus on successive screens appear in different positions the user may not be able to see easily what to do at each step. Some users will report this discomfort, but it can be seen anyway that a good standard is to position menus in a consistent position. Another example arises with mouse-driven systems. I recall being involved with a system that required users to locate the mouse over a button and click merely to continue with no input, an operation which could have been acceler-ated by utilizing a 'Press any key' approach. The users did not complain, but I, as a system tester, complained most bitterly. If the system had gone live in that form I would, one suspects, have been joined by a chorus of protest. The emergence of standards for windows systems such as IBM's CUA has helped greatly with this issue.

There are two ways to proceed in constructing a prototype, and this applies especially to the UI features, either by consensus or confrontation. Consensus con-notes asking the users for their requirements, analysing current working practices and then building the closest approximation the prototyping tools allow to a system that automates the existing task for discussion with all concerned. The confronta-tional approach is potentially far more powerful but also, like a powerful rifle in enthusiastic but unskilled hands, a little dangerous. This requires the analyst to look behind the appearance of current working methods and practices and seek the essence of the business function. Then the prototype is built to show how the world *could be*, not merely modelling how it *is*. The user is 'confronted' with a vision of a brave new world where, conceivably, the computer will benefit the organization by allowing more effective methods of work to emerge. Word processing is already beginning to exhibit this effect in industry at large, as professionals gradually realize that these tools are actually an aid to creative writing and that typing is not 'the secretary's job'. Expert systems may soon change the ways branch bank managers and insurance underwriters, for example, do their work. Hypermedia systems too have the potential to revolutionize the way work is done.

Among the many benefits of prototyping, the one which I claim as the key is that prototypes are an excellent means of eliciting correct, consistent and complete specifications of requirements. Parenthetically, it should be remarked that it seems unlikely that Gödel-like objections to this claim can be raised in such finite domains; that is, claims that infinite formal systems of minor complexity cannot be both complete and consistent, based on Gödel's theorem. As has been indicated above, prototypes also assist with elicitation of the UI and indeed of the contractual agreements upon which a software development project must be founded. I will now argue that eliciting better specifications in this way is a means of reducing maintenance costs.

Both evolutionary and revolutionary prototyping may sometimes speed development, but not always, and the relative length of the project phases will usually be different. However, it nearly always eases maintenance. This is not simply because modern tools, visual programming techniques and code generators mean that changes are implemented at the analysis level and (modulo some tuning) design and coding changes need not always be made and documented. These benefits certainly apply, but the principal reasons for maintenance gains derive from the elicitation of better specifications. Better specifications imply more contented users and fewer change requests. This is not to say that maintenance disappears, only that the burden is mitigated.

It is widely reported (Connell and Shafer, 1989; Lientz and Swanson, 1979) that up to 50% of maintenance requests, principally those which occur in the nine months or so immediately following delivery, result from mis-specification. A typical profile is shown in Figure 9.4. This fact alone justifies the use of any technique that helps produce better, more acceptable, specifications. It cannot be over-emphasized that this sort of maintenance effort is sheer unproductive (and usually unrewarding) labour. Reducing it by any amount will benefit both the corporation and the programmer. As DeMarco (1982) and others have suggested, much of this

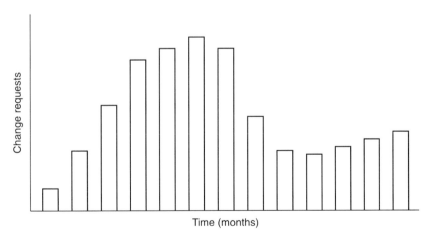

Figure 9.4 Profile of typical monthly volumes of change requests following delivery. (Source: Connell and Shafer (1989))

unproductive labour is partly due to inadequate time spent in the early phases of the project, from estimation onwards. This suggests strongly that project planners should allocate generous time to the prototyping phase with a view to cutting down the length of later phases. Of course, it may be argued that many change requests arise not from mis-specification but from the dynamic character of business, whereby the correctly specified system at the outset of the project is no longer correct when the system is delivered. There are two points to make about this objection. First, we must accept that *some* change requests of this kind are unavoidable, but the evidence suggests (again see Connell and Shafer (1989)) that there is a peak in change requests soon after delivery out of proportion to the design-to-delivery delay. Thus, there is strong evidence that at least some changes are due to mis-specification of functions that are still required. The second point is that the dynamics of the situation strongly suggests an evolutionary approach to systems development, as opposed to a revolutionary one, wherever this is a practical proposition. Hickman *et al.* (1989) have argued against this that evolutionary prototypes may contain designs that, while appropriate for the prototype, are not appropriate for the full-scale system. For this reason a method incorporating evolutionary prototyping must include a design review to address precisely this issue. If such a problem is discovered there is no reason why the evolutionary project, as originally conceived, cannot be converted to a revolutionary one. The design review must therefore allow for some replanning. Furthermore, we have seen how an object-oriented approach makes the merger of analysis and logical design natural and untraumatic. The conventional wisdoms of software engineering therefore may not apply to object-oriented projects so exactly in the presence of extensible code.

Let us examine why it is that prototypes produce better specifications than the traditional methods of functional specification. In doing so, we have an opportunity to look at the rôle of revolutionary prototyping. If this can be demonstrated, then it follows that veritable implementations of the specification will be valid; that is, correct, in that they solve the problem intended and not some pale shadow of it enshrined in a deficient specification.

The prime purpose, as I have emphasized, of prototyping is to help produce an understandable specification that is as correct and complete as possible. The benefits of doing this are as follows.

- Users can understand what is being offered to them.
- Maintenance changes resulting from wrong or incomplete specifications are minimized.
- Development and maintenance teams can work from a specification which has been tested.

A conventional specification consists of a data model and a functional model. An object-oriented specification combines these by encapsulation. I have also argued in Chapter 8 that an object or data model should be complete with all the semantics one would expect to store in a CASE tool. These semantics include not only entity and attribute descriptions, but relationships, subtype and parts hierarchies, relationship modality and multiplicity and business and integrity rules. This is a most important point. These semantics must be stated in explicit form if the prototype is to be useful as a specification. They must be written, as far as possible in implementation-independent form, in the (logical) servers and not 'coded' in the applications. This points to the need to use both object-oriented and rule-based languages for prototyping and away from the use of relatively impenetrable 'codes' such as SQL triggers in their various forms or stored procedures.

A prototype, like a dataflow or entity-relationship diagram or a flowchart, may be used as a means of communication with users, domain experts and management. In many cases, prototypes offer a superior means of communication, because many non-DP personnel are uncomfortable with the huge volumes of text, structured English, screen layouts and diagrams which constitute most functional specifications. No one reads and comprehends complete paper-based functional specifications; they are understood in fragments delegated to specialist teams. No company would commission a new office block or factory that way. The decision maker would expect to grasp the specification and design as a whole, through a mock-up. There can be little argument about what a prototype actually does, and often management is more prepared to approve budgets on such a basis. Of course, many will argue that a structured walk through a well-written specification, replete with dataflow diagrams, is usually understood by users. This can be true in the presence of highly skilled business analysts, but it is evident that (a) the user interface issue is poorly addressed by this method, and (b) that second-order effects will be much more difficult to detect; that is, effects which result from forward chaining or event-driven processes. I am acquainted with users who do not like diagrams and who are not prepared to wade through copious structured English, or at least do not give it their full concentration when so doing. The prototype, if properly constructed, is explicit and ready-to-hand. It may be supported with object, dataflow or entity diagrams, but it provides a dynamic context which all three lack, especially in the UI area.

If analysts ask users what they want, they are making the grave philosophical error of assuming that the two groups share the same perception of the world and what is relevant in it. For example, we could ask an accountant what the ledger system should do. The answer might be that it should store debits and credits in separate columns and insist that entries balance. If we implemented this directly and uncritically by storing both debits and balancing credits, we would be doing violence to the advantages offered by computers. In other words, the system need only appear to behave in a certain way: its internal operation may have a totally different character. This dichotomy between appearance and essence makes prototyping especially important. The problem goes beyond the mere difference between requirements and design: it concerns the difference between perceived wants and actual needs – or sublimated wants. Users may state that they want a system which responds 'immediately', but we know, empirically, that a response within one second will satisfy them. They may ask for a system that is far inferior to the one which can be delivered, and be astounded to find that the system they never imagined was what they wanted all along. If I ask for a device that lets me communicate across distances, I am not yet articulating whether I want the services provided by telegraph, facsimile, two-way radio or television. Show me these media and I will then *know* what I really need.

The outstanding question we have to address is that of why anyone should ever bother with revolutionary prototyping, when the evolutionary approach apparently shares all its advantages and additionally helps build systems that can evolve with businesses. This is chiefly a question concerning the availability of suitable software tools. Suitability here encompasses organizational strategy, efficiency and ease of use.

Revolutionary prototyping is apposite in five situations.

- The organization is committed to software and/or hardware solutions not compatible with rapid prototyping; for example, all programs must be written in PL/1 or COBOL to fit in with existing maintenance staff skills.
- Performance or service-level constraints dictate implementation in a low-level language or TP environment.
- No decision has been taken about the delivery environment.
- Even in the case where the delivery environment is suitable for prototyping, say a relational database and 4GL has been selected, it is felt that business rules must be captured explicitly. This arises when it is expected that the rules may be volatile. Encoding complex business rules as SQL triggers or stored procedures is computationally adequate but they are difficult to read and thus hard to alter.
- A design review has determined that the design used for the prototype will not scale up for the target systems.

The prototyping process has to begin somewhere. It is often inappropriate to begin with a complete prototype. Thus, in concluding this general discussion we will examine two ways to construct exploratory initial prototypes. This concerns the notions of 'broad and shallow' versus 'narrow and deep' prototypes. Generally speaking, a system will cover a number of different functions and cases, corresponding to the layers of object-oriented analysis. For example, a financial system might cover equities, bonds, futures, cash and so on.

A **broad and shallow** prototype records the existence of all the key areas but does not provide depth, in that the detailed functionality for a particular area is not included. A **narrow and deep** prototype takes one subject and explores it in detail. In order for a prototype to be of any use as a specification or for evolution, it must include both these approaches. The initial prototype will normally consist of a broad model outlining the main 'menu' options together with a deep model covering just one subject or layer. This subject should be chosen to be one of those perceived as complex. As the prototype is evolved, either into a full specification or into the final system, other subjects are added. The prototypers should be enjoined to consider carefully the potential for reusability of any module they write, and this is one of the chief reasons for choosing the most complex area for the narrow and deep prototype. In an object-oriented system especially this will pay dividends.

9.3.3 Fitting prototyping into the software life cycle

Once it is accepted that prototyping is beneficial, it has to be realized that a structured approach will be required to avoid the pitfalls of revelationary prototyping and to cope with the managerial problems associated with all large software projects.

The main reasons for this are of course that a prototyping project cannot be allowed to ignore good project management practice. Milestones and deliverables must be defined and the project must be decomposed into manageable chunks for teams and individuals. There is also a need to estimate the time and effort required to produce the prototype accurately. Conventional software engineering has produced many sound guidelines to support these needs and there is no need to throw out this particular baby with the bath water. An additional and often crucial motivation derives from the fact that many organizations have an ineluctable commitment to some standard method such as IE or SSADM. As with object-orientation, being able to demonstrate that the prototyping innovation is merely an extension of these existing standards can make the difference between acceptance and anathema.

As an example of the sort of changes required to a conventional model we may take the conventional Yourdon approach and extend it along the lines suggested by Connell and Shafer (1989), which is summarized in the spiral model illustrated in Figure 9.5. This life-cycle model without prototyping consists of the stages and deliverables shown in Table 9.3.

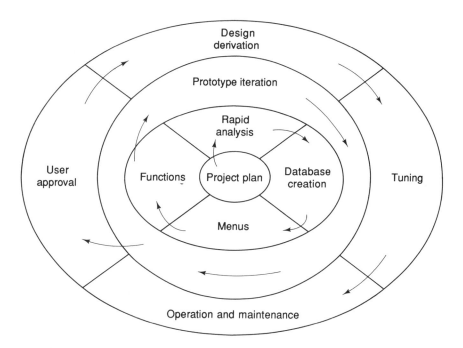

Figure 9.5 A Boehm spiral model of evolutionary prototyping.

Table 9.3 The conventional Yourdon approach.

Stage	Deliverables
Feasibility	Study report, proposal, project plan
Requirements	Software requirements, hardware requirements, system requirements
Analysis	Functional specification
Design	System design, internal design, interface design, criticality report
Coding	System, technical documentation, user guide
Testing	Test plan, test results
Acceptance	Acceptance documents, fault reports

Integrating prototyping into this framework results in a changed life cycle, where the principal changes are the incorporation of a prototype into the analysis phase and the introduction of a tuning phase which subsumes coding of 3GL extensions for greater efficiency. Also notable, from a managerial point of view, is the imposition of a rigid time limit on the prototyping phase, which we refer to as the time-box. This concept will be discussed in more detail below. The changed life cycle consists of the stages and deliverables given in Table 9.4.

Table 9.4 The evolutionary prototyping approach.

Stage	Deliverables
Feasibility	Study report, proposal, project plan
Prototyping within a time-box	Outline requirements, prototype, final software requirements, final hardware requirements, final system requirements
Design review	System design, internal design, interface design, criticality report, amended project plan
Tuning	Tuned prototype
Coding	System, technical documentation, user guide
Testing	Test plan, test results
Integration	Integrated system
Acceptance	Acceptance documents, fault reports

The other changes to be noted are that the lengths of the phases will vary between the two approaches. The analysis and design phases may take a little longer, but testing, integration and most of all maintenance are reduced in length and effort. Testing and integration benefit from being carried out earlier in the project. This is summarized in Figure 9.6, which again is borrowed from Connell and Shafer.

Contrast Table 9.4 with the recommended life-cycle stages, and their deliverables, for revolutionary projects shown in Table 9.5.

Many of the lessons can be extended to the evolutionary approach, but this is left as an exercise to the diligent reader. Revolutionary prototyping starts with the elicitation of user requirements and ends with the production of a specification. Note that we have not yet considered specifically object-oriented issues.

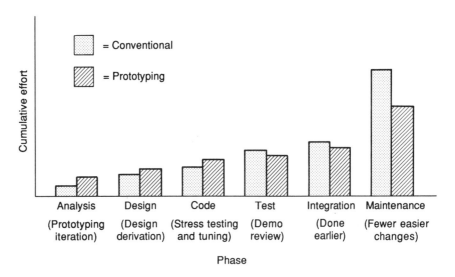

Figure 9.6 Phase length differences for evolutionary prototyping.

Table 9.5 The revolutionary prototyping approach.

Stage	Deliverables
Outline requirements definition	Feasibility report, high-level data and functional models, critical success factors, testing criteria
Prototype within time-box	Prototype, paper model, user documentation, test report
Design review	System design, internal design, interface design, criticality report, service levels
Coding	System, technical documentation, user guide
Testing	Test plan, test results
Acceptance	Acceptance documents, fault reports

MANAGEMENT CONTROL USING TIME-BOXES Now let us shift our attention from prototyping as a technique, whether evolutionary or revolutionary, to its management, focusing on rapid and incremental development.

Prototyping, within large software projects, must be carefully controlled. Iteration cycles should be limited to two or three by the project manager. Documentation, often called a 'paper model', should be produced which is implementation-independent, as far as this is possible. It should state clearly what features of the prototype users may expect to survive to the final version and which may have to be compromised (for example, colour, pop-ups, and rodent operation when a mainframe port is envisaged). Ordinary data modelling or object-oriented analysis and similar techniques should be used to record analysis decisions reached via the prototype. Deliverables and observable milestones must be agreed when the project plan is produced and reviewed regularly. Several rapid development approaches impose what is called a 'time-box', which sets a rigid limit to prototype iterations to ensure management control. The time-box is usually defined as 40–80 elapsed working days. A small team is mandatory, and the tested prototype is both end point and deliverable. The SOMA time-box concept is shown in Figure 9.7.

The time-box tackles the following management issues.

- Wants versus needs – by forcing requirements to be prioritized by negotiation between users and developers. Users and the project team are forced to concentrate on the real needs of the business.
- Creeping functionality – in the traditional life cycle the long delay between specification and delivery can lead to users requesting extra features. The use of a time limit reduces this tendency. The prototyping approach prevents this by setting a time limit on development.
- Project team motivation – the developers can see a tangible result of their efforts emerging.
- The involvement of users at every stage reduces implementation shock.

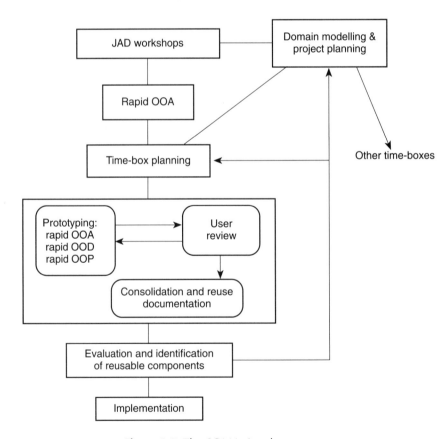

Figure 9.7 The SOMA time-box concept.

The approach recommended consists of the following stages:

- Outline requirements definition and analysis;
- Prototyping within a time-box;
- Evaluation.

Outline requirements definition involves performing an analysis similar to business area analysis (as used in the Information Engineering method), but with a higher-level focus. This is due to the fact that a detailed logical specification is not needed at this stage. A number of well-known techniques exist to support this, such as running joint application design (JAD) workshops as discussed in Section 9.1.2, if appropriate, or holding 'face-to-face-to-screen' sessions with users otherwise, placing special emphasis on time-box slicing and sequencing (that is, not how much is to be achieved but in what sequence) and confirming the suitability of prototyping (using an application grid, say). A critical task is establishing the time-box team. There must be at least one person in the team who is familiar with the outline requirements definition and how it has been drawn up.

Drawing up the outline requirements definition may involve one or more of the following techniques: critical success factors, data analysis, decision trees, dataflow diagrams, object-oriented diagrams, object/objective and task/object matrices, JAD workshops, effect correspondence diagrams, entity life histories, state transition diagrams or state change diagrams. Where a relational database is to be used for evolutionary prototyping, some third normal form (TNF) analysis at the attribute level may be useful.

The time-box provides management control over prototyping. Control is achieved since the time-box sets a rigid time limit on the prototyping cycle, uses a small project team, and demands a system as both end point and deliverable. Tasks in the time-box include time-box planning, which includes establishing the environment, the project team and bringing in specialists in, say, communications, operations, and corporate data administration, if necessary. Time-box planning can involve any analysis technique, including object-oriented ones.

Building a prototype involves building an initial prototype as discussed, testing its functionality, and producing user documentation to guide users through the proto-typing review process.

An additional step is sometimes considered necessary to build in security and/or recovery features and complete documentation. This may only need to be described for revolutionary prototyping, rather than implemented in the prototype.

System and performance testing must be completed within the time-box. It involves testing prototype functionality, including (possibly simulated) interfaces with other systems, and sizing.

It is recommended that walkthroughs should be used wherever possible in the time-box. These enhance the prototyping life cycle because they improve the quality of work, highlight errors early on in development, and can result in the cross-education of team members in the application. Also, application expertise is communicated, work take-over is simplified, and technical progress is readily assessed.

A major deliverable from this process is a specification suitable for use in systems development. The specification should comprise the physical prototype and its paper-based counterpart. The forms of expression of the prototype code and the paper model should be as close as possible to each other.

The final, evaluation or acceptance, stage is the formal review of the prototype and documentation of the lessons learnt. It is a simple matter just to demonstrate the prototype, but to do so is a one-way process, for the most vital element in the whole prototyping approach is obtaining and exploiting user feedback. It is therefore very important that users recognize the need and plan for enough time to review the prototype properly. Thus the prototype review process needs to be highly organized and may even become a major logistical exercise. The review should primarily allow the project sponsor (see the discussion of rôles below) to agree that the deliverables have been produced according to the outline requirements definition and time-box planning documentation. However, representatives from all the users who may be affected by the system need to be present, so that all aspects of the system can be reviewed and feedback obtained.

As a result of the review process, the evaluation team must decide whether to commission the next time-box (if more development is needed), or decommission the project team (if the requirements definition and users are satisfied).

At this stage, a number of questions arise naturally, such as how a team can control endless prototyping. There may be the fear that users will get carried away, constantly changing and rechanging their minds, opening up the spectre of an endless, uncontrolled development. Another common problem is what I call 'user disagreement flip-flop'. This occurs when the team visits several users in turn and makes changes after each visit, without collecting the consensus. The changes made in response to the first user's comments may be reversed by a later user's comments. Such situations should not be allowed to arise, as endless prototyping translates very directly into bottomless budgets. Commercial constraints rapidly take over, and it may be apparent to both users and system builders that enough has been learnt from the first few prototypes to make further interactions unnecessary and economically unjustifiable. Further prototypes may be built in exceptional circumstances if, for example, there is a change in the system's underlying functionality or the object model has changed.

Other questions include how users are to know if the prototype is any good. This can be determined by a number of factors, namely, conformity to company DP standards, tests against task scripts, user reactions, and logical arguments and explanations presented by users, project team members, and so on. Taking the question of user reactions first: the prototyping process helps set the right expectations. As has been mentioned, the prototype can, among its many rôles, be a superbly effective channel of communication between technical and non-technical teams. Providing the user realizes how much is missing from the prototype and the value of the missing parts, the close interaction between user and technical staff that takes place during prototype development can be used to communicate a much deeper understanding of the challenges and details of systems development than has been achieved in the past. The communication is two-way, for the development team also learn a tremendous amount about the real user requirement, but the communication from the technical team to users is often overlooked, and can be a vital part in building a better working relationship.

Finally, how do all teams concerned know that the prototype is finished? Once the prime business paths have been prototyped, by mutual agreement with the users, then the requirements list can be signed off, leaving the tidying up of any loose ends, such as exception-handling rules and routines.

MILESTONES AND DELIVERABLES

Deliverables from the outline requirements definition stage include:

- a non-technical description of the requirements
- a report containing
  - diagrams describing the object model
  - descriptions of each method
  - identified service levels
  - number of users
  - transaction volumes, and so on
  - diagram showing classification, composition and use structures
  - critical success factors
  - the development environment
  - team skill-set
  - project management and control
  - software tools and class libraries required
  - test plan and task scripts

Deliverables from the time-box stage include:

- the physical prototype
- paper-model prototype (including refined object diagrams, business rules, integrity rules, help screens, and so on)
- user documentation
- interview transcripts (optional)
- test report

Deliverables from the evaluation stage include a report detailing the prototype review process, users present, user reactions, changes to be made, candidates for reuse, and the date of the next review.

Typical project management milestones might include the following.

- Receive and agree terms of reference
- Agree project plans, including resource and time constraints
- Complete and document preliminary interviews
- Agree deadlines
- Produce and test first prototype
- Produce user documentation
- Evaluate prototype
- Refine and test second prototype
- Update documentation

- Evaluate prototype
- If necessary, refine and test a third prototype
- Update documentation
- Evaluate prototype
- User sign-off

SKILLS AND TOOLS REQUIRED
The SOMA life-cycle model needs the right people to apply it and the right tools to support them. These skills and tools are different from the traditional approach. The difference is that between the production-line specialization of third-generation methods, and total systems responsibility with fourth-generation or object-oriented methods. When development takes months or years, there is little choice but to specialize, with expensive and experienced staff concentrating on the initial feasibility, design and specification stages, and technical specialists concentrating on the coding and testing.

Experience with the prototyping method described suggests small teams of four or five at the most and having no specialization within the team (there is seniority, and grades of responsibility, but that is a different issue). The staff are not analysts or programmers: they are system builders expected to develop all the skills of building the system from start to finish. One therefore needs to recruit project staff who possess skills or potential in coding, analysis (business and technical) and effective communication with users. This increases job satisfaction but, most importantly, minimizes the risk of misunderstandings arising from multi-stage communication down the 'production line'.

ROLES AND RESPONSI- BILITIES
The following describes the rôles of all those involved in the life cycle including, in detail, those of the system builders or project team. These rôles consist of those of lead user, team member, sponsor and the evaluation team.

The **lead user** is a member of the time-box team. The responsibilities of this member of the team include allocating at least 50% of his or her time to the management issues; resolving most business issues, especially with large projects, where there may not be enough time to keep going back to various managers; sitting on the evaluation team; driving the prototyping in the time-box; organizing user training and documentation; and managing users' expectations.

The time-box stage should utilize a set of full-time **team members**. They are guardians of the prototyping method and, to this end, they must be totally committed to the approach and its time-scales. They contribute to business design, act as visionaries, form part of the evaluation team, build the prototype, involve IT support groups as required, act as primary agents of change, and are flexible rather than dogmatic.

Sponsors are users who initiate the project and should have full commitment to build the system. Their rôle consists in being part of the evaluation team, allocating project funds – although not necessarily 'holding the purse strings', allocating user resources, resolving major business issues, and facilitating easy access to decision makers. Ideally, there should be only one sponsor or a lead sponsor with executive powers.

The **evaluation team** is a small team consisting of the sponsor, lead user, lead developer and the IT controller. The rôle of the latter is to check that the project is consistent with the overall IT view of the organization. The rôle of the evaluation team is to sign off the requirements definition stage; evaluate the completed time-box systems and decide on options such as when to re-enter the time-box or redevelop from the time-box specification; manage diminishing returns by prioritization of essential requirements; and utilize others as needed, such as auditors, operations staff, and so on.

One of the issues that inevitably arises as a control or management issue is the selection of tools. Real, large, commercial systems will almost always involve a database of some sort. Therefore much prototyping will utilize the 4GL features of modern DBMSs. What must be decided is the shape of the final application. Is it to be portable or local? In such a case the PC solution is usually the best. Is it to access the corporate database? Here the choice is not straightforward, since high transaction rates indicate a purely mainframe solution from day one of the proto- type, whereas low update frequencies often mean that the application software can run happily on a PC or workstation with access accomplished across a network: the client/server approach. Here it becomes necessary to evaluate performance charac- teristics very carefully indeed. Further, many organizations have to protect existing software investments and they may construct object wrappers to place legacy systems in a new object-oriented, distributed context (see Graham (1994) for further discussion of this topic).These are some of the considerations which will have a bearing on the cost of the project and its ability to meet the demands of users. In general, tools should be more powerful than seems to be required, because the unexpected is always upon us.

Up to recently, the only suitable tools for rapid or incremental development were 4GLs, usually based on relational databases. For revolutionary prototyping such environments are not sufficiently semantically rich. With the emergence of object-oriented and deductive databases this has changed.

The bullet points below record a number of selection criteria which have been found to be useful in choosing suitable tools for prototyping. It will be noted that they look almost like a set of requirements for object-oriented databases. The fact is that they were prepared without any particular solution in mind.

General requirements:

- Be able to store persistent data structures.
- Permit the import of existing data and schema definitions.
- Support quick changes in front of users, where the changes are simple ones.
- Permit the production of specification documents in the form of
  - diagrams
  - schema descriptions
  - screen layouts
  - rules
  - process outlines.
- Support interactive screen painting or visual programming.
- Contain a high-level computationally rich procedural language.

- Not require the use of macros (as with Lotus) to record complex procedures.
- Not limit the amount or structure of help text.
- Provide a non-procedural enquiry language for the database.
- Provide a non-procedural report generator.
- Provide suitable environmental features: editors, debuggers, and so on.
- Provide a declarative language for business rules.

Requirements which apply to evolutionary projects:

- Support 3GL extensions/interfaces for efficiency.
- Perform at the required service levels on volume data and work load.

Requirements which apply to revolutionary projects:

- Run on a cheap, preferably portable, machine.
- Perform quickly on small data volumes.

Requirements which apply to expert systems projects:

- Provide explanation facilities.
- Support a range of inference techniques (for example, forward and backward chaining).
- Support a range of knowledge representation formalisms (for example, rules and frames).
- Support a range of uncertainty modelling techniques (for example, probability, Shaferian belief, truth maintenance and fuzzy sets).

9.3.4 Prototyping and object-oriented programming

Conventional systems developments can benefit greatly from techniques developed for expert and object-oriented systems. In particular, they can benefit from the controlled use of prototyping, from the explicit representation of business semantics and from principles of software reuse and extensibility. All three issues are interrelated and arise when prototyping is considered. Equally, prototyping is particularly suitable for use with object-oriented programming languages and databases.

As we have seen, there are three kinds of prototyping each with their own distinctive life cycles. Only the evolutionary and revolutionary approaches are commercially viable.

Conventional systems development life cycles can be easily modified to incorporate prototyping and object-orientation. The time-box technique is an important way of imposing management control.

Prototyping, if properly managed, can help produce correct, tested, reversible specifications and thus reduce some maintenance costs.

Specific points relating to object-oriented programming languages as prototyping tools are that:

- reusability with class libraries supports very rapid development;
- extensibility means that prototypes are quick to extend;
- and, most importantly, the explicit capture of semantics makes it possible to use prototypes as full functional specifications; in fact, they should be *better* than the average paper-based functional specification. This demands that object-oriented programming languages should support rule-based extensions if these specifications are to be 'read' by users.

Object-oriented languages are powerful means of building large complex systems and support incremental development through extensibility. However, lack of support for persistent objects or version control in these languages means that object-oriented databases are better prototyping tools.

9.4 On metrics and methods

There is a need for metrics specific to object-oriented methods. These have yet to be developed out of the early project experiences but the topic is attracting a great deal of attention.

Developers should collect metrics from all object-oriented projects from the outset. This will pay dividends later in terms of estimating and resource allocation. Definition of these metrics should be attempted early on. Suggestions for metrics include:

- Number of external objects
- Number of use cases
- Number of domain objects
- Number of application objects
- Number of subscripts (exceptions) per task script
- Number of classification structures, with objects per structure and their depth, breadth and fan-out
- Number of composition structures, with objects per structure and their depth, breadth and fan-out
- Homology of usage structures
- Number of attributes per object
- Number of operations per object
- Number of rules per object
- Error rates in use
- Indices of user satisfaction
- Conventional complexity measures for methods

The costs associated with various sorts of change that may be made to an object-oriented program or design, in order of increasing cost, are as follows.

- Changing the implementation of a class, if that implementation is properly encapsulated, is usually straightforward and easy to estimate. However, if the class participates in a classification structure one should beware of the possibility that subclasses will be affected. Adding or overriding methods is less costly than removing them.
- Adding a new class will usually cost about two man-months' effort, if it is to be reusable.
- Changing a classification structure is usually straightforward, but the whole structure must be tested anew.
- Changing the interface of a class is sometimes required. This can be very expensive, since many clients may be affected and may also have to be changed. Soundly documented use structures are required to minimize the risks.
- Changing a composition structure may affect all the classes below the class which is reclassified in both the old and new structures.

Measure productivity by counting classes that have been accepted. Measure progress by recording how often interfaces change. They should stabilize over time if the project is meeting its objectives.

Do not try to force the project into an unsuitable structured method or follow guidelines, including those given in this chapter, too closely[2]. The wisdom quoted at the head of this chapter is echoed by Booch (1991):

> The amateur software engineer is always in search of some sort of magic, some earthshaking technological innovation whose application will immediately make the process of software development easy. It is the mark of the professional software engineer to know that no such panacea exists. Amateurs often want cookbook steps to follow; professionals know that rigid approaches to design only lead to largely useless design products that resemble a progression of lies, behind which developers shield themselves because no one is willing to admit that poor design decisions should be changed early, rather than late. ...The process of object-oriented design is the antithesis of cookbook approaches.

Booch is talking about design, but his critique applies equally well to analysis and project management. Formal, structured methods cannot possibly be designed to foresee all eventualities. Use them, but use them with a willingness to deviate and adapt to the empirical reality of projects. The valuable resources in a software project are the people, not the shelves full of methods documentation.

Although I have argued against cookbook approaches, this section has been a sort of cookbook. How can this be justified? One of the things I enjoy doing is cooking. I own several cookery books. I look in them for two reasons: when I am concocting something of a type I've never tried or, more frequently, just for ideas. Then I put the books back on the shelves and ignore their recipes. That, I believe, is how object-oriented software engineering methods should be utilized. Bon appetit!

---

[2] Logically minded readers will note that this sentence is self-referential, and may therefore be ignored if it is not ignored.

⊟ 9.5 Summary

Total senior management commitment is essential for object-oriented projects. Appoint lead users and experts who will resolve disputes.

Organize projects into small teams. Layers or classes are the units of configuration management as well as of work packaging.

Adopt a risk-driven spiral model.

Allow more time for analysis and design and less for maintenance.

Tape-recording interviews is highly beneficial. Use questioning techniques covertly.

Reuse does not happen automatically: it is necessary actually to reuse the reusable. The alternative to interviewing people individually is to conduct workshop sessions.

The SOMA approach produces a context model emphasizing message flow between the system and external entities. To this context model, task scripts and subscripts are added. The task script texts are analysed to find entities and their responsibilities. Rough SOMA diagrams are produced including classification and composition structure diagrams. The objects in the model are the basis for preparing modified CRC cards. Rules are also written on these cards. At this point, rôle play may be carried out. The output from this stage consists of the completed cards and a series of event traces documenting the walkthroughs. Object types are divided into those with significant states and others. Where the states are complex a state transition model should be used to discover further operations. The task scripts relate to quality and will be used to produce test plans later.

It is a good idea to work within the context of a standard process model.

The only conventional estimation technique likely to be at all useful is Function Points Analysis.

Use object wrappers to protect investment in existing code.

Incremental compilers, good debuggers and class hierarchy browsers are essential. Build a test harness.

Object-oriented requirements capture and analysis has much in common with HCI design.

Identifying objects is a key skill. The following techniques are recommended.

- Abbott textual analysis
- Protocol analysis
- Task and topic analysis
- Kelly grids, cards sorts, laddering and sorting
- Basden's questioning techniques
- Analysis of judgements

Analysts can learn much from a study of philosophy, HCI design and knowledge engineering. All the techniques used to identify entities in conventional data modelling remain useful for the identification of objects.

Distinguish essential objects that represent universals from accidental objects that represent mere bundles of arbitrary properties. Keep reuse in mind. Practise user-centred design.

Analysts and managers should be trained in knowledge elicitation techniques and object-oriented programming concepts.

There are three kinds of prototyping, each with their own distinctive life cycles. Only the evolutionary are revolutionary approaches are commercially viable.

Conventional systems development life cycles can be easily modified to incorporate prototyping. The time-box technique is an important way of imposing management control.

Prototyping, if properly managed, can help produce correct, tested, reversible specifications and thus reduce some maintenance costs. Use a time-box to control runaway prototyping, expectations and budgets.

Prototyping helps deliver better UIs. Confrontation is better than consensus in discovering innovative functional solutions.

Conventional systems development life cycles can be easily modified to incorporate prototyping and object-orientation. The time-box technique is an important way of imposing management control.

Object-oriented programming languages are suitable for prototyping because of extensibility (inheritance) and the possibility of class libraries. Object-oriented databases are required if data are to be modelled in a prototype. To support semantics, and thus reverse engineering, properly these tools must also support rule-based programming.

CASE tools are as immature a technology as object-oriented programming. Object-oriented databases are the ideal platform technology for CASE.

Use good people and powerful, flexible tools for prototyping.

Define appropriate metrics. Assure quality against published design goals.

Object-orientation is the opposite of the cookbook approach. Methods should be used with imagination and sensitivity, to encourage best practice rather than enforce it. The practice imposed by the bureaucracy may not be truly *best*.

9.6 Bibliographical notes

Managing the design process is discussed in Booch (1991). Design and managerial lessons learnt on several object-oriented programming projects are documented in Pinson and Wiener (1990).

Jacobson *et al.* (1992) gives careful consideration to issues of testing object-oriented software. Berard (1993) discusses requirements capture and testing. Davis (1993) also covers requirements capture. Object-oriented life-cycle issues are also discussed to greater or lesser extents by Alabiso (1988), Bailin (1989), Bulman (1991), Gorman and Choobineh (1989), Ilvari (1991), Johnson and Foote (1988),

Kappel (1991), Lee and Carver (1991), Leiberherr *et al.* (1988) and Scharenberg and Dunsmore (1991).

Booch (1991) lists many useful heuristics for identifying objects. Winblad *et al.* (1990) also provide a summary of such desiderata.

A readable introduction to the history of phenomenology is given by Grossman (1984) although he ignores the influence of Hegel. Hegel's notion of object is analysed in Stern (1990) and a very clear introduction to Hegel's philosophy in general is given by Marcuse (1941).

Lenat and Guha (1990) discuss the identification of objects, the distinction between classes and instances and between attributes and classes, although their terminology is quite different. The context is their work on a huge ten-year research project aimed at building an expert system, Cyc, containing most of everyday knowledge and a good deal of the average encyclopaedia. Although I think the project is ultimately doomed to fail – because thinking is not, as they say it is, 'pushing tokens around' – it has already produced many enormously significant ideas and computational techniques.

Various structured interviewing techniques are described in Scott *et al.* (1991) and several other books on knowledge acquisition and expert systems.

Kelly grids were first introduced by Kelly (1955). Graham and Jones (1988) and Hart (1989) provide an introduction to their use in knowledge engineering. Boose and Gaines' four edited volumes (1988, 1990) provide much that will be of value to the object-oriented analyst willing to learn from her sisters in knowledge engineering.

The fountain model for object-oriented software development is described in Henderson-Sellers (1992) and Henderson-Sellers and Edwards (1993).

The seminal works on prototyping are Brooks (1973) and Boar (1984). Anther useful reference on the evolutionary prototyping of conventional systems is Connell and Shafer (1989). Some of the views expressed here were first put forward in Graham (1991).

For a quick survey of conventional methods, techniques and CASE tools see Gane (1990).

10

The future of object-oriented methods

From fearful trip the victor ship comes in with object won.

Whitman (Oh Captain, My Captain)

In this concluding chapter we will take a broad speculative look at the immediate future for software engineering as a whole, concentrating on those areas where object-orientation has a rôle to play. We will cover projected developments in software, methods, hardware and research directions. Object-orientation is a rapidly developing field and is too broad to admit of a formal characterization. Therefore, we may expect many new and unforeseen developments. However, enough is known to make some educated guesses within a ten-year horizon.

10.1 Trends in languages and software

In terms of software, it is safe to predict that most 3GLs will acquire object-oriented features in the manner that C, LISP, COBOL and Pascal already have. I would go slightly further and predict that, as has already begun to happen with C, these extensions will become standard and the provision of object-oriented features will be delivered willy-nilly with the core compiler and become part of the international language standards. Even COBOL will not be able to resist this trend. An object-oriented COBOL standard is inevitable by 1997, when the next major ANSI release is due. What is not so clear is to what extent Object COBOL will be object-oriented rather than object-based. I suspect the latter is a better bet, partly because of the inherent conservatism of the COBOL community. This would be a pity because in the sort of commercial applications where COBOL has been traditionally used extensibility is likely to be a far more important issue than reuse. The requirement is not to write new reusable code but to reuse the millions of lines of existing

COBOL code and extend or replace it gradually. As hardware gets cheaper it may soon be more cost effective to rewrite, or reverse engineer, applications in a 4GL with suitable extensions in a language such as C++ where efficiency is important, than to persevere with the maintenance of huge unwieldy COBOL systems. This is especially true where the quality of the COBOL code is poor, which is sadly the case for very many systems in use today. The first commercial object-oriented COBOL compilers should be available by the time this book is printed. Object COBOL will significantly affect the state of play in object-oriented applications. As it is used to develop and extend mainstream commercial systems, object-orientation will be able to achieve respectability even in the most Luddite DP organizations.

Paradoxically, it is difficult to see this respectability being widely conferred on Ada. For the time being, C++ will be the language of choice for developments where the performance or single-user limitations of Smalltalk cannot be tolerated. For revolutionary prototyping and educational purposes Smalltalk and – where the declarative semantics and the related issues discussed in this text are important – CLOS will be the languages of choice. Smalltalk will gain in popularity for commercial applications and vie with C++ as the favourite. Eiffel too will gain ground as a public domain language, especially in safety-critical applications.

Open research issues in object-oriented programming languages include the convergence of the functional and object-oriented styles, the relationships between object-oriented programming, logic programming and formal methods, efficiency, the development of type theories for object-oriented programming languages and the possibility of mixed language environments facilitated by small interfaces between languages regarded as encapsulated objects. There are also a number of open questions about object-oriented databases, including those concerned with schema evolution, locking strategies, distributed access and query languages. These products will continue to mature and be fine-tuned, recapitulating the history of their relational predecessors. Relational databases will continue to acquire object-oriented features and within ten years it will be hard to tell the difference. Vendors of applications such as CAD and GIS may agree on a standard object-oriented database on which to base their newer products.

Efficiency must be a prime concern. It is to be hoped that completely new, pure object-oriented languages aimed at improved efficiency will appear as research pushes back the frontiers of our knowledge. Their success will depend not only on overcoming the technical problems this poses (if indeed they can be overcome) but on convincing the business community to make yet another switch to a new language. These new languages will adopt formal semantics through the use of type theories, but there will be no universal agreement on one model or type theory. Each language designer will ride their own hobby horse. As hardware costs come down, the trend to garbage collection and dynamic binding will be reinforced. Parallel implementation will support this trend, but there will be classes of application where efficiency and economy dictate that early binding, strongly typed, garbage-collection-free languages will be important for years to come.

There may well be a convergence of the object-oriented and functional styles of programming. This is hinted at by combinations such as that of the functional AI language Natural Expert with the Adabas Entire entity-relationship database. The Ptech CASE tool also attempts a synthesis of functional specification and programming with object-oriented analysis and design. Again, parallel hardware will be an enabling technology to help overcome the performance problems associated with all forms of logic programming and formal specification languages.

Object-oriented programming and methods have only recently moved out of the universities and research laboratories. The existence of many commercial software development projects at large companies such as IBM, GE and ICI is leading to a much more practical focus.

▤ 10.2 4GLs and expert system shells

4GLs will also acquire object-oriented features. This has already begun to happen with the 4GLs based around relational databases, such as Ingres, and with expert systems development environments, which increasingly take on the character of general-purpose 4GLs in their own right. Several expert system shells already have such features and these will persist and be extended. I think we will see the emergence of hybrid expert system/object-oriented/conventional 4GLs. Of course, object-oriented features will persist as a design feature in expert system shells and become ubiquitous in them. Where the architecture of the systems allows, this will happen to many other high-level languages and systems. One place to expect this is in financial modelling systems and spreadsheets. At least two of these have been designed using object-oriented methods, so it is reasonable to expect the benefits to be transferred to the user via extensions to the high-level languages within these products. Database languages such as Clipper have begun to support the creation of reusable classes.

As we saw in the last three chapters, software engineering methods are already being influenced by ideas from object-oriented programming and expert systems. I firmly believe that prototyping will soon become the norm rather than the exception in commercial software engineering. This has certain implications for the features which must be supported by the new generation of 4GLs. In particular, it posits the synthesis of object-oriented and rule-based styles I have referred to. Object-oriented methods for design and analysis will permeate structured methods thinking for some time to come.

The trends in structured methods and CASE tools have been discussed at length in preceding chapters. In brief, existing methods are embracing object-orientation, new methods are emerging, and CASE tool support follows in train. CASE tools supporting object-oriented analysis and design exist, as has been demonstrated in Chapters 7 and 8, and will continue to emerge as the methods evolve. Repository technology is very similar to that of object-oriented databases and we can confidently expect CASE repositories to be uniformly object-oriented within a few years.

Object-oriented databases will replace relational ones for small systems and for systems involving complex data types such as VLSI CAD, hypermedia and decision support systems. Existing RDBMSs will remain the environments of choice for mainstream commercial projects, but increasingly will include object-oriented features.

10.3 Objects and frames

I have commented on the split in terminology between the artificial intelligence, database and object-oriented communities. Objects for the latter, entities in the middle and frames for the former have so few dissimilarities that I predict a complete convergence of the concepts. This will require two things. First, the object will have to embrace complex attribute structures, procedural attachment, facets, demons, and so on. Second, it will have to be realized that frames are merely data structures and not models of mental representations as originally advocated by Minsky and subsequently by other cognitivists.

The SOMA objects presented in Section 8.3 represent one view of what the converged concept will be like. Also, Appendix I offers a view on another point of convergence between artificial intelligence and object-oriented technology.

The principal points of convergence are as follows.

- Frame systems must have a clearer notion of the way frames encapsulate methods and offer more in the way of information hiding.
- Frames must support the multiple inheritance of explicitly encapsulated methods as well as attribute values.
- Objects must encapsulate declarative semantics and control rules.
- Objects must be able to encapsulate the methods of their attribute's domains in the form of demons which fire if needed to establish an attribute value or when the attribute is updated.
- Object-oriented systems must permit the multiple inheritance of attribute values as well as methods.
- Object-oriented systems should incorporate means of modelling and managing uncertainty.

Objects, entities and frames will converge as concepts to the mutual benefit of object-oriented programming, data modelling and artificial intelligence.

10.4 Handling uncertainty

Very little attention has been paid in the object-oriented literature to problems of handling uncertainty. It has long been recognized that managing uncertainty is a key problem in decision-making and process control problems. Decision makers want answers quickly; their accuracy is not the key issue. Also, several approximately correct solutions may be acceptable and the input data may be irreducibly uncertain or too expensive to collect with absolute precision. Furthermore, it is known that probability theory is not able to represent every kind of uncertainty.

Bellman and Zadeh (1970) put it like this:

> Much of the decision-making in the real world takes place in an environment in which the goals, the constraints and the consequences of possible actions are not known precisely. To deal quantitatively with imprecision, we usually employ the concepts and techniques of probability theory and, more particularly, the tools provided by decision theory, control theory and information theory. In so doing, we are tacitly accepting the premise that imprecision – whatever its nature – can be equated with randomness. This, in our view, is a questionable assumption.
>
> Specifically, our contention is that there is a need for differentiation between *randomness* and *fuzziness*, with the latter being a major source of imprecision in many decision processes. By fuzziness, we mean a type of imprecision which is associated with *fuzzy sets*, that is, classes in which there is no sharp transition from membership to non-membership. For example, the class of *green objects* is a fuzzy set. So are the classes of objects characterized by such commonly used adjectives as large, small, substantial, significant, important, serious, simple, accurate, approximate, etc. Actually, in sharp contrast to the notion of a class or a set in mathematics, most of the classes in the real world do not have crisp boundaries which separate those objects which belong to a class from those which do not. In this connection, it is important to note that, in discourse between humans, fuzzy statements such as 'John is *several* inches taller than Jim', 'x is *much larger* than y', 'Corporation X has a *bright future*', 'the stock market has suffered a *sharp decline*', convey information despite the imprecision of the meaning of the italicized words. In fact, it may be argued that the main distinction between human intelligence and machine intelligence lies in the ability of humans – an ability which present-day computers do not possess – to manipulate fuzzy concepts and respond to fuzzy instructions.

Most uncertainty management techniques originate from work in operational research and expert systems. The methods which have been used or suggested seriously, fall into two broad classes: those offering quantitative numerical representations of degrees of certainty in some way, and those which attempt to model uncertainty in a purely descriptive or qualitative way.

Numerical methods include fuzzy set theory, described in outline in Appendix I, certainty factors and Bayesian probability theory. The certainty factor model of the medical diagnosis expert system MYCIN and its descendants assigns to each proposition a certainty between –5 and +5 and incorporates a calculus, arithmetically similar to that of standard fuzzy sets theory, for propagating those factors through long chains of reasoning. Rules themselves may also be hedged with certainty factors and the calculus takes this into account. A generalization of this approach, and one with a more elaborate mathematical justification, is the Dempster–Shafer theory of evidence. Another system, the one used in the PROSPECTOR expert system, is based on Bayesian probability theory. Here the certainties are interpreted as subjective probabilities and propagated in accordance with Bayes' Rule. Chapter 2 of Graham and Jones (1988) covers these methods in an introductory manner.

There is thus a need to be able to represent uncertain statements in object-oriented programming languages. At present, all the functionality to do this must be handcrafted as no object-oriented programming language has the appropriate constructs built in. Expert systems shells are usually little better, offering usually no means, or at best one or two, of representing uncertain information.

One of the only commercial product offerings in this area which offers fuzzy set-based uncertainty management is ES/KERNEL, which is an object-oriented expert system shell marketed in Japan by Hitachi. It has been used for a number of applications. ES/KERNEL offers the usual facilities of a shell but has a number of novel features. It supports knowledge representation by rules and objects with a noticeably object-oriented style, it has an excellent graphical user and programmer interface – currently using Japanese (Kanji) characters – and it is particularly notable here for incorporating a fuzzy inference capability as an extension to the basic product. It is a powerful system and its unique fuzzy facilities are extremely well implemented and appear very easy to use indeed. I will describe these very briefly.

Membership functions (of fuzzy sets) are defined by choosing from a set of seven graphically displayed templates which can then be modified by the user who changes two, or sometimes more, parameters. These parameters may be changed dynamically during reasoning. The fuzzy part of ES/KERNEL is derived from a successful fuzzy expert control system for the Sendai subway system, mentioned below. This practical application is the basis for confidence in the generality of the seven shapes, but also probably restricts the range of applicability of the system in its present form. The fuzzy rule syntax is typified as follows (in a financial application):

IF *official rate is high* and *average stock price is high*
THEN *buy less pounds*
IF *official rate is low* and *average stock price is low*
THEN *buy more pounds*

I have italicized the phases corresponding to membership functions.

The fuzzy inference engine is essentially an add-on to the basic ES/KERNEL offering. Communication between the fuzzy rule base and the core system is accomplished by message passing between rules or procedures (methods) and the fuzzy system invocation frames. Its background and reasoning methods make it particularly suitable for applications involving real-time control and prediction.

ES/KERNEL currently runs on Hitachi M Series mainframes under VOS3 (similar to MVS/XA), and 2050 workstations running System V UNIX. It is written in C. This system, still being improved and developed, is one of the most significant commercial developments in this area.

One of the most impressive applications of fuzzy expert systems is the automatic train operations system developed by Hitachi for the Sendai municipal subway system. The significant feature here is that Sendai's commuters are prepared to entrust their safety to a piece of mathematics that is often denigrated. The benefits they receive are principally a smoother ride and lower fares as the controller also optimizes fuel consumption and other aspects of the total systems performance. The key to the success of fuzzy control as opposed to numerical control is the elicitation of rules from skilled operators. These rules are, perforce, expressed in vague terms: 'if the speed is *far below* the limit then the power notch is selected'. Also the performance indices such as safety and riding comfort are readily expressed as membership functions. The standard methods of fuzzy sets can then be used to combine elastic constraints and produce control output via the compositional rule of inference and defuzzification methods.

The experiences in the use of fuzzy methods gained by Hitachi engineers on this project led them to incorporate fuzzy methods in the ES/KERNEL product. One of the largest building and civil engineering companies in Japan has used ES/KERNEL's fuzzy set facilities in building a system to support bridge design decisions. At the time of writing this system exists in prototype. A major Japanese bank is also planning to use the technology to construct a sophisticated system for financial chart analysis, with the long-term aim of distributing it for routine use. The application of fuzzy sets in expert system shells is surveyed in Graham (1991a). Object/IQ is a Romanized version of ES/KERNEL but the fuzzy capability has been removed. XShell from Expersoft of San Diego is a set of object-oriented development tools that supports fuzzy systems for process control applications.

Real-world problems, especially decision-making problems, usually involve the management of uncertainty. For this reason object-oriented methods need a notion of fuzzy objects and therefore of inheritance under uncertainty and of uncertainty in the expression of business rules. A fuzzy object could be a fuzzy set, appearing as the value of some attribute, or it could be an object with several fuzzy attributes. At present, uncertainty management in object-oriented methods is an unsolved problem. In inheritance systems, we have the problem of modelling partial inheritance of both crisp and fuzzy properties. For example, we might quantify the extent to which a paper clip is A Kind Of a mental puzzle. The problem is especially complex when multiple inheritance is involved. Here, the problem is how to combine the inherited fuzzy properties. The theory needs to be worked out and agreed. Appendix I is a small contribution to this programme.

⊟ 10.5 Open and distributed systems

The trend towards UNIX and open systems will both require and support object-orientation. Require, because client/server architectures, distributed processing and complex UIs will need the modelling expressiveness and programming productivity delivered by the object-oriented style. Support, because user demands for robust, adaptable, friendly systems will flow from early successes with object-oriented systems. Without reusability, extensibility and semantic richness, true open and distributed systems cannot be delivered at a low enough cost.

The period up until 2001 will be characterized by a continuing trend towards integration and the sharing of resources, despite the best efforts of the major computing corporations. Already, we have seen standards begin to emerge so that different products and applications can have the same 'look and feel' regardless of the machine or network in use and interwork through standards. Seamless integration of languages, databases, UIs and operating systems enables applications which make full use of all these environments. Also, the widespread use of application development systems, such as spreadsheets, modelling packages, expert system shells, word processors, text retrieval systems and hypermedia tools, on distributed systems is forcing these systems to share more data. This means that database management, or perhaps we must say 'information and knowledge-base management' now, will become the central issue in computing. The object-oriented and intelligent databases discussed in Chapters 5 and 6, including perhaps the advanced relational products, are mandatory for the efficient and robust sharing of data. In this sense, OPEN implies OBJECT-ORIENTED.

Complete, multimedia system development databases, or repositories as they are called, are being developed alongside CASE tools. IBM's projected product will be surrounded by a number of application-specific, possibly proprietary, ER databases. Object-oriented databases are the ideal technology for system-wide repositories for reasons which were made clear in Chapter 6, namely, because object-oriented databases support object identity, semantic information, complex data types and version control. Other major and influential manufacturers, such as Amdahl and DEC, have already recognized this in their repository products. I predict that most repositories will be based on object-oriented database models within three years, although the physical implementation may be quite different in some cases. PCTE is emerging as the standard for CASE tool interoperability.

Open systems demand open product philosophies. Any organization that standardizes on a particular manufacturer or product runs a risk. The life of any product is likely to be finite. Also, bureaucratic standardization policies inhibit individual productivity. For example, an organization which standardizes on a word processing package will have to retrain new entrants in that package and may have chosen an inferior package for certain unusual or unforeseen tasks that arise. Far better to permit any suitable word processor to be used, provided that its documents are freely interchangeable with other systems. One way to achieve this is to set a standard that says any word processing package must import and export files in Diff and IBM revisable format, or other, better standards, such as SGML or OLE, as they emerge. This approach maximizes both individual productivity and group communication. It also is a less risk-prone approach. Similar remarks apply to data-bases, spreadsheets, financial modelling systems and engineering packages. In other words: do not standardize on a product, productize on a standard. Let people use what they are most productive with, but within a company-wide discipline.

⊟ 10.6 The rôle of the Object Management Group

A prime requirement for open and distributed systems is to represent applications and services on a network through a common object schema consisting of objects to represent every entity and with all locations and implementations transparent to the user and other objects. Most systems houses have made this aim a part of their strategies for the 1990s. However, not all the theoretical problems have yet been solved and this is a rapidly evolving area. Typical unsolved problems concern abstract models of distributed objects, multi-user servers, security, maintaining locational transparency without overloading the network and lack of standards. However, standards are beginning to emerge.

One important way in which future packages and applications will inter-operate is through the Object Management Group's Common Object Request Broker Architecture (CORBA).

The Object Management Group (OMG) is a group of influential companies committed to establishing broad agreement between vendors on both the terminology of object-orientation and on 4GL style and interface standards – possibly based on existing technology from suppliers such as DEC, Hewlett-Packard and Hyperdesk. Companies involved in the OMG include most of the leading hardware, software and object-oriented suppliers and several major users. Meetings of the OMG Technical Committee rotate between Europe, the USA and the Far East, helping to ensure an international base. The OMG is committed to the fast production of published stan-dards, faster anyway than the official standards bodies can operate, and has already published an architecture guide, a standard for object request brokers (ORB) and a high-level object-oriented abstract data model as part of a reference model for object-oriented analysis and design. Already some suppliers (including Hyperdesk and DEC) have announced CORBA-compliant products and many more will soon follow.

An ORB is a transparent data highway connecting object-oriented applica-tions and object-oriented front-ends to existing applications (Figure 10.1). It is analogous to the X500 electronic mail communications standard wherein a requester can issue a request to another application or node without having to have detailed knowledge of its directory services structure. In this way the ORB removes much of the need for complex RPCs (remote procedure calls) by providing the mechanisms by which objects make and receive requests and responses transpar-ently. It is intended to provide interoperability between applications on different machines in heterogeneous distributed environments and to connect multiple object systems seamlessly.

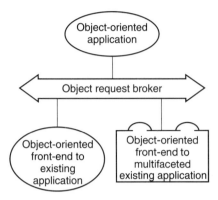

Figure 10.1 The object request broker.

The ORB fits in with the OMG architecture model in which objects are classified as application objects, common facilities and object services (Figure 10.2). Application objects are specific to particular end-user applications such as word processing or spreadsheets. Common facilities are objects which are useful in many contexts such as help facilities, browsers, E-mail and so on. Object services provide basic operations for the logical modelling and physical storage of objects and might include object-oriented databases, directory and file services or transaction monitors. In the ORB, a request names an operations and its parameters which may be object names. The ORB arranges the processing of the request by identifying and running a suitable method and returning the result to the requester.

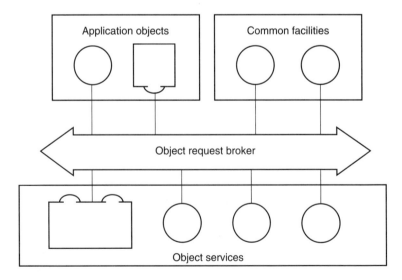

Figure 10.2 The OMG architecture.

Object request brokers work by acting on requests from all other types of object. They bind these to objects and route requests to other ORBs for binding. They can be regarded as either communication managers or systems integrators since they either route requests to the correct destination object or understand the syntax and semantics of each request by maintaining an object model, or both. They replace the need for much complex RPC programming and are a small step towards truly intelligent networks. In future I anticipate expert systems and machine learning techniques being used to take this development even further.

Most users will have to wait for ORB-compliant products to emerge from major suppliers to gain the interoperability benefits potentially on offer. It will be interesting to see how existing products and *de facto* standards such as Microsoft's OLE are positioned in relation to the ORB. One hopes that there will be no conflict but proprietary considerations may dictate otherwise. In the meantime it would be wise to become at least a subscribing member of the OMG, which is not vastly expensive, if you are engaged in the development of any major system which could benefit from interoperation with other systems in future, and perhaps try to comply with the standard in advance. If this strategy takes off it will mean that organizations building object-oriented front-ends to existing applications will benefit even more than they anticipated.

At present this is still a wait-and-see strategy to some extent. Let us try to see what can be achieved now at relatively low cost.

The abstract object model (AOM) sets out to define, at a reasonably high level, the semantics of the main object-oriented analysis and design constructs. Keeping the level high is especially important since, while there is a good consensus about the basic concepts at the programming level, there is still little agreement at the analysis level, as we saw in Chapter 8 especially. Figure 8.56 illustrated the structure of the reference model. Fixing too much too early would stifle innovation. The chief innovation of the abstract object model itself, at least from the standpoint of the object-oriented programmer, is the introduction of constructs from semantic data modelling. Thus visible attributes are recognized as equivalent to two standard methods: Get and Set. Encapsulation is interpreted as the hiding of the implementation of state, not the abstract state itself. Further, relationships between objects are introduced allowing the analyst to express concepts of adding and removing instances and navigating around the model. There are two kinds of entity in the AOM representing objects, their characteristics and concepts concerning them, with various subclassifications as shown earlier in Table 8.1.

The client/server model is not without its problems, as discussed in Chapter 4, but the ORB offers some hope that these problems are not insuperable. In Hyperdesk's implementation, object services manage class, instance, state, security, version and so on for other objects. Different implementations of object services are supported simultaneously, so that multiple database managers and multiple naming systems can execute as required by the network's application and common facilities objects. These object services need not be stored in an object-oriented database although their interfaces must meet the standard; that is, they must be suitably *wrapped*. In this system, definition objects store the system's class structure and object attributes. Life-cycle objects define the intrinsic methods used to manipulate and store objects and manage their values. Naming service objects encapsulate the implementation of object location functions or, in other words, know where all objects are within the network. What is emerging is the spectre of future networks being quite smart as regards what is connected to them. Other ORB products will begin to see daylight very soon and this will alleviate many of the problems of interoperation and of client/server systems in general.

The emergence of the OMG and the almost universal consensus that it commands are among the most important factors ensuring the rapid maturation and widespread adoption of object technology.

▤ 10.7 Concurrency and parallel hardware

Concurrency refers to processes which happen at the same time. If these processes happen outside the computer then we need ways for even conventional Von Neumann machines to cope with simultaneous, multiple demands on their processing power. Multi-user operating systems and locking strategies in databases are two solutions to this kind of concurrency problem. Another kind of concurrency arises when we can have two or more processes executing simultaneously inside the computer. This is parallel computation. We will deal with non-parallel concurrency first.

Models of concurrent computation usually involve a notion of message passing, although these are real messages as opposed to the metaphorical message passing of object-orientation. However, the analogy is so strong that it is difficult to resist the temptation of seeing object-oriented programming as the natural solution to problems of concurrency. Furthermore, as Tomlinson and Scheevel (1989) have pointed out, alternative shared memory models of concurrency do not lend themselves as well to parallel or distributed implementations as do encapsulated models. Object-oriented approaches support the clustering of objects that communicate frequently, and this too helps to support concurrent applications.

Concurrent object-oriented systems have to specify whether objects are synchronous or asynchronous with respect to their various methods. That is, whether the object or actor may continue processing after it has sent or received a message. The usual terminology refers to blocking sends, blocking receives, non-blocking sends, and so on. The notion of message passing combines information transfer into a single construct, whereas the usual shared memory model of concurrency does not and involves the use of complicated semaphores. Furthermore, objects, which encapsulate both data and methods, are a very natural unit of distribution in distributed implementations.

There have been a number of suggestions for concurrent object-oriented programming languages and similar ideas very closely related to objects, such as actor systems. Just as everything is an object in Smalltalk, everything is an actor in actor systems. Actors have unique permanent identity and current behaviour which may change over time and which determines how the actor will respond to the next message it receives. The behaviour is composed of instance variables, called *acquaintances*, and methods, called its *script*. Acquaintances determine the other actors with which the actor may communicate. An actor with no acquaintances is a candidate for garbage collection. On receipt of a message the current behaviour may replace itself. If it does not have a method to handle the message, the actor may *delegate* to a *proxy*, which is an actor nominated among its acquaintances. This notion is similar to that of a superclass, but the methods are not inherited; that is, no code is copied, all that takes place is message passing. Unlike object-oriented programming, there is a well-defined semantics for actor systems, but actor languages are very low-level and difficult to use.

In addition to actor languages, such as Act 3, there are also concurrent versions of pure object-oriented languages, such as ConcurrentSmalltalk (Yokote and Tokoro, 1987), and hybrids such as Orient84/K, which combines the Smalltalk and Prolog styles (Ishikawa and Tokoro, 1987).

Object-oriented concurrent programming is a new field for researchers, but its future importance is assured by two incontrovertible facts: distributed and client/server architectures involve concurrency if effective use of resources is to be made, and no other programming style offers a clear and conceptually economical model for this kind of complex, cooperating concurrent system.

Parallel computation has nothing to do with the number of processors in a machine. A multiprocessor transputer surface can run several programs in parallel, a single transputer can simulate several processors (using a time slicing technique) but a multiprocessor mainframe usually is only able to process one application program instruction at a time, the other processors being devoted to specialized operations such as I/O.

There are several different kinds of parallel computer system. The basic division is between shared memory designs which use a coarse-grained decomposition of processes that each share the same data space, and distributed memory designs. Shared memory designs have up to about 30 processors and give similar price performance to PCs. Distributed memory systems distribute the data storage across several processors and usually implement a more fine-grained decomposition of processes. Distributed memory designs can be of two basic types: either all processors run the same program, as with connection machines and vector processors, or different processors can run different programs, as with database machines, transputer surfaces or hypercube architectures. Neural networks are examples of parallel machines in which all the processors are identical at a low level but which give the appearance of several processes running at a higher level of granularity.

Transputer-based systems can give price/performance figures as low as $800/MIPS[1]. Many parallel machines now run under a parallel version of UNIX, such as Mach. There are several different architectures for parallel machines.

---

[1] The MIPS (million instructions per second) figures quoted in this chapter are approximate measures equivalent to about 0.8 of a VAX MIPS (a VUP) or about 1.6 RISC MIPS.

Up until recently programming parallel machines, such as the transputer, was extremely difficult and was accomplished in extremely low-level languages, like Occam. New parallel languages will be required if widespread commercial use is to occur. Parallel hardware will also require new design methods. These new languages and methods are likely to be object-oriented.

Processors in distributed memory systems communicate by sending messages. The object-oriented metaphor therefore maps directly onto the problem of describing the topology of a process running on such a machine. Object-oriented programming languages and design techniques are therefore likely to become standard for such machines, although this is far from the case at present.

Since Simula, objects have been a way of implementing both data structures and processes where concurrency is involved. Distributed architectures involving networks and remote procedure calls emphasize the need to describe these systems. Once again the object-oriented metaphor applies directly and is likely to become standard in applications of this kind.

Parallel computing is still an intriguing research problem. Many issues have yet to be resolved, before the technology matures and receives wide commercial application. It is a key technology for the 1990s and will mature in close connexion with object-orientation.

It has been mentioned that garbage collection imposes performance limitations for some object-oriented languages. Parallel computing offers the prospect of a happy resolution to this problem. More powerful machines will be more tolerant of dynamic binding and garbage collection, especially the latter where there are already ancillary chips in existence which accomplish garbage collection concurrently with main processing. In the very near future, garbage collection in some language implementations may be supported in parallel by a separate processor.

One option for high-level parallel programming languages is exemplified by Strand and Parlog (Foster and Taylor, 1990), which are logic programming languages in the tradition of Prolog. Prolog is based on the idea of expressing all program statements declaratively in the form of Horn-clause logic, and then applying automatic inference algorithms at execution time, usually a form of backward chaining. This process is thought of as either pattern matching or theorem proving. A Horn clause is a special kind of logical implication rule with only one term in its conclusion or consequent. For example,

If A and B and C then D

is in Horn clause form, whereas

If A and B then C and D

is not. In the Edinburgh Prolog notation, the former would be expressed as

D :- A, B, C

Guarded Horn clauses are an extension of logic programming used in parallel theorem provers, such as Parlog or Strand, which support parallel execution of all the descents of the proof tree.

A guarded Horn clause has the following form:

H :- $G_1, G_2, \dots, G_m$ | $B_1, B_2, \dots, B_n$

where H is the 'head', | is the 'commit' operator, $B_1, B_2, \dots, B_n$ is the 'body' of the clause and $G_1, G_2, \dots, G_m$ is the 'guard'.

The guard specifies the precondition under which a process may execute. This style of programming combines formal specification with parallel execution.

One of the attractive features of Strand is the fact that it is portable from sequential to parallel machines. It has been found that the approach exemplified by Strand is more successful than object-oriented programming in certain application areas, such as telephony (Foster and Taylor, 1990). On the other hand there seems to be no more natural way to model communicating processors than with the object-oriented metaphor. We saw in Chapter 3 that there are current research initiatives aimed at amalgamating functional, logic and object-oriented programming. It is to be expected that the first applications of any successes from this research will be applied to programming parallel computers.

Hardware and operating systems design itself, both conventional and parallel, will be influenced by object-oriented notions. We saw in Chapter 4, with the examples of the AS/400, NeXT and Rekursiv machines, that it already has been to some extent.

The main barrier remaining to the widespread acceptance of parallel machines is lack of compatibility. As systems become more 'open' in general, this will cease to matter. Design notations where concurrency is explicitly recognized, such as OOSD and the Harel state charts used in methods such as OMT, may be particularly suitable for object-oriented design of parallel systems.

▦ 10.8 Formal methods and correctness

Formal methods address the problems of vagueness in specifications and of matching the semantics of specifications to those of source code. While the latter aim is purely laudable, there can be two views on vagueness: either it should be factored out by more formality or it is an essential component of the very act of description. For example, every user knows what an *adequate* response time is, but formal methods require that it should be expressed as so many seconds (or as a function returning so many seconds) to remove all vagueness. More seriously, a requirement for 'a friendly user interface' must be formally stated. I cannot think of a reasonable way to formalize friendliness, and incline to the opinion that vagueness is an essential feature of specification and should itself be captured in the formalism. This view is exemplified in the treatment of inheritance semantics in Appendix I, but is not a fashionable one.

Alan Turing suggested using formal logic to program computers as early as 1948. The idea was taken up by Dijkstra and Hoare in the late 1960s, who showed that the semantics of a programming language could be formally characterized and that specifications could be expressed in a formal language. Formal proof systems enable mathematicians to take a specification, expressed in a formal language based on logic or set theory, and a piece of source code and prove that the code meets the specification. A more sophisticated approach, adopted by methods like Z and VDM, involves starting with a formal specification and then refining it through step-by-step mathematical transformations into a program. The difficulty with this approach is that it takes a great deal of mathematical skill and a great deal of time to produce these proofs of correctness, often skill at the level of a PhD in mathematics.

VDM, IBM's Vienna Development Method, now has a BSI standardization committee and a standard for Z is also projected. Other formal specification methods/languages include OBJ and STC's *me too*. Logic programming languages may also be used to produce executable specifications directly. The problem with this approach is twofold. First, FOPC may not be expressive enough to capture the specification, if vagueness is involved for example. Second, and more seriously, programming in logic is still programming and this approach merely shifts the position of the programming effort forward in the life cycle. Formal logic is not itself entirely 'design-free', for the very act of stating a problem in logic involves a commitment to certain positions about what can be validly expressed. This is why there are several different logics. Another problem is the need to retrain programmers in formal logic, which is a subtle and difficult subject to master. The most sophisticated approach of all is based on AI and proof theory. The philosophy here is that a program is identical to a proof of a theorem which represents the specification. Automatic theorem provers take the specification and search for a proof. If the search terminates, the stored result is executable code. The most successful proof-theoretic methods are based on non-standard logics, such as the Martin-Löf intuitionistic type theory (Martin-Löf, 1975, 1982). At present, and for the foreseeable future, this approach only works on trivially small problems.

Because of the time- and skill-intensive nature of formal methods they are usually only considered worthwhile in safety-critical domains. However, the ideas evolved in formal methods can be adopted informally with considerable practical benefit in commercial systems, especially when combined with object-oriented methods.

Formal specification maps onto object-oriented design through the notion of a contract between client and server objects. This contract is expressible as pre- and postconditions as described in previous chapters. No formal theory is required to make immediate use of this good idea.

An object-oriented approach to the specification of open distributed systems is being developed by the ISO using the international standard specification language LOTOS and the Z notation. At the University of Manchester, work is proceeding on using formal methods to overcome the problems associated with using large object libraries. The basic idea is that programmers need to know what the objects in a library do, so why not attach a formal specification to them so that one can prove theorems about them and even form composite objects constructed from them? The work depends on the notions of pre- and postconditions and effectively extends Smalltalk with these notions from VDM. This gives Smalltalk features which are provided already in Eiffel.

▤ 10.9 How to achieve competitive edge

As George Cox, of the Butler Cox Foundation, has remarked, the age we live in can be characterized as the age of the designable business. In an increasingly competitive and larger world market, competition is not only fiercer within industry sectors, but comes from unexpected directions with increasing frequency. Not long ago, banks competed with other banks and insurance companies with other insurance companies. Now competition for a bank can come not only from anywhere in the financial services sector but from retail companies setting up new financial arms to diversify.

Why has this change come about? If deregulation is blamed for this change, one must immediately ask where the pressures for deregulation originated. I think it is due to two interlinked factors: the tendency to decline of the global average rate of profit on capital, caused by the increasing capital intensity of worldwide production, and the emergence of information technology (IT). Companies are forced to automate to compete and IT automation enables them to adapt to compete.

This rapid adaptation was not possible before the advent of computers, and not effectively possible in the days of batch-processing mainframes. Victorian enterprises retained the same structure across generations. Now we are reorganized every five years or so. The slogan repeated in DP departments used to be: 'whatever you do, you can't beat the system, you can't change the organization'. Now if the organization does not adapt to exploit the full potential offered by IT it may go under. Change becomes more and more rapid as the technology makes it possible. That is the true kernel of all the current fuss about reusable and extensible systems. Only with such systems can the accelerating pace of organizational change be supported without cataclysm.

Competitive edge can only be achieved by organizations that are not only willing to adapt, but use their computers to enable previously unimaginable changes. Reusable and extensible code and specification is not a pious wish but a life and death necessity. If object-oriented methods cannot deliver, then something else will have to be found. I think that object-orientation offers the best bet at present.

A corollary of this position and the fact that there are thousands of millions of lines of ageing, but essential, lines of code in the commercial arena, is that reverse engineering techniques are in demand. For this reason object-orientation is not enough unless it incorporates rule-based, semantically rich features that will support reverse engineering.

One of the dangers of having a distributed corporate database, given the above perspective on the adaptable business, is that reorganization of the business may require redistribution of data. Thus, the topology of the distribution itself may inhibit organizational changes which would be otherwise beneficial. If distributed databases are essential, for whatever reason, then steps should be taken to ensure that redesigning the distribution structure should be easy. I suggest that this implies that the distribution is based on objects: coherent wholes which represent lasting real-world entities (and their properties) which can be moved as a whole between processors with minimal disruption and effort.

Object-oriented methods – analysis, design, databases and programming – offer potentially huge increases in productivity. There are some software development companies, principally in the United States, offering to develop custom applications in certain vertical markets for as little as 25% of price quotations based on conventional development effort. They are only able to do this by utilizing application-specific class libraries.

What is required by companies seeking to survive and prosper, then, if you have followed the argument of this book, is reusable, extensible semantically rich specifications, class libraries, methods which incorporate prototyping and open systems. The adoption and successful utilization and management of these technological developments can lead to significant benefits in terms of competitive edge, because the organization taking this path is more flexible. The specific benefits relevant in this context are:

- lower maintenance costs;
- lower analysis costs;
- quicker response to organizational change; and
- lower upgrade costs.

When a claim is made for lower analysis costs, some care is needed. I have argued that more time must be spent on analysis when using object-oriented methods. Lower *overall* analysis costs will only be achieved when the results of specification are reused. This means that the benefits of reuse have to be discounted at the current money-market rate. Thus in periods of high interest rates these benefits will be perceived to be lower. There is a flaw in this argument, for flexible systems are a matter of survival, not a matter of cost. Nevertheless, it is important that reuse benefits are not over-zealously claimed for objects which will be reused rarely or a long time in the future.

The OMG has already been mentioned as a force for both change and standardization. It represents major suppliers. The Object Interest Group (OIG) was originally founded in early 1990 as a club of users, mainly UK-based companies, including four leading high street banks, two of the larger insurance companies, BP, British Airways, British Aerospace, British Steel, BT, ICI, Ford, Rolls Royce and some governmental bodies. They aimed to evaluate the current state of the technologies of object-orientation and issue a set of requirements that suppliers will be expected to meet. One potential aim of the OIG in its first stage was the setting of industry-wide standards for 'engineering' library objects, using the professional engineering bodies to define them. They found a great deal of secrecy surrounding object-oriented applications, but were not able to determine whether this was due to commercial success and competitiveness or shamefacedness in the face of poor results. They did discover an industry trend towards prototyping and incremental development. However, many of the claims made for object-orientation were validated by the study. In particular, there was evidence that object-orientation supports incremental development, provides enhanced productivity and quality and uses consistent concepts throughout the life cycle, from analysis to implementation. Reuse benefits were not in evidence, and no benefits in terms of improved communication with users were found, especially at a detailed design level. One very significant conclusion of the stage one report was that there is a need for an economic model of object-oriented development of the type provided by Boehm (1981) for conventional projects. Another identified deficit of current methods was the need for sound methods for identifying objects and a process that can be recommended for this purpose. At the time of writing, OIG has begun a second stage and is sponsoring a few pilot projects.

Object-oriented technologies are not the only ones for achieving competitive edge. Notably, the development of so-called groupware or workflow technology will be significant, although this technology itself may be implemented on top of object-oriented programming. Groupware is a generic term describing computer systems which support the way groups of people work together, and covers everything from electronic mail and computer conferencing to systems that keep track of responsibilities and commitments.

Completely separate from the technology of object-orientation is that of high bandwidth communications. This is probably the area where the most revolutionary changes will occur, and this is not the place to discuss them. However, with the commercial advent of Ted Nelson's XANADU hypermedia system, these otherwise separate technologies will be effectively married together in supporting a common purpose.

10.10 Rightsizing: how to reduce hardware costs by an order of magnitude

Computer power is usually measured these days in millions of instructions per second (MIPS)[2] . Of course, this measure is a very rough one. It gives no guide to channel capacity, floating point efficiency, and many other issues. Before an expensive purchase decision is made, it is wise to examine suitable benchmarks based on the type of task envisaged for the machine. However, as a rough measure, MIPS is probably as good as any. On this basis, price/performance or value for money can be measured in pounds, yen, marks or dollars per MIPS ($/MIPS): what some droll Americans, inverting the ratio, refer to as 'bangs per buck'. To a first approximation, mainframes are two orders of magnitude more expensive than workstations on this measure, and even large minicomputers can be more than one

---

[2] MIPS is sometimes said to stand for Meaningless Indication of Performance Statistic.

order of magnitude more. This is illustrated schematically in Figure 10.3. The question that forces itself on us is then: 'Why should anyone ever buy a mainframe?'. Ignoring the important issue of channel capacity, the simple answer is that 200-MIPS mainframes exist and 200-MIPS PCs do not. Thus, if you have a 200-MIPS application the decision is made for you. As the figure shows, PCs go up, in MIPS, to perhaps 12, UNIX workstations may hit the 80 level, although these limits are going up month by month. Whatever the exact figures – and hardware advances are so rapid that anything written about MIPS quickly dates – it is clear that mainframes will be more powerful than workstations for quite a while and likely that they will remain vastly more expensive on the $/MIPS measure.

This argument was all very well until someone invented the local area network. Ten networked 10-MIPS workstations deliver 100-MIPS, provided the workload can be divided in a suitable way or resources shared via remote procedure calls. Naturally, networks have a cost in both computing power and money associated with them, but even allowing for this it looks as though an order of magnitude saving should be possible. This is so only for certain applications where the channel capacity provided by mainframes is not the key issue.

Open systems, networks and shared resources make it possible to deal with problems which admit a coarse-grained partitioning into tasks that can run on separate processors with minimal cooperation, although cooperation among such systems is theoretically possible by means of a separate scheduling machine operating as a sort of blackboard system (see for example Graham (1987)). However, database systems and high-transaction servers do not have this character, and we cannot expect to see the demise of the mainframe, merely a new rôle for it as a server on a network of lower-cost machines.

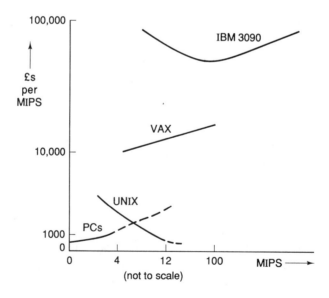

Figure 10.3 Price/performance curves for mainframes, minicomputers and workstations.

Thus, networked workstations may reduce costs by two, or at least one, order of magnitude for a limited, but quite wide, class of problems. Object-orientation has an important rôle in describing systems for such distributed applications.

Workstations and small systems will increase in power as parallelism and optical computing techniques are exploited.

As the cost of MIPS comes down, storage will become relatively more expensive, but optical storage will counteract this tendency too.

☰ 10.11 Getting started with object-oriented methods

The danger with new technologies is that people are either too enthusiastic and unrealistic in their expectations or too pessimistic and obstructive. In the first case they plunge into them with gay abandon, often discrediting the technology if not actually damaging their own careers. In the second, the Luddites are overtaken by companies that take the best aspects of the technology and use it for competitive edge.

The example that springs to mind to support this view is the example of expert systems. In the early 1980s, as expert systems emerged from the AI research labs, there was enormous media hype, much of it ill-informed but a lot taken directly from the propaganda put out by professors of AI who should have known better, but who had research grants to win. Thus, we had a relatively immature technology with modest real capabilities and a market expectation of systems which would, in the words of Herb Simon (1965), be 'capable of performing any task that a man could perform within 20 years'. This is the formula for failure: immature technology + unrealistic expectations.

I will caricature the process of failure in a parable. The DP manager of a large corporation in 1983, say, became excited by the possibilities of expert systems, having read about them in the press. The R&D expert was asked to investigate. The preliminary investigation showed that benefits could be obtained and it was decided to run a pilot project. So far so good, but now things began to go wrong. The DP manager – let's call him Abe S. Traction, wondering whom he could spare for this task, began to survey the corporate horizon. Lo, there was the OR department. Now they hadn't done anything useful for years (OR had been discredited, through a process similar to that I am parodying here, in the late 1960s). So Abe went to see the head of OR who, happy to be needed, offered to help. Who could he spare? Well, those guys in department C weren't doing anything right now, so Bob's your uncle, the expert systems section was created. The new department was given a minuscule budget and told to find a suitable problem for expert systems, buy a couple of shells to play with and report back. As time went on they were directed away from any application that was in any way significant to the business: 'What if it goes wrong? People will notice'. When they did find an application – probably concerned with the help desk – the solution didn't work very well, but that didn't matter because nobody significant noticed. However, after five or six attempts Abe had

had enough and decided that expert systems were a load of hype – he actually used a slightly different word, but that need not detain us here. In this company, and in the world at large, unrealistic expectations gave way to pessimism, and the so-called AI winter commenced in the late 1980s. Expert systems are actually now a mature, powerful and useful technology and many companies are gaining benefits, but they are the companies with very different DP managers from Mr. Traction.

I hope you will see by now that I am constructing a simile between expert systems and object-orientation. The latter is an immature technology which is widely believed to be the solution to many DP ills. How should companies wanting to explore object-oriented systems proceed? The answer is simple: do not do what Abe did. Here are some guidelines.

- Choose the people you can least afford to spare for the development team. Object-oriented methods, just as expert systems, need good people, not leftovers from the corporate elephants' graveyard.
- Choose a business-critical application to test the methods on, but allow time for false starts. By all means choose a small application, but make sure it will be noticed, fail or succeed.
- Allocate a budget in proportion to the importance of the application. This implies carrying out proper cost and business justification exercises.
- Set clear objectives for the project team: not just technical objectives but business objectives.
- Establish clear senior user management commitment to the project. Keep users involved and report back lessons learnt.

From the suppliers' point of view there are some general lessons to be drawn from my simile. They apply to nearly all new technologies. New ideas are characterized by a steady, linear growth in the capability of the technology that supports them. Expectations, on the other hand, tend to peak early on in the lifetime of the technology, far in excess of the real capabilities at that time. When it is shown that this is the case by failed projects, optimism turns to utter gloom and the level of expectation falls far below the real capability curve, which is still rising steadily. At this point a window of opportunity opens for vendors and progressive users (Figure 10.4). Until expectations converge with real capabilities again, which they will gradually, the technology can be purchased at advantageous terms and, more importantly, decisive competitive edge can be gained. User organizations will need to educate themselves on pilot projects before the crossover point in order to reap the benefits thereafter.

The true justification for object-orientation is the production of flexible, friendly and robust systems. It helps us to tackle the maintenance problem through more correct specification based on prototyping in semantically rich languages, and through easier extensibility based on inheritance. It helps us with the development of new systems because we can build those systems from reusable components which encapsulate the state and behaviour of abstractions based on stable objects in the real world of an application or enterprise. It helps us build systems which are more secure, by exploiting further the encapsulation of the state of objects. It helps

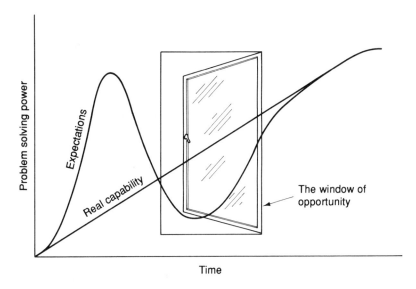

Figure 10.4 The window of opportunity for new technologies.

us build friendly, ready-to-hand, flexible user interfaces. It supports a very high level of modular (reusable) design and easy extensibility of function. Although these ideal benefits may sometimes be limited, as with the tension between abstraction and inheritance discussed in the first chapter, the justification remains convincing for companies who want to survive the corporate rat race.

All this adds up to a very strong requirement for industry to adopt object-oriented methods cautiously but quite wholeheartedly. The outstanding problem then is how to move from where we are now to where we want to be. That is the subject of *Migrating to Object Technology* (Graham, 1994) which picks up where this book leaves off the issues of adaptability, productivity and quality.

Object-oriented methods have reached the stage where the window of opportunity is about to open, although exactly how soon the crack will be wide enough to lean out of is hard to tell. That it is not yet open wide can be seen from the fact that consultants in this area can still charge high fees and that there are still many uncertain IT managers. For the latter, I hope that reading this book has proved both encouraging and anodyne.

10.12 Summary

Object-orientation will become a standard 3GL feature and object-oriented 4GLs will emerge to replace the current generation. Object COBOL marks the start of a new era of respectability and practical application for object-oriented programming.

Otherwise, C++ remains the language of choice for implementation and Smalltalk and CLOS are the preferred languages for prototyping and training, with Eiffel gaining ground rapidly.

The trend in structured methods is towards object-orientation. CASE tools to support object-oriented methods are appearing and existing CASE tools are being rewritten with object-oriented programming languages and databases. Future system development repositories will be object-oriented databases.

Prototyping will become the norm rather than the exception in general software engineering.

Small systems and systems involving complex objects will utilize object-oriented databases, whereas large, mainstream, record-oriented, commercial systems will continue to be built using relational products.

There will be a convergence of ideas from artificial intelligence, semantic data modelling and object-oriented programming, leading to a refinement of the object concept. Decision-making and process control applications demand that uncertainty be modelled. This cannot be done well in current object-oriented systems or expert systems products. A small number of AI products are more advanced in this area.

The open systems movement will both require and support object-orientation.

Open systems demand open product philosophies: do not standardize on a product, productize on a standard.

The OMG is already producing agreed standards which will be very important along with the new interoperation products that support them.

Faster, possibly parallel, machines will support the acceptance of languages that use dynamic binding and garbage collection. Parallel hardware will also require new design methods.

Formal proofs of correctness are still labour- and skill-intensive. They are still important in safety-critical applications. Formal specification maps onto object-oriented design through the notion of a contract between client and server objects. This contract is expressible as pre- and postconditions.

We live in the age of the designable business. Computer systems to support adaptable organizational structures will be object-oriented and rule-based by the end of the decade.

Object-oriented methods offer potentially huge increases in productivity. The adoption and successful utilization and management of these techniques can lead to significant benefits in terms of competitive edge.

Networked workstations may reduce hardware costs by an order of magnitude for a limited, but quite wide, class of problems. Mainframes will become network servers.

When beginning to use object-oriented methods, use the best people and tools. Set a realistic budget, get management commitment and choose small, but business-critical, applications.

The window of opportunity for object-oriented methods is about to open.

⊟ 10.13 Bibliographical notes

Useful, topical reports on emerging technologies are published annually by CSC Index (formerly Butler Cox). Other organizations who publish high-level management summaries of new technologies include BIS Mackintosh Ltd, New Science Associates and Ovum. Frost and Sullivan produce more marketing-oriented reports. Tony Durham's *IT Horizons* is concise, accurate and good value for money among the subscription services.

The weekly computer press (*Computing* and *Computer Weekly* in the UK) and monthlies such as *Byte* are useful sources of information on trends in technology.

Hutchison and Walpole (1991) survey the whole area of the exploitation of object-oriented technology in open and distributed systems.

Hollowell (1993) describes the OMG object model in an introductory fashion. The details are to be found in the various publications of the OMG itself, which are constantly being updated; the original, fundmental reference is Soley (1990).

Turner (1984) provides a popular exposition of Martin-Löf's intuitionistic type theory which is also briefly described in Graham and Jones (1988); the latter also covers AI and uncertainty in some detail.

Foster and Taylor (1990) gives a gentle introduction to the concepts of parallel programming in general, and the ideas behind Strand in particular.

APPENDIX I

Fuzzy objects: inheritance under uncertainty

It is the nature of all greatness not to be exact.
Edmund Burke
(Speech on American Taxation)

This appendix is included to support some of the remarks made in Chapter 8, because the material presented here is not easily accessible in the literature. It is not essential to read the appendix to understand the remainder of the book, and those readers without a background in expert systems, fuzzy set theory or mathematics may find it slightly heavy going.

In Chapter 8 we saw that there was a number of strategies available for dealing with conflicts in the inheritance of values and defaults when multiple inheritance is supported. This technical appendix describes one of the more unusual of these techniques that arises when the data are uncertain or the inheritance links themselves cannot be asserted with complete certainty. This problem either does not arise with the inheritance of methods or, if it does, then needs a very complex method for dealing with the propagation of certainty factors attached to the output variables returned by methods. We thus will restrict ourselves to examining the inheritance of attributes. The partial inheritance of methods, represented by a certainty factor, is taken to mean the possibility that the object can carry out the operation. This clearly has little value for a programmer but may be of immense utility in describing systems in contexts such as enterprise modelling and business process re-engineering.

This appendix describes a computational method of representing uncertain knowledge which was developed as a generalization of the frame notion introduced by Minsky (1975) and others and the object concepts of object-oriented programming. Since the generalization uses, in an intrinsic way, the theory of fuzzy sets due to Zadeh (1965), it is natural to designate the generalized objects *fuzzy objects*. These structures were first introduced, in an AI context, by Graham and Jones (1987) under the name fuzzy frames. Recently, some other, more restricted, notions of fuzzy objects have appeared, such as the one due to Yazici *et al.* (1992).

To begin with, we shall review briefly the AI version of objects – the theory of frames – and the, perhaps less familiar, machinery we will require from fuzzy set theory. At the end of the appendix we explore some of the intriguing questions which the theory raises, some of its problems, and suggest topics for further research. In doing this there is cause to compare this approach with the fuzzy quantifiers of Zadeh (1982) and non-monotonic logic (McDermott and Doyle, 1980; Reiter, 1985). It is suggested that there are important links to current issues in semantic data modelling and object-oriented databases. It is also suggested that fuzzy objects offer a unified framework for the representation of both certain and uncertain knowledge about objects, and, in a sense to be explained, generalize fuzzy relations and, *a fortiori*, relations.

▤ I.1 Representing knowledge about objects in AI

In terms of knowledge engineering, there are many ways to represent knowledge: as rules, by logic, in procedures, and so on. Each of these formalisms is usually better at expressing one particularly suitable type of knowledge. For example, rules are good at describing knowledge about causality, logic at expressing relationships, and there is no better way to describe knowledge about calculating a cube root, say, than as a procedure. On the other hand, describing a bowl of fruit or a beautiful stained glass window in the form of rules would be hopelessly tedious to say the least. See Brachman and Levesque (1985), Shadbolt (1989) or Graham and Jones (1988) for more complete treatments of knowledge representation. The forms of AI knowledge representation which seem to best capture knowledge about objects and their properties (such as bowls of fruit) are generally referred to as semantic networks and frames. We will concentrate on these object-like representations.

Often knowledge is uncertain, and usually some additional mechanism has to be introduced in expert systems to model the uncertainty. This can be done by assigning certainty factors or probabilities to rules in rule-based approaches or to their atomic clauses, or through the use of some truth maintenance procedure, depending on the type of uncertainty involved. Shastri (1988) observes that: 'an agent cannot maintain complete knowledge about any but the most trivial environment, and therefore, he must be capable of reasoning with incomplete and uncertain information.'

In frame-based or object-oriented systems, uncertainty often arises as a side-effect of multiple inheritance. Here we concentrate of the kinds of uncertainty which can be readily modelled with fuzzy sets, but, in principle, the arguments should apply to stochastic problems equally well.

I.1.1 Semantic networks and frames

I must perforce state my philosophical position *vis-à-vis* the notion of a 'frame'. I unrepentantly regard frames as data structures, rather than as models of human cognition of some sort. Further, there is little or no distinction made here between frames and structurally equivalent notions such as semantic networks. This puts this exposition at odds with many workers in AI such as, for example, Brachman, who are concerned with the logical adequacy of the theory rather than the mostly practical issues which motivate this work. It also distances me from those who, likes Hayes (1985), would reduce frames to some sort of first-order logic. For me, the whole point of frames is to facilitate higher-order constructs of the sort found in, *inter alia*, object-oriented databases and semantic data models.

A semantic network consists of a set of nodes and a set of ordered pairs of nodes called 'links', together with an interpretation of the meaning of these. I will restrict myself to describing this interpretation using a descriptive semantics; that is, a set of statements describing the interpretation. Terminal links are called 'slots' if they represent properties (predicates) rather than objects or classes of objects. A frame is a semantic net representing an object (or a stereotype of that object) and will consist of a number of slots and a number of outbound links. Consider, for clarification, the frame for a toy brick shown in Figure I.1 in the form of a network.

It may also be represented in a tabular form as follows.

Brick-12
IsA: Brick,
         Toy
Colour: Red

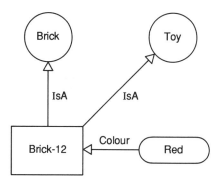

Figure I.1 A frame represented as a semantic network.

A collection of frames, or objects, forming a semantic network will be referred to in this appendix as an *object base*. In the above example, there are implicitly frames for Brick and Toy.

Figure I.2 illustrates the inheritance of properties into slots as shown also in the form of frames below.

Brick   Toy
AKO: Block,Commodity   AKO: Commodity
Shape: Cuboid

Frames can inherit properties through IsA or AKO links, so that Brick-12 inherits the Shape slot's value from Brick in this case, as well as those properties of toys, commodities and blocks which offer no contradiction. IsA is used to stand for membership and AKO to stand for inclusion. Touretzky (1986) has argued that attempts to make the distinction between IsA and AKO founder when systems permit multiple inheritance. This exposition ignores, to some extent, the controversy surrounding the various usages of IsA and AKO links (Brachman, 1983).

Winston (1984) introduces sub-slots (facets) to permit default values, demons and perspectives. This extension to the theory of fuzzy objects is not discussed herein but there seems to be no obstacle to such a development.

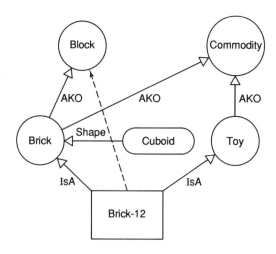

Figure I.2 Multiple inheritance of properties.

I.1.2 Property inheritance

Inheritance provides computer systems with a method of reasoning with implicit facts. Various frame-based languages have been implemented: FRL, KRL, KEE, Leonardo and others as described in Chapter 3. Most of these systems, however, suffer from various problems. They usually have no formal semantics, they are not good at reasoning about exceptions (non-monotonic logic) and they cannot handle partial inheritance, either in the sense of partially inheriting a property or of inheriting a combination of partially true properties. Other authors have discussed partial inheritance, but from a completely different point of view. An example is Khan and Jain (1986). The programme of this appendix aims to remedy all these defects within a single unified framework.

Touretzky (1986) points out that non-monotonic or default logics, while possessing a formal semantics, are hopelessly general for practical purposes because they do not have the facility of inheritance systems to reason with implicit data.

A sort of duality is being asserted here between logics that add extra operators, such as L and N in modal logics and M in non-monotonic logics, and those that expand the truth space, such as many-valued, fuzzy and probability logics. An example of the latter, which is exploited in this appendix, is fuzzy logic with Zadeh's fuzzy quantification given the sigma-count interpretation of his test-score semantics (Zadeh, 1982; Kandel, 1986).

Shastri (1988) has argued cogently that frame systems need to be able to support what he calls 'evidential reasoning'. The solution proposed by Shastri avoids the need to deal with both non-monotonicity and fuzzy truth values. His approach involves a frequency count semantics. I, however, have taken the view that fuzzy truth values have a certain utility and feel that there may be a place for both approaches.

It will be shown later, informally, how the mechanisms of fuzzy objects can be used to overcome some of the problems of non-monotonic reasoning which often arise in inheritance systems or through polymorphism connascence.

Fuzzy objects also provide a computationally efficient means of modelling truth maintenance systems or possible worlds, without the introduction of modal operators.

A certain amount of the machinery of fuzzy logic will be required, and this is introduced as briefly as possible. For the reader with no previous knowledge of fuzzy sets, Graham and Jones (1988) provides an explanation of all the concepts used here.

I.2 Basic concepts of fuzzy set theory

The concept of a fuzzy set is due to Zadeh (1965) and involves the relaxation of the restriction on a set's characteristic function that it be two-valued. This section gives a very fast summary of the techniques from fuzzy set theory which we will require later in this appendix. This is merely to fix terminology, and is not intended as a tutorial. Fuller explanations can be obtained from Graham and Jones (1988) or in some cases from Kandel (1986).

I.2.1 Fuzzy sets

A fuzzy set is a function $f:X \rightarrow I$ whose co-domain is the unit interval, I. It may be interpreted as a linguistic value over the variable represented by the domain. For example, if the domain, X, represents wealth (over an arbitrary monetary scale) we can introduce fuzzy sets to stand for the imprecise linguistic terms 'rich', 'comfortable' and 'poor' as illustrated in the diagram in Figure I.3. The unit interval (vertical axis) is used to represent the degree of truth, so that 'poor' is fully true for wealth zero but falls off as wealth increases until eventually a point is reached when it is entirely untrue: has zero truth. Fuzzy sets are conveniently represented pictorially in this way. They may also be represented as vectors of truth values.

There are several fuzzy logics. In the standard one, which is the one adopted here, the operations of the propositional calculus are defined for fuzzy predicates as follows.

$$f \text{ AND } g = \min(f,g)$$
$$f \text{ OR } g = \max(f,g)$$
$$\text{NOT } f = 1 - f$$

Implication is then defined in the usual way, by:

$$(f \Rightarrow g) = (\text{NOT } f) \text{ OR } g = \max(1-f,g)$$

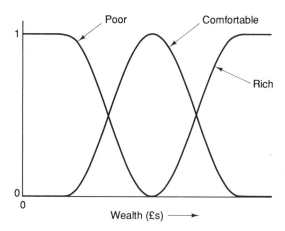

Figure I.3 Fuzzy term set for the variable 'wealth'.

Given a term set of permissible linguistic values, it is possible to extend it using the propositional operators and operations known as *hedges*. As examples the hedges 'very' and 'quite' are often defined by:

VERY $f = f^2$; QUITE $f = \sqrt{f}$

Thus, expressions such as 'very rich' or 'not very poor' receive an interpretation as a fuzzy set. This has evident utility in knowledge representation, and this has been explored in many other works.

I.2.2 Rules of inference

Given these basic definitions it is possible to approach the problem of representing inexact inferences with fuzzy sets. The two kinds of statements we may wish to use are assertions of the form 'X is A' and rules of the form

'If X is [not] A [and|or X' is ...] then Y is B'.

X, X' and Y stand for objects and A and B stand for fuzzy sets. Simple syllogisms such as *modus ponens*:

$$X \text{ is } A$$
$$\underline{\text{If } X \text{ is } A \text{ then } Y \text{ is } B}$$
$$Y \text{ is } B$$

are handled as follows. The extension in the Cartesian product of all linguistic variables appearing as assertions is computed and their intersection E taken. The extension and intersection of two fuzzy sets are illustrated in Figure I.4. This fuzzy set is interpreted as an elastic constraint on the solution. Next, taking the consequent clause of each rule separately, the current scalar value of the variable X is used to determine the truth level of the antecedent fuzzy set, so that the fuzzy set B is effectively truncated at this level. The resultant, truncated fuzzy set is formed by union with the constraint set E. This rule will be used in this appendix, although others have been suggested.

For a simple example of fuzzy inference, consider the rule

If X is A then Y is B.

The fuzzy sets A and B are illustrated in Figure I.5. If the input is the value x from the domain X then the first step in the inference is to determine the truth value of x: its compatibility with A. In Figure I.5(a) this is seen to be 0.6. Therefore, the fuzzy set B is truncated at this level. The output from the inference is this truncated fuzzy set, shown as the shaded area in Figure I.5 (b).

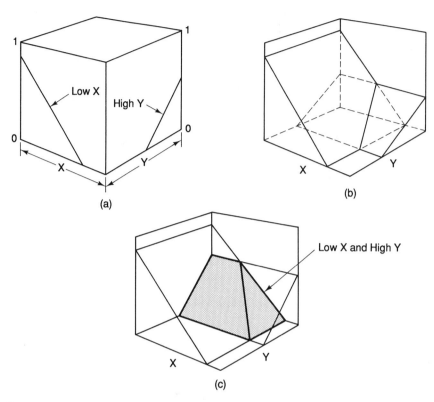

Figure I.4 **(a)** Fuzzy sets over two different domains; **(b)** The extension in the Cartesian product of two fuzzy sets; **(c)** The intersection of two fuzzy sets.

I.2.3 Defuzzification

In case it is not convenient to work with fuzzy sets as output values, the result may be 'defuzzified' to return a scalar value. There are a number of ways this can be accomplished. We will need to know about two. The 'mean of maxima' (or maximum) method involves returning the scalar in the domain of the resultant fuzzy set which maps to the arithmetic mean of its maxima. The 'centre of moments' (or moments) method returns the average of all domain values weighted by their truth in the output fuzzy set; in other words the centre of gravity of a notional cardboard cut-out of the graph of the fuzzy set. The appropriateness of these methods in different applications is discussed extensively by Graham and Jones (1988). Basically, the moments rule is best for control applications where a smooth variation in output is desired, and the maximum method for decision support applications where discrete jumps between output states are preferable. Figure I.6 illustrates that different scalar values will be returned by these two rules for any non-symmetric fuzzy set.

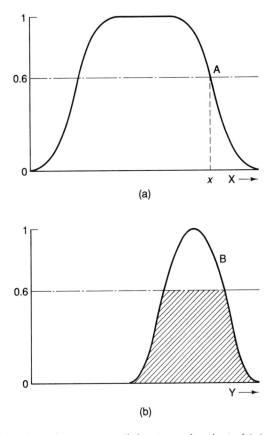

Figure I.5 **(a)** The value x has a compatibility (or truth value) of 0.6 with the fuzzy set A; **(b)** The fuzzy set B is truncated at the truth level of x.

If a fuzzy set is required as output, but some regularity in its form is desirable, then a method known as linguistic approximation may be invoked. This involves the predefinition of an allowed 'term set' of fuzzy sets over the domain, such as the one given in Figure I.3. In the case of fuzzy numbers (fuzzy subsets of the real line) an example term set might be {tiny,small,medium,large,huge}. The term set may be extended by fuzzy set operations (for example, to include 'not very small'). Linguistic approximation returns the term 'closest' to the resultant fuzzy set, according to some stated measure of distance.

I.2.4 Fuzzy quantifiers

Fuzzy quantifiers are represented by words such as 'most', 'almost all', 'some' and so on, as opposed to the crisp quantifiers 'for all' and 'there exists'. They often

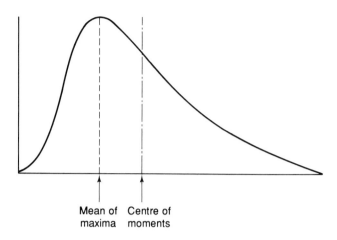

Mean of   Centre of
maxima   moments

Figure I.6 Two methods of defuzzification.

occur implicitly in natural language. Thus, 'birds fly' may be interpreted as 'most birds can fly'. Zadeh (1982) introduces rules of inference and a formal semantics for such statements. His test-score semantics interprets quantifiers as elastic constraints on a family of fuzzy relations, which are regarded as entities. This structure is viewed as a test which scores according to the compatibility of the quantifier with the objects in the world (the database). A typical rule of inference for this system is

$$\frac{\begin{array}{c} \text{Q1 A are B} \\ \text{Q2 (A and B) are C} \end{array}}{\text{Q1 * Q2 A are (B and C)}}$$

where the Qs are fuzzy quantifiers, interpreted as fuzzy numbers, and * stands for the product of fuzzy numbers. For example this justifies the syllogism:

$$\frac{\begin{array}{c} \text{Most (about 90\%) birds can fly} \\ \text{Most (about 90\%) flying birds have feathers} \end{array}}{\text{At least many (about 81\%) birds have feathers}}$$

Of course there are other rules of inference. The exact meaning of the test scores depends on the measure used for the cardinality of a fuzzy set. The usual one is the sigma-count measure, which is to say the arithmetic sum of the grades of membership (the integral in the continuous case). More details may be found in Kandel (1986).

This completes the presentation of the minimal set of concepts from fuzzy set theory which we shall require in this appendix.

☰ I.3 Fuzzy objects

We now come to the main results of this appendix. First, the notion of an object is extended to that of a fuzzy object, in two ways: first, by allowing attributes to contain fuzzy sets as values, in addition to text, list and numeric variables or other objects[1]. Second, inheritance through AKO and IsA attributes is allowed to be partial. Later we will see how to generalize in a third dimension by allowing instances to contain more than one set of attribute values, to facilitate the representation of possible worlds or time-variant objects. To explain the advantages and mechanics of fuzzy objects it is preferable to use an example, rather than to develop the formal mathematics.

Consider the following problem. You are an Aardvark customer faced with the problem of estimating the safety implications following from the purchase of various leisure items. Objects give us a way of representing knowledge about and data concerning key abstractions or concepts in the domain. The most natural way to analyse the problem (remembering that we are thinking of building a computerized adviser here) is to list the physical objects involved. Suppose they include a dinghy and a hang-glider among a number of others. These objects are types of more general objects, and have associated with them various attributes, methods and rules. The methods are not relevant to this discussion. Figure I.7 shows how we can represent this knowledge about some objects interesting in this context using fuzzy objects. Note that the instances are distinguished from the classes by the use of IsA: instead of AKO: attributes, and by icons with sharp corners. We will now consider nine of these objects, in each case annotating them with explanation of a rudimentary syntactic convention, on the way to a solution of the problem. The most general object is referred to as a commodity.

I have divided the figure among essential and accidental classes and instances. Notice, incidentally, the syntactic provision for defaults and backward chaining demons (IfNeeded procedures). Forward chaining (IfUpdated) demons would be dealt with similarly. The way the rules windows are interpreted will become clear later.

First, consider the concept of a vehicle. Our general knowledge about the attributes of vehicles can be summarized in the following structure.

```
O1   Vehicle
     AKO: Commodity
     Uses: (travel,pleasure) [list]
     Keeper: undefined [text]
     Necessity: high [fuzz]
     Safety: high [fuzz]
     Utility: high [fuzz]
     Cost: high [fuzz]
```

---

[1] This is not necessarily a real extension, since fuzzy sets form an abstract data type. It is only an extension if this data type is regarded as primitive.

O1

```
Vehicle

AKO       : Commodity
Uses      : (travel, pleasure) [list]
Keeper    : undefined [text]
Necessity : high [fuzz]
Safety    : high [fuzz]
Utility   : high [fuzz]
Cost      : high [fuzz]

Methods

Rules
  Control rules:
  Inherit by maximum
  Defuzzify by maxima
```

O2

```
Toy

AKO       : Commodity
Uses      : (pleasure) [list]
Keeper    : child [text]
Necessity : low [fuzz]
Safety    : undefined [fuzz]
Utility   : high [fuzz]
Cost      : low [fuzz]
```

O3

```
Dinghy

AKO    : Vehicle [0.4],
           Toy [0.6],
           Dangerous object [0.1]
Safety : undefined [fuzz]
Cost   : undefined [fuzz]
Draft  : 3 [real];
           IfNeeded = depth-calc

depth-calc
```

O4

```
Hang-glider

AKO    : Vehicle [0.05],
           Toy [0.7],
           Dangerous object [0.9]
Safety : undefined [fuzz]
Cost   : undefined [fuzz]
```

O5

```
Car

AKO    : Vehicle [0.9],
           Toy [0.6],
           Dangerous object [0.1]
Safety : undefined [fuzz]
Cost   : undefined [fuzz]
```

O6

```
Toy-car

AKO    : Vehicle [0.3],
           Toy [0.9]
Safety : undefined [fuzz]
Cost   : undefined [fuzz]
```

O7

```
Book

AKO    : Dangerous-object,
           Toy [0.6]
Cost   : undefined [fuzz]
Safety : undefined [fuzz]
Adult  : No [text]
```

O8

```
Magazine

AKO    : Book [0.5],
           Toy [0.3],
           Borrowed object [0.5]
Safety : undefined [fuzz]
Cost   : undefined [fuzz]
```

(a)

O9

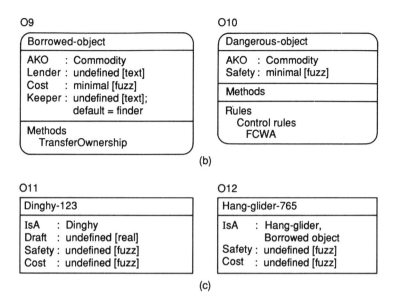

O10

Borrowed-object
AKO   : Commodity Lender : undefined [text] Cost   : minimal [fuzz] Keeper : undefined [text];   default = finder
Methods   TransferOwnership

Dangerous-object
AKO : Commodity Safety : minimal [fuzz]
Methods

Rules
   Control rules
    FCWA

(b)

O11

O12

Dinghy-123
IsA   : Dinghy Draft : undefined [real] Safety : undefined [fuzz] Cost   : undefined [fuzz]

Hang-glider-765
IsA   : Hang-glider,   Borrowed object Safety : undefined [fuzz] Cost   : undefined [fuzz]

(c)

Figure I.7 Some fuzzy objects.

Here the AKO attribute points to another object, in this case the most general one possible. Vehicle, along with the other structures illustrated, is a fuzzy object in two respects. First, the degree of property inheritance from the object(s) in the AKO attribute may be specified as a number between 0 and 1 in square brackets after the name. In this case no value is given and the default value of [1.00] is assumed. Second, the other attributes may contain fuzzy sets (vectors of truth values) as values. The bracketed expressions indicate the type of the value: either [fuzz], [real], [list], [text] or some user-defined abstract data type. The fuzzy set, high, used in the Vehicle object may be represented as in Figure I.8.

We may assume certain attribute values for the general commodity by including an object for it. Let us assume here only that Commodity has known values of high for Safety and Utility.

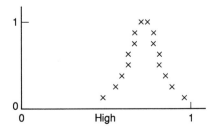

Figure I.8 A fuzzy set representing 'high' on an arbitrary interval scale.

If it is normal to assume that something purchased is safe, the Toy object will inherit the value 'high' for Safety, since the attribute contains 'undefined', the uniform fuzzy set on the interval scale, which is equal to 1 everywhere. The other attributes are unaltered. Inheritance occurs based on the immediately superior object only, and then only when the 'child' has an undefined value. In some applications, it may be preferable to allow inheritance into even those attributes which contain defined values. In such a case the inheritance mechanism is modified in such a way that the intersection (minimum) of the fuzzy sets in the parent and child is taken. This corresponds to what could be designated 'the fuzzy closed world assumption' (FCWA). That is, if the values assigned to attributes represent immutable knowledge about the state of the world and the constraints it imposes, we would not wish to permit a contradictory reassignment that ignored the influence of the value in a parent. This is an interesting variant of overriding, which emphasizes the sharing of information, and compromise, between parent and child objects. The repository for this control information is the *rules* window of the object, where the declarative semantics are encapsulated.

Two more objects representing general classes of objects must now be discussed. They are the accidental objects:

O9 Borrowed-object	O10 Dangerous-object
AKO: Commodity	AKO: Commodity
Lender: undefined [text]	Safety: minimal [fuzz]
Keeper: undefined [text]	
Cost: minimal [fuzz]	

Here we may wish to consider the sad possibility that a borrowed object, such as a book, may pass from *meum* to *tuum* without the transition being too noticeable[2]. Thus, in the case of the borrowed magazine in object O8, only 0.5 of the ownership properties of O9 may be inherited. In particular, the inheritance mechanism attaches a 0.5 certainty factor to the Lender and Keeper values (if they are known). The mechanism for fuzzy attributes is that the fuzzy sets (*minimal* in this case) are truncated at the 0.5 level. Returning to the mainstream of our argument, two new fuzzy sets have been introduced, so their definition is given in Figure I.9, pictorially as before.

Now we come to the objects describing fairly specific items in the scheme. For example, we have:

O3 Dinghy	O4 Hang-glider
AKO: Vehicle [0.4],	AKO: Vehicle [0.05],
Toy [0.6],	Toy [0.7],
Dangerous object [0.1]	Dangerous object[0.9]
Draught: 3 [real]	Wing-span: unknown [real]
Safety: undefined	Safety: undefined [fuzz]
Cost: undefined	Cost: undefined [fuzz]

---

[2] In other words, be (politely) stolen!

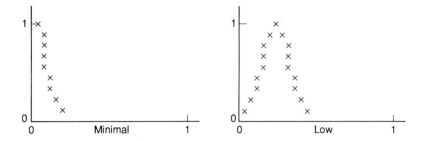

Figure I.9 Fuzzy sets for 'minimal' and 'low'.

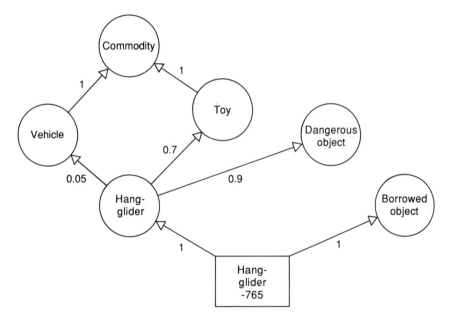

Figure I.10 Partial inheritance network for hang-glider-765.

We now have to understand how the undefined attributes in the lowest-level objects (representing instances) for Dinghy-123 and Hang-glider-765 may be filled. Notice first that we have a non-fuzzy attribute for Draught, and multiple inheritance from higher levels. Let us look at the Safety attribute of Dinghy first.

Since a dinghy is a vehicle the Safety: attribute inherits 'high', but as this is only true to the extent 0.4 the fuzzy set is truncated at this level. It also inherits the value 'minimal' from Dangerous-object, but only to degree 0.1. The inheritance path from Commodity via Toy gives the value 'high' in degree 0.6. These fuzzy sets are combined with the union operator as shown in the diagram in Figure

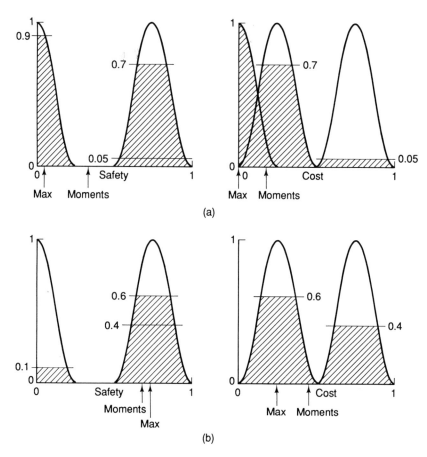

Figure I.11 **(a)** Inherited fuzzy sets for hang-glider-765; **(b)** Inherited fuzzy sets for dinghy-123.

I.11(b). If this were the final result of some reasoning process the resultant fuzzy set would be defuzzified (in this case with the mean-of-maxima operation) to give a truth or possibility value for the term 'safe'. Alternatively, linguistic approximation could be applied to return a word corresponding to a normal, convex fuzzy set[3] approximating the returned value. In a different application, the moments defuzzification method might be applied. This is a control decision in the same category as the fuzzy closed world assumption, and, I feel, should be left to the discretion of the user or systems designer and encapsulated locally within the rules window. The other diagram in Figure I.11(b) shows the fuzzy set for the dinghy's cost. In the absence of evidence to the contrary, Dinghy-123 inherits both these values.

---

[3] That is, a fuzzy set which attains the value of 1 somewhere (normal) and which has only one peak (convex). The fuzzy sets of Figure I.3, I.5 (a), I.6, I.8 and I.9 all have both these properties.

Cost here is being interpreted as the cost that one might be willing to bear, and thus the cost of a dinghy purchased just for fun ought, normally, to be low. The case of the safety attribute of Hang-glider is a little more interesting. The diagrams in Figure I.11(a) illustrate the text.

Here, the Safety attribute inherits the union of the fuzzy set minimal from Dangerous-object [0.9] and high from both vehicle [0.05] and Commodity (via Toy) [0.7]. Applying the operation of union or disjunction to these three fuzzy sets (we of course exclude 'undefined' from this process) to represent the view that AKO attributes are *alternative* viewpoints from which the object may be viewed, we arrive at a resultant fuzzy set. Defuzzification then gives a value close to 0 (or the linguistic approximation 'minimal').

Thus the system is able to deduce correctly that a hang-glider is a very dangerous toy along with the unsurprising conclusion that it doesn't cost much to borrow one in the case of Hang-glider-765.

The choice of the maximum operator here may be regarded as problematical because of the difficulty in assigning a definite semantics to the disjunction operation, OR, in normal speech. However, the system proposed here should allow for this by the provision of a control parameter, or rules, which would allow users to specify the alternative minimum operation to deal with applications wherein the natural interpretation of the combination of values is different and perhaps represents the possibilistic view that only evidence receiving support from all sources should be inherited. This is what the rules in the icon for object O1 in Figure I.7 refer to. This discussion also indicates the need to extend the number of rule types within the rules window listed in Section 8.3 (p.305). This is dealt with in Section I.6.

Clearly, the reason we have adopted the view that a hang-glider is only a vehicle to a small extent is that one usually thinks of a vehicle as a safe-ish means of getting from A to B and, indeed, back again. This is not independent from our assumptions about dangerous objects. This warns of a possible design problem for fuzzy object bases. However, there is a further problem. If, as is quite reasonable, a survey showed that most people actually gave a higher value, say 0.95, to the 'toyness' of a hang-glider then the result would be quite different under the maximum rule of inference, and quite counter-intuitive: hang-gliders would be highly safe. The apparently counter-intuitive nature of this result – which, incidentally only has noticeable, serious consequences under the moments rule – could be due to the incompleteness of this example.

It is worth remarking that all object-oriented, frame and multiple inheritance systems pose a similar dilemma. A property, such as dangerousness, can be associated with an individual either by inheritance or by explicit inclusion in the object's descriptor. A way round this problem is suggested in Section I.7. Currently, the topic of design criteria for fuzzy and indeed crisp semantic models is a research issue. What is required is analogous to the theory of normal forms in database design theory.

To put matters right temporarily, let us now explore an example which does conform to intuition more closely than the one chosen above to explicate the syntax and semantics. The type declarations have been dropped as they are always clear from context.

Immortal
AKO: Category
Goodness: high
Intellect: omniscient

Mortal
AKO: Category

Man
AKO: Mortal
Goodness: fair
Intellect: average

Apollo
IsA: Man[0.4],
     Immortal[0.9]
Goodness: undefined

Lucifer
IsA: Immortal
Goodness: low

Socrates
IsA: Man,Immortal[0.2]
Intellect: bright
Goodness: undefined

Philanthropist
AKO: Man,
     Immortal[0.1]
Goodness: high
Fame: high

JohnpaulgettyIII
IsA: Philanthropist
Goodness: undefined
Fame: undefined
Intellect: undefined

In this case the inheritance mechanism enables us to infer that John Paul Getty III is a nice chap who'll be remembered for quite a while, because philanthropists are usually famous. Apollo, on the other hand, inherits average intelligence as the epitome of manliness and omniscience from his godliness. We know from our Homer that Apollo was in fact only wise on occasion, and this is reflected in the returned fuzzy set for his intellect, whose linguistic approximation is something like 'bright' if we use the moments rule. Apollo's goodness is also reduced by his manliness. In the absence of a richer structure or, in other words, more knowledge and information, we can only deduce average intelligence for John Paul Getty III, although he might be remembered by posterity as brighter owing to the magnifying effect of a degree of immortality (in the sense of living in memory here) on intelligence. Clearly, this kind of object base has considerable application to computerized models of common-sense reasoning. Zadeh (1985) refers to the type of reasoning implied here as that of 'usuality', while Touretzky (1986) (erroneously) calls it 'normative' reasoning (he means 'what is normal').

This example, of course, raises many of the usual questions about inheritance that we find in crisp systems. In addition, we are led to ask what would happen in a more complex object base. In particular, in certain applications it might be necessary to consider that the inheritance of god-like properties by offspring and offspring of offspring should be subject to attenuation but not to complete exception (for example, Leda, Europa). In that case, we would want to invoke the fuzzy closed-world assumption to 'visit the sins of the fathers upon the children unto the third and fourth generation'. The other question raised here, as compared with the previous example, is the evident comparability of the categories represented by the AKO links. This suggests that well-designed object bases should evince this property. I will have more to say on the soundness of designs later.

For some reason, it is apparent that the moments method of defuzzification is the more appropriate one in the example deductions discussed here. This is because we were dealing with the usuality of properties which are subject to combination in reaching a 'balanced view', rather than ones which contribute to either/or decision making. There could be problems if we had mixed objectives in our use of the object base. We would at least have to type the AKO links – using the rules window – were the two strategies to be required over the same object base.

I have thus presented, via a couple of very simple examples, the basic theory of fuzzy objects in SOMA and explained its logic of inheritance. I have concentrated on attributes but operations can have inheritable possibilities attached and rules in SOMA can be fuzzy rules of the sort found in languages such as Reveal (Graham and Jones, 1988). I now want to justify these efforts by presenting a more practical example.

I.4 An application

Consider the problem faced in allocating a marketing budget among the various activities that could lead to higher sales of a product. It is part of the folklore of marketing that different types of product will benefit from different budget allocations. Suppose that the methods at our disposal are:

Advertising   Promotion   Sales Training   Packaging   Direct Mail

Now, suppose that we compare the allocation ideal for breakfast cereals with that for package software. Advertising, promotions and packaging are clearly all useful, but there is not much point in direct mailing to cereal consumers, and the degree of training required by the sales force is not usually considered to be high. In such a situation, we might well represent the allocation of resources in the following matrix of percentages[4].

	Adverts	Promotion	Sales training	Packaging	Direct mail
Breakfast cereal	30	50	5	15	0
Package software	10	5	15	20	50

In the case where knowledge is expressed inexactly we can readily replace these numbers by fuzzy numbers as follows.

	Adverts	Promotion	Sales training	Packaging	Direct mail
Breakfast cereal	about a third	about half	hardly any	a little	none
Package software	less than a little	hardly any	a little	about a fifth	about half

---

[4] Warning to marketing executives: these figures are not meant to represent a truly effective strategy.

Here we have two fuzzy relations, for Breakfast-cereal and Package-software. Presumably they can be regarded as part of a larger database of products: in fact, product classes. Viewing them as classes prompts us to write them down as fuzzy objects and ask about inheritance through AKO links. To see that inheritance (of the attributes under consideration) may be partial, consider the fuzzy object representing the class of commodities called Vending-Machine. A vending machine may be viewed as office furniture, catering equipment or even as packaged food depending on the marketing approach taken. Fuzzy objects give a natural way to build a description of this problem and suggest an implementation which is able to combine evidence and reason with exceptions.

Figure I.12 shows how the combined partial inheritance of fuzzy (that is, linguistically expressed) allocations from general classes of products may be used to infer an allocation for specific types of product. All attributes are fuzzy and undefined attributes are left blank. The fuzzy set which is returned into the DirectMail attribute may be defuzzified and linguistically approximated, to indicate that investment in this area of about a third of the budget will be likely to produce the best results. This result is based purely on the fact that vending machines share features with catering equipment, office furniture and packaged food about which more is known. As it happens, in this example, the moments and maximum methods of defuzzification will give approximately the same result.

Another possible practical application is to 'dotted line' relationships in organizations, where the responsibilities of certain specialists to technically related parts of an organization may override or mingle with those of the formal reporting hierarchy. One application of such an object base is to assist with the decision as to whom should be consulted when the specialist is asked to work overseas for a year. Another concerns the construction of formal models of the sort of loose–tight properties of organizations referred to by Peters and Waterman (1982).

It is my belief that there are a tremendous number of opportunities for the application of fuzzy objects. Among the most promising are enterprise and strategic business modelling. Of course, it may be argued that these applications can be addressed by other technologies, but none that I can think of offer simultaneously the advantages of naturality of expression in a unified representational formalism to the extent that fuzzy objects do.

Let us briefly compare this system with a couple of other methods of representing uncertain statements about objects.

I.5 Fuzzy objects, fuzzy quantifiers and non-monotonic logics

We can now explore the application of fuzzy objects to one of the classical problems in inheritance, using non-standard quantifiers instead of non-monotonic logic. Touretzky discusses (and dismisses) this approach by reference to the work

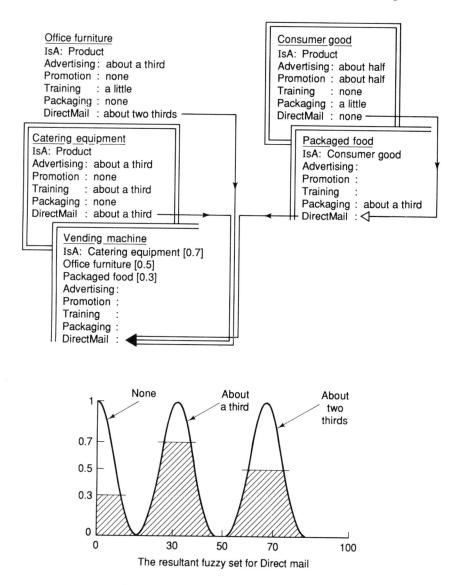

Figure I.12 How to sell vending machines.

of Altham (1971), but seems to be unaware of Zadeh's more encouraging results for the representation of fuzzy quantifiers and their inference properties.

As we have seen, Zadeh's theory of dispositions and fuzzy quantifiers and test score semantics lets us express one of the classical motivating problems of non-monotonic logic as 'Most birds can fly'. It is a part of the folklore of fuzzy sets that this can be neatly expressed with fuzzy inheritance; thus a fuzzy objects approach is indicated. Here is the object base:

Flying-animal
AKO: Animal
Can-fly: true [fuzz]

Bird
AKO: Flying-animal [0.9]
Wings: 2

Penguin
AKO: Bird
Can-fly: false [fuzz]

Tweety
IsA: Bird [1], Penguin [1]
Can-fly: ?

The fuzzy sets involved are illustrated in Figure I.13. The answer is that Tweety is a bird and cannot fly. So far this is the same result as that suggested in McDermott and Doyle (1980) – but we can do better: penguins do sort of fly (they make fluttering movements when diving or running) and the fuzzy set shown in Figure I.14 preserves this information in a way. Another approach to this problem would be to use analogical reasoning, but this is often a very complex approach.

A rather obvious generalization springs to mind at this point. The numerical factor representing the degree of inheritance could be replaced by a linguistic variable (a fuzzy set or fuzzy number). This would mean that the truncation of inherited fuzzy sets would itself be fuzzy. We could call such objects 'Ultrafuzzy Objects' or '2-Fuzzy Objects'. However, finding a formal semantics then becomes much harder, and I suspect that the practical value of such a theory would be severely limited by its complexity. In fact, this generalization would correspond much more closely to the interpretation of fuzzy quantifiers given in Section I.2.4, where fuzzy quantifiers are represented as fuzzy numbers. The inheritance mechanism of 2-fuzzy objects could indeed be modified to exploit the inference rules of approximate reasoning (for example, the intersection-product syllogism given in Section I.2.4). This is certainly worthy of further investigation.

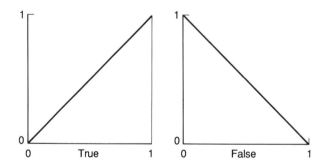

Figure I.13 The fuzzy set 'true' is given by x=x and 'false' by x=-x.

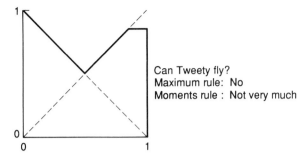

Figure I.14 Fuzzy set for the compatibility of the statement 'Tweety can fly'.

It is useful to interpret a fuzzy AKO link as a most/some-type fuzzy quantifier. In the hang-glider/toy example this is also a natural interpretation. AKO links may be used (or misused) for a variety of conflicting purposes. A good design theory would force us to state the interpretation of the inheritance links and not mix them up. An alternative is to permit fuzzy objects to have a number of 'typed' inheritance links. Then inheritance could take place through a manifold of different networks.

I.6 Control rules for fuzzy multiple inheritance systems

Let us summarize the control regimes available within the theory of fuzzy objects. These are global rules only if stated within the rules window of the most general object, if there is one. Otherwise, they may be subject to local variations.

(1) The default regime: if an attribute is filled, do not inherit into it. If it is not then combine the truncated inherited attributes with the maximum operator. For non-fuzzy variables the maximum of the certainty factors represented by the AKO values is attached to the inherited value. Multiple inheritance of non-fuzzy values may result in multi-valued attributes (lists).

Different fuzzy logics may be used according to the application at hand. The maximum operator may then be replaced with the appropriate t-conorm. The maximum (or conorm) operator may be replaced for individual AKO attributes by the minimum (or corresponding norm). The choice of maximum corresponds to regarding conflicting values as alternative viewpoints. The choice of minimum corresponds to maximal caution and the view that the conflicting sources complement each other.

(2) The fuzzy closed world assumption: inherit all defined values and perform a union. Some theory of attenuation may be added. The control strategy pre-

cludes exceptions, but this is sometimes what is required. For example, when we reason that dogs have four legs because they are mammals and that humans are an exception, having only two, we are plumping for naive physics in contradistinction to a mature biology. Humans (normally) do have four legs: it is merely that two of them have become adapted to other purposes. From such a viewpoint, we want an inheritance mechanism that propagates the mammality in despite of the human exception: that takes account of both factors.

Each regime bifurcates because one of the maximum or moments methods of defuzzification must needs be selected, unless linguistic approximation is employed. This gives the system designer a choice from at least 24 control regimes. It also suggests the need for some experimental work.

Thus, the array of permissible control regimes can be characterized by the following decisions.

(1) Should defined attributes inherit?
(2) Should multiple inheritances be combined with union or intersection?
(3) Which fuzzy logic is appropriate?
(4) Which defuzzification method is to be used?

☰ I.7 Design theory for fuzzy objects

In this section, I examine some of the problems that arise in the design of fuzzy object systems, and suggest some design guidelines.

Fuzzy objects are not alone in raising general problems in terms of multiple attribute or property inheritance. Touretzky (1986) lists the analogous problems with crisp inheritance systems and suggests some very reasonable ways round them in terms of a lattice-theoretic semantics. I suspect that it is possible to use Touretzky's hierarchical distance ordering to provide attenuation of inheritance for fuzzy objects.

As a parenthetical remark at this point, it is worth observing that Touretzky's semantics generate the truth tables of Kleene three-valued logic rather than the Lukasiewitz logic, the multi-valued logic which corresponds to fuzzy logic (Giles, 1976). Lukasiewitz motivation for the uncertain term was contingent statements (about the future): indeterminate values. The motivation behind Touretzky's system is the presence of links which indicate that no conclusion may be drawn (or value inherited). Other three-valued logics (of Bochvar, say) offer interpretations in terms of meaninglessness. The difference therefore between my approach and that of the mainstream, symbolic processing movement as represented by Touretzky here is this: conflict in inheritance is not to be interpreted as undecidability but as possibility: as potentiality.

I.7.1 Completeness of design

It is not just on theoretical grounds that this approach offers some benefits. There are some problems that Touretzky's approach does not address. The problem that the hang-glider is safe because toys are (because the typical commodity is) could be viewed as one of conflict resolution. Perhaps we could decompose the link using an additional class object such as Dangerous-toy in such circumstances. Using an inferential distance-ordering approach assumes that this has not only already been done, but that all possible such decompositions have been explicated in the object base. Otherwise, a slight perturbation of the design could result in totally different behaviour under inheritance. What is therefore required is a procedure which determines whether an object base is 'complete' in this sense. We need to develop a design theory for general object bases. This would appear to be a very difficult problem, since the recognition of a 'good' expansion is clearly a question of relevance. The absence of such a theory forces one to adopt some method of default reasoning under Reiter's closed world assumption (not the fuzzy version mentioned above).

The analogous question of completeness hangs over all attempts to structure knowledge and data. Even in conventional entity-relationship data models it is recognized that a sound design is achieved only by the exercise of great skill. Decomposition is assisted by a theory of normal forms, but completeness can rarely be assured when the model is of a real, dynamic system.

Furthermore, because of the fact that Dangerous-toy is evidently one of the accidental objects we were warned of in Section 9.2, warning bells should be ringing.

I.7.2 Objects versus attributes

A major problem in the area of design criteria arises when we have to decide whether the degree to which an object (whether instance or class) has a property is determined by inheritance or by attribute filling (which in turn can result from inheritance). Thus, the two objects:

```
Object-1                    Object-2
AKO: ?                      AKO:Object-with-property-A [degree]
Property-A:degree [fuzz]
```

are equivalent in all except syntax. The problem is to decide when to choose between the alternative formulations. I will call such objects *tautological*. They are a particularly nasty kind of accidental object.

This is nothing more than the class-attribute problem of database design. Making the choice correctly remains a matter of skill and judgement. The analysis of judgements described in Chapter 9 may help, but is only a guide to good practice in distinguishing accidental from essential abstractions. As a step towards a solution of the problem, the status of such 'tautological objects' is discussed below.

This problem also raises the question of the status of the two kinds of fuzziness: the fuzziness subsisting in the way classes (or instances and classes) are related, and the fuzziness inherent in predicates of description (attributes). It is necessary to ask if we are committing the unforgivable sin of mixing different kinds of uncertainties. This is clearly a danger with poor designs. On the other hand, it may be argued that more expressive power results from allowing the programmer to mix both forms as convenient.

I.7.3 Tautological objects and maximal decomposition

What, we may ask, is the status of tautological objects like the one below?

Dangerous-object
AKO: Object
Danger:not less than high [fuzz]

These objects are recognizable as having only one non-AKO attribute with a meaning predicate and value corresponding exactly to the object's name. The AKO attribute also contributes nothing new. The specification of the object asserts that a dangerous object is an object which has the property of being dangerous to the degree 'high' or more.

In crisp systems we would automatically disallow such perversions. But, in the hang-glider example above, if we disallow all tautological objects on principle, then the only way the low value for safety can ever get into the attribute is if we put it there. This could accord with intuition, because there is really no *a priori* reason (at least not within the confines of our given object base) why we should think a hang-glider dangerous: it just IS. This is a convenient way of resolving the problem, which incidentally begs the same question for the design of crisp object systems. On the other hand it is sometimes unnatural not to include such objects: an elephant is a grey object; a grey object is a drab object. Once again, this issue of the difference between the essential and the accidental comes to the fore.

One interesting angle on this problem is that the presence of a tautological object in a design invariably indicates the presence of a personal construct of the kind used by Kelly grids, for example Danger–Safety, so that the presence of tautological objects in a design naturally results from using the methods of knowledge elicitation derived from Kelly grids.

Another, useful point of view is suggested by the discussion of judgement analysis and the recognition of universals given in Chapter 9.

Other structures which one would naturally disallow in a theory of non-redundant (or normal) forms for object bases include cycles. In the crisp case, the problem raised by the example discussed immediately below does not arise, since a loop of the type below always represents equality and the network may be collapsed. In the case of fuzzy objects it is harder to decide whether there is a need for such relationships.

For example, the phrase 'Most men are avaricious' may be represented by fuzzy objects in the form:

Man   Greedy-man
AKO:Greedy-man [0.8]   AKO:Man [1]

This pair of fuzzy objects contains an irreducible cycle. Crisp inheritance systems usually demand acyclicity. This is certainly computationally convenient, but no theory exists to say that it is strictly necessary for coherent inheritance, except for the collapse argument given above. The problem just pointed out is, however, special to the fuzzy case, because, for fuzzy objects, the cycles do not collapse. One way to remove the problem is to disallow the cycle and expand the network to include a new object representing 'avaricious entity' (for example, a petrol-hungry car). Then, a greedy man is avaricious [1] (or has the attribute avaricious filled with 'high') and a man [1], and a man is avaricious [0.8] and there are no cycles. In doing this we have broken the no-tautologies rule though. Thus, there seems to be a trade-off between cycles and the use of tautological objects.

The intimate relationship between acyclicity in a design and the presence of tautological objects suggests the following design rules.

DR1 Tautological objects should be introduced to break cycles.
DR2 Tautological objects should be used to prevent users asserting a property for an object explicitly. This has the effect of preventing update anomalies where two objects would inherit the same value from the tautological object but may be assigned different values by the user.
DR3 Otherwise, tautological objects should be avoided.

There is one other problem with the hang-glider example worth a mention. Regarding the problem of determining safety as one of conflict resolution in the presence of fuzzy inheritance means that one could look for a mechanism which would recognize the presence of 'very bimodal' distributions in returned fuzzy sets and then prompt the user for a decision. The difficulty with this approach is centred on that of finding a universally acceptable measure of distance between fuzzy sets. It would, however, be worth exploring on an experimental basis.

This completes the exposition of the design theory for fuzzy objects. I should now like to offer some insight into the intuitions that led to the notion and in doing so suggest the place of the theory within knowledge representation as a whole.

▤ I.8 The relationship of fuzzy objects to other concepts

In this final section, I suggest that fuzzy objects are a natural generalization of both relations and objects. The argument is informal, but assumes a mathematical background. It may be omitted without interfering with the main thread of the argument given above.

I.8.1 Fuzzy objects as a generalization of fuzzy relations

The first observation to make is that fuzzy relations generalize relations.

A relation is a subset of some Cartesian product of sets. It can also be regarded as a function from that product into the truth set of classical logic $2=\{0,1\}$. A fuzzy relation is such a function where the co-domain is the truth lattice of a multi-valued logic; in the case we consider, the unit interval fulfils this rôle. Of course a tabular (extensional) representation is also possible.

Now, it is well known (at least in mathematics) that there is a bijective correspondence between functions $A \times B \to I$ and functions $A \to I^B$. This also holds for n-dimensional Cartesian products. The correspondence is given by assigning to every function $f(a,b)$ the function which takes a point a to the function (fuzzy set)

$$g:B \to I:b \mapsto f(a,b).$$

This proves that, in tabular representation, the form

Loves:	Person1	Person2	Degree
	John	Mary	0.9
	Mary	John	0.2
	Jill	Mary	0.4

corresponds to the form

Loves:	Person	Possibility distribution
	John	$\pi1$
	Jill	$\pi2$
	Mary	$\pi3$

The possibility distributions are fuzzy sets (not illustrated here). For example, $\pi1$ shows the degree to which John loves each other person in the universe of discourse. Its truth value for Mary is 0.9.

Thus, the syntax we use in fuzzy objects (ignoring the AKO attributes for a moment) corresponds to an adequate syntax for fuzzy relations.

The next point to notice is that relations may form a category with arrows that preserve some desired properties of relations, such as projections or joins or both. Zadeh's extension principle (see Kandel (1986)) implies that, with a suitable notion of property-preserving arrow, fuzzy relations also may form a category. The exact definition of the arrows is not important for our argument – it would be if we wished to proceed to formal proofs. There is an obvious embedding functor from relations to fuzzy relations:

$$(\text{Rel}) \rightarrow (\text{FuzRel})$$

This gives an exact meaning to the statement that fuzzy relations (fuzzy relational databases) generalize relations (relational databases).

If we now add the inheritance structure to a fuzzy relation we have fuzzy objects (classes) as a generalization of fuzzy relations.

I.8.2 Fuzzy objects as a generalization of objects

In a similar way class objects (regarded as sets of instances) also generalize relations.

Apart from first normal form and object identity, which in any case can be system generated in a relational system, the key differences between objects and relations are that objects do not require atomic values of attributes – there may be sub-attributes (facets), methods, list-valued entries, and (because of inheritance) we cannot predict in advance the number of attributes in the data dictionary definition of an object. The first relaxation is equivalent to saying that the underlying logic is no longer first order (as with fuzzy relations). The second says that we are working in a potentially (countably) infinite Cartesian product. Intuitively, this corresponds to the assertion that an object may be assigned ANY attribute in the world: blueness, hunger, pointedness, and so on. Real objects only have a few relevant attributes, but in the object model they MIGHT inherit anything. Instances are only an exception to this rule when we restrict to single inheritance, since, although instances inherit *all* their parent class properties, they may belong to potentially all classes which may be defined.

Having said this, instance objects are normally thought of as representing single objects. This is the reason we sometimes talk about sets of objects or classes. An n-tuple in a relation corresponds to one filling of a class by an instance; each filling corresponds to a real thing. Of course, there is absolutely no reason why instances themselves should not be multi-valued. There are at least two interpretations of this: (1) each 'filling' corresponds to a 'possible world'; (2) each filling corresponds to a state on some world line. This provides a start on generalizing objects, or fuzzy objects, to contain temporal modelling capabilities. This will not be explored further here.

Regarding classes as abstract data types lets us view them as algebras. Thus, mappings which preserve the algebraic structure, the methods, may exist. Looked at in this way, object sets, classes, may form a category – the arrows preserving the object composition structures (and possibly having something to do with inheritance). Thus again we get the embedding functor:

$$(\text{Rel}) \rightarrow (\text{Class})$$

which takes relations to objects with no (non-attribute) methods; that is, none other than the standard get and put methods.

The practical application of this idea, on its own, is that truth maintenance systems and temporal logic systems acquire a very coherent implementation framework, and many of the techniques of relational database theory can be mapped across to this framework.

Adding the ability for objects to hold fuzzy sets as attribute values shows that fuzzy objects can be viewed as a generalization of objects.

Obviously, the idea has only been sketched here, and much further work remains to be done.

I.8.3 Fuzzy objects as a pushout

Having two functors in the category of categories, as described, naturally leads to the question: what is their pushout? If we could construct it, we would have the universal generalization of both objects and fuzzy relations. I conjecture at this point that fuzzy objects are a very reasonable candidate for this pushout and thus that fuzzy objects generalize all object knowledge representations.

If this result or even a much weaker version of it (that the diagram shown in in Figure I.15 commutes) could be established, then we would have a step towards a unified theory covering the following issues in knowledge representation.

- The relational model of data.
- Object-orientation and inheritance systems.
- Fuzzy relations and fuzzy information retrieval.
- Non-monotonic reasoning.
- Temporal reasoning, possible worlds and modal logic systems.

This is a bold claim. The arguments above are tentative. However, at the very least, it is worthy of further exploration. I hope that researchers will take up some of these ideas as lines of research.

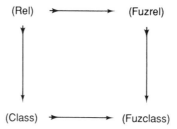

Figure I.15 A conjectured pushout in the category of categories.

▤ I.9 Summary

This appendix informally defined the syntax and semantics of fuzzy objects and the corresponding fuzzy extension to SOMA.

Fuzzy objects in SOMA can have fuzzy attribute values which can be inherited. The theory of how to do this under multiple inheritance was described. Fuzzy objects may also inherit both crisp and fuzzy attribute values *partially*; that is with a defined certainty value. The appendix showed how these numbers could be combined with inherited fuzzy sets to model the partial inheritance of partial properties. The partial inheritance of methods, represented by a certainty factor, is taken to mean the possibility that the object can carry out the operation. Rules can be fuzzy rules.

Several candidate applications were suggested. Fuzzy objects may be of immense utility in describing systems in contexts such as enterprise modelling and business process re-engineering. Among the most difficult of the other applications which suggest themselves is the application to the interpretation of natural language statements. It is to be hoped that other, more academic, researchers will take this up as a research topic. My interest is in the practical issues. Additionally, I have suggested a line of research for mathematicians interested in database theory and the abstract algebra of relations. I hope that this too will be taken up and solved by the academic community.

The design and methodological issues surrounding fuzzy objects were also explored. A number of unsolved problems in this area were suggested as topics for further research. In general, I believe that this research must be predicated on applications. There is a clear resonance between the issues dealt with here and the current interest in object-oriented databases.

The theory described is readily implementable. This makes it possible to move on to the stage of implementation and applications.

▤ I.10 Bibliographical notes

A partial and rudimentary version of this theory appeared in Graham and Jones (1987) and a fuller one in Graham and Jones (1988). The latter is a reasonable guide to the vast literature on fuzzy sets and systems. The classic reference on that subject is Dubois and Prade (1980); Kandel (1986) is a sound introduction to the basic mathematics, while Graham and Jones (1988) is more oriented towards applications and covers fuzzy rule-based systems, including Reveal, in detail. The journals *Fuzzy Sets and Systems* and *The Journal of Approximate Reasoning* are good sources of current research material on both theory and applications.

The literature on AI frame systems is also quite vast. Winston (1984) and Lenat and Guha (1990) give the theoretical view, while Shadbolt (1989) is an informed but gentle introduction.

GLOSSARY OF TERMS

Italicized words in a definition may be found as entries in the glossary. Acronyms may be defined in the Subject Index.

Abstract class   Either the same as *metaclass* or more usually a class whose instances have no concrete interpretation; that is, no subtypes. The opposite of a *concrete* class. Sometimes, a class representing an abstract concept.

Abstract type   The same as *abstract class*. A type designed to supply common behaviour to a set of subtypes, or *abstract data type*.

Abstract data type   An abstraction, similar to a class, that describes a set of objects in terms of an encapsulated or hidden data structure and operations on that structure.

Abstraction   'The act of separating in thought' (OED) – representing the essential features of something without including background or inessential detail.

Access operations   Operations which access the state of an object but do not modify it.

Active object   An object which can initiate message passing.
OR
An object whose methods are activated by a change in its state: *a demon*.

Actor   An object which suffers no operations but only operates on other objects (Booch).
OR
An object with an address and a current state which may communicate with other objects only by message passing. Actors can change their local state, create new actors and send messages. Actor systems replace inheritance with delegation (Hewitt).
OR
A user adopting a rôle (Jacobson).

ADT   Abstract data type.

Agent   An object which performs some operation at the request of another object and may in turn operate upon another object.

Aggregation   The same as *composition*.

AKO   A Kind Of. The inheritance relationship between classes and their superclasses.

Algorithm   A procedure which is guaranteed to terminate in a finite time.

Application framework   A collection of objects designed to solve a particular class of problem. The classes are specialized to deal with specific applications. A common example is an application framework for graphical user interface development.

Applicator   An operation that applies one of its arguments (a reference to a function) to the other arguments.

Assertions   Statements of the form 'A is B' in rule-based languages. Also called 'facts'.
OR
In formal languages a general term for *preconditions, postconditions* or *invariance conditions*.

Attribute
A static, or printable, property of an object. It cannot exist independently of the object.

Attributes may take other objects as values. See *instance variable*.

Backward chaining   A method of search, or inference, with starts with a conclusion and follows a chain of rules backwards to find plausible reasons or causes for the conclusion.

Base class   A class from which the behaviour of other classes is inherited. A *superclass*.

Behaviour   The set of methods of an object defines its behaviour.

Behaviour sharing   A form of *polymorphism*, when several entities have the same interface. This is achieved by inheritance or *operator overloading*.

Browser   A tool to help programmers navigate visually through the classification structures of a system, following the inheritance links.

Class   An abstraction of a set of objects that specifies the common static and behavioural characteristics of the objects, including the public and private nature of the state and behaviour. A class is a template from which object instances are created.

Class-oriented (or -based)   Object-based systems in which every instance belongs to a class, but classes may not have superclasses.

Class method   A method which is inherited by all subclasses of the class it belongs to and which defines the behaviour of the collective of instances rather than individual ones. The values of class variables may be inherited by subclasses and overridden.

Class variable   An attribute which is inherited by all subclasses of the class it belongs to and which defines the state of the collective of instances rather than individual ones. The values of class variables may be inherited by subclasses and overridden.

Classification, AKO or IsA structure   A tree or network structure based on the semantic primitives of inclusion (AKindOf) and membership (IsA) which indicates that inheritance may implement specialization or generalization. Objects may participate in more than one such structure, giving rise to multiple inheritance.

Client   An object which uses the services of another, server, object. That is, clients can send messages to servers.

Collaboration   The relationship of clients to servers via usage or message passing.

Composition (or part-of) hierarchy   A tree structure based on the semantic primitive 'part-of' which indicates that certain objects may be assembled from collections of other objects. Objects may participate in more than one such structure.

Constructor operations   Methods which create and initialize the state of an object.

Container class   A class that defines a data structure for collecting instances of other types; for example, lists, bags, sets, queues and stacks.

Contract   The set of messages that a client can send to a server which defines its responsibilities. Sometimes (in CRC) a coherent subset of this set.

Data semantics   Specification of the meaning of data and their relationships; specifically the multiplicity and modality of relationships, inheritance and composition. These relationships include integrity constraints.

Data type   Same as *type*.

DBMS   Database management system.

Declarative semantics   The same as *functional semantics*.

Delegation   In actor systems, the passing of responsibility to carry out a method to another object. A form of classless inheritance.

Demon   An object or procedure which is activated by a change of state; a data-driven procedure. The same as a *trigger*.

Derived class   A refinement or specialization of an existing class.

Destructor operations   Methods which destroy objects and reclaim their space.

Dialectics   A form of argument based on the resolution of contradictory components, or the view that everything is constantly transformed by the resolution of internal contradictions. The unity and conflict of opposites.

Dynamic binding   The allocation of storage at run time rather than compile time.

Early binding   The same as *static binding* and the opposite of *late* (or *dynamic*) *binding*.

Empiricism   The philosophical position that perception, rather than objective reality, is primary to all knowledge. Empiricism and certain philosophical positions derived from it, such as that of Kant, logical positivism and pragmatism, has been the dominant philosophy in Western science since Bacon.

Encapsulation   The scoping of unrestricted reference to an object. Objects may examine or change their own state, but its accessor methods prevent other objects from making inappropriate requests or updates. Closely related to the concept of *information hiding*.

Epistemology   The science or theory of knowledge.

Forward chaining   A method of search, or inference, with starts with one or more facts and follows a chain of rules forwards to find one or more consequences of the facts.

Frame   A data structure used in artificial intelligence similar to an object. Frames have *slots* which may contain data and procedures.

Framework   See *application framework*.

Friend   In C++, a method of an object with privileged access to the private implementation of another object.

Functional semantics   The specification of the meaning of the procedural and control aspects of an object. In particular, the specification of rules for triggers, conflict resolution, handling exceptions, control regimes and general business rules.

Fuzzy quantifier   A term such as *some*, *a few* or *most* which quantifies an expression inexactly.

Fuzzy object   An object which may contain or inherit attribute values which are fuzzy sets, and which may inherit any attribute with an attached certainty factor, thus modelling partial inheritance.

Fuzzy set   A generalization of a set where membership may be partial. The set of tall men is a fuzzy set.

Garbage collection   The process of reclaiming the core storage occupied by objects no longer in use or reachable from the current task image.

Genericity   The ability to parametrize classes; a special case of *polymorphism*.

Generalization   The opposite of *specialization*. vb. Moving 'up' a *classification structure*. n.sing. A more general class than some other which inherits from it.

Generic package   An Ada package that includes generic parameters.

Implementation   The private or hidden features of an object.

Inferential distance ordering   The partial ordering of an inheritance network according to the number of superclasses through which a value is inherited. The distance is the number of steps in the inheritance chain. For example, in the inference 'Fido has hair because Fido is a dog and dogs are mammals (and mammals have hair)', the distance is 2.

Information hiding   The principle which states that the state and implementation of an object or module should be private to that object or module and only accessible via its public interface. Closely related to *encapsulation*.

Inheritance   The relationship between classes whereby one class inherits all or part of the description of another more general class, and instances inherit all the properties and methods of the classes they belong to.

Instance   A particular object or individual example of a class.

Instance variable   A data-holding attribute contained within an instance that describes the state of that instance. Only the declaration of an instance variable, not its value, may be inherited by subclasses. See also *attribute* and *class variable*.

Instantiation   The creation of a data item representing a variable or a class – giving a value to something.

Interface   The visible methods of an object.

IsA   The inheritance relationship between instances and their classes; as in: 'Jane Gray IsA PERSON'.

Iterator   A method that permits all parts of an object to be visited.

Late binding   The same as *dynamic binding*.

Layer   A partition of a diagram with only a few objects treated as a composite object communicating with other layers.

Level   The same as a *layer*.

Late binding   The same as *dynamic binding*.

Manipulator   A value in an expression that causes side-effects. Usually implemented as references to other methods and often used as the operator argument of an *applicator*.

Member function   A function declared within a class with access to its internal state.

Membership function   The characteristic function of a set, or in particular a fuzzy set, which takes values between 0 and 1. A value of 0 indicates that a member of the domain of the membership function is not in the set and 1 indicates full membership. With fuzzy sets, such as the set of tall men, a member can have a partial membership. For example, a man 5'11" high might be given the value 0.6 in the set 'tall'. For all practical purposes, a membership function is the same thing as a fuzzy set.

Message   A request for an object to carry out one of its operations.

Message passing   The philosophy that objects only interact by sending messages to each other that request some operations to be performed.

Metaclass   In languages like Smalltalk, a class whose instances are classes, as opposed to an abstract class that has no instances, only *subclasses*. Used loosely as a synonym for abstract class in this book. See also *superclass*.

Method   A procedure or function which an object can perform. Strictly the implementation of an operation in some language, but used loosely to mean the same as *operation*.

Milliard   = 1,000 million (Americans use 'billion' for this number).

Mixin   An abstract class containing a package of methods which can be inherited by (mixed into) any class. Normally mixins are associated with CLOS.

Modal logic   The logic of possibility which introduces two extra operators to ordinary first-order logic, L (meaning 'it is possible that') and N (meaning 'it is necessary that') along with new rules to manipulate them.

Monomorphism   The opposite of polymorphism, where a message may only have one, system-wide, interpretation.

Multiple inheritance   Inheritance where a more specialized object can inherit its description from more than one more general class and where contradictions may result.

Non-monotonic logic   A type of formal logic in which theorems can be retracted (unproved) in the light of new facts. Most logic is *monotonic* in the sense that adding new facts always increases the number of provable theorems.

Object   Anything that can be named. Either an object type or one of its instances. A class or an instance of a class. Note that other books use the term *object* solely to refer to instances. This book follows the Smalltalk philosophy where 'everything is an object'.

Object type   This is the standard OMG term. It means an entity type equipped with *operations* which encapsulate its data structure. Usually referred to as a *class*, though strictly classes are implementations of object-types. Sometimes abbreviated to *object*.

Object-based   Systems are object-based when they allow objects to encapsulate both data and methods and which enforce object identity.

Object identity   The rule that objects have unique identity throughout their existence.

Object-oriented   Object-oriented systems are *object-based*, class-based, support inheritance between classes and superclasses and allow objects to send messages to themselves.

Ontology   The science or study of being.

Operation   A procedure that an object knows how to perform and which gives access to the object's data. Operations are implemented as *methods*.

Operator overloading   A special case of *polymorphism*; attaching more than one meaning to the same operator symbol.

'Overloading' is also sometimes used to indicate using the same name for different objects.

Overriding   The ability to change the definition of an inherited method or attribute in a subclass.

Package   An Ada construct that combines a set of declarations into a single program unit which can be used to create an abstract data type.

Persistence   The property of objects to persist in terms of identity, state and description through time, regardless of the computer session which created or uses them. Objects stored, ready for use, on secondary storage.

Phenomenology   A school of thought within modern philosophy which asserts the active rôle of the subject in perception, characterized by the slogan: there is no object without a subject. The term is either used exactly to refer to the idealist positions of Brentano and Husserl and their existentialist followers such as Heidegger and Sartre, or more loosely to include Hegel and some modern materialists.

Polymorphism   Literally: many-formedness. The ability of an object or operator to refer to instances of different classes at run time. Thus, polymorphic messages may be interpreted differently when received by different objects or in different contexts.

Private parts   Those parts of an object, methods or attributes, which may not be accessed by other objects, only by subclasses or instances.

Protocol   The set of public operations of an object.

Public interface   That part of an object, methods or attributes, which may be accessed by other objects. The public part of an object constitutes its interface.

Pushout   In the mathematical theory of categories, the universal object standing at the terminal corner of a square of arrows. Universal here means that any other object in that place could be factored through the universal one. This formalizes the notion of 'the object most easily constructed' or the 'best' or 'most natural' object. For example, Cartesian products are universal with respect to their projections.

Quantification   In logic, setting limits on how many things an expression applies to. Classical logic has two quantifiers, *there exists* (written $\exists$) and for all (written $\forall$).

Responsibility   Something that an object can be regarded as knowing about (an *attribute*) or knowing how to do (an *operation*).

Rule   A rule or constraint that specifies some relationship between two or more attributes and/or operation within an object. Occasionally rules specify the conflict resolution strategy that objects will adopt when there is, for example, a conflict arising from multiple inheritance.

Rule-set   A set of If ... then ... statements. Rules are regarded as independent and their order does not matter. Rule-based languages are non-procedural in this sense.

Selector   A method that evaluates the current state of an object.

Selector operation   A method which can access but not alter the state of an object.

Self-recursion   Being able to send messages to oneself.

Self-reference   The same as self recursion; being able to refer to oneself in a method.

Server   An object which suffers operations but may not act upon other objects. It may only send messages to other objects as a result of a request from them, unless it is also a client of other servers. See *client*.

Set abstraction   Considering concrete instances as belonging to a class defined by abstract properties or predicates.

Specialization   The opposite of *generalization*. *vb*. Going 'down' *a classification structure*. *n. sing*. A more restricted class than some other which it inherits from.

Static binding   The opposite of dynamic binding. Values are bound to variables, or methods to messages, at compile time. Also called *early binding*.

Slot   The word used in AI frame systems for attributes. Note that attributes of frames can contain methods. An instance variable in CLOS.

Strong typing   The property of a programming language which ensures that all expressions are guaranteed to be type consistent.

Structure   In object-oriented analysis, a linked set of objects. Structures are of three main kinds: classification, composition and use. General *associations* also give rise to structures.

Subclass   A class which has an AKO link to a more general class, as in: 'a DOG is AKindOf MAMMAL'.

Subject (area)   In Coad/Yourdon object-oriented analysis, the same as a *level*.

Subsystem   A general term like *level*, *subject* or *subject area* referring to a subdivision of a system description to make it more understandable or tractable.

Superclass   A class which has one or more members which are (more specialized) classes themselves. A *base class*.

Syllogism   A logical or other process whereby two unlinked terms are linked by an intermediate term. A relationship between particular, individual and universal, in any order. The classical example is the deductive syllogism: 'All men are mortal (universal). Gaius is a man (particular). Therefore, Gaius is mortal (individual).'

t-norm   A generalization of the various kinds of 'and' operation in fuzzy logics. *t-conorms* generalize 'or' operations similarly. A typical non-standard t-conorm is the probabilistic sum: a+b+a*b.

Tautology   A statement which is true by definition, such as 'red roses are red'.

Trigger   A *demon*. A rule which fires in response to a change of state.

Type   A set together with operations defined on this set. See *abstract data type*.

Use (or usage) structure   The structure of relationships between clients and servers connected by message passing.

Visibility   The ability of one object to be a server to others.

Weak typing   The opposite of strong typing. Type errors may occur at run time.

REFERENCES AND BIBLIOGRAPHY

Abbott R.J. (1983). Program design by informal English descriptions. *Comm. ACM,* **26**(11), 882–94

Abrial J.R. (1974). Data semantics. In *Data Base Management* (Klimbie and Koffeman, eds). Amsterdam: North-Holland

Ackroyd M. and Daum D. (1991). Graphical notation for object-oriented design and programming. *J. Object-Oriented Programming,* **3**(5), 18–28

Adams M. and Lenkov D. (1990). Object-oriented COBOL: the next generation. *HOOT,* **2**(2) 12–15

Agha G. (1986). *Actors: A Model of Concurrent Computation in Distributed Systems.* Cambridge, MA: MIT Press

Agha G. and Hewitt C. (1987). Actors: a conceptual foundation for concurrent object-oriented programming. In *Research Directions in Object-Oriented Programming* (Shriver B. and Wegner P., eds.) Cambridge, MA: MIT Press

Agha S. (1989). *Hypertext Systems.* MSc Thesis, City University, London

Agrawal R. and Gehani N. (1989). ODE: the language and the data model. *Proc. ACM SIGMOD Conf. on the Management of Data,* Portland, Oregon

Ahmed S., Wong A., Sriram D. and Logcher R. (1992). Object-oriented database management systems for engineering: a comparison. *J. Object-Oriented Programming,* **5**(3), 27–44

Akscyn R.M. and McCracken D.L. (1984). The ZOG approach to database management. In *Proc. Trends and Applications Conference: Making Database Work,* Gartherburg, Maryland

Akscyn R.M., McCracken D.L. and Yoder E.A. (1988). KMS: A distributed hypermedia system for managing knowledge in organisations. *Comm. ACM,* **31**(7), 820–35

Alabiso B. (1988). Transformation of data flow analysis models to object-oriented design. In *OOPSLA'88 ACM Conference on Object-Oriented Programming Languages and Applications.* (Meyrowitz N. 1988) ACM SIGPLAN, **23**(11)

Albana A. *et al.* (1988). The type system of Galileo. In *Data Types and Persistence* (Atkinson M.P., Buneman O.P. and Morrison R., eds.). P.101–19. Berlin: Springer-Verlag.

Albrecht A.J. and Gaffney J.E. (1983). Software function, source lines of code and development effort prediction: a software science validation. *IEEE Transactions on Software Engineering,* **9**(6), 639–47

Aleksander I. and Morton H. (1990). *An Introduction to Neural Computing.* London: Chapman and Hall

Altham J.E.J. (1971). *The Logic of Plurality.* Methuen

Andersen B. (1992). Ellie: a general, fine-grained, first-class, object based language. *J. Object-Oriented Programming,* **5**(2), 35–41

Anderson J.A., McDonald J., Holland L. and Scranage E. (1989). Automated object-oriented requirements analysis and design. *Proc. 6th Washington Ada Symposium,* 265–72

Andleigh P.K. and Gretzinger M.R. (1992). *Distributed Object-Oriented Data-Systems Design.* Englewood Cliffs, NJ: Prentice-Hall

Andrews T. and Harris C. (1990). Combining language and database advances in an object-oriented development. In *Readings in Object-Oriented Database Systems* (Zdonik S.B. and Maier D., eds.). Los Altos, CA: Morgan Kaufman

Apple (1988). *The MacApp Interim Manual.* Cupertino, CA: Apple Computer Inc.

Ashby W.R. (1956). *An Introduction to Cybernetics.* London: Chapman and Hall

Ashby W.R. (1960). *Design for a Brain* 2nd edn. London: Chapman and Hall

Atkinson M.P. and Buneman O.P. (1987). Types and persistence in database programming languages. *ACM Computing Surveys,* **19**(2), 105–90

Atkinson M.P., Bancilhon F., DeWitt D., Dittrich K., Maier D. and Zdonik S. (1989). The Object-Oriented Database System Manifesto, *Deductive and Object-Oriented Databases.* Amsterdam: Elsevier 1990; also in *Proc. 1st International Conference on Deductive and Object-Oriented Databases*, Kyoto, Japan, December 4–6, 1989, 40–57

Attwood T. (1991). At last! A distributed database for Windows 3.0. *Object Magazine*, **1**(1), 36–57

Bachman C. (1977). The rôle concept in data models. In *Proc. 3rd International Conference on Very Large Databases*, IEEE, New York, 464–76

Bailin S.C. (1989). An object-oriented requirements specification method. *Comm. ACM*, **32**(5), 608–23

Barker R. (1990). *CASE*METHOD: Entity Relationship Modelling.* Wokingham: Addison-Wesley

Basden A. (1990). Towards a methodology for building expert systems I. *Codex*, **2**(1), 15–19. Uxbridge: Creative Logic Ltd

Basden A. (1990a). Towards a methodology for building expert systems II. *Codex*, **2**(2), 19–23. Uxbridge: Creative Logic Ltd

Beck K. and Cunningham W. (1989). A laboratory for teaching object-oriented thinking. In *OOPSLA'89 ACM Conference on Object-Oriented Programming Systems, Languages and Applications* (Meyrowitz N., ed.). Reading, MA: Addison-Wesley

Beech D. (1987). Groundwork for an object-oriented database model. In *Research Directions in Object-Oriented Programming* (Shriver B. and Wegner P., eds.). Cambridge, MA: MIT Press

Beech D. (1992). *Relational versus Object DBMS.* Lecture notes, Object World, July 1992, San Francisco

Belcher K. (1991). Object-orientation: the COBOL approach. *Object Magazine,* **1**(1), 74–83

Bell D.A., Shao J. and Hull M.E.C. (1990). Integrated deductive database system implementation: a systematic study. *Computer Journal,* **33**(1), 40–48

Bellman R. and Zadeh L.A. (1970). Decision making in a fuzzy environment. *Management Science*, **17**(4), 141–64

Berard E.V. (1993). *Essays on Object-Oriented Software Engineering.* Englewood Cliffs, NJ: Prentice-Hall

Bezivin J., Hullot J-M., Cointe P. and Leiberman H., eds. (1987). *ECOOP'87 European Conference on Object-Oriented Programming.* Lecture Notes in Computer Science 276. Berlin: Springer-Verlag

Bezivin J. and Meyer B. (1991). TOOLS4: *Proc. fourth International Conference on the Technology of Object-Oriented Languages and Systems.* Englewood Cliffs, NJ: Prentice-Hall

Biggerstaff T. and Richter C. (1989). *Re-usability Framework, Assessment and Directions.* Tutorial: Software Reuse – Emerging Technology, IEEE Computer Society, EH0278–2, 3–11

Birtwistle G.M. (1979). *Discrete Event Modelling On Simula.* London: Macmillan

Black A., Hutchinson N., Jul E. and Levy H. (1986). Object structure in the Emerald system. In *OOPSLA'89 ACM Conference on Object-Oriented Programming Systems, Languages and Applications* (Meyrowitz N., ed.). ACM SIGPLAN Notices, **21**(11) pp. 78–87

Blair G., Gallagher J., Hutchison D. and Shepherd D. (1991). *Object-Oriented Languages, Systems and Applications.* London: Pitman

Blum A. (1992). *Neural Networks in C++: An Object-Oriented Framework for Building Connectionist Systems.* New York:Wiley

Boar B. (1984). *Application Prototyping: A Requirements Definition Strategy for the 80s.* New York: Wiley

Bobrow D. and Stefik M. (1983). *The LOOPS Manual.* Xerox Corporation

Bobrow D., Kahn K., Kiczales G., Masiuter L., Stefik M. and Zdybel F. (1986). CommonLOOPS: merging LISP and object-oriented programming. In *OOPSLA'89 ACM Conference on Object-Oriented Programming Systems, Languages and Applications* (Meyrowitz N. ed.). ACM SIGPLAN Notices, **21**(11) pp.17–29

Bobrow D.G. and Winograd T. (1985). An overview of KRL. In *Readings in Knowledge Presentation* (Brachman R.J. and Levesque H.J., eds.). Los Altos, CA: Morgan Kaufman

Bodkin T. and Graham I.M. (1989). Case studies of expert systems development using microcomputer software packages. *Expert Systems,* **6**(1), 12–16.

Boehm B.W. (1981). *Software Engineering Economics.* Englewood Cliffs, NJ: Prentice-Hall

Booch G. (1982). Object-oriented design. *Ada Letters,* **1**(3), 64–76

Booch G. (1986). Object-oriented development. *IEEE Trans. on Software Eng.,* Vol SE-12(2), 211–21

Booch G. (1987). *Software Engineering with Ada* 2nd edn. Redwood City, CA: Benjamin Cummings

Booch G. (1987a). *Software Components with Ada.* Redwood City, CA: Benjamin Cummings

Booch G. (1990). On the concepts of object-oriented design. In *Modern Software Engineering: Foundations and Current Perspectives* (Ng P.A. and Yeh R.T., eds.). New York, Van Nostrand, pp. 165–204

Booch G. (1991). *Object Oriented Design with Applications.* Redwood City, CA: Benjamin Cummings

Boose J.H. (1986). *Expertise Transfer for Expert Systems Design.* Amsterdam: Elsevier

Boose J.H. and Bradshaw J.M. (1988). Expertise transfer and complex problems: using AQUINAS as knowledge acquisition workbench for knowledge based systems. In *Knowledge Acquisition Tools for Expert Systems* (Boose J.H. and Gaines B.R., eds.). London: Academic Press

Boose J.H. and Gaines B.R., eds (1988). *Knowledge Acquisition for Knowledge Based Systems.* London: Academic Press

Boose J.H. and Gaines B.R., eds (1990). *The Foundations of Knowledge Acquisition.* London: Academic Press

Borenstein N.S. (1990). *Multimedia Applications Development with the Andrew Toolkit.* Englewood Cliffs, NJ: Prentice-Hall

Borning A. and Ingalls D. (1982). A type declaration and inference system for Smalltalk. In *Proc. 9th Annual ACM Symposium on Principles of Programming Languages,* Albuquerque, NM., Jan. New York: ACM, 133–41

Brachman R.J. (1983). What IS-A is and isn't: an analysis of taxonomic links in semantic networks. *IEEE Computer,* **16**(10), 30–6

Brachman R.J. and Levesque H.J., eds (1985). *Readings in Knowledge Representation.* Los Altos, CA: Morgan Kaufman

Braune R. and Foshay W.R. (1983). Towards a practical model of cognitive information processing, task analysis and schema acquisition for complex problem solving situations. *Instructional Science,* **12**, 121–45

Bretl R., Maier D., Otis A., Penney J., *et al.* (1989). The GemStone data management system. In *Object-Oriented Concepts, Databases and Applications* (Kim W. and Lochovsky F.H., eds.). Reading, MA: Addison-Wesley

Brodie M.L., Mylopoulos J. and Schmidt J.W., eds. (1984). *Conceptual Modelling.* Berlin: Springer-Verlag

Brodie M.L. and Mylopoulos J., eds. (1986). *On Knowledge Base Management Systems.* Berlin: Springer-Verlag

Brooks F. (1973). *The Mythical Man Month.* Reading, MA: Addison-Wesley

Brooks F. (1986). No silver bullet: essence and accidents of software engineering. In *Information Processing '86.* (Kluger H.-J. ed.). Amsterdam: Elsevier

Brown A.W. (1991). *Object-Oriented Databases and their Applications to Software Engineering.* London: McGraw-Hill

Buchanan B. and Shortliffe E. (1984). *Rule-Based Expert Systems: The MYCIN Experiments of the Stanford Heuristic Programming Project.* Reading, MA: Addison-Wesley

Buhr R.J.A. (1984). *System Design with Ada.* Englewood Cliffs, NJ: Prentice-Hall

Bulman D. (1991). Refining candidate objects. *Computer Language,* Jan. 1991, 30–9

Burstall R.M., McQueen D.B. and Sannella D.T. (1980). *HOPE: An experimental applicative language.* Internal Report CSR-62-80, University of Edinburgh

Bush V. (1945). As we may think. *Atlantic Monthly,* **176**(1), 101–8

Cameron J. (1992). New ingredients for an object-oriented method. *Object Magazine,* **2**(4)

Cardelli L. and Wegner P. (1985). On understanding types, data abstraction and polymorphism. *ACM Computing Surveys,* **17**(4), 471–522

Cardenas A. and McLeod D., eds. (1990). *Research Foundations on Object-Oriented Databases.* Englewood Cliffs, NJ: Prentice-Hall

Carmichael A. (1994). *Approaches to Object-Oriented Analysis and Design.* New York: SIGS Books

Cattel R.G.G. (1991). *Object Data Management: Object-Oriented and Extended Relational Database Systems.* Reading, MA: Addison-Wesley

Cattel R.G.G. and Skeen J. (1990). *Engineering Database Benchmark.* Technical Report, Sun Microsystems, Mountain View, CA

Champeaux D. de, Lea D. and Faure P. (1993). *Object-Oriented System Development.* Reading, MA: Addison-Wesley

Chan A., Dayal U., Fox S. and Ries D. (1983). Supporting a semantic data model in a distributed database system. In *Proc. 9th International Conference on Very Large Databases,* Very Large Database Endowment, Saratoga, CA., 354–63

Chen P. (1976). The entity-relationship model: toward a unified view of data. *ACM Trans. on Database Systems,* **1**(1), 9–36

Chorafas D.N. and Steinmann H. (1993). *Object-Oriented Databases: An Introduction.* Englewood Cliffs, NJ: Prentice-Hall

Coad P. (1992). Object-oriented patterns. *Comm. ACM,* **35**(9), 152–8

Coad P. and Nicola J. (1993). *Object-Oriented Programming.* Englewood Cliffs, NJ: Yourdon

Press/Prentice-Hall

Coad P. and Yourdon E. (1990). *Object-Oriented Analysis.* Englewood Cliffs, NJ: Yourdon Press/Prentice Hall

Coad P. and Yourdon E. (1991). *Object-Oriented Analysis,* 2nd edn. Englewood Cliffs, NJ: Yourdon Press/Prentice-Hall

Coad P. and Yourdon E. (1991a). *Object-Oriented Design.* Englewood Cliffs, NJ: Yourdon Press/Prentice-Hall

Codd E.F. (1976). A relational model of data for large shared data banks. *Comm. ACM,* **13**(6), 377–87

Codd E.F. (1985). *Is Your Relational Database Management System Really Relational?* Oracle Users' Conference, San Diego, California

Colbert E. (1994). The OOSD Method: Requirements analysis with object-oriented software development. In *Approaches to Object-Oriented Analysis and Design* (Carmichael A., ed.). New York: SIGS Books

Coleman D. and Hayes F. (1991). Lessons from Hewlett-Packard's experience of using object-oriented technology. In *TOOLS4: Proc. Fourth International Conference on the Technology of Object-Oriented Languages and Systems* (Bezivin J. and Meyer B., eds.). Englewood Cliffs, NJ: Prentice-Hall

Coleman D., Arnold P., Bodoff S., Dollin C., *et al.* (1994). *Object-Oriented Development: The FUSION Method.* Hemel Hempstead, UK: Prentice-Hall

Connell J.L and Shafer L.B. (1989). *Structured Rapid Prototyping: An Evolutionary Approach.* Englewood Cliffs, NJ: Yourdon Press

Cook S., ed. (1989). *ECOOP'89 European Conference on Object-Oriented Programming.* Cambridge: Cambridge University Press

Cook S. and Daniels J. (1992). Essential techniques for object-oriented design. *Proc OOPS-59.* London: BCS OOPS Group

Cook W. (1989). A denotational semantics of inheritance and its correctness. In *OOPSLA'89 ACM Conference on Object-Oriented Programming Systems, Languages and Applications* (Meyrowitz N., ed.). Reading, MA: Addison-Wesley

Coplien J.O. (1992). *Advanced C++: Programming Styles and Idioms*. Reading, MA: Addison-Wesley

Cox B.J. (1986). *Object-Oriented Programming – An Evolutionary Approach*. Reading, MA: Addison-Wesley

Cox B.J. and Novobilski A. (1991). *Object-Oriented Programming – An Evolutionary Approach* 2nd edn. Reading, MA: Addison-Wesley

Dadam P. (1988). *Research and Development Trends in Relational Databases (NF2 Relations)*. IBM Scientific Centre, Heidelberg

Dahl O.J. (1987). Object-oriented specification. In: *Research Directions in Object-Oriented Programming* (Shriver B. and Wegner P., eds.). Cambridge, MA: MIT Press, pp. 561–76

Dahl O.J. and Nygaard K. (1966). SIMULA – An Algol-based simulation language. *Comm. ACM*, **9**, 671–78

Dahl O.J., Myrhaug B. and Nygaard K. (1968). *SIMULA 67 Common Base Language*. Norwegian Computing Centre, Oslo

Danforth S. and Tomlinson C. (1988). Type theories and object-oriented programming. *ACM Computing Surveys*, **20**(1), 29–72

Daniels P.J. (1986). The user modelling function of an intelligent interface for document retrieval systems. In *IRFIS 6: Intelligent Information Systems for the Information Society* (Brookes B.C., ed.) pp. 162–176. Amsterdam: North-Holland

Daniels P.J. and Coote S. (1993). Strategies for sharing objects in distributed systems. *J. Object-Oriented Programming*, **5**(8), 27–36

Date C.J. (1981). *An Introduction to Database Systems* 3rd edn. Reading, MA: Addison-Wesley

Date C.J. (1983). *An Introduction to Database Systems*. Vol II. Reading, MA: Addison-Wesley

Davis A.M. (1993). *Software Requirements: Objects, Functions and States, Revision*. Englewood Cliffs, NJ: Prentice-Hall

Dedene G. (1994). M.E.R.O.D.E. and the practical realization of object-oriented business models. In *Approaches to Object-Oriented Analysis and Design* (Carmichael A., ed.). New York: SIGS Books

DeMarco T. (1982). *Controlling Software Projects*. Englewood Cliffs, NJ: Yourdon Press

Demers A.J. and Donahue J.E. (1979). *Revised report on Russell*. TR79-389, Dept. of Computer Science, Cornell University, Ithaca, NY

Desfray P. (1992). *Ingénerie des objets: Approche classe-relation application à C++*. Paris: Editions Masson

Deux O. (1990). The story of O_2. *IEEE Transactions on Knowledge and Data Engineering*, **2**(1), 91–108

Dewhurst S. and Stark K. (1989). *Programming in C++*. Englewood Cliffs, NJ: Prentice-Hall

Dietrich W.C., Nackman L.R. and Gracer F. (1989). Saving a legacy with objects. In *OOPSLA'89 ACM Conference on Object-Oriented Programming Systems, Languages and Applications* (Meyrowitz N., ed.). Reading, MA: Addison-Wesley

Dillon T. and Tan P.L. (1993). *Object-Oriented Conceptual Modeling*, Sydney, NSW: Prentice-Hall

Dorfman L. (1990). *Object-Oriented Assembly Language*. Pennsylvania: Windcrest

Dubois D. and Prade H. (1980). *Fuzzy Sets and Systems: Theory and Applications*. London: Academic Press

Durham A. (1992). BETA: The pattern language. *Object Magazine*, **2**(4), 82–3

Eastlake J.J. (1987). *A Structured Approach to Computer Strategy*. Chichester: Ellis Horwood

Eckel B. (1989). *Using C++*. Osborne, McGraw-Hill

Edwards J. (1989). Lessons learned in more than ten years of practical application of the object-oriented paradigm. *Proc CASExpo-Europe*, London

Ege R., Singh M. and Meyer B., eds. (1993). *TOOLS8: Proceedings of the eighth International Conference on the Technology of Object-Oriented Languages and Systems*. New York: Prentice-Hall

Ehn P. (1988). *Work-oriented Design of Computer Artifacts*. Arbetslivscentrum, Stockholm

Eliëns A. (1992). An object-oriented approach to distributed problem solving. In *Research and Development in Expert Systems IX* (Bramer M.A. and Milne R.W., eds.). Cambridge: Cambridge University Press

Elmasri R. and Navathe S.B. (1989). *Fundamentals of Database Systems.* Reading, MA: Benjamin Cummings

Elmore P., Shaw G.M. and Zdonik S.B. (1989). *The ENCORE Object-Oriented Data Model.* Technical Report, Brown University

Embley D.W., Kurtz B.D. and Woodfield S.N. (1992). *Object-Oriented Systems Analysis: A Model-Driven Approach.* Englewood Cliffs, NJ: Yourdon Press

Englebart D. (1963). A conceptual framework for the augmentation of man's intellect. In *Vistas in Information Handling* Vol 1 (Howerton P.W. and Weeks D.C., eds.) Washington: Spartan Books

Englebart D. and English W.K. (1968). A research centre for augmenting human intellect. In *Proc. 1968 AFIPS Conference,* AFIPS Press – Montale NJ, 395–410

Englemore D. and Morgan A., eds. (1989). *Blackboard Systems.* Wokingham: Addison-Wesley

Ericsson K.A. and Simon H.A. (1984). *Protocol Analysis: Verbal Reports as Data,* Boston: Bradford Books

Feigenbaum E., McCorduck P. and Nii H.P. (1988). *The Rise of the Expert Company.* London: Macmillan

Fiedler S.P. (1989). Object-oriented unit testing, *Hewlett-Packard Journal,* April 1989, 69–74

Firesmith D.G. (1993). *Object-Oriented Requirements Analysis and Design: A Software Engineering Approach.* Chichester: Wiley

Fishman D.H., et al. (1989). Overview of the IRIS DBMS. In *Object-Oriented Concepts, Databases and Applications* (Kim W. and Lochovsky F.H., eds.). Reading, MA: Addison-Wesley

Foster I. and Taylor S. (1990). *Strand: New Concepts in Parallel Programming.* Englewood Cliffs, NJ: Prentice-Hall

Forsythe R., ed. (1989). *Expert Systems: Principles and Case Studies* 2nd edn. London: Chapman and Hall

Fowler M. and Capey A. (1991). The use of object-oriented analysis to define a generic model for health care. *Proc. SCOOP Europe.* London 1991

Futatsugi K., Goguen J., Jouannaud J-P. and Meseguer J. (1985). Principles of OBJ2. *Proc. 12th Annual Symposium on Principles of Programming Languages,* ACM, New York, 52–66

Gaines B. and Shaw M. (1992). Documents as expert systems. In *Research and Development in Expert Systems IX* (Bramer M. and Milne R., eds.). Cambridge: Cambridge University Press

Gane C. (1990). *Computer-Aided Software Engineering: The Methodologies, the Products and the Future.* Englewood Cliffs, NJ: Prentice-Hall

Giles R. (1976). Lukasiewitz logic and fuzzy theory. *Int. J. Man-Machine Studies,* **8**

Gjessing S. and Nygaard K., eds. (1988). *ECOOP'88 European Conference on Object-Oriented Programming.* Lecture Notes in Computer Science 276. Berlin: Springer-Verlag

Glassey C.R. and Adiga S. (1990). Berkeley library of objects for control and simulation of manufacturing (BLOCS/M). In *Applications of Object-Oriented Programming* (Pinson L.J. and Weiner R.S., eds.). Reading, MA: Addison-Wesley

Goguen J. and Meseguer J. (1986). EQLog: equality, types and generic modules for logic programming. In *Logic Programming* (DeGroot D. and Lindstrom G., eds.). Englewood Cliffs, NJ: Prentice-Hall

Goguen J. and Meseguer J. (1987). Unifying functional, object-oriented and relational programming with logical semantics. In *Research Directions in Object-Oriented Programming* (Shriver B. and Wegner P., eds.). Cambridge, MA: MIT Press

Gohil N. (1988). *Object-Oriented Database Management.* Unpublished Bachelor's thesis, Imperial College of Science and Technology

Goldberg A. (1984). *Smalltalk-80: The Interactive Programming Environment.* Reading, MA: Addison-Wesley

Goldberg A. and Robson D. (1983). *Smalltalk-80: The Language and its Implementation.* Reading, MA: Addison-Wesley

Goldberg D.E. (1989). *Genetic Algorithms in Search, Optimization and Machine Learning.* Reading, MA: Addison-Wesley

Goodwin M. (1989). *User Interfaces in C++ and*

Object-Oriented Programming, Cambridge, MA: MIT Press

Gorman K. and Choobineh J. (1989). The object-oriented entity-relationship model (OOERM). *J. Man. Info. Systems,* **33**(9), 41–65

Graham I.M. (1987). Expert systems find an ideal setting. *Banking Technology,* July 1987, 17–24

Graham I.M. (1991). Structured prototyping for requirements specification in conventional IT and expert systems. *Computing and Control Engineering Engineering Journal,* **2**(2) 82–9.

Graham I.M. (1991a). Fuzzy logic in commercial expert system shells: results and prospects. *Fuzzy Sets and Systems,* **40**(3) 451–72

Graham I.M. (1992). A method for integrating object technology with rules. *Proc. Advanced Information Systems* 92, Oxford, Learned Information

Graham I.M. (1992a). Interoperation: combining objects. *Object Magazine,* **2**(4) 36–7

Graham I.M. (1993). Migration using SOMA: a semantically rich method of object-oriented analysis. *Journal of Object-Oriented Programming,* **5**(9), Feb. 1993

Graham I.M. (1993a). Migration strategies. *Object Magazine,* **2**(5)–3(5).

Graham I.M. (1993b). OOPS59 – Conference Report. *Object Magazine,* **3**(1)

Graham I.M. (1994) SOMA: Combining object-oriented analysis with rules and task analysis. In *Approaches to Object-Oriented Analysis and Design* (Carmichael A., ed.). New York: SIGS Books

Graham I.M. (1995). *Migrating to Object Technology.* Wokingham: Addison-Wesley

Graham I.M. and Jones P.L.K. (1987). A theory of fuzzy frames. In *Research and Development in Expert Systems IV* (Moralee, D.S., ed.). Cambridge: Cambridge University Press

Graham I.M. and Jones P.L.K. (1988). *Expert Systems: Knowledge, Uncertainty and Decision.* London: Chapman and Hall

Graham I.M. and Milne R.M., eds. (1991). *Research and Development in Expert Systems X.* Cambridge: Cambridge University Press

Gray P. (1984). *Logic, Algebra and Databases.* Chichester: Ellis Horwood

Gray P.D. and Mohamed R. (1990). *Smalltalk-80: A Practical Introduction.* London: Pitman

Gray P.M.D. and Kemp G.J.L. (1990). An OODB with entity-based persistence: a protein modelling application. In *Research and Development in Expert Systems VII* (Addis T.R. and Muir R.M., eds.) Cambridge: Cambridge University Press

Gray P.M.D., Krishnarao G.K. and Paton N.W. (1992). *Object-Oriented Databases: A Semantic Data Model Approach.* Englewood Cliffs, NJ: Prentice-Hall

Gregory R. (1983). Xanadu: hypertext from the future. *Dr. Dobbs Journal,* **75**, 28–35

Grossmann R. (1984). *Phenomenonology and Existentialism: An Introduction.* London: Routledge and Kegan Paul

Gupta R. and Horowitz E. (1991). *Object-Oriented Databases with Applications to CASE, Networks and VSLI CAD.* Englewood Cliffs, NJ: Prentice-Hall

Halasz F.G. (1988). Reflections on NoteCards: seven issues for the next generation of hypermedia systems. *Comm. ACM,* **31**(7), 836–52

Halliday S. and Weibel M. (1993). *Object-Oriented Software Engineering.* Englewood Cliffs, NJ: Prentice-Hall

Hammer M. and McLeod D. (1978). The semantic data model: a modelling mechanism for database applications. *Proc. ACM SIGMOD*

Hammer M. and McLeod D. (1981). Database description with SDM: a semantic database model. *ACM Trans. on Database Systems,* **6**, 351–86

Hansen T.L. (1990). *The C++ Answer Book.* Reading, MA: Addison-Wesley

Harel D. (1987). Statecharts: a visual formalism for complex systems. In *Science of Computer Programming,* **8** 231–74

Harland D.M. (1988). *Rekursiv: Object-Oriented Architecture.* Chichester: Wiley

Harland D.M. and Drummond B. (1991). REKURSIV – object-oriented hardware. In Object-Oriented programming Languages, Systems and Applications (Blair G., Gallagher J., Hutchison D. and Shepherd D., eds.) London: Pitman

Harmon P. and Taylor D.A. (1993). *Objects in Action: Commercial Applications of Object-Oriented Technologies.* Reading, MA: Addison-Wesley

Hart A. (1989). *Knowledge Acquisition for Expert*

Systems 2nd edn. London: Kogan Page

Hayes P.J. (1985). The logic of frames. In *Readings in Knowledge Presentation* (Brachman R.J. and Levesque H.J., eds.). Los Altos, CA: Morgan Kaufman

Heeg G., Magnusson B. and Meyer B., eds. (1992). *TOOLS7: Proc. seventh international conference on the Technology of Object-Oriented Languages and Systems.* New York: Prentice-Hall

Heitz M. (1988). HOOD: A hierarchical object-oriented design method, *Proc. 3rd German Ada Users Congress,* Munich, 12-1 – 12-9

Henderson-Sellers B. (1992). *A Book of Object-Oriented Knowledge.* Brookvale NSW: Prentice-Hall

Henderson-Sellers B. and Constantine L.L. (1991). Object-oriented development and functional decomposition, *J. Object-Oriented Programming,* **3**(9), 11–17

Henderson-Sellers B. and Edwards J.M. (1990). The object-oriented systems life cycle. *Comm. ACM,* **33**(9), 143–59

Henderson-Sellers B. and Edwards J.M. (1994). *Book Two of Object-Oriented Knowledge: The working object.* Brookvale, NSW: Prentice-Hall

Hewitt C. and de Jong P. (1984). Open systems. In *Conceptual Modelling* (Brodie M.L., Mtlopoulos J. and Schmidt J.W., eds.). Berlin: Springer-Verlag

Hickman F.R., Killen J., Land L. *et al.* (1989). *Analysis for Knowledge-based Systems.* Chichester: Ellis Horwood

Hoare C.A.R. (1974). Monitors: an operating system structuring concept. *Comm. ACM,* **17**(10), 549–57

Hodgson R. (1990). Finding, building and reusing objects. *Proc. Object Oriented Design,* Unicom Seminars, Uxbridge

Hollowell G. (1993). *Handbook of Object-Oriented Standards: The object model.* Reading, MA: Addison-Wesley

Hood R., Kennedy K. and Muller H. (1987). Efficient recompilation of module interfaces in a software development environment. In *Proceedings of the ACM SIGSOFT/SIGPLAN Software Engineering Symposium on Practical Software Development*

Environments. (Henderson, P. ed.) pp. 180–9 ACM Press,

HOOD Working Group (1989). *HOOD Reference Manual.* Issue 3.0. European Space Agency, Noordwijk, Netherlands

Hook J. (1984). Understanding Russell – a first attempt. In *Semantics of Data Types.* (Goos G. and Hartmanis J., eds.), Berlin: Springer-Verlag

Horty J.F., Thomason R.H. and Touretzky D.S. (1990). A skeptical theory of inheritance in nonmonotonic semantic networks. *Artificial Intelligence,* **42**, 311–48

Hu D. (1989). *C/C++ Expert Systems.* Cambridge, MA: MIT Press

Hughes J.G. (1991). *Object-Oriented Databases.* Englewood Cliffs, NJ: Prentice-Hall

Hull R. and King R. (1987). Semantic database modelling: survey, applications and research issues. *ACM Computing Surveys,* **19**(3), 201–60

Hutchison D. and Walpole J. (1991). Distributed systems and objects. In *Object-Oriented Languages, Systems and Applications* (Blair G. *et al.*, eds.), London: Pitman

Ilvari J. (1991). Object-oriented information systems analysis: a framework for object identification. *Trans. of the IEEE,* 205–18

Ince D. (1991). *Object-Oriented Software Engineering with C++.* London: McGraw-Hill

Ingalls D.H.H. (1978). *The Smalltalk-76 Programming System: Design and Implementation.* Fifth Annual ACM Symposium on Principles of Programming Languages, Tucson, Arizona

International Business Machines (1991a). *Common User Access: Guide to User Interface Design.* Cary, NC: IBM

International Business Machines (1991b). *Common User Access: Advanced Interface Design Reference.* Cary, NC: IBM

Ishikawa Y. and Tokoro M. (1987). Orient84/K: an object-oriented concurrent programming language for knowledge representation. In *Object-Oriented Concurrent Programming* (Yonezawa A. and Tokoro M., eds.). Cambridge, MA: MIT Press 159–98

Jackson M.A. (1983). *System Development.*

Englewood Cliffs, NJ: Prentice-Hall

Jacobson I., Christerson M., Jonsson P. and Övergaard G. (1992). *Object-Oriented Software Engineering: A Use Case Driven Approach.* Wokingham: Addison-Wesley

Jagannathan D. *et al.* (1988). SIM: A database system based on the semantic data model. *Proc. ACM SIGMOD 88 Conf.,* 46–55

Jeffcoate J., Hales K. and Downes V. (1989). *Object-Oriented Systems: The Commercial Benefits.* London: Ovum Ltd.

Johnson P. (1992). *Human Computer Interaction: Psychology, Task Analysis and Software Engineering.* London: McGraw-Hill

Johnson R.E. and Foote B. (1988). Designing reusable classes. *J. Object-Oriented Programming,* **1**(2)

Kaehler T. and Krasner G. (1983). LOOM: large object-oriented memory for Smalltalk-80 systems. In *Smalltalk-80: Bits of History, Words of Advice* (Krasner G., ed.) Reading, MA: Addison-Wesley

Kandel A. (1986). *Fuzzy Mathematical Techniques with Applications.* Reading, MA: Addison-Wesley

Kappel G. (1991). Using an object-oriented diagram technique for the design of information systems. In *Dynamic Modelling of Information Systems* (Sol H.G. and van Hee K.M., eds.) Amsterdam: Elsevier

Kay A. and Goldberg A. (1977). *Personal Dynamic Media.* IEEE Computer 1977 – originally a 1976 Xerox technical report.

Keene S. (1989). *Object-Oriented Programming in Common LISP.* Reading, MA: Addison-Wesley

Kelly G.A. (1955). *The Psychology of Personal Constructs.* New York: W.W. Norton

Khan N.A. and Jain R. (1986). Explaining uncertainty in a distributed expert system. In *Coupling Symbolic and Numerical Computing in Expert Systems* (Kowalik, J.S., ed.) Amsterdam: North Holland

Khoshafian S. and Abnous R. (1990). *Object Orientation: Concepts, Languages, Databases, User Interfaces.* New York: Wiley

Khoshafian S., Baker A.B., Abnous R. and Shepherd K. (1992). *Object-Oriented Multi-Media Information Management in Client/Server*

Architectures. New York: Wiley

Kilov H. and Ross J. (1994). *Information Modeling: An Object-Oriented Approach.* Englewood Cliffs, NJ: Prentice-Hall

Kim W. (1990). *Introduction to Object-Oriented Databases.* Cambridge, MA: MIT Press

Kim W., Ballou N., Chou H.T. *et al.* (1989). Features of the ORION object-oriented database. In *Object-Oriented Concepts, Databases and Applications* (Kim W. and Lochovsky F.H., eds.) Reading, MA: Addison-Wesley

Kim W. and Lochovsky F.H., eds. (1989). *Object-Oriented Concepts, Databases and Applications.* Reading, MA: Addison-Wesley

King R. (1989). My cat is object-oriented. In *Object-Oriented Concepts, Databases and Applications* (Kim W. and Lochovsky F.H., eds.). Reading, MA: Addison-Wesley

Kirkerud B. (1989). *Object-Oriented Programming with SIMULA,* Wokingham: Addison-Wesley

Kitagawa H. and Kunii T. (1989). *The Unnormalized Relational Data Model for Office Form Processor Design.* Berlin: Springer-Verlag

Knolle N.T., Fong M.W. and Lang R.E. (1990). SITMAP: a command and control application. In *Applications of Object-Oriented programming* (Pinson L.J. and Weiner R.S., eds.). Reading, MA: Addison-Wesley

Knudsen J.L., Lofgren M., Lehrmann-Madsen O. and Magnusson B., eds. (1994). *Object-Oriented Environments: The Mjølner Approach,* Hemel Hempstead, UK: Prentice-Hall

Koenig A. and Stroustrup B. (1990). Exception Handling for C++. *J. Object-Oriented Programming,* **3**(2), 16–33

Korson T., Vaishnavi V. and Meyer B., eds. (1991). *TOOLS5: Proc. Fifth International Conference on the Technology of Object-Oriented Languages and Systems.* New York: Prentice-Hall

Kristensen B.B., Madsen O.L., Moller-Pedersen B. and Nygaard K. (1987). The BETA programming language. In *Research Directions in Object-Oriented Programming Systems, Languages and Applications* (Meyrowitz N., ed.). Reading, MA: Addison-Wesley

Kurtz B., Woodfield S. and Embley D. (1991).

Object-Oriented Systems Analysis and Specification: A Model Driven Approach. Englewood Cliffs, NJ: Prentice-Hall

LaLonde W.R. and Pugh J.R. (1990). *Inside Smalltalk: Volume I.* Englewood Cliffs, NJ: Prentice-Hall

LaLonde W.R. and Pugh J.R. (1991). *Inside Smalltalk: Volume II.* Englewood Cliffs, NJ: Prentice-Hall

Lang K. and Perlmutter B. (1986). Oaklisp: An object-oriented scheme with first class types. In *OOPSLA '89 Conference on Object-Oriented Programming Systems, Languages and Applications* (Meyrowitz N., ed.). ACM SIGPLAN Notices, **21**(11)

Langham A. (1993). On the impossibility of artificial intelligence. *The International* (to appear)

Laranjeira L.A. (1990). Software size estimation of object-oriented systems. *IEEE Transactions on Software Engineering,* **16**(5), 510–22

Leathers B. (1990). Cognos and Eiffel: a cautionary tale. *Hotline on Object-Oriented Technology,* **1**(9), 1–8

Lecluse C., Richard P. and Velez F. (1988). O_2, an object-oriented data model. *ACM International Conference on the Management of Data,* Chicago

Lee S. and Carver D.L. (1991). Object-oriented analysis and specification: a knowledge based approach, *J. Object-Oriented Programming,* **3**(9), 35–43

Leiberherr K., Holland I., Lee G. and Riel A. (1988). Object-oriented programming: an objective sense of style. *IEEE Computer,* **21**(6)

Lenat D.B. and Guha R.V. (1990). *Building Large Knowledge Based Systems: Representation and Inference in the Cyc Project.* Reading, MA: Addison-Wesley

Lenzerini M., Nardi D. and Simi M., eds. (1991). *Inheritance Hierarchies in Knowledge Representation and Programming Languages.* Chichester, UK: Wiley

Lientz B.P. and Swanson E.B. (1979). Software maintenance: a user/management tug of war. *Data Management,* April 1979, 26–30

Linnemann V. (1987). Non first normal form relations and recursive queries: an SQL-based approach, *IEEE Conference on Data Engineering,* 591–98

Lippman S. (1989). *C++ Primer.* Reading: Addison-Wesley

Liskov B., Snyder A., Atkinson R. and Schaffert C. (1977). Abstraction mechanisms in CLU. *Comm. ACM,* **20**(8)

Lloyd D. (1990). LISP is no impediment! *Systems International,* Jan 1990, 43–5

Loomis M.E.S. (1991). Objects and SQL. *Object Magazine,* **1**(3) 68–78

Lorenz M. (1993). *Object-Oriented Software Development: A Practical Guide,* Englewood Cliffs, NJ: Prentice-Hall

Love T. (1992). *Object Lessons.* New York: SIGS Books

MacLennan B.J. (1982). Values and objects in programming languages. *SIGPLAN Notices,* **17**(12), 70–9

MacQueen D. (1986). Using dependent types to express modular structure. In *Proc. 13th Annual ACM Symposium on Principles of Programming Languages,* St. Petersburg Beach, Fla, Jan. New York: ACM, 277–86

Madsen O.L. and Moller-Pedersen B. (1988). What object-oriented programming may be – and what it does not have to be. In *ECOOP'88 European Conference on Object-Oriented Programming* (Gjessing S. and Nygaard K., eds.). Lecture Notes in Computer Science 276. Berlin: Springer-Verlag

Madsen O.L., Moller-Pedersen B. and Nygaard K. (1993). *Object-Oriented Programming in the BETA Programming Language.* Wokingham, UK: Addison-Wesley

Maier D. and Stein J. (1987). Development and implementation of an object-oriented DBMS. In *Research Directions in Object-Oriented Programming* (Shriver B. and Wegner P., eds.). Cambridge, MA: MIT Press

Mandrioli D. and Meyer B. (1992). *Advances in Object-Oriented Software Engineering.* Englewood Cliffs, NJ: Prentice Hall

Manola F. and Dayal U. (1986). PDM: an object-oriented data model. *International Workshop on Object-Oriented Database Systems,* California

Marcuse H. (1941). *Reason and Revolution: Hegel and the Rise of Social Theory.* London: Oxford University Press

Marden R.J. (1990). *Object-Oriented System Development: Notation and Method.*

(Unpublished manuscript)

Martin J. and O'Dell J. (1992). *Object-Oriented Analysis and Design*. Englewood Cliffs, NJ: Prentice-Hall

Martin-Löf P. (1975). An intuitionistic theory of types: predicative part. In *Logic Colloquium 1973* (Rose H.E. and Shepherdson J.C., eds.), 73-118 Amsterdam: North-Holland

Martin-Löf, P. (1982). Constructive mathematics and computer programming. In *Logic, Methodology and Philosophy of Science VI* (Proceedings of the 6th International Congress, Hanover 1979). Amsterdam: North-Holland, 153–75

Marx K. (1961). *Capital* Vol. I. Afterword to the second German edition, translated by Moore and Aveling. Moscow: Foreign Languages Publishing House

Masiero P. and Germano F.S.R. (1988). JSD as an object-oriented design method. *Software Engineering Notes*, **13**(3), 22–3

Matthews D. (1983). *Programming Language Design with Polymorphism*. PhD Dissertation, Computer Lab., University of Cambridge, England

McCabe F.G. (1992). *Logic and Objects*. Englewood Cliffs, NJ: Prentice-Hall

McCarthy J. (1960). Recursive functions of symbolic expressions and their computation by machine, Part 1. *Comm. ACM*, **3**(4)

McDermott D. and Doyle J. (1980). Nonmonotonic logic I. *Artificial Intelligence*, **13**(1,2)

McGregor J.D. and Sykes D.A. (1992). *Object-Oriented Software Development: Engineering Software for Reuse*. New York: Van Nostrand

McInnes S.T. (1988). *The Generic Relational Model*. PhD Thesis, Department of Computer Science, University of Strathclyde, Glasgow

Meersman R.A., Kent W. and Khosla S., eds. (1991). Object-oriented databases: analysis, design & construction (DS-4). *Proceedings of the IFIP TC2/WG2.6 Working Conference*, Windermere, UK, 2-6 July 1990

Meyer B. (1988). *Object-oriented Software Construction*. Englewood Cliffs, NJ: Prentice-Hall

Meyer B. (1990). *Eiffel: The Language and the Environment*. Englewood Cliffs, NJ: Prentice-Hall

Meyer B. and Mandrioli D., eds. (1992). *Advances in Object-Oriented Software Engineering*, Englewood Cliffs, NJ: Prentice-Hall

Meyrowitz N., ed. (1986). OOPSLA'86 ACM conference on object-oriented programming systems, languages and applications. *ACM SIGPLAN Notices*, **21** (11)

Meyrowitz N., ed. (1987). OOPSLA'87 ACM conference on object-oriented programming systems, languages and applications. *ACM SIGPLAN Notices*, **22** (12)

Meyrowitz N, ed. (1988). OOPSLA'88 ACM conference on object-oriented programming systems, languages and applications. *ACM SIGPLAN Notices*, **23** (11)

Meyrowitz N., ed. (1989). *OOPSLA'89 ACM Conference on Object-Oriented Programming Systems, Languages and Applications*. Reading, MA: Addison-Wesley

Meyrowitz N., ed. (1990). *OOPSLA'90 ACM Conference on Object-Oriented Programming Systems, Languages and Applications*. Reading, MA: Addison-Wesley

Milner R. (1978). A theory of type polymorphism in programming. *J. Comput. Syst. Sci.*, **17**, 348–75

Minsky M. (1975). A framework for representing knowledge. In Haugeland J. (1981) *Mind Design*, Cambridge, MA: MIT Press

Mitchell J. and Plotkin G. (1985). Abstract types have existential type. In *Proc. 12th Annual ACM Symposium on Principles of Programming Languages*, New Orleans, LA, Jan. New York: ACM, 37–51

Mock M. (1990). Doublevision: a foundation for scientific visualization. In *Applications of Object-Oriented Programming*. (Pinson L.J. and Weiner R.S., eds.). Reading, MA: Addison-Wesley

Monarchi D.E. and Puhr G.I. (1992). A research typology for object-oriented analysis and design. *Comms. ACM*, **35**(9), 35–47

Moon D. (1986). Object-oriented programming with Flavors. In *OOPSLA'89 ACM Conference on Object-Oriented Programming Systems, Languages and Applications* (Meyrowitz N., ed.). ACM SIGPLAN Notices, **21**(11)

Moon D. (1989). The Common LISP object-oriented programming language standard. In *Object-Oriented Concepts, Databases and*

Applications (Kim W. and Lochovsky F.H., eds.). Reading, MA: Addison-Wesley

Mullin M. (1989). *Object-Oriented Program Design.* Wokingham: Addison-Wesley

Myers G.J. (1979). *The Art of Software Testing.* New York: Wiley

Nelson T.H. (1980). Replacing the printed word: a complete literary system. In *Information Processing 80.* (Lavington S.H., ed.). 1013–23. Amsterdam: North-Holland,

Nelson T.H. (1981). *Literary Machines.* Nelson, Swathmore PA

Nerson J. (1992). Applying object-oriented analysis and design. *Comms. ACM,* **35**(9), 63–74

Nguyen G.T. and Rieu D. (1989). Schema evolution in object-oriented database systems. *Data & Knowledge Engineering,* **4**(1), 43–68

Nierstrasz O. and Tsichritzis D.E. (1989). Integrated office systems. In *Object-Oriented Concepts, Databases and Applications* (Kim W. and Lochovsky F.H., eds.). Reading, MA: Addison-Wesley

Nierstrasz O., Gibbs S. and Tsichritzis D.E. (1992). Component-oriented software development. *Comms. ACM,* **35**(9), 160–5

Norman D.A. and Draper S.W. (1986). *User Centred System Design.* Hillsdale NJ: Lawrence Erlbaum

Object Management Group (1992). *Common Object Request Broker Architecture.* Framington MA: Object Management Group

Object Management Group (1993). *Object-Oriented Analysis and Design Reference Model.* Framington, MA: Object Management Group

Paepcke A., ed. (1991). *OOPSLA'91 ACM Conference on Object-Oriented Programming Systems, Languages and Applications.* Reading, MA: Addison-Wesley

Page-Jones M. (1992). Comparing techniques by means of encapsulation and connascence. *Comm. ACM,* **35**(9), 147–51

Page-Jones M. and Weiss S. (1989). Synthesis: An object-oriented analysis and design method. *American Programmer,* **2**(7) 64–7

Page-Jones M., Constantine L.L. and Weiss S. (1990). Modelling object-oriented systems: the uniform object notation. *Computer Language,* Oct. 1990, 70–87

Parnas D. (1972). On the criteria to be used in decomposing systems into modules. *Comm. ACM,* **15**(2), 1053–8

Parsaye K., Chignell M., Khoshafian S. and Wong H. (1989). *Intelligent Databases: Object-Oriented, Deductive Hypermedia Technologies.* New York: Wiley

Peckham J. and Maryanski J. (1988). Semantic data models. *ACM Computing Surveys,* **20**(3), 153–89

Perry D.E. and Kaiser G.E. (1990). Adequate testing and object-oriented programming. *J. Object-Oriented Programming,* **3**(5) 13–19

Peters T.J. and Waterman R.H. (1982). *In Search of Excellence.* New York: Harper & Row

Peuquet D.J. and Marble D.F., eds. (1990). *Introductory readings in Geographic Information Systems.* London: Taylor and Francis

Pinson L.J. and Weiner R.S. (1988). *An Introduction to Object-Oriented Programming and C++.* Reading, MA: Addison-Wesley

Pinson L.J. and Weiner R.S., eds. (1990). *Applications of Object-Oriented Programming.* Reading, MA: Addison-Wesley

Pinson L.J. and Weiner R.S. (1990). Object-oriented design of a branch path analyzer for C-language software systems. In *Applications of Object-Oriented Programming* (Pinson L.J. and Weiner R.S., eds.). Reading, MA: Addison-Wesley

Pohl I. (1989). *C++ for C Programmers.* Redwood City, CA: Benjamin Cummings

Potter J. and Takoro M., eds. (1992). *TOOLS6: Proceedings of the sixth international conference on the Technology of Object-Oriented Languages and Systems.* New York: Prentice-Hall

Pountain D. (1988). Rekursiv: an object-oriented CPU. *Byte,* **13**(11), 341–9

Prieto-Diaz R. and Freeman P. (1987). Classifying software for reuseability. *IEEE Software,* **4**(1), 6–16

Quillian M.R. (1967). Word concepts: a theory and simulation of some basic semantic capabilities. *Behavioural Science,* **12**, 410–30

Raghavan R. (1990). Building interactive graphical applications using C++. In *Applications of Object-Oriented Programming.* (Pinson L.J. and Weiner R.S., eds.). Reading, MA:

Addison-Wesley

Reenskaug T.M.H. (1981). User-oriented descriptions of Smalltalk systems. *Byte,* Aug 1981, 149–66

Reenskaug T. and Skaar A.L. (1989). An environment for literate Smalltalk programming. In *OOPSLA'89 ACM Conference on Object-oriented Programming Systems, Languages and Applications* (Meyrowitz N., ed.). Reading, MA: Addison-Wesley

Reenskaug T., Anderson E.P., Berre A.J. *et al.* (1991). Seamless support for the creation and maintenance of object-oriented systems. *Taskon A/S, Gandstadalteen 21, N-0371 Oslo 3*

Reiter R. (1985). On reasoning by default. In *Readings in Knowledge Presentation* (Brachman R.J. and Levesque H.J., eds.). Los Altos, CA: Morgan Kaufman

Rentsch T. (1982). Object-oriented programming. *SIGPLAN Notices,* **17**(9), 51–79

Roberts R.B. and Goldstein I.P. (1977). *The FRL manual.* AI Memo. No. 409, MIT Artificial Intelligence Laboratory

Robinson P., ed. (1992). *Object-Oriented Design.* London: Chapman and Hall

Rosenberg J. and Koch D., eds. (1990). *Persistent Object Systems.* Berlin: Springer-Verlag

Rubin K.S. and Goldberg A. (1992). Object behaviour analysis. *Comms. ACM,* **35**(9), 48–62

Rumbaugh J., Blaha M., Premerlani W. *et al.* (1991). *Object-Oriented Modelling and Design.* Englewood Cliffs, NJ: Prentice-Hall

Rummelhart D.E. and McClelland J.L. (1986). *Parallel Distributed Processing: Explorations in the Microstructure of Cognition* (2 vols.). Cambridge, MA: MIT Press

Saeki M., Horai H. and Enomoto H. (1989). Software development process from natural language specification. *Proc. 11th International Conference on Software Engineering.* New York: IEEE Computer Society

Sakkinen M. (1988). Comments on "the Law of Demeter" and C++. *SIGPLAN Notices,* **23**(12), 38

Schaffert C., Cooper T., Bullis B., Kilian M. and Wilpot C. (1986). An introduction to Trellis/Owl. In *OOPSLA'89 ACM Conference on Object-Oriented Programming Systems, Languages and Applications* (Meyrowitz N., ed.). ACM SIGPLAN Notices, **21**(11)

Schank R.C. and Abelson R.P. (1977). *Scripts, Plans, Goals and Understanding.* New York: Lawrence Erlbaum Associates

Scharenberg M.E. and Dunsmore H.E. (1991). Evolution of classes and objects during object-oriented design and programming. *J. Object-Oriented Programming,* **3**(9), 30–4

Schlageter G., Unland R., *et al.* (1988). OOPS: An object-oriented programming system with integrated data management facility. *Proc. IEEE 4th Int. Conf. on Data Engineering,* Los Angeles, 118-25

Schmid H.A. and Swenson J.R. (1975). On the semantics of the relational data model. *Proc. 1975 ACM SIGMOD International Conference on Management of Data*

Schmucker K. (1986). *Object-Oriented Programming for the Macintosh,* Hayden Book Company

Scott A.C., Clayton J.E. and Gibson E.L. (1991). *A Practical Approach to Knowledge Acquisition.* Reading, MA: Addison-Wesley

Seidewitz E. and Stark M. (1986). *General Object-oriented Software Development. Software Engineering Letters,* 86-002

Servio Logic (1989). *Programming in OPAL.* Beaverton OR: Servio Logic Development Corp.

Shadbolt N. (1989). Knowledge representation in man and machine. In Forsythe R., *Expert Systems: Principles and Case Studies* 2nd edn. London: Chapman and Hall, 1989

Shastri L. (1988). *Semantic Networks: An Evidential Formalization and its Connectionist Realization.* London: Pitman

Shaw M. and Gaines B. (1992). On the relationship between repertory grid and term subsumption knowledge structures: theory, practice and tools. In *Research and Development in Expert Systems IX* (Bramer M. and Milne R., eds.). Cambridge: Cambridge University Press

Shipman D. (1981). The functional data model and the data language DAPLEX. *ACM TODS,* **6**(1)

Shlaer S. and Mellor S.J. (1988). *Object-Oriented Systems Analysis – Modelling the World in*

Data. Englewood Cliffs, NJ: Yourdon Press

Shlaer S. and Mellor S.J. (1991). *Object-Lifecycles: Modelling the World in States.* Englewood Cliffs, NJ: Yourdon Press

Shneiderman B. (1987). User interface design for the hyperties electronic encyclopedia. In *Proceeding of the Hypertext '87 Workshop,* University of North Carolina at Chapel Hill

Shriver B. and Wegner P., eds. (1987). *Research Directions in Object-Oriented Programming.* Cambidge MA: MIT Press

Simon H. (1965). *The shape of Automation for Men and Management.*

Skarra A.H. and Zdonik S.B (1986). The management of changing types in an object-oriented database. In *OOPSLA'89 ACM Conference on Object-Oriented Programming Systems, Languages and Applications* (Meyrowitz N., ed). ACM SIGPLAN Notices, **21**(11)

Smith J.M. and Smith D.C.P. (1977). Database abstractions – aggregation and generalization. *ACM Trans. on Database Systems, 2*, 105–33

Snyder A. (1987). Inheritance and the development of encapsulated software systems. In *Research Directions in Object-Oriented Programming* (Shriver B. and Wegner P., eds.). Cambridge, MA: MIT Press

Soley R.M., ed. (1990). *Object Management Architecture Guide.* Framington, MA: Object Management Group

Sommerville I. (1989). *Software Engineering* 3rd edn. Wokingham: Addison-Wesley

Stern R. (1990). *Hegel, Kant and the Structure of the Object.* London: Routledge

Stoecklin S.E., Adams E.J. and Smith S. (1988). Object-oriented analysis. *Proc. 5th Washington Ada Symposium.* ACM, New York, 133-8

Stonebraker M.R. and Rowe L.A., eds. (1987). *The Postgres Papers.* Research memo. UCB/ERL M86/85, University of California, Berkeley

Stonebraker M.R., Rowe L.A., Lindsay B., Gray P., Carey Brodie M.L., Bernstein P. and Beech D. (1990). The third generation database system manifesto. *Proc. 1990 SIGMOD Conference,* ACM

Stroustrup B. (1986). *The C++ Programming Language.* Reading, MA: Addison-Wesley

Stroustrup B. (1988). What is object-oriented programming? *IEEE Software*, May 1988, 10–20

Sully P. (1993). *Modelling the World with Objects.* Englewood Cliffs, NJ: Prentice-Hall

Swaffield G.E. (1990). *Development of a Structured Method for Knowledge Elicitation.* PhD Thesis, Thames Polytechnic, London

Symbolics (1988). *Statice.* Cambridge, MA: Symbolics Inc.

Taylor D. (1992). *Object-Oriented Information Systems: Planning and Implementation.* New York: Wiley

Taylor D. (1992a). *Object-Oriented Technology: A Manager's Guide.* Reading, MA: Addison-Wesley

Tello E.R. (1989). *Object-oriented Programming for Artificial Intelligence: A Guide to Tools and System Design.* Reading, MA: Addison-Wesley

Ten Dyke R.P. and Kunz J.C. (1989). Object-oriented programming. *IBM Systems Journal,* **28**(3)

Teorey T.J., Yang D.Q. and Fry J.P. (1986). A logical design methodology for relational databases using the extended entity-relationship model. *ACM Computing Surveys,* **18**(2), 197–222

Tesler L. (1981). The Smalltalk Environment. *Byte* Aug 1981, 90–147

Thimbleby H. (1990). *User Interface Design.* New York: ACM Press (Addison-Wesley)

Tomlinson C. and Scheevel M. (1989). Concurrent object-oriented programming languages. In *Object-Oriented Concepts, Databases and Applications* (Kim W. and Lochovsky F.H., eds.) Reading, MA: Addison-Wesley

Touretzky D.S. (1986). *The Mathematics of Inheritance Systems.* London: Pitman

Turner D.A. (1985). Miranda: a non-strict functional language with polymorphic types. In *Functional Programming Languages and Computer Architectures* (Jouannaud J-P., ed.). Berlin: Springer Lecture Notes in Computer Science 201, 1–16

Turner R. (1984). *Logics for Artificial Intelligence.* Chichester: Ellis Horwood

Ullman J.D. (1981). *Principles of Database Systems.* Maryland: Computer Science Press

Ullman J.D. (1988). *Principles of Database and Knowledge-base Systems.* Vol. I. Computer

Science Press

Ullman J.D. (1989). *Principles of Database and Knowledge-base Systems.* Vol. II – The New Technologies. Rockville, MD: Computer Science Press

Wand Y. (1989). A proposal for a formal model of objects. In *Object-Oriented Concepts, Databases and Applications* (Kim W. and Lochovsky F.H., eds.). Reading, MA: Addison-Wesley

Ward P. (1989). How to integrate object-orientation with structured analysis and design. *IEEE Software,* **6**, March 1989

Wasserman A.I., Pircher P.A. and Muller R.J. (1990). The object-oriented structured design notation for software design representation. *IEEE Computer,* March 1990, 50–62

Wegner P. (1987). The object-oriented classification paradigm. In *Research Directions in Object-Oriented Programming* (Shriver B. and Wegner P. eds.). Cambridge: Cambridge University Press

Weiner R. and Pinson L. (1990). *The C++ Workbook.* Reading, MA: Addison-Wesley

Weiser S.P. and Lochovsky F.H. (1989). OZ+: an object-oriented database system. In *Object-Oriented Concepts, Databases and Applications* (Kim W. and Lochovsky F.H., eds.). Reading, MA: Addison-Wesley

Weiskamp K. and Fleming B. (1990). *The Complete C++ Primer.* London: Academic Press

Whitewater Group (1989). *Actor Language Manual.* Evanston IL: The Whitewater Group Inc.

Wilkie F.G. (1993). *Object-Oriented Software Engineering: The Professional Developer's Guide.* Wokingham: Addison-Wesley

Wilson D. (1990). Class diagrams: a tool for design, documentation and teaching. *J. Object-Oriented Programming,* **3**(9), 38–44

Wilson P. (1991). *Computer Supported Cooperative Work.* Oxford: Intellect Books

Winblad A.L., Edwards S.D. and King D.R. (1990). *Object-Oriented Software.* Reading, MA: Addison-Wesley

Winder R. (1993). *Developing C++ Software.* 2nd edn. Chichester: Wiley

Wing J.M. amd Nixon M.R. (1989). Extending Ina Jo with temporal logic. *IEEE Transactions on Software Engineering*, Feb 1989

Winograd T. and Flores F. (1986). *Understanding Computers and Cognition.* Reading, MA: Addison-Wesley

Winston P.H. (1984). *Artificial Intelligence* 2nd edn. Reading, MA: Addison-Wesley

Wirfs-Brock R., Wilkerson B. and Wiener L. (1990). *Designing Object-Oriented Software.* Englewood Cliffs, NJ: Prentice-Hall

Woods W.A. (1985). What's in a link. In *Readings in Knowledge Presentation* (Brachman R.J. and Levesque H.J., eds.). Los Altos, CA: Morgan Kaufman

Wu C.T. (1990). Development of a visual database interface: an object-oriented approach. In *Applications of Object-Oriented Programming* (Pinson L.J. and Weiner R.S., eds.). Reading, MA: Addison-Wesley

Wulf W.A., London R.L. and Shaw M. (1976). An introduction to the construction and verification of Alphard programs. *IEEE Transactions on Software Engineering,* SE-2

Yazici A., George R., Buckles B.P. *et al.* (1992). A survey of conceptual and logical data models for uncertainty management. In *Fuzzy Logic for the Management of Uncertainty* (Zadeh L. and Kacprzyk J., eds.). New York: Wiley

Yokote Y. and Tokoro M. (1987). Concurrent programming in ConcurrentSmalltalk. In *Object-Oriented Concurrent Programming* (Yonezawa A. and Tokoro M., eds.). Cambridge, MA: MIT Press 129–158

Yonezawa A. and Tokoro M., eds. (1987). *Object-Oriented Concurrent Programming.* Cambridge, MA: MIT Press

Young J.Z. (1986). *Philosophy and the Brain.* Oxford: Oxford University Press

Yourdon E. and Constantine L.L. (1979). *Structured Design: Fundamentals of a Discipline of Computer Program and Systems Design.* Englewood Cliffs, NJ: Prentice-Hall

Zadeh L.A. (1965). Fuzzy Sets. *Information and Control,* **8**

Zadeh L.A. (1982). *A Computational Approach to Fuzzy Quantifiers in Natural Languages.* University of California (Berkeley) Memo. UCB-ERL M82-36

Zadeh L.A. (1985). Syllogistic reasoning in fuzzy logic and its application to usuality and reasoning with dispositions. *IEEE*

Transactions **SMC-15**(6)

Zdonik S.B. and Maier D., eds. (1990). *Readings in Object-Oriented Database Systems.* Los Altos, CA: Morgan Kaufmann

Zdonik S.B. and Wegner P. (1985). *A Database Approach to Languages, Libraries and Environments.* Technical Report CS-85-10, Department of Computer Science, Brown University

Zdonik S.B. and Wegner P. (1985a). *Language and Methodology for Object-Oriented Database Environments.* Technical Report CS-85-19, Department of Computer Science, Brown University

NAME INDEX

SUBJECT INDEX

NOTES

NOTES

NOTES

NOTES

NOTES

NOTES

NOTES

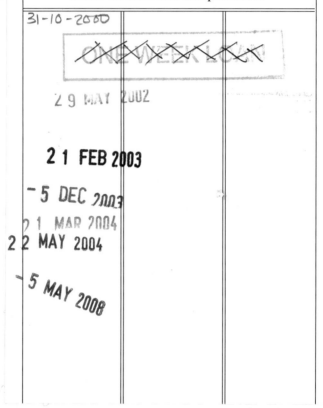